Harold C. Schonberg was the senior music critic of *The New York Times*. In 1971 he was awarded the Pulitzer Prize for criticism. He has written two previous books: *The Great Conductors* and *The Great Pianists*.

HAROLD C. SCHONBERG

The Lives of
The Great Composers

Again, to Rosalyn

An Abacus Book

First published in Great Britain by Davis-Poynter Ltd
Published by Futura 1980, reprinted 1982, 1986, 1989
Published in Cardinal 1991
Published in Abacus 1992

ISBN 0 349 10340 2

Printed and bound in Great Britain by
BPCC Hazells Ltd
Member of BPCC Ltd

Abacus
A Division of
Little, Brown and Company (UK) Limited
165 Great Dover Street
London SE1 4YA

Contents

Preface

I have written this book for the intelligent layman, and have tried to organize it so that the consecutive line from Johann Sebastian Bach to Arnold Schoenberg has been traced. Music is a continually evolving process, and there has been no genius, however great, who has not taken from his predecessors.

Also, in the process of writing this book, I have tried to humanize the great composers, to give an idea of what they felt and thought. This approach is somewhat unfashionable today. Many musical scholars insist that the work rather than the man is the thing; that a piece of music can best be explained *as music*; that thorough harmonic and structural analysis is the only valid "explanation." The rest is sentimental program-note writing and has no real application to the music. I happen to disagree. I firmly believe that music can be explained by the man; indeed, *must* be explained by the man and his times. For a man's music is a function of himself, and is a reflection of his mind and his reaction to the world in which he lives. Just as we see the world through the eyes and mind of a Rembrandt, Cézanne, or Picasso when we look at their paintings, so we experience the world through the ears and mind of a Beethoven, Brahms, or Stravinsky when we hear their music. We are in contact with a mind, and we must attempt an identification with that mind. The closer the identification, the closer it is possible to come to understanding the creator's work. That is why the French pianist Alfred Cortot insisted that his pupils, while studying a piece of music, also read biographies of the composer, his letters, and the letters of his contemporaries. Then the pupil had to relate the piece of music to the composer's entire life and work.

Hence this book is greatly concerned with the biographical aspects of the great composers. There is little on form and analysis. Technical terminology is kept to a minimum, though sometimes it is unavoidable, especially in a discussion of twentieth-century dodecaphonic and serial music. It is easy to make a mystique out of form and analysis; but are not these topics best left to the student and the professional? I have always been amused by books supposedly for the layman which are full of complicated musical examples. Some of those examples—score reductions and the like—Vladimir Horowitz himself would find difficult to play. A reader who is an able enough musician to play them does not need them, while a reader who has trouble following a single line in C major on a G clef—and that includes the majority —cannot use them.

A glance at the Table of Contents will reveal that most of the greatest composers receive a complete chapter devoted to themselves. Other great composers whose contributions to the history of music are better understood when compared with one or more contemporaries are bracketed with them within a single chapter. And, finally, there is a third kind of chapter devoted to an entire period or a specific time and place, offering general material to supplement the succession of biograhical chapters.

I have started with Bach in volume one, not because there were no great composers before Bach, but because Bach is where the active repertoire really begins. The book ends in volume two with the Second Viennese School. It had to cut off *somewhere*, and the trinity of Schoenberg, Berg, and Webern seemed the logical place. A postlude briefly discusses major trends since 1945. This may be a cowardly evasion, but the development of serial, postserial, electronic, stochastic, aleatoric, and mixed-media music is so complicated and so lengthy a subject that it demands a book in itself.

Orthographical problems always arise in books on music. I have followed normal American professional usage in spelling and terminology Some British writers have accused my previous books of being too "American" in style Did they think I was Mongolian? American usage, for example, dictates "twelve-tone music" instead of the British "twelve-note," for reasons explained in the chapter on Schoenberg. American usage dictates, to give two examples. *Harold in Italy* yet, inconsistently, *Symphonie fantastique.* Never have I heard the former work referred to as *Harold en Italie,* just as one rarely if ever hears reference to the Berlioz *Fantastic Symphony.* Generally it is just *Fantastique.* "Bernstein conducted the Berlioz *Fantastique* last night."

Russian and other foreign names pose their familiar problems The "v" endings are used for Prokofiev, Balakirev. and the others. Yet Rachmaninoff is spelled with the double "f" because that is how he himself signed his name, just as Schoenberg insisted on that spelling and not Schönberg Similarly, Handel rather than Händel. If there are inconsistencies throughout the book, I apologize.

Some of the material in the following pages originally appeared as Sunday articles in my weekly New York *Times* column, and several appeared as

Times magazine pieces. All have been revised and amplified. I wish to thank the New York Times Company for permission to use that material. A substantial portion of the chapter on Charles Ives originally appeared in the December 1958, issue of *Esquire*, and is reprinted by permission of Esquire Magazine, Inc. I would like to thank my wife for her constant help and encouragement. Eric Schaal was kind enough to supply several rare photographs of composers from his famous collection, and Rosemary Andersen was extremely helpful in gathering others. And Robert E. Farlow, my editor at W. W. Norton, gave the manuscript a stupendously thorough scrutiny, one unparalleled in my fairly wide experience. In more than one respect it is "our" book.

THE LIVES OF
THE GREAT COMPOSERS
Volume One

Transfiguration of the Baroque

JOHANN SEBASTIAN BACH

There was a tradition in Leipzig that the body of Johann Sebastian Bach had been interred near the door of the Church of St. John, approximately six paces from the south wall. In 1894, St. John's readied itself for alterations—alterations that would have destroyed the traditional site of Bach's grave. Whereupon a group of scholars, headed by an anatomist named William His, started looking for the grave. They had one piece of information with which to work: in 1750, the year of Bach's death, only twelve persons had been interred in oak coffins. One of those twelve was Bach.

Three coffins were dug up near the south wall. Two of them were of pine. One was of oak and contained a male skeleton in good condition. Every possible test was made, and a facial mask to cover the skull was contributed by the sculptor Karl Seffner. The mask corresponded closely to the known portraits of Bach. In his report, published in 1895, Dr. His summarized all evidence and concluded, along with the scientists who had worked on the project, that the skeleton was indeed Bach's. The remains were then transferred to a tomb beneath the altar of St. John's.

If the skeleton was indeed Bach's, and there is no good reason to doubt it, the composer was a man about 5 feet, 7½ inches tall, with a rather massive head, a strong physique and a solid body, all physical characteristics suggested by the few portraits from life that have come down to us. Bach iconographers have bemoaned the fact that there is so little pictorial evidence, and a few believe that there is no way of telling what he looked like. But whatever pictures we do have, all with Bach wearing a wig, according to the custom of the day (though some scholars have wondered if it covers a bald head), show many points in common. There are the prominent nose, the fleshy cheeks, the outthrust chin, the severe lips. It is a tough, strong masculine face, the face of a man who will stand up for his rights. It is an uncompromising face· not with the look of a fanatic, but certainly with the look of one who is determined to have his own way.

All of this tallies with whatever is known about Bach the man. He was stubborn, he had a temper, he had the reputation of being a hard person to get along with. His pupils, and most likely his children, may have feared this stern figure. He was a religious man, a practicing Lutheran whose library contained an extraordinarily (for the day) large number of ecclesiastical volumes. He seems to have been obsessed with the idea of death, and worried about it far more than his contemporaries even in those days when Heaven and Hell were not abstract concepts but fearful truth. Handel, for instance, was a profoundly religious man, but he *knew* he would be going to Heaven. So, one gathers, did Haydn. Those two men felt that they were friends of God. Not Bach, who stood much more in awe of the Deity. He once said that the aim and final reason of music "should be none else but the glory of God and the recreation of the mind." That he had a strong sexual drive, his family attests; he had twenty children, of whom nine survived him. It was the largest family, by far, produced by any of the great composers: large even for Bach's day, when large families were not unusual. There also is the reproof handed him by the Arnstadt authorities in 1706: "Thereupon ask him further by what right he recently caused the strange maiden to be invited into the organ loft and let her make music there." Victorian biographers of Bach were thrown into sheer consternation by the implication that their saintly hero, the composer of the B minor Mass, could have been interested in strange maidens. It was decided that the strange maiden was his cousin, Maria Barbara, whom he married the following year. But there is no evidence one way or the other.

Bach was a solid burgher, twice married, and as thrifty as a peasant. He never suffered want. Of all the Bachs of his day he was the most affluent and most respected, but he was not above pinching every penny and watching grimly over every expense. Some of his correspondence with his cousin, Johann Elias, is rather amusing in this respect. Indeed, it is virtually the only amusing thing in Bach's humorless life. Did the man ever smile? One wonders. Certainly his music has less humor than the music of any of the other great composers. Even Wagner composed a *Meistersinger* Bach's musical humor—his *Coffee Cantata*, his *Capriccio on the Departure of a Beloved Brother*, one or two other pieces—bulk infinitesimally small in his output. Anyway, getting back to Johann Elias, Bach writes about a gift of wine that Elias had sent. Some of it was lost in transit, and Bach lamented mightily "that even the least drop of this noble gift of God should have been spilled." Then Bach hastily says he is in no position "to make an appropriate return." Then, finally, there is a postscript: "Although my honored Cousin kindly offers to oblige with more of the *liqueur*, I must decline

14

his offer on account of the excessive expenses here. For since the carriage charges cost 16 groschen, the delivery man 2 groschen, the customs inspector 2 groschen, the inland duty 5 groschen, 3 pfennig, and the general duty 3 groschen, my honored Cousin can judge for himself that each quart costs me almost 5 groschen, which for a present is really too expensive."

Bach was born in Eisenach, Germany, on March 21, 1685, the youngest of the eight children of Johann Ambrosius Bach, who was the son of Christoph Bach, who was the son of Johannes Bach, and so back to Veit Bach, whose birth date is unknown but who died in 1619. Johann Sebastian, who like all the Bachs took great pride in the accomplishments of the family, once started a genealogy named "Origin of the Musical Bach Family." He traced it back to Veit, "a white bread baker in Hungary," who "in the sixteenth century was compelled to escape from Hungary because of his Lutheran faith." In this genealogy, Bach draws a charming picture of old Veit, who "found his greatest pleasure in a little cithern which he took with him even into the mill and played while the grinding was going on. (How pretty it must have sounded altogether! Yet in this way he had a chance to have the rhythm drilled into him.) And this was, as it were, the beginning of a musical inclination in his descendants." Bach always believed he was of Hungarian descent, but most scholars now think that Veit had been born in Germany, had moved to Hungary, and then returned.

In Veit's day there were also Hans Bach and Caspar Bach. Veit fathered Johannes and Lips. From Johannes sprang Johanna, Christoph, and Heinrich. From Lips came the Meiningen line of Bachs. The family was industriously fertile, and for over two centuries bred true, producing one respected musician after another. There were musical Bachs in Arnstadt and Eisenach, in Ohrdruf, Hamburg, and Lüneburg, in Berlin, Schweinfurt, and Halle, in Dresden, Gotha, Weimar, Jena, Mühlhausen, Minden, and Leipzig. They were a close-knit, clannish group who loved to visit one another, making music, exchanging gossip, trying to place members of their own family in important musical posts. Whenever an opening presented itself anywhere in Germany, news raced through the ganglia of the great Bach family, causing twitches and responses. As often as not, the Bachs got their man in.

Johann Sebastian's father, Johann Ambrosius, was a highly regarded church organist in Eisenach. He died when Sebastian was ten (his mother had died the preceding year). Sebastian and his brother Jakob were taken in by their older brother Johann Christoph, who was organist at Ohrdruf. Not much is known about the five years Sebastian spent there. He must have been a gifted child. He was what we would call a senior in the local school at the age of fourteen, and at that time the average age of seniors was nearer eighteen He also was a good organist and clavier player (the clavier is the generic term for keyboard stringed instruments: harpsichord, clavichord, spinet), a singer, a good violinist, presumably already a composer. But we are not discussing any talented young musician. We are discussing Johann Sebastian Bach, perhaps the most stupendously gifted figure in the history of music, and there is so much more we would like to know about his childhood. When did his extraordinary talent first show itself? Did he have absolute pitch? (He must have had.) The Bach family being what it was, a genetic factor must be taken into consideration. What went on in the boy's head, what kind of musical and physical reflex operated, exactly what kind of training did his father and elder brother give him? We do not know.

We do know the main external events of his life. We know that at the age of fifteen he went to St. Michael's school in Lüneburg; that he visited Hamburg; that already he was a contentious young man; that his life was a series of positions in the service of the court or the church: Arnstadt, Mühlhausen, the ducal court of Anhalt-Cöthen, his final position, which he held for twenty-seven years, as cantor (teacher) of St. Thomas's Church in Leipzig. We know that he was highly respected in his day, though more as an organ player and organ technician than as a composer. Bach, who carried the baroque movement to its peak, lived during a time when radical new concepts were undermining the edifice that to a large extent had been built on polyphony. Indeed, Bach lived to find himself considered an old-fashioned composer, a pedant, whose music was pushed aside in favor of the lighter, homophonic, melodic music of the *style galant*—the elegant, graceful, rather superficial music that made his son, Johann Christian, so popular in London.

The chances are that this did not bother Bach very much. He lived before the romantic notion of art for art's sake, of music composed for eternity. Bach was as practical and as level-headed a composer as ever lived. Like all composers of the day, he regarded himself as a working professional, one who ordinarily wrote to fill a specific need—a cantata for Sunday, an exercise book for the children, an organ piece to demonstrate a particular instrument. He did publish certain pieces of which he was especially proud, but by and large he fully expected the bulk of his music to disappear after his death. When he became cantor in Leipzig, he disposed of all his predecessor's music, and he knew that his successor would just as summarily get rid of whatever Bach manuscripts were around. It was a cantor's job to present music that *he* had composed, not the music of another man.

Of course, he knew his worth. He must have known from the beginning, and if there was anything that drove him out of his mind it was slovenly musicianship, or musicianship of a kind that did not meet his own standards. And those standards were—well, Bachian. His whole life is dotted with episodes that attest to his determination to make music on his own level. As early as 1705, in Arnstadt, he got involved in an argument with a student named Geyersbach. The upshot was that Bach drew his dagger and went for Geyersbach; and, in a trice, the future composer of the *St. Matthew Passion* was rolling on the ground. attempting mayhem on his opponent. On examination it turned out that Bach had once disdainfully called his colleague a *Zippelfaggotist*—a bassoonist who produced sounds like those of a nanny-goat. Bach was reproved, especially as he "already had the reputation of not getting along with the students."

But Bach was incorrigible. It would seem that he knew his potentialities and was determined to have his own way. Nothing could interfere with his vision of music and his drive—no, his compulsion—to saturate himself in his art, to improve himself, to study, to absorb everything that could be absorbed. If somebody interfered, *tant pis!* He is reproved in 1706 for staying away from his duties (he had walked to Lübeck to hear Buxtehude play the organ). He is reproved for his strange harmonies at the organ during services. He is reproved for playing too long and, in defiance, "he had at once fallen into the other extreme and made it too short." He is reproved for being a "loner," for his standoffish, superior attitude. "For if he considers it no disgrace to be connected with the Church and to accept his salary, he must not be ashamed to make music with other students assigned to do so."

At Weimar he is actually sent to jail, in 1717, for "too stubbornly forcing the issue of his dismissal." Bach wanted to go to Cöthen. In Leipzig he is constantly complaining to the Elector about money matters and his perquisites, and soon becomes very unpopular with the town council, which accuses him of neglecting his duties. Bach's duties were numerous. In his application to Leipzig in 1723 he had written out what he promised to do:

(1) That I shall set the boys a shining example of an honest, retiring manner of life, serve the School industriously, and instruct the boys conscientiously;

(2) Bring the music in both the principal Churches of this town into good estate, to the best of my ability;

(3) Show to the Honorable and Most Wise Council all proper respect and obedience, and protect and further everywhere as best I may its honor and reputation; likewise if a gentleman of the Council desires the boys for a musical occasion, unhesitatingly provide him with the same, but otherwise never permit them to go out of town to funerals or weddings without the previous knowledge and consent of the Burgomaster and Honorable Directors of the School currently in office;

(4) Give due obedience to the Honorable Inspectors and Directors of the School in each and every instruction which the same shall issue in the name of the Honorable and Most Wise Council;

(5) Not take any boys into the School who have not already laid a

foundation in music, or are not the least suited to being instructed therein, nor do the same without the previous knowledge and consent of the Honorable Inspectors and Directors;

(6) So that the Churches may not have to be put to unnecessary expense, faithfully instruct the boys not only in vocal but also in instrumental music;

(7) In order to preserve the good order in the Churches, so arrange the music that it shall not last too long, and shall be of such a nature as not to make an operatic impression, but rather incite the listeners to devotion;

(8) Provide the New Church with good scholars;

(9) Treat the boys in a friendly manner and with caution, but, in case they do not wish to obey, chastise them with moderation or report them to the proper place;

(10) Faithfully attend to the instruction in the school and whatever else it befits me to do;

(11) And if I cannot undertake this myself, arrange that it be done by some other capable person without expense to the Honorable and Most Wise Council or to the School;

(12) Not to go out of town without the permission of the Honorable Burgomaster currently in office;

(13) Always so far as possible walk with the boys at funerals, as is customary;

(14) And shall not accept or wish to accept any office in the University without the consent of the Honorable and Learned Council.

In addition, Bach was responsible for musical programs—the actual music and its performance—in all four of the city's churches. He had to compose a cantata for the weekly service and conduct the performance. He had to provide Passion music for Good Friday. All this was the normal part of any cantor's post. There were extracurricular activities, such as providing motets for weddings and funerals, or festival compositions for the city. From these extracurricular tasks he derived income, and he once pointed out in all seriousness that "when there are rather more funerals than usual, the fees rise in proportion; but when a healthy wind blows, they fall accordingly, as for example last year, when I lost fees that would ordinarily come in from funerals to an amount of more than 100 thaler."

In Leipzig, Bach found neither the co-operation, the income, nor the appreciation he had hoped for, and soon he was as usual at odds with the officials. City Councilor Steger was provoked into saying that not only did the Cantor do nothing, "but he was not even willing to give an explanation of that fact." This probably confirmed the council's secret suspicions about Bach, for he had come to Leipzig because no other candidates who suited the council were available. As Councilor Platz had put it, "since the best man could not be obtained, mediocre ones would have to be accepted." Thus did Councilor Platz assure himself of a footnote in history. The "best man" to whom he referred was Georg Philipp Telemann (1681–1767), an incredibly prolific composer who had some 3,000 works to his credit at his death. Telemann, a fine musician and an admirable composer, was very popular in Germany—far more than the less fashionable Bach ever was. Then, in 1736, came Bach's great battle with Johann August Ernesti, the rector of St. Thomas's School. It was an affair that rocked the school, drove the council frantic, and brought out every bit of the considerable stubbornness and fighting instinct of Bach. Ernesti had chosen one Johann Gottlieb Krause to be prefect of the St. Thomas School. But Krause was a poor musician, and Bach was infuriated. He protested to the council. Ernesti answered back. There were charges and countercharges. Bach would not quit. He carried the fight to the consistory and, when he could get no satisfaction, "to His Most Serene Highness, the Mighty Prince and Lord, Frederick Augustus, King in Poland, Grand Duke in Lithuania, Reuss, Prussia, Mazovia, Samogitia, Kyovia, Vollhynia, Podlachia, Lieffland, Smolensk, Severia and Czernienhovia, Duke of Saxony, Jülich, Cleve, Berg, Engern and Westphalia, Archmarshal and Elector of the Holy Roman Empire, Landgrave of Thuringia, Margrave of Meissen, also of Upper and Lower Lausiz, Burgrave of Magdeburg, Prince and Count of Henneberg, Count of the Marck, Ravensberg and Barby, Lord of Ravenstein, My Most Gracious King, Elector and Master." Nobody knows how the affair finally came out. It is assumed that Bach finally won.

The point is that Bach was not a man to be pushed around, and he carried this attitude into his music-making. How he chafed at the mediocrity with which he was surrounded! This complete musician, this incomparable executant, this composer whose vision embraced the then-known musical universe, this titan had to work in Leipzig with wretched students and with personnel far below the strength he needed and wanted. In 1730 he outlined his minimum requirements for church music forces. Every musical choir, he told the town council, should contain at least twelve singers, though it would be better if sixteen were available. For the orchestra there should be eighteen and preferably twenty players. But, complained Bach, what did he have? A grand total of eight—four town pipers, three professional fiddlers, and one apprentice; and "Modesty forbids me to speak at all truthfully of their qualities and musical knowledge." Bach threw up his hands. Such conditions were intolerable, and on top of everything else, most of the students were untalented. This accounted, Bach said, for the decline of performance standards in Leipzig. At the end, he summarizes the quality of the students. Seventeen were "unusable," twenty "not yet usable," and seventeen "unfit." These fifty-four boys constituted the choruses of the four churches in Leipzig. Poor St. Peter's Church got the worst of the lot, "namely those who do not understand music and can only just barely sing in a chorale."

(Note the reference to the "town pipers." Those gentlemen could be well-rounded musicians, and in 1745 Bach examined one of them, a worthy named Carl Friedrich Pfaffe. "It was found," Bach wrote, "that he performed quite well, and to the applause of all those present, on all the instruments that are customarily employed by town pipers, namely: violin, oboe, transverse flute, trumpet, and horn, and the remaining brass instruments, and he was found quite suited to the post of assistant which he seeks.")

That, then, was what Bach had to work with. Every once in a while, for special occasions, he could get more. For the *St. Matthew Passion* he scraped together over forty participants. Bach evidently craved large forces, and it is a mistake today, in the name of "authenticity," to present such large-scale works as the B minor Mass and the two big Passions with a tiny number of participants in line with Bach's memo of 1730. Of course, Bachian textures must be preserved whatever the forces involved, and the music must be presented with perfect clarity. But that does not preclude a big sound.

Bach did his best with the raw material. He could probably play most of the instruments in the orchestra, and he took his forces in charge much as a modern conductor does. Generally he conducted from the violin or the harpsichord. Very little scholarly work has been done in the early history of conducting, and the general assumption is that not until the nineteenth century did a leader actually beat time. Yet there is plenty of evidence from Bach's own day that the person in charge of an ensemble most definitely did beat time. Indeed, when Bach examined the unfortunate Krause, he specifically mentions that the student could not beat time correctly; that "he could not accurately give the beat in the two principal kinds of time, namely even, or four-quarter, and uneven, or three-quarter."

From all eyewitness accounts, Bach at the head of an orchestra was a dominating figure. He was a brilliant score reader. "His hearing was so fine that he was able to detect the slightest error even in the largest ensembles." While conducting, he would sing, play his own part, keep the rhythm steady, and cue everybody in, "the one with a nod, another by tapping with his feet, the third with a warning finger, giving the right note to one from the top of his voice, to another from the bottom, and a third from the middle of it—all alone, in the midst of the greatest din made by all the participants, and, although he is executing the most difficult parts himself, noticing at once whenever and wherever a mistake occurs, holding everybody together, taking precautions everywhere and repairing any unsteadiness, full of rhythm in every part of his body." Thus has Johann Matthias Gesner.

the Rector who preceded the troublesome Ernesti, described the great man at work. His son, Carl Philipp Emanuel, remarks that Bach was especially finicky about tuning. To this he paid the greatest attention, both in the orchestra and in his own instruments at home. "Nobody could tune and quill his instruments to please him. He did everything himself. . . . He heard the slightest wrong note even in the largest ensembles." The concept of the conductor, in the modern sense of the word, had not been invented; but, it is interesting to note, Bach was a modern conductor in everything but name —and probably, with his quick temper, a fearsome one.

Exactly how he conducted, we do not know. What were his tempos? Ideas about rhythm? Expressive devices? Today many of the fine points of Bach performance practice have been lost. We can only speculate about things like pitch, instruments, ornaments, embellishments, balances, even the rhythms and tempos. Take the subject of pitch. Scholars have determined that it was often as much as a full tone lower in Bach's day than it is in ours. But there also are organs of Bach's day, still in operation, in which the pitch is *higher*. How Bach himself tuned his instruments we do not know. As for embellishments, books have been written on the subject of written-out embellishments in Bach's music, and often the authorities disagree. Which is not surprising, for authorities in Bach's own day disagreed. In addition there seem to have been many conventions that were not written out, such as holding notes for a longer length of time than they were actually written. At best the conscientious musician can, after much specialized study, make an informed guess.

But where performance practices are transitory, changing from generation to generation, Bach's music remains stronger than it ever was. Stronger, indeed, for we can look at it in historical perspective, comparing it with the music of the other great men of his day—Handel, Vivaldi, Couperin, Alessandro Scarlatti. By any measurement Bach eclipses all. His vision was greater, his technique unparalleled, his harmonic sense frightening in its power, expression, and ingenuity. And while he is not considered one of the great melodists, he could nevertheless spin out tunes of ineffable rapture, such as the aria *Bist du bei mir*, or the slow movement of the Trio Sonata in E minor, which proceeds in calm, immense, noble phrases in a kind of tidal ebb and flow.

Bach was a composer of the Baroque. In music, the Baroque Era runs from about 1600 to 1750. Baroque music, as practiced by its greatest figures, has pronounced mannerist qualities: mysticism, exuberance, complexity, decoration, allegory, distortion, the exploitation of the supernatural or grandiose, all commingled. Where the Renaissance period (and later the Classic) stood for order and clarity, the Baroque (and later the Romantic) stood for movement, disturbance, doubt. The musical baroque started in Italy with such figures as Claudio Monteverdi (1567–1643) and the Florentine group that "invented" opera, and rapidly swept through Europe. The Baroque saw the rise of four-part harmony and the figured bass, in which numerals indicate the harmonies to be used. Another name for figured bass is thorough bass, and to Bach it was equivalent to a system handed down from On High. The thorough bass, he was quoted by a pupil as saying, "is the most perfect foundation of music, being played with both hands in such a manner that the left hand plays the notes written down while the right adds consonances and dissonances, in order to make a well-sounding harmony to the Glory of God and the permissible delectation of the spirit; and the aim and final reason, as of all music, so of the thorough bass should be none else but the Glory of God and the recreation of the mind."

The Baroque also saw the disappearance of the old church modes and the consolidation of the scale and its associated keys that have remained in use to this day. It also saw the development of rhythmic ideas that broke music into accented bar lines. It saw the rise of the forms that were to lead directly into sonata, symphony, concerto, overture, and variation. But the Baroque also had its own free forms—toccata, fantasia, prelude, ricercar.

It was a period that saw the rise of a cultured middle class. Music began to spread from court and church into the city, where many middle-class citizens started demanding musical entertainments. These were the forerunners of today's public concerts. Musicians began to supply those demands, sometimes, as in the case of Handel, on a spectacularly successful financial basis. Musical academies were formed, and even coffeehouses put on musical programs to satisfy their patrons. Bach was involved in such a project, and for many years conducted the weekly concerts at Zimmermann's coffeehouse in Leipzig, on Friday evenings from 8 to 10. The participants (so ran the announcement in 1736) "are chiefly students here, and there are always good musicians among them, so that sometimes they become, as is well known, famous virtuosos."

With Bach the baroque in music came to fulfillment. Bach was all that had gone before, and he anticipated much that was to come. He was not only a learned musician when it came to his own music; he also was a learned musician in all music. He certainly was one of the most cultured musicians of his day, with a tremendous knowledge of what was happening in the European scene. He had a sheer lust to know and to assimilate all of the music then available, ancient and contemporary. It was not that he was a scholar interested in musical history. There is no evidence that he made any great effort to unearth medieval music, for instance. That probably would not have interested him. What did interest him, overwhelmingly and even compulsively, was technique. How did composers put things together? What was the quality of their ideas? In matters like these, Bach seems to

22

have had insatiable professional curiosity. Was it because, consciously or unconsciously, he wanted to measure himself against other composers? He went to hear new music, wherever it was possible for him to attend, and was constantly reading what he was not able to hear in person. Bach, of course, could read a printed score as easily as an accountant reads a ledger or a commuter the evening newspaper. As a youth he would absent himself from his duties to listen to the great organists—Vincent Lübeck and Buxtehude, among others—and it was one of the great regrets of his life that he never heard the famous Handel. He knew the old music by Palestrina, Frescobaldi, and Legrenzi; new music by Vivaldi, Telemann, and Albinoni. He was familiar with the music of the French school, from Lully to d'Anglebert and Couperin. (There is no evidence that he was acquainted with the music of the English school.) Of the German composers he esteemed the music of Froberger, Kerll, Fux, Schütz, Theile, Pachelbel, Fischer. He knew the sonatas of Domenico Scarlatti and the choral works of Alessandro Scarlatti. As a child he had grown up with an unquenchable musical appetite, and was never able to satisfy it.

To a large extent he probably was self-taught. Musicians on the order of genius possessed by a Bach, a Mozart, or a Schubert do not need much instruction. They have minds like blotters that immediately soak up and assimilate every musical impulse. They merely have to be pointed in the right direction and be given a little push. So it was with Bach. From the very beginning he took from all sources and made them his own. And he did this in every known musical form with the exception of opera. Bach's music has endless variety. At its worst—and Bach could write *dull* music, though never *bad* music—Bach's music bears signs of haste and impatience, and clearly he was dashing off a formula piece to meet the demands of a specific occasion. But his average is very high, and at its best his music is at the summit of the art. Bach could use formulae of the day and make them sound fresh and original, because they were *his* formulae. The forty-eight preludes and fugues of the *Well-Tempered Clavier* are as different from one another as are the Chopin Études. *The Art of Fugue* (*Die Kunst der Fuge*), unanimously hailed as one of the great intellectual *tours de force* of Western man, is a colossal work, an unfinished series of contrapuntal variations, again with unfailing variety and imagination.

Nobody knows how Bach intended the *Art of Fugue* to be played—as an organ work, as an orchestral work, or anything in between. The instrumentation is unspecified, and the German scholar, Friedrich Blume, even suggests that Bach himself was not interested in whether such works as the *Art of Fugue* were ever performed, or were capable of being performed. "In them," Blume writes, "he wanted to continue a tradition of consummate contrapuntal skill, which he had inherited from the Roman school of the

Palestrina period by way of Berardi, Sweelinck, Scacchi, Theile, Werckmeister and G. B. Vitali. It was   an 'esoteric' activity, this disinterested transmission of a purely abstract theory." Perhaps, but was there ever a composer who wrote abstract music not to be played? One doubts it. In any case, the *Art of Fugue* carries pure counterpoint to its height. To give an idea of the complexity of the work: it starts with four fugues, two of which present the theme, the others presenting the theme in contrary motion (that is, back to front). Then there are counterfugues, in which the original subject is inverted (turned upside down) and combined with the original. There are double and triple fugues, several canons, three pairs of mirror fugues. In Karl Geiringer's description, "Bach presents all the voices first in their original form and then, like a reflected image, in complete inversion. To make the mirror reflection doubly realistic, the treble of the first fugue becomes the bass of the second fugue, the alto changes into a tenor, the tenor into an alto, and the bass into a treble, with the result that No. 12:2 appears like 12:1 standing on its head."

Musicians for over 200 years have been awed by the incredible technique and ingenuity with which Bach, in the *Art of Fugue*, summarized everything known about counterpoint and then added the full measure of his own mighty genius, creating a score that in its majesty and poetry stands unique. It is Bach's last major composition, and he never finished it. While working on an enormous triple fugue he decided to add as a counterpoint the letters of his own name (B = B flat, and H = B natural in German nomenclature). Just as his name appears, the autograph stops. Some musicians—Tovey, Riemann, and others—have worked out a completion, but those are never played in concert, nor should they be. The emotional shock of hearing the B-A-C-H theme, and then abrupt silence just as the fugue is getting started, is an overwhelming experience.

Polyphony is but one side of Bach. He could write collections of dance movements under the titles of Suite or Partita; or devotional cantatas; or music with the bracing athletic vigor of the *Brandenburg* Concertos; or music as titanic as the B minor Mass and *St. Matthew Passion*, or out-and-out virtuoso pieces for the organ, of grand design, overwhelming sonority, and uninhibited finger and foot display (these organ works should be played on a baroque and *never* on a romantic organ); or involved pieces for solo violin or cello; or a long set of harpsichord variations called the *Goldberg*, which in chromatic intensity (that twenty-fifth variation!) has hardly a peer until Chopin and Wagner.

It is harmonic intensity above all that sets Bach's music apart from that of his contemporaries. Bach had anything but a conventional musical mind. His work is always full of surprises: something unexpected, something that departs from the norm, something that only Bach could have dreamed from

24

the material. A Vivaldi concerto grosso, for example, goes along primarily in tonic, dominant and subdominant harmonies, and any exploration of keys is within safely charted courses. In Bach's music a completely new harmonic language is forged. A superior harmonic sense is the mark of nearly all the great composers, the one thing that sets them off from their more timid and less inventive contemporaries. Where most composers of his day would confine themselves to the rules, Bach *made* the rules. Even as a young man he was industriously investigating the harmonic potential of music. It was for this that he would be reproved. His listeners were not used to such daring. At Arnstadt, the twenty-one-year-old Bach was rebuked "for having hitherto made many curious variations in the chorale, and mingled many strange tones in it, and for the fact that the congregation has been confused by it." As he grew older, his harmonic adventurousness became more and more pronounced.

Taking the forms bequeathed to him, Bach was constantly expanding, refining, improving them. He developed the clavier concerto. His music for solo string instruments has never been surpassed for ingenuity, complexity, and difficulty. One wonders how good a violinist Bach was. Surely none but a master of the instrument could have conceived such figurations. One also wonders how many violinists in the world at the time could have played, with any degree of accuracy, such phenomenally taxing writing. The immense chaconne from the D minor Partita for solo violin is the best-known of these solo string pieces, but the fugue of the C major Sonata is as powerful and magnificent a conception. The fugal movements of the solo suites for cello are also of extreme complexity and difficulty. As one of the outstanding performers of the day, Bach clearly enjoyed an occasional workout. There are bursts of exhilarating virtuosity in his music, as in the clavier cadenza of the D major *Brandenburg* Concerto. And many of his organ works are finger-twisters and foot-tanglers. "There!" one can imagine Bach saying, after the conclusion of the D major Prelude and Fugue for organ. "Beat *that!*"

Bach was the one who, once and for all, established the well-tempered scale used today. Composers had been working in that direction, but it remained for Bach to demonstrate the practicality and, indeed, inevitability of the system. Up to his time, mean-tone temperament was in general use, which meant half tones of different sizes. The problem was how to arrange the tones within the octave so that the scale would have consistent harmonic ratios from tone to tone. In mean-tone temperament, the ratios of the scale in any given key could be worked out, but what was good for, say, C major was not good for F minor. The German theoretician and writer on music, Friedrich Wilhelm Marpurg (who lived in Bach's time), put it this way: "Three scales were made ugly in order to make one beautiful." Or, in the words of the British musicologist, Percy A. Scholes, "It is not possible to tune any keyed instrument *perfectly* for more than one key; if you tune it correctly for key C, the moment you play in another key some of the notes will be out of tune. On the mean-tone temperament just a single key was perfect, but, by a compromise, a certain number of keys were made near enough perfect for the ear to tolerate them, the rest being outside the pale." The compromise mentioned by Scholes involved raising or lowering individual pitches of the scale so that several keys could be accommodated. But, as Scholes points out, certain keys were so outside the mean-tone patterns that they could not be used. In early music such common keys as B major or C sharp minor are very seldom found—except in Bach. Following the lead suggested in Andreas Werckmeister's *Musical Temperament* (1691), Bach divided the octave into twelve approximately even tones. No one key was perfect in this kind of compromise, and there were slight imperfections in all keys, but those were small enough for the ear to tolerate. Bach's system made it practicable to modulate into any other key, and any of the twelve keys could serve as the tonic. He composed the *Well-Tempered Clavier* as an illustration of what could be done with this kind of tuning. The two books of the *Well-Tempered Clavier* contain forty-eight preludes and fugues, two each in all of the major and minor keys.

In recent years a good deal has been written about Bach's use of musical symbolism. Albert Schweitzer was one of the first proponents of the idea. He maintained that not only was Bach essentially a painter in tones, but also that Bach as often as not incorporated into his music specific motives of terror, grief, hope, weariness, and so on. Schweitzer insisted that it is impossible to interpret a Bach work unless the meaning of the motive is known. Most of Schweitzer's ideas along this line are discounted today, though it is still a parlor game among a handful of Bach specialists to read ecclesiastical and even numerical symbolism into Bach's music. The substitution of numbers for the letters of the alphabet seems to have been an occasional practice in Bach's day. Thus, to quote from Karl Geiringer's 1966 biography of Bach, "14, for instance, is the number symbolizing Bach [B=2, A=1, C=3, H=8]; inverted, it turns into 41, which stands for J. S. Bach, as J is the ninth, S the eighteenth letter, and 9 plus 18 plus 14 makes 41. In Bach's very last chorale arrangement this symbolic method is significantly used."

The temptation is great to say that if this was indeed Bach's method, the less Bach he. Fortunately, his music can be enjoyed without such artificial props, stimulating as such exercises may be to a certain kind of mind. There is no music in the literature that has Bach's kind of *rightness*, of inevitability, of intelligence, of logically organized sequences of notes. And there is scarcely any music by any major composer that is so tied up with religion, specifically, Lutheranism. Bach honestly believed that music was an expression of divinity. He began his scores of sacred music with JJ (*Jesu Juva*, "Jesus, help") and ended with SDG (*Soli Deo Gloria*, "To God alone the Glory"). Unconvincing attempts have been made by one or two scholars to prove that Bach was not really a religious composer. It is hard to follow the reasoning. Bach composed a great deal of church music (including much that has been lost), and in the motets and cantatas, the masses and passions, there is so religious a feeling that the music cannot fully be understood except by one whose religious roots, feeling, and very background run closely parallel to Bach's. In the appreciation of any art, the responder's identification with the mental processes of the composer is critical: the closer the identification, the greater the appreciation. Any of us can get the obvious message of *Christ lag in Todesbanden* or the B minor Mass. But the niceties and refinements of the music in relation to the spiritual message and the actual religious service that it represents are fully open only to those who can identify with the church and the spiritual life of Bach's day. Nor are these remarks necessarily confined to Bach's church music. Certainly a work like the *Art of Fugue* means more to one who has himself struggled with counterpoint, and thus is in a position to recognize the diabolically ingenious way Bach solved the problems, than it means to a listener who cannot even read music. But at least the secular music poses fewer difficulties. It is abstract, and following the lines of Bach's thought, sharing in his mental processes, is one of the intellectual and emotional treats music has to offer.

One of the great problems posed by Bach's music in the twentieth century involves matters of performance practice. Obviously, it is impossible to re-create a performance that would duplicate one in Bach's day. Too many factors have changed. And every age has its own performance style. The romantics, as they did in everything, took a very free attitude toward Bach, and played him in their image. Romantic performance practice has extended into our own day, and it has been only within the last few decades that serious attempts have been made to come to grips with the problem. Musicians, thanks to intense musicological research, now know much more than previous generations did about the salient points of Bach's style in performance. Not enough, however, is known. As a corrective to romantic performance practice, a generation of young artists grew up playing, singing, and conducting Bach with mechanical rigidity, using approved editions and relatively small forces in an attempt to be "authentic." The trouble has been that the music then sounds sterile—a Bach robbed of humanity, of grace, of style, of line. If we know one thing about Bach, it is that he was a passionate man and a passionate performer. He undoubtedly played and conducted his own music with infinitely more dash, freedom, and spontaneity than modern performance practice will admit. Bach himself told a pupil, one Johann Gotthilf Ziegler, that an organist should not merely play the notes. He should express the "affect," the meaning, the emotional significance of the piece. By a strange irony, it might eventually turn out that the derided romantics, even though lacking today's scholarship, were instinctively closer to the essential Bach style than the severe, note-perfect, and literal musicians of today.

After Bach's death, most of his music was shelved, though he himself and a handful of his scores were not forgotten. It seems to be an article of faith among Bach biographers that he was neglected for some seventy-five years. That simply is not true. For one thing, his sons, who had a rather ambivalent attitude toward their father (and toward his second wife, too; they let Anna Magdalena all but starve, and she was buried in a pauper's grave), nevertheless did something to propagandize his music. Johann Christian may have once referred to his father as "the old perruque;" but it was Johann Christian who introduced Bach's music to many of the performers of the day. Carl Philipp Emanuel, who seems to have been a little embarrassed by the old-fashioned quality of Bach's music, and who disposed of the plates of the *Art of Fugue*, nevertheless supplied invaluable material to Johann Nicolaus Forkel, Bach's first biographer (1802).

Indeed, all of Bach's sons spread his name and fame. They all took up music, as was expected. "All born musicians," the proud father said of his boys. But several died young and another was feeble-minded. Four, however, went on to important careers.

Wilhelm Friedemann (1710–1784) went to Halle, then started a wandering life, and finally settled in Berlin. He was eccentric and ill-adjusted and, it is believed, a drunkard. He was very talented, and his father's pride, but he lived an unfulfilled life. Carl Philipp Emanuel (1714–1788) was at the court of Frederick the Great for twenty-eight years, achieving great fame—more than his father ever did—as keyboard player, composer, and teacher. In 1768 he succeeded Telemann in Hamburg. As a composer, Carl Philipp Emanuel represented the new style that was sweeping Europe—the elegant, noncontrapuntal *style galant* that was developed by the Mannheim composers and led into Haydn and Mozart. One curious thing about C. P. E. Bach: he could not play the violin because he was left-handed. Johann Christoph Bach (1732–1795), known as the Bückeburg Bach, served in that city from the age of eighteen until his death, carrying on his father's tradition. Finally, there was Johann Christian (1735–1782), the London Bach, who was one of the few traveling members of the family. He went to Italy, where he called himself Giovanni Bach, and he became a Catholic. His father would not have liked that. Then, in 1762, he went to England, where he was known as John Bach. A big social and artistic success, he composed operas, gave piano recitals and conducted orchestras, taught, was mentor to the young Mozart when the child visited London, went bankrupt and died leaving many debts. He, too, represented the *style galant*.

These four sons of Bach, two of them known all over Europe, helped keep old Bach's memory alive. Several things should be kept in mind when discussing Bach's reputation after his death. The institution of the public concert was in its infancy. When concerts *were* given, at whatever kind of hall could be pressed into service (a nobleman's salon, or a dance hall, or an opera house, or whatever, for there were almost no concert halls as such), it was generally through the efforts of a composer who wanted to introduce his own music. The idea of a concert artist playing other men's music was still in the future. Music until the romantic period was very much a contemporary art, concerned primarily with what was going on, not with what had been. Little interest was paid to music of the past. In any case, it was extremely difficult to hear, or to study, music of the past. Scores were hard to find, performances all but nonexistent.

Yet so great was the power of Bach's music that it remained known to many professional musicians. It even came to pass that Bach's music broke tradition by remaining in the repertory at Leipzig. Johann Friedrich Doles, Bach's pupil and successor as the cantor at St. Thomas, from 1756 to 1789, continued to perform Bach's music at the services. Doles also acquainted Mozart with some Bach scores, and Mozart was entranced. He studied them, arranged some of the music, and was strongly influenced by Bachian counterpoint. Baron Gottfried van Swieten in Vienna was the leader of something that amounted to a Bach cult. He showed Bach scores to Mozart and Haydn, and had musicales at which Bach's music was played. Haydn was well acquainted with the *Well-Tempered Clavier* and the B minor Mass, owning the printed music of both. Beethoven was brought up on the *Well-Tempered Clavier*. The English organist and composer Samuel Wesley (1766–1837), long before Mendelssohn revived the *St. Matthew Passion*, was studying, playing, and preaching Bach—and Wesley had been introduced to Bach by a group of dedicated amateurs and professionals. Johann Baptist Cramer (1771–1858), composer and pianist, was playing Bach in public before 1800, and was followed by such other pianists as Alexander Boëly, Joseph Lipavsky, and John Field. Anybody who takes the trouble to go through European musical periodicals and books of the late eighteenth and early nineteenth centuries can dig out innumerable references to "the famous Bach." Many musical histories state that Bach was forgotten after his death, and not rediscovered until the Mendelssohn *St. Matthew* revival of 1829. But that is a myth. Bach most definitely was not forgotten. Indeed, he bulked large. Not so large, perhaps, as Handel, or Johann Adolf Hasse (1699–1783), the popular composer of now-forgotten operas, but large; and the myth of his "total neglect" should be laid to rest.

With Bach's sons, the great stream exhausted itself. The last male Bach descended directly from Johann Sebastian was Wilhelm Friedrich Ernst (1759–1845), a grandson through the Bückeburg Bach. The strain is still alive. Bachs of the Meiningen and Ohrdruf branches are in existence today, and as late as 1937 there was started a *Bach'ser Familienverband für Thüringen*—the Bach Family Association for Thuringia. But none of the twentieth-century Bachs is a professional musician.

Zenger Collection, Municipal Archive, Augsburg

St. Thomas Church in Leipzig, where Bach worked from 1723
to the end of his life

2

Composer and Impresario

GEORGE FRIDERIC HANDEL

Where Bach was a provincial, a German who never left Germany, his great contemporary George Frideric Handel (so he spelled his name in England, where he spent most of his life) was a cosmopolite, a man of the world, an independent figure, one of the first great composers to be also a business man of music. George Frideric Handel: a big man and a lusty one; a naturalized British subject who spoke English with a heavy accent; a man with an explosive temperament and withal a sweet-tempered and even generous philanthropist; a man who made and lost fortunes in his musical enterprises; the owner of a good art collection, including some Rembrandt paintings; one of the greatest organists and harpsichord players of his day; a man with a simple, uncomplicated faith and an equally simple and uncomplicated view toward life.

Handel first came to London in 1710 and made a shattering impact upon the city. That was no easy thing to do in those days. What an age it was! The London of Handel's day had a collection of wits, litterateurs, eccentrics, dandies, perverts, poets, essayists, politicians, and courtiers that made it one of the great intellectual centers of Europe. It was a closed society and a gossipy one. John Gay would write to Alexander Pope, who would relay the information to Dr. Arbuthnot, who would pass it on to Jonathan Swift. Joseph Addison and Richard Steele were delighting London with their *Tatler* and *Spectator* papers. Sir Isaac Newton, having overturned many mathematical concepts and introduced new ones that would keep scientists busy for generations, was brooding about religion. The wits were running all over London, maliciously telling stories about one another. There were no secrets, especially at court; and when Lord Hervey got into one of his frequent scandals, or when one of the Duchess of Queensbury's ladies-in-waiting flirted with a member of the royal family, or when Lord S. was observed slipping from Lady B.'s boudoir, tongues started to wag simultaneously all over London. But the wits did not claim to be retailing gossip.

Never that, they said, licking their lips. As Swift once wrote to Sir Charles Wogan, "You see, Pope, Gay and I use all our endeavours to make folks merry and wise, and profess to have no enemies except knaves and fools."

Into this society, Handel, the burly stranger from Saxony, simply erupted. Domineering, tactless, he immediately started to make enemies, beginning with Addison and Steele. Addison's position was not exactly disinterested. Shortly before the arrival of Handel, Addison had written a libretto that was set to music by a nonentity named Thomas Clayton. The opera was named *Rosamond,* and seldom has the lyric stage given birth to such a failure. Addison, who had hoped to establish a school of opera-in-English, was still smarting, and when that foreigner Handel made his debut with enormous success, and with an Italian libretto, Addison unleashed his heaviest artillery. The *Spectator* papers dealing with Italian opera are still among the funniest and most venomous contributions to the British polemic style.

Handel set the pace, and for years turned out Italian opera after Italian opera. No composer could stand up against him for very long. Handel made Italian opera the rage; and, as a by-product, he made a great deal of money. The impact was overwhelming. Gay wrote about the fad to Swift, with great disgust: "There is nobody allowed to say *I sing* but an eunuch or an Italian woman. Every body is grown now as great a judge of singing as they were in your time of poetry; and folks, that could not distinguish one tune from another, now daily dispute about the different stiles of Handel, Bononcini and Attilio. . . . In London and Westminster, in all polite conversations, Senesino is daily voted to be the greatest man that ever lived." Senesino, born Francesco Bernardi, was one of the important castrato singers active in London. Of the castratos, more later.

The public, and society, took to Handelian opera, but there were fearsome attacks upon him in the press. Nevertheless, by and large, it was believed by most cultivated Englishmen—and Europeans, too—that Handel was the greatest musician who ever lived. He did not suffer from lack of appreciation in his own time. "Hendel from Hanover, a man of the vastest genius and skill in music that perhaps has lived since Orpheus." That was the entry of Viscount Percival in his diary of August 31, 1731. (Percival, like many in that free and permissive orthographic day, spelled words as they were pronounced. Handel dropped the umlaut from his name after he settled in England, but the pronunciation remained "Hendel," and so it was frequently spelled.) Antoine Prévost, he who wrote *Manon Lescaut,* gave an estimate of Handel in his *Le Pour et Contre* (1733): "Never has perfection in any art been combined in the same man with such fertility of production." These reactions of Percival and Prévost were typical. Few composers in history have been so eulogized in their own time, and few were more written about.

And of none of the famous composers in history, except Franz Schubert, have we such scant personal information. There is an enormous amount of material *about* Handel, as anybody can see glancing through Otto Erich Deutsch's massive *Handel: A Documentary Biography*. But no composer has been so secretive about himself. Gaps exist in the Handel chronology, especially during the years he spent in Italy. We know how much money he made, we know how his music was received throughout his life, but we know almost nothing about what he thought. The few Handel letters that have come down to us are formal, stilted affairs in which he reveals nothing about his personal life. For a man so much in the public eye—as composer, as impresario, as executant, as one of the more colorful figures in a colorful period—this cannot be entirely accidental. It is almost as though the man had some secret to hide. Handel guarded his privacy and went out of his way to keep his public life divorced from his private life.

The main contemporary source of information about him comes from the biography by the Reverend John Mainwaring. This was published in 1760, the year after Handel's death, and was the first biography ever written about a musician. That alone is extraordinary testimony to Handel's fame. (Bach's first biography came in 1802, fifty-two years after his death.) But Mainwaring never even knew Handel. He got much of his information from Handel's secretary, John Christopher Smith (born Johann Christoph Schmidt), and the book is full of inaccuracies. Much Handel material can be found in Charles Burney's *A General History of Music* (1776–1789), which has a sketch of the composer's life and a good deal of miscellaneous information. Burney at least knew Handel, and has given a physical description that can be accepted with confidence. Handel, he says, was large, corpulent (Sir John Hawkins, another British writer on music, says that Handel's thick legs were bowed), unwieldy in his motions, and "his general look was somewhat heavy and sour; but when he *did* smile, it was his sire the sun bursting out of a black cloud. . . He was impetuous, rough, and peremptory in his manners and conversation, but totally devoid of ill-nature or malevolence." That appears to be a fair judgment. The great composer could go into terrible rages, but there never was any malice in him, and his dealings with all people were invariably honest. Burney says that Handel had "a natural propensity to wit and humor," and was a good raconteur even with his heavily accented English. "Had he been as great a master of the English language as Swift, his *bons mots* would have been as frequent, and somewhat of the same kind." Johann Mattheson, the then-famous composer who as a young man had been very close to Handel in Hamburg, attests to Handel's wry sense of humor. Handel "behaved as if he could not count to five. . . . He had a dry way of making the most serious people laugh, without laughing himself." He retained his sense of proportion and could even joke about the affliction that cursed his late years. During his blindness—he lost his sight in 1752, though that did not stop him from composing and playing the organ—his surgeon, Samuel Sharp, suggested that John Stanley participate in one of the Handel concerts. Stanley was a famous blind organist. Handel is supposed to have burst out in a roar of laughter. "Mr. Sharp, have you never read the Scriptures? Do you not remember, if the blind lead the blind, they both fall into the ditch?"

Much traveled, in contact with many great men of the day, Handel must have been a well-rounded personality. It is known that he was a connoisseur of painting. He studied at the University of Halle, which means that he must have received a good humanistic education. But because of his secretiveness, many guesses have to be made about the breadth of his culture. Also guesses are anything that has to do with his sex life. He never married, and whatever associations he had with women he kept to himself. In his early days there were vague rumors about his liaisons with Italian singers. In a copy of the Mainwaring biography is a scribbled bit of marginalia: "G. F. Handel . . . scorned the advice of any but the Woman he loved, but his Amours were rather of short duration, and always within the pale of his own profession." The handwriting is believed to be that of George III.

Judging from his activities, Handel was a gambler, as all impresarios must be. His temper was legendary, especially with singers who crossed him. The most famous occurrence along that line came when the soprano Francesca Cuzzoni refused to sing an aria—*Falsa immagine* from *Ottone*—as written. Handel lost control, grabbed her and made as if to throw her out of the window, bellowing meanwhile: "Madame, I know you are a true she-devil, but I will show you that I am Beelzebub, the chief devil."

What else? He was religious, but not fanatically so, and he told Hawkins of his delight at setting the Scriptures to music. He was an enormous eater, and the famous caricature by Joseph Goupy shows him with the face of a pig, seated on a wine barrel, surrounded by food. (For this it seems that Handel cut Goupy out of his will.) He moved comfortably in the highest society. He was not one of those art-for-art's-sake musicians (that was, in any case, almost unheard-of in Handel's day). He could easily be persuaded to entertain. There is the charming account of a party, on April 12, 1734, which he attended. Lord and Lady Rich were there, and Lord Shaftesbury, and Lord and Lady Hanmer, and the Percivals. Handel played the harpsichord, accompanied amateur singers, and was at the keyboard from 7 to 11, enjoying himself immensely.

Handel was born in Halle on February 23, 1685, the year Bach was born. Little is known about his boyhood, though by the age of ten he was playing the organ well enough to attract the attention of Duke Johann Adolf of Weissenfels. Handel was sent to study with Friedrich Zachow, organist at the Lutheran church at Halle. If Handel had any teacher other than Zachow, he is not known. By 1702, Handel was organist at the cathedral. But he was not cut out to be a church organist. From the very beginning he was attracted to the theater, and in 1703 he went to Hamburg, one of the busiest and most famous opera centers in Europe. It was there that he made friends with the young German composer Johann Mattheson (1681–1764), and it was there that he started composing in earnest. It was there, too, that his life almost came to an end. Mattheson was as strong-minded and stubborn as Handel, and the two young men got into an argument. *Cleopatra*, an opera by Mattheson, was being produced in Hamburg. In addition, Mattheson sang one of the leading roles. Then, presumably to show his versatility, he descended into the orchestra, where Handel was presiding at the harpsichord, and attempted to relieve him of that task. Handel was not the kind of young man who could be pushed aside. There were words, and the two hotheads marched out and drew their swords. Mattheson lunged at Handel, and the sword broke on a metal button of his opponent's coat. A half-inch in any other direction . . . The two made up, and Mattheson even took the tenor lead in Handel's first opera, *Almira*, composed in 1707.

That same year, 1707, Handel went to Rome. He spent the next three years in Italy, where he was called *Il Sassone*—the Saxon—making a big impression there, as he did everywhere. Very little is known about this Italian sojourn. There are anecdotes. Legend has it that he had a harpsichord and organ duel with Domenico Scarlatti, his exact contemporary (Scarlatti also was born in 1685) and the composer of those remarkable keyboard sonatas or "exercises." Scarlatti composed over 550 of these short, glinting masterpieces. The Handel-Scarlatti encounter took place in the house of Cardinal Ottoboni. As harpsichordists, both were declared equal. As organist, Handel won easily. "Scarlatti," says Mainwaring, "himself declared the superiority of his antagonist, and owned ingenuously, that till he had heard him on this instrument, he had no conception of its powers." Something has gone out of musical life with the disappearance of those duels—the appearance on one program of two major instrumentalists who would try to play each other under the table. Mozart and Clementi fought to a draw before the King of Prussia. Beethoven demolished the Abbé Gelinek and anybody else who came his way. Liszt and Thalberg had it out at the salon of Princess Belgiojoso in Paris.

Another anecdote involves the great violinist-composer Arcangelo Corelli. A work by Handel was being played, and Corelli was having trouble in the high positions. Handel, always impulsive, snatched the violin from the hands of the greatest virtuoso in Europe and demonstrated how the passage should go. Corelli, a sweet-tempered and generous man, took no offense. "My dear Saxon, this is music in the French style, of which I have no knowledge." The point is that Handel achieved the respect of all musicians with whom he came into contact. He met everybody, studied everything, and was influenced by the sunny flow of Italian melody. The music of Alessandro Scarlatti (1660–1725), Domenico's father, made a particular impression on him.

From Italy, Handel went to Hanover in 1710 as court musician to the Elector. Later that year he went on leave of absence to England, where Italian opera was the most fashionable of musical entertainments, and where the castrato singers were astonishing everybody with their vocal power and brilliance. Handel composed an opera for the English. It was named *Rinaldo,* was produced in 1711, and was a tremendous success. He went back to Hanover, and it is easy to guess what went on in his mind: a sleepy little court, with little opportunity, versus the great city of London and the chance to become famous and wealthy. So in 1712, Handel obtained permission to go back to England, with the proviso that he return within a reasonable time. In this case, a reasonable time was forever. On his arrival in England he composed an opera, *Il Pastor Fido,* and, soon after, a grand official piece, the *Utrecht Te Deum,* celebrating the Peace of Utrecht. He also wrote a birthday piece for Queen Anne, who settled upon him a yearly pension of £200. Two years had passed, and Handel definitely was absent without leave from the Hanover court. He may or may not have had thoughts of going back. But matters were taken out of his hands when Queen Anne died in 1714. His employer, the Elector of Hanover, succeeded Anne as George I of England. Handel must have spent some uneasy hours wondering what would happen to him.

Nothing did happen. Before long, he was back in George's favor, with a doubled pension. There is a pleasant story, now considered apocryphal, that Handel was restored to the royal confidence through his *Water Music.* As the story goes, the King so admired the score, which was played in 1717 on the occasion of a royal barge trip on the Thames, that a reconciliation immediately took place. There was such a trip, and it is a matter of record that a suite of Handel's music was played during the festivities. And the *Daily Courant* of July 19, 1717, states that George liked the music so well "that he caus'd it to be plaid over three times in going and returning." Unfortunately for the pleasant legend, however, the reconciliation appears to have taken place before 1717.

In London, mentally at ease now that his relations with the King were established, Handel began his long series of operas, becoming as much tangled up in the economic and producing end as in the creative side. He established permanent liaisons with British nobility, especially with Lord Burlington and the Duke of Chandos. For a time he lived in Burlington's great house in Piccadilly, a fact of which John Gay took careful note. The

British wits always were greatly interested in the sponsorship any creative figure enjoyed. Burlington House was an artistic and literary center, and Gay commemorated it in his *Trivia*.

> Yet *Burlington's* fair Palace still remains;
> Beauty within, without Proportion reigns
> There *Hendel* strikes the Strings, the melting Strain
> Transports the Soul, and thrills through ev'ry Vein

Handel plunged into London's social life, aided not only by the £400 pension from George I but by an additional £200 from the Princess of Wales. He headed opera companies that were underwritten by the nobility, and went to Europe to search for singers. In the meantime, a stream of operas was flowing from his pen: *Il Pastor Fido* (1712), *Teseo* (1712), *Silla* (1718), *Radamisto* (1720), *Floridante* (1721), *Ottone* (1723), *Giulio Cesare* (1724), *Tamerlano* (1724), and *Serse* (1738), among others. He turned these out with amazing speed. The Italian librettist, Giacomo Rossi, was amazed at the way Handel dashed off the music for *Rinaldo* in 1711. "Mr. Hendel, the Orpheus of our century, while composing the music, scarcely gave me time to write, and to my great wonder I saw an entire opera put to music by that surprising genius, with the greatest degree of perfection, in only two weeks." What Rossi did not know was that Handel used for *Rinaldo* some music he had previously written for another opera. But Handel was a very, very fast workman. Before he was through, he was to compose over forty operas. All were in Italian, and all were what today is called baroque opera.

Handelian baroque opera was as strict a form as such later art forms as the sonata and the cowboy film. It was marked by certain conventions. Almost always the libretto was based on a classical or mythological subject. Characters in Handel operas sport names like Bradamante, Oronte, Melissa, Morgana, Alcina. They are as artificial as their names. Little attempt at characterization was made by librettists of baroque opera. Handel's music to these librettos may be gay, or martial, or heartbreaking in its pathos, but it is music that more often defines mood than character. The plots had almost no action, and baroque opera has been described as a concert in costume. Handel's operas were no exception. Dramatically they are close to being entirely static.

Basic to the operas was the *da capo* aria. In the *da capo* aria the singer goes through all of the musical material and then returns to the first section. On the return the singer was expected to show off his bag of vocal tricks, embellishing, adorning, and ornamenting the melody. Handelian opera is largely a succession of *da capo* arias, with a few duets and occasional larger ensembles thrown in. Choruses and orchestral interludes were few. One other aspect of baroque opera might be noted—the behavior of the audience. Opera-going in Handel's day was not the sedate experience it is today. People went to the opera to be seen, and to follow the vocal gyrations of a favorite singer. At performances they would play cards, chat, move around, eat oranges and nuts, spit freely, hiss and yowl at a singer they did not like. The singers themselves would go out of character, greeting friends in the boxes, or talking to one another while they were not singing. Nobody on stage pretended to act.

For this kind of opera, spectacular singing was needed. Handel had those singers, and vocal art has been in decline ever since the disappearance of the castratos. A great castrato was the vocal wonder of all time: a singing machine, virtually a musical instrument. Even before Handel's time the castratos were idols. They were spoiled, pampered figures of great wealth and vanity, and even greater eccentricity. They were the first performers in musical history to achieve star status.

Castratos are what the name implies—castrated males. They were known to antiquity, and reappeared in the service of the popes in the twelfth century. Women's voices had been banished from the church, and the castratos replaced them. The operation took place before puberty. After years of rigorous training, the singers were sent into the service of the church, having female voices and male lungs. Such was the accomplishment of their singing that they began to appear in public, outside of the church. Baldassare Ferri (1610–1680) was the first of the stars. They could do incredible tricks. Some of them had ranges of *four* octaves, up to the A or even B above high C in full voice. And those were voices that lasted. Caffarelli sounded youthful at seventy. Orsini caused a furor with his beautiful singing in Prague when he was seventy-three, and ten years later was singing before Maria Theresa. Bannieri, who died at the age of 102, was singing at the age of ninety-seven. Often these singers were physical freaks, oversized, fat, with barrel chests and yet with skinny arms and legs. They had a sexless kind of woman's voice, but from all reports the sound they produced was of exceptional sweetness. One of their vocal tricks, and one that astounded audiences every time, was their ability to hold a tone. Some of them could sustain a note for well over a minute, and part of the fun of going to the opera in those days was to cheer an encounter between a castrato and a trumpeter or flutist. All would turn blue in the face, holding on to a single note, but the castrato always won. It is related of the young Farinelli that an oboe player once held on to a note, in unison with the singer, much longer than he had done at rehearsal. Farinelli, still singing, let him run out of breath, after which Farinelli continued on and on, still in the same breath. While the audience sat transfixed, waiting for him to explode, Farinelli added a difficult extempore cadenza; and not until then did he have to pause for air.

The great period of castrato singing was from about 1720 to 1790, a period dominated by such singers as Nicolo Grimaldi (called Nicolini), Francesco Bernardi (Senesino), Gaetano Maiorano (Caffarelli), and the greatest of all, Carlo Broschi (Farinelli). All flourished within the period of about a hundred years—from 1673, when Nicolini was born, to 1783, when Caffarelli died. The last of the operatic castratos was Giovanni Battista Vellutti, for whom Meyerbeer wrote a part in *Il Crociato in Egitto* (1824). The breed became extinct, as far as is known, with the death of Alessandro Moreschi (1858–1922). Moreschi was a member of the Sistine Chapel Chorus and actually made a few phonograph records in the first decade of the twentieth century. The sound on those records makes one shiver. The voice has a timbre like that of an alto who is neither male nor female, and with a strange, sad, pleading quality.

What the castrato stood for, vocally, was control and flexibility. A glance at the score of any Handel opera reveals coloratura passages of running thirty-second notes that seem to continue forever without giving the singer a chance to take a breath. The parts do not run especially high, and in any case, audiences of the day did not care for high notes. The tenor's high C is a romantic invention. As a matter of fact, the starring tenor was largely a romantic invention. In baroque opera, tenors sing secondary roles. It is true that most of the castratos could easily take a high C, and if the flutist-composer Johann Quantz (1697–1773) is to be believed, Farinelli could take an F above high C in full voice. But the castratos did not normally go in for such effects. What they were proud of was their incredible breath control and the ability to negotiate any kind of complicated figuration without a break in register or any evidence of vocal strain.

The women singers of Handel's day also had this ability. Most famous were Francesca Cuzzoni and Faustina Bordoni. Both sang in Handel operas in London, often in the same cast. Cuzzoni was short, fat, ugly, ill-tempered, and no actress at all, just as the castratos tended to be tall, fat, ungainly (the absence of secondary sex characteristics prevented the growth of their beards and often gave them the breasts of a woman), and were no actors at all. Bordoni, on the other hand, was attractive and, for the day, an accomplished actress. Naturally, the two women hated one another, and things came to a climax on June 6, 1727, with a performance of Bononcini's *Astianatte*. Spurred by their supporters in the audience (Bordoni was a favorite of the Burlington faction, and Cuzzoni's admirers were part of Lady Pembroke's circle), the two women made for each other with curved talons, and a great fight ensued, complete with screams and hair-pulling. The newspapers had a great time with it, and a pamphlet was published giving a blow-by-blow report of the "full and true Account of a most horrible and bloody Battle between Madame Faustina and Madame Cuzzoni." The pamphlet proposed that the two ladies fight it out in public. Handel happened to be the impresario that immortal evening. He roared that Cuzzoni was a she-devil, that Faustina was "Beelzebub's spoiled child," and that both were hussies.

Audiences in Handel's day were willing to accept the castrato and the conventions of baroque opera. Later audiences did not. Today, no singer could begin to handle the vocal writing as did the singers of Handel's day, nor can the impossibly stilted librettos compensate for the wonderful music. Highly stylized productions are necessary. Some scholars suggest that the castrato roles be transferred to baritones or basses. In any case, the vocal line has to be simplified today, and much of the *raison d'être* of Handelian opera is thus lost. It can still give pleasure, as revivals of *Julius Caesar* and *Alcina,* among others, have shown, but these modern productions can only be called adaptations of the original.

A surprisingly large part of some Handel operas is not original music. Audiences of Handel's day were prepared to accept his appropriations of other men's music. This always has been a touchy subject in Handel biography, and writers have turned themselves inside out trying to explain it, or apologize for it. To put it bluntly, Handel was a plagiarist, and was known as such in his own day. Early in his career he was drawing upon the music of such composers as Keiser, Graun, and Urio and passing it off as his own. From 1737, the year he became ill, Handel more and more drew on the music of other men. His contemporaries took a lenient view of this practice. The Abbé Prévost wrote in 1733: "Some critics, however, accuse him of having borrowed the matter of many beautiful things from Lully, especially from our French cantatas, which he has the skill, so they say, to disguise in the Italian style. But the crime would be venial, were it certain." One charitable explanation would be that the busy Handel, faced with the administration of an opera house, faced with the personality clashes of his singers, faced with the necessity of turning out new operas, faced with the necessity of writing occasional pieces for the court, simply did not have the time to do everything. So he took other material, generally improving it in the process, and passed it off as his own. A list of Handel plagiarisms would be appallingly large. (Bach rewrote other men's music, but these works were in the nature of adaptations or arrangements, and there is no evidence that Bach ever tried to profit from material not his own. Gluck was a self-plagiarist who plundered his own music rather than the music of other men.)

By the late 1720's, the craze in London for Italian opera began to fall off, and was almost killed by the success of *The Beggar's Opera*—a ballad opera sung in English, full of satire addressed against the Walpole administration. *The Beggar's Opera,* with words by John Gay and music arranged by John Christopher Pepusch (1667–1752), has had a more consistent life than any Handel opera, and has never been out of the repertoire since its premiere in

1728. It is an authentic minor masterpiece. It also contributed to the bankruptcy of Handel's Italian opera company. But Handel had made a great deal of money in the enterprise and was able to put £10,000 of his own funds into his next operatic venture at the King's Theater—a venture that lasted until 1737. It might have lasted longer had not a rival opera company been established at Lincoln's Inn Fields. London was not big enough to support two houses, and this time Handel lost a great deal of money.

Italian opera seemed dead, and Handel turned to something else—oratorio in English. He found a ready public for this. He composed *Saul* in 1738, *Israel in Egypt* in 1739, *Messiah* in 1741. In all he composed close to twenty oratorios, ending the great series with *Jephtha* in 1752. Had not total blindness set in by 1751 he doubtless would have composed many more. Recent years have seen an increasing interest in the Handel oratorios, but most of them still remain unknown.

Why did Handel turn to the oratorio? Older biographers liked to believe that after a stroke and some mental disturbance in 1737, Handel became very religious. The truth is probably more mundane. He was a professional composer largely on his own. He was a businessman-composer. If Italian opera was played out, he would turn to something else. Discovering that audiences would flock to his oratorios, he supplied oratorios. Some Handel scholars, notably Paul Henry Lang, insist that the oratorios are not devotional religious works at all; that they are dramatic works on Biblical subjects, completely divorced from the church. In any case, Handel found that composing oratorios was a most profitable enterprise. He was, after all, one of London's most famous figures, and also extremely popular as a performer. So he saw to it that he appeared as organ soloist on every one of his oratorio presentations, playing a concerto or two as added lure. His blindness aroused pity, and that too helped. When *Samson* was presented, and tenor John Beard stood next to the blind composer to sing:

> Total eclipse—no sun; no moon.
> All dark, amid the blaze of noon

there must have been an audible gulp from the audience.

The neglect today of most of Handel's operas and oratorios—indeed, of most of his music except for *Messiah*—raises some perplexing questions. In his own time Handel was considered one of the greatest musicians who ever lived, and posterity has seen no reason to change the opinion. His reputation in England immediately after his death and during the nineteenth century remained constantly high, though it was primarily as a composer of oratorios that Handel was held in esteem. His powerful influence had a stifling effect on English music; and, indeed, not until the emergence of

41

Edward Elgar did England produce an internationally famous composer. Thanks to Handel, any British composer had to write elaborate choral pieces to prove himself, and, in effect, England went oratorio-crazy. The craze lasted to the end of the nineteenth century, prompting George Bernard Shaw to observe that "The British public takes a creepy kind of pleasure in Requiems." Choral music was considered the property of the people. Only a year after Handel's death a writer named William Mann was saying that village musical groups all over England "since the rage of oratorio has spread from the Capital to every Market Town in the Kingdom, can by no means be satisfied unless they introduce Chaunts, Services, and Anthems into their British Churches. . . ." A great bourgeois pall descended upon British music, and annual Handel festivals became almost a religious event. Whether or not Handel meant his oratorios as a religious exercise, they were taken as such by the public. The *Chester and North Wales Magazine* of April, 1813, had this to say: "The music of Handel is, indeed, admirably adapted to fill the mind with that sort of devotional rapture which, with the commemoration of our blessed Lord and Saviour, as men we ought to admire, and, as Christians, to *feel*." For well over 150 years, music in England was clutched by Handel's enormous fist, with only Mendelssohn making any other kind of impact. No British composer was strong enough to break free.

But after the turn of the twentieth century Handel's reputation declined even in England. Today it is amazing how little of his music actually is heard in public. His operas were forgotten in his own lifetime. Throughout the nineteenth and most of the twentieth century only one of his works achieved great popularity outside of England. That was, of course, *Messiah*. Seldom did an orchestra perform one of his concerti grossi, and seldom do they do so today. His most popular orchestral work, the *Water Music*, is most often heard in an arrangement by Hamilton Harty. Violinists, if they bother to play Handel at all, turn to such souped-up romanticisms as the Nachez arrangement of the A major or D major Sonatas. His organ concertos contain magnificent music, but almost never are they introduced into the concert hall. Most of his operas remain unknown. In Germany before World War II there was an attempt at a revival of the Handel operas, but the works did not take hold. In effect he turned into a one-work man, and it can be said with complete truth that almost everything by Handel except *Messiah* is out of the permanent repertory, with just a handful of works on the periphery. This is in sharp contrast to Bach, whose music is constantly being presented by orchestras, soloists, and choruses the world over.

The reason for Handel's neglect is hard to determine. Naturally, any performance of one of the operas does pose sizable problems. But no problems are involved with his oratorios, his concerti grossi, his harpsichord suites, his anthems, and cantatas. And this is great music. Through all of it breathes an unusual kind of vigor, breadth, confidence, and invention. It also has a peculiarly British quality, some of it derived from Henry Purcell. Handel's music is, in many ways, more accessible than Bach's: easier to understand, more direct in statement, less complex, more strongly melodic and virile. He did not have Bach's harmonic ingenuity or mastery of counterpoint—who had?—but Handel's counterpoint is nevertheless confident and secure. Handel biographers used to worry about Handel's counterpoint and would compare it unfavorably with Bach's. Comparison is meaningless, for the two composers were after different things. Bach *thought* contrapuntally, as naturally and inevitably as he breathed. Handel used a freer, less textbookish kind of counterpoint only as a tool, for certain effects.

Handel's music awaits rediscovery, a fact that would have come as an overwhelming surprise to his contemporaries. For *they* knew his worth, and Handel himself knew, even unto requesting that he be buried in Westminster Abbey. He died at the age of seventy-four on April 14, 1759, and there was real grief all over England. Handel became the subject of innumerable and elaborate obituaries, of which the one in the *Public Advertiser* of April 17 is typical, complete with acrostic on Handel's name:

> *H*e's gone, the Soul of Harmony is fled!
> *A*nd warbling Angels hover round him dead.
> *N*ever, no, never since the Tide of Time,
> *D*id music know a Genius so sublime!
> *E*ach mighty harmonist that's gone before,
> *L*essen'd to Mites when we his Works explore.

Reproduced by permission of S. Karger, Basel/New York
from Moses, P.J.: The psychology of the castrato
voice. Folia phoniat. 12:204–216 (1960).

CONTEMPORARY CARICATURES OF THE GREAT CASTRATO FARINELLI

❧ 3 ❧

Reformer of Opera

CHRISTOPH WILLIBALD GLUCK

Christoph Willibald Gluck's greatest claim to historical fame is as the man who initiated the first great reform in opera. Indeed, he is more famous as a reformer than as a composer. He wrote about fifty operas, of which only one —*Orfeo ed Euridice*—is steadily in the repertory, though *Alceste* and the two *Iphigénie* operas are revived once in a while. Working almost exclusively for the stage, he composed no instrumental music to speak of. Very few, if any, of his early operas have survived. Gluck was a late developer, and not until the age of forty-eight did he compose *Orfeo*. Up to then he had uncomplainingly written a long series of works that followed the established conventions. There was no hint that he was dissatisfied, no indication that in *Orfeo* he would come up with something so spectacularly and radically new.

Had he not met a librettist who stimulated him, Gluck in all probability would never have composed music on the level of an *Orfeo*, nor would he have reformed anything. Ranieri da Calzabigi (1714–1795) was to Gluck what Lorenzo da Ponte was to Mozart. And those two poets had a great deal in common. Both were adventurers, travelers, intriguers, politicians, and rather unscrupulous operators. Both were playwrights with a thorough understanding of, and appreciation for, the musical theater. Both turned up in Vienna just at the right moment. Calzabigi arrived there in 1761 and, in effect, handed Gluck his reform in the libretto of *Orfeo ed Euridice*. Gluck was generous enough to pay full tribute to his collaborator:

> If my music has had some success, I think it is my duty to recognize that I am beholden for it to him, since it was he who enabled me to develop the resources of my art. . . . No matter how much talent a composer has, he will never produce any but mediocre music unless the poet awakens in him that enthusiasm without which the productions of all the arts are but feeble and drooping.

44

Up to 1762, the year of the *Orfeo ed Euridice* premiere, Gluck had achieved some success, but was regarded as a good professional rather than as the (middle-aged) *enfant terrible* he turned out to be. He was born in Erasbach, in the Upper Palatinate, on July 2, 1714. His father was a forester in the service of great nobles, and the family was constantly on the move. Not much is known of Gluck's early years. He appears to have been well educated, and could play the violin, cello, and clavier. There is evidence that he went to the university in Prague. At the age of twenty-two he went to Vienna, and then to Milan, where he studied with the famous Giovanni Battista Sammartini (1701–1775). Italy claimed Gluck for eight years, and it was there, in 1741, that he composed his first opera, *Artaserse*. It was produced in December of that year in Milan, was a success, and was followed by a series of operas that today are completely forgotten. Even the scores of some of them are lost.

Like Handel, Gluck was a cosmopolite. He drifted to Paris for a brief stay, then to London in 1745. In London he composed two works for the Italian Opera, *La Caduta de' Giganti* and *Artamene*. These were commissioned by Lord Middlesex, proving that Gluck already must have enjoyed a certain amount of fame. In London, too, he made friends with Handel, who is reported to have jeered that his cook knew more counterpoint than Gluck. Considering that Handel's cook, Gustavus Waltz (or Walz), was a bass singer and a well-trained musician, there may have been some truth in the statement. But certainly Gluck, with his kind of training, must have been able to handle the intricacies of fugue. The point is that he was never particularly interested in counterpoint, which is different from saying that he could not manage it. Because Gluck thought homophonically (as opposed to contrapuntally), it has become an article of faith in certain circles that his technique was inferior. Thus Sir Donald Tovey, while pointing out Gluck's constant inspiration, insisted that "his routine technique was and remained poor." Which it was, when measured against the infinite resource of a Bach or Handel. But it wasn't in relation to what Gluck was trying to do. Gluck may or may not have heard Handel's gibe. Certain it is that they remained on good terms, and later in life Gluck had a painting of Handel in his bedroom. He would point to it, saying: "There is the portrait of the most inspired master of our art. When I open my eyes in the morning I look upon him with reverence and awe, and acknowledge him as such."

Gluck's peregrinations took him next to Hamburg, where he directed a touring Italian opera company that visited, among other cities, Leipzig and Dresden. In 1749 he was back in Vienna, and the following year he married the daughter of a rich merchant. From that time he never had to worry about money, which put him in a unique position among the composers of his day. The financial security doubtless accounted for his growing independence—some called it arrogance—and stubbornness. It is easy to tell the world to go to hell when you do not have to worry about the consequences. Gluck composed steadily, and also made a name as a conductor. In 1752 he was appointed kapellmeister of the Imperial Court in Vienna, and in 1754 the director of Prince Hildburghausen's orchestra. In 1756 he received a knighthood from Pope Benedict XIV. After that he insisted upon being called Ritter von Gluck or, in France, the Chevalier Gluck. During these years he composed a series of operas completely forgotten today. They sport such names as *Ezio, Issipile, Le Cinesi, La Dansa,* and *Antigono.*

If his acquaintance with Calzabigi sparked his reform, it can also be said that reform was in the air. Opera had become sheer formula, solidified on the one side by the librettos of Metastasio and disintegrated on the other by the antics of the singers. Pietro Metastasio (1698–1782) was a writer who was especially famous in musical circles for his twenty-seven *drammi per musica.* Most of these were written while he was the Imperial Court Poet of Vienna, a position he held from 1730 until his death. These twenty-seven musical dramas were set by eighteenth-century composers over *a thousand* times. Some of them were so highly regarded that they were set by as many as seventy different composers. No wonder audiences would attend a new opera with the feeling that they had seen it all before. The Metastasian librettos were based on mythology and ancient history, had many characters, and were carefully put together. Tovey describes them as well-constructed and logical, "a very rational musical scheme, according to which each situation was arrived at by a natural and smooth progress of dialogue and action, in order to be marked at every emotional crisis or possible point of repose by a tableau during which the emotion could be expressed in an aria and set to a few lines of pregnant poetry so designed that the words would bear repetition with good musical effect in a musical scheme."

That might have been. But Metastasian opera, and indeed all Italian opera of the time, was a succession of solos and duets dominated by singers who incessantly bawled improvised roulades on a few vowels. And the singers those days were lords of creation who loftily told the composer what to do, and who had no hesitation about altering the music to fit their individual egos and vocal styles. All stage action would come to a stop while they approached the footlights and astounded the audience with vocal pyrotechnics. From the composers, poor things, came occasional objections and pleas for reform. As early as 1720 the Italian composer Benedetto Marcello, in a prose sketch entitled *Il Teatro alla Moda,* satirized Italian opera. One paragraph in it sets forth the relationship between composer and singer: "In working with singers, especially castratos, the composer will always place himself on their left and keep one step behind, hat in hand.   He will quicken or retard the tempo of the arias set to the genius of the virtuosos, covering up whatever bad judgment they show with the reflection that his own reputation, credit and interests are in their hands, and for that reason, if need be, he will alter arias, recitatives, sharps, flats, naturals, etc."

It was time for reform. There were factors other than the built-in absurdities of baroque opera. The age of the baroque was being superseded by a new classicism, and the trend was toward simplicity rather than ornateness. Musicians by 1760 had broken completely away from the complicated baroque splendor and were writing in the *style galant*, a simple and melodic style devoid of counterpoint. The thinking of the age was influenced by Rousseau, who came out with his ideal of nature and naturalness in his *Nouvelle Héloïse* (1760) and *Émile* (1762). Johann Joachim Winckelmann, in his famous history of Greek art (1764), reintroduced the classic ideal to Europe. His conclusions, that beauty was a subjugation of details to the whole, that true art consisted of harmony and graceful proportion, greatly influenced the aesthetic thinking of the Enlightenment. Gluck, stimulated by the Calzabigi librettos, did for opera what Winckelmann preached for art and Rousseau for man (Gluck, who obviously had read Rousseau, was always talking about returning to nature in his music, nature meaning not merely trees and sky but life as it actually is lived). Discarding baroque opera, with its embellishments, ornateness, and vocal show, he turned to the classical ideals of purity, balance, simplicity, and even austerity. He was not, however, altogether consistent in his thinking. In the twenty-five years following *Orfeo ed Euridice*, he composed thirteen more operas. Of those, six were "reform" operas and the others in the earlier baroque style. Nevertheless it was Gluck who changed the course of opera, and his ideas did lead to Wagner and even beyond.

His first step was to put the singers in their place, and he did this in two ways. One was by insisting that they remain in character throughout the opera. The other was by modifying or abolishing the da capo aria. No longer could singers insanely improvise on the return to the first section. They had to sing what was written; and the hot-tempered and imperious Gluck, the most demanding conductor of his day, invariably conducted his own operas to make sure that was exactly what would happen. In the Gluck reform operas, arias are much shorter than they were in baroque opera, and there is an increased amount of recitative. Recitative is heightened speech, declamatory in nature, as opposed to sung aria. It is used as a device to further the stage action and characterization, bridging the sung portions of the opera. Gluck all but discarded the old *recitativo secco*, in which the accompaniment is reduced to a chord or two played on the harpsichord. Instead, he used the much more expressive *recitativo stromentato*, with its rather elaborate instrumental accompaniment. He established the overture as part of the drama, strove for emotional realism and development of character, and tried to achieve a complete dramatic unity.

All of this was new in operatic thinking. In a letter to the *Mercure de France* in 1773, Gluck neatly outlined what he was trying to do: "The imitation of nature is the acknowledged goal to which all artists must set themselves. It is that which I too try to attain. Always as simple and natural as I can make it, my music strives toward the utmost expressiveness and seeks to reinforce the meaning of the underlying poetry. It is for this reason that I do not use those trills, coloraturas and cadences that Italians employ so abundantly." Gluck repeated the point to the *Journal de Paris* in 1777: "I believed that the voices, the instruments, all the sounds, and even the silences [in my music] ought to have only one aim, namely that of expression, and that the union of music and words ought to be so intimate that the libretto would seem to be no less closely patterned after the music than the music after the libretto."

Orfeo ed Euridice adheres to these ideals more closely than any other Gluck opera does. The plot lines are clear (even below a minimum of action, some writers have complained), the poetry is simple but elevated, the music is stripped of all superfluities, even of harmonic superfluities. Gluck never was a very inventive harmonist, and was timid about modulations and key changes.

The original 1762 version of *Orfeo* was in Italian, with a male alto as Orfeo. That was the only conventional thing about the score. Musicologists have pointed out that never in the history of opera had such a drastic change in style been accomplished. At first, *Orfeo* was too novel for the Viennese public, but it did not take long before it had enthusiastic adherents. Gluck's next reform opera was *Alceste*, in 1767, again in Italian. It is in the preface to *Alceste* that Gluck fully set forth his theories. As one of the most famous documents of music, it deserves to be reprinted here in a substantially complete version·

When I undertook to write the music for *Alceste*, I resolved to divest it entirely of all those abuses, introduced into it either by the mistaken vanity of singers or by the too great complaisance of composers, which have so long disfigured Italian opera and made of the most splendid and most beautiful of spectacles the most ridiculous and wearisome. I have striven to restrict music to its true office of serving poetry by means of expression and by following the situations of the plot, without interrupting the action or stifling it with a useless superfluity of ornaments; and I believed that it should do this in the same way as telling colors affect correct and well-ordered painting, by a well-assorted contrast of light and shade, which serves to animate the figures without altering their contours. Thus I do not wish to arrest a performer in the greatest heat of dialogue in order to wait for a tiresome *ritornello*, nor to hold him up in the middle of a word on a vowel favorable to his voice, nor to make display of the agility of his fine voice in some long-drawn passage, nor to wait while the orchestra gives him time to recover his breath for a cadenza. I did not think it my duty to pass quickly over the second section of an aria of which perhaps the words are the most impassioned and important, in order to repeat regularly four times over those of the first part, and to finish the aria where its sense may perhaps not end for the convenience of the singer who wishes to show that he can capriciously vary a passage in a number of guises; in short, I have sought to abolish all those abuses against which good sense and reason have cried out in vain.

I have felt that the overture ought to apprise the spectators of the nature of the action that is to be represented and to form, so to speak, its argument; that the concerted instruments should be introduced in proportion to the interest and the intensity of the words, and not leave that sharp contrast between the aria and the recitative in the dialogue, so as not to break a period unreasonably nor wantonly disturb the force and heat of the action.

Furthermore, I believed that my greatest labor should be devoted to seeking a beautiful simplicity, and I have avoided making displays of difficulty at the expense of clarity; nor did I judge it desirable to discover novelties if it was not naturally suggested by the situation and the expression; and there is no rule which I have not thought it right to set aside willingly for the sake of an intended effect.

Such are my principles. By good fortune my designs were wonderfully furthered by the libretto, in which the celebrated author, devising a new dramatic scheme, for florid descriptions, unnatural paragons, and sententious, cold morality had substituted heartfelt language, strong passions, interesting situations and endlessly varied spectacle. The success of the work justified my maxims, and the universal approbation of so enlightened a city has made it clearly evident that simplicity, truth and naturalness are the great principles of beauty in all artistic manifestations. . . .

The third Calzabigi-Gluck collaboration was *Paride ed Elena* in 1770. Then Gluck turned his attention to Paris, where there was great curiosity about his operas. *Iphigénie en Aulide*, with a libretto by François du Roullet, was produced at the Opéra in 1774. Gluck in Paris had the not inconsiderable support of Marie Antoinette. She had been one of his singing pupils in Vienna, and he had no hesitation about dropping her name. Once, dissatisfied at an *Iphigénie* rehearsal, he loudly said: "I shall go to the Queen and tell her that it is impossible to produce my opera. Then I shall get into my coach and go straight back to Vienna." Gluck had his way, as he always did. *Iphigénie* was followed a few months later by the French version of *Orfeo*, in which a tenor replaced the castrato. (The original Italian version, with a mezzo-soprano or contralto replacing the male alto, is the

49

one customarily heard today.) Gluck also put *Alceste* into French.

His years in Paris were enlivened by his rivalry with Niccolò Piccinni (1728-1800), a skillful Italian composer who came to Paris in 1776. Piccinni had immediately attracted a group of followers who felt much happier with his traditional operas than with the classical austerities of Gluck. There were great polemics, and Paris enjoyed the controversy as much as it had enjoyed the *Guerre des bouffons* in the early 1750's. That earlier controversy also had to do with opera. Some maintained that the old French opera of Jean-Baptiste Lully (1632-1687) was the only logical course for French opera to take; others insisted with equal fervor that salvation lay only through Italian opera. Rousseau favored the latter, saying that the French language was unmusical and that French opera therefore necessarily had to be an absurdity. Parisians entered the Gluck-Piccinni controversy with equal seriousness. It was reported that men, meeting for the first time, would say: "Sir, are you a Gluckist or Piccinnist?" Benjamin Franklin, in Paris at the time as Commissioner of the new United States of America, listened with amazement to the two factions, who, he wrote:

> were disputing warmly on the merit of two foreign musicians, one a *cousin*, the other a *moscheto;* in which dispute they spent their time, seemingly as regardless of the shortness of time as if they had been sure of living a month. Happy people! thought I, you live certainly under a wise, just and mild government, since you have no public grievances to complain of, nor any subject of contention but the perfections and imperfections of foreign music.

Through all this, Gluck and Piccinni remained on good terms, though a note of asperity crept into their relations toward the end of the *affaire.* The consensus was that Gluck had carried the field, especially after *Armide* of 1777 and *Iphigénie en Tauride* of 1779. Some diplomatic observers, however, attempted to smooth things over by saying that Gluck was superior in tragedy, Piccinni in comedy. *Echo et Narcisse,* also produced in 1779, was Gluck's last major work. He had a stroke in 1781 and spent the last years of his life in Vienna, holding court but composing no more.

Gluck was a tough, domineering man with an explosive temper and a genius for self-promotion. In the memoirs of Johann Christoph von Mannlich, a court painter in Paris, there is a good description of Gluck. Mannlich was a little disappointed at first. "Anybody meeting Gluck, wearing his round wig and his large overcoat, would never have taken him for a prominent person and a creative genius." Gluck, says Mannlich, was a little above medium height (which in those days would have put him about 5 feet, 6 inches), "stocky, strong and muscular without being stout. His head was

50

round, his face ruddy, broad and pock-marked. The eyes were small and deeply set.' (Dr. Charles Burney agreed, saying that Gluck was "coarse in figure and look.") Mannlich comments on Gluck's "excitable" nature and his devastating frankness or even rudeness. "He called things by their name and therefore, twenty times a day, offended the sensitive ears of the Parisians, used to flattery." The French considered him a very impolite man. "He was a hearty eater and drinker," continues Mannlich. "He never denied being grasping and fond of money, and displayed a goodly portion of egotism, particularly at table, where he was wont at sight to claim first right to the best morsels."

Not only did the Parisians consider him uncouth. As a conductor he was the Toscanini of his day, an irascible martinet, and musicians trembled before him. Or they refused to play in his orchestras. He was a perfectionist who would have the players repeat a passage twenty or thirty times before he was satisfied. Such was the antagonism between Gluck and his players in Vienna that more than once the Emperor himself had to intervene. The gossip was that when Gluck was preparing one of his operas, he had to bribe musicians by offering them double rates. Gluck must have had an extraordinary ear, and the sloppy playing prevalent in his day drove him crazy. He said that if he received twenty livres for composing an opera, he should be paid 20,000 for rehearsing it. Mannlich, who attended the *Aulide* rehearsals, gives an idea of what went on:

He tore around like a madman. Now the violins were at fault, then the wind instruments had failed to give proper expression to his ideas. While conducting, he would suddenly break off, singing the part with the desired expression. Then, after conducting for a while, he would stop them, screaming at the top of his lungs: "This isn't worth a hoot in hell!" I mentally saw the violins and other instruments flying at his head. . . .

But although Gluck hated to do so, he invariably insisted on preparing his own operas. He knew what would happen if he entrusted them to other hands. As he pointed out to the Duc de Bragance in the dedication of *Paride ed Elena,* "The more one strives for truth and perfection, the more necessary are precision and exactitude." Only the composer, Gluck justly observed, can attain this. "It requires little for my aria, *Che farò senza Euridice,* to turn into a saltarello by Burattini—no more, in fact, than a slight change of expression. . . . Thus the composer's presence at the performance of such music is as necessary as the presence of the sun in the works of nature. He is its very life and soul, and without him everything is confusion and darkness."

To his singers, Gluck was equally abrupt, constantly charging them with screaming, with lack of taste and musicianship. Indeed, to everybody the strong-minded, independent, tactless Gluck was a trial. He always seemed to be saying the wrong things. In retrospect, they have proved to be the right things. Gluck was far ahead of his time as a sociological phenomenon. But that did not make it any easier for his friends to live with him. There was the time he was invited to visit the King at Versailles. On his return to Paris, he dined at the home of a duke. "Were you not pleased at the King's reception?" the grandee wanted to know. Gluck growled that he supposed he should be flattered, but "if I write another opera in Paris, I should prefer to dedicate it to the general collector of taxes, because he may give me ducats instead of compliments." There was consternation among the guests, and the duke quickly changed the subject. Gluck had something remarkably Beethovenian in his nature, and was prepared to dictate to life on his own terms. Thus, in his dealings with the Opéra, he did not ask for but demanded certain conditions. "I must be given at least two months after I arrive in Paris to train my cast; I must have complete authority to call as many rehearsals as I think necessary; there will be no understudies, and another opera shall be held ready in case one of the singers is indisposed. These are my conditions, without which I shall keep *Armide* for my own pleasure." No other composer in Europe could have gotten away with such a *Diktat*.

It was generally realized in Gluck's day that he had revolutionized opera. Dr. Burney, who visited Gluck in 1772, noted that "The Chevalier Gluck is simplifying music . . . he tries all he can to keep his music chaste and sober." Elsewhere: "His invention is, I believe, unequalled by any composer who now lives or has existed, particularly in dramatic painting and theatrical effects." Burney was overwhelmed, as much by the man as by his music, and he relates a charming episode on the occasion of his, Burney's, *adieux*. He visited the Chevalier to say good-bye, "and it was near eleven o'clock when I arrived, yet, like a true great genius, he was still in bed."

Other composers envied Gluck his success, and also were somewhat afraid of him. He was a dangerous infighter. Leopold Mozart told his son to keep away from Gluck. Their paths crossed during Mozart's visit to Paris in 1778. Later, Wolfgang and Gluck met once again in Vienna, and Mozart called him a "great man." It was an indication of the relative position of the two in official eyes that Gluck received 2,000 florins as Royal and Imperial Court Composer of Vienna. When Mozart succeeded Gluck, it was at a pittance of 800 gulden. Leopold Mozart, always a suspicious man who saw conspiracies under the corner of every tablecloth, was convinced that Gluck was jealous of Wolfgang, and was at the head of a cabal to keep his son down.

Gluck's influence turned up only peripherally in Mozart. It is noticeable primarily in Mozart's *opera seria*, *Idomeneo*. Once in a while a melody, such as the one in the slow movement of the D major Flute Quartet, suggests Gluck. The Gluckian spirit was much more pronounced in the works of Spontini, Cherubini, and, to a point, the classicism of Berlioz' *Les Troyens*. Debussy noted that influence in the Berlioz opera and wrote that it was "reminiscent of Gluck, whom he passionately loved." Berlioz did indeed worship Gluck, and as a student he spent hours copying and memorizing the Gluck operas. "The Jove of our Olympus was Gluck." At the Opéra, Berlioz was the watchdog who barked and howled when the conductors touched up a Gluck opera, or otherwise departed from the score. After Berlioz, the direct influence of Gluck is scarcely discernible in European music. Romantic color and Gluck's white classicism did not go together. Modern scholars tend to take Gluck as the end rather than the beginning of a period. Donald Grout's summation (in his *A Short History of Opera*) is representative: "Gluck was, like Handel, the end of an epoch rather than the beginning. He sums up the classicism of serious opera as Handel does of baroque opera." But there is more to Gluck and his influence than that. He did point the way to opera as music drama, as an all-in-one synthesis where song, text, action, dance, and décor were to be united on more or less equal terms. As such, he is the spiritual ancestor of Richard Wagner.

❧ 4 ❧

Classicism par excellence

FRANZ JOSEPH HAYDN

The age in which Franz Joseph Haydn was the most celebrated musical figure was an age that prided itself on its civilization, on its logic, on its emotional restraint, on its *politesse*. It was the golden age of the aristocracy; and also an age in which philosophers honestly believed that reason could direct the working of man and his society. Blood and revolution were to come, near the end of the century, followed by new concepts of society and the role of the artist. But in the eighteenth century, young intellectuals and artists did not walk around wrapped in a mental toga, glorying in their unique gift, making a great to-do about their visions, their sufferings, their ideals and aspirations. That remained for the young romantics of the nineteenth century. The second half of the eighteenth century was an age that looked for proportion in all things. In music, it did not care for fugue or for the immense, complicated forms of the Baroque. It demanded melodic music, homophonic music, music that would entertain, music that would not put too great a strain on the intellect.

Joseph Haydn was *the* composer of the period—the most respected, the most honored, the one closest to the tastes of his public. He was the classic composer *par excellence*, and in his long life, from 1732 to 1809, he grew up with the new musical ideas and, more than any one man, shaped them. In his way he was the typical figure of the Enlightenment, religious but not too religious, daring but not too daring, intelligent but not aggressively so, adventurous but not nearly so revolutionary as Mozart (a much more suppressed, dangerous, rebellious man). With Haydn, everything was in intellectual and emotional proportion.

Physically he was not a prepossessing figure. He was short and dark, his face was pitted by smallpox, his legs were too short for his body. His nose had a polyp that threw it out of shape, and he appears to have been sensitive about it. The famous Haydn never commissioned a portrait. But he must have been a very nice man to know. A person of singularly sweet, kind disposition, he made virtually no enemies at any time. He was even-tempered, industrious, generous, had a good sense of humor, handled his love affairs like a gentleman, enjoyed good health except for some eye trouble and rheumatism toward the end. He may not have been well educated, he was not much of a reader, but he was a practical man with good common sense. He had integrity and intellectual honesty—the kind of honesty that could allow him to say, when Mozart's name came up, "My friends often flatter me about my talent, but he was far above me." He liked to dress well. A Bohemian musician, Johann Wenzel Tomaschek, described the old master receiving guests toward the end of his life: "Haydn sat in an armchair, all dolled up. A powdered wig with side locks, a white neckband with a gold buckle, a white, richly embroidered waistcoat of heavy silk, in the midst of which shone a splendid jabot, a dress coat of fine coffee-colored cloth with embroidered cuffs, black silk breeches, white silk hose, shoes with large silver buckles curved over the instep, and on the little table next to him a pair of white kid gloves."

Haydn lived in a period of patronage. When he entered the service of the Esterházy family—and he was to remain with the Esterházys for a good part of his life—he never did question his position as a servant who wore his master's livery and ate with the help. Yet that never inhibited his strong streak of independence. He was not particularly impressed with nobility and, not being a snob, did not seek contacts with the great. It was not that he felt inferior or knew his position. He simply was not interested, and his feet were too firmly on the ground. "I have had converse with emperors, kings and great princes, and have heard many flattering remarks from them, but I do not wish to live on a familiar footing with such persons, and I prefer people of my own class." Primarily he was interested only in musicians or those who loved music; he was completely apolitical and wanted to be left alone to do his own work. There he was fully aware of his superiority and had no hesitation exercising his authority. One of his masters, Prince Nicholas II, once interfered with a Haydn rehearsal. Haydn all but threw His Grace out. "That, your Highness, is *my* affair." It is reported that Nicholas stomped away in a rage, but made no effort to discipline his famous Kapellmeister. Had he done so, Haydn might have left for good. There were plenty of rich princes eager to have the great Haydn in their employ. Haydn was just as independent with his publishers. He got into a dispute with the firm of Artaria in 1782 and, when matters were not satisfactorily resolved, sent a curt note: "So finish the affair and send me either my music or my money." But there was nothing small or petty about Haydn. He was an authentically big man, a secure man, and never worried about competition. He not only had infinite praise for Mozart, but as early as 1793 he knew enough about the young Beethoven, whom he had briefly taught, to send a tremendous endorsement to the Elector of Cologne: "Beethoven will in time fill the position of one of Europe's greatest composers . . ."

In short, Haydn was a well-adjusted man, and it shows in his music. It is hard to think of the music of any composer that is so free of the neurotic (probably the only comparable body of music in this respect would be Dvořák's). Haydn's music is always sane and healthy. It may have lacked the passion of Mozart's, but a good case can be made that Haydn's music is as consistently on as high a plane as Mozart's, perhaps higher, even if he never reached the mighty levels of Mozart at his greatest. From about 1780 to his death there is scarcely a Haydn symphony, quartet, mass, or oratorio that cannot legitimately be called a masterpiece. The fertility of the man was breathtaking.

But had he died at Mozart's age, thirty-six, he would be all but unknown today. Haydn developed slowly, in a straight line. He was very talented as a child, but was not a Wunderkind, and never dashed off music the way that Mozart, Schubert, or Mendelssohn did. "I was never a quick writer, and composed with care and diligence," he indicated. His career is one of slow growth. He moved along, consolidating his gains. When he started his work, the new music—the music of the *style galant*—was in its infancy and Haydn put everything together. It is not for nothing that he is called The Father of the Symphony. With equal justice he could be called The Father of the String Quartet, or The Father of Sonata Form.

Franz Josef Haydn was born on March 31, 1732, in the town of Rohrau, just on the border of Austria and Hungary. It was formerly believed that the family was Croatian. Modern research has established the fact that the Haydns were Austrian. Mathias Haydn, Joseph's father, was a wagon-maker. The boy grew up virtually as a peasant. But from the beginning he showed unusual musical aptitude. There are pleasant stories of the five-year-old Joseph playing make-believe violinist, sawing at his left arm with a stick. His parents hoped he would become a clergyman, and it was with this aim that Joseph, shortly before he was six years old, was sent to nearby Hainburg at the instigation of a cousin. There he learned to read and write, studied the catechism, and, because of his musical ability, received instruction in wind and string instruments. Haydn himself wrote, in an autobiographical sketch, "Our Almighty Father had endowed me with such fertility in music that even in my sixth year I stood up like a man and sang masses in the church choir and I could play a little on the clavier and violin." But it was not all easy going. Haydn had a miserable life as a child. "More floggings than food," he later remembered. For the most part he had to teach himself. "Proper teachers I never had. I always started right away with the practical side first in singing and playing instruments, later in composing. I listened more than I studied, but I heard the finest music in all forms that was to be heard in my time. Thus little by little my knowledge and my ability were developed."

It was in Vienna that Haydn heard the "finest music." At the age of eight he was recruited into the choir of St. Stephen's Cathedral, where he became one of the star pupils. In 1749 his voice broke, and he was dismissed. Legend has it that his dismissal was accelerated by a schoolboy prank. He is supposed to have cut off a fellow student's pigtail. Haydn was seventeen at the time, and his sole possessions were three old shirts and a worn coat. When he left, the new star pupil was his younger brother, Michael (1737–1806), of whom great things were predicted. Michael seems to have been more gifted than Joseph in everything but composition. He did go on to have a fine career, taking Mozart's place at Salzburg as director of the Archbishop's orchestra. He also composed a large quantity of church music. None of his work, however, has remained in the active repertoire.

For several years after leaving St. Stephen's, Haydn all but starved. As a pianist and violinist he was not on a professional level. He himself admitted that he was "a wizard on no instrument, but I knew the strength and working of all; I was not a bad clavier player or singer, and could also play a concerto on the violin." But many musicians could do that. For eight years Haydn had to "eke out a wretched existence." He lived a Bohemian life, playing at social functions, teaching, arranging music; and, "in my zeal for composition, composed well into the night." He studied the music of C. P. E. Bach and had a few lessons with Nicola Porpora (1686–1767), a famous composer of the day. Little by little he made headway. Possibly his piano and violin playing improved. Certainly his reputation grew. In 1758 he was appointed music director and composer for Count Ferdinand Maximilian von Morzin. Two years later he made the greatest single mistake of his life He married Maria Anna Aloysia Apollonia Keller.

She was the daughter of a hairdresser, and Haydn was really in love with one of her sisters. Here there is a strong parallel with Mozart, who was in love with Aloysia Weber and then married her sister Constanze on the rebound. Haydn, searching for a wife, was probably talked into marriage by the Keller family. Maria Anna was three years older than Haydn, ugly, ill-tempered, jealous, and a shrew. She did not like music, she was a poor housekeeper, she could not manage money, and she was not thrifty. Small wonder that Haydn quickly became disenchanted, referring to her as "that infernal beast," and turned elsewhere for relaxation. He later rationalized his extramarital affairs by telling his first biographer, Georg August Griesinger, "My wife was unable to bear children, and for this reason I was less indifferent toward the attraction of other women."

It was in 1761 that Haydn made the most significant move of his life, entering the service of the Esterházy family as vice-Kapellmeister. Prince Paul Anton Esterházy was head of the greatest and richest family in Hungary, and was a lover of art and music. His castle at Eisenstadt had 200 rooms for guests, and also contained parks and theaters. Haydn moved in, congratulating himself. The terms of his contract are interesting. They give an idea of what was expected from a musician in the service of a great lord:

1st. For many years there has been in Eisenstadt a Kapellmeister Gregorius Werner, who has rendered faithful service to the princely house, but on account of his great age and the incapacity often resulting therefrom can no longer fulfill his duties. He, Gregorius Werner, in consideration of his services of many years, will remain head Kapellmeister, and the aforementioned Joseph Heyden [so his name is spelled throughout the contract] will be Vice-Kapellmeister, subordinate to and answering to Gregorius Werner in choir music; but in all other matters, where music has to be made, everything pertaining to music will at once become the responsibility *in genere* and *in specie* of the Vice-Kapellmeister.

2nd. Joseph Heyden will be considered an officer of the house. Therefore, His Serene Highness graciously trusts that he will, as befits an honest house officer, behave soberly and, to the musicians directed by him, not brutishly but gently, modestly, calmly and honestly, especially when music is to be made in front of His Highness, and not only shall the Vice-Kapellmeister Joseph Heyden together with his subordinates, appear at all times clean and in livery, but he will also see that all those answering to him follow the instructions given to them and appear in white stockings, white shirt, powdered and pigtails dressed alike. Therefore:

3rd. All musicians are subordinated to the Vice-Kapellmeister, consequently he will behave himself in an exemplary manner, so that his subordinates can follow the example of his good qualities. He will avoid any undue familiarity in eating and drinking or otherwise in his relations with them, lest he should lose the respect due him. . . .

4th. At the command of His Serene Highness is required to compose such music as His Serene Highness may require of him. Such compositions are not to be communicated to any person, nor copied, but remain the property of His Serene Highness, and without the knowledge and permission of His Serene Highness, he is not to compose for any person.

5th. Joseph Heyden shall appear daily . . . in the morning and the afternoon in the antechamber and will be announced and will await the decision of His Serene Highness whether there should be music; and having received the order, will inform the other musicians, and not only appear himself punctually at the appointed time but also ensure that the rest appear, and should a musician either come late for the music or even be absent, he will take his name.

6th. Should, regrettably, quarrels or complaints occur among the musicians, the Vice-Kapellmeister shall attempt in accordance with the circumstances to settle them, so that His Grace will not be importuned with trifling matters; but should a more important incident occur that he, Joseph Heyden, cannot himself settle by mediation, he shall faithfully report it to His Serene Highness.

7th. The Vice-Kapellmeister shall survey and take care of all musical instruments.

8th. Joseph Heyden is obliged to instruct the female singers, so that they shall not forget in Eisenstadt what they have learned in Vienna . . . and since the Vice-Kapellmeister has experience of various instruments, he will allow himself to be employed in playing all those instruments with which he is acquainted.

9th. The Vice-Kapellmeister will receive herewith a copy of the convention and norms of behavior of his subordinate musicians, so that he will know how to make them behave in service, in accordance with these regulations.

10th. As it is not considered necessary to commit to paper all the services that he is obliged to perform, His Serene Highness graciously hopes that Joseph Heyden will in all matters spontaneously carry out not only the above-mentioned services but also all other orders of His Grace that he may receive in the future, and also maintain the music in good order.

11th. The Vice-Kapellmeister will be accorded by His Lordship four hundred guilder annually, payment to be made quarterly by the Chief Cashier. In addition to this,

12th. Joseph Heyden shall receive his meals at the officers' table or half a guilder for board daily. Finally,

13th. This convention was concluded in the 1st May, 1761, with the Vice-Kapellmeister for at least three years, provided that if Joseph wishes to continue in this honor after having served for three years, he must announce his intention to His Lordship six months in advance . . . Similarly,

14th. His Lordship promises not only to keep Joseph Heyden in his service for the agreed period, but if he gives full satisfaction, he may expect the position of Principal Kapellmeister; should the contrary be the case, however, His Serene Highness is free at any time to dismiss him from his service.

But Haydn served with Prince Paul for only a year. Paul died in 1762 and was succeeded by Prince Nicholas, called the Magnificent. Nicholas promptly built himself a new castle and named it Eszterháza. Completed in 1766 at a cost of millions, it was the greatest palace in Europe except for Versailles. It contained a marionette theater and a 400-seat theater for opera. The royal box of the opera house was supported by red marble Roman columns decorated with golden rods, according to a contemporary report, which further went on to say (after describing the lavishness of the building and its surroundings) that German comedies and Italian opera alternated from day to day. "The Prince is always present, and six o'clock is the usual time. The delight for eyes and ears is indescribable. It comes first from the music, since the entire orchestra resounds as a complete entity: now the most moving tenderness, now the most vehement power penetrates the soul—because the great musician, Herr Haiden, who serves the Prince as Kapellmeister, is the director." The Empress Maria Theresa was impressed. "If I want to enjoy a good opera, I go to Eszterháza," she said.

Werner died in 1766 and Haydn became kapellmeister. It was a busy job. He had to direct the orchestra, compose music, be the librarian, take on all administrative duties pertaining to music, hire and fire personnel, be the copyist, arbitrate disputes. He did all this in an unruffled, level-headed manner, stern but always just, often going directly to the Prince to plead for his men. They adored him and called him "Papa."

Nicholas and Haydn got along very well. The Prince, as ardent a music lover as his predecessor, played the baryton, a now obsolete instrument related to the cello. Haydn was expected to compose a great deal of music for Nicholas himself to play, and he obliged with almost 200 pieces for the Prince's favorite instrument, most of which were scored for baryton, viola, and cello. He knew how lucky he was. "My Prince was always satisfied with my work. Not only did I have the encouragement of constant approval, but as conductor of an orchestra I could make experiments, observe what produced an effect and what weakened it, and was thus in a position to improve to alter, to make additions or omissions, and be as bold as I pleased. I was cut off from the world; there was no one to confuse or torment me, and I was forced to become original."

At Eszterháza, Haydn presided over an orchestra that numbered between twenty and twenty-three players. That was fair-sized for its day. Only a few orchestras in Europe were larger. The finest in the world was at Mannheim, which boasted some fifty players. There was a school of Mannheim composers, represented notably by Johann Stamitz (1717–1757) and Christian Cannabich (1731–1798), both active in Haydn's day and who may have influenced him. Stamitz and later Cannabich directed the Mannheim Orchestra, a group described as "an army of generals." Such precision, power, and virtuosity had been unknown up to then, and even the supercilious Mozart was carried away. Christian Schubart, the composer and critic, was rapturous in his description: "Here the forte is thunder, the crescendo a cataract, the diminuendo a crystal streamlet bubbling away in the far distance, the piano a breeze of spring." This was the famous "Mannheim crescendo," rising from triple pianissimo to crashing fortissimo.

Haydn's orchestra was not on that level, but he made it one of the best in Europe. He was its conductor, and he called himself that. It must be realized that his function as conductor was somewhat different from what is today meant by that term. The day of the virtuoso time-beater with the baton was yet to come. Haydn would have conducted from the clavier or as head of the violin section. In his day it was customary to have two conductors, one leading from the keyboard, the other from the violins. The clavier player would keep the rhythm and correct errant players or singers. The violinist would attend to the general ensemble and the nuances. In Haydn's case there were many nuances, and he insisted on fine degrees of shading, as evidenced in one of his letters explaining how his music should sound. In any orchestra he directed he would have assumed complete control, divided leadership or not, and in effect he would have led his orchestra much as modern conductors lead theirs, dominating the players, setting the tempos, keeping the ensemble together. Only he would have done this seated within the body of the orchestra.

Haydn supplied music for two weekly concerts, Tuesdays and Saturdays, from 2 to 4 in the afternoon. He also was in charge of the opera performances and composed many for the Eszterháza theater (none of the Haydn operas has held the stage, though a few are occasionally revived as novelties). In 1786 alone there were given at Eszterháza seventeen operas (including eight premieres) for a total of 125 performances. The Haydn authority, H. C. Robbins Landon, has estimated that in the course of the ten-year period from 1780 to 1790 Haydn conducted 1026 performances of Italian operas, not to mention the marionette operas and the incidental music to plays. It was hard work, but there were compensations. Haydn had a good salary, a maid, a coachman, a carriage and horses, lived in one of the showplaces of Europe, and had absolute authority over a group of skillfull musicians he himself had selected. He could also pursue his favorite pastimes, hunting and fishing, and to the end of his days would tell of the great occasion when he brought down three birds with one shot.

A considerable spur to his development was his meeting with the twenty-five-year-old Mozart in 1781. The two geniuses admired each other. Not only did Mozart dedicate his great set of six string quartets (Nos. 14-19) to Haydn, but he also defended him in word and deed. Thus when Leopold Kozeluch, a pianist active in Vienna, sneered at a passage in a Haydn quartet, saying "*I* would not have written it that way," Mozart cut him short with "Neither would I. And you know why? Because neither of us would have had so excellent an idea." Haydn reciprocated, and when *Don Giovanni* was criticized in his presence, he said: "I cannot settle this dispute, but this I know: Mozart is the greatest composer the world possesses now." From Mozart, Haydn got new ideas about organization, about key relationship, and, above all, about the expressive possibilities of music. Certain it is that after exposure to Mozart's music, Haydn's became broader than it had ever been, deeper, more expressive. It worked both ways. Mozart learned a great deal about structural organization from Haydn.

By the time of his meeting with Mozart, Haydn already was one of the most famous composers in Europe. As early as 1776 his music was being received with rapture, and one review referred to "Herr Joseph Haydn, the darling of our nation, whose gentle character is marked in each of his pieces. His compositions have beauty, order, clarity, a fine and noble simplicity. . . ." France, Italy, Russia, Spain—all countries admired his music. It was published, then copied and pirated. Invitations for the great Haydn to appear in person came from all the musical capitals. Haydn held fast at Eszterháza. But in 1790 Nicholas the Magnificent died and his successor, Anton, who was not very interested in music, dismissed the orchestra except for a few musicians. Haydn, of course, was kept on. There was little for him to do; and as he was free to go wherever he wished, he moved to Vienna. Late in 1790 he accepted an offer to appear in England. Johann Peter Salomon, a violinist and impresario who had settled in London, made a trip to Vienna to court Europe's most famous composer. All Haydn had to do was go to England, compose music for the public there, make personal appearances, and return to Vienna a rich man. So Salomon assured Haydn, and he was correct. Haydn arrived in England on January 1, 1791, and remained for eighteen months.

No capital in Europe had as much music as London, and the arrival of Haydn created much excitement. Dr. Charles Burney, Handel's old friend, wrote for the new hero a long poem in stately couplets. *Verses on the Arrival of Haydn in England,* it was titled, and it contained such flattering stanzas as:

> HAYDN! Great Sovereign of the tuneful art!
> Thy works alone supply an ample chart
> Of all the mountains, seas, and fertile plains,
> Within the compass of its wide domains.—
> Is there an Artist of the present day
> Untaught by thee to think, as well as play?
> Whose head thy science has not well supplied?
> Whose hand thy labors have not fortified?

Newspapers made much of the event. The *Public Advertiser* of January 6, 1791, discussed Haydn and also gave a list of the musical events to be found in the city, under the heading: *Musical Arrangements for every Day in the Week Through the Winter Season.* The list is impressive:

. . . Our Readers may be pleased to see what will be the arrangements of musical pleasures for the week; even if the coalition of the two Operas should not take place . . .

SUNDAY: The Noblemen's Subscription is held every Sunday at a different house.

MONDAY: The Professional Concert—at the Hanover-square Rooms—with Mrs. Billington.

TUESDAY—The Opera.

WEDNESDAY: The Ancient Music at the Rooms in Tottenham Street, under the patronage of Their Majesties.

THURSDAY—The Pantheon.—A Pasticcio of Music and Dancing, in case that the Opera coalition shall take place; if not, a concert with Madama Mara and Sig. Pacchierotti. Academy of Ancient Music, every other Thursday at Free-Mason's Hall.

FRIDAY—A Concert under the auspices of Haydn at the Rooms, Hanover Square, with Signor David.

SATURDAY—The Opera.

Haydn was taken to the bosom of London society. "My arrival," he wrote to a friend in Vienna, "caused a great sensation throughout the whole city, and I went the round of all the newspapers for 3 successive days. Everybody wants to know me. I had to dine out 6 times up to now, and if I wanted, I could dine out every day; but first I must consider my work, and 2nd my health." The work consisted of a group of six symphonies that turned out to be the first half of his last twelve (Nos. 93-104), all known as the *London* symphonies. (To complicate matters, No. 104 in D is known as the *London Symphony*.) Haydn's first concert took place on March 11, 1791. He conducted an orchestra of forty from the piano. It was the largest group he had ever directed, and he was thrilled by it. His success was tremendous, and the reaction of the *Morning Chronicle* was typical. "Never, perhaps, was there a richer musical treat," the critic wrote, and went on to compare Haydn with Shakespeare. The critic also put out a feeler that was to be re-echoed: "We were happy to see the concert so well attended the first night, for we cannot suppress our very anxious hope that the first musical genius of the age may be induced, by our liberal welcome, to take up his residence in England."

Haydn had a very good time in England. Two of the high spots were his award of an honorary doctorate from Oxford, and his romance with Mrs. Rebecca Schröter, the widow of a well-known pianist. His impressions about musical and social life in England can be found in his diary, the so-called *London Notebooks*, which he religiously kept up.

This diary makes delightful reading, and a good deal about the workings of Haydn's mind can be learned from it. A very attractive personality comes through. Haydn was insatiably curious, and he loved statistics. "The national debt of England is estimated to be over two hundred millions. Recently it was calculated that if they had to make up a convoy to pay this sum in silver, the wagons, end on end, would reach from London to York, that is, 200 miles, presuming that each wagon could not carry more than £600." Or, "The City of London consumes 8 times one hundred thousand cartloads of coal each year; each cart has 13 sacks, each sack holds 2 dry measures: most of the coal comes from Newcastle. Often 200 loaded ships arrive at once. A cartload coats £2½." There are also critical notes: "On 21st Giardini's concert took place in Renelag [Ranelagh Gardens]. He played like a pig." Haydn goes to the races at Ascot on June 14, 1792, and writes down a full description. The observant, curious Haydn was a fine reporter. It is fascinating to read his account of the afternoon he spent, which is, incidentally, one of the earliest descriptive accounts of racing:

. . . When they are ready, the bell is rung a second time, and at the first stroke they ride off at once. Whoever is the first to traverse the circle of 2 miles and return to the platform from which they started receives the prize. In the first heat there were 3 riders and they had to go around the circle twice without stopping. They did this double course in 5 minutes. [Impossible. Haydn's timing is much too fast.] No stranger would believe this unless they had seen it themselves. The second time there were seven riders. When they were in the middle of the circle, all 7 were in the same line, but as soon as they came nearer some fell behind, but never more than about 10 paces; and just when you think that one of them is rather near the goal, and people make large bets on him at this moment, another rushes past him at very close corners and with unbelievable force reaches the winning place. The riders are very lightly clad in silk and each one has a different color, so that you recognize him more easily; no boots, a little cap on his head, they are all as lean as a greyhound and as lean as their horses. Everyone is weighed in, and a certain weight is allowed him, in relation to the strength of the horse, and if the rider is too light he must put on heavier clothes, or they hang some lead on him.
. . Among other things a single large stall is erected, wherein the Englishmen place their bets. The King has his own stall at one side. I saw 5 heats the first day, and despite a heavy rain there were 2000 vehicles, all full of people, and 3 times as many common people on foot. Besides this, there are all sorts of other things—puppet plays, hawkers, horror plays—which go on during the races; many tents with refreshments, all kinds of wine and beer. . . .

Haydn does not say if he came out a winner. He could have afforded a flutter or two, for his London trip was, as Salomon had promised, very lucrative. So lucrative was it that there was every inducement for him to make a return trip, and he did, early in 1794, to remain until August 15, 1795.

Returning to Vienna after the second London visit, he found a new Ester-házy. Prince Anton had died, and the new head of the family, Nicholas II, wanted to restore the orchestra, to be used mostly for church services. Haydn agreed to take it over, and composed a series of great masses, but otherwise he had plenty of time for himself.

It was during these years that he composed the Austrian National Anthem. Haydn had been impressed by the dignity and simplicity of *God Save the King,* and decided that Austria should have an equivalent. The matter was discussed at court, and the imperial chancellor commissioned the poet Leopold Haschka to write a patriotic text. *Gotte erhalte Franz den Kaiser* —"God save Emperor Franz"—was the result, and Haydn set it to music. On February 12, 1797, it was sung in all the theaters of Vienna and the provinces. Later that year, Haydn used the theme for a set of variations in his C major Quartet (Op. 76, No. 3), which of course was promptly nicknamed the *Emperor* Quartet.

In 1802 Haydn was released from his official duties. He lived quietly in Vienna, one of the most celebrated figures in Austria. His wife had died in 1800. Illness plagued the last years of his life, and Haydn, who had never complained of anything, who had never had a serious ailment, was largely confined to his house. Rheumatism swelled his legs so that it was painful to walk. He liked to sit at home, the grand old man of European music, and receive visitors. On May 31, 1809, he died. His last musical act was to be carried to the piano, where he played the Austrian hymn three times. That was a day or two before his death. His last reported words were "Children, be comforted. I am well." At the funeral the Mozart Requiem was played. That would have pleased Haydn.

Like so many of the pre-Beethoven composers, Haydn went into eclipse during the nineteenth century. Mozart at least interested the romantics, and *Don Giovanni* was never far from them. But very little of Haydn's music was played in the concert halls except for *The Seasons, The Creation,* and an occasional symphony. It remained for the classic revival after World War I and the extraordinary classic and baroque renaissance after World War II to re-establish Haydn. Up to then he had been largely an admired textbook figure, represented on programs by a few—no more than a half-dozen—of his more than 100 symphonies, and on chamber music programs by a handful of string quartets, and in piano recitals by two works, the F minor Variations and the big E flat Sonata. All of a sudden came the realization of just how significant a creator and innovator Haydn was, and how bracing, inventive, and wonderful his music is.

In his steady output there is surprisingly little change after the early 1780's, in that no matter how much an individual work differs from another individual work, all the music is animated by much the same approach: a pure and perfect technique, a feeling of optimism, a clear layout, masculine-sounding melodies, a surprisingly rich harmonic texture, and a sheer joy in composition. Rococo is left far behind; this is classicism of the purest kind, and the music is big. Emotionally it is uncluttered and uncomplicated. It does not lack feeling or even passion, but the impression it always gives is one of buoyancy. This is true of the symphonies, the chamber music, the masses, and the two great oratorios—*The Seasons* and *The Creation*, both of which also abound in some of the most charming nature painting music has to show.

Haydn's greatest technical contribution was his consolidation of sonata form. In his early years he was content to write tuneful music that had little or no development: arias for instruments, as it were. But as he developed, as he became familiar with the work of the Mannheim school and the early Viennese school, as his vision became bigger and his technique more encompassing, he worked out the sonata principle better than anybody in Europe at the time. Sonata form is essentially contrast and development. That is, the first movement of a sonata is divided into three sections—exposition, development, and recapitulation. The exposition presents the material on which the movement is built. There is a strong theme (first subject), and a more lyric, contrasting theme (second subject). Sometimes, especially in the romantic period, these were called the masculine and feminine elements. In the development one or both of those two themes are manipulated. The quality of the development is the test of the composer's resource, imagination, and technique. After the themes are put through their paces, the recapitulation brings back the two original themes, more or less in their original form. Thus an arch is rounded out. In many classic symphonies the first movement starts with a slow introduction and ends with a snappy coda. A slow, lyric second movement follows; then a dancelike third movement (sometimes this is omitted); and then a finale. Often the finale is a rondo, a form in which subsidiary themes revolve around a main one, in a pattern of ABACA.

Haydn invented none of this, but no composer in Europe so refined the principle. From the 1760's and 1770's to the end of his life he turned out work of miraculous inventiveness, charm, and life, though it was not until after 1780 that he shone with full maturity. He was one of the most prolific composers in history. Standard listings give 104 symphonies, 83 string quartets, 52 piano sonatas, many concertos, much miscellaneous chamber music, a large number of choral works, 23 operas, many songs, 4 oratorios, and many masses. There was no form of music to which Haydn did not turn his industrious pen. And all Europe knew him for the master he was. There was a tendency in some professional circles to underplay his music. It was thought too light, too mellifluous. Haydn never challenged the Establish-

66

ment, as did Mozart and Beethoven, and there was a tendency to take his music for granted. His lusty peasantlike minuet movements, which so influenced the Beethoven scherzos, were often looked down upon as "common" or "vulgar." So graceful and assured was his writing that some of its remarkable aspects went unnoticed—the daring key structure, for example. In the 1770's Haydn went through what is known as the *Sturm und Drang* period —a period in Europe where creators tried to express a more personal kind of feeling. It was a preromantic urge. *Empfindsamkeit*, it was called in Germany and Austria. Those were the years when Haydn composed music in unusual keys—F minor, E minor, F sharp minor, B major—all "romantic" keys. His choice of keys, indeed, is more adventurous than even Mozart's, though Mozart is more adventurous *within* the key. And Haydn's later music often contains even more anticipations of romanticism. But above all there is that direct, clear, good-natured, un-neurotic view toward life and art. "Since God has given me a cheerful heart, He will forgive me for serving him cheerfully," Haydn once wrote. And that sums it up.

❧ 5 ❧

Prodigy from Salzburg

WOLFGANG AMADEUS MOZART

Wolfgang Amadeus Mozart was the greatest composer of his day. As a composer he was supreme in all forms of music—opera, symphony, concerto, chamber, vocal, piano, choral, everything. He was the finest pianist and organist in Europe, and the finest conductor. Had he worked on it he could also have been the best violinist. There was literally nothing in music he could not do better than anybody else. He could write down a complicated piece while thinking out another piece in his head; or he could think out a complete string quartet and then write out the individual parts before making the full score; or he could read perfectly at sight any music placed before him; or he could hear a long piece of music for the first time and immediately write it out, note for note. He lived but thirty-six years, from January 27, 1756, to December 5, 1791, and in that short span gave the world a legacy of music that shines as bright today as it did in the last years of the eighteenth century.

Mozart was one of the most exploited child prodigies in the history of music, and he paid the price. Child prodigies seldom grow up to lead normal lives. They develop as children cultivating a specific talent at the expense of all others, most of their time is spent with adults, their general education is neglected, they are overpraised. A warped childhood results, and as often as not this leads to a warped manhood. The tragedy of Mozart was that he grew up reliant on his father and was unable to meet the demands of society and life. This was generally recognized in his own day. Thus Friedrich Schlichtegroll, Mozart's first biographer, could write in 1793: "For just as this rare being early became a man so far as his art was concerned, he always remained—as the impartial observer must say of him—in almost all other matters a child. He never learned to rule himself. For domestic order, for sensible management of money, for moderation and wise choice in pleasures, he had no feeling. He always needed a guiding hand." Or, five years later, Franz Niemetschek in his biography of 1798 wrote: "This man, so exceptional as an artist, was not equally great in the other affairs of life." The men who wrote these comments were not Philistines lamenting the fact that Mozart led an unconventional life. They knew what many knew, that Mozart was his own worst enemy.

That Mozart was indeed an exceptional musician, nobody in his day would dispute. At the age of three he started picking out tunes on the piano. His ear was so delicate that loud sounds would make him physically ill. And it was not only delicate, but perfect in pitch. At the age of four he was telling his elders that their violins were a quarter tone out of tune. At that age he also could learn a piece of music in about half an hour. At five he played the clavier amazingly well. At six he started composing, and his father, Leopold, took him on tour with his sister Maria Anna (Nannerl). Nannerl, five years older than Wolfgang, was also a child prodigy, though not nearly as gifted as her brother. Leopold was a good musician, a violinist, vice-kapellmeister in the archiepiscopal court at Salzburg, and the author of a famous treatise on violin playing. But the elder Mozart had not made a great success of his life and was determined to see that his genius of a son should find the best possible position and, incidentally, enrich the Mozart coffers. Leopold wanted security for his old age, a goal about which he kept constantly reminding his son later in life.

Thus from the age of six young Wolfgang was steadily on the road in his formative years, being exhibited to the courts of Europe, to the learned musical academies, to the public. As an adult he made further concert tours, with the result that fourteen of his thirty-six years were spent away from home. In one respect, they were not wasted years. Mozart came in contact with every important musician of the day, and with every kind of music, all of which his incredible brain soaked up and retained. His name was constantly in the news, especially when he was amazing Europe with his fantastic feats as a child. A spate of learned articles was written about the fabulous boy by the musical and scientific community. When Mozart played in Paris, shortly before he was seven years old, Baron Friedrich Melchior von Grimm, writing in the *Correspondance Littéraire*, all but went out of his mind. Mozart went through some of the tricks his father had devised for him, such as playing a clavier whose keyboard was covered with a cloth (not really a very hard task, but one calculated *pour épater le bourgeois*), reading at sight, improvising, harmonizing melodies at first hearing, demonstrating his absolute pitch, and so on. "I cannot be sure," wrote Grimm, "that this child will not turn my head if I go on hearing him often; he makes me realize that it is difficult to guard against madness on seeing prodigies. I am no longer surprised that Saint Paul should have lost his head after his strange vision." All Europe resounded with the praise of this marvelous boy.

A musician with such gifts should have had no trouble landing a lucrative position. But Mozart never succeeded in doing this, though he spent his whole life looking for one, preferably a position at court, with a large and guaranteed salary. He grew up a complicated man with a complicated personality and an unprecedented knack for making enemies. He was tactless, spoke out impulsively, said exactly what he thought about other musicians (rarely did he have a good word to say), tended to be arrogant and supercilious, and made very few real friends in the musical community. He had the reputation of being giddy and lightheaded, temperamental, obstinate. We can look back upon all this and sympathize. He was Mozart; he *was* better than any musician of his time; he *did* unerringly spot the mediocrity around him (and also the great figures: he had nothing but respect for Haydn), and in his musical judgments he was never wrong. But that did not make things any easier for him while he was alive. In addition he was not a glamorous figure physically. He was very short; his face, with a yellowish complexion, was pitted from smallpox; his head was too big for his slight frame. He was nearsighted, and had blue eyes that tended to protrude, a thick head of hair, a large nose, and plump hands. (Most great pianists have had plump hands with wide palms and a big stretch between thumb and forefinger. The romantic notion of a great pianist's hand being long, tapered, and beautiful seldom is borne out in actual life.)

For many years Mozart struggled to escape the domination of his father. The full story of the relationship between the two remains to be told by a competent psychiatrist who understands Mozart's music and his time. Leopold Mozart was not a complicated man. He was intelligent but unimaginative and unbending: a precise, pedantic, well-organized, cautious, prudent, and rather avaricious man. Being a good musician, he immediately recognized the genius of his son. But, much to his grief, he discovered that as Wolfgang grew older he seemed ill-equipped to meet life on equal terms—at least, according to Leopold's views about life. Wolfgang, who had constantly been leaning on his father during all those early years, seemed to collapse as soon as the prop was removed. Perhaps there was unconscious resentment. Perhaps Wolfgang wanted to express himself as a human being and did not know how. Perhaps it was inevitable that he run wild once the reins were removed. Whatever the reason, Wolfgang turned out to be the emotional antithesis of his father—easygoing, gregarious, undisciplined, and a soft touch.

Leopold was constantly bombarding his son with sage advice. Respect money. Do not trust strangers. Never go out walking at night. Plan ahead. Cultivate the right people. Act with dignity. But just as there was a great deal of Polonius in Leopold, so Wolfgang was Hamlet, with a great deal of Micawber as well. He never could make up his mind, or strike when the occasion was right. That did not seem to worry him. Everything was going to turn out all right. Tomorrow. With Wolfgang it was always tomorrow. "Little by little my circumstances will improve." Wolfgang was always writing these words to his father, but the pot of gold remained eternally at the end of the rainbow. What a trial Wolfgang turned out to be for Leopold! He wasted money, frittered away his talents, cultivated the wrong people, and never learned to assess character. Time and again Leopold writes to his son, warning him about his tendency to like everybody. "All men are villains! The older you will become and the more you associate with people, the more you will realize this sad truth." He begs Wolfgang not to be so easily swayed by flattery.

But Wolfgang goes his merry way. He probably is afraid of his father. Certainly his letters are evasive. Everything will be all right soon. Yes, he has lost money. No, he has not made any decent contacts. But he has prospects, great prospects. In vain Leopold tells his son that "flattering words, praises, cries of 'Bravissimo' pay neither postmasters nor landlords. So as soon as you find there is no money to be made, you should get away at once." Often Leopold loses his temper, especially when Wolfgang writes vague letters full of pious moralizing. "Blast your oracular utterances and all the rest!" Leopold does not want to know what his son thinks of life. He wants to know whether or not a good job is coming up, and where those gold ducats disappeared. He also worries that Wolfgang's loose social habits will make him an object of ridicule. Especially, he warns, keep away from musicians. They are low in the social order and it does not pay to be too friendly with them. That includes composers as important as Gluck, Piccinni, and Grétry. To them, be polite and nothing more. "You can always be perfectly natural with people of high rank, but with everybody else behave like an Englishman. You must not be so open with everyone." Poor Wolfgang probably flinched when he received a letter from his father. Nag, nag, nag. Leopold, of course, meant well. "The purpose of my remarks is to make you into an honorable man. Millions have not received that tremendous favor which God has bestowed upon you. What a responsibility! And what a shame if such a great genius were to founder!"

The upshot was that Leopold all but drove his son from him. Leopold could not change or bend his set of values; and Wolfgang, pushed by a musical genius that demanded a certain kind of evolution, could not be the sober, industrious, thrifty bourgeois his father so earnestly desired him to be. Leopold represented the golden mean. How could a Wolfgang Amadeus Mozart, with the dreams of *Don Giovanni* and the C minor Piano Concerto in his head, represent a prudent golden mean? So Leopold knew his son and did not know his son. Leopold could see nothing but the flaws in his character, and could not respond to an order of genius far beyond his comprehension. He failed utterly to realize how high-strung Wolfgang was, how badly he needed encouragement, sympathy, and support instead of homilies and lectures. Of course, Wolfgang did have those character flaws that Leopold was constantly reminding him of. But many of those flaws can be traced to the unnatural childhood imposed upon him by his father. And so the two, father and son, tortured each other for years in a classic love-hate relationship.

Leopold would have been happy had his son settled in Salzburg as a court musician. That was security. Wolfgang, on the other hand, hated the idea of Salzburg and everything connected with it. He knew his powers and knew they would be wasted in a provincial city. Wolfgang was not one to fight against patronage. Almost every composer had an employer—the church, the court, a rich patron. But he wanted a patron with the imagination and resources to let him exploit the ideas racing through his head. Lacking that kind of patron, he tried to achieve his artistic goal on his own, one of the first musicians in history to make the break. It took determination and courage. Artistically he succeeded, though he died penniless. Throughout his letters, beneath all the nonsense that frequently occurs, is the picture of a creative artist with a goal that had to be achieved. No matter what, he adhered to his vision. He could and did write to order, he could write light music, but he could not write cheap music. Mozart never prostituted himself.

His letters are amazing, and they make wonderful reading. In them everything is laid bare. Traveling as much as they did, the Mozarts were constantly in touch with each other by letter. At first, of course, it was Leopold who wrote home. Then, as Wolfgang grew older, he too took the pen. His life and thought can be traced in his letters—those psychologically complex, bright, observant letters, written in so lively a manner; those nervous letters, so full of bravado; those sad last letters, when he is reduced to abject begging for loans. Mozart was a highly intelligent man. In his youthful letters he could be boyish and affectionate: "Kiss Mama's hands for me 100000000 times." There are ebullient, high-spirited letters to his sister: "If you see Herr von Schiedenhofen"—a family friend—"tell him that I am always singing 'Tralaliera, Tralaliera,' and that I need not put sugar in my soup now that I am no longer in Salzburg." Mozart was fourteen when he wrote this, and already an experienced veteran of the musical circuit. His travels never stopped. There are letters to Salzburg from Vienna, Munich, Coblenz, Frankfurt, Brussels, Paris, London, Lyons, Milan, Bologna, Naples, Venice, Innsbruck, Mannheim. Always he was making music, listening to music, talking with musicians. Even at the age of thirteen he was completely mature when it came to writing about music. Already he is the complete professional, as witness the manner he dissected a performance in Mantua in

72

1770: "The prima donna sings well, but very softly; and when you do not see her acting, but only singing, you would think that she is not singing at all. For she cannot open her mouth, but whines out everything . . . The seconda donna looks like a grenadier and has a powerful voice, too, and, I must say, does not sing badly. . . . The primo uomo, il musico, sings beautifully, though his voice is uneven." From Bologna he sends home a letter in which he writes out, note for note, a cadenza sung by the soprano Lucrezia Agujari (who, he says, went up to a C above high C in full voice).

In 1777, Wolfgang went on a long tour with his mother. The object was to find a good job. It was his first trip without his father, and thus his first touch of independence. He kept coming up with wildly impractical suggestions, driving his father out of his mind. An air of bravado can be found in these letters from Munich, Mannheim, and Paris; and as one project or another failed, the bravado increased. In Mannheim he made friends with the Weber family, and they were not the kind of friends to Leopold's liking. They had little money, they lived a Bohemian life, and they had been tied up with shady business deals and lawsuits. The father, Fridolin, was a bass singer, prompter, and music copyist at the court theater. There were the mother, a son, and four daughters. Aloysia Weber, eighteen years old when Mozart met her, had a beautiful voice and a promising future as an opera singer. He fell in love with her. Even Mozart's mother, a gentle soul, protested. "When Wolfgang makes new acquaintances, he immediately wants to give his life and property to them." Mozart's ardent friendship with the Webers was temporarily broken when he and his mother continued on to Paris. His mother died there in 1778, and Mozart had to break the news to his father, which he did in a roundabout way. The old man was not deceived. As soon as he read his son's letter, in which he stated that Mama was very ill, he had a feeling that she was gone.

There was no longer any reason for Mozart to remain in Paris, and he returned to Salzburg in 1779—after a long stay with the Webers in Munich. Aloysia had become a prima donna at the opera there, and things were looking up for the Weber family. When Mozart finally reached home, he was a dejected young man. Aloysia had jilted him. She had bigger fish to net. No, there was little to make Mozart happy in Salzburg. He had warned his father in a sort of declaration of independence from Paris: "A fellow of mediocre talent will remain a mediocrity whether he travels or not; but one of superior talent (which without impiety I cannot deny I possess) will go to seed if he always remains in the same place. If the Archbishop would trust me, I should soon make his orchestra famous; of this there is no doubt. . . . But there is one thing more I must settle about Salzburg, and that is that I shall not be kept to the violin as I used to be. I will no longer be a fiddler. I want to conduct at the clavier and accompany arias."

73

At Salzburg Mozart settled in as court organist, with a chip on his shoulder. He was sullen, truculent, and insubordinate. "I shall certainly hoodwink the Archbishop, and how I shall enjoy doing it!" This was not the frame of mind to endear him to the archiepiscopal court. Nevertheless, bored and dejected as he was, he composed steadily. From this period came the first great works of his young maturity. Up to then his music had been fluent and masterfully constructed, but not much had been very striking. Now, however, came the *Coronation* Mass and some other fine church music, the lovely E flat Concerto for two pianos, and the equally lovely *Sinfonia Concertante* for violin, viola, and orchestra. Suddenly Mozart was a great master. He even received a major opera commission, and *Idomeneo* had its premiere in Munich in 1781. It is an *opera seria*—a serious opera along Gluckian and Metastasian lines. Much of it is stiff and formal, but it contains some magnificent music, including a vocal quartet that is as deep and imaginative as anything he ever wrote. *Idomeneo* never has been one of Mozart's more popular operas. During the nineteenth century and much of the twentieth it was out of the repertoire. In recent years, however, it has been picked up by many opera houses.

The year of *Idomeneo* was also the year Mozart broke with the Archbishop, whose secretary, Count Karl Arco, sped his departure with a kick on the backside. Mozart breathed revenge—from a safe distance. "I shall feel bound to assure him in writing that he may confidently expect from me a kick on his arse and a few boxes on the ear in addition. For when I am insulted I must have my revenge." Of course, he never wrote the letter. Poor Mozart was not cut out to be a hero.

After his dismissal, Mozart settled in Vienna. He had no money, and begged his father not to add to his worries by writing unpleasant letters. The Webers were in Vienna, and Mozart moved in with them. On December 15, 1781, he wrote his father a long letter. After a tremendous preamble about the necessity of a young man getting married, he broke the news that he was in love: "Now then, who is the object of my love? Certainly not a Weber? Yes, a Weber, but not Josepha, not Sophie, but Constanze, the middle one. . . . She is not ugly, but by no means a beauty. Her whole beauty consists in two small black eyes and a winsome figure. She is not witty but she has enough sound common sense to enable her to fulfill her duties as a wife and mother. . . ." Leopold's worst fears had come true, and he must have exploded with rage and frustration. His son was to marry a penniless girl from a family of dubious character. Married they were, in August, 1782. Constanze turned out to be a giddy and flirtatious girl, a bad manager, and no help at all to Mozart. But he loved her, and the marriage seems to have been happy, even if Leopold was not. Relations between Mozart and his father cooled off considerably after 1781.

For a while, things looked promising. Mozart got pupils and commissions. His opera, *Die Entführung aus dem Serail—The Abduction from the Seraglio*—was a decided success when it was produced at the National Theater in 1782. He followed this with masterpiece after masterpiece in all forms. In 1786 he met Lorenzo da Ponte, poet for the imperial theaters, and three great operas resulted—*Le Nozze di Figaro* (1786), *Don Giovanni* (1787), and *Così fan tutte* (1790). The first two were immediate successes in Prague, and Mozart had the greatest public acclaim he had ever achieved. How he loved it! On December 2, 1787, he was appointed Chamber Composer to Emperor Joseph II, with a salary of 800 gulden (as against the 2,000 that Gluck had received). At a rough guess (monetary conversions from two centuries back are highly speculative), 800 gulden in Mozart's day would be equivalent to about $1,000 in 1970 American currency. Mozart took the title but was disgusted. "Too much for what I do, too little for what I could do." The subject of Mozart and his income has never been fully investigated. As a successful opera composer and acclaimed piano virtuoso, he *should* have made a great deal of money. For all we know, it was a great deal, but nobody really knows. If he did make a great deal of money, he and Constanze frittered it away. He was constantly on the move, changing residences eleven times in nine years. He became a Mason. He began to run short of money in the last years of his life and constantly was asking his friend and fellow Mason, the rich merchant Michael Puchberg, for a loan. Puchberg generally came through, even though he must have known he would never be repaid. In 1788 Mozart asked Puchberg for 2,000 gulden for a year or two "at a suitable rate of interest." But if that was inconvenient, "then I beg you to lend me until tomorrow at least a couple of hundred gulden as my landlord in the Landstrasse has been so importunate that in order to avoid such an unpleasant incident I have had to pay him on the spot, and this has made things very awkward for me." Later on, Mozart's requests for loans became almost hysterical. In the last year of his life he composed *Die Zauberflöte—The Magic Flute*—which was first performed on September 30, 1791 and which became a smash hit and presumably would have brought in some money. But a combination of overwork and kidney disease sent him to an early death. He received the cheapest funeral available and is buried not in a pauper's grave, as legend has it, but in an unmarked common grave in St. Marx cemetery. Today nobody knows where the body lies.

Mozart's music is at once easy and hard to listen to: easy, because of its grace, its never-ending melody, its clear and perfect organization; hard, because of its depth, its subtlety, its passion. It is strange to say of a composer who started writing at six, and lived only thirty-six years, that he developed late, but that is the truth. Few of Mozart's early works, elegant as they are, have the personality, concentration, and richness that entered his music after 1781 (the year of his final break from Salzburg, significantly). Such works as the little G minor Symphony (K. 183), with its *Sturm und Drang* drama, or the A major (K. 201) and C major (K. 338) Symphonies are exceptions. (The "K" found after Mozart's works refers to a listing by Ludwig Köchel, who in 1862 made a complete chronological catalogue of Mozart's music.) But 1781 marks the period of Mozart's maturity, and virtually every work thereafter is a masterpiece.

Mozart was on his own in Vienna, and it is as if a great psychological block was lifted. He began to write music of much greater depth, confidence, brilliance, and power. This music was not universally admired. There were those who found it turgid, too complicated, hard to follow. Even such professionals as Karl Ditters von Dittersdorf (1739–1799), an eminent violinist and composer who on the whole admired Mozart, was worried. His conventional mind was shaken, even shocked, and he wrote: "I have never yet met with any composer who had such an amazing wealth of ideas. I could almost wish he were not so lavish in using them. He leaves his hearer out of breath, for hardly has he grasped one beautiful thought than another of greater fascination dispels the first, and this goes on throughout, so that in the end it is impossible to retain any one of these beautiful melodies." (We in the late twentieth century, with recordings and radio and concerts in which Mozart is a staple of the repertoire, are apt to forget that in the 1780's even a professional musician could not be sure that the first time he was hearing a work might not also be the last. There were not that many concerts. A new piece of music had to be grasped immediately. It probably would not even be printed. Not until Beethoven and the romantics could a composer be reasonably sure that all of his major works would be published.) Dittersdorf was not the only one a bit puzzled. Others considered Mozart's music too "highly spiced," too "discordant," his operas too richly scored. "Too beautiful for our ears, and far too many notes, my dear Mozart," as Joseph II said.

Mozart's musical development was conditioned by his father and by such composers as Johann Schobert, C. P. E. Bach, and J. C. Bach. Those were the years when the young Mozart was turning out an enormous amount of music in the *style galant*, graceful, well contoured, melodious, and not particularly striking. The first composer who really meant something to Mozart was Haydn, and the younger man studied the six quartets of Haydn's Op. 33 very carefully, using them as a model for the superb series of six quartets he composed between 1782 and 1785. Mozart gratefully dedicated the six to the Austrian master. "I have learned from Haydn how to write quartets," he said. When Haydn heard these quartets, at Mozart's home in Vienna, his reaction was typically unselfish. "Before God and as an honest man," he exclaimed to Leopold Mozart, "I tell you that your son is the greatest composer known to me, either in person or by name."

Later came the influence of J. S. Bach and Handel, especially the former. Mozart came to know Bach's music through the enthusiast Baron Gottfried van Swieten. The Baron, as ambassador to Prussia, had been introduced to Bach's music and brought back to Vienna copies of many Bach works. (He also was a Handel enthusiast.) It was in 1781 that Mozart became friendly with van Swieten, and he writes to his father the following year: "I go every Sunday at 12 o'clock to Baron van Swieten, where nothing is played but Handel and Bach." The Baron lent Mozart some of the music. "When Constanze heard the fugues she fell absolutely in love with them. Now she will listen to nothing but fugues. . . . Well, as she had often heard me play fugues out of my head, she asked me if I had ever written any down, and when I said I had not, she scolded me roundly for not recording some of my compositions in this most artistic and beautiful of all musical forms." It was after this exposure to Bach that a polyphonic texture entered Mozart's music. Mozartean polyphony is not Bachian polyphony, but Mozart was inspired by Bach to introduce all kinds of contrapuntal devices, all used with perfect security and confidence. The culmination is the last movement of the *Jupiter* Symphony, where contrasting themes are lined up, harnessed, and sent galloping down the final stretch in one of the most glorious, tingling, and overwhelming passages in music.

Mozart and opera requires a book in itself. All his life Mozart was interested in opera. He started composing operas at the age of thirteen with *La Finta Semplice,* and a constant stream followed: *Bastien und Bastienne, Mitridate,* and a half-dozen or so more up to *Idomeneo* of 1781. None of these, except the large-scale *Idomeneo,* is a repertory work of the twentieth century, though they do enjoy occasional revivals. The Mozart operas that are in the repertoire of opera houses all over the world are *Die Entführung aus dem Serail* (1782), *Le Nozze di Figaro* (1786), *Don Giovanni* (1787), *Così fan tutte* (1790), and *Die Zauberflöte* (1791). All of these are comedies, including *Don Giovanni,* which Mozart called a "*dramma giocoso,*" or humorous drama. A good deal of comic opera had been written before Mozart's time, but very little of significance. Mozart was the first to make comic opera transcend mere entertainment. He was able to do so because he himself liked people, because he himself had a gay, bubbling, irrepressible streak within him, and because he tried to make his music explain mood, situation, and character. He was the first psychologist of opera.

Mozart realized the supremacy of music. In a letter to his father he wrote that "in an opera poetry must be altogether the obedient daughter of the music." But he did not mean that the libretto was unimportant. Mozart

77

spent a great deal of time looking for workable librettos. More than anything else he wanted to compose operas. To his father, in 1778: "Do not forget how much I desire to write operas. I envy anyone who is composing one. I could really weep for vexation when I see or hear an aria." In 1781 he set to work on *Entführung*, and his letters give an illuminating insight into his approach. He is discussing Osmin's aria and explains to his father that as the character's rage increases, "there comes (just when the aria seems to be at an end) the allegro assai, which is in a totally different measure and in a different key; this is bound to be very effective. For just as a man in such a towering rage oversteps the bounds of order, moderation, and propriety and completely forgets himself, so must the music too forget itself. But as passions, whether violent or not, must never be expressed in such a way as to excite disgust, and as music, even in the most terrible situations, must never offend the ear, but must please the hearer, or in other words must never cease to be *music*, I have gone from F (the key in which the aria is written) not into a remote key, but into a related one, not, however, into its nearest relative D minor, but into the more remote A minor."

Then Mozart discusses Belmonte's aria, *O wie ängstlich* ("Oh, how anxiously"). "Would you like to know how I have expressed it—and even indicated his throbbing heart? By the two violins playing octaves. This is the favorite aria of all those who have heard it, and it is mine also. I wrote it expressly to suit [Johann Valentin] Adamberger's voice. You feel the trembling—the faltering—you see how his throbbing breast begins to swell; this I have expressed by a crescendo. You hear the whispering and the sighing—which I have indicated by the first violins with mutes and a flute playing in unison." In another letter, Mozart ruminates on opera in general: "Why do Italian comic operas please everywhere—in spite of their miserable librettos—even in Paris, where I myself witnessed their success? Just because there the music reigns supreme and when one listens to it all else is forgiven. Why, an opera is sure of success when the plot is well worked out, the words written solely for the music and not shoved in here and there to suit some miserable rhyme. . . . The best thing of all is when a good composer, who understands the stage and is talented enough to make sound suggestions, meets an able poet, that true phoenix . . ."

Mozart at that time (1781) did not know it, but he was shortly to meet his true phoenix. Lorenzo da Ponte, born in 1749 as Emanuele Conegliano, was an Italian priest who had fled Italy because of a scandal. An adventurer and intriguer, he settled in Vienna and in 1783 became poet of the Court Theater in Vienna for Italian opera. (His life ended in New York City in 1838, where he was the first professor of Italian at Columbia College. He wrote an autobiography, mentioning Mozart hardly at all.) Da Ponte and Mozart came together for an operatic adaptation of the Beaumarchais play,

The Marriage of Figaro. It was surprising that the opera which has such an explosive subject—the routing of an aristocrat by a pair of quick-witted plebeians—was allowed to be staged at all. The original play did contain the seeds of revolution, as more sensitive observers, such as the Baroness d'Oberkirch, realized. She watched great lords and ladies chortling at the Beaumarchais comedy and observed: "They will be sorry for it one day." Did Mozart secretly see himself as Figaro? It is not impossible.

The Marriage of Figaro opens the door to a new world of opera. It is a scintillating work with real people in it, and the music exposes them for what they are—lovable, vain, capricious, selfish, ambitious, forgiving, philandering. Human beings, in short, all brought alive by the alchemy of a surpassingly inventive and sympathetic musical mind. In *Figaro* there is not one flawed note, not one situation that rings false. *Così fan tutte*, for instance, has a score on the musical level of *Figaro*, but the libretto written by da Ponte is frankly a farce—a farce with a deep underlying meaning, to be sure, but nevertheless a libretto with an artificially arranged construction. It is an adorable work, but without the humanity of its predecessor. Similarly *The Magic Flute*, in which many see the quintessence of Mozart's music, has a fairy-tale libretto by Emanuel Schikaneder which is full of Masonic symbolism but which, read in cold blood, is as naïve and awkward a pageant as ever disgraced the operatic stage. (The general plan was that of the spectacular comedies popular with Viennese audiences of the time.) All kinds of theories have been advanced about the opera. In 1866 one Moritz Alexander Zille insisted that *The Magic Flute* was an allegory striking back at Leopold II, who was persecuting the Masons. In this interpretation, Sarastro represented Ignaz von Born, leader of Austrian Freemasonry. The Queen of the Night was Empress Maria Theresa, the foe of Masonry. Tamino was Joseph II, Leopold's predecessor, who had been hospitable to the Masons. And so on. Other theories have been advanced. But no matter what is read into it, the libretto is silly and inconsistent. Nevertheless, the Viennese public took it to its heart. It was by far the biggest success with which Mozart had been associated.

The Mozart opera that meant the most to the romantic nineteenth century was *Don Giovanni*, and it is the most romantic of Mozart's operas, just as it is the most serious, the most powerful, and the most otherworldly (the romantics especially loved the graveyard scene and the final appearance of the Commandant). Many consider *Don Giovanni* to be the greatest opera ever composed. The overture sets the mood. With a few diminished seventh chords and a D minor scale, Mozart creates a feeling of anxiety, intensity, anguish, oncoming horror. Near the end of the opera the scale reappears, and one's hair stands on end. It is a colossal effect with the simplest of means. Small wonder the romantics rejoiced. The opera had a moral, and the sentimental romantics liked that too, even if many of them missed the point. What makes the dissolute, cynical, decadent, and rather unsavory Don Giovanni an authentic hero, and a modern hero at that, is the fact that he is willing to die for his principles. "Repent!" cries the apparation of the Commandant. "No!" says the Don. "Repent!" "No!" and Hell opens wide. Carmen was later to be the same kind of heroine. She knows Don José will kill her, but that is less important than giving in to a man she despises. Like Don Giovanni, she dies for a principle.

It was not only in opera, of course, that Mozart's genius shone; it was in every form. The piano concerto is a musical form developed by Mozart into symphonic breadth, and there is not one of his concertos after K. 271 in E flat without its special kind of eloquence, finish, and virtuosity: some gay and happy, as the B flat (K. 595) or the A major (K. 488), even with its ele- giac slow movement; some dark and romantic, such as the D minor; some classic and noble, such as the C minor.

The works of Mozart's maturity read like an honor roll: the Clarinet Quintet, the E flat Divertimento, the unfinished Mass in C minor and the unfinished Requiem, the two piano quartets, the last ten string quartets, the five great string quintets, the Sinfonia Concertante for Violin and Viola, the Serenade for Thirteen Winds, the last six symphonies, the Clarinet Con- certo, the Adagio and Fugue in C minor. These works stand together as a body of music in which form, expression, technique, and taste are raised to unprecedented heights.

Mozart was constantly talking and writing about "taste," and he had nothing but scorn for the musician who indulged in cheap or meretricious effects. That was one reason why he had hard words to say about the pianist Muzio Clementi—"a charlatan"—for Clementi was out to impress with his technique, with his double thirds, octaves, and virtuosity. (Another reason for Mozart's distaste may have been the realization that Clementi possessed an order of execution as good as his and probably superior.) Mozart was an apostle of proportion. This does not imply sterility or inhibition for Mozart was a very practical composer who was as much interested in the effect of a piece as Verdi or Liszt. He composed his piano concertos as vehicles for himself, and some were frankly virtuoso exercises calculated to make the public—and competing pianists—sit up and take notice. Talking about his Concertos in B flat (K. 450) and D (K. 451) he said that he regarded both as works "bound to make the performers perspire." Similarly as an opera com- poser he had no hesitation in tailoring an aria for a particular voice, or sim- plifying the music as necessary to accommodate a singer, as he did for Anton Raaff in *Idomeneo*. Raaff was unhappy about some of the settings and Mozart was only too glad to oblige him. But what always sets Mozart's music apart is its proportion and *rightness*—its taste, if you will. That, and an inexhaustible fund of melody joined to an extremely daring harmonic sense. A fully developed harmonic sense, a feeling for modulation, is the infallible mark of the important composer. It is the mediocrity who sits close to home, who does not have the imagination or the daring to go from key to key. The lack of harmonic richness is what makes so much eighteenth-century music so boring today, that incessant tonic-dominant harmony. Bach had harmonic imagination, and so did Mozart. Mozart's constant and unexpected deviations from the textbook help make his music so entrancing and ever fresh. In a work like the E flat Violin Sonata (K. 481), the first movement touches on the keys of A flat, F minor, D flat, C sharp minor, A major, and G sharp minor. Some of his late piano works, such as the B minor Adagio, have a harmonic texture that actually anticipates Chopin, so varied is the key structure.

Relatively little of Mozart's music was published during his lifetime—144 works in all, a good deal of it light music. He left a very large mass of autographs, and suddenly his widow, who had never been much of a help to him when he was alive, developed into a first-class businesswoman, selling off publication rights for excellent prices, but holding on to the autographs themselves. Thanks to the great success of *The Magic Flute*, there was a Mozart boom at his death, and his music received many performances, though not always as he would have liked. *The Magic Flute*, for instance, was staged in Paris in 1801 as *Les Mystères d'Isis*. The text was changed, harmonies were altered, and sections of other Mozart operas and even of Haydn symphonies were introduced into the score. As far as the age was concerned, however, there was nothing unusual about such a procedure. The concept of fidelity to the printed score was to come much later, in the twentieth century. In any case, Mozart was constantly misunderstood by the nineteenth century. He was called the Raphael of music, and was considered an elegant, dainty rococo composer who just happened to have composed *Don Giovanni*. The humanity and power that animate his music went largely unnoticed.

Nor was Mozart played very much during the Romantic period. When he was, it was with all the exaggerations and trappings of romanticism—inflated dynamics, super-legato phrasings, balance obscured under the heavy color of massed strings. It was not until after the First World War that a serious effort was made to return to the performance practices of Mozart's own day. The battle has not yet been won, however, for orchestras still tend to be out of balance, ruining Mozart's delicate instrumental adjustments. It is not a matter of the size of orchestras. Mozart, like any other composer, was thrilled when he heard his music played by large forces, but he expected the conductor to compensate by adding low-voiced instruments to counterbalance the violins. In 1781 he heard one of his symphonies played by a very large group, and he wrote to his father about it with glee: "The symphony went magnifique and had the greatest success. There were forty violins; *the wind instruments were all doubled,* there were ten violas, eight cellos *and six bassoons.*" (Italics added.) The point is that twentieth-century conductors are still apt to lose the sounds, balances, and adjustments Mozart had in his ear, just as no brilliantly voiced concert grand piano, with its roaring bass and unlimited power, can give an idea of Mozart's piano music, which was composed for a light-actioned Walther piano with a modest dynamic range.

Of course, it is impossible to duplicate exactly the conditions under which Mozart heard his music played. For one thing, pitch has gone up a full half tone since Mozart's day. If he, with his perfect ear, were to hear his G minor Symphony in what to him would be G sharp minor, he would become physically ill. (Musicians with highly organized aural equipment have trouble listening to music played in wrong keys. They hear both keys at once, a semitone or whatever apart, and it is a discordantly unnerving experience.) Instruments, too, have changed. Tempos in Mozart's day are still a mystery. What, exactly, did he mean by "allegro" or andante?" Another problem is that of improvisation. The piano parts of Mozart's concerto scores sometimes are little more than a skeleton of what he actually did on stage. The slow movement of the *Coronation* Concerto as it has come down to us is a good example. It is written in a kind of shorthand, with single notes in the treble and bass. Mozart would have filled in the harmony and embellished the bare melody while playing it. Like all performing musicians of the day, Mozart constantly improvised not only cadenzas but also embellished the melodic line as he went along. It is a mistake to approach Mozart's music with the attitude that the printed note is the final word. Often it is, or should be, just the beginning. If recent research into eighteenth-century performance practice has demonstrated one thing, it is that our forefathers used much more freedom in interpreting the music than many twentieth-century musicians are prepared to admit.

In any case, the music of Mozart today stands rehabilitated, largely freed from the misconceptions of previous eras. The little man from Salzburg was a miracle. More protean than Bach, musically more aristocratic than Beethoven, he can be put forward as the most perfect, best equipped, and most natural musician the world has ever known.

๕ 6 ๖

Revolutionary from Bonn

LUDWIG VAN BEETHOVEN

The difference between Beethoven and all other musicians before him—aside from things like genius and unparalleled force—was that Beethoven looked upon himself as an artist, and he stood up for his rights as an artist. Where Mozart moved in the periphery of the aristocratic world, anxiously knocking but never really admitted, Beethoven, who was only fourteen years Mozart's junior, kicked open the doors, stormed in and made himself at home. He was an artist, a creator, and as such superior to kings and nobles. Beethoven had decidely revolutionary notions about society, and romantic notions about music. "What is in my heart must come out and so I write it down," he told his pupil Carl Czerny. Mozart would never have said a thing like this, nor Haydn, nor Bach. The word "artist" never occurs in Mozart's letters. He and the composers before him were skilled craftsmen who supplied a commodity, and the notion of art or writing for posterity did not enter into their thinking. But Beethoven's letters and observations are full of words like "art," "artist," and "artistry." He was of a special breed and he knew it. He also knew he was writing for eternity. And he had what poor Mozart lacked—a powerful personality that awed all who came in contact with him. "Never have I met an artist of such spiritual concentration and intensity," Goethe wrote, "such vitality and great-heartedness. I can well understand how hard he must find it to adapt to the world and its ways." Little did Goethe understand Beethoven. With Beethoven, it was not a matter of adapting himself to the world and its ways. As with Wagner later on, it was a matter of the world adapting its ways to *him*. With this high-voltage personality, coupled to an equally high-voltage order of genius, Beethoven was able to dictate to life on his own terms in almost everything except his tragic deafness.

He was able to achieve this despite character flaws and deplorable manners. Never a beauty, he was called *Der Spagnol* in his youth because of his swarthiness. He was short, about 5 feet, 4 inches, thickset and broad, with a massive head, a wildly luxuriant crop of hair, protruding teeth, a small rounded nose, and a habit of spitting wherever the notion took him. He was clumsy, and anything he touched was liable to be upset or broken. Badly co-ordinated, he could never learn to dance, and more often than not managed to cut himself while shaving. He was sullen and suspicious, touchy as a misanthropic cobra, believed that everybody was out to cheat him, had none of the social graces, was forgetful, was prone to insensate rages, engaged in some unethical dealings with his publishers. A bachelor, he lived in indescribably messy surroundings, largely because no servant could put up with his tantrums. In 1809 he was visited by the Baron de Trémont, and this is how that shocked worthy describes Beethoven's quarters:

> Picture to yourself the darkest, most disorderly place imaginable—blotches of moisture covered the ceiling; an oldish grand piano, on which the dust disputed the place with various pieces of engraved and manuscript music; under the piano (I do not exaggerate) an unemptied chamber pot; beside it a small walnut table accustomed to the frequent overturning of the secretary placed on it; a quantity of pens encrusted with ink, compared with which the proverbial tavern pens would shine; then more music. The chairs, mostly cane-seated, were covered with plates bearing the remains of last night's supper, and with wearing apparel, etc.

The Baron de Trémont's description is one of many along those lines. Beethoven was disorganized in everything but the one thing that really mattered—his music.

His genius was recognized almost from the beginning. A provincial from Bonn, where he was born on December 16, 1770, he was brought up by his father, a dissolute court musician. As a child prodigy, Ludwig was subjected to a severe regimen, and as so often happens in the history of prodigies, it affected his life. Richard and Edith Sterba, who have written a psychiatric study of Beethoven, maintain that "An early rebellion against his father's arbitrariness and unjust strictness laid the foundation for the revolt against every kind of authority which appears in Beethoven with an intensity which can only be described as highly unusual." His father hoped that he would be able to duplicate the feats of the young Mozart. It did not work out that way. The boy was certainly talented enough, and when he was twelve one of his teachers, Christian Gottlob Neefe, said that if he continued as he began, "he will surely be a second Mozart." But although Ludwig was a skilled pianist, violinist, and organist, he was something more than that. From the beginning he was a creator, one of those natural talents, full of ideas and originality.

It was this originality that set him apart. He was a force of nature, and nothing could contain him. He had a few lessons with prominent composers of the day, including Haydn and Mozart, but was dissatisfied with both of those great men and nothing much came of those lessons. It made no difference. Beethoven was not the kind of pupil who can be easily taught. He was too confident of his own genius. Once he made up his mind about something, he *knew* he was right. He always looked with suspicion on "rules" of harmony, and one of his friends once pointed out a series of parallel fifths in his music. In classical harmony, this is the unforgivable sin. Beethoven bridled. Who forbids parallel fifths, he wanted to know. A list of authorities was cited: Fux, Albrechtsberger, and so on. Beethoven dismissed them with a wave of his hand. *"I* admit them," he said. And there exists a notebook in which one harmony exercise is worked out seventeen times to show that one of the "rules" was wrong. Disproving the rule to his own satisfaction, Beethoven added *Du Esel*—you ass—as a comment on the authority who had made the "rule."

He first came to fame as a pianist. By 1791 a critic named Carl Ludwig Junker heard Beethoven play and had a few perceptive remarks to make: "'His style of treating the instrument is so different from that usually heard that it gives one the idea that he has attained that height of excellence on which he now stands by a path of his own discovery." When Beethoven settled in Vienna, in 1792, his style of playing made an overwhelming impression. The Viennese were conditioned to the smooth, fluent style of a Mozart or Hummel. Here came young Beethoven, hands high, smashing the piano, breaking strings, aiming for a hitherto unexploited kind of orchestral sonority on the keyboard. In his quest for more power, Beethoven begged the piano manufacturers to give him a better instrument than the light-actioned Viennese piano, which he said sounded like a harp. Beethoven was the greatest pianist of his time, and perhaps the greatest improviser who ever lived. In the Vienna of his time there was a group of able pianists, in residence or constantly passing through—Hummel, the Abbé Gelinek, Joseph Wölffl, Daniel Steibelt, Ignaz Moscheles. All these Beethoven at one time or another played under the table. None could stand up to him, though the admirable Wölffl, with his classic style, had a strong following among the conservatives. In many respects, Beethoven was the first of the modern piano virtuosos. Where pianists before him suavely and elegantly wooed an audience, Beethoven planted bombs under their seats.

Beethoven was all but adopted by the aristocracy. Fortunately for him, it was a liberal, enlightened, and music-loving aristocracy. Many of the noblemen maintained private orchestras and nearly all had musical salons. Great figures like the Princes Lobkowitz, Schwarzenberg, and Auersperg, Count Heinrich von Haugwitz, and Count Batthyany actually traveled with their orchestras. Prince Grassalkowich had a small wind orchestra. Beethoven moved in these circles and was not in the least awed. "It is easy to get on with the nobility if you have something to impress them with." Haydn and Mozart were expected to dine with the servants. Not Beethoven, who was mighty insulted if he was not at the host's side.

He not only moved in this society. He even had love affairs with its ladies, though the subject of Beethoven and women has been largely unexplored. He is credited by one of his contemporaries with having made conquests that an Adonis could not have made, and he seems to have been in and out of love all his life. Yet there is no real evidence that his amours were ever crowned with physical success. The Sterbas flatly say that Beethoven hated women; that even though he often said he wanted to be married, he subconsciously fled the idea. That is why he fell in love with women who under no circumstances would marry him—women who were already married, or far above him in social station. Nevertheless, there are ardent Beethoven letters to this or that lady, including the famous one to the mysterious Immortal Beloved, whoever she may have been. "My angel, my all, my very self . . . can you change the fact that you are not wholly mine, I not wholly thine . . . Ah, wherever I am, there you are also. . . . Much as you love me, I love you more. . . . Is not our love a heavenly structure, and also as firm as the vault of Heaven . . ." There seems to be no more chance of identifying her than there is of identifying the Dark Lady of the Sonnets, though scholars for generations have been working on those shadowy figures in Beethoven's and Shakespeare's life. However, George Marek, in his biography of Beethoven (1969), has found new evidence that points to Dorothea von Ertmann. She was the wife of an Austrian army officer and a gifted pianist. Beethoven, by the way, was very prudish. He even objected to *Don Giovanni* on the basis of its plot, which he said was immoral.

It is an oversimplification to say, as some music histories do, that Beethoven made his way without patronage. He probably could have been able to do so, but the fact remains that as early as 1801 Prince Lichnowsky settled some money on him. Later, when Beethoven was offered a position in the Westphalian court, the Archduke Rudolf, Prince Lobkowitz, and Prince Kinsky got together and put up 4,000 gulden to keep him in Vienna. That was in 1808. Because of the devaluation of the currency in 1811, that annuity was dissipated. Then Kinsky was killed in an accident and Lobkowitz went bankrupt. Nevertheless, the two noblemen and the Kinsky estate made up the difference, and from 1815 until his death Beethoven received 3,400 florins annually. He was not ashamed to take the money. Quite the contrary. He actually went to court to make the Kinsky estate uphold its obligation. Beethoven did not ask for the money, he *demanded* it. He felt it was his due.

During Beethoven's early years in Vienna, all was rosy. The world was at his feet. He was successful, honored, admired. He had swept all before him as a pianist, and his compositions were beginning to make their mark. His list of pupils boasted some of the most famous names in Vienna. Financially he did very well. "My compositions bring me in a good deal," he wrote to Franz Wegeler, his old friend from Bonn, in 1801, "and I may say that I am offered more commissions than it is possible for me to carry out. Moreover, for every composition I can count on six or seven publishers and even more, if I want them. People no longer come to an arrangement with me. I state my price, and they pay."

But something terrible was beginning to happen. Beethoven's hearing was going.

"My ears buzz continually day and night," he wrote Wegeler. "I can say that I am living a wretched life because it is impossible to say to people: 'I am deaf.' . . . In order to give you an idea of this singular deafness of mine, I must tell you that in the theater I must get very close to the orchestra in order to understand the actor. If I am a little too distant I do not hear the high notes of the instruments, singers, and if I am a little further back I do not hear at all. Frequently I can hear a low conversation, but not the words, and as soon as anybody shouts, it is intolerable." Beethoven tried everything to arrest the aural decay. He even was willing to attempt a cure by galvanism, or by quack doctors.

Naturally, he went through a traumatic experience, and the famous Heiligenstadt Testament, written in 1802 and addressed to his brothers to be read after his death, is a *cri de coeur:* "Oh you who think or say that I am malevolent, stubborn or misanthropic, how greatly do you wrong me. You do not know the secret cause which makes me seem that way to you. . . . Ah, how could I possibly admit an infirmity in the *one sense* which ought to be more perfect in me than in others, a sense which I once enjoyed in the highest perfection, a perfection such as few in my profession enjoy or have enjoyed . . ." There is page after page of lamentation.

He refused to bow to his affliction, though every year saw a further deterioration. By 1817 he was all but stone deaf, though he had his good days in which he could hear some music or speech without an ear trumpet. The cause of his affliction has not been established. It could have resulted from an attack of typhus. Or it might, as some otologists believe, have resulted from syphilis, acquired or congenital. Beethoven's battle with deafness was heroic, epic. He continued to play the piano, and he insisted on conducting his own music even though his wild gestures, coupled with an inability to hear well, completely threw the orchestra off course. The players learned not to look at him, paying attention instead to the first violinist. However, Beethoven, being the musician he was, could actually let sight substitute for hearing. Joseph Böhm, leader of a string quartet, has left us a description of Beethoven at work, and it is heartrending. In 1825, Böhm worked on the E flat Quartet (Op. 127) with the composer present. "It was studied industriously and rehearsed frequently under Beethoven's own eyes: I said Beethoven's *eyes* intentionally, for the unhappy man was so deaf he could no longer hear the heavenly sounds of his own compositions. And yet rehearsing in his presence was not easy. With close attention his eyes followed the bows and therefore he was able to judge the smallest imperfections in tempo or rhythm and correct them immediately."

Nonmusicians find it next to impossible to imagine how a deaf composer can function. But with musicians of a high order of ability, deafness involves only external sounds, not internal ones. Beethoven had absolute pitch, the ability to hear any note or combination of notes and instantly name them; or, on the opposite side, the ability to sing correctly any note without the artificial aid of a piano or tuning fork. That ability is not particularly rare. Any good musician, or even a talented nonprofessional, for that matter, can pick up a score and read it, "hearing" everything that goes on. A good composer does not need a piano to work. Indeed, Beethoven once told his English pupil, Cipriani Potter, never to compose in a room in which there was a piano, in order to resist the temptation to consult an instrument. To many nonmusicians, this ability is on the order of black magic, but professionals take it as a matter of course. Thus Beethoven, with his incredible musical mind, would have had no trouble, no more than Bach or Mozart had, writing music guided only by the sounds in his inner ear.

At the height of his depression, Beethoven was working on the *Eroica* Symphony, which had its premiere in 1805. The *Eroica* is one of the turning points in musical history. Up to then Beethoven had been a composer with roots in the eighteenth century. His music, to be sure, was more rugged than that of Haydn and Mozart. The six quartets of Op. 18 had a lustiness that hinted, but only hinted, at a new world. The first two symphonies pushed the classic symphony to new lengths, both in actual duration and size of the orchestra. The early piano sonatas, especially the *Pathétique*, *Moonlight* (not so named by Beethoven), and D minor, went farther than any of Mozart's or Haydn's piano music in their massive sonority, romantic expression, unconventionality of form, and a new kind of virtuosity. But nevertheless, on the whole, the pre-*Eroica* music is the language of Beethoven's great predecessors. Then came the *Eroica*, and music was never again the same. With one convulsive wrench, music entered the nineteenth century.

The background of the *Eroica* is well known. Beethoven set to work on it in 1803, intending the score to be a tribute to Bonaparte. When Bonaparte proclaimed himself Emperor, legend has it that Beethoven, who preached a kind of democracy, tore up the title page containing the dedication. By May, 1804, the score was finished, and the premiere took place on April 7, 1805, at the Theater an der Wien. History does not relate the quality of the performance. Beethoven's gigantic score must have imposed unprecedented difficulties on the musicians, and the chances are that they played raggedly and out of tune. One wonders, too, what went through the mind of the audience on that historic occasion. It was faced with a monster of a symphony, a symphony longer than any previously written and much more heavily scored; a symphony with complex harmonies; a symphony of titanic force; a symphony of fierce dissonances; a symphony with a funeral march that is paralyzing in its intensity.

Sensitive listeners realized they were in the presence of something monumental. The critics were worried. They recognized the power of the *Eroica*, but very few could grasp its stringent logic and organization. "This long composition," wrote the critic of the *Allgemeine Musikalische Zeitung*, "extremely difficult of performance, is in reality a tremendously expanded, daring and wild fantasia. It lacks nothing in the way of startling and beautiful passages, in which the energetic and talented composer must be recognized; but often it loses itself in lawlessness. . . . . This reviewer belongs to Mr. Beethoven's sincerest admirers, but in this composition he must confess that he finds much that is glaring and bizarre, which hinders greatly one's grasp of the whole, and a sense of unity is almost completely lost." Musical Vienna was divided on the merits of the *Eroica*. Some called it Beethoven's masterpiece. Others said that the work merely illustrated a striving for originality that did not come off. In those circles the feeling was that Beethoven should not continue on this track but should go back to writing music like the celebrated Septet and the first two symphonies. The latter faction outnumbered the admirers of the *Eroica*. At the premiere the audience was not as responsive as Beethoven would have liked to have seen, and he was unhappy, but he refused to change a note. "If *I* write a symphony an hour long, it will be found short enough," he was quoted as saying. His only concession was to suggest that the *Eroica* be played near the beginning of a program, before the audience got weary. The *Eroica* runs about fifty minutes, and even longer if all the repeats are taken. Few, if any, Mozart or Haydn symphonies are over a half-hour long.

The next seven or eight years saw a succession of masterpieces: the first version of *Fidelio* in 1805 (it was not a success until its revision in 1814), the three *Razumovsky* Quartets, the Violin Concerto, the Piano Concertos Nos. 4 in G and 5 in E flat, the Symphonies Nos. 4 through 8, several of the most famous piano sonatas (including the *Waldstein* and *Appassionata*). But around 1811 there was a falling-off in Beethoven's productivity. Several things happened. As his deafness became total, he retired more and more into his inner world. It was a period of gestation from which were to come the *Missa Solemnis* and the final string quartets and piano sonatas—those gigantic, mysterious, mystic creations. Beethoven knew he was in the process of conception even though his pen was idle. "It has always been one of my rules: *Nulla dies sine linea,*" he told Wegeler, "and if I let the Muse sleep, it is only in order that she shall wake up the stronger." In addition, his health was not good. He was bothered by liver and intestinal trouble. But the major factor in his life, one that took up much of his time and conceivably might have robbed the world of some masterpieces, was his relationship with his nephew, Karl.

When Beethoven's brother Caspar died in 1815, the will appointed Caspar's wife, Johanna, and his brother Ludwig, guardian of the nine-year-old child. Beethoven's opinion of Johanna was low to begin with, and to get Karl away from her he resorted to the courts, acting like a wild man, accusing her of character defects and immorality. He did get her guardianship annulled, but she fought back and in 1819 was successful. Beethoven went to a higher court and in 1820 finally won his case. Karl seems to have been a bright, receptive boy, but he could not have found a worse guardian than his doting Uncle Ludwig, who meant well but was alternately strict and easygoing. Karl was driven out of his mind. He learned to take the easy way out and flatter his uncle, but nothing worked. The boy found dubious friends, tried to break away, was unsuccessful and finally, in 1826, attempted suicide. One bullet missed, the other gave him a scalp wound. On recovery, he said that he wanted Beethoven to keep away. "If only he would stop nagging me!" He told the police that Beethoven tormented him. Beethoven took it very badly, and friends said he aged twenty years in those weeks. Eventually Karl, a maligned and misunderstood figure, went into the army. He resigned in 1832, married, inherited the estate of Uncle Johann (Beethoven's other brother), and died in 1858.

Thanks to Beethoven's endless litigation over Karl and his psychopathic determination to thwart his sister-in-law, the period from 1815 to 1820 saw very little music, only six major works in six years. These included the last two cello sonatas, the song cycle *An die ferne Geliebte,* and the Piano Sonatas in A (Op. 101), B flat (Op. 106), and E (Op. 109). The B flat is the *Hammerklavier,* the longest, grandest, and most difficult sonata in history, with a last movement consisting of an all but unplayable fugue. Would he have composed so murderous (technically) a movement had he not been deaf? One wonders. From 1818 he was occupied with the *Missa Solemnis* and Ninth Symphony, finishing the former in 1823 and the Ninth in the following year. The Ninth Symphony had its premiere on May 7, 1824—with only two rehearsals! It must have been a catastrophe. The chorus had trouble singing the music and pleaded for the high notes to be taken down, just as the contralto soloist, Caroline Unger, also begged for changes. Beethoven refused. At the concert, those singers who could not reach the high notes simply omitted them. The scherzo made a big impression, however, and Unger turned Beethoven around so he could see the applause he could not hear. As the *Eroica* was a pivotal point in nineteenth-century music, so the Ninth Symphony was the Beethoven work that above all captured the imagination of the later romantics. Beethoven's last great contributions to music were five string quartets and a fugue for string quartet, the *Grosse Fuge,* originally intended as the last movement of the B flat Quartet (Op. 130).

In his Vienna he was as famous a figure as ever, universally conceded to be the greatest composer in the world, greater even than the composer-pianist Johann Nepomuk Hummel. He also was admired by the Viennese as one of the great eccentrics. His fame, of course, was universal, and people came from all over the continent and England to visit him. He saw them all. He was a familiar figure in the taverns and coffeehouses, where he would hold forth pontifically on all subjects. Self-educated, he was not what could be called an intellectual, and outside of music his mental processes were anything but remarkable. This can be seen in his letters, those infuriating letters, most of which consist of dealing with publishers, or short notes inviting friends for dinner—everything but the things we most want to know: what he thought about music, about his contemporaries, about life. Mozart's letters are revelatory, illustrative of a sharp, quick mind and an endearing, if weak, personality. Beethoven's for the most part (there are exceptions) tell us virtually nothing about himself.

He died on March 27, 1827, after a long illness. If contemporary accounts are to be believed, there was a flash of lightning, a clap of thunder, and the dying man raised himself and defiantly shook his fist at it. The story sounds too pat, too much a romantic invention, to be true, but one hopes it is. Beethoven went through life defying everything. Why not at the end of the struggle, defy the elements and God himself? It is reported that some 20,000 people turned out for the funeral.

This was the man who was the most powerful musical thinker of music. He is often considered a bridge between the classical and romantic periods, but that is merely a label, and not a very accurate one. Indeed, there is surprisingly little romanticism in his music, much less than in the work of Weber and Schubert, two composers active in his time (Weber died in 1826, Schubert in 1828), and much less than in the work of some of the minor figures, such as Ludwig Spohr and Jan Ladislav Dussek. Certain exceptions in Beethoven's music can be cited. The slow movement of the E major Piano Sonata (Op. 109), with its almost Chopinesque melody, has some romanticism in it, for example. But Beethoven simply did not speak the language of the romantics. He had started as a composer in the classic tradition and ended up a composer beyond time and space, using a language he himself had forged: a language compressed, cryptic, and explosive, expressed in forms of his own devising.

Beethoven was a very slow worker. Where Mozart took days or weeks over a work, Beethoven took months and years. Mozart composed his three greatest symphonies within six weeks in the summer of 1788. Beethoven took at least three years, polishing and rewriting, before he thought his Op. 1, three piano trios, was ready for publication. He carried ideas in his head for a long time, and then there was the struggle of getting them on paper. His sketchbooks reveal that he would refine and refine, changing a phrase note by note until it had that definitive quality we recognize as Beethovenian. The theme of the slow movement of the Fifth Symphony must have passed through at least a dozen transformations before Beethoven settled on its final shape. Maturity did not bring relaxation. As Beethoven's musical vision grew, so did his struggles with the material.

Beethoven's music falls into three periods. At the beginning he worked mostly within the forms of the day. His first twenty works or so test the old forms, expanding them, hinting at the explosive power that was to come. Even there, the rough humor and the high degree of expressivity that was to mark the mature Beethoven were already in evidence. The galloping minuet of the First Symphony points the way to the powerful scherzos of the later ones. The intense, beautiful slow movement of the D major Piano Sonata (Op. 10, No. 3) is a minature tone poem. Already Beethoven was a poet in tone, and there is a personal quality to this kind of writing, a direct emotional involvement, a kind of near-romantic melody that is something new in music. The difference between the first movement of the *Pathétique* Sonata and the equally great and powerful C minor Fantasy (K. 475) by Mozart is the difference between the eighteenth and nineteenth century, the difference between a society dominated by the idea of aristocracy and a society dominated by the concept of individuality. In Beethoven's music, the concepts put into motion by the French Revolution and the Industrial Revolution are shaping the destiny of man and art. Beethoven's music has much more personal quality than Mozart's. It is more concerned with inner states of being and the desire for self-expression. Mozart holds himself in classic restraint, while Beethoven bares his soul for all to see.

After the turning point of the *Eroica*, the second period sets in. Beethoven was confident, a master of form, with a fertile mind and an individuality that made its own rules. Under his pen, sonata form underwent a metamorphosis. Beethoven took the sonata form of Haydn and Mozart, and the majority of his great works—the symphonies, concertos, quartets, piano and violin sonatas, trios and other chamber music—are expressed in sonata form, *his* sonata form, not textbook sonata form. The lesser composers of his day used sonata form much as a builder uses a standard architectural plan for a prefabricated house, and the result had as much individuality: Theme A, Theme B, a routine and mechanical development (breaking no rules and using no unconventional harmonies), a recapitulation. But Beethoven bent and twisted sonata form to suit himself and his material. His invention and resource never flagged. He could, in the Fifth Symphony, erect an entire structure on four notes—hammerblows, more a motif than a theme. He could, in the *Appassionata* Sonata, devise a work that breaks all classic rules and erupts wildly all over the keyboard. Lacking the superrefined harmonic sense of a Mozart, he could and did bring something different to music—a propulsive kind of rhythm, a broadening of all musical structures, a kind of development that wrings everything out of the material, a kind of accentuation, often off the beat, that throws the music into uneasy and unexpected metrical patterns, a sheer independence. Beethoven's music is not polite. What he presented, as no composer before or since, was a feeling of drama, of conflict and resolution. But this is conflict expressed purely in musical terms. Beethoven thought only in tone, in musical architecture. He derided program music. While composing the *Pastoral* Symphony he thought about the problem and set down some observations: "All painting in instrumental music is lost if pushed too far. . . . Anyone who has an idea of country life can make out for himself the intentions of the composer without many titles. . . . Also, without titles, the whole will be recognized as a matter more of feeling than of painting in sounds."

Thus, whatever the emotional state of being that any Beethoven score suggests, it is held together by purely *musical* logic, by the composer's ideas of development, contrast, thematic linkages, and rhythm. The music may be a yelp of sheer exultation, as in the last movement of the C major Quartet or most of the Seventh Symphony; or it may be gnarled and cryptic, as in the curious Piano Sonata in F sharp, or it may be a combination of electric virtuosity and pure lyricism, as in the *Emperor* Concerto; or it may be ravishing lyricism throughout, as in the G major Piano Concerto. Whatever it is, it is music governed by the inexorable logic of a great technician and musical thinker.

Then comes the fallow period, followed by the so-called last-period works —the last five string quartets and piano sonatas, the *Diabelli* Variations, the *Missa Solemnis*, the Ninth Symphony. Here we are on a rarefied plane of music. Nothing like it has been composed, nothing like it can ever again be. It is the music of a man who has seen all and experienced all, a man drawn into his silent, suffering world, no longer writing to please anybody else but writing to justify his artistic and intellectual existence. Faced with this music, the temptation is to read things into it in some sort of metaphysical exegesis. The music is not pretty or even attractive. It merely is sublime. At this stage of his career, Beethoven seemed to be dealing as much in concepts and symbols as in notes. Themes can be terse and abrupt or, in such works as the cavatina of the B flat major String Quartet, a long effusion without end. Even silences play a part in this music. Suddenly the trill assumes a menacing importance. The music of Beethoven's last period is full of long, vicious trills that must have had some kind of extramusical significance to him. Form is now not what the professors or the age dictate, but only what the music dictates. The C minor Piano Sonata (Op. 111) has only two movements, the last movement a series of variations ending with a sustained, hushed, mysterious chain of trills. The C sharp minor Quartet has seven clearly defined movements played without a break. The Ninth Symphony has a final movement that uses a chorus and vocal soloists. All of this is music turned inward, music of the spirit, music of extreme subjectivity and extraordinary grandeur.

To this day the last quartets pose problems. Those who will not or can not enter Beethoven's world find them bleak, cold, and incomprehensible, and this is especially true of the great trinity, Opp. 130 in B flat, 131 in C sharp minor, and 132 in A minor. In a way, these three string quartets can be looked upon as one superquartet. They have themes in common, share the same language and feeling, are interrelated texturally and harmonically. Each of these quartets is very long (just as, contrariwise, the last three piano sonatas are relatively short), and each defies description. They are a mystic state of mind as much as music. Their organic developments, the convulsions of the *Grosse Fuge,* the ineffable unfolding of the Lydian slow movement of the A minor Quartet, the fugal introduction to the C sharp minor, the Cavatina of the B flat—all this and much more carry music to a height that actually seems to transcend music.

This concept of Beethoven's musical transcendentalism may have been felt during Beethoven's lifetime, and was certainly adopted by the musicians of the romantic period. In 1859 a scholar named Adolf Bernhard Marx wrote a book about Beethoven that introduced the concept of *Idealmusik,* the idea being that the music of Beethoven had as much to do with ethics as with pure tone. Music as revelation; music as an ideal force (in the Platonic sense); music as manifestation of the Divine. The romantics eagerly embraced the concept. The last five quartets did not mean so much to the romantics, and it remained for the twentieth century to make them its own. But to the romantics, the Ninth Symphony was the beacon. It represented everything the romantics thought to be the essence of Beethoven—a defiance of form, a call for brotherhood, a titanic explosion, a spiritual experience. The Ninth Symphony was the Beethoven work that most influenced

Berlioz and Wagner. It was the Ninth Symphony that remained the unapproachable, unachievable ideal of Brahms, Bruckner, and Mahler. To the romantics, and to many today, the Ninth Symphony is something more than music. It is an *ethos,* and Debussy was not entirely wrong when he said that the great score had become a "universal nightmare." It pressed too heavily on the music of the century. Only within the last generation have there been those who dare criticize the last movement, but not even those critics have anything but awe for the other three movements. And, indeed, the coda of the first movement, with its slippery, chromatic bass and the awesome moans above it, remains a paralyzing experience. *That* is the way the world ends. It is absolute music, but it clearly represents struggle, and it is hard to hear so monumentally anguished a cry without reading something into it. The trouble is that, faced with such music, all of us tend to become sentimentalists, reading into it the wrong message.

Perhaps the true, extramusical interpretation of any Beethoven work would be a long way from what most listeners believe. It might represent nothing more than the strong-minded, even arrogant, reflection of a phenomenal musical intellect who was driven by illness and mental suffering to retreat completely into his own world, his own silent world, the result being sheer solipsism far removed from the lofty ideals attributed by later ages. Beethoven had vague ideas about universal brotherhood and a perfect society, but he would have nothing to do with those abstract concepts when it came to himself. "I don't want to know anything about your system of ethics," he wrote to a friend. "Strength is the morality of the man who stands out from the rest, and it is mine." These are frightening words: a dangerous, ominous, prophetic utterance. But the man was redeemed by his music, and it is the most powerful body of music ever brought together by one composer.

7

Poet of Music

FRANZ PETER SCHUBERT

Franz Schubert, who died at the age of thirty-one, lived all his life under the shadow of Beethoven. To the Viennese, and indeed to all of Europe, Beethoven was the great man, and only a few composers—Hummel, Spohr, perhaps Weber—deserved to be mentioned in the same breath. Schubert was not one of them. It is not that he was considered a nonentity. In his own country he had a tidy reputation, though it was primarily as a composer of songs. But his reputation was mostly local. He never moved far from Vienna, except for two short trips to neighboring Hungary, where he taught the children of Count Johann Karl Esterházy, and he was rather shy and retiring. The first great composer in history *not* to be a conductor or public instrumentalist, he could not achieve fame as an executant or push his music through his own virtuosity. He never asked much from life, was something of a Bohemian, and seemed content to pour out page after page of music whether or not it ever was performed. His mission was to create music; that was the only thing he was made for. "The state should keep me," he told his friend Josef Hüttenbrenner. "I have come into the world for no purpose but to compose."

Despite all that has been written about Schubert, he remains a rather vague and even mysterious figure. A great deal is known about the external aspects of his life, but there is surprisingly little about what he said, thought, felt. He left very few letters, and the abortive diary he started in 1816 consists mostly of charming adolescent musings of a general nature. "Man resembles a ball, to be played with by chance and passion." Or, "Happy he who finds a true man friend. Happier still he who finds a true friend in his wife." All very engaging, but nothing specific, nothing that tells us much about the writer. Some forty years after his death, when the world woke up to the fact that Schubert was one of the colossal creative figures of music, efforts were made to get reminiscences from all who knew

96

him. A flood of material resulted, all of which has to be screened with great care. Naturally at that date, anybody who had been associated with Schubert wanted to share in the reflected glory. But of Schubert during the actual period of his short life—January 31, 1797, to November 19, 1828— there remains material only for a superficial biographical sketch. That is why most Schubert biographies concentrate on the music rather than the man. His character is very hard, and perhaps impossible, to evoke.

The main outlines of his life are, of course, documented. He was the twelfth of fourteen children, of whom five survived. His father was the head of his own school, conducted in his own house, where Schubert was born. In 1808, young Franz became a soprano in the choir of the court chapel at the Imperial and Royal Seminary, where he also received a general education. As a seminary student he wore the official uniform: an old-fashioned three-cornered hat, white neckerchief, a dark-colored cutaway coat, a small gold epaulette on his left shoulder, shiny buttons, an old-fashioned waistcoat that reached below the stomach, short breeches with buckles, shoes without buckles. A bright boy, Franz did well in all of his studies, and in music immediately established his superiority. He was the "big man on campus"—a good pianist and violinist, and already a prolific composer. This at the age of eleven. The principal music teacher at the seminary, one Wenzel Ruzicka, found that he had nothing to teach the boy. "This one's learned from God!" he is reported to have said. Another teacher, Michael Holzer, later wrote: "If I wanted to instruct him in anything new, he already knew it. Therefore I gave him no actual tuition but merely talked to him and watched him with silent astonishment." Also in 1808 Schubert made a big enough impression to attract the attention of Antonio Salieri, the court musical director, and became a composition student of that important figure. (Salieri was one of the best-known composers of the day and also was Mozart's *bête noire*. Salieri had all the contacts and guarded them jealously. Mozart could make little headway against him. After Mozart's death there were weird rumors that Salieri had poisoned him. There is no proof to that absurd contention, but it worked on poor Salieri's mind, and on his very deathbed he kept protesting that he was innocent.) At the seminary Schubert made many friends, and one of them, Joseph von Spaun, remained close to Schubert all his life. From the little that is known about Schubert in the Imperial and Royal Seminary, he was a sweet, uncomplicated boy with a spectacular musical talent. At home he would play chamber music with his brothers and his music-loving father, timidly correcting Papa when the elder man made one of his frequent mistakes.

His voice broke in 1813, but he was kept at the seminary on a scholarship. Later in that year, however, he resigned and started training as a schoolmaster. He loathed the studies and the work, though from 1814–1818

97

he was an assistant at his father's school. During his years as a teacher he composed steadily, turning out song after song, writing symphonies, chamber music, and masses, and also trying to break into the Viennese theater. The time was against him for that. He composed German opera, and Vienna was in the throes of a Rossini craze. It was toward the end of 1816 that Rossini's *L'Inganno felice* created a furor in Vienna, and a succession of Rossini operas followed. Schubert, who never let personal considerations interfere with an objective evaluation of anybody else's music, called Rossini an "extraordinary genius," and some Rossinisms crept into his own music. Perhaps had Schubert found a decent librettist, he might have had a chance. His operas are full of lovely ideas. But seldom has a composer had to set the kind of nonsense Schubert was constantly being saddled with.

In the first two decades of the nineteenth century, music had come out of the courts and salons into the market place. All of a sudden it started to become a bourgeois phenomenon. There was a craze for the waltz, and that influenced serious music. Schubert, like Mozart and to a lesser extent, Beethoven, wrote a very large amount of dance music. Up to the second decade of the century, the minuet, Ländler, and contradance were the popular forms. Then came the waltz. The waltz became fashionable during the Congress of Vienna in 1814–15, and from that time Vienna was the Waltz City. In the 1820's, on the Thursday before Carnival Sunday, the city would offer as many as 1,600 balls in a single night. The bourgeoisie as well as the aristocracy danced to the waltz. The bourgeoisie also heavily supported the Italian opera craze and the German drama. Vienna, not a large city, had four theaters to supply the demand—the Burg Theater, for spoken drama; the Kärntnertor Theater, for opera and ballet; the Theater an der Wien, for drama, concerts, and opera; and the Leopoldstadt Theater for drama and opera. In addition, there were smaller halls—the Josefstadt Theater, the Redoutensaal, the court ballrooms of the Hofburg, the Great Hall of the University, and the County Hall. Many members of the aristocracy maintained their own orchestras and musical salons. Above all, a large group, the cultivated middle class, began to participate in music, associating with composers and making music an essential part of its life.

It was the music-loving, art-loving, intellectual middle-class group with which Schubert was associated all his life. He seldom mixed with the aristocracy, as Beethoven did. He felt comfortable only among the bourgeoisie and the artistic Bohemians of Vienna. When he left schoolteaching for good in 1818, he entered that Bohemian circle and it was for its members that he composed his music. It was a circle of musicians, artists, and literary figures, and most of them were his close friends. There were the poets Johann Mayrhofer and Franz Grillparzer, the painter and illustrator Moritz von Schwind, the composer and conductor Franz Lachner, the singer Johann

Vogl, the dilettante Franz von Schober, and many others. "Our circle," Schubert called them.

He lived *la vie de bohème*, seldom having money, moving in with friends, spending much time at cafés. After 1818 he was on his own, though two years previously he had become a professional. An entry in his diary, dated June 17, 1816, reads: "Today I composed for money for the first time. Namely, a cantata for the name day of Professor Wattrot [Watteroth], words by Dräxler. The fee is 100 florins, V.C." That would be around $50. The chances are that he did not keep the money long. Schubert was always short of cash, and never had enough even to rent a piano, much less buy one. It made no difference, for he did not need a piano for composition. He said it made him lose his train of thought. If he needed a piano, he would go to a friend's house. Among Schubert's closest friends were Schwind and Eduard von Bauernfeld, and the three of them formed a tiny communistic enclave in which there was no such thing as private property. Hats, shoes, clothes, money—all was communal. Whoever was in funds for the moment took care of the bills. Money meant nothing to Schubert, and he was an unaggressive businessman when it came to selling his music and dealing with publishers. Nor did time mean much to him. He would drive his friends to desperation by not turning up when he was expected. A letter from Schwind in 1825 chides him for not showing up for a party, and the letter also gives a clue to the complexity of Schubert's character: "Had you thought of how much affection was waiting for you, you would have come. . . . I am almost afraid of getting as much pleasure from you, seeing how ill I have succeeded all these years in overcoming your mistrust and your fear of not being loved and understood." It could be that Schubert, like many shy persons, was apt to imagine slights and was extremely sensitive about peoples' reaction to him.

Yet there was something in him that made his friends fiercely loyal. And women wanted to mother him. He was a Kewpie doll of a man: tiny (about 5 feet, 1½ inches), dumpy enough to be nicknamed *Schwammerl* (Tubby), with curly brown hair, a stubby rounded nose, a round face, and dimpled chin. His eyesight was bad and he always wore glasses. Generally he was good-natured and could easily be cajoled to the piano to play and improvise waltzes at parties. Sometimes, however, he was moody and irascible, especially during his illness. He contracted venereal disease and went through a bad period in which he temporarily lost his hair and all but retired from society. In Beethoven's conversation book of 1823 there is a note in his nephew Karl's handwriting: "They greatly praise Schubert, but it is said that he hides himself." Schubert's friend Leopold von Sonnleithner said that Schubert "never laughed openly and fully, but only managed a chuckle which sounded toneless rather than bright." His way of life was completely irregular. From about 9 in the morning (unless he was suffering from a hangover) until 2 in the afternoon, he composed. Then he was on the town. Unless invited somewhere to dinner, or to a party, he frequented the cafés. The Anchor, and Bogner's, were among his favorites. There he would stay until midnight, smoking, drinking coffee and wine, reading the papers, holding court with his circle. On the whole he was a taciturn man. He had affairs with women, but kept them to himself, and not even his friends knew the particulars. He never married. Although never an alcoholic, he sometimes drank more than he could handle. Undoubtedly there were aspects of his life unknown to us. Josef Kenner, another friend, has left some dark hints: "Any one who knew Schubert knows he was of two natures foreign to each other, how powerfully the craving for pleasure dragged his soul down to the slough of moral degradation . . ." This may be mere pious Victorian moralizing; and, then again, there very well may be something to it.

The tentative efforts of Schubert to find a publisher did not get very far. In 1817 he sent Breitkopf and Härtel one of his greatest songs, the *Erlkönig*. Breitkopf and Härtel could not have been less interested, and returned it to the only Franz Schubert they knew, a composer of that name who lived in Dresden. The Dresden Schubert was insulted, and sent a stiff note back to the publishers. Who was the upstart making free with his name? Schubert of Dresden said he would keep the song. "I shall retain it in my possession to learn, if possible, who sent you that sort of trash . . ." In the meantime, Spaun sent to Goethe a group of Schubert songs set to that master's poetry. Spaun hoped to arouse his interest, but Goethe did not even answer. It was not all frustration, however. Little by little Schubert's name became known. Such singers as Anna Milder and, especially, Johann Vogl began to present his music in public; and Schubert's circle, small but influential, made propaganda for their hero. Vogl was of great importance in Schubert's life. When the composer first met him, in the spring of 1817, the baritone was nearly thirty years older and nearing the end of a distinguished operatic career. He looked at some Schubert songs, hemmed and hawed, but was attracted to them and became Schubert's first great interpreter. Vogl was a stout, stern majestic figure, and he and the diminutive Schubert were a sight marching along the streets of Vienna. There is an amusing caricature, believed to be by Franz von Schober, of the two. The fact that so important a singer as Vogl specialized in Schubert was very important for the young composer. Reviewers began to take notice of him, and the notices generally were flattering. A long and understanding review in the *Wiener Zeitschrift für Kunst* flatly called him a genius in 1822; and the following year he was referred to in that publication as "this popular master." Schubert never achieved the fame he deserved, but neither did he work in a vacuum.

The "Schubertiaden" in Vienna were well known. These were evenings sponsored by Schubert's friends in which nothing but his music was performed. With Schubert at the piano, there would be songs, chamber music, four-hand and solo piano pieces. It was this Schubert circle that saw the first group of his songs off the press. As no publisher was willing to print the music, Schubert's admirers got together and raised the money for publication. Franz von Hartmann, a member of the circle, wrote about many Schubertiads in his diary. The entry of December 15, 1826, is characteristic:

> I went to Spaun's, where there was a big, big Schubertiad. On entering I was received very rudely by Fritz and very saucily by Haas. There was a huge gathering. The Arneth, Witteczek, Kurzrock and Pompe couples; the mother-in-law of the Court and State Chancellery probationer Witteczek; Dr. Watteroth's widow, Betty Wanderer, and the painter Kupelwieser and his wife, Grillparzer, Schober, Schwind, Mayrhofer and his landlord Huber, tall Huber, Derffel, Bauernfeld, Gahy (who played four-hand music gloriously with Schubert), and Vogl, who sang almost thirty splendid songs. Baron Schlecta and other Court probationers and secretaries were also there. . . . When the music was over, there was grand feeding and dancing. But I was not at all in a courting mood. I danced twice with Betty and once with each of the Witteczek, Kurzrock and Pompe ladies. At 12:30, after a cordial parting with the Spauns and Enderes, we saw Betty home and went to The Anchor, where we still found Schober, Schubert, Schwind, Derffel and Bauernfeld. Merry. Then home. To bed at 1 o'clock.

As Schubert's reputation grew, a few publishers approached him, but very few of his important works were printed during his lifetime. None of the symphonies appeared in print, only one of the nineteen string quartets, three of the twenty-one piano sonatos, one of the seven masses, none of the ten operas, 187 of the more than 600 songs. From this, according to the estimate of the Schubert authority, Otto Erich Deutsch, Schubert netted an estimated $12,500 spread over twelve years. Not much; but, in Deutsch's words, "Schubert never starved." In the very last years of Schubert's life there were indications that matters would improve. In 1828 the firm of Schott sent him a letter—the address was to "Franz Schubert, Esq., Famous Composer in Vienna"—asking for music. The firm of Probst also was interested. Something might have come of those overtures, especially from Schott, who was looking for a composer to take the place of Beethoven.

Had Schott pursued negotiations in the last year of Schubert's life, the company would have made a great deal of money in the long run. What a tremendous year it was! It was the year of the C major Symphony, the C major String Quintet, the last three piano sonatas, and some remarkable songs. It also was the year of the one and only public concert he had during his lifetime. Again it was the result of his friends, who got together and rented a hall. The concert, given on March 26, 1828, never was reviewed. Paganini happened to be in town and gave his first concert on March 29, following it with thirteen more. Those took up all the space in the papers. As if Schubert was not occupied enough, that last hectic year of his life, he arranged with the theorist Simon Sechter for lessons in counterpoint. Schubert had been reading the music of Handel and decided to study strict counterpoint. "Now for the first time I see what I lack." It was a decision that has amazed later Schubert scholars and admirers, though nobody has raised an eyebrow about Mozart's immersion in Bachian counterpoint, and his enthusiasm for it. But Schubert's lessons were not to be. Early in November he took to his bed and died on the nineteenth of that month from typhoid fever (not typhus, as some biographies have it). He left nothing—no books, no money, no furniture, no estate at all. All that remained were manuscripts scattered all over Vienna. Schubert was buried near Beethoven. His friends were desolate. Schwind wrote to Schober: "Schubert is dead, and with him all that we had of the brightest and fairest." Grillparzer wrote the epitaph on the tombstone: "The art of music here entombed a rich possession, but even far fairer hopes."

In his thirty-one years, Schubert wrote an enormous amount of music. He was a very fast writer, incredibly fast, and while recent scholars cast doubt on some of the stories of his speed, there is no reason to disbelieve the contemporary accounts. They all agree. When Schubert worked, he worked at white heat. Said Schober: "If you go to see him during the day, he says 'Hello, how are you?—Good!' and goes on working, whereupon you go away." Awed friends told story after story of his speed, and those stories are true in essence if not always in detail. Sonnleithner reports that "At Fräulein Fröhlich's request, Franz Grillparzer had written for the occasion the beautiful poem *Ständchen,* and this she gave to Schubert, asking him to set it to music as a serenade for her sister Josefine (mezzo-soprano) and women's chorus. Schubert took the poem, went into an alcove by the window, read it through carefully a few times and then said with a smile, 'I've got it already, it's done, and it's going to be quite good.' " Spaun tells of the composition of the *Erlkönig.* He and Mayrhofer visited Schubert and found him reading the poem. "He paced up and down several times with the book, suddenly he sat down, and in no time at all (just as quickly as you can write) there was the glorious ballad finished on the paper. We ran with it to the Seminary, for there was no piano at Schubert's, and there, on the very same evening, the *Erlkönig* was sung and enthusiastically received." For many years it was believed that Schubert never made sketches even for major compositions like symphonies. Modern research has established otherwise. But there is no doubt at all that Schubert, like Mozart, was one of the fastest writers in musical history: a composer who could conceive a whole work in his head and immediately write it down.

His music is highly original. No composer of the day could entirely escape the influence of Beethoven, Mozart, and Haydn; but Schubert, once his style was formed, broke away more than any composer of the time. Schubert admired Beethoven—from a safe distance. If the two met more than once, history has not recorded it. Beethoven, who knew what was going on everywhere, read through some of the Schubert songs and was impressed. According to Schindler, he said that Schubert had the divine spark. That does not make it a true statement. Schindler often was the victim of his own imagination. But we know from Karl's entry in the conversation books that Beethoven was very much aware of Schubert and his music. Apparently Schubert got up enough nerve to visit Beethoven only once, when Beethoven was on his deathbed. Nothing about the visit is known. But there was really, in Schubert's music, as little Beethoven influence as there was actual personal contact. After experimenting with the forms and textures of Mozart and Haydn in his early music, Schubert proceeded to go along a road of his own without ever turning back.

In his specialty, the song literature, he had relatively little precedent. There were a few composers who had previously added to the German song literature. Among them were Johann Friedrich Reichardt, Carl Friedrich Zelter, and Johann Rudolf Zumsteeg. As a young man, Schubert directly imitated a few Zumsteeg songs. Haydn, Mozart, and Beethoven had given some lovely songs to the world. But Schubert, while he may not have been the first composer to specialize in song (there had been the Elizabethan, John Dowland, for example), nevertheless was the first of the great composers to write a large body of art songs that have remained a permanent part of the active repertoire.

From the very beginning something propelled Schubert into the art song, or lied. He was only seventeen years old when he composed *Gretchen am Spinnrade,* one of the most perfect songs ever written. That was in 1814, and the following year he wrote 145 songs. For his poetry he ranged over the entire field of contemporary German literature. Goethe he found especially attractive, and of his more than 600 songs, about seventy are set to poems by Goethe. He set poems by Schiller, Heine, and Klopstock; poems by his friends Mayrhofer and Schober; poems by Ludwig Gottfried Kosegarten and Wilhelm Müller. In all, lyrics by ninety-one poets are represented. Schubert's basic song forms are strophic or *Durchkomponiert* (through composed). In the strophic song the same melody is used for all the verses. (There also are modifications of the strophic song.) A song that is *Durchkomponiert* follows the poem from beginning to end in a single dramatic or lyric continuity. Often *Durchkomponiert* song suggests the ballad form. It so happens that a composer named Karl Loewe (1796–1869), born a year before Schubert, specialized in the narrative ballad and composed some masterpieces in the form, including a setting of the *Erlkönig*. Schubert's own familiar setting is also a ballad, as purely descriptive as it is emotional, and it strikes far deeper than Loewe's, fine as the latter's is. Schubert was never dogmatic about his song forms. Often he would mix strophic and through-composed writing.

"He bade poetry sound and music speak," said Grillparzer. Schubert's songs are of infinite variety—long and short, lyric and dramatic, simple and complex, strophic and through-composed. Some are ballads. Generally speaking, the ballad is purely narrative while the lied is lyric. Some are declamatory, almost recitations, while others are tiny jewels that flicker gaily through existence. The essence of the lied is the same as the essence of lyric poetry—to heighten an emotion in a brief span. Schubert took his poems and by his own magic illustrated the moods of the words through music so that both elements are heightened.

It is a commonplace statement that Schubert is one of the greatest melodists of music. No song writer can work without an inexhaustible fount of melody, and Schubert above all composers tossed off an extraordinary number of unforgettable melodic ideas—*Auf dem Wasser zu singen, Du bist die Ruh', Horch! Horch! die Lerch!, Liebesbotschaft, Ungeduld, Der Musensohn, Ave Maria*—one after the other in a steady outpouring. Schumann, in an 1829 letter to Friedrich Wieck, used an unforgettable phrase to describe Schubert's melody: "compressed, lyrical insanity." Allied to that fount of melody was a brilliant feeling for modulation. Melodies have to be harmonized, and in his harmonic ideas Schubert was supreme. He would move from key to key in the freest manner, hitting just the inevitable-sounding chord to underline a word or phrase, linking the key changes within a song with rich and unexpected moves that hit the listener with visceral impact. Schubert is a master of the unexpected. It is safe to say that no great music is without the element of the unexpected: the departure that is so original, yet so inevitable. A great composer's mind never works in conventional ways.

Among Schubert's songs are two cycles—*Die schöne Müllerin* and *Die Winterreise*. Many believe *Die Winterreise* (*The Winter's Journey*), composed in 1827, the year before his death, to be the greatest single series of songs in the literature: sad, plaintive haunting, mounting in melancholy and even desperation to the shattering last song, *Der Leiermann*. This song is about an organ-grinder playing his machine in the winter. Nobody gives him any money, nobody listens to his music, nobody cares. Snarling dogs chase him, but he continues to smile and show no disappointment. "*Wunderlicher Alter,*" ends the song, "*soll ich mit dir geh'n? Willst zu meinen Lieder dei-*

ner Leier dreh'n?"—meaning, "Mysterious old man, shall I go with you? Will you crank your hurdy-gurdy to my songs?" All this is expressed in a mood of total desolation, with bare fifths in the bass and a scrap of melody, more a motto, really, above it. It is a song that sends icicles of despair through the listener, and it is hard to escape the notion that the words by Wilhelm Müller had an autobiographical significance for Schubert.

Schubert composed in every medium except one. He never wrote a concerto, which is not surprising. For in those days and, indeed, in all music up to then, concertos were composed by musicians who themselves would play the work, and Schubert, though an able pianist, was no virtuoso. A good deal of Schubert's music still goes unheard. His operas are unknown quantities today, and experts say that the librettos are so poor that they cannot be staged. This was also felt in Schubert's time. The reviewer in the *Conversationsblatt* pointed out in an 1820 article on *Die Zauberharfe* that the plot was ridiculous. "What a pity that Schubert's wonderfully beautiful music has not found a worthier subject!" The operas aside, several representative examples of Schubert's work in every form are in today's permanent repertory.

There used to be a tendency to look down on Schubert as a technician. The argument seemed to be that since his ideas of sonata form departed from the classic ideal, since his developments undeniably did have a tendency to wander and become diffuse, since his constructions lacked the organization and power of a Beethoven—ergo, he knew nothing about "sonata form."

Schubert, it is true, was pulled two ways when he engaged sonata form. In the Vienna of his day, a period dominated by Beethoven and the memory of Mozart, all composers wrote sonatas, concertos, and symphonies. Schubert's lyric instinct did have some trouble lacing itself into the corset of the sonata. But he felt obliged to comply. The demands of the day pressed on him. Even though he was one of the most original composers in history, he did not have the kind of mind that gloried in breaking conventions of form. Thus many of his early symphonies, sonatas, and quartets dutifully go through the motions of the sonata mystique. Later, as in the *Unfinished* Symphony and the big C major, he was able to unite content with his own kind of form, and the result is a kind of sonata form just as perfect in its way as Beethoven's was for Beethoven.

There is some confusion about the numbering of Schubert's symphonies. The correct sequence is: No. 1 in D major (1813); No. 2 in B flat major (1815); No. 3 in D major (1815); No. 4 in C minor (1816); No. 5 in B flat major (1816); No. 6 in C major (1818); No. 7 in E major (1821; sketched out and never completed); No. 8 in B minor (the *Unfinished*, 1822); and No. 9 in C major (1828). There also is a mysterious work, of which no real evidence exists, called the *Gmunden-Gastein* Symphony, so named because Schubert worked on it during a summer vacation at those two cities. The manuscript never has turned up. One theory was that Schubert's *Grand Duo* for piano four hands is a reduction of the *Gmunden-Gastein* Symphony, but nobody takes that idea very seriously today. Another theory is that the *Gmunden-Gastein* Symphony later developed into the Ninth in C major. But all that is known is that Schubert did work on a symphony that has been lost.

The first three symphonies are prentice works, though No. 2, bouncing and tuneful, already breathes the essential Schubert. No. 4 in C minor (which he himself named the *Tragic* Symphony), is an underrated work. It is supposed to be Schubert's bow toward a symphony in the Beethoven style, and scholars tend to be condescending about it. As a matter of fact, the music has very little Beethoven in it, and it has a slender, elegiac quality, especially in the last movement, that is of extreme beauty: Schubertian beauty, not Beethovenian. It is amazing how consistently Schubert managed to avoid the influence of his titanic contemporary. Haydn was much more of an influence, and the Fifth Symphony, elegant and lightly scored, is a throwback to the Haydn style. No. 6, with moments of great beauty and also a Rossinian *joie de vivre,* is not a complete success and does not hang together too well—but it is still Schubert.

The *Unfinished,* that universal favorite, is a torso, and millions of words have been written trying to explain it. If the truth about the work has not been discovered by now, it never will be. Schubert gave the score to Anselm Hüttenbrenner in 1822. It was dedicated to the Graz Musical Society, which had just elected Schubert an honorary member, and Hüttenbrenner was supposed to deliver it to the members. Whether or not he did, nobody knows. Whether or not Schubert gave him more than the two movements, nobody knows. The score remained in Hüttenbrenner's possession until 1865, when the conductor Johann Herbeck bribed him out of it by promising to play one of his, Hüttenbrenner's, works in Vienna. Why only two movements? One theory is that Schubert intended to send the other two movements later. Another theory maintains that Schubert felt he could never improve the two existing movements, and thus dropped work on the symphony. It is an unlikely theory. Schubert did not work that way; and the extant manuscript does have sketches for a third movement. Still another suggestion is that Hüttenbrenner lost the final two movements, and this makes the most sense of all.

It was Robert Schumann who unearthed the Ninth Symphony, the "Great" C major. Schumann had known of its existence and on New Year's Day of 1838 he visited Schubert's brother Ferdinand, who showed him piles of manuscripts. Ferdinand allowed Schumann to depart with the score of the C major Symphony, and on March 29, 1839, Mendelssohn conducted the world premiere in Leipzig. There is some evidence that the work was tried out in Vienna in 1828, under Schubert's supervision, and was shelved as being too difficult. In a letter to Clara Wieck, Schumann raved about the score: "It is not possible to describe it to you. All the instruments are human voices. It is gifted beyond measure, and this instrumentation, Beethoven notwithstanding—and this length, this heavenly length, like a novel in four volumes, longer than the [Beethoven] Ninth Symphony." (Schumann was a little too exuberant here. The Schubert Ninth was about fifty minutes, the Beethoven Ninth a little over an hour.) Then Schumann reviewed the Leipzig premiere with his typical understanding and big-heartedness: "The symphony produced such an effect among us as none has produced since Beethoven. . . . Years must pass, perhaps, before the work will be thoroughly understood in Germany, but there is no danger that it ever will be overlooked or forgotten. It bears within it the core of everlasting youth." Schumann, as nearly always, was right. The C major Symphony, in its breadth and passion, has a claim to stand near the Beethoven Ninth. Schubert, in his last year, expanded tremendously. His music is packed with ideas, is enormous in scale, is starting to head in a new direction. On his deathbed he is said to have cried that new ideas were running through his head. What would he not have done had he lived!

Wherever one looks in Schubert's music there is something to love. Always the music is intensely, even piercingly, melodic, the melodies often tinged with a kind of melancholy that can only be described as—well, Schubertian. There are the direct, simple, and lovable waltzes for piano. There are the two piano trios, of which the B flat is the more popular. The slow movement of the B flat Trio contains a wonderful example of Schubert's magic in modulation. The music is going along in the key of A flat and by a twist the music is suddenly in a far remote E major. It takes Schubert exactly a fourth of a measure to get there, and the effect is of the heavens opening up. But all of his music has strokes like this. The last three string quartets (A minor, D major, and G major) are full of them, and so is the great F minor Fantasy for piano duet; and so is the *Trout* Quintet, and so is the lovely and spirited Octet for Winds. The C major String Quintet, one of Schubert's last works, occupies a special niche. Its first two movements have the serene melancholy (there is no other way to describe it) of the *Unfinished* Symphony, that tensile, flawless layout enmeshed in supreme poetry.

It is only in recent years that the piano sonatas have become popular concert-hall pieces. Romantic pianists, by and large, avoided them, and if they played Schubert it was the big *Wanderer* Fantasy or the *Moments Musicaux* (Schubert's own bad French). As far as pianists were concerned, the music was ungratefully written, difficult without any obvious virtuosity, hard to organize. And the music demanded as much from the audience as the player. Not until the 1930's did pianists, following the lead of Artur Schnabel, begin to play the Schubert sonatas with regularity. Today the sonatas have become staples. It took an antiromantic age to make them popular. In Schubert's piano writing—it is true of all his instrumental writing—the piano is merely the medium, not the Thing Unto Itself. The pianist is concerned with music, not with technical tricks (though in order to play the music well, a substantial technique is needed, especially for the three gigantic posthumous sonatas).

It took about forty years after Schubert's death for the world to realize his genius. Today his place is permanently fixed. Although he exerted little influence on the early romantic school, he nevertheless anticipated romanticism in the subjective way he approached music. Schubert was not the first of the romantics, for Carl Maria von Weber was a much more romantic composer, and exerted infinitely more influence on the oncoming generation. But if Schubert was not the first of the romantics, he occupies another and even more significant place. He was the first lyric poet of music.

⚞ 8 ⚟

Freedom and a New Language

WEBER AND THE EARLY ROMANTICS

By the time Beethoven had died in 1827 and Schubert in 1828, the forces that had been set in motion by the French Revolution and the Industrial Revolution had transformed Europe. Everything was in the process of change. Networks of railroads were beginning to carry people and goods with unheard-of speed. A new class of citizen, the industrial bourgeois, started to amass enormous wealth. Science and medicine were advancing in multiple jumps. Poets were breaking away from couplets, alexandrines, and hexameters, and were writing a new, intensely personal and lyrical kind of verse. New attitudes about life, religion, economics, and politics were in the air. In the arts, everybody was talking about romanticism. Modern man came into being.

Music, of course, reflected the new age. Beethoven had expanded the orchestra to unprecedented size, and the new composers expanded it even further. Hector Berlioz in France dreamed of an orchestra of 467 players supplemented by a chorus of 360. Technology improved the unreliable wind instruments of the eighteenth century, adding keys and valves, and for the first time horns and bassoons could consistently play in tune. As the orchestra grew and as music became more complicated, there evolved the necessity for a controlling force—a man who would undertake all the responsibilities of interpreting a Beethoven symphony. A Vivaldi concerto grosso could run along pretty much by itself, helped by the first violinist and the player at the clavier, but not the complex symphony of Beethoven and his successors. Around 1820 the virtuoso conductor arrived—the man who could stare down the individual egos of the orchestral players and weld them into a single unit. Ludwig (Louis) Spohr (1784–1859), Carl Maria von Weber (1786–1826), and Gasparo Spontini (1774–1851) were among the pioneers of the baton, along with François-Antoine Habeneck (1781–1849), who founded the Paris Conservatory Orchestra in 1828 and led it with a violin bow in lieu of a baton.

Just as technology improved the instruments of the orchestra, so it improved the piano. The delicate Viennese instrument of Mozart's time and the more robust instrument of Broadwood that so delighted Beethoven gave way to a massive engine with a steel frame, and hosts of virtuosos rushed to take advantage of it. They wanted to do on the piano the equivalent of what Nicolò Paganini could do on the violin. Paganini, a graceful but unimportant composer, has an unusually high position in musical history as one who inspired all instrumentalists and instrumental writing of the romantic movement. He was the first of the supervirtuosos, and may have been the greatest violinist who ever lived. Something of a genius, something of a charlatan, Paganini (1782–1840) from 1805 was creating untold excitement wherever he went. There was a feeling of Satanism about this tall, dark, emaciated Italian who could do undreamed-of things on his Guarnerius. Musicians swarmed to his concerts trying to figure out how he achieved his effects. The public also flocked, and many of the more superstitious listeners believed him in league with the Devil. Paganini did nothing to dispel the notion. A great showman, he played up the diabolical quality of his concerts and did everything but come on stage wrapped in a blue flame. He gave saturnalia rather than concerts. One of his tricks was to break a string in the middle of a composition and continue to the end on three strings. Or he would produce a scissors, cut three of the strings, and perform miracles on the G string alone. He greatly expanded the technique of the violin, with new bowings, fingerings, harmonics, double stops of incredible virtuosity. There was not a professional instrumentalist who in his way did not try to duplicate Paganini's hold over an audience. Liszt and Schumann wrote variations on Paganini's famous Twenty-fourth Caprice, trying to achieve the equivalent of Paganini's transcendental technique. Later Brahms, Rachmaninoff, and others used the Twenty-fourth Caprice as a basis for extended piano works.

Paganini was the archetype of the Virtuoso-as-Hero, though there had of course been famous virtuosos before him. Any time an instrumentalist or singer does something better than anybody else, he can count on fame and fortune. Italy in the eighteenth century had some extraordinary violinists, and one of them, Giuseppe Tartini (1692–1770), anticipated Paganini, in a way, by writing a satanically difficult work named *The Devil's Trill*. The great castrato singers also were matinee idols. Toward the end of the eighteenth century appeared a group of pianists, headed by Johann Baptist Cramer, Ignaz Moscheles, Jan Ladislav Dussek, and John Field, who linked the classic school with the oncoming romantic. But no instrumentalist in history caused the sheer mania that Paganini did, nor had anybody else ever brought such a element of calculated, brilliant showmanship to his work. To Liszt fell Paganini's tradition, and those two mighty instrumentalists helped make the nineteenth century an era of rampant virtuosity. The public demanded virtuosity—the heroic virtuosity of Liszt as well as the tinkling, top-of-the-keys virtuosity of Henri Herz, that popular pianist who charmed audiences for several decades. Liszt, a trail-breaker in so many ways, was the first pianist in history to give a concert entirely on his own, unassisted by fellow artists who occupied the program while the Great Man was resting.

To take care of the demand, concert halls were being built all over Europe. Musical associations were created, permanent orchestras formed. In the opera houses, Rossini, Bellini, and Donizetti, starting shortly after the turn of the century, were writing music in which the emphasis was on the voice: *bel canto*, beautiful singing. Again there had been precedents for this kind of singing, but the term *bel canto* is applied specifically to the operas of those three composers. In *bel canto* singing, the emphasis is on flexibility, purity of line, ease of technique in coloratura passages, and careful shaping of vowel sounds. As the century progressed, the emphasis shifted to a more dramatic type of singing, much to the distress of Rossini and other lovers of the *bel canto* style. To them, Meyerbeer, Verdi, and Wagner had murdered pure vocalism. Such great singers as Giovanni Rubini, Luigi Lablache, Maria Malibran, Wilhelmine Schröder-Devrient, Pauline Viardot-Garcia, Gilbert-Louis Duprez, and Enrico Tamberlik were as popular as the pianists and violinists. Duprez was the first tenor consistently to sing a high C in full voice. Rossini, with great disgust, described that note as sounding "like the squawk of a capon whose throat is being cut."

In the first half of the nineteenth century, as before, the great instrumentalists were also the great composers. Weber, Mendelssohn, Chopin, and Liszt were the four greatest pianists of their time. Berlioz, Mendelssohn, Weber, and Wagner were the four greatest conductors. Midway in the century came something new in history—executants who were not themselves composers. Such pianists as Hans von Bülow and Karl Tausig made arrangements of music by other men, but they themselves did next to no serious composing. They were pure virtuosos. Today, virtuosity is something of a dirty word. It carries the implication of vulgarity, of excess, of exploitation of the composer for the performer's nasty little ends. But the nineteenth century did not look on virtuosity in that respect. Nobody has ever written a definitive history of musical virtuosity and its implications, but it seems clear that the great performers of the nineteenth century had considerable influence on the thinking of the composers. Music is no good on the printed page. It has to sound, and it can only sound through the fingers, voices, and brains of performers. In the eighteenth century and before, composer and performer of instrumental music were almost always the same. In the nineteenth century, with the advent of the specialist-virtuoso, a composer's music began to be refracted through the prism of a different mind. That could, and did, create problems. There always have been virtuosos willing to submerge beautiful music in a welter of cheap effects. But the composers of the nineteenth century, by and large, were perfectly willing to ally themselves with the virtuoso, even if they occasionally grumbled. Composers, on the whole, are more permissive about their music than many modern musicians realize—certainly the romantic composers were—and they above all realize that notation is an inexact medium.

The early romantics were especially permissive. With romanticism came the burgeoning of the Ego, a striving for an intensified kind of personal expression, the ideal of art for art's sake. Beethoven may have been the first composer to work on that premise. Jean-Jacques Rousseau had stimulated his own age with his doctrine of the natural man and the concept of a man's individual worth. Man's feelings, said Rousseau, serve us more reliably than reason. Express yourself and your feelings, said Rousseau. The romantics, who took him very seriously, did exactly that. Johann Paul Friedrich Richter, the great German writer known to the world as Jean Paul, had laid down some ground rules of romanticism as early as 1804 in his *Vorschule der Aesthetik*. The decisive element of romanticism, he said, is expanse. "Romanticism is beauty without bounds—the beautiful infinite." Or, "If poetry is prophecy, then romanticism is being aware of a larger future than there is room for here below."

Much has been written about romanticism, and the subject often is befogged, but its main lines are clear enough: content more important than classical form; alliance of literature with the other arts; an expanded horizon; an interest in the supernatural; a constant experimentation with new forms, new colors, new textures. Within one decade, roughly 1830–1840, the entire harmonic vocabulary of music changed. It seemed to come from nowhere, but all of a sudden composers were using seventh, ninth, and even eleventh chords, altered chords and a chromatic as opposed to classical diatonic harmony. Generally speaking—exceptions, of course, can always be pointed out—composers from Bach through Schubert wrote in diatonic harmony, with a sparse use of accidentals. They might range far afield in their key structures, but the basic tonality always was clear, and the actual chord structure seldom exceeded an octave. Nor was there much in the way of augmented or diminished intervals.

But the romantics reveled in unusual tonal combinations, sophisticated chords, and dissonances that were excruciating to the more conventional minds of the day. Chopin had no hesitation about using minor ninths, and musicians of an older generation were appalled. Ignaz Moscheles (1794–1870) was a fine composer, and he was one of the best pianists in Europe; and he also was as noble and dedicated a musician as ever lived.

When he first encountered Chopin's music he did not know what to make of it. "My thoughts, however, and through them my fingers, stumble at certain hard, inartistic and to me inconceivable modulations." Musicians brought up as Moscheles had been, with the emphasis on clarity, purity, proper voice leading, and spare use of the pedal, could not understand romantic music because they did not understand its aesthetic and acoustical premises. Pure *sound*, sound as sound, was very important to the romantics, and they brought new ideas of technique and composition to express those new concepts. It was not until Moscheles actually heard Chopin play that he realized his error, and handsomely admitted it. For Chopin's new kind of technique, his kind of legato playing supported by nuances of the pedal, enabled him to smooth out those dissonances.

Romantic music thus had its own sound—a rich, sensuous, colorful sound —and that is probably the most important single aspect of the period. Of course there were many other aspects that set romanticism off from the previous periods. Romantic music to a surprisingly large extent is nonabstract music. It might be that the composer followed a specific program in his music, as Berlioz and Liszt so often did. Or more often the program was there but unspecified. In the idealistic age of romantic music, with its close alliance to literature, and with the broader general culture of most composers, one of the favorite games was to read implied programs into music. No music was exempt, and the finest musical minds of the day read the most incredible things into any score. Music, it was felt, expressed specific states of mind and feeling. Schumann was always reading things into music, and the greater the piece, the more he read into it. "The more special a work is, the more individual pictures it spreads before the listener, and the more lasting it will be for all time. Such special traits are especially common to Beethoven and Franz Schubert." Wagner also was constantly reading things into music, portentously so. So did most of the performing artists. In one of the more delirious episodes in this kind of exegesis, Hans von Bülow saw in Chopin's E major Prelude the composer striking his head with a hammer. "The sixteenth and thirty-second notes are to be carried out in exact time, indicating a double stroke of the hammer." And Wagner interpreted the *Eroica* as a dialogue between Man and Woman, ending with the overwhelming power of Love. "Once more the heartstrings quiver, and tears of pure humanity well forth; yet from out the very quick of sadness there bursts the jubilant cry of force—that force which lately led itself to Love and—helped by that—the whole, the total Man now chants to us in avowal of his godhead." Reconstructions like this were common throughout the nineteenth century, and not until the objective outlook of a later age was there a change. Arturo Toscanini was to have his comment about the *Eroica*, contemptuously dismissing the romantic outlook: "Some say this is

Napoleon, some Hitler, some Mussolini. Bah! For me it is simply allegro con brio." Almost everybody today would take the Toscanini point of view.

Toscanini's remark was made in the 1920's and represented an attitude that more and more took hold, to a point where, by mid-century, the principles of romanticism had been all but forgotten—as forgotten as the principles of Mozartean performance practice were in the 1840's. The subject deserves mention, for the relationship of romanticism to the late twentieth century is a complicated one. Much of the present-day repertory is romantic or late romantic, and it seems to be an article of faith that musicians understand this kind of music but are less equipped to handle the classic and baroque repertory. As a matter of fact, the reverse is true. Thanks to a generation of concentrated musicological research, from Mozart back to the Renaissance, young musicians today have a better idea about preromantic music than about music from 1830 to 1900, which means the bulk of the repertory.

This is ironic but true. Today, every educated musician knows a good deal about performance practice in Mozart's time, but the Liszt tradition has all but vanished. Next to nothing has been written about the performance practice of the romantics, for most musicological research centers on problems (and mostly archival problems) in early music. And musicians of the middle third of the twentieth century were brought up in an antiromantic era, one in which the traditions of romanticism were suspect. Many young musicians today do not even know how to realize the notes of a romantic piece. A composer like Schumann, for instance, took great pains to indicate inner-voice relationships, carefully marking the phrases, notating the flags of individual notes so that they stand out clearly, putting legato phrase marks over bass or tenor lines. Schumann did not do this idly. There is a harmonic and polyphonic meaning. But hardly any musician notices those markings when he plays the *Carnaval* or *Kinderszenen*, just as he fails to bring out stepwise bass notes, a convention universally practiced by the romantic pianists and expected by the romantic composers. The romantics expected a slowdown between first and second themes; they expected contrasting sections to be carefully set off; they expected a great deal of rubato and dynamic extremes; they expected constant fluctuation of tempo. Above all, they did not object to discreet tampering with the text, which was anything but sacrosanct. The better musicians, from all that can be gathered, never were anarchic about their modifications, but there was not one who would not unhesitatingly change or reinforce a passage for optimum effect or for the grand gesture. He did this because he honestly believed it was in the spirit of the meaning of the music. In short, the romantics approached music with a freedom forbidden a hundred years later.

With the attitude of the romantics toward music as free and as literary as

114

it was, and with the kind of freedom the nineteenth century gladly gave its vocal and instrumental virtuosos, it was no wonder that all preromantic music was misrepresented during the nineteenth century and especially during the earlier period of romanticism. The early romantics had a tendency to see everything in their own image. There was no concern for scholarship, nor was there a discipline of musicology. When Mendelssohn revived the *St. Matthew Passion* in 1829, it was shortened, revised, reorchestrated, and, in sections, recomposed. Mozart was a heavy sufferer, as was Beethoven. The romantics idolized Beethoven, but again in their own image. They considered him the greatest of all revolutionaries and ascribed an ethical ideal to his music, but that did not deter them from altering his scores to bring them "up to date." Wagner reorchestrated Gluck, and Liszt "improved" Schubert's piano music. They honestly considered it an act of homage. As Wagner put it, in his Beethoven revisions, "I never carried my piety to the extent of taking his directions absolutely literally." A mind as musically sensitive as Wagner's could not commit mayhem on the Beethoven symphonies, certainly not the mayhem that Mahler committed on the Schumann symphonies later in the century, but Wagner and Mahler both did try to "improve" the music. The conducting of both might sound startling to today's ears.

Many things entered music with the romantics. Sentimentalism appeared. Nationalism became firmly fixed, first with Chopin and his mazurkas and polonaises, then with Liszt and his Hungarian rhapsodies, and later with the Bohemian and Russian nationalists. Opera changed, and the formula *bel canto* operas gave place to the grand spectacles of Meyerbeer, the red-blooded melodrama of Verdi, and the music drama of Wagner. Along with these came a new and dramatic style of singing and acting. All this took place within twenty-five years, beginning with the first group of romantics, born within five years of one another: Mendelssohn in 1809, Chopin and Schumann in 1810, Liszt in 1811, Wagner and Verdi in 1813. But in music, as in life, nothing springs full-grown. Everything has its predecessors, and the romantic period had some interesting and important precursors.

One of the significant figures was E. T. A. (for Ernst Theodor Amadeus) Hoffmann, a legend to the German romantics, especially Schumann. Hoffman (1776–1822) was everything—poet, painter, novelist, theater manager, singer, composer, conductor, critic, public official, and he seems to have been good and even distinguished in everything. He was one of those people who are always interested in the avant-garde, a sort of Cocteau of his time. Long before the musical romantics appeared on the scene he was writing about romanticism, insisting that "music is at home only in the realm of romanticism," calling music "the most romantic of the arts—in fact, one might almost say, the only genuinely one . . ." This was in 1813, in an essay on Beethoven's instrumental music. "Every passion," Hoffmann continued, "love, hatred, anger, despair, and so forth, just as the opera gives them to us, is clothed by music with the purple luster of romanticism." There is much in Hoffmann's writings about "the faraway spirit realm of sound," "the unknown realm," "the spirit world of the infinite," "the monstrous and immeasurable," "the eternal dances of the spheres," "endless longing," "jubilant song," "inner being." The romantics loved it. Hoffmann's writings about music are high-blown, sentimental and, by modern standards, all wrong; but he was a standard-bearer well in the vanguard, and the romantics were enthusiastically guided by his ideas. He preached a break from the past, looking forward to an idealistic, personal kind of music. In 1815 he composed *Undine,* an opera that in its supernatural subject matter links up with Weber's *Der Freischütz.* Weber praised it as "one of the more spirited works that the newer period has given us."

Another precursor was Muzio Clementi (1752–1832), a pianist-composer who set modern piano technique on its way. He specialized in virtuoso work, especially thirds and octaves, then new, and pianists followed his lead rather than the classical style of Mozart, who was an infinitely greater artist but not as exciting an executant. John Field (1782–1837), a pupil of Clementi, was also an important pianist of the day, representing an incipient romanticism. His graceful series of nocturnes were directly imitated by Chopin. Another fascinating transitional figure was Johann Nepomuk Hummel (1778–1837), whose roots were in the eighteenth century (he was a pupil of Mozart), but who composed some music that strongly verges on romanticism. In Vienna, he was considered Beethoven's only real rival, and for the first half of the nineteenth century it was taken for granted that Hummel was one of the immortals. His Septet for Piano and Winds introduced a harmonic vocabulary much more "modern" and sophisticated than Schubert's, and a style of piano writing that led directly into Chopin. Hummel composed several piano concertos, notably one in A minor; and Chopin's E minor Piano Concerto owes a strong debt to the Hummel. Very little of Hummel's music is in the twentieth-century repertoire, but he was an inventive composer and his work deserves revival.

The music of Ludwig (Louis) Spohr (1784–1859) also warrants a hearing. Spohr lives today by a single violin concerto, the *Gesangszene,* but in his time he experimented with chromatic textures and his music was considered extremely daring. There was a curious dichotomy in Spohr's career. He was the greatest classical violinist of his time, he was of the Mozart school, and he was no great friend of the romantic composers (though late in his career, when he was court conductor at Cassel, he espoused the cause of Wagner). Yet much of his own music looks forward rather than back, and in one of his operas, *Kreuzfahrer* (1845), he anticipated Wagner by "through-composing" the work "somewhat as a musical drama, without superfluous textual repetitions and ornaments, and with ever-increasing action." Previously he had composed an opera, *Jessonda* (1823), that was greeted with almost as much enthusiasm as Weber's *Der Freischütz*, and he had also composed a popular opera on the Faust legend. Spohr was one of the most admired and respected composers of his time.

History is apt to judge a period only by its greatest figures, but at any single time most people are uncomfortable in the presence of greatness and flock to a host of lesser figures who will satisfy their unsophisticated needs. In the 1830's, for example, the average music lover would have said that Beethoven, Mozart, and Hummel were the three greatest composers; but, at the same time, the average music lover was much more comfortable with the music of such as George Onslow (1784–1853), Ferdinand Ries (1784–1838), Henri Herz (1803–1888), Franz Hünten (1793–1878), and Friedrich Kalkbrenner (1785–1849). *Those* were the composers most often played—the commercial men of the period. They provided the music that offered no problems for anybody. They cooked up tasteful overtures, potpourris, and paraphrases, and they supplied the young ladies of Europe with appropriate music to place on their pianos. They wrote the battle pieces and the sentimental ditties and the arrangements for flute, harp, and piano that graced the music rooms of the bourgeoisie and enriched the music publishers.

Kalkbrenner can be taken as a representative example. He was an elegant, flawless pianist whose high reputation was exceeded only by his fine opinion of himself. It was to Kalkbrenner that young Chopin turned when he arrived in Paris. *This,* Chopin exulted, was piano playing! Kalkbrenner's music was extremely popular, and he turned out piece after piece. Probst, his publisher, could not waste much time with Schubert because the firm was engaged in bringing out the complete works of Kalkbrenner. The poet Heinrich Heine, who was a brilliant and acerbic reviewer, has left an amusing description of a Kalkbrenner concert: "On his lips there still gleamed that embalmed smile which we recently noticed on the lips of an Egyptian pharaoh when his mummy was unwrapped at the museum here." And Clara Schumann has left an even more penetrating description of Kalkbrenner "smiling sweetly and highly satisfied with himself and his creation. He always looks as if he was saying 'Oh, God, I and all mankind must thank Thee that Thou hast created a mind like mine.' " The point is that Kalkbrenner was rich, famous, and everybody had to take notice of him. Composers like Kalkbrenner are always around, forgotten a generation after their death, but extremely popular until then. It is that kind of composer who makes up the bulk of the active repertoire of his time, not the four or five geniuses who happen to be active at the same time.

To the early romantics the big man—Beethoven always excepted—was

Carl Maria von Weber, and a good case can be made for him as the first of the true romantics. He met most of the specifications. He was a major pianist and a touring virtuoso; his music was in advance of the day; he wrote operas on supernatural subjects; he dabbled in literature; he had the fashionable disease, consumption. Today very little Weber remains in the repertoire except for *Der Freischütz*, the overtures to three operas, and once in a while the *Concertstück* for piano and orchestra or one of the sonatas. There also is the *Invitation to the Dance*, but that is almost never heard in its original form as a piano solo. Thus it is hard to realize the overwhelming impact of Weber on the oncoming romantics—on Mendelssohn, Berlioz, Liszt, Marschner, and, especially, Wagner. Heinrich Marschner (1795–1861) was a once-popular opera composer—two or three of his operas still hold the stage in Germany—who in such works as *Der Vampyr* took his cue from *Der Freischütz* and raised the hair of audiences in the 1830's and '40s with his ghosts and demons.

The full influence of Weber on Wagner remains to be told, though anybody can listen to those strange harmonies in Weber's *Euryanthe* Overture and hear in them anticipations of the *Ring* cycle. At one time, in 1813, Weber was about to write an opera on the Tannhäuser legend. That would have anticipated Wagner by thirty years. Weber anticipated Wagner in other ways. As a conductor, he was one of the first to demand full control over all aspects of an operatic production, one of the first to institute section rehearsals, one of the first to exercise full authority. Wagner adopted many of his ideas. Weber, too, like Wagner, had pronounced pan-Germanic ideas about opera. He sought, as he explained in 1817, "a fully rounded and self-contained work of art in which all the ingredients furnished by the contributing arts disappear in the process of fusion, and in thus perishing help to form an entirely new universe." This is much the Wagnerian concept of the *Gesamtkunstwerk*—total art work—forty years before Wagner expounded *his* theories.

To the romantics, Weber was the one who unleashed the storm. If any single composition can be said to have set off the Romantic age of music, it was *Der Freischütz*. The scene in the Wolf's Glen, with its mystery and enchantment, its evocation of the power of evil, its nature painting and sheer color, its power and imagination—all this hit Europe with tremendous force, and helped launch the new movement.

Weber was born on November 18, 1786, and died on June 5, 1826, at the age of forty. He died a year before Beethoven and two years before Schubert. He had composed *Der Freischütz* in 1820, and it was unlike any other opera that had ever been written. *Oberon* and *Euryanthe*, which followed, suffered from impossible librettos and are not staged very often today, but those two operas also dealt with the supernatural and the exotic, and to the

118

romantics they opened a new world. Around 1840 the English critic Henry Fothergill Chorley wrote an estimate of Weber that can stand as the typical reaction (and it should be emphasized that Chorley was a reactionary who promptly frothed at the mouth when the names of Schumann and Wagner were brought up). Weber's music, wrote Chorley, "is instinct with the spirit of that olden time, when there were omens whispered in the woods, and battles foretold by the blood-red phantoms that brandished their arms and waved their banners in the West. The fancy of it is not untinctured with superstition; the hue upon it is either the pearly tent of Dream-land, or that gorgeous tint which streams through some blazoned window garnished 'WITH MANY A QUAINT DEVICE.' " Chorley fancied himself as a literary stylist. But his response is genuine. Weber was all that to the romantics. His piano music was as popular as his operas. When Wilhelm von Lenz, that pushy young man who collected names and piano teachers and later wrote books about them, introduced Liszt to the *Invitation to the Dance* and the Sonata in A flat, in the 1820's, the great pianist all but shrieked his admiration to the skies. Liszt and the other romantic pianists were constantly playing Weber.

Weber was a slim, sickly, consumptive man who had been born with a diseased hip and walked with a limp throughout his short life. When he died, it was as much from overwork as anything else. But in his forty years he contributed much to music. His talents were manifold. He was one of the great pianists of the day, and the layout of his piano music is far beyond anything that Beethoven and Schubert conceived. Much of it is frankly virtuosic, with a few technical idiosyncrasies. The short Weber had an enormous pair of hands, and some of the stretches he wrote cannot be played by normal human beings. As a touring pianist very much aware of the public, Weber could be guilty of some meretricious effects, and a good deal of his piano music has more glitter than substance. But when everything came together, as it did in the *Concertstück*, the music approaches sublimity. Today his four piano sonatas, his variations, and such virtuoso pieces as the *Polacca brillante* are almost out of the repertoire, but during the entire nineteenth century they enjoyed enormous popularity.

It was not only as a pianist and composer that Weber achieved fame. As the most important conductor of his period he opened the gate to a group of followers, and it was not long before conductors were the dominating musical forces in the world. As early as 1804, when he was eighteen, Weber became chief conductor at the opera house in Breslau, where he encountered tremendous opposition, for both his youth and his novel ideas about leadership. The first violinist, a great dignitary named Joseph Schnabel, even left the orchestra rather than submit to the indignity of being directed by a "child." Weber left Breslau in 1806 and after various minor appointments and some concertizing, became director of the opera house in Prague in 1812. From there he went to Dresden where he was summoned by the king of Saxony late in 1817 specifically to found a German opera house as a counterattraction to the Italian opera craze. Rossini had swept Germany, and in 1820 in Berlin the redoubtable Spontini had established a dictatorship as conductor and as composer of such popular operas as *La Vestale* (so beloved by Berlioz) and *Fernand Cortez*. Weber, a brilliant organizer, turned the Dresden opera house upside down and reconstructed it in his own image, even having Italian and French librettos translated into German. He made himself the dominating force. Wagner not many years later was conducting at Dresden, and picked up many of Weber's ideas. Weber, at Dresden, was a fierce disciplinarian who had to have everything right. He went through all the scores, correcting errors; his demands at sectional rehearsals were legendary; he took charge of all aspects of production, from scenery and staging to casting, rehearsing, and conducting. When he conducted the finished performance, it was indeed a finished performance.

Then in 1821 came *Der Freischütz*, which made Weber the founder of romantic German opera. Before him there was very little German opera—at least, very little that was in the repertoire. Three of the four great Mozart operas were in Italian, and the German *Die Zauberflöte* no more started a school of opera than Beethoven's *Fidelio* did. Schubert's operas lay forgotten, gathering dust, and they still do. But *Der Freischütz* led directly into the very popular, though mostly forgotten, operas of Marschner, Spohr, and Lortzing, and thence to Wagner.

Weber had the kind of restless mind typical of the romantics. He dabbled in lithography, was one of the first virtuosos on the guitar, and he was a passably good singer, though he permanently ruined his voice in 1806 by accidentally drinking a glass of nitric acid. For a time his life was in despair. He found time for some lusty love affairs and spirited dissipation. He turned to literary work and, from 1809 to 1818, wrote book reviews, poems, an unfinished novel, and a large amount of journalism, including some music criticism. Weber had the reputation of being a stringent, uncompromising critic, and even had some derogatory words to say about Beethoven. He went into criticism with the same energy and enthusiasm he applied to everything, and was one of the founders of an association named *Harmonischer Verein*. The idea was to introduce and explain the principles of romanticism. All the members of the *Verein* (meaning society or club) were required to be a combination of composer and literary man, and the motto was "The elevation of musical criticism by musicians themselves." Each member adopted a pseudonym. Weber's was Melos. He also wrote under the signatures of "Simon Knaster" and "B.f.z.Z.," meaning *"Beharrlichkeit führt zum Ziel,"* or "Perseverance leads to the goal"—his own motto. Not many years later, Schumann was to operate his musical journal on much the same premise, pseudonyms included. Schumann called his group the *Davidsbünd-ler*. None of Weber's prose has been translated into English. He was a fascinating figure, this aristocratic, intelligent, forceful man: an authentic genius whose greatest tragedy was that he was born about thirty years ahead of his time.

✲ 9 ✲

Romantic Exuberance and Classic Restraint

HECTOR BERLIOZ

Hector Berlioz was the first important composer in the history of music *not* to come up by way of being either a prodigy or an immensely gifted child. That goes far toward explaining his strengths and weaknesses. Child prodigies, instinct in music from babyhood, develop a certain kind of aural and digital response, and before they arrive at their teens they already are masters of technique. They have imbibed the literature from the cradle, have physically grappled with it, have become secure craftsmen, can do anything they want to do as easily as breathing. As they mature, they go as far as their imaginations allow, but always they develop into masters of form. Some remain merely technicians; some become innovators; some constantly grow; some disappear. But always there is the sense of professionalism in their writing.

But Berlioz! Berlioz never even learned to play a useful instrument correctly. All he could do was pluck a few chords on the guitar or tootle a few notes on the flute or flageolet. Not very much is known about Berlioz' childhood at Saint-André in Isère, where he was born on December 11, 1803, but it is clear that his musical education was sketchy. His father, a physician with a liberal bent, saw to it that the boy was well educated; but when it came to music, neither Dr. Berlioz nor anybody in the vicinity could help Hector very much. There was an old flageolet in the house, and Dr. Berlioz showed his eager son how to finger it. Then he got a flute for the boy and arranged for lessons. Hector also learned the fingering of the clarinet. That was about all. A mighty impulse was present, and there are notebooks filled with rudimentary compositions. From the beginning Hector wanted to be a composer, and he taught himself everything he could about composition. His father would not have encouraged these experiments. Hector was to be a doctor.

Thus Berlioz never did have the ease in manipulation of one who has grown up from the beginning with the materials of music. As a result, the forms he used were different and self-evolved. Sometimes his ideas turned out brilliantly successful, and sometimes they did not come off very well. Often there is a feeling of struggle as he tried to shape his materials. Or there may be a lack of point to his writing. But he did have one thing working for him: genius. If he lacked certain ABC's of his craft, his super-heated imagination could turn that very lack to advantage by making him think differently from all other composers.

He was aware of this. He realized how useful a tool the piano is to a composer. "But when I consider the appalling number of miserable platitudes to which the piano has given birth, which would never have seen the light had their authors been limited to pen and paper, I feel grateful to the happy chance that forced me to compose freely and in silence, and this has delivered me from the tyranny of the fingers, so dangerous to thought, and from the fascination which the ordinary sonorities always exercise on a composer, to a greater or lesser degree. Many amateurs have pitied me for this deprivation, but that does not bother me very much." In any case, if he could not play an instrument, he could play on a hundred instruments—the symphony orchestra.

So he developed into the first French romantic and the first true exponent of what Europe later was to call The Music of the Future. It was Berlioz who, by creating the modern orchestra, demonstrated a new kind of tonal power, resource, and color. It was Berlioz who was the first to express himself autobiographically in music, bringing a new dimension to the psychology of the art. It was Berlioz who, in the detailed program of his autobiographical *Symphonie fantastique,* led to the symphonic poems that so afflicted the latter part of the nineteenth century. It was Berlioz who broke away from the classic rules of harmony to explore hitherto forbidden chord progressions and an entirely new kind of melody. It was Berlioz who emerged as one of the seminal forces of the nineteenth century—the composer studied by Liszt and Wagner, by the new Russians, by Mahler and Richard Strauss, by the new generation of French composers. He had no direct followers, for his ideas were too unorthodox for his immediate contemporaries to absorb; but later composers did absorb his message, and his influence extended to every sector of the musical avant-garde.

Liszt realized this. When he sent Berlioz a copy of Wagner's *Tannhäuser* Overture he wrote on it: "You will rediscover your own." And Wagner, whose *Tristan und Isolde* stems in a way from Berlioz' *Roméo et Juliette*—sections of the latter achieve a *Tristan*-like intensity and unbroken melodic stream—sent Berlioz a score of his masterpiece with the inscription: "To the dear and great composer of *Roméo et Juliette,* the grateful composer of

Tristan und Isolde." Gounod, who turned out to be the new leader of the French school after Berlioz, was another composer influenced by *Roméo et Juliette.* He heard it in 1839 and called it "a strange, passionate, convulsive music that opened up such new and colored horizons for me."

Berlioz was not only the first true French romantic but also the first of music's true romantics anywhere, anticipating Chopin and Schumann by a few years. He was an enthusiast, a natural revolutionary, the first of the *conscious* avant-gardists. Weber would not have considered himself of the avant-garde, nor would have Schubert. But Berlioz was the first of the young Turks, the wild men of music. Uninhibited, highly emotional, witty, mercurial, picturesque, he was very conscious of his romanticism. He loved the very *idea* of romanticism: the urge for self-expression and the bizarre as opposed to the classic ideals of order and restraint. It is romanticism that animates his music and runs riot through his wonderful autobiography, that revealing, magnificently written document. Fancy sometimes outran fact in this book, and some of it indeed is downright fiction. But in all his writing —Berlioz wrote an enormous amount of criticism in his day—he was a brilliant stylist, one who added something not only to musical but also to world literature. His prose as well as his life presents a man with a vivid imagination, a lust for life and battle, and a degree of self-revelation unique in musical annals. (Mozart's letters were not written for publication.) Compared to this, Wagner's autobiography is a dull, gray compilation, part fact, part metaphysics, entirely lacking the civilized, ironic style of Berlioz.

He was an unusual man. Everything about him was unusual. Almost singlehandedly he broke up the European musical establishment. After him, music would never be the same. And what he did, he did all by himself, impatiently brushing aside convention and the old way of doing things. Only a genius could have overcome his lack of basic knowledge. But only his lack of basic knowledge could have led him into the paths he took.

It was in Paris that his genius blossomed. His father had sent him there to study medicine. How Berlioz hated it! At his first dissection, he fled. He is very funny about it in his autobiography:

When I entered that fearful human charnel house, littered with fragments of limbs, and saw the ghastly faces and cloven heads, the bloody cesspool in which we stood, with its reeking atmosphere, the swarms of sparrows fighting for scraps, and the rats in corners, gnawing bleeding vertebrae, such a feeling of horror possessed me that I leaped out of the window and fled home as though Death and all his hideous crew were at my heels. It was twenty-four hours before I recovered from the shock of this first impression, utterly refusing to hear the words anatomy, dissection or medicine, and firmly resolved to die rather than enter the career that had been forced on me.

. . . I consented to return to the hospital and face the dread scene once more. How strange! I now felt merely cold disgust at the sight of the same things that had before filled me with such horror. I had become as callous to the revolting scene as a veteran soldier. It was all over. I even found some pleasure in rummaging in the gaping breast of an unfortunate corpse for the lungs, with which to feed the winged inhabitants of that charming place.

"Well done!" cried Robert, laughing. "You are growing quite humane! Feeding the little birds!"

"And my bounty extends to all nature," I answered, throwing a shoulder blade to a great rat that was staring at me with famished eyes.

It did not take long for medical studies to take second place to music. Berlioz spent much more time at the Opéra and the library of the Conservatoire than in the medical school at the Hospital of Pity. Finally he managed to overcome the resistance of his father and, equally important, his mother. She was a pious woman who sincerely believed that anybody becoming a professional musician was automatically on the road to Hell. Berlioz was admitted to the Conservatoire, overcoming the objection of the director, Luigi Cherubini, and on his fifth attempt won the Prix de Rome in 1830.

Even as a student he was unforgettable. Berlioz shocked people in his day. "He believes in neither God nor Bach," said the composer-pianist-conductor Ferdinand Hiller, properly scandalized. Hiller has left us a fine description of Berlioz: "the high forehead, precipitously overhanging the deep-set eyes; the great, curving hawk nose; the thin, finely-cut lips; the rather short chin; the enormous shock of light brown hair, against the fantastic wealth of which the barber could do nothing—whoever had seen this head would never forget it." Berlioz was a striking figure and, consciously or unconsciously, was always attracting attention to himself. At the Opéra, where he held court in the balcony surrounded by fellow students, he would rise in wrath and let the world know if something foul was going on. Ernest Legouvé, the dramatist, was at a performance of *Der Freischütz* one evening when there was a commotion in the gallery. As Legouvé described it:

One of my neighbors rises from his seat and bending towards the orchestra shouts in a voice of thunder: "You don't want two flutes there, you brutes! You want two piccolos! Two piccolos, do you hear? Oh, the brutes!" Having said this, he simply sits down again, scowling indignantly. Amidst the general tumult produced by this outburst, I turn around and see a young man trembling with passion, his hands clenched, his eyes flashing, and a head of hair—such a head of hair. It looked like an enormous umbrella of hair, projecting something like a moveable awning over a beak of a bird of prey.

There were those who found Berlioz objectionable. Mendelssohn, a reserved and rather prissy man, was repelled on their first encounter, which took place in Rome. He thought Berlioz affected. "This purely external enthusiasm, this desperation in the presence of women, this assumption of genius in capital letters, is insupportable to me." But even Mendelssohn had to admit that Berlioz was interesting. Schumann was more sympathetic. "Berlioz does not try to be pleasing and elegant. What he hates, he grasps fiercely by the hair; what he loves, he almost crushes in his fervor."

Berlioz was far from being a mere braggart. He had the authentic big vision, and in certain areas the twentieth century has not even started to approximate it. Take his vision of the symphony orchestra. In the 1830's the orchestra seldom went over sixty players. Berlioz, the greatest orchestral innovator in history, had in mind an ideal orchestra, the only orchestra that could properly play his music. As early as 1825 he had brought together an orchestra of 150, but that was as nothing to his dream orchestra. It numbered 467 (to which would be added a chorus of 360); and in addition to the 242 strings there were to be such groupings as thirty harps, thirty pianos, twelve cymbals, sixteen French horns, and an exotic variety of percussion. No wonder his friends considered him impractical and his enemies crazy. Berlioz was unperturbed. "Vulgar prejudice," he said, "calls large orchestras noisy, but if they are well balanced, well trained and well led, and if they perform true music, they should rather be called powerful."

From the beginning his big orchestral conceptions startled Europe. Somehow this relatively untrained composer, this ex-medical student who could not play a respectable musical instrument, had the ear to conceive tonal combinations undreamed-of until then. The *Symphonie fantastique*, whatever it may have owed to Beethoven, had concepts of color and sonority that forced all future composers to revise their estimates of orchestral sound and of the capabilities of the symphony orchestra. The *Fantastique* was Berlioz' first major work. He finished it in 1830 before graduating from the Conservatoire.

Certainly none of the early romantics—the prim and classic Mendelssohn; Chopin and Schumann, who thought primarily in terms of the piano; Liszt, also a pianist who did not compose any significant orchestral works until the middle 1850's—certainly none of those men were thinking along such lines. Berlioz, so far ahead of his time, influenced Wagner and Richard Strauss much more than his contemporaries. Even today the last two movements of the *Fantastique*, which depict a march to the scaffold and a hallucinated witches' Sabbath, remain shockers.

The five-movement symphony is music of youth, of abandon, music that received its initial impetus from De Quincey's *Confessions of an Opium Eater*, music in which the classic emotional amenities are discarded. Berlioz had an imagination that ran as much along literary as musical lines, and it could be triggered very easily. From any other composer the descriptive effects that abound in his music would be superficial. They are not in Berlioz because he was so original, so much his natural self. Defiantly he set about expressing *himself* in his music: *his* loves, *his* attitude toward the world, *his* kind of experience. Not even Schumann, that most personal of composers, ever attempted so graphic a picture of the artist as a young man as Berlioz did in the *Fantastique*.

Here the problem of program music enters. The *Symphonie fantastique* is the first great piece of program music (*i.e.*, a piece of music that tells a story), though there had been many precedents. Even Bach had written a piece on the departure of a beloved brother. How does one listen to program music? Must the story be constantly in mind? Can the story be disregarded and the music listened to merely as music? Aestheticians for a century and a half have been arguing about the problem. It so happens that for the *Fantastique*, Berlioz used some music he had composed long previously for other purposes—music that had nothing to do with the program of the *Fantastique*. It also happens that the *Fantastique* divorced from its program is in many respects an orthodox symphony, with an allegro in sonata form, an adagio, scherzo, and finale. So what price program music? There is no easy answer. Everybody listens to music his own way. The less sophisticated listener often needs some kind of prop and he tends to "see" pictures in all kinds of music. The professional listens differently, concentrating on form, line, and shape, and, as often as not, he completely ignores any program in any type of music. (Arnold Schoenberg has confessed that for years he listened to, and loved, the Schubert songs—songs are in essence a kind of program music—without having the slightest idea of their texts.) In any case, no music can specifically describe anything. Anybody hearing the *Symphonie fantastique* for the first time—or Liszt's *Les Préludes*, or Strauss's *Till Eulenspiegel*, or Debussy's *La Mer*—without knowing the superimposed literary content of the work, would find it impossible to guess the program. At best, music can express only mood and emotion. It would take a dull listener indeed who did not realize that the second movement of the *Fantastique* is a waltz; or that the last movement is a wild, snarling, and turbulent evocation of *something*. And that is as far as anybody can go. A program may give an idea of what went on in the composer's mind, but music succeeds or fails on purely *musical* terms, and this is true even in opera, where extramusical associations necessarily play a part. No opera has ever remained in the repertoire because it has a great libretto. It remains because the music is great.

Berlioz needed some extramusical stimulus to set him off. In the *Fantastique* he expressed his own fantasies, and the thing that triggered them was his affair with the Irish actress Harriet Smithson. To say merely that he was in love with her would be like saying that the oceans have some water in them. It was more than love on Berlioz' part; it was a force of nature that all but drove him out of his mind. He wept to his friends. He raved. He disappeared into the fields outside of Paris, and on one of those occasions Liszt, Mendelssohn, and Chopin went out looking for him, convinced that he was going to destroy himself. Berlioz wrote about his "anguish," his "interminable and inextinguishable passion," his body shuddering with pain. "If she could for one moment conceive all the poetry, all the infinity of a like love, she would fly to my arms though she were to die through my embrace."

Miss Smithson did not reciprocate his great love, and for a good reason. She did not know Berlioz. They had not met, and all she knew about him was contained in the violent letters he sent her. They scared her to death. She thought he was mad and would not see him. He went to the theater to watch her. When he saw her in the arms of her stage lover, he screamed in pain and rushed from the house. Out of all this came the *Fantastique*. He heard rumors that she was carrying on with another man. Very well. He would show her. He put her into the last movement of the symphony as a whore at the witches' Sabbath. Later, learning the rumors were false, he removed the reference to her as a courtesan, but she still attends the Sabbath.

There had been program music before, but nothing like this. The *Fantastique* was first performed in 1830, and bemused listeners followed the progress of Hector and Harriet through five movements of tumultuous upheaval. Naturally, few understood what was going on. Liszt of course knew, and promptly made a piano arrangement of the work, movements of which he played at concerts. One of his tricks was to have the orchestra play the *March to the Scaffold*. Then Liszt would grandly dismiss the orchestra and play his solo version of the movement, building to immense sonorities that made an even grander effect.

One technical idea in the *Fantastique* made a big impression. The hero of the symphony, the young musician in love with Her, never thinks of his beloved except as associated with a musical thought, and Her theme runs through the entire symphony, presenting for the first time the *idée fixe* that eventually was to lead into the Wagnerian leitmotif. The *Fantastique* has its flaws. There is some overwriting, some self-conscious posing, some melodic material less than stimulating, some awkward transitions. But these shrink to nothing before the power and originality of the work, its brilliant orchestration, its ardent romanticism.

This mixture of flaw and genius is true of almost any Berlioz work. Moments of inspiration can alternate with banalities or interminably stretched-out passages. Even by Berlioz' own loose standards his forms sometimes are

128

unsatisfactory. Some composers can get away with deficiencies of form. Schubert and Schumann could because of their extraordinary melodic gifts and the intrinsic quality of the material. Berlioz could because of his hypersensitive imagination and unparalleled ear for color. He never was the most disciplined of composers, nor was he the most facile of melodists, though occasionally he could come up with an inspired tune, as in the love music of *Roméo et Juliette* or the first song of the *Nuits d'Eté* cycle.

Berlioz eventually married his Harriet, after six years of siege, but not without a few interesting intervening episodes. There was, for instance, the Marie Moke caper. After the fuss created by the *Fantastique* Berlioz went off to Rome, having temporarily forgotten about his Harriet. His new love was a talented pianist named Marie Moke. In Italy he learned that Marie had married the piano manufacturer Pleyel. Berlioz in his autobiography has some fun with this episode. "I was beside myself with passion, and shed tears of rage; but I made up my mind on the spot what to do. My duty was clear. I must at once proceed to Paris and kill two guilty women"— Marie's mother was the other—"and one innocent man. After that, of course, it would be incumbent upon me to commit suicide." He arranges for a coach, first taking time out to orchestrate an unfinished work. Business before pleasure. He procures a dress and accessories so that he can disguise himself as a lady's maid, gets a pair of pistols, a bottle of laudanum and a bottle of strychnine. Loaded with this conspicuous example of overkill, breathing fire, he reaches Nice and suddenly finds himself cured. At Nice he spends the three happiest weeks of his life. Berlioz narrates all this with high good humor. He is playing a part and poking fun at himself, and he wants the reader to join the fun. It is utterly charming.

In 1832 he returned to Paris and the following year married Harriet. She turned out to be a shrew and, soon, an alcoholic. They fought like Balin and Balan. At intervals between bouts, Berlioz plunged into the European musical life and immediately became the leader of the avant-garde. He was interested only in the future. "If you were to produce one of Sebastian Bach's works I probably should take flight at one of his fugues." Many of the romantic composers either disliked classic music or paid mere lip service to it. Berlioz in his dislike of the early composers was more frank than most. He did not care for the music of Haydn and ignored most of Mozart. The big musical inspiration of his life, as to all the romantics, was Beethoven. Before Beethoven, little music existed for Berlioz, except for the operas of Gluck and Spontini. Yet, paradoxically, in literature he had a great love for the past: Homer, Virgil, Dante, Shakespeare. Shakespeare above all. "Next to God, it is Shakespeare who has created most." At parties he would declaim *Hamlet* for hours to his bored friends. "To have reached the age of 45 or 50 and not to know *Hamlet*—it's like having lived all one's years in a coal mine!" Berlioz could be an inconsistent man. With all of his screams against tradition, there nevertheless was a great deal of tradition in his music, as recent scholars have been pointing out. As he grew older, the classical tradition in his music became ever more pronounced, and sections of his last opera, *Les Troyens*, are as chaste as anything in Gluck. It was not, of course, an eighteenth-century classicism. Rather it was a classicism in which the uncontrollable instincts of youth are tempered by restraint, clarity, and proportion. Berlioz was French, with all the logic and mental organization that implies.

Even with that classically controlled current running beneath his frequently wild music, the important thing about Berlioz was that he was in every way a revolutionary, a man fully prepared to throw established and even sacred notions into a garbage can. The nineteenth century knew it. "He sought the impossible and would have it at any cost," Saint-Saëns said. Théophile Gautier, in his *Histoire du romanticisme* (1854), placed Berlioz with Hugo and Delacroix as the three great French romantics. To Gautier, Berlioz represented "the romantic musical idea." In his comparison of Berlioz with Hugo, Gautier pointed out that "Their first thought . . . has been to free themselves from the old classical rhythm with its unending drone, its obligatory cadences and its predetermined pauses. Just as Victor Hugo replaces caesuras, uses enjambment and varies, by all kinds of devices, the monotony of the poetic phrase, Hector Berlioz changes rhythm, deceives the ear, which was expecting a symmetrical occurrence, and punctuates as he sees fit the musical phrase. . . . With both there is . . . the same disdain for the too bare, the too simple, line of classical art." Berlioz represented an anti-German type of romanticism: less thick, less sentimental, more aristocratic. As he grew older he shunned such extroverted fantasies as the *Fantastique* and said that "one must try to do coolly the things that are most fiery."

His unique series of scores came in steady progression—*Harold in Italy* in 1834 (where Byron had gone, the romantics were not far behind), the Requiem (1837), *Roméo et Juliette* (1839), *La Damnation de Faust* (1846), the *Te Deum* (1849), the oratorio *L'Enfance du Christ* (1854), the operas *Benvenuto Cellini* (1838), *Les Troyens* (1859), and *Béatrice et Bénedict* (1862). These are the major scores; there also were many choral works, songs, and other material. Often the music is in bastard forms of Berlioz' own devising. *La Damnation de Faust*—what is it? Oratorio? Opera? Berlioz called it "a concert opera." *Roméo et Juliette*—what is it? A choral work? Berlioz called it a "dramatic symphony." No matter. Each work must be judged on its own, not on *a priori* concepts of what constitutes "form." In the case of the *Damnation* the listener, only too conscious of some awkward settings and interminable recitative, can nevertheless thrill to the *Rákoczy* March and feel his skin prickle during the ride to the abyss. Those snarling trombones and bassoons under the whistling of the wind: what a stroke! Or, quite different, the intimate *L'Enfance du Christ*, with its quiet sounds and infinitely appealing tenderness. Or the power of the Requiem, with its secondary brass orchestras, its sensuousness of sound (Berlioz was the first composer to use sound for its own sake—to make an aesthetic of pure sound). No normal set of values can be put to much of this music, for normal values do not apply. The constructions are too unconventional, the melodies too asymmetrical, the harmonic language too personal. The music has a peculiar kind of *essence* that is immensely meaningful to some listeners and rather negative to others. The ever-increasing classic strain in Berlioz involves something more internal than external: quality of line rather than sound. As Gerald Abraham, in *A Hundred Years of Music*, puts it, "The history of music records few more striking paradoxes than this: that when the romantic movement had conquered the whole world of music in the nineteenth century, the only important composer who went on composing serenely beautiful music, filled with the classical spirit and fulfilling the classical ideal, was he who a quarter of a century earlier had been considered the most extravagant of the romantics."

Through these years Berlioz was in constant trouble: trouble at home with his wife (it did not take him long to find a mistress, a second-rate singer named Marie Recio, and he eventually married her after Harriet's death in 1854), trouble with his colleagues, trouble with the French public, which was puzzled by his music. He did have a following. Great composers have always had a following. There is no such thing as a completely misunderstood genius. But it was a small and predominantly professional following, nothing like what the mighty Giacomo Meyerbeer, the hero of the Opéra, could command. Berlioz had to fight every inch of the way, enmired in debt, trying to make the world understand his idiom. Paganini once bailed him out with a gift of 20,000 francs (probably close to $20,000 in 1970 American currency). Paganini said that Berlioz was the only man capable of making Beethoven come alive again.

Musicians of an older school resisted Berlioz' innovations or simply ignored them. His relations with Habeneck were typical. François Habeneck was a nice old boy who had founded the Concerts du Conservatoire in 1828. But he was a conservative and Berlioz had little respect for him. In 1836, Berlioz obtained one of the few official commissions of his career. The Minister of the Interior appointed him to compose a Requiem, and it was scheduled for performance on the day of the annual service commemorating the dead of the 1830 Revolution. The premiere took place the following year, Habeneck conducting. Berlioz was disturbed. Habeneck was the last man he wanted. As he explains the situation, Habeneck had not spoken to him for years. "His behavior to me was rude and incomprehensible." But there was little Berlioz could do, for the premiere was under government auspices, and Habeneck was in charge of the music at all important state musical occasions. The day of the premiere came, and in his autobiography Berlioz described what happened:

My forces had been divided into several groups spread over a wide area; necessarily so because of the four brass bands which I use in the *Tuba mirum,* and which have to be placed beyond the main body of performers, one at each corner. At the point where they enter, at the beginning of the *Tuba mirum*—which follows the *Dies Irae* without a pause —the music broadens to a tempo twice as slow. First, all four groups break in simultaneously—at the new tempo—then successively, challenging and answering each other from a distance, the entries piling up, each a third higher than the one before. It is therefore of the utmost importance to indicate the four beats of the slower tempo very clearly the moment it is reached; otherwise the great cataclysm, a musical representation of the Last Judgment, prepared for with such deliberation and employing an exceptional combination of forces in a manner at the time unprecedented and not attempted since—a passage which will, I hope, endure as a landmark in music—is mere noise and pandemonium, a monstrosity.

With my habitual mistrust I had stayed just behind Habeneck. Standing with my back to him, I supervised the group of timpani (which he could not see), as the moment approached for them to join in the general tumult. There are perhaps a thousand bars in my Requiem. In the very bar I have been speaking of, the bar in which the tempo broadens and the brass proclaim their tremendous fanfare—the one bar, in fact, in which the conductor's direction is absolutely indispensable—Habeneck laid down his baton and, calmly producing his snuffbox, proceeded to take a pinch of snuff. I had been keeping my eye on him. In a flash I turned on my heel, sprang forward in front of him and, stretching out my arm, marked out the four great beats of the new tempo. The bands followed me and everything went off in order. I conducted the piece to the end. The effect I had dreamed of was attained. When, at the final words of the chorus, Habeneck saw that the *Tuba mirum* was saved, he said: "God! I was in a cold sweat. Without you we would have been lost."

"I know," I replied, looking him straight in the eye. I did not say another word. Had he done it deliberately? Was it possible that this man, in collusion with X (who hated me) and with Cherubini's friends, had actually planned and attempted to carry out an act of such base treachery? I would rather not think so. Yet I cannot doubt it. God forgive me if I am doing him an injustice.

Ernest Newman, in his edition of the Berlioz memoirs, doubts that any such incident ever took place. Newman is wrong. Charles Hallé, the pianist and conductor, specifically mentions Habeneck's lapse in his reminiscences. Berlioz to the end of his life believed that Habeneck had tried to sabotage him.

To have some sort of steady income, Berlioz turned to criticism. In 1853 he became critic of the *Journal des Débats,* a position he held for ten years. He also contributed to other publications. Berlioz was the greatest music critic of his time, possibly of all time, but he hated the idea of criticism and he hated to write, even though his prose flows so easily and with so fresh a style that it always appears spontaneous. He was voluble on the subject of his mental blocks when it came to writing, and his memoirs are filled with great moanings about the unhappiness of his lot. He said that he could spend eight consecutive hours on his music, but that he had to fight with himself to begin a piece of prose, and he describes the state of mind so many writers get into:

About the fourth line or so I get up, walk around the room, look out into the streets, take up a book. . . . My brain seemed ready to burst. My veins were burning. Sometimes I remained with my elbows on the table, holding my head in both my hands. Sometimes I strode up and down like a soldier on guard in a frost 25 degrees below zero. . . .

And when, on turning around, my eyes fell on that accursed title inscribed at the head of that accursed sheet of paper, still blank and obstinately waiting for the words with which it was supposed to be covered, I felt simply overcome by despair. There was a guitar standing against the table. With one kick I smashed it in the center. . . . On my chimney two pistols were looking at me with their round eyes. I stared at them for a long time. I went so far as to bang my head again and again with my fist. At last, like a schoolboy who cannot do his homework, I tore my hair and wept with furious indignation.

There have been music critics (not many) with Berlioz' technical expertise. There also have been critics (even fewer) with a livelier writing style. But the combination of knowledge and vivacity makes his writing unique. He was very conscious of style. The fear of being dull or monotonous, he said, "makes me try to vary a little the turn of my poor sentences." On the passing musical scene he wrote with warmth, fairness, and good humor. Unfortunately, most of his reviews remain untranslated and have to be dug out of the *Journal des Débats* or the *Gazette Musicale.* Some of his pieces have been reproduced in the volume *Soirées de l'Orchestre,* a collection that contains some of his funniest essays. One of them is a feat of imagination that would have done credit to E. T. A. Hoffmann. It is an account of a piano competition at the Conservatoire. Thirty pianists are assembled to play the competition piece, Mendelssohn's G minor Concerto. After thirty performances the piano, a noble Érard, starts playing the concerto by itself. Nobody can stop it. They send for the manufacturer and Érard himself rushes over. The piano has gone berserk and will not listen to orders. Érard sprinkles the piano with holy water. That does not help. They remove the keyboard, which continues to play, throw it in the courtyard, and Érard has it chopped up with an axe. Now each piece of the keyboard dances around. Finally they throw it into a fire. "There was no other way to loose its grip. But, after all, how can a piano hear a concerto thirty times in the same hall on the same day without contracting the habit of it? M. Mendelssohn won't be able to complain that his music isn't being played. But think of the damage!"

In the latter part of his life, Berlioz spent much time conducting. He turned to the podium because nobody seemed capable or desirous of conducting his music. After a conductor—his friend, Narcisse Girard—messed up the premiere of *Harold in Italy* in 1834, Berlioz resolved in the future to conduct himself. As a musician with ideas, as a forceful personality, as a man with a vision of how music in its ideal state should sound, he was able to get more from an orchestra than anybody of his time. Wagner heard Berlioz conduct in 1839 and was more than impressed; and Wagner was not the man to pass compliments around: "I was simply all ears for things of which I had not dreamed until then, and which I felt I must try to realize." Berlioz was a volatile and extravagant figure on the podium, one of the first of the choreographic conductors. But no matter how much he gyrated, his beat remained clear and his interpretations must have been lucid, logical, and proportioned. As a conductor he was at the opposite pole from Wagner. Wagner stood for egocentricity, constant fluctuation of tempo, expression of self as much as expression of the composers' ideas. Berlioz did not admire this approach and once remarked of Wagner's conducting that it was in much too free a style, "like dancing on a tightrope, *sempre tempo rubato*." Wagner, on the other hand, thought Berlioz superficial in everything except his own music. (German musicians have always had a tendency to regard French musicians as superficial, and that remains true today.) The odds are that Berlioz' style rather than Wagner's would be much more palatable to twentieth-century tastes.

Berlioz and Wagner: two of the biggest men of the avant-garde. Their careers only slightly intersected, for Wagner came to maturity in the 1860's, after Berlioz had stopped writing. Berlioz never heard any of Wagner's great works, the *Tristan* Prelude being the only work of Wagner's maturity he came across. Berlioz was puzzled and did not like it. Reviewing the piece, he called it "a sort of chromatic moan, full of dissonant chords, of which the long appogiaturas that replace the real note only increase the cruelty." Yet both composers were of the vanguard, and Berlioz of all people should have been responsive to the new speech of his great contemporary. He himself had been knocked from pillar to post, and in his lifetime did not achieve even the slightest foothold in Paris.

It was in London, in 1855, that the two men got to know each another. Both were there on conducting assignments. Wagner has left a record of one evening, not realizing how unconsciously funny it was. Wagner was always a compulsive talker, full of ideas about everything, and his pontifical speech was governed by an underlay of Kantian, Schillerian, and Schopenhauerian aesthetics and metaphysics. On this particular evening in London, Wagner was holding forth in grand and unintelligible manner: "Life's impressions hold us captive, as it were, until we rid ourselves of them by the formation of inner soul forms, which are by no means called forth by those impressions, but are only aroused by them from their deep slumbers so that the artistic image is not the result of the impressions but, on the contrary, a liberation from them." Wagner talked, Berlioz gravely listened. Whereupon, Wagner says, Berlioz smiled in a "condescending, sagacious sort of way," and said: *Nous appelons cela digérer.* Wagner had no sense of humor at all, and did not see the point of Berlioz' remark, "We call that digestion." But how deftly it pricks Wagner's inflated and self-satisfied theorizing!

No, the two men could not ever come together. Berlioz had too much of a classic feeling, was too realistic, too urbane, too witty—as urbane and witty as Wagner was egocentric, selfish, and philosophically muddle-headed. As the two most publicized leaders of the avant-garde, it probably was inevitable that they be set up against each other. Liszt and his group solved the problem by joining with Wagner and following him, all united under the banner of The Music of the Future. Berlioz could never have joined that party. He had been first in the field, to begin with, and his style was fully formed long before *Tristan.* He also may have felt, and resented, the fact that the wave of the future was with Wagner. Berlioz was a loner. He left no disciples, and it was Wagner to whom most of the younger generation flocked. Yet in 1860 Wagner, writing to Liszt, shows that he was perfectly aware of Berlioz' high and lonely position. To Wagner, there were only three composers worth taking notice of—Liszt, Berlioz, and Wagner. Or, as Wagner put it, "In the present period we alone are on a par—that is, You, He and I." Characteristically, Wagner omitted the name of Verdi. Otherwise, he was completely accurate. In 1860 Schumann, Mendelssohn, and Chopin were dead, and the great postromantic composers had yet to make their mark.

Berlioz found himself living too long. Ill, dejected, he spent the last half-dozen years of his life waiting for death in a small apartment he named Caliban's Cave. Once in a while he made public appearances, as when he went to Vienna to attend performances of his *Damnation de Faust* and *Harold in Italy*. But music was passing him by, and the great romantic became an anachronism. Liszt, Meyerbeer, Auber, Gounod, Thomas—these were the new heroes in Paris. Berlioz attempted to relieve his physical and emotional pain by taking opium. On March 8, 1869, he died. Thomas and Gounod were among the pallbearers. Cherubini, Gluck, Mozart, and a part of the Berlioz Requiem figured in the funeral service. If Berlioz had not been popular during his life, at least his death attracted some notice. According to newspaper reports, the way to the Montmartre Cemetery was lined with considerable crowds. A band of the National Guard played funeral marches during the passage of the procession. Musical pundits all over Europe wrote estimates of Berlioz' life and work. He was condemned by some as being an evil influence on the development of music. But there was one sensitive and appreciative estimate by Oscar Comettant, the critic of *Le Ménestral*. Among Comettant's observations was a paragraph on what Berlioz' music meant when it was first heard:

Roméo et Juliette, when I first heard it many years ago, with an imposing orchestra and a numerous chorus, under the direction of the composer himself, produced in me one of those profound but indeterminate sensations which do not command enthusiasm though they inspire respect. I saw before me a great artist; I felt I did; my reason told me that I was listening to grandiose music, full of poetry; but it was only with difficulty that my ear, then inexperienced, could follow its ingenious and bold development. On the other hand, the accents of the melody, chaste, voluptuous, fantastic, gloomy, brilliant, ardent, impassioned in turn, but always bearing the stamp of genius, that is to say of originality, merely glided lightly over my heart without penetrating it. In the presence of this original work I remained cold but dazzled, as an inhabitant of the plains of Texas, or of the volcanic mountains of Peru, would be if suddenly transported without any preparation from those solitary and distant regions to the midst of a city like Paris, on some grand fête day.

To this day listeners first coming into contact with the music of Berlioz still have the feelings described so accurately by Comettant in 1869.

Although Berlioz was never entirely out of the repertoire after his death, he was represented only by a handful of works, and only one large-scale piece, the *Symphonie fantastique*. He had some champions, such as Felix Weingartner, but on the whole was a marginal figure until his rediscovery after World War II. In England especially there was a strong revival, and even his operas were staged, to vast acclaim. The Berlioz revival has not spread as strongly in the United States, though much more of his music has been heard since 1950 than ever before. Perhaps Berlioz will always remain the object of veneration by a strong and articulate minority. He could not speak to Everyman. But there is not one piece of his that lacks its incandescent moments. And then Berlioz is seen plain, his eagle beak defiantly thrust at the heavens, glorifying in a kind of tonal magnificence and an ideal of self-expression that make the concept of romanticism very clear.

10

Florestan and Eusebius

ROBERT SCHUMANN

With Robert Schumann romanticism came to full flower. Every aspect of romanticism was reflected in him. He was introspective, idealistic, closely allied spiritually with the literary aspects of the age, an innovator, a critic, a propagandist for the new—and a great composer. His music at first almost entirely dispensed with old forms (later he was to write more orthodox symphonies and quartets). He was the first of the completely anticlassic composers, and form as it previously existed meant little to him, though he was a superior theorist and as well informed as any musician then alive. While composers of his day were writing sonatas, symphonies, and variations, Schumann was writing music named *Intermezzi, Arabesque, Davidsbündlertänze, Kreisleriana, Carnaval, Kinderszenen*. These are caprices bundled together; they are spiritual diaries as well as music. A critic once rebuked him for not writing orthodox sonatas. Schumann's response was fervid, and it represented the romantic attitude: "As if all mental pictures must be shaped to fit one or two forms! As if each idea did not come into existence with its form ready-made! As if each work of art had not its own meaning and consequently its own form!" This is a very important, and very modern, statement. For the first time in music is found the expressed statement that content and idea dictate form, not the reverse. More than any composer, more even than Chopin, whose forms also to a large extent were anticlassic, Schumann established an entire aesthetic that verged on impressionism. In this concept, a short statement can be as valid as a long speech, and perhaps more so. Schumann, along with Chopin (the two worked independently of each other), demonstrated that forms existed not for the academicians but for the creative mind: that pure idea could impose its own forms, and that a small but perfect form, one that captured and exploited a single idea, could be its own aesthetic justification.

Mood, color, suggestion, allusion—these were important to Schumann, much more important than writing correct fugues, rondos, or sonatas. Invariably his music has a capricious and unexpected turn, a kaleidoscopic texture and emotion, an intensity of personal utterance that can be measured only in astronomical units. Naturally every pedant and academician in Europe promptly set Schumann up as a whipping boy. To them his works were the end of music, a sign of the degeneracy of the times. His music appeared strange, formless, anarchic, from the void. It was a music tied up with poetry, painting, personal allusions, and romantic aesthetics. To Schumann it was all one. "The esthetic experience," he once wrote, "is the same in any art, only the materials differ." Few major composers have been so disliked in their own time, and even fewer have been so little performed. Wagner, for instance, was hated in many quarters, but he received plenty of performances, and his work was discussed all over Europe. Wagner knew how to promote himself. The gentle Schumann never did. A quiet man, medium-sized, with a sensitive face and lips that were always pursed as though he were whistling to himself, he never really fought back, as Wagner and Berlioz did. When he did fight, and he did so as a critic, it was for the new music and not for himself. Big-hearted, generous, dedicated, in love with music, he lent a helping hand to all young talent. In the meantime his pungent harmonies, his unusually strong dissonances and syncopated rhythms, his new concept of free but functional form—all were being described by the conservatives as the work of a madman. To Henry Fothergill Chorley, the critic of the *Athenaeum* in London, Schumann's music represented the art of "covering pages with thoughts little worth noting and of hiding an intrinsic poverty of invention by grim or monotonous eccentricity." Chorley smelled the end of civilization as he knew it. "Decadence!" he thundered. Fortunately, Schumann had friends and disciples, and his admirers saw to it that his music was spread around. He also had a wife who was one of the best pianists in the world. Little by little his music made progress, though it was not until after his death that he was accepted as one of the immortals.

If ever a composer was doomed to music it was Robert Schumann. There was something of a Greek tragedy in the way music reached into his cradle, seized him, nourished him, and finally destroyed him. From the beginning his emotions were overstrung, abnormally so. His mind was a delicate seismograph upon which music registered violent shocks—shocks that would not even be noticed by people with less sensitive receiving apparatus. He himself once described how, as a child, he stole at night to the piano and played a series of chords, weeping bitterly all the while. He was so moved by the writings of Jean Paul that the intensity of the pleasure drove him (in his own words) to the verge of madness. When he heard of Schubert's death he wept the whole night. Anybody with sensibilities refined to such a pitch is apt to lose control, and Schumann eventually did. Sometime around 1851, five years before his death, he began having hallucinations. He would hear harmonies from heaven. One night he imagined that the spirits of Schubert and Mendelssohn had brought him a theme, and he leapt out of bed to write it down. Like William Blake, he had visions. Unlike Blake, he could not live with them, and his mind finally gave way.

But he accomplished much in the forty-six years of his life. His daemon dictated to him a kind of music that no composer up to that time had begun to visualize. The derivative forces in the music of Bach, Haydn, Handel, Mozart, and Beethoven can easily be traced. Berlioz owed a large debt to Beethoven. Even in so amazing a genius as the young Chopin there can be found influences of earlier composers—Field, Weber, Hummel. But Schumann from the beginning struck off entirely on his own, and it is hard to find a precedent for his music.

Basically he was a self-taught composer. Certainly there were no musical antecedents in his family. He was born on June 8, 1810, in the little town of Zwickau in Saxony. His father, August, was a bookseller and, like Robert, a rather shy and retiring person. In addition to selling books, he undertook publication, in German translation, of the complete works of Scott and Byron. But most of all he liked to sit in his study, smoking pipe after pipe, and writing romances. There was a bad strain in the family. August had what was called a nervous disorder, and was anything but normal in his last years. His daughter, Emilia, was a mental and physical defective who committed suicide. Many years later, Robert was also to try to kill himself. Even as a young man, Robert was afraid that he too would become insane, and the thought plagued his whole life. August died when Robert was sixteen.

With all the books in his father's shop, and with his natural, eager intelligence, it was no wonder that Robert was constantly reading. He especially loved reading the romantics—Ludwig Tieck, Jean Paul, Novalis (the *nom de plume* of Georg Friedrich Philipp von Hardenberg), E. T. A. Hoffmann, Klemens Brentano. Robert grew up conditioned by literature, and in no other composer is there such an attempted fusion of sound with literary idea. His favorite writer was Jean Paul, and that great romantic and visionary was constantly making remarks about music—remarks that the young Schumann devoured. "Sound," wrote Jean Paul, "shines like the dawn, and the sun rises in the form of sound; sound seeks to rise in music, and color is light." Or, Jean Paul would write, it is music alone "which can open the ultimate gates to the Infinite." To Schumann, romantic literature in general and Jean Paul in particular were governing processes of life itself. "If everybody read Jean Paul," he wrote to a friend when he was eighteen, "we should be better but more unhappy. Sometimes he almost clouds my mind, but the rainbow of peace and the natural strength of man bring sweet tears, and the heart comes through its ordeal marvellously purified and softened."

Inspired by his literary heroes, Schumann tried his hand at poetry and fiction. He also attempted composition. Indeed, he had been doing so from the age of seven. He had easily learned how to play the piano and had a strong talent for improvisation. But his musical education was almost nil, and he had to pick everything up by himself. There were musicales and literary readings in Zwickau, and Schumann was the star at those affairs. In music and literature, however, he could be called only an amateur.

At the death of his father he was still wavering between a career in music or literature. His mother had different ideas. She could see no future for Robert in either field, and she sent him to Leipzig to study law. Leipzig was the wrong place for so impressionable a young man as Robert. There was too much music in the city. He would go to concerts at the Gewandhaus, or to the musical services at St. Thomas (Bach's old church), or to the performances of the Euterpe choral society. Or he would get up early and, in a spasm of activity, practice the piano eight or nine hours a day, smoking innumerable cigars in the process. At night he would summon his friends and play for them. Or he would read Goethe, Shakespeare, Byron, and of course Jean Paul, committing to memory page after page of their work. He was a romantic *par excellence*, affecting a Byronic pose, falling in and out of love, dabbling in the arts, arguing about music, life, and aesthetics through the night and well into the morning. He did not study much law in Leipzig. Nor did he study much more in Heidelberg, where he went for a year. One of his closest friends was there, and there also was a law professor, one Justus Thibaut, who had written a book on musical aesthetics and was a great music lover.

All this was very fine, but musically speaking it was not very professional. Not until Schumann was eighteen did he take his first serious musical instruction. In 1830, on his return to Leipzig, he came across a piano teacher named Friedrich Wieck. The best testimonial to Wieck's pedagogical theories was his daughter, the nine-year-old Clara. She was a formidable prodigy and she developed into one of history's outstanding artists. Wieck was enthusiastic about Schumann's potential. He wrote to Schumann's mother, promising that Robert would "be one of the greatest pianists within three years. He shall play with more warmth and genius than Moscheles, and on a grander scale than Hummel." Mrs. Schumann was not happy about the turn events had taken, but there was little she could do about it. Schumann moved into Wieck's house, practiced hard, started composing, and also took lessons in composition with Heinrich Dorn, conductor of the Leipzig opera. But his career as a professional pianist ended before it started. Trying to achieve a short cut to finger independence, the impetuous Schumann invented a contraption that permanently ruined one of his fingers. He does not appear to have been greatly distressed by the accident. Already he must have known that his future was in composing. In 1831 his first published composition appeared, the *Abegg* Variations. Characteristically, he constructed the theme on the letters of a girl's name. Soon came his Op. 2, the *Papillons*, a musical rendering of the ballroom scene from Jean Paul's *Flegeljahre*. This appeared in 1832, and Schumann saw the whole world opening up to him:

> On sleepless nights I am conscious of a mission which rises before me like a distant peak. When I wrote *Papillons* I began to feel a certain independence. Now the butterflies [papillons] have flown off into the vast and magnificent universe of spring; the spring itself is on my doorstep looking at me—it is a child with celestial blue eyes.

His head was full of new music, and he started putting it on paper. He also started reviewing concerts and new music for the *Allgemeine Musikalische Zeitung* and the *Komet*. One of his first reviews in the *Zeitung*, in 1831, brought Chopin to the attention of German readers. Schumann came across the *Là ci darem* Variations (Op. 2), and wrote an enthusiastic review that contained the famous line: "Hats off, gentlemen! A genius!" The review, written in Schumann's best Jean-Paulese, is an amazingly sympathetic and prescient summary of Chopin's startling new music and what it stands for. In 1833 he decided to start his own music magazine, and the first issue of the *Neue Zeitschrift für Musik* appeared in 1834. And he fell in love with Clara.

They became engaged in 1837. Old Wieck took it hard. More than that, he did everything in his power to stop the marriage. History has labeled him the prototype of the hard-hearted, selfish, ambitious father. Yet one can see his point of view. He had made Clara the outstanding pianist of her sex. Now, just when he was ready to reap the financial rewards, she was throwing herself away on a penniless composer, a vague idealist, a radical musician whose theories were being called mad, an impractical and disorganized man. Wieck looked around and could find plenty of material to support his arguments. Nobody thought much of Schumann's music. In Paris, Chopin was poking fun at it. Mendelssohn, who was the strongest musical power in Germany, and who liked Schumann personally, could find little to praise about his music. (Later, when Schumann started composing symphonies, Mendelssohn did bring them to the public.) Liszt himself, the great Liszt, had tried to play some Schumann music in public and had failed. If Liszt, the greatest of matinee idols, could not establish Schumann's music, who could?

But, much as one can see Wieck's point of view, his tactics in trying to stop the marriage were distressing. He spread rumors that Schumann was a dipsomaniac, unreliable, incapable of taking care of a wife. He used every trick to tear the lovers apart, maligning him, lying, growing frantic with rage, anxiety, and frustration. He would tell Clara that Schumann was lazy, and she would relay that bit of information to him. Schumann answered her letters. "Your father calls me phlegmatic. *Carnaval* and phlegmatic! F sharp minor Sonata and phlegmatic! Being in love with such a girl and phlegmatic! And you can listen calmly to all this? He says that I have written nothing in the *Zeitschrift* for six weeks. In the first place, that is not true. Secondly, even if it were, how does he know what other work I have been doing? . . . Up to the present time, the *Zeitschrift* has had about eighty sheets of my own ideas, not to mention the rest of the editorial work, besides which I have finished ten major compositions in two years, and they have cost me some heart's blood. To add to everything else, I have given several hours of hard work every day to Bach and Beethoven, and to my own work, and conscientiously managed a large correspondence, which was often delicate and complicated. I am a young man of twenty-eight, with a very active mind, and an artist in addition. . . . And you mean to say all my industry and simplicity, all that I have done, is quite lost upon your father?" Finally the lovers had to go to court for permission to marry without Wieck's consent. They were married in 1840.

It turned out to be an idyllic marriage, the union of two extraordinary minds. She was the stabilizing force in his life; he was the spiritual beacon in hers. Adjustments had to be made. His work came first, even if it meant that she had to go long periods without practicing; and she worried about that. Practicing, to the professional instrumentalist, becomes compulsive, and there can be a psychic wrench if the normal six or seven hours a day are missed. But Clara had to forego her practicing while *Der Meister* was at work. And Schumann was difficult when he was in one of his moods. At such times he could be the Prussian type of husband. Once he accompanied Clara to Russia on a concert tour, and they were taken on a sightseeing tour of St. Petersburg by the great pianist Adolf Henselt. They came to a tower that gave a fine view of the city, but Schumann refused to climb. "No, it will make me dizzy." Schumann was deathly afraid of heights; he always lived on the ground floor of any house. Mme. Henselt then invited Clara to ascend. "No," Schumann growled. "Clara does not go where I do not go." Mme. Henselt, who told the story, said that Clara apologized meekly and quickly sat next to Robert with a scared look. He still may have been smarting about the remark of the nobleman to whom he was introduced at one of Clara's musicales in St. Petersburg. "Are you, too, musical?" the nobleman wanted to know.

In one respect Clara was a bad influence on Robert. Musically she had been brought up "correctly," and was conditioned to believe that the "best" composers wrote symphonies and operas. Much as she loved Robert and his music, she nevertheless felt that he would not fully realize himself until he entered the arena in competition with Beethoven and the other symphonic heroes. Perhaps it was also a subconscious wish for Schumann to be "respectable." So she pushed him into areas for which he was emotionally, intellectually, and technically unfitted. She wrote in her diary before they were married: "It would be best if he composed for orchestra. His imagination cannot find sufficient scope on the piano. . . . His compositions are all orchestral in feeling. . . . My highest wish is that he should compose for orchestra—that is his field. May I bring him to it!" Clara was monumentally wrong. She was also blind to many of his other musical lapses, and became infuriated when it was suggested that her Robert had better refrain from conducting. This was in Düsseldorf, where he went as musical director and promptly ran the orchestra and chorus into the ground. Clara fought for him, though by then she must have realized his problems. She meant well, but her interference in his life was not always for the best.

Even with his mental handicap, which became progressively worse during the last fifteen years of his life, Schumann did an enormous amount of work. Composition was but a part of his activity. He taught at the Leipzig Conservatory, appeared here and there as a conductor of his own music, made his house one of the centers of progressive musical activity in Europe, and carried on his duties as editor of the *Neue Zeitschrift für Musik*. The journal continued to be run on personal, romantic lines; it was a reflection of Schumann himself. When he and his friends decided to put out the magazine, the idea was to provide a forum in which good music could be praised and bad music spanked. The early 1830's were dominated by a good deal of inferior commercial junk, and the popular composers were such footnotes to history as Henri Herz and Franz Hünten, who industriously provided titillating potpourris for the salons of Europe. As Schumann explained the aims of the magazine in 1834, Rossini reigned on stage, "and at the piano nothing was heard but Herz and Hünten; and yet only a few years had passed since Beethoven, Schubert and Weber lived among us. Then one day awoke the thought: 'Let us not look on idly, but also lend our aid to progress. Let us again bring the poetry of art to honor among men!' "

In his own publication, Schumann could indulge his fancy for romantic byplay. He invented a society known as the *Davidsbund*—the band of David—and gave pen names to the members who would discuss music and write reviews. Schumann himself had two names—Florestan, reflecting the exuberant side of his nature, and Eusebius, the reflective side. There were Master Raro, Chiara, Jonathan, and so on. All were real people. Chiara was Clara; Master Raro was Friedrich Wieck; Jonathan was Ludwig Schunke. All of the Davidites were leagued together to combat the Philistines, those unimaginative bourgeois or pedants or musical tricksters who immersed themselves in safe or meretricious music.

As a critic Schumann was knowledgeable, conscientious, and open-minded. He did not have the flash, brilliance, and wit of Berlioz, but a more generous critic never lived. He was ready to praise a composer unreservedly if he detected any sign of talent. Schumann has been censured for his praise of composers who today are considered second-raters. But men like Niels Gade (1817–1890), William Sterndale Bennett (1815–1875), and the others he helped launch are second-raters only in retrospect. In their own day they achieved big reputations, and they *were* talented and honest musicians, the best of the crop. As a matter of fact, Gade was a really fine composer, and his music deserves to be heard. His String Quartet in F minor, for one, is something of a masterpiece.

Schumann was merciless toward sham and pretentiousness in music, and he was not afraid to engage those current heroes, Rossini and Meyerbeer, in combat. The test of a great critic, in any case, is not how many talents he overpraises, but how many geniuses he fails to recognize. On these grounds, Schumann's record is near-perfect. One of his very first reviews introduced Chopin, and his very last introduced Brahms. He had some reservations about Berlioz, but his long and detailed critique of the *Symphonie fantastique* is a model of fairness and understanding. Mendelssohn he adored, and Liszt he respected, though he told Clara that Liszt's world was not his. Some think that he did not understand Wagner, but that is not true. He did point out the weaknesses of *Tannhäuser*, which indeed does have weaknesses. However, he did not hear any of the music of Wagner's maturity, and thus should not be criticized for something out of his control. As for his writings on past composers, Schumann's appreciative and enthusiastic articles helped clarify the music of the late Beethoven and the virtually forgotten Schubert; and his many articles on Bach were a vital part of the Bach renaissance. In short, here was a writer on music with vast knowledge and impeccable taste, doing what a critic should do—conveying his enthusiasms and educating the public. "It is not enough that a newspaper mirrors the present," he wrote. "The critic must be ahead of his times and ready armed to fight for the future." That was Schumann's credo as a critic, and he adhered to it, as he adhered to all of his principles. "I love not the men whose lives are not in unison with their works," he once made Florestan say.

Schumann's last years were sad, and his illness must have left a permanent scar on Clara, who outlived him by forty years, dying in 1896. As his mind became progressively unbalanced, Schumann withdrew into his own world. He kept hearing in his inner ear an incessant A that prevented him from talking or thinking. Always taciturn, he said less and less, and visitors could not get a word out of him. Wagner once came to his house and, as was his custom, inundated him with talk. But even Wagner, who was notably insensitive, and who liked to hear his own opinions and nobody else's, was bothered. "An impossible person," he indignantly said of Schumann. "You can't always talk *alone*." Toward the end, the Schumann family was in trouble. It was a large family (the Schumanns had eight children, of whom five lived), and there was not much money around. Schumann was not able to work, and he started having hallucinations. Early in 1852 he went through an entire week during which he said that angels were dictating music to him while devils in the form of tigers and hyenas were threatening him with Hell. On February 27 he attempted suicide by throwing himself off a bridge into the Rhine. At his own request he was placed in an asylum. Clara had to leave him and go on tour to bring money home. She was called back from a concert at his last moments. There are harrowing accounts of Schumann's last days, written by Clara and friends of the family; and also by Johannes Brahms, who had been living with the Schumanns. At least there was the consolation that at the time of Schumann's death, on July 29, 1856, his music had started to make an international reputation. The A minor Piano Concerto was popular, and other works were beginning to enter the repertoire.

Although Schumann, as a critic, could well understand and explain to the public the views of other composers, few could understand his. His message was too unconventional and too personal. He realized this, but could write only the way his genius dictated. He was, after all, one of the great melodists and he easily could have turned out pretty, salable items. The thought never once occurred to this most uncompromising of idealists. How wistful is one of his letters to Clara: "I confess it would be a great delight to me if I succeeded in writing something which, when played by you, would make the public dance with delight." But as a young man he had taken up the fight against the Philistines, and to his own self he had to be true.

The unconventionalities aside, what made his music hard to understand fully—the same is true today—is the personal nature of the content. It is almost autobiographical. "I am affected by everything that goes on in the world—politics, literature, people—I think it over in my own way, and then I long to express my feelings in music. That is why my compositions are sometimes difficult to understand, because they are connected with distant interests; and sometimes unorthodox, because anything that happens impresses me and compels me to express it in music." These are the words of a true romantic, and in writing them, Schumann was merely expressing a romantic article of faith. Novalis, one of the leaders of the early German romantic movement, had previously expressed the same thought: "The soul of the individual should be one with the soul of the world." Or Henrik Steffens, the German natural philosopher: "The external world is itself an aspect of our internal being." Schumann was only dropping the small change of the intellectual currency of the time. But he not only echoed it. He applied it.

Nearly everybody, for instance, loves Schumann's *Carnaval,* and pianists love to play it. But it also has to be heard on a secondary level, with a knowledge of the vast extramusical symbolism it contains. This has nothing to do with program music. It merely explains what was going on in the composer's mind. *Carnaval* cannot be fully understood without realizing that it is a picture gallery in which are painted the two sides of Schumann's own nature (Florestan and Eusebius), in which appear Clara, Chopin, Wieck, Paganini, Mendelssohn, and others; that the entire work is based on four notes—ASCH (in German, E flat = S and B natural = H)—Asch being a city in which a lady friend of the composer lived, and also a city that contained four letters that occur in the composer's last name; and that the final march is a musical illustration of Schumann's determination to lead his band of righteous musicians into the enemy camp of Meyerbeer, Herz, and Hünten and demolish them. There are other symbols in *Carnaval,* but this is the general idea. Many of Schumann's works were conceived this way, and many of the allusions he makes have long since lost their meaning. We can only guess, building on a knowledge of Schumann's style and symbolism.

He himself often did not know what his music meant. Some of it was written in what amounted to a trance. First he wrote it. *Then* he looked it over, giving the work a title. That was his standard practice, and nearly all of his pieces were named after they were written. The name merely gives a clue to the mood, and is not to be taken as a guide to a story. "In my latest songs," he told Clara, "I often hear many things that I can hardly explain. It is most extraordinary how I write almost everything in canon and then only detect the imitation later, and often find inversions, rhythms in contrary motion, etc." Schumann's rich, complicated harmony did indeed have a strong polyphonic texture, a fact not generally realized, especially by the young pianists who play his music today. Schumann's careful indications of secondary and inner voices pass largely unnoticed by modern pianists. One musician who did realize the density and polyphonic complexity of the seemingly simple Schumann compositions was Alban Berg. In 1920, Berg had been attacked by the conservative composer-critic Hans Pfitzner for his "lack of melody." Why, asked Pfitzner, could not Berg, Schoenberg, and Webern write a pretty, uncomplicated, melodic work like Schumann's *Träumerei?* Berg demolished Pfitzner by publishing, in a Viennese music magazine, a structural and harmonic analysis of the *Träumerei.* Far from being uncomplicated, Berg demonstrated, the Schumann piece is not only amazingly sophisticated harmonically but is also "a strict piece of four-part writing," so rich in its polyphony that it "could easily be given to a string quartet or wind ensemble, or even to the four singing voices."

Like Chopin, Schumann started as a composer of piano music, and his first twenty-three works are for solo piano. In this series are three sonatas and the three-movement Fantasy in C major, which can loosely be called a sonata. The rest are, for the most part, small pieces bundled together under a name. Sometimes, as in the *Études symphoniques* or *Carnaval,* a unifying structural idea runs through the work, but more often there is no pretense at unity. It was a kind of piano music that had little to do with the pianistically more graceful, glittering piano music that Liszt, Thalberg, and Henselt were turning out. Their piano music was virtuoso material, and the concert hall and audiences were always in mind. Schumann's piano music can be equally difficult, but it is normally not showy. There are exceptions, as in the second movement of the Fantasy, but even there the bravura element is dictated by the content. The Fantasy, Schumann's greatest and largest work for solo piano, is, with Chopin's B flat minor Sonata and the Liszt B minor Sonata, one of the trinity of pieces upon which all romantic piano music rests. In Schumann's piano music are no show-off passages, none of the flashy octaves and finger work characteristic of the age. Schumann had nothing but scorn for virtuosity as an end in itself. "As if there were nothing higher than the art of pleasing the public!"

Not that the music is reticent. Quite the opposite. The Schumann piano works are exuberant, poetic, introspective, grand, and intimate in turn. Schumann's particular musical charm is hard to describe, even with its pronounced idiosyncracies—those syncopations, those altered seventh chords, that thick texture. It is a soaring kind of music, imbued with the romantic ideal, out to do for music what Jean Paul did for literature. In his piano music, Schumann is never far from Jean Paul. To Jean Paul, music represented man's efforts to achieve the infinite. "So life fades and withers behind us, and of our sacred and vanished past, only one thing remains immortal —music," Jean Paul wrote. Schumann had the same feeling. Music was the mysterious art, the art that picked up after poetry and, indeed, life itself had ceased. In expressing all this in his music, Schumann approached mysticism, composing in a state of what might be described as ecstasy, a vision always before him. This sounds sentimental, but it was not sentimental to Schumann. It was what made him go.

From piano music Schumann turned to song, and in 1840 composed a remarkable series of cycles and individual songs—the two *Liederkreis* sets, *Myrthen, Frauenliebe und Leben*, and, above all, the *Dichterliebe* to Heine poems. The sixteen songs of *Dichterliebe* rank with Schubert's *Winterreise* in the hierarchy of song cycles. Schumann took up where Schubert left off, broadening the concept of the art song, making the piano an even more subtle partner, adding piano preludes and postludes. Schumann and the lied were made for each other, for his gift was essentially lyric, his melodic ideas were unique in their taste, imagination, and refinement, and he thought naturally in small forms. In all, he composed over 250 songs throughout his career, including a series of ravishing vocal duets.

When Schumann started to explore a new form of writing, he dropped everything else. Thus, after piano and song, came symphony, and the year was 1841. Clara's dearest wish came true. It took Schumann only four days to sketch out his First Symphony, in B flat, which he himself called *Spring*. Three months later, in March, the scoring was complete, and Mendelssohn conducted the world premiere in Leipzig. In April Schumann finished a score that he called an Overture, and the next month he added two more movements, naming the work at first a suite and later referring to it as a "symphonette." Today the work is called Overture, Scherzo, and Finale, and it lacks only a slow movement to be a full-scale symphony. It is a beautiful piece of music that, for some reason, has been passed over by conductors. In May came a one-movement Fantasy for Piano and Orchestra. Clara played it, and then Schumann put it aside for four years. It eventually emerged as his most popular work, the A minor Piano Concerto.

Immediately after completing the Fantasy, Schumann set to work on a symphony in the key of D minor. This was finished in September and also put aside, emerging ten years later as the Symphony No. 4. Then Schumann started another symphony, this one in C minor. It, too, was put aside, and nothing came of it. The work we know as the Second Symphony was published in 1846, and the Third (*Rhenish*) in 1850. Schumann seems to have spent himself on orchestral writing in 1841. The following year he turned to chamber music, and within six months wrote all of his important works in that form—the three String Quartets, the E flat Piano Quartet, and, above all, the radiant Piano Quintet in E flat.

All four Schumann symphonies are very much in the repertoire, and this despite structural and orchestral flaws that commentators have been pointing out ever since they were composed. There is no argument that Schumann was a weak orchestrator; he thought pianistically rather than in terms of the orchestra, and conductors have always found it necessary to touch up the scoring. Today those emendations are done in a discreet manner, which was not true at the turn of the century, when such conductors as Mahler decided to help Schumann by virtually rewriting his music. It also is conceded that Schumann was unhappy working within the strictures of the sonata form. His transitions can be labored and his developments very awkward. At that, Schumann was full of original ideas in his symphonies, including ideas about thematic linkages. This was carried to its ultimate in the one-movement Symphony No. 4 in D minor, in which four movements are packaged into one, and in which a kind of theme transformation is used that foreshadows the Liszt B minor Sonata. What keeps the Schumann symphonies alive is their special glow, the high quality of the musical ideas. Each of the symphonies has its special characteristic: the ebullience of the *Spring* Symphony; the flaming romanticism of the Second (with its mournful adagio movement, one of the most beautiful ever written by any composer); the bigness and pride of the *Rhenish* Symphony, in which Schumann, like Berlioz in the *Fantastique,* composed five movements; and the innovations of the Fourth Symphony, which is also the most "feminine" of the four. Pedants may worry about certain inaccuracies in the scoring, and foolish writers may downgrade the Schumann symphonies by putting them on a scale weighted on the other end by the Beethoven symphonies. But if listeners are content to accept the Schumann symphonies for what they are, they are among the most inspired creations of the nineteenth century.

Schumann achieved success in all musical forms except one, opera. He spent much time over *Genoveva,* which achieved no fame in its day and has had very few performances since. He also wrote a large quantity of choral music, including *Paradies und die Peri,* the *Requiem für Mignon,* and *Der Rose Pilgefahrt,* none of which is much encountered any more. Indeed, a surprisingly large amount of Schumann's music is no longer played. He is not a composer to everybody's taste. As the arch-romantic, the most personal and least objective of the great composers, his message ran counter to the aesthetic that dominated the Western world after 1918. To many of the intellectuals in the period from 1920 to 1940, Schumann was a rather embarrassing relic of the early romantic period. He was considered sentimental, self-indulgent, and one step above a salon composer—at best, a sweet singer without emotional discipline. The whole point of his music was missed—that perfect weld of form and content in his shorter works, that overwhelming daring and originality, that basic purity even in moments of extravagance. Purity is not a word normally used in association with Schumann, but everything about him was pure—his life, his love, his dedication, his integrity, his mind, his music.

11

Apotheosis of the Piano

FRÉDÉRIC CHOPIN

Most of the romantic composers had a *parti pris* about romanticism. They were propagandists; they played or conducted one anothers' music; they wrote reviews and articles about the new styles and theories; they helped one another as best they could; and as teachers, some of them passed their aspirations to the oncoming generation. Not Frédéric Chopin. He would have none of it. Indeed, he disliked romanticism. He thought Liszt's music vulgar, did not like Schumann's music at all, had nothing to say about the works of Berlioz or Mendelssohn, though he was the friend of all of those great men. He approached Beethoven with a mixture of admiration and dislike; the thunderer was too big and uncouth, and Chopin felt uncomfortable in his presence. If he heard any music by Schubert, he did not mention it. The only two masters who meant anything to him were Bach and Mozart. For them he had nothing but praise. He also adored the operas of Bellini.

He was not widely read, nor did he respond to romantic art. Delacroix was one of his best friends, but Chopin would look at a Delacroix painting and mumble something noncommital, not wanting to hurt Delacroix' feelings. His teaching—which was how he supported himself in grand style—was private and largely confined to society. Elegant pupils would enter Chopin's studio and put their twenty or thirty francs on the mantelpiece while he looked out of the window. He was a gentleman, and gentlemen did not soil their hands with anything as vulgar as business transactions. He liked to move in aristocratic circles, and was greatly concerned with style, taste, clothes, and *bon ton*. He could be witty, malicious, suspicious, ill-tempered, charming. There was something feline about Chopin.

One of the greatest pianists in history, he gave very few concerts during his life and was primarily a salon pianist. Short, slim, fair-haired, with blue-gray (some say brown) eyes, a prominent nose, and an exquisite bearing, he was physically frail and his playing at best never had much sonority. Toward the end it was a whisper. Early in life he learned that he should never play in large halls, and his last public appearance in Paris took place on April 26, 1835, when he was twenty-six. For the rest of his life—he died in 1849—he gave only three more recitals, and those were semiprivate, at the salon of the piano manufacturer Pleyel, before a carefully selected audience that never numbered more than 300. He did do a great deal of playing at musical parties. What evenings those must have been! Chopin and Liszt playing four-hand music (Chopin playing the bass; Liszt was not going to drown *him* out), perhaps Mendelssohn turning pages while awaiting his turn at the keyboard. Around the piano might be Berlioz, Meyerbeer, Eugène Sue, Delacroix, Heine, and George Sand, with Ary Scheffer making sketches in the background.

Chopin fit beautifully into the mad, bad, sad, glad Paris of the 1830's and 40's. Although he did not have many close friends, he knew everybody, and everybody liked and respected him. They knew he was a genius. And Paris those days was highly experienced in judging genius. It was the intellectual and artistic capital of the world. Hugo, Balzac, Sand, Vigny, Lamartine, Heine, Gautier, and Musset were among the literary figures living there. Delacroix and Ingres were at the height of their careers. Liszt, Meyerbeer, Rossini, Berlioz, and Luigi Cherubini made Paris their home. Mendelssohn was in and out. Paris had three good orchestras and the greatest opera house in Europe. Malibran, Pasta, Lablache, Rubini, and Nourrit could be heard in opera, and they supplied a kind of florid, virtuosic singing that must have been hair-raising. Paris was the headquarters of European pianism, with Kalkbrenner, Thalberg, Herz, Heller, Litolff, and Prudent in residence. Politically Paris was temporarily stabilized. *Les Trois Glorieuses* of July, 1830, had put Louis-Philippe on the throne and, as the uprising had been a popular movement, there were concessions to popular taste. The *bourgeoisie* was raised to power; and while the lower classes did not have much more than they ever had, there was a kind of national revival and prosperity that manifested itself in a sudden flowering of the arts. Paris in the 1830's was experiencing the kind of renascence that London had experienced in the latter days of Elizabeth I.

Chopin had arrived in Paris in 1831. He spent the rest of his life there. When he came to Paris, it was as a provincial from Warsaw. His birthplace was in Zelazowa Wola, near the Polish capital, and there is some confusion about the date. The parish register says February 22, 1810, but Chopin's mother insisted it was March 1, and that was when she celebrated her famous son's birthday. Some scholars have dug up evidence that suggests 1809 as the year of Chopin's birth. The matter has not yet been resolved. Chopin's father was an émigré from France, his mother a Pole. Frédéric was the second of four children and the only son. His musical talent showed up early and he was a good pianist at the age of six. Adalbert Zywny, his teacher, was a cultivated musician who fed his genius of a pupil plenty of Bach. (Bach in Warsaw in 1816! And they say he was forgotten after his death!) At the age of eight, Chopin saw his first composition in print. It was a polonaise. From 1826 to 1828 he studied composition with Joseph Elsner, a man who had the wisdom to realize that Chopin was something special, to be treated with special care. As an academician, Elsner fervently wanted Chopin to compose symphonies, sonatas, and perhaps Polish national opera. But he never forced Chopin's style and did everything he could to let the young man develop naturally. That may have been his biggest contribution, and one for which posterity must be grateful. For in a way Chopin was a musical freak, more so than even most prodigies. He was not only a genius as a pianist, he was creatively a genius, one of the most startlingly original ones of the century.

From where did he get his ideas? Warsaw was a little removed from the cosmopolitan centers of Europe, though it was visited by important artists. Chopin did have the opportunity of hearing some—Hummel, Paganini, and the soprano Henrietta Sontag among others. The genesis of some of Chopin's music can be traced in the work of Moscheles, Hummel, and Czerny. But that does not explain the revolutionary qualities of Chopin's thinking—his development of an altogether new kind of piano playing; his daring, yet refined, harmonic sense; his experimentation with a kind of piano sonority that once and for all released the instrument from the past. All that can be said was that in the young Chopin a musical fermentation went on, and he found that he had to change the rules. How much was conscious in his new way of thinking, how much unconscious, is anybody's guess. He was a genius, and was born with certain reflexes in fingers, ears, and mind that less fortunate musicians never attain. Certainly he came to full maturity earlier than most composers, and everything seemed to come easy to him. "You know," his father wrote, "that the mechanics of piano playing occupied little of your time, and that your mind was busier than your fingers. If others have spent whole days working at the keyboard, you rarely spent an hour playing other men's music." Thus as a musician Chopin was one of the lucky ones—a natural technician with an easy style, a composer who decided early to write only for the instrument that he loved. His work turned out to be mostly in the smaller forms, but he helped change the face of music, and most of his contemporaries recognized him for the revolutionary he was. "Cannon buried in flowers," said Schumann of Chopin's music.

In Warsaw it was realized that young Chopin was something exceptional, though nobody could have guessed to how fantastic an extent. The first inkling came when Chopin left Poland for Vienna, to put himself on exhibition as a pianist-composer. This was in 1829, and he gave several concerts, startling the experts with the novelty of his music and his approach to the keyboard. Like all virtuosos of the day, Chopin concentrated on his own music. In his letters home he wrote modestly and even deprecatingly about his reception, though he did say that "the journalists have taken me to their hearts," and that when he improvised on some Polish tunes, "my spies on the floor of the house declare that people were dancing up and down in their seats." Among the reactions of the Viennese was one expressed again and again. How, they kept asking, could Chopin have learned so much in *Warsaw?*

Back in Poland, he had a puppy-love affair, composed steadily, went to the opera, was feted and pampered, and then decided to make his career in Paris. On November 2, 1830, he left Poland for good, with very little money and supreme confidence in his ability. He played in Vienna once again, made contacts, visited musicians, and listened to competing pianists. Sigismund Thalberg, the new pianistic lion, was one, and Chopin had left a devastating pen portrait of him: "Thalberg plays famously but he is not my man. He is younger than I, popular with the ladies, plays potpourris on themes from *Masaniello,* produces *piano* with pedal rather than the hand, takes tenths as easily as I take octaves, wears diamond shirt-studs." Chopin could have made a career in Vienna, but Paris was his goal, and he arrived there late in 1831, awed by the great men around him. Almost immediately he involved himself in one of the more delirious episodes of musical history.

Chopin, twenty-one years old, a genius with a perfectly formed and original pianistic style, heard Friedrich Kalkbrenner play and was overwhelmed. Kalkbrenner was undoubtedly a wonderful pianist, but he was a classicist of the old school. Preromantic pianists like Kalkbrenner, Moscheles, Hummel, and Clementi would run well-drilled notes up and down the keyboard, with little or no pedal. Using high finger strokes, playing from hand and wrist rather than elbow and arm, they had little idea of the coloristic resources of the piano (an instrument that by 1830 was very close in action and sonority to the concert grand of today). As a group, the classic pianists had no sympathy with romantic music. Kalkbrenner was probably the most proficient of the group. He was one of the most popular pianists of his day, and a conceited popinjay to boot. For some reason Chopin became entranced with his way of playing. He hastened to Kalkbrenner for lessons, and the great man gravely listened to his younger colleague. Then he told Chopin that he had talent, and that he would develop into a fine artist if he spent three years at the Kalkbrenner studio. Chopin promptly notified his family of the step he was going to take. His father and Elsner, both horrified, sent frantic letters from Poland. Fortunately, Chopin came to his senses and made his Paris debut on his own, early in 1832. Liszt and Mendelssohn were present, and the recital was the talk of Paris. After that there was no more nonsense about Kalkbrenner.

Chopin began to move in the highest circles. Through his titled Polish friends he became acquainted with the Rothschilds, and that alone was a passport. Almost immediately he had more pupils than he could handle—Princess this, Countess that. From that time the pattern of his life was set until he met George Sand. He traveled a little. In 1834 he visited Aachen and renewed his friendship with Mendelssohn; the following year he made a trip to Dresden and met Schumann, who idolized him. There was another meeting with Schumann in Leipzig in 1836. Chopin owed a good deal to the generous Schumann, whose review of the *Là ci darem* Variations had introduced him to Germany, and who, in the *Neue Zeitschrift für Musik*, was enthusiastically reviewing every Chopin piece that came his way. (Chopin had been, or pretended to be, vastly amused when, in 1831, he read Schumann's famous review of the Variations. "In the fifth bar of the adagio he declares that Don Giovanni kisses Zerlina on the D flat. Plater [Count Ludwik Plater, a friend in Paris] asked me yesterday where her D flat was, etc.!") But for the most part Chopin stayed in Paris, composing, socializing, making important friends. "I have found my way into the very best society," he wrote home with great satisfaction in 1833. "I have my place among ambassadors, princes, ministers. I don't know by what miracle it has come about, for I have not pushed myself forward. But today all that sort of thing is indispensable to me: those circles are supposed to be the fountain-head of taste. . . . I have five lessons to give today. You will imagine I am making a fortune—but my cabriolet and white gloves cost more than that, and without them I should not have *bon ton* . . ." Chopin was in a position to charge as much as thirty francs a lesson, an enormous sum in those days. He lived in luxury. He also had the quota of love affairs that any spirited and unattached male has. Before tuberculosis weakened him, his sexual habits were perfectly normal. He was neither effeminate nor chaste, though he kept his love affairs to himself and could be prudish.

Chopin's life changed when he was introduced to George Sand by Liszt. He was twenty-six and she was thirty-two years old, already a famous novelist, equally notorious for her independence and her disdain for the proprieties. Her real name was Aurore Dudevant, but she adopted the pen name of George Sand for her novels *Indiana* (1831) and *Lélia* (1833). Both books attracted wide attention for their attacks on conventional morality, especially marriage. She was a short, rather dumpy woman of sharp intelligence, and she was constantly in the public eye. For a time she wore men's clothes, smoked cigars, and had a succession of lovers. The woman who had been the mistress of Jules Sandeau, Prosper Mérimée, Alfred de Musset, Michel de Bourges, Pietro Pagello, and, most likely, Franz Liszt, did not lack experience. By her husband, Casimir Dudevant (they were separated in 1836), she had two children, Maurice and Solange. If a letter of one of Chopin's friends is to be believed, he was repelled at first by George Sand. The love affair progressed slowly, but by 1838 they were living together, and they spent the winter of 1838–39 in Majorca.

The trip had been intended as an idyll, and it turned out to be pure hell. The weather was bad, there was constant rain, the house in which they lived was eternally damp, and Chopin's weak lungs acted up. He all but died. As Sand admitted, the trip was a fiasco. She had to nurse him back to health, and brought him to Marseilles more dead than alive. Chopin sent a wry note to a friend: "The three most celebrated doctors on the island have seen me. One sniffed at what I spat, the second tapped where I spat, the third sounded me and listened as I spat. The first said I was dead, the second that I am dying, the third than I'm going to die." Despite his ill health, Chopin did some important work at Majorca. It was there that he finished his set of twenty-four préludes. One of them, the *Raindrop,* is supposed to be a musical interpretation of the rain dropping relentlessly on the villa in which the lovers were staying. But that title is a later invention, and nobody knows which prélude it is—even if the story were true, which it probably isn't. Some plump for No. 15 in D flat, with the reiterated notes in C sharp minor section, while others with equal insistence say that the *Raindrop* is really the B minor Prélude, with its regular, mournful left-hand pattern.

The relationship between Chopin and George Sand lasted until 1847. During the years of their liaison they were never far apart. In Paris they lived in adjoining houses. In the summer they went to Sand's house at Nohant, staying there about four months. It was at Nohant that Chopin composed his greatest music. Sand babied him, mothered him, looked after him. It seems that after a short time the relationship between them was platonic. Sand appeared content, and there is no evidence that she had any lovers during her long affair with Chopin. The breakup was sad. Sand's children, spoiled and undisciplined, were the agents. Maurice and Chopin did not get along very well, and his favorite was Solange. In 1847 she married a sculptor of dubious reputation named August Clésinger, after breaking off an engagement with a young man that both Chopin and Sand liked. Within the family there were fights and recriminations, lies and charges of bad faith. Solange actually accused her mother of having an affair with one of Maurice's friends. Sand did not want to have anything to do with Solange and her husband, while Chopin took Solange's side. When the smoke cleared away, Sand and Chopin were permanently estranged. During all this she carried herself with great dignity, and she cuts a better figure than Chopin, who seemed eager to believe the lies Solange poured into his ears. After the break they met once, by accident. Chopin was leaving a party, Sand entering. They had a few words in front of the door. "She asked me how I was," Chopin wrote to Solange. "I said I was well, and then I called for the concierge to open the door. I raised my hat and walked home to the Square d'Orléans." With these banalities they parted forever.

Chopin had only a year to live. He was already in a terminal stage, and was spitting blood. In 1848 he visited England at the urging of Jane Stirling, a friend and pupil. She was a very rich maiden lady from Scotland who probably was in love with Chopin. He thought he had nothing to lose by accepting her invitation. The Revolution of 1848 had broken out in Paris and Chopin's pupils had fled, leaving him without a steady source of income. So he dragged himself to England and Scotland. He was in dreadful shape, and was so weak that he had to be carried to his bedroom and undressed by his valet. In England he played for the best society, observed the people and their customs, and hated every bit of it. His letters to Paris give the picture of a man exasperated beyond endurance. He describes a party in his honor given by a titled Scots lady: "After I had played, and other Scottish ladies had sung various songs, they brought a sort of accordion and she [his hostess], with the utmost gravity, began to play the most horrible tunes on it. But what can you expect? It seems to me that every one of these creatures is crazy. . . . The ones who know my compositions ask 'Play me your *Second Sigh* [the Nocturne in G] . . . I love your bells.' And every comment ends with the words: 'Leik Water,' meaning that the music flows like water. I have never yet played to an Englishwoman without her saying: 'Leik Water!!' They all look at their hands and play wrong notes most soulfully. What a queer lot! God have pity on them."

Back in Paris, away from the suffocating clutches of Miss Stirling, Chopin did almost no work, waiting for the end. He was mentally depressed. "I have not yet begun to play, and I cannot compose. God knows what sort of fodder I shall have to live on before long." He was helped by Miss Stirling and her sister who, learning of Chopin's desperate condition, sent him an anonymous gift of 25,000 francs. His sister Louise came from Warsaw to nurse him during his final illness. George Sand sent Louise a letter that she would like to see Frédéric before it was too late. Louise did not answer. It was not George Sand but Solange Clésinger who was at Chopin's side when he died on the morning of October 17, 1849. Also at the bedside were Louise and Princess Marcelline Czartoryska, a friend of the family. In later years there were legends about Chopin's last hours, and wonderfully romantic stories about this or that countess singing sad songs while he died.

Chopin had no false modesty about himself and his work. As early as

1831 he was writing about his "perhaps too audacious but noble wish and intention to create for myself a new world." He did precisely that. As a pianist he created a style that dominated the entire second half of the nineteenth century and was not substantially changed until Debussy and Prokofiev came along. It was a style that broke sharply from everything that went before it. For the first time the piano became a *total* instrument: a singing instrument, an instrument of infinite color, poetry, and nuance, a heroic instrument, an intimate instrument. Schumann's piano music, wonderful as it is, original as it is, sounds thick by comparison. Chopin's music flowed naturally out of his own way of playing the piano, and as a pianist he was light-years ahead of Schumann, exploiting the instrument in an idiomatic and completely modern manner. In any case, the piano music of Schumann exerted relatively little influence in its day, whereas the new ideas about pedaling, fingering, rhythm, and coloristic resource that Chopin invented were immediately taken up by every one of the younger pianists.

Many professionals of the day could not follow him. Moscheles was not the only one who was perplexed. Even so fine a musical mind as Mendelssohn's was disturbed at first. Mendelssohn, who had been trained by Moscheles in a classic style—hands close to the keyboard, little pedal, a minimum of rubato or tempo change—had to become seasoned to Chopin by exposure before he was won over. But Mendelssohn surrendered, as did everybody else. "There is," Mendelssohn wrote, "something entirely original in his piano playing and it is at the same time so masterly that he may be called a perfect virtuoso. . . . He produces new effects, like Paganini on the violin, and accomplishes things nobody could formerly have thought practicable."

Even the great Liszt was not too proud to learn from Chopin. Between the two was an uneasy friendship. They saw a great deal of each other, but there may have been an unconscious hostility. Chopin envied Liszt his strength, his extroversion, his virility, his power to hypnotize large audiences. "Liszt is playing my études," he wrote to Stephen Heller, "and transporting me outside of my respectable thoughts. I should like to steal from him the way to play my own études." But there was an element of vulgarity and fakery to Liszt that repelled Chopin. Occasionally Chopin burst into spitefulness, as in a letter to Jules Fontana: "One of these days he'll be a member of parliament or perhaps even the King of Abyssinia or the Congo —but as regards the themes from his compositions, well, they will be buried in the newspapers."

Liszt, on the other hand, sincerely admired Chopin's pianism and adopted many of his ideas. Chopin showed that the piano could be much more than a virtuoso instrument even in virtuoso music; and, more important, Chopin's music showed that even the wildest flights of virtuosity could have a musical meaning. Chopin's filigree and bravura, in his mature works, never are merely show-off. He introduced the concept of functional ornamentation. Up to the time he met Chopin, Liszt was primarily a banger. After exposure to Chopin's playing and music, he tried to modify his bravura into a more poetic style. But could Liszt have felt a little uncomfortable in Chopin's company? The elegant Pole was an aristocrat, while there was something about Liszt that made him a social climber rather than a natural inhabitant of the great salons. He dressed too flashily, spoke a little too loudly, bragged too much, could not hold his liquor as a gentleman should. Definitely he did not have *bon ton*. Occasionally the sparks flew between him and Chopin. Liszt, who was always "improving" somebody else's music, once played a Chopin nocturne, adding all kinds of embellishments. Chopin, according to an anecdote that appears in Josef Nowakowski's study, snapped at Liszt, telling him to play the music as written or not play it at all. But the two greatest pianists of their time nevertheless did continue to see each other, and as late as 1848 Chopin was referring to "my friend Liszt."

Two things about Chopin's piano style—and by extension, as always, his music—are of extreme importance: his ideas about rubato, and his classic bent. Rubato, which had been the subject of much discussion by performers as far back as Mozart and C. P. E. Bach, is a kind of displacement in which the rhythm is delicately altered but never the idea of the basic meter. It gives variety and added interest to a phrase. Every sensitive musician uses it; the device is equivalent to variation of line in a drawing by a master. Chopin, with his Polish dance heritage, used such a pronounced rubato that listeners unaccustomed to it were taken aback. Meyerbeer, himself a fine pianist, was convinced that Chopin played two-four instead of three-four in his mazurkas. Charles Hallé, another fine pianist, noted that a remarkable feature of Chopin's playing "was the entire freedom with which he treated the rhythm, but which appeared so natural that for years it had never struck me." Hallé also insisted that Chopin in some of his mazurkas played in duple rather than triple time.

Yet despite his romantic rubato and his extremely romantic music, Chopin had a strong classic streak in him. He always had a metronome on his piano, insisted that his pupils play in strict time, gave them plenty of Bach and Mozart, and went into a tantrum when rhythmic liberties were taken. His own playing was pure, and he insisted on purity from his pupils. That, and complete flexibility plus a singing line. "Yesterday we heard Henri Herz," wrote Joseph Filtsch to his parents. "His execution is elegant, agreeable and coquettish, but without subtlety. What a difference between him and Chopin, whose fingers sing and bring tears to your eyes, making anybody who is sensitive tremble with emotion. His delicate and slender hands cover wide stretches and skips with a fabulous lightness, and his finger agility is so marvelous that I am ready to believe the amusing story that he has been seen to put his foot around his neck! Moreover, it is thanks to this flexibility that he can play black notes with his thumb, or a whole series of notes with two fingers only, passing the longer finger over the shorter and sliding from one note to another." These were practices condemned by the classic teachers. Black notes were not to be played with the thumb. Filtsch goes on to describe Chopin's rubato. "To his pupils he says: 'Let your left hand be your conductor and keep strict time.' And so his right hand, now hesitant, now impatient, is nevertheless constrained to follow this great rule and never weaken the rhythm of the left hand." (Mozart had said almost the exact same thing over a half-century previously.) Joseph Filtsch, incidentally, was a pianist who had come from Hungary with his younger brother Karl to study with Chopin. Karl was enormously gifted and was by far the best pupil Chopin ever had. Liszt heard him and said that when the youngster started playing in public, then he, Liszt, would shut up shop. Poor Karl died at the age of fifteen.

As a composer, Chopin has survived all changes of fashion and is as popular today as he ever was. Almost everything he composed is in the active repertoire. Can this be said of many other composers? He found his style very early—before he left Poland for Paris, in fact. In later years a greater depth was to enter his music, but very little in the way of technique, harmonic ideas, or melody. After the Études of Op. 10, many of which had been completed before his arrival in Paris, there was no substantial change. He also had worked out the basic style of his mazurkas and nocturnes in Poland. The nocturnes were derived from John Field's compositions. Chopin took the form of the Field nocturnes and refined it into something much more aristocratic, with a more interesting arpeggiated bass and melodies resembling the long-breathed cantilenas that can be found in Italian bel canto opera. If there was one thing Chopin loved, it was beautiful singing, and many of his melodic ideas came from the great vocal stylists of the day.

Another aspect of his musical style was Polish nationalism, as represented by the mazurkas and polonaises. To Europe, these were strange and exotic. Chopin was the first of the great nationalists. The great nationalists do not copy folk melodies. They do not have to. The folk tradition is part of their background, their racial subconscious. It emerges as an evocation of homeland, even if (as in the case of so many nationalists) no actual folk-tune quotations are used. In his mazurkas and polonaises, Chopin echoed the melodies with which he had grown up. In his other music he was much more a cosmopolitan, though here and there, as in the middle section of the B minor Scherzo, a folk tune can make its appearance.

Chopin was an "absolute" composer, and never gave anything but abstract titles to his music. In this he was different from the other romantics. Even the classicist Mendelssohn supplied descriptive titles to some of his *Songs Without Words* and other pieces. Chopin, never. *Black Key* Étude, *Winter Wind* Étude, *Little Jew* Mazurka, *Raindrop* Prélude, *Military* Polonaise—all these are romantic inventions, generally supplied by publishers. In none of Chopin's music are there any programmatic implications, though it is claimed that the four ballades were inspired by poems by Adam Mickiewicz, the Polish patriot. If this is true, Chopin was remarkably quiet about it. The supposed Mickiewicz background to the ballades is probably another romantic invention. The only names Chopin gave to the overwhelming majority of his music (the Polish songs, of course, excepted) were generic: waltz, mazurka, étude, polonaise, nocturne, scherzo, prélude, fantasy, impromptu, ballade, variations, sonata, concerto.

In his youth his music was graceful, exuberant, inventive, full of brilliance, marked by a decided predilection for virtuosity. Like all composers up to then, Chopin composed his music as vehicles for public performance, and naturally he tailored it to his own pianistic specifications. There are the two concertos, the *Là ci darem la mano* Variations for piano and orchestra, the early études, the *Krakoviak* for piano and orchestra (seldom played, but it is a haunting work). All are marked by an extension of piano technique as it was then known. Schumann, working independently in Germany, was writing piano music in which the *music* was the thing. Chopin turned out music in which there was more of a balance between music and the piano as thing-unto-itself. His music is much more idiomatic than Schumann's in terms of the keyboard. It fits the hand, where Schumann often is awkward. It is often breath-taking music, sparkling and coruscating, taking complicated figurations and breaking them up or spreading them over the keyboard so that the notes scatter like pinpoints of flame.

Now, there were composers around who could come near matching Chopin in mere technical display. Moscheles and Kalkbrenner were among them, and so was the young Liszt. What immediately set Chopin's music off and made it different was a combination of melodic and harmonic resource of unprecedented charm and richness. Few composers have had Chopin's ear, his gift for modulation, his taste in combining pure virtuosity with an aristocratic and poetic kind of melody. That could be heard from the beginning, and he never changed his approach. But as he grew older his forms became tighter. There was less padding, and every note had a point. The music could be difficult, but it also was condensed and under perfect control. It had dissonances, including harsh seconds and ninths, that sounded intolerable as the classic pianists played them, and the new generation of pianists had to learn how to handle them, how to make them glint and resolve through a skillful use of the pedal. Those chromatic and daring harmonies were a seminal influence on nineteenth-century musical thinking. Chopin as a harmonist influenced Wagner and even later composers. The *Barcarolle* actually anticipated Debussy, with its free-floating pedal effects and near-impressionist harmonies. The delicate, sickly Polish composer put a mighty hand on the future of music.

Delicate and sickly; but that does not mean his music lacks power. The scherzos and ballades, the F minor Fantasy, the last polonaises (especially the heroic one in F sharp minor, an even more thrilling and masterly work than the popular A flat Polonaise), the last two sonatas (he composed three, but the C minor is a student work no longer in the repertoire), all contain majestic utterances. These are clothed in forms perfectly appropriate to the material, forms that were dictated by the music. Except in the sonatas, he did not try to impose form on idea. Lyric and spontaneous as his music often sounds, it was the product of much work and thought. He did not rush his ideas to paper, as Mozart and Schubert so often did. Chopin was a slow worker who would not let a piece of music be published until he was satisfied that it was as jeweled, as flawless, as logical as he could make it. His initial ideas came fast, but working them into the appropriate form could be excruciating. Many of his compositions resulted from improvisations, and Filtsch has described the way Chopin worked: "The other day [this was in March, 1842] I heard Chopin improvise at George Sand's house. It is marvellous to hear Chopin compose in this way. His inspiration is so immediate and complete that he plays without hesitation as if it had to be thus. But when it comes to writing it down and recapturing the original thought in all its details, he spends days of nervous strain and almost frightening desperation. He alters and retouches the same phrases incessantly, and walks up and down like a madman." Even when a work was published, Chopin was not satisfied. He would make changes whenever he could, and in many of his works there are differences between the French and German editions, some of them significant.

His music is all of a piece. Whether tiny, as in the Prélude in C sharp minor of Op. 28, which lasts no more than twenty seconds (is there a shorter piece in the entire literature?), or extended, as in the B minor Sonata, it is highly idiosyncratic music characterized by graceful, often melancholy, melodies and a richness of harmonic texture almost Franckian in its chromaticism. But it is not a cloying kind of chromaticism. Chopin's mind was too precise to allow color to dominate form. It is for the most part a highly precise, condensed form of music in some of which a single idea is exploited. The single-idea aspect of Chopin comes in the études, preludes, mazurkas, and nocturnes, though in the longer mazurkas and nocturnes subsidiary ideas make their appearance. The works in larger form—the scherzos, ballades, F minor Fantasy—are Chopin's own solution of the problem of sonata form. Classic sonata form did not interest him very much. In the B minor Sonata he dutifully goes through the motions of exposition, development and recapitulation, achieving a copybook form that just passes. What saves the sonata, and has made it so popular, is the wealth of its ideas and the freedom with which it moves once the first movement is past. The earlier B flat minor Sonata, the one with the *Funeral March,* is completely alien to the concept of the classic sonata, and even so dedicated an admirer as Schumann threw up his hands. This is not a sonata, he said. Chopin has merely assembled for his four movements "four of his wildest children." Ironically enough, the first movement happens to be Chopin's most successful experiment with sonata form. It is tidy, well organized, and consistent all the way through. After that movement, Chopin and sonata part company. Most puzzling of all is the finale, a sotto-voce, murmuring mystery in fast unison scale passages that lasts no more than a minute and a half. It could have been one of the préludes, and for all we know was originally intended as one. The Prélude in E flat minor (No. 14) is close enough in mood, layout, and technique to be a sister of the finale of the B flat minor. Both were composed about the same time. The B flat minor Sonata dates from 1839, and the Préludes between 1836 and 1839.

Toward the end of his life Chopin began to introduce polyphonic textures into his music. There always had been a classic strain in this most romantic of composers, classic in the sense that his forms were tightly organized, classic in their elegant workmanship, classic in that the works of his maturity avoided empty passagework. No matter how effective, glittering, and even spectacular the writing may be (as in the last section of the Impromptu in F sharp major or the cascading figurations of the Scherzo in C sharp minor), each note has an expressive or coloristic meaning that far transcends mere display. Never is it vulgar, never is it effect for effect's sake. There are other things in Chopin's music that suggest classicism and, in particular, his beloved Bach. The twenty-four Préludes follow the idea of the *Well-Tempered Clavier,* going through all the major and minor keys in the circle of fifths. (Hummel had done the same, also in a series of tiny préludes composed at least fifteen years before Chopin's.) Could the very first Prélude by Chopin, the C major, be an implied compliment to the C major Prelude that opens Bach's great series? If Chopin's is played at a very slow tempo, there is a startling relationship between the two. And in the Études Chopin also started an interrelated key scheme, but never carried it out. Later, as in the F minor Ballade or the ending of the Mazurka in C sharp minor (Op. 63, No. 3), are passages in canonic imitation. Polyphonic writing occurs in many of Chopin's late works. To Chopin, fugue was the ultimate in musical logic, and he said as much to Delacroix, who dutifully noted Chopin's comments in his diary: "To know fugue deeply is to be acquainted with the element of all reason and consistency in music." This is a side of Chopin unknown to many. He composed only one known fugue; it is a student work and not in the repertoire.

Once Chopin had established himself, there was remarkably little criticism of his music. It was accepted as the work of a master, and even such doubters as Ludwig Rellstab, the critic from Berlin, and James William Davison, the pundit from London, eventually came around. As Liszt wrote in 1841, "This exquisite, lofty and eminently aristocratic celebrity remains unattacked. A complete silence of criticism already reigns about him, as if posterity already had come." Liszt was only stating a fact. Certainly the informed men of the day—Liszt, Mendelssohn, Schumann, Berlioz—knew that Chopin was an immortal; that within his self-imposed limitation he was perfection itself. To be a great pianist in the nineteenth century, it was necessary to be a great Chopin pianist. This was even true in the antiromantic days after World War I. It is less true today, now that romantic performance practice is almost a lost art. Yet even today, Chopin's music figures as strongly on piano recitals as the work of any other composer, and certainly much more than the music of the other romantics Other composers have had their ups and downs. Chopin goes steadily along, and the piano literature would be inconceivable without him. He seems impervious to changing tastes.

✾ 12 ✾

Virtuoso, Charlatan—and Prophet

FRANZ LISZT

If Chopin was the pianist's pianist, Franz Liszt was the public's pianist—the showman, the Hero, the one who made inarticulate apes of his audiences. He had everything in his favor—good looks, magnetism, power, a colossal technique, an unprecedented sonority, and the kind of opportunism (at least in his early years) that could cater to the public in the most cynical manner. He had the Aura. Before Liszt, pianists kept their hands close to the keyboard, playing from wrist and finger rather than arm or shoulder. But not after Liszt. He established once and for all the genre of the bravura pianist, the pianist who would haughtily come out, cow the audience, lift hands high, and assault the instrument. Even musicians who hated everything he represented, the "pure" musicians, could not but be impressed. Mendelssohn, who was the South Pole to Liszt's North, had to admit that Liszt was unparalleled, that he could play with "a degree of virtuosity and complete finger independence and a thoroughly musical feeling that can scarcely be equaled. In a word, I have heard no performer whose musical perceptions so extend to the very tips of his fingers." Contemporary pianists, such as Charles Hallé, heard Liszt and were in despair. They could not possibly begin to compete with that combination of brilliance and sheer aura. Clara Wieck, no mean technician herself, was completely taken aback because "Liszt played at sight what we toil over and at the end get nowhere with."

It was as a pianist that Liszt made his initial impact on Europe. Later he became everything—composer, conductor, critic, littérateur, Don Juan, abbé, teacher, symbol, and, at the end, The Grand Old Man of Music. He was born on October 22, 1811, about the same time as the other early romantics, but he far outlived them all. Mendelssohn died in 1847, Chopin in 1849, Schumann in 1856, Berlioz in 1869. Liszt died on July 31, 1886, the last of the great musicians who had been a close friend of the early heroes, the man who had met Beethoven and had actually (so it was believed) been kissed by the lips of the Immortal. Franz Liszt: a great man, a complicated man, a man all things to all men. He had genius, yet there was a great deal of the charlatan about him. He was pulled to the church, yet even after becoming an abbé continued the sexual escapades that were the talk of Europe. He had a fine musical mind, one of the strongest in history, yet in his recitals he could not keep from tampering with other men's music, cheapening even Beethoven by added effects. He could be kind and generous, yet could turn around and be arrogant and capricious. He was vain and needed constant adulation, yet he could be genuinely humble in the presence of a genius such as Wagner. Yes, he was all things to all men, and as a result not many have been able to see him whole. Perhaps Liszt himself never could. To many he was the Renaissance Man of music. His admirers could see only his good points. To others he was all tinsel and claptrap—" a talented humbug," as the conductor Hermann Levi scornfully said. His enemies could see only his bad points.

It would take volumes to sift fact from fancy, and it would take a battery of psychiatrists to attempt an explanation of Liszt's motivations. But the general outlines are clear enough. Born in Raiding, Hungary, he was playing the piano very well at the age of seven, composing at eight, making concert appearances at nine, studying with Czerny and Salieri in Vienna at ten. On all of these trips he was accompanied by his father. Adam Liszt, a steward in the service of the Esterházy family, was a skilled musical amateur who fully realized the enormous talent of his son. So did a group of Hungarian noblemen, who subsidized the studies of young Franz. Musical Europe fully endorsed their high opinion of the young genius. The boy startled audiences wherever he appeared. Only a few years after his work with Czerny in Vienna he was a veteran of the concert stage, having made his debut in Paris and London, and having toured Europe. At the age of sixteen he was experiencing doubts and nervous exhaustion, and was talking of quitting everything and joining the church. Throughout his life he was always talking about joining the church; that was part of the romantic posture. Of course it was mostly talk. Even when Liszt did join, late in life, he had the best of both worlds, and probably never took his religion very seriously. He only made a great show of taking it seriously.

Not until the age of nineteen did he more or less settle down. He made Paris his headquarters in 1827, after the death of his father, and worked to remedy gaps in his education. Like most Wunderkinder, he had had only a sketchy general education, and he had an immense amount of study and reading to do once he decided to catch up. Liszt eventually was to pass as a cultured man, and that was a triumph of his industry, for he did it all by himself. "My mind and fingers," he wrote in 1832, "have worked like the damned. Homer, the Bible, Plato, Locke, Lamartine, Chateaubriand, Beethoven, Bach, Hummel, Mozart, Weber are all around me. I study them, I devour them with fury." He moved in intellectual circles, welcome because of his genius and good looks. He mowed down the nubile young ladies of Paris. And he heard the three musicians who so decisively influenced his development.

Berlioz was the first. From Berlioz, Liszt discovered the meaning of color, and also the meaning of Thinking Big. The Berlioz approach was congenial to Liszt. It introduced him to the visionary kind of romanticism, its stirrings and yearnings, its subjectivity and love of the monumental. Liszt tried to do on the piano what Berlioz did with the orchestra, and even transcribed for solo piano several major orchestral works of Berlioz. Among them was the *Symphonie fantastique*. He actually played it in concert, and one of his tricks was to follow an orchestral performance of the *Fantastique* with his piano version of the *Marche au supplice*, the fourth movement, with an effect (wrote Hallé) "surpassing even that of the full orchestra and creating an indescribable furor." Liszt was the first to *orchestrate* on the piano, achieving the wildest of dynamic extremes, the maximum of color, and using the entire compass of the keyboard in a pile-up of sonorities. For all this he was in debt to Berlioz.

The second influence was Paganini. Here the impact was purely instrumental rather than aesthetic or philosophical. In 1831 Liszt heard Paganini for the first time, listened carefully, and was thunderstruck. He immediately decided to transfer Paganini's effects to the piano. There were two goals to this quest: transcendental technique and showmanship. One of the first things he did was to transcribe for the piano six of the Paganini *Caprices* for solo violin, heaping difficulty upon difficulty. Probably nobody but Liszt himself could play them at the time, and very few can today. Liszt's *Paganini Études* are an amazing pianistic equivalent of the original violin pieces. In addition the music, played as only Liszt could play it, drove audiences to a wild excitement comparable to that exerted by Paganini himself.

Finally, Liszt heard Chopin, and realized that there was poetry as well as bravura to piano playing, that the instrument was capable of subtle washes of color as well as of heroic storms, that decoration could be functional to the musical ground plan rather than flashy and vulgar excrescences.

Thus when Liszt resumed his European tours, it was as a finished artist, and he swept all before him. His recitals were a series of triumphs. Women were especially attracted to his concerts, as they later were to Paderewski's, and there were scenes of actual frenzy in which impressionable ladies fainted or would fight over the gloves he negligently tossed on the stage. Heinrich Heine, attempting to describe the phenomenon, spoke of "magnetism and electricity; of contagion in a sultry hall filled with innumerable wax lights and some hundred perfumed and perspiring people; of histrionic epilepsy; of the phenomenon of tickling; of musical cantharides; and other unmentionable matters." Liszt well knew the impression he was making. Everything was calculated. That included his programs, which seldom had much meat on them. In his own studio he played everything. He probably had the entire literature, as it was then known, committed to memory. But at his big public concerts he would play sure-fire, attention-getting music, for the most part. Generally the music was his own. He would enter the stage, clanking with decorations suspended on chains. His hair was down to his shoulders. He would survey the audience and slowly remove his gloves, tossing them to the floor. Until 1839 he followed the established format for concerts, which meant that he shared the time with other artists or an orchestra, and he would be heard only for part of the program. A typical Liszt contribution to one of his recitals would be his transcription of Rossini's *William Tell* Overture, his fantasy on Mozart's *Don Giovanni,* his transcriptions of Schubert's *Erlkönig* and Beethoven's *Adelaide,* and his *Galop chromatique.* This was the actual program he once played in St. Petersburg.

Naturally it would have had to be Liszt, that great egomaniac, who in 1839 invented the solo recital as it is known today. Why should he share a program with anybody else? At first he called his purely solo appearances "soliloquies," and he described them to the Princess Belgiojoso: ". . these tiresome *musical soliloquies* (I do not know what other name to give these inventions of mine) with which I contrive to gratify the Romans, and which I am quite capable of importing to Paris, so unbounded does my impudence become! Imagine that, wearied with warfare, not being able to put together a program that would have common sense, I have ventured to give a series of concerts all by myself, affecting the Louis XIV style and saying cavalierly to the public, *le concert, c'est moi.*" Later the soliloquies began to be called recitals, and the term aroused great merriment in England. "What does he mean? How can one *recite* upon the piano?"

If Liszt came early to maturity as a pianist, most likely the greatest pianist the world has ever known, he was somewhat late in his development as a composer. His early music no longer has any interest. Most of it is empty virtuoso material. He did compose an opera, *Don Sancho,* at the age of fourteen. That too has been forgotten. From 1829 to 1834 he was busy transcribing various material—Berlioz orchestral works, the Beethoven symphonies—or making operatic paraphrases. Not until 1835 did he start the series of works that were to remain in the repertoire. The four years after 1835 are the years of the *Transcendental Études,* the *Paganini Études,* the first two books of the *Années de Pelérinage,* the arrangements of Schubert songs, the series of Bach organ works transcribed for piano. After 1840 came many of the Hungarian Rhapsodies, the large-scale operatic paraphrases, and a remarkable series of songs that are seldom sung today but should be.

In 1847 Liszt stopped being a "professional" pianist—that is, touring and giving concerts for money. Up to that time his life had been a hectic musical and emotional outburst, and it had included a love affair that had all Europe wagging its head in disapproval (a disapproval perhaps tinged with secret envy). Liszt had met the Countess d'Agoult in 1834, and the following year she deserted her husband and ran off with Liszt to Switzerland. Three children resulted from the union. Two died young, but Cosima, born in 1837, later married Liszt's first great pupil, Hans von Bülow, and then deserted *him* for Wagner. She was a chip off the old block and, like her father, she enjoyed a long life, dying in 1930 at the age of ninety-three.

The Countess d'Agoult had literary aspirations, and it was due to her urging—and, most likely, with the assistance of her editing and rewriting— that Liszt started writing criticism and essays. He and the countess settled in Geneva, where he taught, and it was the headquarters from which he set out on tour after tour. In 1842 he was appointed Grand Ducal Director of Music Extraordinary at the Weimar court, but did not take up serious duties there until 1848. In the meantime, his relations with the countess were cooling, and they separated in 1844. She returned to Paris and, under the pen name of Daniel Stern, wrote a novel named *Nélida*. Liszt cuts a pretty poor figure in it.

On his last tour as a virtuoso, Liszt played in Russia. In Kiev he met the Princess Carolyne Sayn-Wittgenstein. He was thirty-six years old. She was twenty-eight, the daughter of a Polish landowner, and had been married at the age of seventeen to Prince Nicolas of Sayn-Wittgenstein. After a few years they separated, and she lived alone on the estate in Kiev. Not very attractive physically, she was something of a religious fanatic, strong-minded and rather masculine. But she *was* a princess, if only by marriage, had immense wealth, and Liszt made of her still another of his conquests. She was not going to let him go. She joined him at Weimar in 1849, scandalizing the court. Try as she could, she could never get a divorce. In any case, there was very little sexual relationship between Liszt and her after a few years. She was one of those women who wants to guide a man's mind, not his body, and she took Liszt in hand. A writer herself, and a pompous, inferior one, she probably wrote a good part of the material that appeared under Liszt's name. Thanks to her, and her ideas about literary style, Liszt's biography of Chopin, which could have been a primary source about the man and his piano playing, degenerated into a series of vague, purple-prose passages in which Chopin plays a minor role. History has good reason to dislike Carolyne Sayn-Wittgenstein. In the latter years of her life she lived in Rome, working on her great project, a series of books named *Causes intérieures de la faiblessse extérieure de l'Eglise* ("Interior Causes of the Exterior Weakness of the Church"). It was published in twenty-four volumes, most of the volumes over 1,000 pages each. In her room were a printing press, fourteen busts of Liszt, and hundreds of strong cigars made especially for her. The tobacco, so ran the report, was dipped in iron filings to make it stronger.

At Weimer, Liszt plunged into work and made the little city the headquarters of the progressive musical movement. He presented the music of Wagner, Berlioz, Schumann, and such composers of the oncoming school as Raff, Cornelius, and Verdi. Pianists from all over Europe flocked to Weimar to study with him. The most outstanding was Karl Tausig, who died in 1871 at the age of thirty. Tausig, from all accounts, was a stupendous pianist who could do anything Liszt could do, though without Liszt's flair. It was at Weimar, too, that Liszt started conducting. The importance of Liszt as a conductor has not been generally realized. He brought to the podium many of the characteristics of his piano playing. It was free conducting that he represented. Rather than confining himself to the bar line and conducting with regular accents, as so many conductors did and still do, Liszt looked for metrical pliancy, drama, and color. His highly unorthodox beat outlined the rise and fall of a phrase rather than coming down heavily on the first beat of the bar. "We are pilots and not mechanics," he would say. Wagner was another conductor more interested in phrase than accent, and Wagner, like Liszt, took great liberty in matters of tempo. There was no *one* tempo when Liszt or Wagner conducted; there was a series of fluctuating tempos linked by an over-all conception. The chronology is hard to establish, and it is impossible to determine how much Liszt influenced Wagner as a conductor, and how much Wagner influenced Liszt. The two were constantly leaning on each other. But Liszt was there first, as a pianist, and his free ideas about interpretation were carried over into his conducting. The chances are that Liszt, as in so many things, influenced Wagner more than Wagner influenced Liszt.

Because of a hostile demonstration at the premiere of *The Barber of Baghdad* by Peter Cornelius, in 1858, Liszt resigned his position at Weimar. At least, that was the reason he gave. Liszt was no longer happy at Weimar. His first employer, the Grand Duke Charles Frederick, had given him complete authority and a generous budget. But Charles Frederick died in 1853 and his successor, the Grand Duke Charles Alexander, showed little interest in music. Nor was the Grand Duke happy with the expense of the orchestra and opera house. Liszt's position was not improved by the presence of his mistress. When the Cornelius opera was booed, Liszt knew that the demonstration was as much directed against himself as against the composer.

But although Liszt relinquished his duties as director of music, he retained close ties with Weimar. For the rest of his life he established a routine that had him alternating between Rome, Budapest, and Weimar, but also turning up anywhere and everywhere in Europe to lend his services to a good cause. Always he was followed by pupils and adoring young ladies. He took four minor church orders in 1865 and henceforth wore a cassock and was addressed as the Abbé Liszt. "Mephistopheles in a cassock," was one description. He composed steadily, he taught up to the last year of his life, he moved among royalty as royalty.

From the beginning of his career he had insisted on being accepted as an equal by the aristocracy. When young, he had played in the great salons and noted that "artists of the first rank, such as Moscheles, Rubini, Lafont, Pasta, Malibran and others are forced to enter by the service stairs." Liszt would have none of that. If he could not mingle on equal terms with the guests, whoever they were, he would not play. In the course of his career he insulted nobles and even kings when their manners were rude while he was playing. He was Liszt, the only one of his kind, and royalty had to bow to his will. As Liszt grew older, he actually acted like royalty and expected the perquisites. But once homage and adulation were given—Liszt unfortunately was a snob—he could be sweet and generous, and there were very few talents who crossed his path and did not go away rejoicing. Young composers from all over Europe and even the United States brought him their music. He would go through it with unfailing politeness, encouraging such composers as Grieg, Smetana, Borodin, Rimsky-Korsakov, Balakirev, MacDowell, and, for a while, even Brahms. That flirtation with Brahms, who visited Weimar in 1853, did not last long. Brahms represented the "pure" classical school that stood for the old forms of symphony and the sonata principle. Liszt and his group stood for free forms, romantic excess, and a kind of music triggered by extramusical associations. In 1860 Brahms, Joachim, and several others signed a proclamation against the Music of the Future represented by the Weimar school. Brahms was to emerge as the leader of the opposition, the Keeper of the Faith, but history was not on his side. He and his followers, such as Max Reger, had very little impact upon twentieth-century music, whereas Liszt and Wagner led directly into Strauss, Mahler, the young Arnold Schoenberg, and, eventually, the twelve-tone school and its derivations.

As a piano teacher, too, Liszt's influence was to extend far. He turned out two generations of epigones, all of whom spread the style and the teachings of the master all over the world. After von Bülow and Tausig there were such pianistic giants as Sophie Menter, Eugene d'Albert, Moritz Rosenthal, Alfred Reisenauer, Alexander Siloti, Arthur Friedheim, Frederic Lamond, Rafael Joseffy, Emil von Sauer, and Bernhard Stavenhagen—all Liszt products, and most of them teachers who passed on the Liszt tradition. There were, literally, hundreds of others, all trained by Liszt, all representing a now-departed school of romantic pianism.

During the first Weimar period, 1848 to 1858, Liszt was at his creative peak. With an orchestra at his disposal, he started a new phase of composition. At first he had his scores orchestrated for him by August Conradi, Joachim Raff, and other talented young composers in his circle. By 1854 he was confident enough to do his own orchestration. From this period come the twelve symphonic poems, a new musical form invented by Liszt. These are examples of program music, in one movement, inspired by an external stimulus—a poem, a play, a painting, anything. The name of the symphonic poem and, often, a literary excerpt published in the score, supply the clue: *Les Préludes, Orpheus, Hamlet, Mazeppa*. The music specifically illustrates the program, though it may be as strictly organized in its way as a sonata is in its. After Liszt set the example, the vogue of writing symphonic poems swept Europe. Another Liszt contribution was a concept that involves thematic transformation. In such works as the massive one-movement B minor Sonata, or the E flat Piano Concerto, a theme is made to do multiple duty. It may be altered to turn up as a second subject, it may later serve in still another form as the subject for a finale, but it remains recognizably the same theme throughout. Liszt was very inventive in this kind of thematic juggling, and it often served as a formal principle with him, giving his music its own kind of unity without falling back on old forms. Liszt and the classic style had nothing to do with each other, ever. Even Chopin, in his three sonatas and the Cello Sonata, made a bow toward the old sonata principle. Liszt never did. He always invented his own forms.

His tremendous operatic paraphrases for solo piano were also something new. Composers like Herz and Hünten made a good living by filling the demand for operatic paraphrases. They would write a flashy introduction—difficult, but not too difficult for the young ladies who were their customers—and then introduce the theme of the work, following it with a series of standard and uninventive variations, ending with a coda full of scales and arpeggios. Compared to these, Liszt's paraphrases and fantasies on operas are as a bolt of lightning against the flicker of a candle. He threw themes together in a contrapuntal mélange, he changed harmonies, he exploited to the utmost every technical resource of his pianistic genius. The result is music for supervirtuosos only: original compositions (whatever the source) on a heroic and even explosive scale. Music like this has fallen into disfavor during the twentieth century, though recently there have been signs that it is beginning to edge back. The music does contain great ingenuity, and it does bring to life as no other music a specific period in musical history, a period in which the virtuoso was king and virtuosity an end in itself.

The Weimar period also brought forth such ambitious works as the *Faust* Symphony, the *Dante* Symphony, the astounding *Totentanz* for piano and orchestra, a large amount of organ and religious music, and many extended works for solo piano, including an intense, fascinating set of variations on a theme from Bach's cantata *Weinen, Klagen, Sorgen, Sagen*. All of this music is as hard to describe as the man himself, for it is a combination of nobility and sentimentality, poetry and vulgar effect. But one thing the music of his maturity uniformly has, and that is a harmonic outlook of the most original, daring, and even extreme order. Underneath all the effects, underneath the emphasis on manner over matter, is a startlingly unusual musical mind. Liszt's chromaticism could be more extreme even than Chopin's, and it was to lead directly into Wagner. There is a Liszt song, *Ich möchte hingehn*, that contains the famous *Tristan* chords note for note, with one slight change (D natural in the very first chord instead of D sharp). It was composed in 1845, long before Wagner had started thinking of *Tristan und Isolde*. One story, possibly apocryphal, has Liszt and Wagner sitting in a box as the *Tristan* Prelude starts. "That's *your* chord, Papa," Wagner says. To which Liszt answers, sourly, "At least, now it will be heard." Wagner admitted his debt to Liszt. "Since my acquaintance with Liszt's compositions," he wrote in 1859, "my treatment of harmony has become very different from what it was." Liszt's bold strokes and frequent dissonances were copied by young composers everywhere, and between Liszt and Chopin, a new language entered music. Chopin was the pioneer, first in the field. Liszt's harmony, which does owe something to Chopin's, was much more extroverted than the more refined, subtler harmony of the Polish composer. But it was just as personal, just as idiosyncratic, just as far-reaching.

Otherwise Liszt's music is music of dash and bravura, of carefully calculated effect, of defiant pose, of the triumphant resolution of massive technical difficulties. It is kinetic music. It is music intended to amaze. Later in his life, there were to be some significant changes. But to describe Liszt's music as pure effect and little substance, as some have done, misses the point. No music of such harmonic daring can be entirely superficial. Nor can many of Liszt's long-breathed melodies be dismissed. He was a superior melodist, even if his tunes pose just a shade too long, are just a little too determined to attract attention. The music has genuine fascination, but one of the difficulties in understanding it is that it is so heavily dependant on performance. This is especially true of the piano music. The romantic tradition of Liszt playing began to disappear after World War I, and today there are very few who have the combination of *diablerie* and imagination to bring it off successfully. If a pianist approaches the notes literally, he is lost. The music then sounds like empty, rattling, scales and arpeggios. If a pianist uses too much leeway, on the other hand, the music can sound vulgar and self-indulgent. Liszt's piano music needs pianists of unbounded technique, of daring (those careful pianists who never take a chance because they fear to hit a wrong note can never be convincing Liszt players), of great sonority, of delicate shadings, of exhibitionism and extroversion tempered with an ability to float an aristocratic line, of steady yet flexible rhythm. It is not only the pianistic layout that is difficult. Much more difficult these days is an identification with Liszt's mind and world.

Late in life Liszt began a group of curious experiments. In such piano pieces as the *Czardas macabre* and *Nuages gris,* virtuosity is all but eliminated. Harmonies are dissonant, bare, and open. Impressionism and even expressionism are suggested. In recent years there has been considerable study of these late pieces of Liszt. In them are the seeds of Debussy, Bartók, and the other moderns. They remain largely unknown, for very few pianists play them in public. Many are sketches rather than fully worked-out compositions. But they are prophetic and even spooky: the old Liszt idly sketching music that hints at a world still unknown, merely to amuse himself, not caring if the music was ever played or, indeed, ever saw the light.

Liszt in his old age was an institution. He was constantly surrounded by young pianists, young composers, journalists, sycophants, and hangers-on. Occasionally he would appear in public, and he still had the ability to make his listeners swoon. Nor did age, white hair, and a notable collection of warts dim the ardent lover in him. Women remained attracted to the great man, and there was a fine scandal when his pupil, the rich Olga Janina ("the Cossack Countess") tried to shoot him and then herself. His life was constantly being discussed. Everything about the man was of interest to a gossip-hungry world. The hands of the greatest of all pianists received special attention. Plaster casts were made of them, and his pupils wrote prose poems about them. The prevailing notion was that he had a tremendous hand, which was not true. He could span comfortably only a tenth. Just as phrenologists were anxious to examine the bumps on Liszt's head, palmists were eager to look at Liszt's hand, and one American lady, Anne Hampton Brewster, actually did. She sent a report to the Philadelphia *Evening Bulletin,* dated March 22, 1878, and part of it is worth reproducing as a curiosity:

What a proof of Desbarolle's theory is to be found in the hand and fingers of this celebrated artist! It is a mixed one; that is, the fingers are varied, some are round, some square and some flat or spatula; this is the true hand of an artist, for it betokens form and idea. The palm is covered with rays, betraying that his life has been an agitated, eventful one, full of passion and emotion—but the philosophic and material *noeuds,* or knots, on the Apollo and Mercury fingers, the logic and will on that wonderful long thumb, which extends beyond the middle joint of the forefinger, shows how this remarkable man has been able to conquer instincts and govern temperament. According to palmistry this self-control is shown in the palm lines, which are a little defaced. Serious, severe work, and study of a high and noble character, have effaced the impressions of a stormy youth and placed him in old age on a lofty plane where he enjoys serenity and peace. The line of life is the strongest I ever saw; and numberless lines start out from the Jupiter mount. The fingers are remarkable. The Jupiter and Saturn fingers are square; the ring, or Apollo, and little, or Mercury fingers are spatula, flat and broad. The second phalange of the Jupiter finger is longer than the first, which denotes ambition. The Saturn finger is full of knots. There is a wart on the Apollo finger of the right hand. The force of the little finger on both hands is tremendous; the knuckle seems as if made of iron. The knuckle of the Apollo finger is very strongly developed. The knuckle of the Saturn finger is like a hinge. A line starts from the root of the Apollo finger and traverses all the joints; it is strongly marked; this means great reknown.

But there also were those who found Liszt's posturings, and his affectations as an abbé, intolerable. Le Charivari in 1877 described his profile as that of a Mephistopheles "who, touched by the death of Marguerite, was meditating a slow conversion." Liszt, said Le Charivari, feigns an aged and impoverished air, but "Do not believe in it; it is merely the affectation of humility, and his cassock can scarcely contain the bounding of his still youthful soul. . . You should see him issue from the Pasdeloup concerts with lowered eyes and modestly enter a princely equipage that a great name has placed at his disposal." Le Charivari goes on to describe Liszt's way of life, his eating habits, the small and very bad Roman cigars to which he was partial, the café noir he was sipping all day, the oysters he ate for breakfast. "One last word," the article concludes. "Liszt's face is adorned with some moles, politely called grains of genius. Formerly he had four, now their number is more than doubled. It is said that it is his faith coming out."

Yes, they could poke fun at Liszt, and his foibles were fair game. But when he died, genuine sorrow swept the world. It was not only that the last great link with the days of early romanticism had gone. Liszt, as teacher and composer, as pianist and matinee idol, had been an inspiration—the archromantic, the man who had made his own rules, the exceptional figure who could have his cake and eat it. He was everything his friends and his enemies had always said he was. Look at him one way, and he was a genius. Look at him another, and he was a poseur. But one had to look and make up his own mind. From the moment Liszt broke upon the world, he could not be ignored.

To many today, Liszt's music remains vulgar and second-rate. To others it is eternally fascinating. It is so much like Liszt the man—always original, always full of ideas, often flawed in character, often with a pseudonobility. It is eternally varied music, from the delicate intimacy of that delicious piano piece Au bord d'une source to the Mephistophelean posturings of the enormous *Faust* Symphony. With Liszt there is always flesh and the devil on one side, the angelic choir on the other. His works of diabolism are consistently more interesting than his religious works (as has constantly been pointed out, sin is more interesting than virtue). Liszt's music can be as empty-headed as the *Grand galop chromatique,* as visionary as the B minor Sonata, as simple as the *Canzonetta del Salvator Rosa,* as complicated as the *Don Juan Fantasy,* as muted as *Il Pensieroso,* as glittering as *Les Jeux d'eaux à la Villa d'Este.* It can be nationalistic, as in the often-derided *Hungarian Rhapsodies* (somebody once pointed out that nobody would have ever objected had Liszt named them *Gypsy Rhapsodies*), or Bachian, as in the various transcriptions of Bach's organ music, or saintly, as in the oratorio *Christus.*

Above all there were the new concepts of form and harmony that Liszt brought to music. Béla Bartók, in an essay on Liszt, pointed out certain obvious deficiencies in his music. But, said Bartók, those were not important. "The essence of these works we must find in the new ideas, to which Liszt was the first to give expression, and in the bold pointing toward the future. These things raise Liszt as a composer to the ranks of the great." Among Liszt's contributions, Bartók cited:

> . . . the bold harmonic turns, the innumerable modulatory digressions, such as the juxtaposition, without any transition at all, of the two keys most distant from each other, and to many other points that would require the use of too many technical terms. But all these are mere details. What is more important is the absolutely new imaginative concept that manifests itself in the chief works (the Piano Sonata and the two outer movements of the *Faust* Symphony, for instance) by reason of which these works rank among the outstanding musical creations of the nineteenth century. Formally, too, though he did not break with tradition completely, Liszt created much that was new. Thus one finds in him, in the E flat Piano Concerto for instance, the first perfect realization of cyclic sonata form, with common themes treated on variation principles. . . . It is humanly very understandable that he did not reject his romantic century, with all its exaggerations. From this comes his own exaggeratedly rhetorical pathos, and no doubt it also explains the concessions he makes to the public, even in his finest works. But whoever picks out only these weaknesses—and there are still some music lovers who do—does not see the essence behind them.

Bartók was one of the first to hail Liszt as the seminal force he was. Brahms and Wagner were to eclipse Liszt as a creative figure during the nineteenth century, and he was all but ignored during the second quarter of the twentieth century. But it may yet turn out that the prophetic Liszt had more to do with music as it actually developed than any single composer of his time. The full story of his majestic place in musical history has yet to be told.

❦ 13 ❦

Bourgeois Genius

FELIX MENDELSSOHN

Of the early romantics, it was the most natural musician of them all who turned into the neoclassicist, the upholder of the traditions, the "pure" musician. Berlioz, Schumann, Chopin, Liszt—all were geniuses, but as a musician Mendelssohn was something unparalleled, and none but Mozart was born with such gifts. Indeed, Mendelssohn developed faster than Mozart, for he composed the fine Octet in E flat at the age of sixteen and the *Midsummer Night's Dream* Overture at seventeen, far eclipsing Mozart—or anybody else in musical history, for that matter—at an equivalent age. Mendelssohn was no musical specialist. Like Mozart, he could do anything. He was one of the finest pianists of the day, the greatest conductor (he was active on the podium before Liszt and Wagner), perhaps the greatest organist. Had he wanted to, he could have been one of the great violinists. His ear was perfect, his memory all-encompassing. In addition, he was a humanist —cultured, widely read, interested in poetry and philosophy. As has been pointed out many times, he would have made a resounding success in anything to which he turned his attention.

But he never lived up to his initial creative promise. A certain conservatism, an emotional inhibition, kept him from reaching the heights. His music, always skillful, became more and more a series of correct, polite gestures as he grew older. For this we can blame his background. Coming as he did from a distinguished, wealthy, conservative Jewish banking family, he was taught from childhood to be correct, to observe good form, to avoid offense. A young man, no matter how ardent and full of genius, does not grow up in great wealth, dominated by a sensitive but patriarchal father, without having conservatism ingrained within him. Mendelssohn grew up a cautious man, one who sniffed suspiciously at anything that threatened the established order of things. "Do not," he told his sister, "commend what is new until it has made some progress in the world and acquired a name, for

178

until then it is a mere matter of taste." Caution, caution. It could also be that the combination of wealth and Jewishness in a strongly anti-Semitic Berlin kept Mendelssohn unconsciously overcareful, hesitant to obtrude, anxious to be accepted. Perhaps, too, his blood pushed him into a kind of avowed German nationalism that later came to fruition in Wagner. Mendelssohn was a German and proud of it, a patriot who was convinced of German supremacy in music and the other arts. German Jews have always, when allowed, tried to be more German than the Germans; and certainly Mendelssohn regarded himself more a German than a Jew. Only once is he known to have referred to his ancestry. In any event, his parents, Abraham and Leah, were not orthodox, and had their children baptized under the name of Mendelssohn-Bartholdy. (Leah's brother had taken the name of Bartholdy on becoming a Christian.)

The Mendelssohns were integrated within Berlin society; they were "accepted," and their home was a center of musical and intellectual thought —but musical and intellectual thought of an accepted order. Felix Mendelssohn's background was not conducive to revolutionary ideas. And so he grew up to be the epitome of the wealthy German *bourgeoisie,* and he grew up with nature on his side, for he was a handsome, high-spirited young man, lithe and active, with an aristocratic bearing, a high forehead, curly black hair, and a refined, expressive face. He was well-bred, somewhat snobbish, rather priggish later in life, distrusted exuberance, enjoyed a quiet family life, had a dutiful wife, worried about his children, worked constantly, and he differed from the other wealthy *bourgeoisie* only in that he happened to be a genius.

What an extraordinary child this grandson of the great philosopher Moses Mendelssohn was! He was born in Hamburg on February 3, 1809, but the family moved to Berlin three years later, and it was there that Felix grew up in an atmosphere of almost grim culture. Grim, because both parents were determined to see that their children had every advantage money and position could provide. Leah herself was an amateur musician and artist, a student of English, French, and Italian literature, and she could also read Homer in the original. Abraham loved music and was in general a cultured, literate man. He and Leah not only directly supervised their children's education, but were also determined that the children be serious about it. This meant a great deal of work, and it was no picnic. Felix would be up at 5 A.M., ready to work at his music, his history, his Greek and Latin, his natural science, his contemporary literature, his drawing. (He was to retain that early rising hour all his life.) He thrived on the regimen, as did his talented sister Fanny. She was four years older than Felix. When Fanny was born, her mother looked at the baby's hands. "Bach fugue fingers!" she delightedly exclaimed. That was the kind of family the Mendelssohns were. Fanny and Felix: another parallel with Mozart, for Fanny was a good pianist and composer, just as Mozart's sister Nannerl was. But where Mozart later drifted away from his sister, Felix was close to Fanny all his life.

By the age of nine, Mendelssohn was playing the piano in public. Ignaz Moscheles, one of the best pianists of the day, put the finishing touches on his style. There was no question of exploiting Felix' talent, as there had been in Mozart's case, and Felix did not make many public appearances as a child. Quite the contrary. Mendelssohn's parents had doubts about Felix becoming a professional musician, and there were great family conferences about it. But it soon became evident that so enormous a gift had to be encouraged and developed. Not only did Felix have a natural instrumental talent, but by 1825, when he was sixteen, he had written four operas, concertos, symphonies, cantatas, and piano music, much of it still in manuscript. Felix tried this music out with an orchestra engaged by his parents. No wonder he developed into a flawless technician. He could grow up writing music for his own orchestra and then conducting it. On Sunday mornings there were musicales at the Mendelssohn home, attended by celebrities of European intellectual and social life. All of the children participated— Felix conducting or at the piano, Fanny also at the piano, Rebecca (born in 1811) singing, Paul (born in 1813) at the cello. Occasionally one or another of these early Mendelssohn pieces are resurrected, and they are impressive for their surety of form, their vivacity, and sheer professionalism. Already the boy was one of the better composers in Europe. When he composed the E flat Octet in 1825, he showed that he was one of the great ones.

The Octet in many ways is typical of Mendelssohn as a composer. It adheres to the established principles of sonata form and never attempts to break new ground in that respect. Never is there a suggestion that in the writing of this sixteen-year-old boy is there a revolutionary trying to break free. But with what confidence and logic is the broad opening theme presented and developed! It is a theme that contains no metrical irregularity of the kind that Berlioz, Chopin, and Schumann were to employ. Mendelssohn's mind did not run in those directions, and the opening theme of his Octet prefigures the calmly flowing, classically configured themes of his maturity, just as the working-out of the Octet theme already has the refinement, elegance, and smoothness of the later works. In the third movement, the scherzo, of the Octet, Mendelssohn did bring something new to music. That graceful, tripping, light-as-air writing was a miracle then and is a miracle now. Older writers on music invariably referred to this as "Mendelssohn's fairy music;" and there is indeed something elfin about it. This kind of writing came to its apex the following year, when Mendelssohn composed the *Midsummer Night's Dream* Overture. He was seventeen years old, and he never wrote a more perfect work. Oberon, Titania, the lovers, Bottom—all stroll through this fairy landscape. The music has remained eternally fresh, and is a perfect example of content wedded to technique. That includes the orchestration. Mendelssohn as an orchestrator, as well as a composer, represented the golden mean. He used exactly what he had to use, and no more; but what he did use, he used with taste, skill, and imagination.

Mendelssohn's early years in Berlin came to a climax with his preparation and public performance of Bach's *St. Matthew Passion* (two performances, on March 11 and March 21, 1829). The work had not been heard since Bach's day, though Bach might have had trouble recognizing his score as presented by Mendelssohn. He used a chorus of 400 and a greatly augmented orchestra. He cut some sections and modified others to make the music palatable to Berlin audiences, and he did not hesitate to supply new orchestrations when he felt they were necessary. The twenty-year-old Mendelssohn did no more or less than other composers and conductors did to early music at that time. The revival did much to spark the Bach renaissance. Throughout his life Mendelssohn was never far from Bach, and probably had all of his then-known music committed to memory. All good musicians have superior memories, but Mendelssohn's was exceptional. As a child he knew the nine Beethoven symphonies by heart and could play them on the piano. He most likely could hear a piece of music once and never forget it. Charles Hallé in a burst of extravagance said that he was convinced that Mendelssohn knew every bar of music ever written, and could reproduce it immediately.

Like all wealthy young men of breeding, Mendelssohn had to make the Grand Tour, and he started out in 1829. The trip was to last three years. He went to Italy, France, and England, meeting everybody and being liked by everybody. He wrote long, articulate letters, often illustrating them with pencil drawings. Mendelssohn has been overpraised as an artist. His drawings are all tight in line and very careful, devoid of personality, merely copies of what he had seen. When he tried to draw the human figure, his deficiencies as a draftsman showed up, though at least those figure drawings have a kind of charm that the carefully copied landscapes lack.

In 1831 he was in Paris, meeting Liszt, Chopin, Berlioz, and Kalkbrenner, listening to the first flush of romantic music and not liking it very much. Chopin, he thought, was the best of the new crop, though it took a little time for Mendelssohn to overcome his initial mistrust of Chopin's radical harmonies and his new way of playing the piano. Mendelssohn also had a high regard for Schumann as a man, but here again was distrustful of his music. It made him uncomfortable, and the conservative Mendelssohn did not like to be made uncomfortable. "He loves the dead too much," gibed

Berlioz. Mendelssohn represented the Biedermeier period: comfortable, homelike, heavy in sentiment, bourgeois, functional. But even though Mendelssohn was temperamentally opposed to romanticism, that did not keep him from conducting romantic music when he became musical director at Leipzig in 1835. It is also interesting to note that where later generations looked down upon Mendelssohn's music as being too precious, too thin, too much on the surface, the early romantics had a completely different idea about him. To Schumann, for instance, Mendelssohn was perfection itself. "I consider Mendelssohn *to be the first musician* of our time, and take off my hat to him as a master." The avant-garde Berlioz had a high regard for Mendelssohn as a composer, and so did Liszt. Part of the admiration may have been a response to Mendelssohn's phenomenal accomplishments as a practicing musician. Musicians always respond to craftsmanship, and Mendelssohn had more craftsmanship than anybody around. But there is also plenty of evidence to show that Mendelssohn's music made a decided impact on his romantic contemporaries. And the public could not get enough of it. Indeed, it is doubtful if any other composer was so universally accepted by the public as a master in his own lifetime.

Mendelssohn's standards were very high, and he had an opportunity to put them into effect in 1833, when he became director at Düsseldorf. He promptly started to program such sixteenth- and seventeenth-century composers as Lassus, Palestrina, and Leo, and directed a revival of *Don Giovanni* at the opera. Mendelssohn, however, was too sophisticated a musician for the sleepy and provincial town of Düsseldorf. When he was invited, in 1835, to take over the Gewandhaus concerts in Leipzig—Bach's town!—he was only too eager to accept. In a short time he made Leipzig the musical capital of Germany, and he also revolutionized orchestral playing in his own country. He increased the orchestra from forty to fifty players, engaged Ferdinand David as concertmaster, and saw to it that his players had ease of mind by securing a pension for each member of the orchestra. One of the first conductors to use a baton, Mendelssohn made his orchestra a precision unit. As a conductor he was sparing in gesture, inclined toward fast tempos, and insistent on accurate rhythm and smooth ensemble. Mendelssohn was probably the first modern conductor as the term is understood today. Spirited, high-strung, dictatorial, he demanded obedience from his players and was known to lose his temper if he did not get what he wanted.

He also revised the repertoire. Before he took over the Gewandhaus concerts, the most-played composers were such now-forgotten figures as Anton Eberl, Ignaz von Seyfried, Karl Reissiger, Alexander Fesca, Sigismund Neukomm, Ferdinand Ries, and other such worthies. Mendelssohn changed all that. He made Mozart and Beethoven the backbone of the repertoire, with Haydn, Bach, and Handel not far behind. Among the newer composers he introduced to Leipzig audiences were Spohr, Cherubini, Moscheles, Gade, Rossini, Liszt, Chopin, Schumann, and Schubert. He got rid of the variety programs that were customary, and began to organize programs much as they are organized today, starting with an overture, proceeding to a large-scale work, then to a concerto or another large-scale work, and ending with a shorter piece. Nor would he separate the movements of a symphony with a divertissement. Often, in programs of the day, a Beethoven symphony would be stopped after two movements, and a harpist, or cellist, or singer would entertain the audience, after which the symphony would be resumed. Sponsors of concerts clearly felt that no audience could survive the intellectual strain of listening to a Beethoven symphony straight through.

Mendelssohn worked very hard at Leipzig, but managed to find the time to get married. His wife was Cécile Jeanrenaud, daughter of a clergyman of the French Reformed Church. The marriage was happy, and was blessed with four children, but surprisingly little is known of Cécile. The Mendelssohns kept their home life to themselves, and Cécile remained in the background. She must have been an intelligent, helpful woman, and she made a good impression on Mendelssohn's sister when the two women finally met, in Leipzig. Fanny wrote home to Berlin:

> At last I know my sister-in-law, and I feel as if a load were off my mind, for I cannot deny that I was very uncomfortable and out of sorts at never having seen her. She is amiable, childlike, fresh, bright and even tempered, and I consider Felix most fortunate for, though inexpressibly fond of him, she does not spoil him, but when he is capricious treats him with an equanimity which will in the course of time most probably cure his fits of irritability altogether. Her presence produces the effect of a fresh breeze, so bright and natural is she.

In addition to the Leipzig concerts, Mendelssohn took over the concerts of the Berlin Academy of Arts in 1841. As a guest conductor he appeared all over Europe and was particularly favored in London, where he was friendly with Queen Victoria and Prince Albert. The Queen liked comfortable music, and her Mr. Mendelssohn was the one to give it to her. Mendelssohn's letters are full of references to musicales and music-making at Windsor Castle. The royal family specially liked to hear Mr. Mendelssohn play the piano. Mendelssohn as a pianist represented the pure, classic style as opposed to the romantic thunderings of the Liszt school or the delicate nuances and color effects of the Chopin style. His playing was like his music—clear, elegant, precise, logical, with little use of the pedal. Probably it sounded like the playing of a Kalkbrenner with brains.

On top of all his conducting and concertizing, not to mention composing, Mendelssohn established the Leipzig Conservatory late in 1842, and it opened on April 3 the following year. He and Robert Schumann taught composition and piano. Among the faculty members was Ferdinand David, in charge of violin teaching. David, one of the best violinists in Europe, had been brought by Mendelssohn to Leipzig as concertmaster of the Gewandhaus orchestra. The two men were close friends, and Mendelssohn consulted David on a number of technical points while he was composing the E minor Violin Concerto.

And thus the middle 1840's saw Mendelssohn active as composer, conductor, pianist, teacher, administrator, family man, and traveler. He also carried on an enormous correspondence, and was instrumental in founding music festivals—at Cologne, Düsseldorf, Schwerin, Birmingham. In 1845 he asked to be released from his duties in Berlin, and that gave him more time for activity in London. He kept at his various activities day and night, constantly traveling, constantly working, constantly more irritable. His family worried about his health. Mendelssohn was physically and emotionally exhausted, but he had a compulsion to work. Early in 1847, for instance, he conducted his *St. Paul* in Leipzig and went to London, where he conducted four performances of *Elijah*. Then he conducted *Elijah* in Birmingham and Manchester. He had other obligations in England, including appearances as a pianist. He looked ill and tired when it was all over, and is reported to have said that another week in London would have killed him. He left London and arrived in Frankfort for conducting appearances.

It was there that in May, 1847, he received the news of his beloved sister's sudden death. She had had a stroke in Berlin, and died on May 14. When Mendelssohn learned about it he himself had a stroke from which he never recovered. He had to stop work—finally!—and went off with his family to Switzerland, where he tried to relax by painting water colors and working on a string quartet and other pieces. In September he returned to Leipzig, saying he was feeling better, but he had another stroke that left him partially paralyzed. He died on November 4, 1847, at the age of thirty-eight.

Mendelssohn's romanticism was by far the most restrained of any of the great composers active in the 1830's and 1840's. He had none of the romantic aspirations, none of the high-flying concepts that so delighted the romantics. "People often complain," he once wrote, "that music is too ambiguous, that what they should think when they hear it is so unclear, whereas everybody understands words. With me it is exactly the opposite. . . . The thoughts that are expressed to me by music I love are not too indefinite to be put into words, but on the contrary too definite." This is the remark of one who responds to logic in music, and most of Mendelssohn's music is nothing if not logical. Instinctively he shrank from excesses of any kind—in music, in art, in life. Naturally the extravagant-sounding music of Berlioz repelled him: "a frightful muddle, an incongruous mess . . . one ought to wash one's hands after handling one of his scores." In some of his earlier works Mendelssohn did experiment with a few advanced harmonies, but soon withdrew as though frightened. His music has almost none of the textural richness of Schumann, Chopin, and Liszt. It is devoid of those altered chords, unorthodox key relationships, irregular metrical groupings. Mendelssohn's music is largely diatonic. He and the romantics did not speak the same language.

It was this lack of harmonic bite in his music that helped make him so popular. Conventional-minded listeners, disturbed by the wild dissonances of the other romantics, were able to sit back and relax with Mendelssohn's music. It had a strong relationship with the then-popular music of Hummel, Cherubini, and even some of the salon composers. What put it miles above their music, however, was the peculiarly Mendelssohnian grace and elegance it displayed, and its clear-cut construction. Later generations would find that kind of perfection boring; would find Mendelssohn's melodies cloying and his rhythms too regular and predictable. Mendelssohn's music has less of the element of surprise in it than the music of any of the great composers. But the first half of the nineteenth century regarded Mendelssohn as close to divine. Especially in England his influence held strong throughout the century, dominating the entire British school. Mendelssohn loved England from the moment he first arrived in London, and the admiration was reciprocated. Sir George Grove, indeed, all but claimed Mendelssohn as a British national. "He has been for long looked on as half an Englishman. He spoke English well, he wrote letters and familiar notes in our tongue freely; he showed himself in the provinces; his first important work was founded on Shakespeare . . . and his *Scotch* Symphony and *Hebrides* Overture showed how deeply the scenery of Britain had influenced him."

In the twentieth century Mendelssohn's reputation took a sharp dip. Yet there never was a time when his music was not in the repertoire, and this despite the disparaging remarks of the intellectual critics. Not only was romanticism generally out of fashion, which threw Schumann, Liszt, and even Chopin into the shadow, but avant-garde critics also decided, almost to a man, that Mendelssohn's music was too unoriginal and even lacking in taste. Paul Rosenfeld, the American critic, had nothing but contempt for such scores as *Elijah* and *St. Paul.* He wrote articles suggesting that Mendelssohn was a Jewish snob trying to pass into Christian society with religious scores as his passport. Rosenfeld's view was generally accepted by avant-garde thinkers. The public, however, paid no attention to the diatribes. The Violin Concerto, the *Italian* and *Scotch* Symphonies, the *Midsummer Night's Dream* and *Hebrides* (or *Fingal's Cave,* as it is also known) Overtures were as popular as ever. Wherever there was a chamber group, the D minor and C minor Trios and several of the string quartets were never far away. The *Variations sérieuses* never left the piano literature, nor did the G minor Piano Concerto.

On the face of it, it was strange that so many musicians and critics in the period from 1920 to 1940 had so low an opinion of Mendelssohn. One can understand listeners who grew up with the antiromanticism of Stravinsky and Bartók feeling uncomfortable with the extroverted flamboyance of a Liszt or the secret soul-states of a Schumann. But Mendelssohn's music has clear lines and beautiful organization; and for the most part it completely avoids the sweeping romantic gesture. Mendelssohn should have been enthusiastically adopted by the twentieth-century antiromantics. Perhaps it was the lack of adventure in his music that made it unpalatable for a time.

In any event the latter part of the twentieth century is busy rediscovering Mendelssohn. Even the once-derided *Songs Without Words* are beginning to be regarded with respect as flawlessly written period pieces with a great deal of personality. Pianists once more are looking at the three Études, the six Preludes and Fugues and such effective virtuoso works as the F sharp minor Fantasy (Op. 28). Recent years have seen an exploration of music that Mendelssohn composed in Berlin when he was twelve years old, and listeners are amazed at the dash, sweetness, and technical expertise of the music—those symphonies for strings, concertos for two pianos, and chamber works. His songs are beginning to come back. Even—*mirabile dictu!*—the oratorios are no longer automatically regarded as stuffy examples of moralistic Victorian piety. Mendelssohn is beginning to be seen in true perspective. He was much more than a polite composer with an enormous technique. His music has sensitivity, style, and a great degree of personality; and he did compose at least one flawless specimen in each of a multiplicity of musical forms—symphony, concerto, piano, chamber music, the lied, the concert overture, oratorio. Everything, indeed, except opera. His influence can be found in music of the French school (especially Gounod and Fauré), in the young Richard Strauss, in the youthful works of Tchaikovsky. Today, there is still a little suspicion of the sentiment implicit in much of Mendelssohn's music. But as serial and postserial music runs its course and neoromanticism returns, as it seems to be returning in the 1970's, Mendelssohn's music, like Liszt's, will be accepted once again, and Mendelssohn will be recognized as the sweet, pure, perfectly proportioned master he was.

❦ 14 ❧

Voice, Voice, and More Voice

ROSSINI, DONIZETTI, AND BELLINI

From 1810, the date of Gioacchino Rossini's first opera, to 1848, the year Gaetano Donizetti died, three composers dominated Italian opera—that is, opera composed in Italy, bel canto opera, as opposed to the stately operas in Italian turned out by such composers as Cherubini in Paris. The three composers were Rossini, Donizetti, and Vincenzo Bellini.

In their kind of opera, singers and singing were the thing. Their operas for the most part aimed frankly at entertainment. Weber may have been concerned with the German people in his operas, and Beethoven in *Fidelio* was aiming at spiritual values. None of this concerned the bel canto composers. Their emotional and exhibitionistic art did not call upon listeners to think deeply. As a result, their operas were immensely popular. "Music for the Italians," complained Berlioz, "is a sensual pleasure and nothing more. For this noble expression of the mind they have hardly more respect than for the art of cooking. They want a score that, like a plate of macaroni, can be assimilated immediately without their having to think about it, or even to pay attention to it." Later, the spectacle operas of Meyerbeer, the psychological operas of Verdi, and the music dramas of Wagner pushed bel canto opera off the stage, though a handful of works survived the international circuit—Rossini's *Il Barbiere di Siviglia*, Donizetti's *Lucia di Lammermoor, Don Pasquale,* and *L'Elisir d'Amore,* and Bellini's *Norma.* In Italy, another half-dozen might have occasionally been heard. But considering that Rossini composed thirty-nine operas, Donizetti about seventy, and Bellini eleven, it was not a large representation.

After World War II there was a sudden revival of interest in bel canto opera all over Europe and America, thanks largely to two singers—Maria Callas and Joan Sutherland. Operas that had been forgotten for a hundred years or more were dragged from the shelves, and music lovers eagerly investigated the curiosities. But very few of those operas turned out to have

187

much more than antiquarian value. Nor was it possible to give an adequate idea of what the operas sounded like. Bel canto opera demands coloratura tenors, contraltos, and baritones as well as coloratura sopranos. (There is a mistaken idea that coloratura pertains to high soprano alone.) But the tradition was gone, much as Callas and Sutherland tried to revive it, and there were no tenors or baritones anywhere in the world who could begin to sing the parts as the tenor Rubini or the bass Lablache did in the first half of the nineteenth century.

A great deal of bel canto opera was formula opera, hastily turned out, based heavily on the device of the cavatina and cabaletta. The cavatina, slow and lyric, was intended to show off a singer's line, to demonstrate the singer's ability to hold a long phrase with beauty of tone, nuance, and color. The cavatina was followed by a fast section called the cabaletta, in which the virtuosity of the singer was called into play. Bel canto, which means "beautiful singing," reflected to a large extent the eighteenth-century ideal of taste in improvisation. A singer was expected to have a flawless technique. A singer was also expected to have taste in embellishment, decoration, and cadenza. The combination of pure tone and brilliant technique constituted bel canto singing. Much of this kind of singing descended from the castrati. Baldassare Ferri, a castrato virtuoso of the seventeenth century, could insert consecutive trills for two octaves, up and down, in one breath. Such passages could take fifty unbroken seconds. Farinelli also was timed at fifty seconds in one phrase. Rossini had heard some of the great castrati and knew what they could do. He knew, too, that the great ones were not mere show-offs. Those with taste could melt their listeners with the purity, beauty, and even passion of their delivery.

The ideal—technique plus taste—did not show up very often. Opera singers above all musicians tend to abuse their prerogatives. In Rossini's early days they did whatever came into their heads. They were spoiled and pampered, and were considered much more important than the composer. The composer had to have the diplomacy of a Talleyrand to satisfy them. If two popular prima donnas were in the same opera, there would be intense rivalry and suspicion, tears and hatred. Each would count the bars of her arias to make sure she was not being cheated. Then she would go ahead and change the music to suit herself. So cavalier an attitude did the singers of Rossini's day have toward the printed note that often the baffled composer was hard put to recognize his own music. Rossini was always fighting the tastelessness of singers. He even wrote out many of the embellishments, and demanded they be closely followed. But not even Rossini expected a star soprano to follow everything exactly as written. Years after his retirement, Rossini accompanied the young Adelina Patti in *Una voce poco fa* from *Il Barbiere di Siviglia*. She embellished the aria out of recognition.

and after congratulating her on her brilliant singing Rossini icily wanted to know who the composer was. A few days later Rossini told Saint-Saëns that he had no objection to his arias being altered or embroidered. "They were made for that. But to leave not a note of what I composed, even in the recitatives—well, that is too much."

In Italy during the first third of the century, the composer would arrive at an opera house, compose an opera in three weeks or so, conduct the first three performances, and move on to the next town. Italian opera had always worked this way; it was a business, and the faster the turnover, the better. Seldom were the operas published, and Rossini, for one, knowing that the next town would not have heard his last opera, would calmly appropriate sections from it and pass them off as new. Rossini's most famous opera, *Il Barbiere di Siviglia* of 1816, uses arias and ensembles from *La Cambiale di Matrimonio* of 1810, and in addition material from four other of his operas. Even the now-famous overture was lifted from a previous work. It was typical that *Il Barbiere* took the composer no more than thirteen days to finish. "I always knew Rossini was a lazy man," joked Donizetti, when told of this feat. Donizetti knew whereof he spoke, for it had taken him no more than eight days to compose *L'Elisir d'Amore*. Felix Mendelssohn, traveling in Italy, looked, marveled, and was amused at the Italian way of composing opera. "Donizetti," he wrote home, "finishes an opera in ten days. It may be hissed, to be sure, but that doesn't matter, as it is paid for all the same, and then he can go about having a good time. If in the end his reputation should be endangered, in that case he would have to work real hard, which he would not like. Therefore he sometimes spends as much as three weeks on an opera, taking considerable pains with a couple of arias in it, so that they may please the public, and then he can afford to amuse himself once more, and once more write trash." Mendelssohn, the industrious German ant, and Donizetti, the Italian grasshopper.

The bel canto composers were able to turn out scores at such speed because they were in effect composing formula operas, all constructed much the same way. An opening chorus was followed by carefully meted-out arias and ensembles, each placed with the rigidity of men in an army platoon at attention, everybody and everything in its appointed place. Each of the two acts would end with a thundering chorus, in which the principal singers advanced to the footlights and sang along, staring the audience down. In a letter to a composer, Rossini was devastatingly frank about his method of work·

Wait until the evening before the opening night. Nothing primes inspiration more than necessity, whether it be the presence of a copyist waiting for your work, or the prodding of an impresario tearing his hair

In my time, all the impresarios of Italy were bald at thirty. . . . I wrote the overture to *La Gazza Ladra* the day of its opening in the theater itself, where I was imprisoned by the director and under the surveillance of the stagehands who were instructed to throw my original text through the window, page by page, to the copyists waiting below to transcribe it. In default of pages they were ordered to throw me out the window bodily. I did better with *Il Barbiere*. I did not compose an overture but selected for it one which was meant for a semi-serious opera called *Elisabetta*. The public was completely satisfied. [What Rossini did not add was that he had also used the *Barbiere* overture for his *Aureliano* and *L'Equivoco Stravagante* in addition to *Elisabetta*.]

Bellini, who did not have the happy-go-lucky temperament of Rossini and Donizetti, and who took his art more seriously, did break away from formula, but only slightly. His two facile contemporaries never bothered to alter their successful formula. In virtually every Rossini and Donizetti opera, and in several of Bellini's, there is slipshod work, self-plagiarism, and cynicism. That is the reason why most of their operas are dead. Donizetti: who has heard, or ever will hear, his *Chiara e Serafina*, his *L'Ajo nell'imbarazzo*, *Parisina*, *Torquato Tasso*, *Rosamonda d'Inghilterra*, or *Belisario*? Rossini: his *Elisabetta, Regina d'Inghilterra, Torvaldo e Dorliska, Adelaide de Borgogna*? Bellini: his *Bianca e Gernando*, or *Zaira*?

Rossini, who outlived Bellini and Donizetti, was the big man of the three. He had genius, he had wit and sparkle, and he had a never-failing melodic gift. "Give me a laundry list and I will set it to music," he bragged. He was born on February 29, 1792, in Pesaro, an Adriatic port. Later in life Rossini was to be called "The Swan of Pesaro." As a child he had immense facility, as so many of the great composers have had, and could play the piano, violin, and viola. He also sang in opera before his voice broke, and he was composing prolifically while a teen-ager. In 1807 he began his studies at the conservatory in Bologna. It was there that he met the Spanish soprano Isabella Colbran, who later became his wife and the great interpreter of his music. The first of his operas to be staged was a one-act farce, for Venice in 1810, named *La Cambiale di Matrimonio*. The dash, spirit, irrepressible humor of the music and its real personality immediately set it apart as something special. Rossini's first big hit, *L'Inganno felice*, was staged the following year also in Venice. Then followed such operas as *La Scala di Seta, Il Signor Bruschino, Tancredi, L'Italiana in Algeri, Semiramide, Il Turco in Italia, La Cenerentola*, and *Le Comte Ory*. At the age of twenty-one Rossini was already world-famous, and as they came out, his operas immediately entered the international repertory.

It was, above all, melody that made Rossini famous, and Wagner ruefully admitted as much. "Rossini," he wrote, "turned his back on the pedantic lumber of heavy scores and listened where the people sang without a writ ten note. What he heard there was what, out of all the operatic box of tricks, had stayed the most unbidden in the ear: *the naked, ear-delighting, absolutely-melodic melody*, that is, melody that was just melody and nothing else." Wagner, with mingled exasperation and irony, concluded that with Rossini "the real life history of opera comes to an end," for all pretense at drama was swept away and the performer was allotted showy virtuosity as his only task. Wagner was determined to correct the situation.

Il Barbiere di Siviglia, that greatest of all buffa operas, made Rossini's music the rage of every opera house in Europe. Rossini had a certain amount of nerve writing an opera on this subject. Giovanni Paisiello, an important and very popular composer, had written a *Barbiere di Siviglia* in 1782 that was loved, admired, and immensely popular. Today, the Paisiello opera is a curiosity, one with a faded charm but essentially unadventurous harmonically and melodically. Rossini's opera, which uses almost the same libretto, sent it into rapid oblivion. Yet Rossini's *Barbiere* was a failure at its first performance, in Rome, on February 20, 1816. Apparently it was poorly sung, and there were some weird accidents that took the public's mind away from the music. A singer tripped and had to sing with a bloody nose; a cat wandered in and upstaged everybody. But the second act went well, and the work soon established itself as *the* comic opera of all time. Only nine years after its premiere it was heard in New York (though an abridged version had been presented in that city as early as 1819) in Manuel Garcia's first season at the Park Theater. Garcia had been the original Almaviva.

Rossini is remembered today primarily as a writer of opera buffa, but his serious and tragic operas were highly esteemed in their day. *Otello, Le Siège de Corinth, Moïse, William Tell*—all made the rounds to great admiration. In 1822 there was a Rossini festival at the Kärntnertor Theater in Vienna, and the city experienced a Rossini delirium. Beethoven himself admired the *Barbiere* and told Rossini to give the world many more. Schubert incorporated the famous Rossini crescendo, and other devices, into some of his scores. In Paris the Rossini operas were constantly being given at the Théâtre des Italiens and the Opéra. London in 1824 had a "Rossini season." Rossini went to London (as he had gone to Vienna) to superintend performances, and his presence added materially to the receipts. Europe was Rossini-mad. Things went very well for the volatile Italian. He married his Colbran, after having lived with her for many years, then took up with Olympe Péllisier and married her when Colbran died. Everywhere he went he was envied, feted, admired. He became corpulent, worked up some interesting ailments, was one of Europe's most famous gourmets (tournedos Rossini are one of his bequests to humanity), and when *William Tell* was performed at the Paris Opéra in 1829 the adulation was all but hysterical.

At that point Rossini stopped composing and although he lived for another thirty-nine years never wrote another note for publication.

His retirement is a mystery that has been the object of endless speculation. He did compose two large-scale religious works, the *Stabat Mater* and the *Petite Messe Solennelle* (which, as has been observed many times, is neither petite nor solennelle), and he amused himself by composing a large number of short piano and vocal pieces. But to all intents and purposes his career was over in 1829, at the height of his fame.

Several guesses can be made. For one thing, Rossini had a great deal of money. At his death he left an estate valued at approximately $1,420,000. There was no financial necessity for him to write; and Rossini was not the kind of idealist who composed from aesthetic conviction or spiritual necessity. For another, his health was not good. He had uremic troubles and on top of that was a hypochondriac and insomniac. "I have all of women's ills," Rossini told a friend. "All that I lack is the uterus." A certain amount of natural laziness, too, entered into his decision to retire.

But more than that, Rossini was distressed at the direction opera was heading. He honestly believed that with the disappearance of the castrati the art of singing was dying. As early as 1817—he was only twenty-five at the time—he was bewailing the corruption of singing: "Many of our singers, born outside of Italy, have renounced purity of musical taste. . . . Warblings, leaps, trills, jumps, abuses of semitones, clusters of notes, these characterize the singing that now prevails." At that time Rossini was also concerned about what he considered the deleterious influence of the German school. In a letter dated February 12, 1817, he sounds as conservative as the strictest academician in any conservatory:

Haydn had already begun to corrupt purity of taste by introducing strange chords, artificial passages and daring novelties. . . . But after him Cramer and, finally, Beethoven, with their compositions lacking in unity and natural flow, and full of artificial oddities, corrupted taste in instrumental music completely. And now, for the simple and majestic styles of Sarti, Paisiello and Cimarosa, Mayr has substituted in the theater his own ingenious but vicious harmonies in which the main melody is strangled in deference to the new German school.

There is no evidence that Rossini changed his mind as he grew older. His own operas, even *William Tell* with its Meyerbeerian elements, are basically classic, with elegance of melody, clarity, modesty of orchestration, and predominantly diatonic harmonies. By 1830 romanticism was on its way, and Rossini was an antiromantic. He detested the loudness, the "eccentricities,"

192

the "affectations" of the new movement. Above all he hated the new style of singing. A new breed, tenors with high notes, was the rage, and Rossini despised everything they represented. Enrico Tamberlik was astounding operatic audiences with his famous high C sharp, and there was the occasion when Tamberlik visited Rossini. "Have him come in," Rossini said. "But tell him to leave his C sharp on the coat rack. He can pick it up on the way out."

Even before *William Tell*, Rossini was thinking of quitting, and it was general knowledge. Stendhal saw Rossini in Milan. "Next April," Stendhal wrote, "Rossini will be 28 and he is eager to stop composing at 30." Then there is a letter from Rossini's father: "Gioacchino has given me his word that he wants to retire home from everything in 1830, wanting to enjoy acting the gentleman and being allowed to write what he wishes, as he has been exhausted enough " The magazines picked up the rumors and, in 1828, the *Revue musicale* in an article about the forthcoming *William Tell* noted that "he himself has asserted . . . that this opera will be the last to come from his pen."

By the 1840's Rossini, even if he had been thinking of resuming his career, must have asked himself whether or not his public would desert him in favor of the new gods, especially Giacomo Meyerbeer. Rossini, who had been the king of European opera for so many years, would not have relished the possibility of being called a has-been. Herbert Weinstock, Rossini's biographer, sums it up: "Nothing about him suggests that he would have competed—or would have wanted to compete—with the composer of *Les Huguenots* and *Le Prophète* and the composer of *Nabucco* and *Ernani* in order to supply audiences whose tastes he did not share with operas that he could not wholly like." The Rossinian opera world, in short, no longer existed.

So Rossini retired. He had homes in Bologna and Paris and a summer home in Passy. He found a new mistress. He busied himself with the Liceo Communale in Bologna, trying to raise the standards of that provincial conservatory of music. He was courted and flattered, and was recognized as The Grand Old Man of music. Witty, civilized, urbane, sharp-tongued, he was feared for his opinions, and his offhand remarks were gleefully quoted everywhere. "I have just received a Stilton and a cantata from Cipriani Potter. The cheese was very good." Or, "Wagner has some fine moments but some bad quarters of an hour." He said, after hearing the *Symphonie fantastique* by Berlioz, "What a good thing it isn't music." Another comment by Rossini about Berlioz concerned the *Song of the Rat* from *La Damnation de Faust*. It did not please, Rossini explained, because there was no cat in the house. Or—he loved making puns—when he overheard somebody praising the Credo of Liszt's *Gran* Mass as the fairest flower in the garland, Rossini said: "Yes, in fact a *fleur de Liszt.*" The tiny piano pieces and songs that he composed—many are still unpublished—he called the sins of his old age. These pieces have a Chabrier and Satie kind of surrealism, especially in the titles: *Les Hors d'oeuvres*, with individual pieces in the set named radishes, anchovies, butter, and so on; or *Mon Prélude hygienique du matin*, or *Gymnastique d'écartement*, or *L'Innocence italienne suite de la candeur française*.

In Paris he established one of the most glittering salons in Europe. On Saturday nights he formally entertained. There would be music, and often Rossini himself would go to the piano to accompany a famous singer. He was a pianist of the old school, using little or no pedal, letting his fingers drift elegantly over the keys. Printed invitations were sent to guests, and there were printed programs for the musical part of the evening. Rossini had a few talented pianists on call, to play or to accompany when he was not in the mood. Charles Camille Saint-Saëns was one of them, and the brilliant Louis Diémer was another. Eduard Hanslick, writing for the *Neue Freie Presse* in Vienna, described one of Rossini's soirées. Hanslick said that the house was too small to accommodate the number of guests:

> The heat was indescribable and the pressure so great that the most desperate efforts were always necessary whenever a fair vocalist (especially one of the weight of Madame Sax) had to make her way from the seat to the piano. A host of ladies, sparkling with jewels, occupy the entire music room; the men stand, so jammed together as to be unable to move, at the open doors. Now and then a servant with refreshment worms his way through the gasping crowd, but it is an odd fact that only very few persons (and those mostly strangers) take anything worth mentioning. The lady of the house, it is said, does not like their doing so.

When Rossini died, on November 13, 1868, it was the death of an emperor.

In his operas, Rossini was never part of the romantic world. But he listened to everything, and in such works as the *Stabat Mater* or the *Petite Messe Solennelle*, he used harmonies much more adventurous than anything that can be found in his operas. The *Messe*, with its chromaticisms alongside its classic melodic outline, is a fascinating amalgam of the old and the new. In its original scoring, for chorus, four soloists, two pianos, and organ, the work exerts a peculiar charm. It is a masterpiece just as the *Péchés de vieilesse—Sins of My Old Age*—are masterpieces in miniature. As for those bubbling pre-1829 operas, there remains the *Barber*. But who today can sing it, or sing those other enchanting frivolities? What would Rossini, the ultimate connoisseur of singing, have had to say had he encountered the strained, throaty, hooty, spread, loud, vulgar, heavy, maladroit singing that today passes, *faute de mieux*, as "the Rossini style?"

Gaetano Donizetti (November 29, 1797–April 7, 1848) was even more prolific than Rossini. He studied in Bergamo, the city of his birth, went to Bologna, returned to Bergamo, and then started to turn out operas with the fluency of a matchstick machine. In addition to some seventy operas there came from his pen twelve string quartets, seven masses, songs, piano music, cantatas, motets, and psalms. He had flair, he had style, and he constantly was abusing his talent, writing too much too fast. Yet *Lucia* (1835), *Don Pasquale* (1843), and *L'Elisir d'Amore* (1832) remain very much with us, and *Anna Bolena* (1830), *La Fille du Régiment* (1840), and *La Favorite* (1840) are occasionally revived. Donizetti's mad scenes were especially admired. Audiences liked to hear his heroines expiring in showers of trills, arpeggios, scales, leaps, and high notes, all augmented with interpolated cadenzas. French opera adopted the Donizetti mad scenes. And Donizetti was a strong influence on the young Verdi, much more so than were Rossini and Bellini. Throughout the century, great singers from Pasta, Rubini, Lablache, and Duprez to Lind, Sontag, Grisi, Patti, Mario, and Albori, loved the Donizetti operas. In those mid-nineteenth-century days of great singing, *Anna Bolena* (1830) was regarded as Donizetti's masterpiece.

Like all Italian opera composers, Donizetti was constantly on the move. He went up and down Italy, staging his operas. Many were enthusiastically received, and after *Anna Bolena* he was famous. *L'Elisir d'Amore* illustrates the conditions under which Donizetti had to work, and the speed with which he filled his commissions. The manager of the Teatre della Canobbiana in Milan needed a new opera at short notice because of the failure of a composer to deliver a promised work. Donizetti was approached two weeks before the scheduled premiere. The desperate manager suggested that Donizetti patch up an old work and pass it off as new. Donizetti probably took this as a challenge. What? Do you think I cannot compose an opera in two weeks? He sent for the librettist, Felice Romani, and is supposed to have said: "I am obliged to set a poem to music in fourteen days. I give you one week to prepare it for me. We'll see which of us two has more guts!" Romani supplied the libretto in time, and Donizetti dashed off the music. It was a success at the premiere and has remained one of his most popular operas. Berlioz heard it in Milan shortly after the premiere. His account gives an idea of the behavior of Italian audiences. He found the theater full of people, but they were "talking in normal voices with their backs to the stage. The singers, undeterred, gesticulated and yelled their lungs out in the strictest spirit of rivalry. At least I presumed they did, from their wide-open mouths; but the noise of the audience was such that no sound penetrated except the bass drum. People were gambling, eating supper in their boxes, etc., etc. Consequently, perceiving it was useless to expect to hear anything of the score, which was then new to me, I left."

The years after *L'Elisir d'Amore* saw Donizetti in Paris, in Vienna, still constantly on the move. *Lucia di Lammermoor* was produced in Naples in 1835. It turned out to be one of the most popular operas of the century. In 1837 Donizetti lost his wife, whom he adored, and he never recovered from the shock. In addition, he had periodic bouts of ill health. He had a stroke in 1845, slowly lost control of his mind, and died three years later. There was general sorrow. Not only had the world lost a talented composer, but also a gentle, good-natured man of whom it was said he never had the least trace of jealousy or viciousness. At his best, he was a composer of grace, and his comic operas have the kind of melodic invention, gusto, and brio that only Rossini has brought to music.

Vincenzo Bellini (November 3, 1801–September 23, 1835) composed an opera semiseria, *La Sonnambula* (1831), a tremendous favorite in its day and still in the repertoire. It has its moments of charm, but the works more representative of Bellini are *Norma* (1831) and *I Puritani* (1835). These are full of the arias that are the essence of Bellini—the long, arched, slow melody over an arpeggiated bass. Bellini was obsessed by melody. Once, playing through Pergolesi's *Stabat Mater,* he told a friend: "If I could write one melody as beautiful as this, I would not mind dying young, like Pergolesi." Even Wagner, who detested most Italian music, responded to *Norma.* He said of Bellini's operas that they were "all heart, connected with words." Rossini and Donizetti had also written long, slow melodies, but without Bellini's peculiar intensity. Rossini's melodies, for instance, are classically oriented, while Bellini's are romantic, and it was with good reason that Bellini and Chopin were close friends. They had something musically in common, and a Chopin nocturne has a type of melody and bass that comes very close to the Bellinian kind of melody. (They had other things in common. Both were slim, slight, aristocratic-looking men. Both had the fashionable romantic disease, tuberculosis, and both died young.) Even in the early Bellini operas, such as *Il Pirata* of 1827 and *La Straniera* of 1829, a new, long-breathed, somewhat sentimental voice was heard. Verdi was to exclaim over Bellini's "long, long melodies, such as no one before has written."

His music attracted the great singers more than the music even of Rossini. They responded to the romanticism implicit in the Bellini arias. And he had some remarkable voices with which to work, notably the heroic tribe of mezzo-sopranos active in the first half of the nineteenth century. It was for them that Rossini, Donizetti, and Bellini wrote many of the roles now sung by sopranos (the role of Rosina in *Il Barbiere,* for instance, was created for low voice). But those bel canto mezzos were protean. They could sing the lightest coloratura role one night and at their next performance sing Norma or the heaviest Meyerbeer role. Maria Malibran, who died in 1836 at the age of twenty-eight after a fall from a horse, was confidently thought by her contemporaries to have been the greatest singer who ever lived. She was a mezzo-soprano who could go down to a low F and up to an easy high C. The same was true of Marietta Alboni and Giulia Grisi. The high sopranos, such as Giuditta Pasta and Henriette Sontag, could reach an F or G. Then there were tenors like Mario (he was known by this name alone), baritones like Antonio Tamburini, and basses like Luigi Lablache, who has come down in history as the greatest of his tribe. Luigi Lablache: he with the voice of thunder and yet the flexibility of "a coiled snake." Bellini wrote for those singers. Probably what was the greatest vocal quartet of all time—Grisi, Rubini, Tamburini, and Lablache—would appear all together in his operas. The great Jenny Lind also achieved her first fame as a Bellini exponent, as did Adelina Patti.

Not necessarily the best, but surely the most electrifying of all Bellini singers, was Giovanni Battista Rubini, the tenor who also had been identified with some of the Rossini and Donizetti operas. "Rubini and Bellini were born for each other," said the *Musical World*. Rubini was especially famous for his interpolated F above high C in *I Puritani*. He sang it falsetto. Léon Escudier, the French critic, once heard Rubini, in Donizetti's *Roberto Devereux*, "leap even to G. He himself has never ascended so high, and he himself, after that *tour de force*, appeared astonished at the feat." He was not a good actor, but nobody went to any of his performances expecting to be thrilled by his acting. They went to be thrilled by his singing. *La Revue des Deux Mondes*, in the obituary notice of Rubini (who died in 1854), gives an idea of his powers:

> The astonished ear followed the singer, in his triumphal ascent, to the highest limits of the tenor register without noticing any interruption of continuity in this long spiral of notes. . . . To this almost incredible power of passing without a break from chest to head register, Rubini added another no less important—namely, a breath control, the force of which he had learned to economize. Gifted with a broad chest, where his lungs could dilate with ease, he took a high note, filled it successively with light and warmth, and when it was completely expanded, threw it forward into the house, where it burst like a Bengal rocket in a thousand colors.

The writer goes on to rhapsodize over Rubini's "prodigiously flexible" coloratura technique—scales, arpeggios, trills taken on the highest notes, grupetti, appogiaturas. Small wonder that the Bellini operas are unable to make their full effect in the twentieth century. The breed of singers for whom they were composed is extinct.

Bellini spent some years in Paris, where he was one of the most romantic figures in a city of romantic figures. Slight, delicate, handsome, languishing, talented, he attracted worshipers, mostly of the opposite sex. Heinrich Heine, sharp and cynical as always, saw Bellini as

> . . . a tall, up-shooting, slender figure who always moved gracefully; he was coquettish, ever looking as though just removed from a bandbox; a regular but large, delicately rose-tinted face; light, almost golden hair worn in many curls; a high, very high, marble forehead, straight nose, light blue eyes, good-sized mouth and rounded chin. His features had something vague in them, a want of character, something milk-like; and in this milk-like face flitted sometimes a painful-pleasing expression of sorrow. This expression in his face took the place of the fire that was lacking; but it was that of a sorrow without depth. It glanced, but unpoetically, from his eyes. It played, but without passion, upon his lips. It was this poutless, shallow sorrow that the young maestro seemed most anxious to represent in his whole appearance. His hair was dressed so fancifully, his clothes fitted so languishingly around his delicate body, he carried his cane so idyll-like, that he reminded me of the young shepherds we find in our pastorals with their crooks decorated with ribbons. . . . The whole man looked like a sigh, in pumps and silk stockings. He has met with much sympathy from women but I doubt if he ever produced strong passion in any one. . . .

Norma is conceded to be his greatest work, though *I Puritani* has more brilliance (including the high D's for Rubini). A poised, infinitely long melody like the *Casta Diva* from *Norma*, building from measure to measure, perfectly proportioned, chaste yet full of passion, makes an unforgettable impact when well sung. Norma is not an easy role. It calls for a dramatic soprano of unusual flexibility. Later in the century the German soprano, Lilli Lehmann, was to say that she would rather sing three Brünnhildes in a row than one Norma. *Norma* is the only Bellini opera steadily in the international repertory. To many it is the very essence of the bel canto tradition.

✥ 15 ✥

Spectacle, Spectacle, and More Spectacle

MEYERBEER, CHERUBINI, AUBER

While the Germans were concentrating on sonata form and absolute music, the French were providing a form of music that the public and the aristocracy from Lisbon to St. Petersburg found titillating and agreeable enough to keep in the active repertory throughout the nineteenth century and even a little beyond. The French grand opera of Meyerbeer and his contemporaries, which succeeded the bel canto operas of Rossini and Bellini, swept the world. Wagner may have had his theories, his great orchestra and his leitmotifs, his daring harmonies and far-reaching vision, but the French knew how to satisfy the palate. This was music to enjoy! Meyerbeer, Auber, Halévy, Hérold—these were composers who could give you melody and singing! And the Opéra in Paris could supply the spectacle.

The Académie Royale de Musique had been founded in 1671 as an institution for serious lyric drama. By the turn of the eighteenth century it had developed into an outlet for opera. Some important composers were active there (and elsewhere in Paris theaters), and many of the operas they produced were markedly preromantic, and much more anticipatory of romanticism than the instrumental music of the time. As early as Jean Jacques Rousseau's *Le Devin du village* (1752) a feeling towards nature was expressed. André Grétry's *Zémire et Azor* (1771), *La Caravane du Caire* (1783), and *Richard Coeur de Lion* (1784), went in for the kind of medievalism and interest in exotic subjects so beloved by the romantics. The operas of Nicolas Dalayrac, especially *Les deux petits Savoyards* (1788) and *Adolphe et Clara* (1799), were popular. Luigi Cherubini, in his *Lodoiska* (1791), *Médée* (1797), and *Les deux journées* (1800), anticipated spectacle opera, with great fires and other natural phenomena simulated on stage. These three Cherubini operas were first presented at the Théâtre Feydeau and later were done at the Opéra. At the Théâtre Favart, François Boieldieu was setting to music such exotic librettos as *Zoraïne et Zulnar* (1798) and *Le Calife de Bagdad* (1800). No comparable operatic school existed anywhere else in the world at the time. German opera was isolated, and only a few works —Mozart's *Die Zauberflöte* and *Don Giovanni*, Weber's *Der Freischütz*, and, later, Nicolai's *Die Lustigen Weiber von Windsor* (1849) attracted much international attention. The operas of Heinrich Marschner, Ludwig Spohr, and Albert Lortzing, popular in Germany, were local phenomena, whereas French opera and light opera captivated all of Europe.

During the 1830's, with Meyerbeer riding high, the Opéra was big business. It was a bourgeois affair. In 1831 the businessmen who had come in with the Citizen King turned the Opéra over to a director-entrepreneur "who should manage it for six years at his own risk and fortune." In effect, it was his house. He could pocket the gains, bear the losses, select repertory and casts. With all that, he enjoyed a subsidy from the State—710,000 francs in the 1830's. The director ran the Opéra as a business enterprise. He supplied a commodity in hope of a profit. Naturally he too was bourgeois, with bourgeois tastes. Louis Véron, the first of the great directors of the Opéra, actually entitled his autobiography *Mémoires d'un bourgeois de Paris*. In that, he reflected the complacency of the real ruling class—the bankers, industrialists, and *bourgeoisie* who ran Paris and the country. The King himself prided himself on being bourgeois, and to many the reign of Louis-Philippe was intolerably dull. "*La France s'ennuie,*" complained Lamartine.

Véron, born in 1798, was trained as a physician and actually practiced medicine. Then he went into journalism and founded the *Revue de Paris*. Shrewd, publicity-conscious, knowing what the people wanted, he also knew what was expected of him. This fat man lived in extreme elegance, dressed like a fop, wore expensive clothing and jewels, went in heavily for advertising, and paid off the critics with a lavish hand. Appointed director of the Opéra in 1831, he straightened out the administration and brought in his own people. He also had some new ideas about repertory, and for the four years he was there, Véron made the Paris Opéra the most prestigious house in Europe. In those days the Opéra was in the Rue Le Peletier. The building had been erected in 1821, and the auditorium seated 1,954.

Composers such as Meyerbeer, Auber, and Halévy supplied the music for many of the operas in Véron's administration. Eugène Scribe was the official librettist. As chief conductor there was François Habeneck, the Beethoven specialist who also was conductor of the Conservatoire concerts. The dancers were headed by the great Marie Taglioni, later to be joined by the equally great Fanny Elssler. Edmond Duponchel and Pierre Cicéri were the stage directors. Among the singers were such stars as Adolphe Nourrit, Louis Duprez, and Cornélie Falcon. There was strong vocal competition from the Théâtre des Italiens, which specialized in Italian opera and had such giants as Malibran and Sontag. But not even they attracted as much attention as Duprez, one of the first great dramatic tenors. He sang high notes from the chest instead of in falsetto; and, says a contemporary report, when "he brought out the high C in the chest voice with all the might of his colossal organ, it was all over with the fame of all his predecessors. Nourrit, till then the favorite of the Parisians, a distinguished tenor, recognized his rival's power. His day was over, and in despair over his lost and irrecoverable glory, he flung himself from an upper window down upon the pavement, and so made an end to his life."

Heading the *corps de claque* was an imposing man known to the world simply as Auguste. His full name was Auguste Levasseur. Of Auguste it was written: "He lived—indeed, he could only live—at the Opéra. . . . Large, robust, a veritable Hercules in size, gifted with an extraordinary pair of hands, he was created and put into the world to be a claqueur." No singer, no composer, not Véron himself, felt safe unless Auguste was directing the applause, creating a success on the spot. The claque remained an institution in Paris throughout the century, and the position of *chef de claque* was eagerly sought after. It was a profitable job. The *chef de claque* could make money by being engaged by singers and composers, and he could also sell the forty free seats he received gratis for each performance. By 1860 the *chef de claque* was no longer paid by the Opéra; instead, he was paying the manager for the job. Not only the opera but every theater had its *chef de claque*. Each made a café his headquarters. As the *Musical World* in London explained the operation, the *chef de claque* would put in an appearance towards 5 or 6 o'clock, "and is mobbed by the forty or fifty people anxious to be enrolled for the evening. As a rule, the first thing the *chef de claque* looks at is the dress of his candidates. He accepts no blouses and no slovens. If he sees a man well arrayed, hearty looking and florid of countenance, endowed with broad shoulders and big hands, he enlists him at once." The *Musical World* went on to say that it would be folly for a new singer to appear without engaging the *chef de claque*. "So long as the French mind evinces a sly relish for furtive hisses and takes overt pleasure in dramatic rows, so long will the *chef de claque* be at his post, crying in a stage whisper to his honorable troops, '*Allons, mes enfants, tous ensemble; chaudement, et à bas la cabale.*'"

Just as the singers felt they needed Auguste, so many composers of French opera would have felt naked without a Scribe libretto. Eugène Scribe (1791–1861) took a law degree in 1815, but never practiced. He was too busy writing successful plays and becoming rich and famous. As early as 1811 he was on the boards, and between 1820 and 1830 about a hundred of his plays were given. During his life he turned out an incredible amount of material, and his complete works fill seventy-six volumes. He had been engaged as librettist for the Opéra in 1828, before Véron's appointment, and he supplied the librettos for some of the most sensational successes of the period.

Scribe's material was largely original and did not follow classical models. He had little to do with the mythology and the classic subjects of lyric tragedy so dear to the heart of the Académie. He echoed the new, popular romantic taste. He wrote about the supernatural, he could supply Gothic romances, and he dealt also with medieval legends. He delighted above all in historical melodrama. Among the famous librettos he wrote were *Robert le Diable, Le Prophète, Les Huguenots,* and *L'Africaine* (Meyerbeer); *La Juive* (Halévy); *La Dame Blanche* (Boieldieu); *Le Comte Ory* (Rossini); *I Vespri Siciliani* (Verdi); *Ali Baba* (Cherubini); *La Favorite* (Donizetti); and *Fra Diavolo* (Auber). Scribe wrote thirty-eight librettos for Auber alone. In addition, many librettos, such as Verdi's *Un Ballo in Maschera,* were fashioned from Scribe plays.

Today his writing is faded, but contemporary audiences saw social significance in his plays and librettos about oppressed peoples and minority groups. Working closely with his composers, Scribe developed a formula. Generally, as in Italian opera, his librettos opened with a chorus. Arias and ensembles were carefully allotted. Everything was calculated to lead to some kind of superspectacle, such as the great ballroom scene in Auber's *Gustav III* or the festival scene in Halévy's *La Juive.* In 1835 the *Courier Français* wrote of *La Juive* as the eighth wonder of the world. "The costumes of the warriors, civilians, and ecclesiastics are not imitated but reproduced in their smallest details. The armor is no longer pasteboard; it is made of real metal. One sees men of iron, men of silver, men of gold! The Emperor Sigismond, for instance, is a glittering ingot from head to foot. The horses, not less historically outfitted than their riders, turn and prance."

That was grand opera. That was Scribe. That was Véron.

Scribe's first libretto was written for Auber in 1828. The opera, *La Muette de Portici* (also called *Masaniello*), was a turning point in the history of the lyric stage. It was grand opera, more elaborate by far than anything hitherto produced. Among its technical features were a cyclorama and mobile panoramas. *La Muette* also had a fine, tuneful, richly instrumented score, one that held the stage throughout the century. The next great hit after the Auber was Rossini's *William Tell,* in 1829. This too was a tremendous stage spectacle, and many listeners thought it contained Rossini's best music. Véron, when he took over the Opéra, wanted to duplicate those two smash hits, and he came up with Meyerbeer's *Robert le Diable* in 1831. It was a romantic opera in that it had to do with medieval knights and the Devil. The costumes outdid even those in *La Muette de Portici;* and for the first time, gas

202

illumination was used on a French stage. *Robert le Diable* was a success that eclipsed anything ever seen in Paris up to that time. So popular was it, and the following Meyerbeer operas, that they all but wiped out the Rossini craze in Europe. Up to then Rossini had been *the* opera composer; but, *William Tell* excepted, how could Rossini's slender, thinly scored music stand up against the cannonades of the heroic Meyerbeer orchestra? It couldn't. Having seen *Robert le Diable*, the public demanded that all other new operas come up to its level as a spectacle.

Meyerbeer, who achieved such fame in Paris, was born in Berlin on September 5, 1791. His real name was Jakob Liebmann Beer. Like Mendelssohn, he came from a rich Jewish banking family. Like Mendelssohn, too, he was a prodigy and one of the most talented pianists in Europe. But unlike Mendelssohn he had a flair for the theater and was only happy composing operas. He went to Italy, where he came under the influence of Rossini, and in 1824 composed a successful opera named *Il Crociato in Egitto*. Then he went to Paris, where the important men were Auber, Méhul, Cherubini, and Spontini. Gasparo Spontini (1774–1851) was a sort of pre-Meyerbeer composer whose two most famous operas, *La Vestale* and *Fernand Cortez*, had been produced at the Opéra in 1807 and 1809 respectively. Berlioz always thought *La Vestale* to be the greatest opera since Gluck. Every once in a while it enjoys a revival, even today. It is an early specimen of grand opera. Musically it is noble and static, very Gluck-like in its diatonic harmonies and lack of modulation.

On Meyerbeer's first visit to Paris, in 1826, opera was in the doldrums. The opera house was the plaything of the aristocracy. Productions were shabby, performances listless, and the previously popular operas by François Philidor, Pierre Monsigny, and André Grétry seldom played. So miserable was the Opéra that François Castil-Blaze in 1824 used the Odéon Theater to stage operas by Mozart, Weber, and Rossini. His intentions were good, but he tampered so heavily with the scores, even inserting his own or some other new music, that the results were monstrous distortions. Rossini in 1826 was called in by the Opéra as a consultant, and he supervised productions of his own *Le Siège de Corinthe, Moïse,* and *Le Comte Ory*. But even he could not overcome the inertia and bureaucracy. It was Véron who had the flair and administrative ability to revitalize the Opéra and bring new works into its repertoire. When Meyerbeer returned to Paris in 1830, he had almost a clear field. All he had to do was compose something on the order of *Muette* or *Tell*. It is to the credit of Véron's imagination that he was willing to take a chance on this little-known composer.

Meyerbeer was not a fast worker. *Robert le Diable* of 1831 was followed by *Les Huguenots* in 1836, *Le Prophète* in 1849, *L'Etoile du Nord* in 1854 (this one at the Opéra-Comique), *Dinorah* in 1859, and the posthumously produced *L'Africaine* in 1865. There was no reason for Meyerbeer to be in a rush. Every one of his operas took Europe by storm, and never had a composer achieved such incredible popularity, not even Rossini. *Robert le Diable* in its first eight years was performed in 1,843 European theaters. "We could fill a library," a British magazine writer said, "with the pieces arranged by a thousand composers from the airs of this opera. . . . Everywhere, at the theater, in the tavern, at military parades, in the churches, at concerts, in the cottage and in the palace, was and is to be heard the delicious music of *Robert*.. . . In London it has been played in four theaters at the same time." Not until the great Verdi successes in the early 1850's was there a composer of operas who could compete with Meyerbeer.

Meyerbeer knew what the public wanted, and he put his operas together determined to satisfy them. There had to be spectacle. There had to be brilliant vocal parts, but the arias were not to last very long. Nobody should be bored. To bore the public was the worst sin. Leave characterization and developments to the Germans. Leave bel canto to the Italians. The orchestration had to be glittering and powerful, with massed superfortissimos. There had to be imposing choruses. There had to be a ballet. Scribe was most accommodating, and gave Meyerbeer exactly what he wanted. The *Journal pour Rire* presented an imaginary dialogue between Meyerbeer and his librettist:

M. MEYERBEER: I should like a libretto for a comic opera having for its subject the amours of Czar Peter the Great and the vivandière [canteen manager] Catherine.

M. SCRIBE: . . . First let us find our three acts. Nothing easier. In the first, Peter the Great, simple ship carpenter, loves Catherine, simple vivandière; in the second, Peter the Great, in the tumult of camps, continues to love Catherine; in the third, Peter the Great, in the bosom of grandeur, always loving Catherine, decides to marry her. Let us occupy ourselves, if you please, with the first act. It is the only important one. Good or bad, the public is obliged to see the other two. We say then that Peter the Great, simple carpenter, loves Catherine, simple vivandière. Here we have the motive for: (1) a chorus of carpenters at the rising of the curtain; (2) a grand aria for Peter's declaration to Catherine; (3) a finale of carpenters. . . .

M. MEYERBEER: I should like to introduce in the first chorus a chanson or ballade like that in *La Dame Blanche*.

M. SCRIBE: Nothing easier. We will bring in some chocolate or cake merchant, who shall offer his refreshments and gay refrains. And then?

M. MEYERBEER: I should also like a wedding like that in the first act of *Macon*.

M. SCRIBE: Nothing easier. We'll celebrate the wedding of one of Peter's companions.

M. MEYERBEER: With an arietta for soprano.

M. SCRIBE: Expressive of the bride's beating heart: tic, tac, tic, tac.

M. MEYERBEER: And a drinking song for the basses.

M. SCRIBE: Chorus of drinking guests: glu, glu, glu, glu. It's done. And then?

M. MEYERBEER: We must find some variation, some military song, like that of Max in *Le Chalet*.

M. SCRIBE: Nothing easier. A troop of recruiters, beating the drum, shall break into the wedding. . . .

M. MEYERBEER: And do you think that will suffice for the intelligence of the public?

M. SCRIBE: Oh, mon Dieu! For the public, the important thing is not to comprehend but to be amused. Besides, if a comic opera contained common sense, it would not be a comic opera.

M. MEYERBEER: And how much time will you require to put all that into verse?

M. SCRIBE: Only a few hours. . . .

The better musicians of the day realized that the Meyerbeer operas were nothing more than skillful collages. Mendelssohn sneered. Yes, he said, the Meyerbeer operas are full of great effects. But of what did they consist? "Melodies for whistling, harmony for the educated, instrumentation for the Germans, contra dances for the French, something for everybody—but there's no heart in it." Something for everybody: Mendelssohn put his finger directly on it. Some doubted if the Meyerbeer operas were even music. The composer-pianist Ferdinand Hiller was asked what he thought of the Meyerbeer operas. "Oh," Hiller said, "let us not talk politics." Others took a stronger view. George Sand said of *Les Huguenots* that she did not care to go to the opera to see Catholics and Protestants cut each other's throats to music set by a Jew. She also said that there was more music in Chopin's tiny C minor Prélude than in the four hours of the trumpetings in *Les Huguenots*. (Claude Debussy, many years later, got off a gibe close to Sand's. He wrote of *Les Huguenots*: "The music is so strained that even the anxiety to massacre unfortunate Protestants does not altogether excuse it.") Berlioz, who never completely made up his mind about the Meyerbeer operas, described them testily (but with a certain amount of respect and even envy) as consisting of

high C's from every type of chest, bass drums, snare drums, organs, military bands, antique trumpets, tubas as big as locomotive smokestacks, bells, cannon, horses, cardinals under a canopy, emperors, queens in tiaras, funerals, fêtes, weddings . . . jugglers, skaters, choirboys, censers, monstrances, crosses, taverns, processions, orgies of priests and naked women, the bull Apis and masses of oxen, screech-owls, bats, the five hundred fiends of hell and what have you—the rocking of the heavens and the end of the world interspersed with a few dull cavatinas and a large claque thrown in.

To the pure Robert Schumann, Meyerbeer was the archfiend of composers, the perverter of taste. When Schumann first became acquainted with *Les Huguenots* he brought up his heaviest artillery: "I am no moralist, but it enrages a good Protestant to hear his dearest chorale shrilled out on the boards, to see the bloodiest drama in the whole history of his religion degraded to the level of an annual fair farce . . ." Schumann concluded that *Les Huguenots* exemplified "commonness, distortion, unnaturalness, immorality and unmusicality." The Germans were not the only opponents of the Meyerbeer operas. Almost to a man the lovers of bel canto accused Meyerbeer of ruining the art of singing. "Meyerbeer," said one critic, "has on his conscience all this screaming and unlovely exaggeration of the effects of song, all ths feverish excitement of the nerves in over-refined decla mation. . . To the consequences of his operas must it be ascribed that our singers no longer sing but scream."

But criticism was to the Meyerbeer operas what the sting of a hornet is to an armored car. For most of the century, even through Wagner's day, Meyerbeer was one of the two most popular operatic composers. Verdi was the other.

Naturally Meyerbeer became rich and famous, moving with great dignity between Berlin (where he was head of the opera) and Paris, with frequent trips to London to supervise productions there. He had more decorations, more orders from nobility, than any man not of royal blood. For one of his influence and wealth, he had surprisingly few personal enemies, though of course many musicians attacked the art he represented. Heine called Meyerbeer "the man of his age," and Heine as usual was correct. Meyerbeer's music, as Heine pointed out, was more social than individual. "Rossini would never have acquired his great popularity during the revolution and empire. Robespierre would have accused him perhaps of being anti-patriotic. . . Men in the old time had convictions; we moderns have only opinions." Meyerbeer had a notoriously thin skin, and with some glee Heine relates how Meyerbeer would try to mold critical opinion: "As the Apostle thinks neither of toils nor sufferings to save a single lost soul, so Meyerbeer, when he learns anybody rejects his music, will expound it to him indefatigably until he has converted him; and then the single saved lamb, were it only the most insignificant soul of a feuilletonist, is to him more dear than the whole flock of believers who have always worshipped him with orthodox fidelity." The careful Meyerbeer, anxious to keep the press on his side, always would invite the critics, before every one of his premieres, to a splendid dinner at the Hotel des Princes or the Trois Frères Provençaux. No critic is on record as ever having turned down the invitation. They staggered away from those meals with grand feelings of fellowship. "How can a chap of decent feeling," Spiridion in the *Evening Gazette* wanted to know, "write harshly of a man who has been pouring the choicest vintages of France and the most delicate tidbits of sea, air, forest, orchard and garden down one's throat? Try it. You will find the thing impossible. . . . There were few music critics in Paris who were not in receipt of annual pensions of several hundred dollars, and in one or two instances they exceeded $1,000 annually. There were critics here who had been in receipt of large pensions from Meyerbeer since 1831. Meyerbeer did not content himself with giving them pensions and good dinners. He also made it a point of duty to give them costly presents on their birthdays and on New Year's Day. Meyerbeer used to defend this by saying that he did not put these gentlemen under obligations. He was the person obliged, and he could not see anything wrong in giving evidence of his gratitude to them." (The critic who above all carried extortion to a fine art was P. A. Fiorentino, who wrote for *Le Moniteur, La France*, and *L'Entr'acte*, among others. Again quoting Spiridion: "He left an estate of over $300,000, although he lived expensively. . . . He levied blackmail with a ferocity unknown even in this capital of blackmail. . . . The managers of the Italian, Lyric and Opéra-Comique paid him considerable sums annually, and as for the costly presents he received there was no end of them. Meyerbeer always paid him a large pension with government punctuality." Fiorentino died in 1864.)

Today, on the rare occasions we hear a Meyerbeer opera, it is difficult to see what all of the excitement was about. Meyerbeer's admirers to the contrary notwithstanding, the music is extremely conventional, all the more so in that there are no heroic singers around who can trumpet forth the music as Caruso, the de Reszkes, Schumann-Heink, and Nordica used to do at the turn of the century. The music sounds synthetic, flabby, and overcalculated, and the melodic ideas are second-rate. Even the once-brilliant orchestration and the once-daring harmonies sound pallid because they are used for so cynical a purpose. The Meyerbeer operas are period pieces. But in their day, great musicians and critics took them very seriously. Bizet all but equated Meyerbeer with Beethoven and Mozart, and called him "a thundering dramatic genius." Heine wrote that the mother of Meyerbeer was the second woman in history to see her son accepted as divine. All over Europe, composers rushed to imitate the Meyerbeer formula. Wagner did, in *Rienzi*, and Verdi as late as *Aïda* in 1871. Gounod and Massenet also were influenced by the Meyerbeer operas.

But Meyerbeer was a dead end. Nobody could seem to imitate him with much success, try as they did. Nobody could follow him, and he had a monopoly on spectacle opera. As Berlioz ruefully said—Berlioz, whose *Troyens* never had any success—"Meyerbeer's influence and the pressure exerted on managers, artists, critics and the public as well by his immense fortune, at the very least as great as that exercised by his genuine eclectic talent, makes any serious success at the Opéra almost impossible." Berlioz also said that Meyerbeer not only had the luck to be talented, but also the talent to be lucky. And Berlioz burst out in genuine admiration over *Les Huguenots*. He was so moved by "this masterpiece" that he longed to be a great man "in order to place one's glory and one's genius at the feet of Meyerbeer."

Wagner, too, soon decided that Meyerbeerian opera was not his line. "It is impossible to surpass him." Wagner hated Meyerbeer—a competitor, a wealthy and successful competitor, and worst of all a wealthy, successful, and *Jewish* competitor. Meyerbeer seems to have been a rather retiring man, interested in the work of young composers, and generous with his money (he helped Wagner among others), but Wagner made him an object of derision. Meyerbeer, he wrote, was "like the starling who follows the plowshare down the field and merrily picks up the earthworm just uncovered in the furrow." Or, "Meyerbeer . . . wanted a monstrous, piebald, historico-romantic, diabolico-religious, fanatico-libidinous, sacro-frivolous, mysterio-criminal, autyloco-sentimental dramatic hodgepodge, therein to find material for a curious chimeric music—a want which, owing to the indominatable buckram of his musical temperament, could not be quite suitably applied." And on, and on, page after turgid page. Wagner's prose was much worse than Meyerbeer's music. It so happens that Wagner was largely correct in his opinions, but his writings about Meyerbeer drip such venom that they are uncomfortable to read. Yet Wagner used many of Meyerbeer's devices as building blocks for his own music. In a curious way Meyerbeer, who died on May 2, 1854, was one of the seminal forces of nineteenth-century operatic music.

Luigi Cherubini (1760–1842) is as little played today as Meyerbeer, though in his day he was considered by many, including Beethoven, to be not merely one of the masters but one of the immortals. The only one of his thirty operas holding the edge of the twentiety-century repertory, however, is *Médée*. And every once in a great while his *Anacreon* Overture turns up on a symphony program.

In the Louvre hangs a portrait of Cherubini painted by Ingres in 1842. Ingres, his good friend, shows him seated deep in thought, accompanied by his constant companion, the Muse of Music. She is giving him her benediction. He accepts it as a matter of course, like accepting dinner from his cook. Ingres has painted the face of a strong man—Roman nose (Cherubini was Italian-born and settled permanently in Paris in 1788), firm thin lips, cold eyes: a face of character, determination, and power.

But others saw him differently. He had a reputation for intolerance, for a temper and a cutting tongue, and he could be cruel. Adolphe Adam, later an important composer, was presented to the great Cherubini as a young boy. Cherubini's only remark was: "My! What an ugly child!" Berlioz, who considered Cherubini his complete enemy, tells about his run-in with the *directeur du Conservatoire*. Cherubini had been appointed the head of that institution in 1822. He was a martinet, and his rules extended even to such piddling details as having separate entrances for men and women. When Berlioz once entered the Conservatory through the wrong door, the porter told Cherubini, who burst into the library and confronted Berlioz "looking more wicked, cadaverous and dishevelled even than usual." The two got into an argument, and Cherubini chased Berlioz around the tables. At least, that is the way Berlioz tells the story. The two men could never hit it off, and Berlioz writes, with satisfaction, that if Cherubini chastized him with whips, "I certainly returned the compliment with scorpions."

If ever there was a textbook teacher and composer, it was Cherubini. That was his trouble. Everything in his music is unutterably, definitively, pulverizingly correct. Chordal progressions move exactly as the books say they should move. A glance at any one of his scores—the operas, the D minor Requiem, the chamber music—shows severe and correct melodies over a very conservative harmonic framework. When he modulates it is to a safe, closely related key. His most daring harmony is the diminished seventh chord, and that already was threadbare in his own day. As a result, his "white-key" music seldom moves. It is this harmonic timidity that afflicts even his most famous work, *Médée*. To attempt to explain his lack of vitality by saying that Cherubini was a classicist will not do. Mozart, just as much a classicist, achieved in *Don Giovanni* what Cherubini could not begin to envision in *Médée*. Basically Cherubini (and also his contemporary, Spontini) merely followed Gluck. After four or five hearings, *Médée* becomes more and more a Gluckian façade, a set of frozen attitudes in which the figures are permanently congealed.

Cherubini's mind was too rigid, and at basis too commonplace, ever to allow him to depart from the rules. What Beethoven, of all people, saw in him is hard to conceive. Probably it was technique. Beethoven, a consummate technician himself, respected technique in others. And in the one area where Beethoven was relatively weak—the human voice and opera (imagine Cherubini writing such an impossible-to-sing chorus as the *Et vitam venturi* from the *Missa Solemnis!*)—Cherubini moved with technical surety and, even, brilliance. Beethoven was far too good a musician not to respond with admiration. He and his contemporaries had no doubt about Cherubini's sublimity. The Director of the Conservatory was considered on a par with the other great composers of the day—Ignaz Moscheles, Ludwig Spohr, Johann Nepomuk Hummel, and Friedrich Kalkbrenner. All were destined for immortality.

The composers of the 1830's and 1840's who were able to write operas that held the stage even against the competition of Meyerbeer include, in addition to Auber, Ferdinand Hérold, with *Zampa* (1831; the overture is still played), and Fromental Halévy, with *La Juive* (1835). Halévy was a one-opera man who turned out work after work without ever coming near his great success. But that one success made him world-famous. For that one opera he was so venerated that his face was in every print-shop window and every photographer's showcase. At Halévy's death the Baron de Rothschild settled upon the widow of the composer of *La Juive* an annuity; and, reported Spiridion in the *Gazette*, "M. Rodriques, a wealthy stockbroker, sent her 8000 francs for the dowry of her two daughters, which sum, he said, was raised by several friends as a tribute of admiration and respect for her husband's memory. . . A few days ago the Emperor sent a bill to the Council of State conferring upon her an annuity." *La Juive* remained extremely popular through the century and up to the death of Enrico Caruso in 1921. Bizet married Halévy's daughter; and Ludovic Halévy, a nephew, was one of the *Carmen* librettists.

At the Opéra-Comique, a house with a history that goes back to 1715, there was equal activity. During the 1830's and 40's, the repertoire of the Opéra-Comique was light in nature and the operas had spoken dialogue. (Spoken dialogue was the one requisite of a work for the Opéra-Comique.) Later in the century the line became obscured, and at the Comique there were operas, such as *Carmen* in 1875, that actually were tragedies. Even spoken dialogue was sometimes dropped. The better composers of the Opéra-Comique turned out a witty, skillful, civilized product. Works like Adam's *Le Postillon de Longjumeau* (1836), Boieldieu's *La Dame Blanche* (1825), Auber's *Fra Diavolo* (1830) and *Domino Noir* (1837) were played everywhere, and some of them still are.

Daniel François Auber (1782–1871) was the dominating force of his time at the Opéra-Comique. His first work there came out in 1805 and his last, forty-four operas later, in 1869. What with turning out this large number of works and in addition active as the head of the Conservatory, he was a busy man. After his death a critic had some recollections:

Auber was always composing. You met him sauntering down the boulevards: he was working. At the theater you had a stall next to his, and in which he was soon asleep: he was working. You pass along the Rue St. Georges after midnight. The street looked black on all sides except for a window through which the light of a modest lamp percolated: he was working. You knocked at his door at 6 A.M. A concierge as decrepit as the fairy Urgéle directed you to the first floor. A housekeeper old as Baucis referred you to a valet as old as Philemon. The valet showed you into a hospitable drawing room where the sounds of the piano already reached you: he was working.

At the age of eighty-seven he was still turning out stage works. He died rich and showered with honors, and not from overwork. He contributed to the lyric stage a handful of charming light operas. In the long run, the grace and sophistication of music like Auber's and Adam's have proved more durable than Meyerbeer's spectacles and big orchestral sounds; more durable, indeed, than anything produced at the Opéra or other grand opera stages in Paris until *Faust* came along in 1859, though nobody at the time would have thought so; or, having thought so, would have had the nerve to say it aloud.

16

Colossus of Italy

GIUSEPPE VERDI

As opera composers go, Giuseppe Verdi made his success early in life. He was born on October 10, 1813, in Le Roncole (almost five months after the birth of Richard Wagner in Leipzig). His first opera, *Oberto*, was well received in Milan in 1839, and his third, *Nabucco*, made him famous in 1842. Thirteen years after that, with *Rigoletto, Il Trovatore,* and *La Traviata* on the boards, he was the most popular composer of operas in the world, edging out even the fabulously successful spectacle operas of Meyerbeer. Verdi was a specialist who gave the public a commodity, and he never pretended to be a learned musician. Even when he was at the height of his fame he claimed that he was a pragmatist. In a letter of 1869 he said that "There is hardly any music in my house. I have never gone to a music library, never to a publisher to examine a piece. I keep abreast of some of the better contemporary works not by studying them but through hearing them occasionally at the theater. . . . I repeat, therefore, that I am the least erudite among past and present composers." This was true; it was not a *façon de parler.* Nor did Verdi speak much about his own work, except to those directly concerned—his publisher, conductors, singers. He wanted his music to do the talking, and he almost indignantly turned down a request for an autobiography. "Never, never will I consent to write my memoirs!"

Certain it is that as a child he gave no indication that he would develop into the musical colossus in the Italy of his time. He did display talent, but not a spectacular talent on the order of a Mozart or a Mendelssohn. In his town of Le Roncole, near Busseto in the duchy of Parma, he had studied with the village organist. His father, an innkeeper and grocer, was pleased with his son's talent and managed to purchase a used spinet for him. When Giuseppe was ten, his father sent him to live with a cobbler friend in Busseto. There he was noticed by Antonio Barezzi, a rich local merchant and a generous man. Barezzi took him into his own house as an apprentice, and also saw to it that the boy received the best musical training Busseto had to offer. It was not much. Verdi worked with the local organist, who also was the conductor of the local orchestra, and soon was deputizing for him. Then Barezzi saw to it that Verdi was sent to Milan, to study at the conservatory. At the age of eighteen the young musician arrived in that city—a short, intense, taciturn person, with brown hair, black eyebrows and beard, a very pale complexion, and a pock-marked face.

Whatever hopes he may have had were immediately dashed. The kind of training he had received in Busseto was not enough to get him into the conservatory. His piano playing was weak, his knowledge of theory insufficient. For two years he remained in Milan, studying privately. He even started work on an opera, *Oberto*. In 1834 he returned to Busseto, and two years later married Barezzi's daughter, Margherita. He finished *Oberto* and it was brought to the attention of Bartolomeo Merelli, the impresario of La Scala. Merelli took a chance on the opera by an unknown composer, and was rewarded when *Oberto* was well received. In a farsighted move, Merelli offered Verdi a contract to compose three operas at eight-month intervals. *Un Giorno di Regno* was the first commission. It was a comic opera, and Verdi had to turn it out during a period in which he lost both of his children and then his wife. Small wonder that *Un Giorno di Regno* failed. The failure not only left a mark on Verdi; it almost stopped his career for good. He seriously thought of giving up composition. It is clear that he had completely lost faith in himself. A dour man, he hid his disappointment about the *Giorno di Regno* disaster, but for years it rankled, and it also helped establish his own inner relations with the public. "It may be," he wrote, "that it is a bad opera, though many no better are tolerated and even applauded. Had the public not applauded, but merely endured my opera in silence, I should have had no words enough to thank them!   I do not mean to blame the public, but I accept their criticisms and jeers only on condition that I do not have to be grateful for their applause." Verdi lived up to this statement all his life.

Un Giorno di Regno fiasco or not, Merelli saw something in the young composer. He pressed on Verdi a libretto that Otto Nicolai, the promising German composer, had refused. Verdi reluctantly set to work. Then came idea after idea, and the opera was finished in three months. It had its premiere on March 9, 1842, and a new operatic hero was hailed by Italy.

The opera was *Nabucco*, short for *Nabucodonosor*. Today it may sound like unformed Verdi, and in many ways it is. It straddles the bel canto school and the coming dramatic school. Donizetti's influence can be heard in *Nabucco*, and also the Rossini of the serious operas. But the formulae take on new breadth, new life, in Verdi's opera. It is hard to put ourselves back in time and realize the impact that *Nabucco* made in 1842. What to day sounds derivative came then as an explosion. During the rehearsals of *Nabucco* the theater was, according to contemporary accounts, "turned up-side down." Nobody had ever dreamed of this kind of music. It was "so new, so unknown, the style so rapid, so unusual, that everybody was amazed. . . . It was impossible to work offstage while the rehearsals were going on, for employees, workmen, painters, machinists, excited by the music they were hearing, left their tasks to stand open-mouthed and watch what was taking place on stage."

Naturally word-of-mouth reports flooded Milan, and the public was be-side itself to hear the opera. The connoisseurs—and everybody in the city considered himself a connoisseur of opera—immediately realized that a new and original talent had arrived. "With this opera," Verdi said, "my artistic career can truly be said to have begun." Verdi's competition also real-ized it. Some of his colleagues were jealous, and some took it gracefully. Donizetti was one of the latter. "The world wants new things," he said. "Others, after all, have yielded the place to us, so we must yield it to others. . . . Delighted to yield it to people of talent like Verdi." Donizetti predicted that his new rival would soon occupy "one of the most honored places in the cohort of composers."

What Verdi did in *Nabucco*, and what struck musical Italy, was to open up and expand the formula bel canto opera. He used a larger orchestra, with a consequently larger tonal thrust. The music itself is much broader and more forceful than in any bel canto opera, and it moves more directly. There is no lingering over empty vocal display. There are, to be sure, plenty of vocal fireworks, but always for an emotional rather than exhibi-tionistic reason. The role of Abigaille is one of the most difficult in the rep-ertory; it needs a dramatic coloratura soprano with a mezzo-soprano ability to take chest tones and an ability to project raw power—the power of the character itself, and the power of Verdi's writing. There is terrific personal-ity all through *Nabucco*. Even when Verdi touched on the bel canto con-ventions and mannerisms, he made them sound bigger and stronger. In this opera he found himself, and the music contains many anticipations of later Verdi. Zaccaria's "D'Egitto là sui lidi" anticipates the elder Germont's arias in *La Traviata*, just as the third-act duet between Nabucco and Abigaille brings to mind the Aïda-Amonasro duets.

In addition, there were political implications in *Nabucco*, and the opera made Verdi a symbol of the resistance to the Austrian domination. The "Va, pensiero" chorus, which concerns the longing of the Jewish exiles for home, was identified by all Italian listeners with their own longing for free-dom. Whether or not Verdi deliberately set this chorus as a politically ori-ented message is not known. He himself was strongly nationalistic, as pro-Italian as Wagner was pro-German. Verdi lived in hope of a united Italy, and he lived to see it. But whatever his motivation for the "Va, pensiero" chorus, the tune immediately made its way through Italy and was sung as a symbol of the resistance. To many Italians, Verdi himself symbolized that spirit, and years later an acrostic was made on his name: *Vittorio Emmanuele, Re d'Italia.*

Verdi followed *Nabucco* with two more hits—*I Lombardi* in 1843 and *Ernani* in 1844. The latter made him known outside of Italy. In Paris it was staged at the Théâtre des Italiens and Verdi went there to supervise the production. Now in a position to demand large fees, Verdi did not hesitate to do so. He was a solid businessman, determined to make the best bargain he could. Several lesser hits or even failures followed *Ernani*, and then came *Macbeth* in 1847. Verdi, who was to conclude his career with two settings of Shakespeare plays, took special pains with *Macbeth*, which had its premiere in Florence. It was the drama of the play he wanted to emphasize; and even if his librettists distorted Shakespeare, Verdi strove with all his power to approximate Shakespeare's kind of terror and pity. It is a strange opera, dark and moody, unconventional and often unsatisfactory. But it does have the "Sleepwalking Scene," an episode that ranks with the great ones of his later operas. At the time he wrote *Macbeth*, Verdi had all but broken free from the Italian operatic conventions. He did not even *want* pretty singing in *Macbeth*. He wanted song to be subsidiary to situation; he wanted the sounds produced by the singers to reflect their inner turmoil and psychological stresses. This was unheard-of in opera at the time. When *Macbeth* in 1848 went into rehearsals in Paris, Verdi write a long letter to the director, and it is a revealing document, telling a great deal of what Verdi was looking for:

> I know you are rehearsing *Macbeth*, and since it is an opera that interests me more than all the others, you will permit me to say a few words about it. They gave the role of Lady Macbeth to [Eugenia] Tadolini, and I am very surprised that she consented to do the part. You know how much I admire Tadolini, and she knows it herself; but in our common interest we should stop and consider. Tadolini has too great qualities for this role. Perhaps you think that is a contradiction! Tadolini's appearance is good and beautiful, and I would like Lady Macbeth twisted and ugly. Tadolini sings to perfection, and I don't wish Lady Macbeth to sing at all. Tadolini has a marvellous, brilliant, clear, powerful voice, and for Lady Macbeth I should like a raw, choked, hollow voice. Tadolini's voice has something angelic. Lady Macbeth's voice should have something devilish.

The point is that Verdi was, in his way, moving toward the direction of music drama. The difference between his approach and Wagner's, musical considerations aside, is that of melodrama opposed to drama. Many Verdi operas are outright melodramas, of wretched literary quality: studies in black and white, with characterization down to a minimum. Sophisticates have always sneered at the Verdi librettos. The subject of Verdi and his librettos is an interesting one. He was not a sophisticate, not an intellectual (though he had as much common sense as any composer in history), and until the end of his career did not seem very concerned about the literary qualities of his librettos. To put it bluntly, he set some ridiculous stuff to music. Or was it that his choice of librettos was conditioned by the taste of the public? Verdi always was responsive to public opinion. "In the theater the public will stand for anything but boredom," he said. He never pretended to be more than a craftsman, giving the public what it wanted. Perhaps Verdi himself believed that he could set only blood and thunder librettos. Whatever the reason, Verdi only too often used librettos that are no credit to his taste. An argument has been advanced that Verdi's librettos are not that bad; that they "work," that they depict raw emotion in great primary colors: love, hate, revenge, lust for power. But this is the stuff of melodrama, and is anything but a subtle literary form. Fortunately, Verdi's power as a composer was such that he could take a melodramatic situation and set it to unforgettable music. This music makes one ignore how conventional and wretched the words can be. Looked at dispassionately, a large number of Verdi librettos are literary trash. It makes no difference. The operas continue to live because they *do* have drama, no matter how primitive, and most of all because they do have great music.

Macbeth was followed by a series of operas that, except for *Luisa Miller* (1849), no longer hold the stage. Then, in 1851–1853, came the first three operas of his maturity—*Rigoletto* (1851), *Il Trovatore,* and *La Traviata* (both 1853). They were epoch-making in their day, and they made Verdi the only opera composer who could approach Meyerbeer in popularity. The public could not seem to get enough of those three operas. As an example: the Théâtre des Italiens in Paris gave eighty-seven performances in the 1856–57 season. Of those, fifty-four went to the three Verdi operas. In London, the clamor for Verdi was so great, and those three operas were done so often, that *Punch* objected:

> Three Traviatas in different quarters,
> Three Rigolettos murdering their daughters,
> Three Trovatori beheading their brothers,
> By the artful contrivance of three gypsy mothers.

The London *Musical World* pondered the phenomenon in 1855 and presented a more considered view than many critical journals were prepared to give. Verdi, the article pointed out, "has revolutionized the musical stage in his native country; for his operas, all others are forgotten. In time he made himself a name on the other part of the Alps. Other mobs caught up the enthusiasm, which spread from kingdom to kingdom, until new countries were invaded and conquered, and the mob-idol of one land became the mob-idol of all. Is this, or is it not, the secret of Signor Verdi's career? Could this have been effected without talent, and is Verdi the nonentity that musicians make him out?"

Singers fell in line as enthusiastically as the public. Marie Wieck, Clara Schumann's sister and herself also a prominent pianist, had a few words to say on the subject in 1855. She describes the glories of bel canto singing as practiced by the old exponents, Sontag, Lind, and the others, and then writes: "This style of singing is seldom heard. . . . The youthful, vigorous singers of today have only *one* name on their lips, and that is Verdi. Upon his operas rests the whole art of music—for the present time as well as for the future—and for this reason many singers under certain circumstances sacrifice the remains of their voices, sometimes even their health and constitution. All are ambitious only to be called Verdi singers, and they claim their title with glorious pride." Wieck, in this discussion of the Verdi operas in relation to singing, was more even-tempered than many critics. In their early years Verdi and Wagner were lumped together as irresponsible creators at whose feet lay the bleeding body of the Muse of Singing. Traditionalists sighed for the good old days of Bellini where—gad, Sir!—a singer was a singer and not a bellows. Meyerbeer had been attacked for his role in the death of singing, but those attacks were as nothing compared to the artillery brought up against Verdi and Wagner. Henry Fothergill Chorley in England wrote venomously of "the years during which singers' music was being stamped into such trash by the Wagners of New Germany and bawled into premature destruction by the Verdis of infuriate Italy."

It is interesting to note that while the public went crazy over the Verdi operas, and while singers jostled one another in their eagerness to be heard in the juicy Verdi roles, the conservatives and the critics were unhappy. They were used to the old conventions, and the furious dramatic onrush of Verdian movement made them uncomfortable. They were also used to mythological and historical characters in their operas, not hunchbacked jesters, consumptive courtesans, and dirty gypsies. Chorley scoffed. "Consumption for one who is to sing! A ballet with a lame Sylphide would be as rational." Sensibilities were offended. In New York, in 1855, two gentlemen started legal action against the impresario Max Maretzek. They sought to prevent the showing of *Rigoletto* on the ground that it was a lewd and licentious work, and that "by its singing, its business, and its plot, was then and there such an exhibition of opera as no respectable member of the fair sex could patronize without then and there sacrificing both taste and modesty." In Boston, where *La Traviata* was given in 1857, John S. Dwight attacked the opera on moral grounds before concluding that in any case it was no good musically: ". . . his old effects tried over and over again, as if with a nightmare inability to move beyond them. Nowhere, in one single point, of song or instrumentation, does this opera add a little to what we all know of Verdi. Invention seems exhausted, and only an intense craving for production left." But the young composers of Europe knew better, and Bizet put his finger on the essential Verdi: "He has marvellous bursts of passion. His passion is brutal, true, but it is better to be passionate that way than not at all. His music is sometimes exasperating but never boring."

Had the ex-Unitarian minister John S. Dwight known more about Verdi's private life, his darkest suspicions would have been proved. During the years that brought forth his three great operas of 1851–1853, Verdi was living with a woman named Giuseppina Strepponi. She was a soprano, and he had met her as early as 1839, when she sang in his very first opera, *Oberto*. Two years younger than Verdi, Strepponi in the 1830's and 1840's was recognized as one of the best singers in Italy—a soprano with a pure, clear voice, a good actress, and a musician of sensitivity. She shared his great triumph in *Nabucco*, singing the role of Abigaille at the premiere, she later sang other Verdi roles, she advised him on contractual and monetary matters, and in 1848 they began to live together. Three years later they moved into a new home, near Busseto. Verdi had purchased property there, had a house built, and named it the Villa Sant' Agata. There was head-wagging, finger-pointing, and soon an open scandal. In Busseto, in 1851, man and woman did not live openly together unless they were married. Verdi was outraged at the gossip. He got off a letter to his old friend and ex-father-in-law, Antonio Barezzi, and it reveals an independent, strong, scrappy, and unconventional man. In effect, Verdi told Barezzi and the town of Busseto to mind its own damn business. "In my house lives a lady, free and independent, and possessed of a fortune that places her beyond reach of need, who shares my love of seclusion. Neither she nor I need render account of our actions to any man." And, "In my house she has the right to be treated with even greater respect than is due to myself, and nobody is allowed to forget it." And, "This long and rambling letter is only designed to establish my claim to that liberty of action to which every man has a right. My nature shrieks against submitting to the prejudices of other people." Some writers suggest that there were two reasons for Verdi's defiant flaunting of the conventions. One was his strong anticlericalism. Who was the Church to tell *him* what to do? Verdi never was a believer, and Frank Walker, whose researches into Verdi's life and thought have opened more areas than those of any previous biographer, flatly says that Verdi was an atheist. The other reason might have been Giuseppina's diffidence. Her past life had not been beyond reproach, and it has been hazarded that she had guilt feelings about marriage.

In any case, having established his point, Verdi finally married Giuseppina in 1859. It was a happy though childless marriage. To compensate for the lack of children, there were animals: cats, dogs, parrots, peacocks, and the undisputed ruler of Sant' Agata—the Maltese spaniel, Loulou.

After the 1851–1853 trinity, the Verdi operas began to change in style. They grew broader, richer in sound, longer, more ambitious. Instead of turning out an opera every year, Verdi took much more time. No longer was there the "guitar" accompaniment of the orchestra that so amused the Germans. Verdi was feeling his way toward something bigger, and he experimented along that line. There was the Meyerbeerian *I Vespri Siciliani*, composed in 1855 for Paris. *Simon Boccanegra*, composed for Venice in 1857, was a failure. The impossibly disjointed libretto did not help. Yet *Simon Boccanegra* had a brooding quality, and some ravishingly sensuous ensembles, which Verdi had not achieved up to then. The year 1859 saw *Un Ballo in Maschera*, which had its premiere in Rome. This was a singing opera, full of bubbling ideas: one of the most sustained flights of lyricism in the entire Verdi canon. *La Forza del Destino*, composed for St. Petersburg, came in 1862 and turned out to be one of Verdi's most popular operas, wretched libretto and all.

The libretto of *Don Carlo* (Paris, 1867) is equally confused. Verdi tinkered with this opera for years. It never has been one of his most popular ones, and not until after World War II did it enter the repertoire with any degree of regularity. But it is a masterpiece. A feeling of black fate lies over the work—a work dominated not by the hero but by the tormented Philip of Spain. The auto-da-fè scene has unparalleled intensity and even a type of chromaticism rare for Verdi. When those trombones come in, heavy, marchlike, and menacing, it is as if the weight of the Inquisition were pressed on the listener's shoulders. The justly admired Inquisitor's scene that follows, with its great "Dormirò sol" for Philip, his confrontation with the blind Inquisitor, and Eboli's "O don fatale," ranks with anything Verdi ever composed. *Don Carlo* is a panorama that swirls around Spain and The Netherlands and, different though it is from Mussorgsky's *Boris Godunov* (which came out only a few years after the Verdi opera), the two works have points in common. Both deal with the responsibilities of rule, aspiration for freedom, countries being ripped apart. They are epic works.

Don Carlo is, indeed, a more striking and original work than *Aïda* of 1871. *Aïda*, composed for Cairo as part of the festivities attendant on the opening of the Suez Canal, is in a way a throwback. It may be the most popular of the Verdi operas, and it is the opera most people think of when the expression "grand opera" is used, but the Meyerbeerian panoply of the first two acts contains some of Verdi's weakest music, and the marches and ballet music of the second act can be listened to, these days, at best with indulgence. Not until the "Nile Scene" does Verdi show what he can do, and from that point to the end the opera is a masterpiece. Mussorgsky, for one, fell in love with *Aïda* and raved about Verdi: "This one pushes ahead on a grand scale; this innovator doesn't feel shy. All his *Aïda* . . . outdistances everyone, even himself. He has knocked over *Trovatore*, Mendelssohn, Wagner."

Even that arch-Teuton, Hans von Bülow, finally came around. Bülow at first had a low opinion of Verdi. After hearing the Requiem in 1874—the Requiem was the next important work by Verdi to follow *Aïda*—he called it rubbish. But shortly after, Bülow sent a hysterical *mea culpa* letter to Verdi (Bülow was never the one to do things by halves), casting dust on his head, beating his breast, and asking for forgiveness. The Requiem, he had now decided, was one of the greatest works of the century.

Bülow never wrote a truer word. Verdi composed the Requiem in honor of Alessandro Manzoni, the poet and novelist. To Verdi, Manzoni could be equated with that other "gloria d'Italia," Rossini. At Rossini's death in 1868, Verdi proposed that the most important Italian composers, including himself, collaborate on a requiem mass in his honor. Nothing came of the project, though Verdi did write a "Libera me" as his contribution. After Manzoni's death in May, 1873, Verdi decided to compose a Requiem Mass, to be performed in Milan, where Manzoni was buried, on the first anniversary of the death. For this work Verdi used—or said that he used (some authorities doubt it)—the "Libera me" that had been composed for Rossini. The long Requiem turned out to be all blazing passion: a colossal work, glorious in sound. Some attacked it for being too theatrical, and even today there are those who feel uncomfortable about its frank drama, which to them suggests opera rather than a religious experience. Giuseppina sprang to Verdi's defense:

> They talk a lot about the more or less religious spirit of Mozart, Cherubini, and others. I say that a man like Verdi must write like Verdi, that is, according to his own way of feeling and interpreting the text. The religious spirit and the way in which it is given expression must bear the stamp of its period and its author's personality. I would deny the authorship of a Mass by Verdi that was modeled upon the manner of A, B, or C.

Critical remarks after the premiere of the *Manzoni Requiem*—remarks to the effect that the music was tawdry, sensational, cheap, unreligious, irreligious, melodramatic—were representative of the critical attitude that faced

Verdi most of his life. His operas received unprecedented critical attack, especially in England and America. Many critics simply could not take Verdi seriously as a composer. The more the public loved his music, the more the critics screamed and lectured about the "obvious" nature of the writing, its "unvocal" quality, its "primitive" orchestration. They assured one another and the public that this music had only a temporary appeal and could not live. The critic of the London *Telegraph* had to take notice of the tremendous reception that the Requiem received at its Milan premiere. But, he gravely explained, that had nothing to do with the music. The ovation occurred because Verdi was so loved as a man, because of Manzoni, because Italians were so proud of Verdi's fame. "Now that the Peninsula is one State, every inhabitant of the most remote district assumes with pride his share in the honor paid to every Italian celebrity." It could not occur to the *Telegraph* critic that the music of the Requiem could have had a bearing on the case. He had been brainwashed for too many years.

Verdi was not disturbed by the negative reaction from some of the critics. He seems to have been one composer who honestly cared little about what critics said. He faced failure and success with equanimity. "You are wrong," he wrote to a friend, "to defend *Ballo in Maschera* from the attacks of the press. You should do as I always do: refrain from reading them and let them sing what tune they please. . . . For the rest, the question is this: Is the opera good or bad? If it is good and they have not thought so owing to their prejudices, etc., one must let them have their say and not take it to heart." And, elsewhere: "As for the newspapers, does anybody force you to read them? . . . The day of justice will come, and it is a great pleasure for the artist, a supreme pleasure, to be able to say: 'Imbeciles, you were wrong!' "

After the *Manzoni Requiem*, about fourteen years passed before Verdi's next major work. He spent some time visiting Vienna, Paris, and London, supervising productions of his operas, then returned to Sant' Agata to lead a life of retirement. He could look at the world and be pleased about certain things. Italy was now united. The Kingdom of Italy had been created in 1860, Venice was restored after Austria was defeated by the Prussians in 1866, and then Garibaldi freed Sicily and Naples. Rome became Italian in 1870. As one who had always hoped for the independence of Italy, Verdi was happy. For a few years he even sat in the Parliament as a member from Busetto. At first, in 1860, he took the job seriously and attended every session in Turin. He did not participate in the debates, but did try to push through a scheme for government subsidy of lyric theaters and conservatories. But soon the political mind started to bother him, and he did not like the politicians with whom he was in constant association. Once, at a session in Turin, he amused himself by setting to music a couple of parliamentary outbursts. One wonders what happened to that manuscript. It might be fun.

Verdi, in retirement at Sant' Agata, could also look at the musical scene in Italy and well realize his place in it. Never in the history of music has an era and a country been so dominated by one man. Wagner in Germany, the opposite number to Verdi in Italy, at least had a Brahms as a counterpoise. Verdi had nobody. Between the death of Donizetti and the emergence, in the 1870's, of Amilcare Ponchielli, there was only *one* important composer in Italy, and that was Verdi (Boito composed the impressive *Mefistofele* in 1868, but he was really a one-work man). No other Italian music survives. The Italian opera houses dutifully staged new operas every year, and the operas were invariably forgotten after a few performances. Take 1869. There were new operas by Sampieri, Mancini, Ricci, Monti, Petrella, Morales, Vera, Montuoro, Marchetti, Perelli, Vezzossi, Battista, Germano, Alberti, Seneke, Zecchini, Tancioni, Libani, and Grondona, among others. Not one of those composers rates even a footnote in any history of music. No; for about thirty years in Italy there was one giant, and then there was nobody— nobody at all.

Verdi in retirement also might have considered his place vis-à-vis Wagner. Certainly he must have heard about Wagner's glorious success with his first Bayreuth season in 1876. It is surprising that the two men never met, for they traveled much and they lived long lives. And they were the most important and famous composers of operas of their time. But Wagner's attitude toward Verdi was one of complete indifference—a lion shrugging off a gnat. Wagner must have heard some of the Verdi operas, but in all his vast correspondence there is virtually no mention of them except for a few slighting references expressed in terms of detached Olympian amusement. Verdi was more generous. Apparently he never heard a note of Wagner's music until 1865, when he encountered the *Tannhäuser* Overture (and did not like it very much). Later he had some words of praise for Wagner, though he detested Wagnerism and was bothered by the theories of symphonic development surrounding the Wagner operas. "Opera is opera," he said, "symphony is symphony."

One charge that strongly irritated Verdi was to hear his operas accused of "Wagnerism," and that kept happening more and more as the Verdi operas grew longer, more powerfully scored, and cunningly put together. Verdi insisted that there was such a thing as an Italian temperament, as opposed to a German temperament, and he looked with dismay as such young composers as Arrigo Boito attempted a style of composition that had Wagnerisms in it. In Verdi's opinion, those composers were imitating Wagner's structure, harmony, and leitmotif development without fully understanding what they were doing. "If the Germans, setting out from Bach and arriving at Wagner, write good German operas, well and good. But we descendants of

222

Palestrina commit a musical crime when we imitate Wagner. We write useless, even deleterious music. . . . We cannot compose like the Germans, or at least we ought not to; nor they like us. . . . If we let fashion, love of innovations, and an alleged scientific spirit tempt us to surrender the native quality of our own art, the free natural certainty of our work and perception, our bright golden light, then we are simply being stupid and senseless." Yet when he heard of Wagner's death in 1883, Verdi wrote to his publisher: "Sad, sad, sad! Frankly, when I received the news yesterday, I was crushed. Let us say no more about it. A great personality has gone, a name that will leave a most powerful impression on the history of art."

During the period following the *Manzoni Requiem* it was assumed that Verdi was finished with composition. He let the world know that he would never again write another work for the stage. And he might have kept his promise had he not been thrown into close association with Arrigo Boito.

Boito (February 24, 1842–June 10, 1918) was a literary man and composer. To most non-Italian music-lovers he is known as the man who furnished Verdi with librettos for *Otello* and *Falstaff*. Others know him as the composer of *Mefistofele*, his only musical work of any importance. But in his youth, around 1865, he was one of the Young Turks of Italian music, and this even though he composed next to nothing. He was always torn between literature and music, wavering uncertainly between the two for many years. *Mefistofele*, composed in 1868 and revised seven years later, was his only completed opera. He worked on another called *Orestiade* but never offered it to the public. A third, *Ero e Leandro* got only as far as a libretto. There remains *Nerone*, which Boito started thinking about in 1862. All his life he worked on that opera, and it remained unfinished at his death in 1918.

Yet Boito had immense talent and perhaps genius. Was it the overpowering force of Verdi that held him down? The two men crossed in the early 1860's. When Boito was twenty years old, fresh from his studies at the Milan Conservatory (where great things were expected of him), he wrote the text for Verdi's *Hymn of the Nations*. But relations between the two men were touchy for a long time. Verdi was notoriously sensitive, and he got the idea that Boito was an enemy.

No doubt this stemmed from Boito's critical writings, in which he kept agitating for a reform in Italian opera. Boito was an intellectual, and one of the very few Italians of his day to propagandize for Beethoven, Wagner, and German music. He wrote a great deal about the necessity for "true form" in opera. As practiced in Italy, opera, he insisted, was merely formula. "The hour has come for a change in style. Form, largely developed in the other arts, must develop too in our own." Boito was thinking in terms of Wagnerian operatic form, and to Verdi this was treason. The Italian spirit, Verdi felt, could never accommodate itself to German form and metaphysics. And as Verdi was in effect the only major composer of Italian opera from the death of Donizetti to the 1890's, even a less sensitive figure than Verdi would have felt that Boito's attacks were directed against him. Verdi grumbled to his publisher, Tito Ricordi, "If I too among the others have soiled the altar, as Boito says, let him clean it and I shall be the first to light a candle."

Thus, when *Mefistofele* had its premiere at La Scala in 1868, many in the audience had a chip on their shoulder. Between Boito's admirers and enemies, the performance ended in the kind of riot so dear to the hearts of the emotional Latins. There was screaming in the theater, fights broke out, and there were demonstrations in the streets. After a second performance the chief of police banned all further presentations in the interests of public safety. Verdi did not hear the opera until more than ten years later. In 1879 he attended a performance in Genoa and had some tart remarks to make: "I had always heard it said, and always read, that the Prologue in Heaven was cast in a single piece, a thing of genius . . . and I, listening to the harmonies of that piece, based almost entirely on dissonances, seemed to be . . . not in *heaven*, certainly."

But Verdi was being cruel. Even for its time the harmonies of *Mefistofele* were not very adventurous, though it is true that the Prologue is an altogether original conception. Boito was trying for higher things than Gounod in his saccharine *Faust* of 1859. Gounod composed a French formula opera, whereas Boito, true to his tenets, was aiming for a kind of intellectual synthesis that would draw together both parts of the Goethe play. Boito's Devil is not a stock figure of evil. He is an elemental force who confronts his Adversary with dignity. In his preoccupation with new operatic forms, Boito anticipated some writing of a future era. The Prologue, for instance, is in classic form, with a scherzo and trio predominating. (Much later, in *Wozzeck*, Alban Berg was to write an opera in which classic forms—variation, sonata, suite, passacaglia, invention—are the actual basis on which the entire opera is constructed.) Boito's entire approach was different from Verdi's, and considering that Boito was only twenty-six years old when *Mefistofele* was staged, one would have thought that the world was his, that the great Verdi would be faced with some real competition. That was not to be. Boito, who on the evidence of so tremendous an achievement at so young an age could conceivably have gone on to magnificence, in effect put down his musical pen. He contributed to intellectual journals, he taught, he became director of the Parma Conservatory, he wrote librettos (*La Gioconda,* for Ponchielli, is his under a pseudonym), he occupied himself with *Nerone*. Something in him held back his musical creativity, and his was one of the strange psychological blocks in musical history. He could not write music, and toward the end he was unable to write so much as a letter.

This was the man who became Verdi's incomparable librettist. The idea for *Otello* came in 1879. At a dinner in which Verdi and Boito were guests, Giulio Ricordi (who had succeeded his father, Tito, as head of the publishing firm), turned the conversation to the Shakespeare play, and Verdi reacted as Ricordi had hoped. Boito and Verdi were brought together to discuss the possibility of an opera on *Othello*. Verdi seemed encouraging, and Boito dropped everything to provide a libretto. He gave it to Verdi later that year, and Verdi put it aside. Then he read it again, made some suggestions, received a new libretto, and again put it away. Finally he set to work, in 1884, at the age of seventy. Everybody concerned with the project walked on tiptoe. Boito wrote to Ricordi: "I have good news for you, but for charity's sake, don't tell anybody, don't tell even your family, don't tell even yourself. I fear I have already committed an indiscretion. The Maestro is writing, indeed he has already written a good part of the opening of the first act and seems to be working with fervor." There were some hitches along the way. Boito had to write and rewrite. There was a silly misunderstanding that had to be cleared up. Finally the opera had its premiere, at La Scala on February 5, 1887, and the seventy-three-year-old composer shared the applause with his librettist.

In *Otello*, the greatest of his tragic operas, Verdi brought to fusion everything that he had learned in a lifetime. He had the best libretto ever submitted to him, and he poured into it a combination of drama, rapture, and compassion unprecedented even for him. There is not a single weak passage in *Otello*, not one false gesture, nothing but a fusion of word, action, and music. Even such normally melodramatic episodes as Iago's "Credo" or the Otello-Iago "Si, pel ciel" duet fall naturally within the movement of the drama. Verdi's musical impulse had deepened and richened. The first-act love duet is all ardor and sensuousness, expressed in music that is the essence of desire. It is not the exultant music of young lovers. Rather it is the radiant music of man and wife. Iago's is two-faced music: hearty and bluff, or subtle, insinuating, and of shattering venom. The last act, with Desdemona's hushed "Salce, salce" and "Ave Maria," is all impending doom suggested by the simplest of means. *Otello* is much more than a collection of arias and ensembles. It is a through-composed opera, every element carefully joined to make a unity. Nor had Verdi ever before handled his orchestra with such mastery. It does not merely accompany singers. It underlines the action, hints at the tragedy to come, describes what the characters are thinking and feeling. Often there are mottos and figures instead of themes. *Otello* is to Italian opera what *Tristan* is to German.

Nevertheless *Otello* is a logical continuation of what Verdi had done from *Nabucco* through *La Traviata*, *Don Carlo*, and *Aïda*. With his last opera, something new enters the picture. *Falstaff* is almost a freak, what the biologists call a sport. Nobody had expected Verdi to compose another opera. And, even granting that there might be another work, who would have expected it to be a comedy, and the most atypical opera Verdi ever wrote?

Falstaff is an opera that always has been part of the standard repertory, but never an integral part. Musicians keep crying its praises. The word customarily used with this opera is "miracle." Yet it has never fully captured the public imagination as *Otello* and the others have. Audiences, for the most part, listen politely, waiting for something to happen, for the big arias that never come. The opera has always been more a *succès d'estime* than anything else, even in Italy, where Verdi is a god.

Admittedly *Falstaff* does not have the immediate emotional appeal of *Otello* or *Aïda*. Verdi's wife, Giuseppina, described it as "a new combination of poetry and music." Indeed it was new. Nowhere in opera had there been an equivalent type of condensation in which words and music are so intertwined. What *Otello* had merely hinted at, *Falstaff* accomplishes. Gone are the arias in which the tenor advances to the footlights, glares down the audience, and stuns it with a high C. Gone is the broad canvas. Gone is the melodrama. Gone are the primary colors. Instead, all is subtle, fast-moving, full of glints, mocking laughter, high humor. *Falstaff* is a commentary on life, a summation of a career, a jest—and such a civilized one!—with its undertone of sadness. Verdi knew it was to be his last opera. "*Tutto è finito. Va, va, vecchio John . . .*"

Verdi had been persuaded by Boito to undertake the task after the success of *Otello*. In 1889 the two men were deep in the Shakespeare comedy. The failure of Verdi's one comic opera, *Un Giorno di Regno* in 1840, had continued to be a sore spot with him all his life. Perhaps he undertook *Falstaff* with the idea of erasing that failure. And, deep down, could he have undertaken *Falstaff* to show the world that Wagner had no monopoly on music drama, that another composer could write an opera with continuous melody and inner development—but in the Italian and not the German manner? Anyway, Verdi worked on *Falstaff* with great enjoyment. He played it down, pretending that he was working on it only to pass the time. Almost eighty, he could spend no more than two hours a day on the opera. But that does not mean he approached *Falstaff* with anything less than his usual thoroughness. From the very beginning he did his homework. Before reading Boito's first script he read the three *Henry* plays and the *Merry Wives of Windsor*. Then he carefully went through the Boito draft, worrying about the last act, which "in spite of its touch of fantasy will be trivial." There was an exchange of letters with Boito in which Verdi actually became coquettish, putting up some token resistance against the idea of writing another opera. Was he too old for such a task? Would he live to complete it? Boito brushed this aside as "not valid and no obstacle to a new work."

226

A letter from Verdi to Boito in 1889 is interesting. "You are working, I hope? The strangest thing is that I am working too. I am amusing myself by writing fugues. Yes, sir, a fugue—and a comic fugue." This must refer to the conclusion of the opera. So Verdi, the old rascal, already had the end of *Falstaff* in mind. By March, 1891, Verdi was all involved with the fat man. "Big belly is going crazy. There are days when he doesn't move, but sleeps and is in a bad humor. At other times he shouts, runs, jumps, causes a devil of a rumpus. I let him indulge his whims a bit. If he continues, I'll put on a muzzle and a strait-jacket."

The world premiere took place on February 9, 1893, at La Scala. It was a success, of course. Verdi was such a revered figure that any opera of his would have been enthusiastically received. He was an Old Master, and long gone were the days when the critics snapped at him. Notables from all over Europe attended the premiere, and also the performance in Rome that followed soon after. The critics wrote learned reviews. Many of them did wonder if an opera with so little in the way of clear-cut melody would ever attract the public. But the critics also were entranced with the translucence of the writing, the wit of the music, the technical mastery evident in every measure. The shades of Mozart (*Figaro*) and Wagner (*Meistersinger*) were invoked, as they are to this day. For *Falstaff* is the third in that trinity of great comic operas, and it is in no way inferior to either.

In 1893, George Bernard Shaw, the music critic for the *World* in London, looked through the score of *Falstaff* and had some observations to make:

> I have noticed one or two exclamations of surprise at the supposed revelation in *Falstaff* of a "hitherto unsuspected" humorous force in the veteran tragic composer. This must be the result of the enormous popularity which *Il Trovatore* and *Aïda* afterwards attained in this country. I grant that these operas are quite guiltless of comic relief; but what about *Un Ballo* with its exquisitely light-hearted *È scherzo od è follia*, and the finale to the third act, where Renato is sarcastically complimented on his domestic virtue. . . . Stupidly as that tragi-comic quartet and chorus has always been mishandled on our wretched operatic stage, I cannot understand anyone who knows it denying Verdi's gift of dramatic humor.

Shaw may not have been surprised at the humor in *Falstaff*, but the public remained perplexed. *Falstaff* does have arias and ensembles, but they move so fast that no sooner does the listener start to enjoy them than they are gone. Falstaff's "Quand'ero paggio" lasts thirty seconds—the entire aria. The duet between Nannetta and Fenton takes a minute and a half (though it is later repeated). Wonderful melodic inspirations seem to be dropped as soon as they are introduced. It is almost as though Verdi is writing a kind

227

of musical shorthand. As a result *Falstaff* gives many listeners the feeling of an opera without development, without anything to seize.

What the listener comes to realize, if *Falstaff* is given a chance, is that the opera is not only continuously melodic from beginning to end, but that it is also full of related melody. *Falstaff* is full of thematic linkages, and that is what gives the work its extraordinary unity. When, at her first appearance, Alice sings "Escivo appunto," it is accompanied by a little six-note motto that is immediately dropped—only to turn up prominently an act later when the words "Dalla due alla tre" are used. As one becomes familiar with the music, linkages like this spring into high relief.

The orchestra plays a more important role in *Falstaff* than in any Verdi opera, *Otello* included. The vocal line of *Otello* is primarily song; in *Falstaff* it is a mixture of song and song-speech (parlando). But when the characters in *Falstaff* are using a parlando line, the orchestra picks up the melody or somehow manages to supplement the action. Nowhere is this better illustrated than in Falstaff's "Honor" monologue. Singer and orchestra are one. When Falstaff builds up to "Che ciancia! Che baja!" the orchestra laughs with a trill: all the strings and lower winds. Then, as if suddenly waking up, the oboes, clarinets, and bassoons suddenly start trilling too, all alone. The effect, if one realizes what is going on, is indescribably witty. When Falstaff sweeps his precious retainers out of the way at the end of the act, the orchestra again his its say. Once more comes a trill, but what a trill! An impolite horse laugh, a Bronx cheer in music, as the orchestra razzes Falstaff and the world.

Everywhere in *Falstaff* come surprises, and the biggest of all is kept for the end. The opera concludes with a fugue. Verdi had been building up to this. *Aïda,* for example, has an unusual amount of polyphony. But nowhere else in the Verdi operas is there a full-fledged fugue, and there is something symbolic in the fact that the old Verdi rounded off his greatest and most revolutionary opera with one of the oldest and severest of musical forms. Only this fugue has nothing severe in it. "Everything is a farce," sing the characters, their voices rising and rising until abruptly cut off. Verdi was having his little joke.

Although *Falstaff* completed his cycle of operas, Verdi was not through writing. He composed a *Te Deum* and finished four religious pieces (two of them written before *Falstaff*), later published under the title of *Quattro Pezzi Sacri.* Boito kept urging him to write another Shakespeare opera. *Antony and Cleopatra? King Lear?* All his life Verdi had toyed with the idea of setting *Lear* to music. Giuseppina fended off Verdi's beseechers. "Verdi is too old, too tired." So was Giuseppina, and she died in 1897. When Verdi received the news he stood erect, mute, refusing to sit down. Most of his remaining years he spent at Sant' Agata, but occasionally visited Milan to be near Boito and other old friends When death came, it was in Milan. He had a stroke, lingered unconscious for a week, and died on January 27, 1901. Several months later Boito wrote to a friend describing Verdi's last hours. "Poor Maestro, how brave and handsome he was up to the last moment! No matter; the old reaper went off with his scythe well battered. Now it is all over. He sleeps like a King of Spain in his Escurial, under a bronze slab that completely covers him."

17

Colossus of Germany

RICHARD WAGNER

If it was Beethoven who dominated music in the first half of the nineteenth century, it was Richard Wagner who loomed over the second half. It was not only that Wagnerian opera changed the course of music. There was also something messianic about the man himself, a degree of megalomania that approached actual lunacy—and that raised the concept of the Artist-as-Hero to an unprecedented degree. He was a short man, about 5 feet, 5 inches tall, but he radiated power, belief in himself, ruthlessness, genius. As a human being he was frightening. Amoral, hedonistic, selfish, virulently racist, arrogant, filled with gospels of the superman (the superman naturally being Wagner) and the superiority of the German race, he stands for all that is unpleasant in human character.

No composer ever demanded so much from society, and Wagner was altogether unblushing about his needs. "I am not made like other people. I must have brilliance and beauty and light. The world owes me what I need. I can't live on a miserable organist's pittance like your master, Bach." His egoism approached madness. He thought nothing of writing to a young man he hardly knew, asking for money. "It would be rather hard for you to provide me with this sum, but it will be possible if you *wish* it, and do not shrink from such a sacrifice. This, however, I desire. . . . Now let me see whether you are the right sort of man!" Then follows an inducement: "The assistance you give me will bring you into very close touch with me, and next summer you must be pleased to let me come to you for three months at one of your estates, preferably in the Rhine district." The young man Robert von Hornstein, refused to give the money to Wagner, who actually was surprised. How could such a pipsqueak refuse to subsidize a man like him? He sent a note to Hornstein, writing him off for good: "It probably will not happen again that a man like me will apply to you."

No composer, and few human beings, have had Wagner's sense of mission. "I let myself be guided without fear by my instinct. I am being used as the instrument for something higher than my own being warrants. . . . I am in the hands of the immortal genius that I serve for the span of my life and that intends me to complete only what I can achieve." Such was Wagner's ego that it is not stretching a point to suggest that he secretly regarded himself as a god. He was sent to earth by mysterious forces. He gathered disciples unto Himself. He wrote holy scriptures in word and music (the Sacred Writings eventually to be gathered in ten large volumes of prose and twenty more of letters). He caused a temple at Bayreuth to be created, in which His works could be celebrated and He Himself worshiped. He cast out all who did not agree with His divinity.

But his egomania was supported by genius; and, after him, music was not the same.

Richard Wagner was born in Leipzig on May 22, 1813. Some mystery attaches to his paternity. There is strong evidence that his true father was an actor named Ludwig Geyer. There is indirect evidence that Geyer was a Jew. The true facts may never be known. In any case, Wagner's legal father died when he was six months old, and his mother married Geyer the following year. The family moved to Dresden, where Richard went to school. From childhood he was surrounded by actors, musicians, and artists, but he showed no unusual aptitude in any direction. Not until he was fifteen, when he heard the Beethoven Ninth Symphony and *Fidelio*, did he decide to become a composer. The Ninth Symphony seems to have shaken him psychically, releasing all the latent musical ferment that was bottled up in him, and the Ninth Symphony remained his ideal throughout his life. Wagner was to maintain that his operas were a continuation of the Ninth Symphony. "The last symphony of Beethoven," he wrote, "is the redemption of music from out of her peculiar element into the realm of universal art. It is the human evangel of the art of the future. Beyond it no further step is possible, for upon it the perfect art work of the future alone can follow: the universal drama for which Beethoven forged the key."

When Wagner at fifteen decided to become a composer, he was completely untrained. In many respects he developed into a self-taught composer, and like many self-taught composers, or composers who came to music late in life, he always lacked certain requirements that normally are considered basic. Like Berlioz, he had no professional skill on any instrument. Even when he was a conductor and a great composer, he could do little more than pick at the piano, and he admitted that he was an indifferent score reader. He made up for his deficiencies by instinct and a profound musicality. His learning seemed to be automatically absorbed. While a teen-ager, he did take a few harmony lessons with a local musician in Leipzig, but he learned much more by himself during the hours he spent poring over scores of the Beethoven symphonies. Then he started composing. His early works show no talent, and of all the great composers he was the one who developed latest in life.

In 1831 he was for a brief time at the University of Leipzig, where he made himself well known by his compulsive, nonstop talking, his dogmatism, and his drinking and gambling. Yet underneath was that enormous pool of musicality, ever rising, finally to overflow. Soon everything was neglected in favor of music. Wagner finally decided he needed discipline, and in 1831 he worked with Theodor Weinlig, the cantor of St. Thomas. Weinlig stopped the lessons because, he said, he could teach Wagner nothing more about harmony or counterpoint. Once Wagner decided to concentrate, he learned with amazing rapidity. As far as is known, the short time he spent with Weinlig constituted his only professional instruction. No great composer has had as little formal training. When Weinlig dismissed him, Wagner immediately started a series of compositions, most of them academic juvenilia, including a piano sonata and a symphony. An opera named *Die Hochzeit* was started but never finished, but in 1833 came *Die Feen*, and Wagner was launched as a composer of operas. (*Die Feen* was never produced in his lifetime, and not until 1888 did it receive a performance.) It was around this time, 1834 to be exact, that Wagner started his series of polemical writings. He wrote an article praising the French style of opera composition ("facile . . . melodious") over the German ("too learned and intellectual"). With that in mind he worked out a libretto based on Shakespeare's *Measure for Measure*, named it *Das Liebesverbot*, and started composing the music. Later that year he accepted a position as musical director of a company in Magdeburg. Now he was a professional. His career had started.

In Magdeburg he established a pattern that was to be his normal way of life. He ran up enormous debts, made many enemies, and tried to impose his will on the musical life of the company and the city. In Magdeburg, too, he fell in love with an actress in the company. Her name was Minna Planer, and he frightened her with his intensity. He had great plans. He would marry her; his opera, *Das Liebesverbot* would achieve a great success and wipe out his debts; he had been promised a position with the opera company at Riga, where he would make a great reputation. *Das Liebesverbot* was produced, in 1836. It failed. Nevertheless Wagner and Minna got married, in November of that year. They lived in Königsberg, where she had an engagement. Wagner ran up more debts. His creditors from Magdeburg pursued him to Königsberg. This frightened the Königsberg creditors, who also presented bills. Minna could not stand it. She left him, to go to her parents in Dresden. Fortunately the position in Riga came through, and Wagner went there in September, 1837, to be joined by Minna.

The pattern repeated itself in Riga. Wagner started work on another opera that would make him famous. This was *Rienzi*, modeled on the grand-opera formula that Meyerbeer had established. More debts were run up, more enemies made. Wagner tried to vitalize the musical life of the city, demanding more rehearsal time, an expansion of the repertoire, and the inclusion of symphony concerts into the musical program. In 1839 Wagner was discharged. He fled to France by boat (legend has it that the trip was the inspiration for *Der fliegende Holländer*), leaving his creditors behind. He and Minna settled in Paris, where he tried to make himself known. Meyerbeer received him, looked at the first act of *Rienzi*, and introduced him to important members of the musical establishment. Nothing happened, and soon the Wagners ran out of money. They pawned everything, and Wagner had to resort to hack work to keep alive. He put the final touches to *Rienzi* toward the end of 1840, and started work on *Der fliegende Holländer*. Then came good news. *Rienzi* was accepted by the Dresden Opera. Meyerbeer had recommended it, as had several other musicians, and the opinion of Meyerbeer carried enormous weight. Wagner and Minna had to borrow still more money to leave Paris. He was, literally, on his uppers; his shoes had no soles, and he had to stay indoors, working on *Holländer*. Finally they were able to say good-bye to Paris. He and Minna went to Dresden for the premiere, which took place on October 20, 1842. Wagner well knew how much was at stake, and he must have been a frightened man on opening night. Heinrich Heine was there and sent off a report to Paris. Wagner, Heine said, "looked like a ghost; he laughed and wept at the same time and embraced everybody who came near him, while all the time cold perspiration ran down his forehead." *Rienzi* turned out to be an enormous success, and Wagner was suddenly a famous man. The Dresden Court Theater immediately secured rights to *Der fliegende Holländer*, which was staged early in 1843. It did not make as big an impression as *Rienzi*, and ran for only four performances. But Wagner made enough of an impression to be appointed second kapellmeister at the Dresden Opera. He was given a salary that would have been comfortable for anybody but a Wagner. As usual he was able to hold on to none of it, spending far more than he earned. In addition, as word of his appointment got out, he was bedeviled by creditors from his previous travels—creditors from Leipzig, Magdeburg, Königsberg, Riga, Paris. It was a story that was to be repeated throughout much of his life.

Wagner settled into his duties and began to conduct some of the operas in the Dresden repertoire. Inevitably he ran into trouble. Trying to do away with the seniority system, he antagonized the entire orchestra. Trying to conduct such great works as *Don Giovanni* according to his inner vision, he alienated the public. The Dresden public was used to comfortable tempos in *Don Giovanni,* and Wagner's dashing attack unsettled the listeners. He was reproved, and he had to promise, in his own words, "to alter nothing in the hitherto accepted interpretation of tempo, etc., when conducting older operas, even when it goes against my artistic judgment." But there were compensations. In Dresden he was admired and respected, and he started work on a new opera, *Tannhäuser,* finishing the libretto in 1843 and the score two years later. The premiere took place on October 19, 1845, and audiences at first were bewildered. Soon, however, *Tannhäuser* achieved popularity, and Wagner started to think about a new opera, *Lohengrin.* The next two years saw *Lohengrin* come into shape and Wagner's financial position disintegrate. He was desperate for money. He also supervised a production of *Rienzi* in Berlin. It failed, and that added to his gloom.

A few years later he got into political in addition to his financial trouble. Stimulated by the collapse of the French monarchy, and influenced by the theories of the anarchist Mikhail Bakunin, Wagner came out on the side of the revolutionaries during the uprising in Dresden. Perhaps he was sincerely interested in the plight of the working man. Or perhaps he looked for a social upheaval that would wipe out the capitalists, thus automatically eliminating his enormous debts. He made speeches demanding the end of money and the abolition of royalty, and he wrote violent tracts: "I will destroy the existing order of things. . . . So up, ye peoples of the earth! Up, ye mourners, ye oppressed, ye poor!" When the Dresden uprising was put down in 1849, Wagner fled to Weimar and his friend Liszt, one of the few musicians who had encouraged him. (Schumann and Berlioz never were attracted to Wagner's music.) After a short stay in Weimar, Wagner made his home in Zurich. *Lohengrin* had been completed in 1848, and Liszt conducted the world premiere in Weimar, 1850. Wagner was not present. He was thinking about new projects in Zurich. His revolutionary period was over. Soon he was writing about "the vulgar egotism of the masses."

Rienzi had been a huge spectacle opera. *Der fliegende Holländer, Tannhäuser,* and *Lohengrin* went to German myth for their subject. But none of these operas fully expressed what Wagner was trying to do. For six years Wagner lay fallow, thinking about the problem, working out his artistic theories, writing a big libretto based on the Teutonic *Nibelungenlied,* and turning out one treatise after another: *Art and Revolution* (1849), *The Art Work of the Future* (1850), *Judaism and Music* (1850), *Opera and Drama* (1851), *A Communciation to My Friends* (1851), and assorted essays.

He arrived at the concept of a unified art work, the *Gesamtkunstwerk,* and decided that all great art must be based on mythology. As early as 1844 he was writing: "It is the province of the present-day dramatist to give expressive and spiritual meaning to the material interests of our own time; but to the operatic poet and composer falls the task of conjuring up the

holy spirit of poetry as it comes to us in the sagas and legends of past ages."
He wrote that "God and gods are the first creations of man's poetic force."
Myth, then, was the ideal stuff of which poetry was made. It was necessary
to go to a pre-Christian period, for Christianity had diluted the *mythos*.
"Through the adoption of Christianity the folk had lost all true understand-
ing of the original, vital relations of the *mythos*."

But how to get back to the *mythos*? What kind of language should be
used? A new speech had to be created, Wagner decided. The poet must use
Stabreim, which resembles the poetry found in the sagas. This is a highly al-
literative kind of poetry, with "a kinship of vowel sounds." Soon Wagner, in
his *Nibelung* libretto, was writing like this:

> Mächt'ger Müh'
> müde nie,
> stau'ten starke
> Stein' wir auf;
> steiler Thurm,
> Thur' und Thor,
> deckt und schliesst,
> im schlanken Schloss den Saal.

The language once secured, the music must meet it on equal terms. The
music must grow out of the libretto. There must be no pandering to the
public, no vocal display for its own sake, no set arias and ensembles in
which the action comes to a halt. Leitmotifs can be used as an organizational force. Leitmotifs are short descriptive tunes, capable of being meta-
morphosed, that describe characters or states of mind. These leitmotifs are
put through a process of constant manipulation and quasi-symphonic development. (Debussy later was to jibe that "the leit-motif system suggests a
world of harmless lunatics who present their visiting cards and shout their
names in song.") Because in this style of composition there is no stop for
arias, and because there is none of the feeling of transition that there had
been in previous opera, mention began to be made of Wagner's "endless
melody." Unbroken drama expressed in unbroken music was his goal, and
as early as *Lohengrin* he was pleased to be able to point out that nowhere
in the opera "have I written the word *recitative* over a passage. The singers
are not to know there are any recitatives in it."

Above all, there was the new use of the orchestra. More than any composer in history up to that point, Wagner made the orchestra an equal part
of the drama. It is in Wagner's big, resonantly scored orchestra where much
of the action of the opera is explained—where psychological changes of the
characters, their motivations, drives, desires, loves, hates, are all underlined.

Singers had to learn how to carry over an operatic orchestra of this unprecedented size. During the last half of the century there were great arguments about Wagner and the human voice. Many professionals cried that Wagner, even more than Verdi and Meyerbeer, was killing the singer by imposing such "unnatural" demands. George Bernard Shaw took Wagner's part, pointing out that Verdi's habit "of taking the upper fifth of the compass of an exceptionally high voice and treating that fifth as the normal range, has a great deal to do with the fact that the Italian singer is now the worst singer in the world." Wagner, Shaw said, used the voice all over its compass, with the result that Wagnerian singers "are now the best in the world."

Not only did Wagner work out the main lines of the *Gesamtkunstwerk* during his years in Zurich, but in the process he also changed his musical style. Up to then his music had tended to be rhythmically four-square, but with *Tristan und Isolde* and the *Ring* cycle came a kind of rhythm that depended more on the phrase than on the bar line. In addition, Wagner's harmonic ideas became intensely chromatic, and key relationships began to become very vague. Wagner was an eclectic who synthesized the techniques of early romanticism. He took ideas about the orchestra from Berlioz. Weber's operas, especially *Der Freischütz*, played a great part in Wagner's final synthesis. He took harmonic ideas from Chopin, Mendelssohn, and, above all, Liszt, and he was even influenced to a certain extent by Meyerbeer. And there was the overriding ethical idea implicit in Beethoven's last works. Wagner welded all of this material into something uniquely his own, creating his own world, a world of myth surrounded by the most advanced music known at the time. It is interesting to note that he himself did not fully carry through on his own theories of the *Gesamtkunstwerk. Das Rheingold* comes closest, whereas *Die Meistersinger* breaks most of his own rules. When a musical idea collided with Wagner's theory of the music drama, it was music that always won over theory. Indeed, the three most "Wagnerian" operas, the three that most closely approach the *Gesamtkunstwerk* that Wagner was talking about, are Verdi's *Falstaff*, Debussy's *Pelléas et Mélisande*, and Berg's *Wozzeck.*

In the meantime, the years that Wagner spent in Zurich were also years that saw the early Wagner operas making their way through Europe. Wagner's genius was recognized almost from the beginning, and it would be a mistake to assume that he was working in a vacuum. From *Rienzi* on, the Wagner operas were the talk of Europe. Verdi's operas were more popular, but there was one significant difference. The Verdi operas did not excite the avant-garde, nor did they drive a wedge into the public. When a Wagner opera was given, it generally was to great excitement and polemics. People may have gone around *whistling* the famous Verdi tunes, but they were constantly *talking* about the Wagner operas—in derogation, in admiration, in

236

derision, in praise, but always talking, and loudly talking. It was realized that Wagner was an elemental force—a destructive force, to some, and the ultimate hope of music to others. The impresario Max Maretzek joked about the furor: "I never discuss politics, religion, or Wagner. It always makes for bad blood and originates quarrels." Not only was Wagner's music a subject for heated conversation. His prose writings achieved very wide circulation, and were even being read in the United States as early as the 1850's. They were promptly translated and published in *Dwight's Journal of Music.* Liszt and his friends loudly beat the drum for Wagner, and the conservatives thought there was an international conspiracy under way. The French writer, François Joseph Fétis, summed up the anti-Wagner feeling in 1855:

> . . . A party has been formed only a few years ago that has the audacity to proclaim itself as the creator of the only true and complete art, and anything previous to it has been mere preparation. . . . The disdain which they affect towards form proceeds from the difficulty they have adhering to it without betraying poverty of matter. Disorder, phrases merely sketched and without construction, are more to their liking because nothing is more irksome to the logic of ideas for sterile and lazy imaginations. . . . In Germany they have taken control of magazines to ensure the triumph of their revolutionary attempt. A silence as of death reigns in these same writings about the work of artists who follow other ways. Some serious men have tried to enlighten public opinion by a rational criticism of this shameful socialism, but have not been able to make their voices heard. All approaches to the press have been closed to them. It would take too long to relate the means used by the brethren and friends for the glorification of their chief: their maneuvers to get possession of theaters; their falsehoods to smother truth when it tries to make itself heard; their concerted plans to blacken and eliminate those not with them . . .

The British critics, headed by the ineffable Henry Fothergill Chorley, were especially vicious. Chorley fought every Wagner opera as it appeared. *Rienzi* he called "simply noise." *Der fliegende Holländer* left "an impression of grim violence and dreary vagueness." Chorley wrote of *Tannhäuser* that he had "never been so blanked, wearied, *insulted* even (the word is not too strong) by a work of pretension as by this same *Tannhäuser.*" Chorley also predicted the "utter ruin which must overtake vocal art if composers followed in the wake of their idol [Wagner] and, for the sake of the orchestra, like him utterly debased and barbarized the cantilena under pretext of truth in declamation." But, ending his description of *Tannhäuser,* Chorley found a ray of hope: "There is comfort, however, in thinking that beyond

Herr Wagner in his peculiar manner it is hardly possible to go. The saturnal of licentious discord must have here reached its climax." Chorley never reviewed the later operas, unfortunately. They would have inspired him to inimitable outbursts of prose. The British critics, more than any in Europe, continually attacked Wagner, even in the 1870's, after his battle obviously was won.

During his years in exile, Wagner lived mostly off other people's money. Often the money came from impressionable women. Julie Ritter and Jessie Laussot helped him in 1850. (He planned to leave Minna and elope with Laussot, but she became frightened and returned to her husband.) To augment his income Wagner did a great deal of conducting, and he turned out to be the strongest influence on conducting in his time. At the beginning of his career, he had been an opera-house conductor. Later he conducted only symphony orchestras. His interpretations were original and highly personal, with insistence on nuanced playing and a complete range of dynamics. Never a purist, he was always more concerned with the spirit than the letter of the score. He also introduced the concept of tempo fluctuation. Most conductors of his period were time-beaters of the Mendelssohn school. Wagner substituted a rise and fall, slowing and speeding, a constant variation of tempo with the use of ritards to link contrasting passages. It was an approach that drove academicians out of their minds. From all evidence, it was also an approach that would sound extremely eccentric to twentieth-century ears. The more classic, restrained conducting of a Mendelssohn or a Berlioz would be preferred. Nevertheless it was the Wagner style of conducting that dominated the last half of the nineteenth century. Not only did Wagner himself set the example on the podium, but the world was full of Wagner-trained conductors. The most famous were Hans Richter, Anton Seidl, Hans von Bülow, Felix Mottl, and Hermann Levi. Probably the most popular conductor of the day was Artur Nikisch, and while he had not worked directly under Wagner's supervision, he had been weaned on the Wagner operas, and his first big assignment was as a conductor of the Wagnerian repertoire. Not until a classic reaction set in, with the advent of such conductors as Felix Weingartner and Arturo Toscanini, was there a counterrevolution. At that, the Wagner type of highly personal conducting continued until 1954 when Wilhelm Furtwängler died.

It was during his Swiss exile that Wagner started work on the four operas of the *Ring des Nibelungen*. An opera on the death of Siegfried was his original conception. Unable to contain the story in one opera, he started a series. In 1852 he finished the complete libretto, and *Das Rheingold* was composed in 1854. A conducting tour to London in 1855 broke into the composition of the *Ring*, but Wagner managed to finish *Die Walküre* in 1856. During these years Wagner was having an affair with Mathilde Wesendonk. She was the young wife of a silk merchant. Otto Wesendonk not only had money, but he also was a patron of the arts. It was a combination very pleasing to Wagner. Mathilde and he had met in 1852, and by 1854 they were in love. She inspired him, while her husband supplied Wagner with money. Matters came to a head when Minna intercepted a love letter. She sent some bitter words to Mathilde: "Before my departure I must tell you that you have succeeded in separating my husband from me after nearly twenty-two years of marriage. May this noble deed contribute to your peace of mind, to your happiness." The Wagners and Wesendonks remained neighbors in Zurich, but relations began to grate. Finally, in 1858, Minna, who was suffering from a heart condition, went to Dresden, ostensibly to be treated. Wagner went to Venice and worked on *Tristan und Isolde*. He had temporarily dropped the *Ring* cycle. The Wesendonk affair had given him a different kind of inspiration, and the shadow of Mathilde hovers over *Tristan*, which was started in 1857. (There are autobiographical elements in many Wagner operas. In the *Ring*, Wagner identified himself with Siegfried. In *Der fliegende Holländer*, the first draft has the heroine named Minna. Wagner changed it to Senta, and the inference is that he felt that Minna could not redeem the Holländer [Wagner]. In *Die Meistersinger*, he is Walther von Stolzing, just as Beckmesser is the Viennese critic, Eduard Hanslick. It was with difficulty that Wagner was talked out of naming the character Hans Lich.)

Nothing Wagner had done had hinted at the operatic miracle named *Tristan und Isolde*. Never in the history of music had there been an operatic score of comparable breadth, intensity, harmonic richness, massive orchestration, sensuousness, power, imagination, and color. The opening chords of *Tristan* were to the last half of the nineteenth century what the *Eroica* and Ninth Symphonies had been to the first half—a breakaway, a new concept. Nor is the impact of the opera yet over. *Tristan und Isolde* has been analyzed and psychoanalyzed almost as much as *Hamlet* (Wagner has been written about more than any composer in history, and *Tristan* occupies a major share of the bibliography). The very opening chords, with their harmonic vagueness, create a certain amount of controversy to this day, and analysts dispute their "spelling." Are they fourths or sevenths? In *Tristan*, harmonic relationships are pushed to their breaking point, and twentieth-century scholars see in the opera the beginnings of atonality. Wagner claimed to have been in something like a trance when he wrote it: "Here, in perfect trustfullness, I plunged into the inner depths of soul-events and from the innermost center of the world I fearlessly built up to its outer form. . . . Life and death, the whole meaning and existence of the outer world, here hang on nothing but the inner movements of the soul." What *Tristan*, that most static of operas and yet the most relentless in building up to its doom, does is to describe inner states, with a kind of power and imagination that peels off layer after layer of the subconscious. It abounds in symbols—symbols of Night, Day, Love, eroticism, the dream world, Nirvana. Whatever its meaning or meanings, *Tristan und Isolde* brings together man and woman, and probes their deepest impulses.

The influence of Schopenhauer was a strong factor in *Tristan und Isolde.* Wagner started to read the German philosopher in the early 1850's, and Schopenhauer's ideas about music entered into a good deal of Wagner's thinking. Schopenhauer wrote that music "is entirely independent of the phenomenal world, ignores it altogether, could to a certain extent exist if there was no world at all, which cannot be said of the other arts." Music, continued Schopenhauer, "is the copy of the will itself. . . . That is why the effect of music is so much more powerful and penetrating than that of the other arts, for they speak only of shadows, but music speaks for the thing itself." In melody Schopenhauer found "the unbroken significant connection of *one* thought from beginning to end representing a whole." This Schopenhauer equated with "the objectification of will, the intellectual life and effort of man." The creator of music "reveals the inner nature of the world." Schopenhauer claimed that if music is too closely connected to word, "it is trying to speak a language not its own." By 1855 Wagner was echoing Schopenhauer and writing that music was "the proto-image of the world itself." Wagner eventually was to assign to music the highest hierarchy in his operas; he decided, as had Schopenhauer, that music was, after all, more important than the Word. Another aspect of Schopenhauer that interested Wagner was his doctrine of the redemption of the soul through the medium of art, and also through renunciation and the ascetic life. Wagner was no more ready to live the ascetic life than Schopenhauer himself had been, but in theory it was a grand and ennobling revelation. The concept of renunciation and redemption, which was present in the Wagner operas as early as *Tannhäuser*, is greatly intensified in the *Ring* and *Parsifal*.

Tristan und Isolde was finished in 1859, but no productions were in sight. The last measures of the opera were written in Lucerne, where Wagner settled—alone, for Minna was still in Dresden—after leaving Venice. They were corresponding, however, and Wagner decided to go to Paris with her. Wesendonk supplied the money for the move by purchasing the completed portion of the *Ring* for 24,000 francs, and the Wagners arrived in Paris toward the end of 1859. It was characteristic that in Paris he rented an expensive house, paid the rent for three years in advance, paid for repairs on the house, had all his furniture sent from Lucerne, and hired a servant for Minna and a valet for himself. Wesendonk's money did not last long. A performance of *Tannhäuser* was arranged for the Opéra in 1861, and it ended in one of the most famous of all operatic scandals, with the Jockey Club booing the opera off the stage. Much has been made of this disaster, but while it might have hurt Wagner's pride, it meant little in the long run. Wagner had gone far beyond *Tannhäuser*.

The next few years were difficult. Vienna promised to stage *Tristan und Isolde* and then backed down: a bitter blow. Wagner ran out of money, had to give up his big house, and moved into menial quarters on the Quai Voltaire, where he started working on a new opera, *Die Meistersinger*. The publishing firm of Schott advanced him money for it, and he soon ran through that. An amnesty allowed him to go back to Germany, and he and Minna moved to Biebrich, on the Rhine. Again his money ran out. He raged: "Mine is a highly susceptible, intense, voracious sensuality, which must somehow or another be indulged if my mind is to accomplish the agonizing labor of calling a non-existent world into being." His next move, in 1862, was to Vienna. Again he was alone. Minna had left him for good. Conducting engagements in Russia, 1863, brought in a good deal of money, but his spending was on a cosmic scale, and what would have sufficed to keep most men happy could not begin to keep Wagner in furs, silks, and perfume. Creditors pressed him, and he had to flee to Switzerland in 1864. The alternative was going to a debtors' prison.

In the darkest hours of 1864, salvation appeared to the desperate Wagner in the person of the homosexual King Ludwig II of Bavaria, who was in love with Wagner's music and very possibly with Wagner himself. Ludwig gave Wagner carte blanche to produce his operas in Munich under ideal conditions. The entire resources of the opera house there—more, the entire resources of Bavaria, as it turned out—were turned over to Wagner. There is no record of any surprise from him. He thought it was his due. "I am the most German of beings. I am the German spirit. Consider the incomparable magic of my works."

Wagner immediately summoned Hans von Bülow to Munich and made him the conductor of the Munich Court Opera. Bülow, trained as a pianist by Liszt, had come under Wagner's spell as early as 1850. In 1857 he married Liszt's daughter, Cosima. One of the best pianists in Europe, Bülow also was a brilliant conductor and one of the sharpest musical minds of his period. His tongue was as sharp as his mind. A tiny, tart, driving, dyspeptic man, he was famous for the intellectual vigor of his interpretations. Some called him all mind and no soul. Wagner, as a friend of Liszt, had seen much of Bülow through the years. He knew that Bülow, who idolized him, would work night and day in his behalf. And Wagner was very, very interested in Cosima. She became his mistress soon after the arrival of the Bülows in Munich, in the spring of 1864. If Bülow knew that he was being made a cuckold, he gave no sign. When a girl, named Isolde, was born to

Cosima in April, 1865, Bülow accepted the infant as his own child.

Rehearsals for *Tristan und Isolde* started. There is an amusing caricature of Wagner and Cosima, who towers over him, walking down the street, with a tiny Bülow, clutching the score of *Tristan*, creeping humbly behind them. Bülow antagonized the musicians with his demands and his tantrums, but from all accounts he conducted brilliantly at the premiere, on June 10, 1865. Three performances rapidly followed.

It took time for *Tristan und Isolde* to establish itself in the European repertoire. The opera was too long, too "uneventful," too "dissonant," too "modern." All many critics could see were two large people screaming at each other. Another reason for the slow progress of *Tristan* was the inability of most singers to cope with the two major roles. At the Munich performances the role of Tristan was sung by Ludwig Schnorr, a tenor who was Wagner's ideal as a singer—young, handsome, heroic in build, intelligent, with a bronzelike, steady voice. Three weeks after the fourth performance of *Tristan und Isolde*, Schnorr was dead at the age of twenty-nine. Rheumatic fever carried him away. Wagner, Ludwig, and all musical Europe grieved.

Wagner was busily engaged in digging his own grave in Munich, and he did not have many months to remain there after the *Tristan* premiere. Faced with an unlimited supply of funds for the first time in his life he ran wild, indulging himself with an incredibly lavish hand. Had he shown any finesse, he could have lorded it over King and court, but his combination of arrogance, recklessness, selfishness, and dishonesty was too much. He even started to dabble in politics, and that really scared some of the most important members of the Bavarian establishment, who gathered together to stop him. They whipped up a public outcry over Wagner's spending, his insane extravagance, his morals (everybody at court knew about his relationship with Cosima, and now the public was told), and his domination over the King. On December 10, 1865, Wagner was forced to leave. It was banishment. Ludwig suggested that it might be better if he disappear for a while—on full allowance, of course. Wagner went to Geneva, where he worked on *Die Meistersinger* In January, 1866, he learned of Minna's death. Cosima joined him, and they found a palatial estate at Triebschen, on Lake Lucerne. It was there that she bore him their second child, Eva, in 1867.

At Triebschen, Wagner lived surrounded by the luxury he needed. The living room, which contained portraits of Beethoven, Goethe, and Schiller, had walls covered with yellow leather traced with gold. The gallery was a long, narrow room hung in violet velvet, lined with statues of Wagnerian heroes, and draped with tapestries portraying scenes from the *Ring*. In one corner of the gallery was a butterfly collection; in another, a gilded Buddha, Chinese incense burners, and other Orientalia. In the carefully kept gardens lived a great dog, a Newfoundland named Russ. (Wagner always had a dog or dogs. In more or less chronological order, there were two black poodles, Dreck and Speck; the Newfoundland, Robber, who accompanied Wagner and Minna from Riga to London and Paris; a spaniel named Peps; another spaniel, Fips; a brown hound, Pohl; two more Newfoundlands, Mark and Brangäne; several terriers; and a Spitz named Putzi. Wagner idolized them.)

Now and then Cosima, for the sake of appearances, joined her husband in Munich, where *Die Meistersinger* was in rehearsal. Bülow and Hans Richter were preparing the opera. Richter, a Hungarian, had come to Triebschen in 1866 as Wagner's secretary and copyist. Later he became, with Mottl and Seidl, the first of the Wagner-trained conductors to emerge from Bayreuth. Many considered him the greatest. It was to Richter that the honor of conducting the *Meistersinger* premiere fell, on June 21, 1868. A few months later, Richter resigned from the Munich Opera, claiming that rehearsals of *Das Rheingold* were scandalously inadequate. Everybody knew that Richter would not have resigned without Wagner's blessing, and Ludwig for once was furious. Franz Wüllner conducted the *Rheingold* premiere (and also the premier of *Die Walküre* in 1870).

Bülow meanwhile was in an intolerable position. All Germany by now knew of his marital problems. Cosima refused to return to him, and in 1869 she bore Wagner a third child, Siegfried. Bülow had enough. Divorce proceedings were set in motion, and the decree became final in 1870. On August 25 of that year, Wagner and Cosima were married. *Siegfried* was finished in 1871 and *Götterdämmerung* substantially completed in 1872 (though the scoring was not finished until 1874).

The early 1870's saw two other major events in Wagner's life—his relationship with Nietzsche, and the inception of Bayreuth.

Friedrich Nietzsche had met Wagner in 1868 and had all but drowned himself in worship of the man and his music (especially *Tristan und Isolde*). In 1872 he published *The Birth of Tragedy from the Spirit of Music*, in which Greek tragedy was interpreted along Wagnerian lines. Nietzsche's concept of Apollonian (pure, classic) and Dionysian (wild, romantic) opposites, as set forth in his book, made a deep impression on contemporary aesthetic thinking. Later, Nietzsche was to reconsider his adoration of Wagner and eventually swung out of the orbit, calling Bizet's *Carmen* the perfect opera. But for a long time Wagner had the support of the most widely read German philosopher.

As early as 1870 Wagner was thinking seriously about a festival theater that would be dedicated to his works alone. He found his ideal site at the quiet little Bavarian town of Bayreuth. Ludwig at first was cold to the idea. But Wagner Societies were formed all over Germany, and Wagner's friends exerted themselves to raise money for the cause. Wagner sent out a circular, dated November 12, 1871, advising that the *Ring des Nibelungen* would open Bayreuth in 1873. Those who donated money "will receive the name and rights of patrons of the festival stage play at Bayreuth, while the carrying-out of the enterprise itself will be left exclusively to my knowledge and my exertions. The real estate accruing from this common enterprise shall be placed at my disposal and subject to such future arrangements as I shall consider most appropriately serviceable to the sense and ideal character of the undertaking." Wagner left Triebschen, had a villa built near the festival theater in Bayreuth, and supervised the work. In Vienna, Hanslick was amazed. "Wagner," he wrote, "is lucky in all things. At first he raves against all monarchs; and a magnanimous King meets him with flattering love and prepares for him an existence free from care and even lavish. Then he writes a pamphlet against the Jews; and all Jewry, both in and outside of music, pays him all the more zealous homage, through newspaper criticisms and purchase of Bayreuth promissory notes."

The Bayreuth project received world-wide publicity, but money was slow coming in. Wagner had to cancel his plans for an 1873 season. Less than half the necessary funds were on hand. Wagner put all his hopes in Ludwig, and was not disappointed. In 1874 the King advanced enough money to start things moving again. There was a great deal of opposition in Bavaria to the project. It was attacked as folly, as a testament to Ludwig's madness. When Ludwig's money ran out, Wagner embarked on conducting tours to raise funds. For a while the future of Bayreuth was in doubt. Nevertheless the building was completed, and the first Bayreuth Festival was given in 1876. *Der Ring des Nibelungen*, Richter conducting, was given three times. The first season showed an enormous deficit, and the future of Bayreuth was once again in doubt. Not until 1882 could a second Bayreuth Festival be undertaken.

The first Bayreuth season was the musical event of the decade. Some 4,000 visitors, including sixty newspaper correspondents from all over the globe, inundated the tiny village. In attendance were the Emperor of Germany, the Emperor and Empress of Brazil, the King of Bavaria, Prince George of Prussia, a Hohenzollern prince, Prince Wilhelm of Hesse, Grand Duke Vladimir of Russia, the Grand Duke of Mecklenburg, the Duke of Anhalt-Dessau, and other nobility. Such was the interest in the festival that the two critics from New York—both the *Times* and the *Tribune* sent reporters—were allowed to use the new transatlantic cable to get their stories through instantly. Among the things they reported was the unhappiness about creature comforts. "The great distance from the town over a dirty road with no shade and no restaurant accommodations caused much discontent. The discontent in these regards is daily increasing," said the *Times*. Audiences listened to the music with some puzzlement but also with honest enthusiasm. At the end of each opera there was an ovation, but no singer was allowed to take a curtain call. "The reason for so declining was explained by Herr Wagner and the leading artists, who said that appearances before the curtain would tend to violate the unity of the representation." At the end of the festival there was a great party for over 500 people. Wagner made a long speech, was cheered, and bent his head to receive a silver crown of laurel leaves. Wagner then paid tribute to Liszt, saying he owed everything to him; whereupon Liszt got up to make *his* speech. "Other countries," he said, "greet Dante and Shakespeare. So," turning to Wagner, "I am your most obedient servant."

Musically the Bayreuth season was the turning point in Wagner's European fortunes. Not only did the audience consist largely of Wagner admirers, but the critics (including the ones from New York) were also for the most part supporters. (Brahms and his group ostentatiously stayed away.) They spread the word about the glories of the new music; and the many composers who came to Bayreuth, especially the French contingent, were overwhelmed. For the first time words like "melodious," "tuneful," "lyric" and "beautiful" began consistently to appear in reviews of the Wagner operas. The chorus of praise drowned out the cries of the doubters. Even Hanslick hedged, though he was bothered by the underlying aesthetic of Wagnerism. "The plastic energy of Wagner's fancy, his astonishing mastery over the orchestral technique, and numerous musical beauties reign in the *Nibelungen* with a magical power to which we willingly and thankfully yield ourselves captive. These single beauties that creep, as it were, behind the back of the system do not prevent this *system,* the tyranny of the word, of unmelodious dialogue, from planting in the whole the seeds of death." Joseph Bennett, in the London *Musical Times,* echoed Hanslick, saying that the music might very well be beautiful, full of genius, full of melody—but "Something of Milton's Fallen Spirit surrounds Wagner, with a strange mixture of attraction and repulsion. Among the gods of his native heaven he might have been great, and in that which is now his own place he lifts himself in Titanic grandeur. But let us not forget he is powerful chiefly for evil." Bennett, like the other old critics, could feel the ground slipping from him, but he went down bravely, firing as he went.

Stimulated by the furor, *Punch* added its contribution. It ran a long imaginary interview on "Music—of the Present and of the Future." Mrs. Hazy Highfaluter was being questioned. "Will you define the tone-art of the future?" Her answer: "It defies definition. I should describe it as a mighty system of spiritual aëronautics, meant to lift up the soul to the sublime regions of supersensuous harmony, above the gross and earthly restraints of received form in composition, and the vulgar attractions of sustained melody."

Everybody in Europe was writing or talking about Wagner. But, more important, the opera houses were staging his works, and not only the early ones After Bayreuth there was a run on Wagner At the Berlin Opera, for example. there were 223 performances during the 1877–78 season Wagner headed the list with thirty-eight performances of five operas Next was Mozart. with twenty-nine of six works. followed by Verdi with nineteen of four works These ratios were to prevail for many years in German opera houses Within a decade after Bayreuth, opera houses in Germany. Austria, England, and the United States were bidding eagerly for the Wagnerian operas, and Wagner was beginning to show up even in such unsympathetic centers as France and Italy

Die Meistersinger quickly made its way as the most "human" of the Wagner operas. German audiences especially identified with medieval Nuremberg, and with Hans Sachs's plea for German art. This is the sunniest of Wagner's operas, and if the humor is heavy-handed and all the cards stacked against poor Beckmesser, the glorious sweep of the music is irresistible The message of *Die Meistersinger* is clear and direct, altogether different from the murky symbolism of the *Ring* The four operas of the *Ring* may outwardly be concerned with gods, goddesses, earth-mothers, and Aryan heroes, all manipulated so that the theme of redemption through love wins out, but the characters end up being archetypes, capable of being interpreted any number of ways. George Bernard Shaw, for one, took the *Ring* in terms of capitalism versus Fabian Socialism. The post-World War II stagings at Bayreuth present the *Ring* in terms of sun-god myths, mother-images, father-images, closed and broken circles, and the whole Jungian apparatus. But a miracle happens when the *Ring* is heard. Exegesis disappears, and the listener is swept into something primal, timeless, and is pushed by elemental forces. The *Ring* is a conception that deals not with women but Woman; not with men, but Man; not with people, but with the Folk; not with mind, but with the subconscious; not with religion, but with basic ritual; not with nature, but with Nature.

Wagner had triumphed. He had had his way Now he was the most famous composer in the world. He could, with relative peace of mind, spend much of his time at the Villa Wahnfried in Bayreuth and devote himself entirely to the things that interested him. That included working on *Parsifal* and writing pamphlets and articles for the official Wagner publications. His personal life became even more eccentric. Among other things, he became a vegetarian and came to the conclusion that the world would be saved if everybody ate vegetables instead of meat. He lived like an Oriental pasha, bathed in incense, dressed in violently clashing colors, with only the softest silk touching his skin Secure in his all-embracing wisdom, he wrote reams of prose on every conceivable subject. Sometimes his articles approached idiocy, as in the section of an essay on Beethoven dealing with the composer's cranial characteristics.

If it is held to be an axiom of physiology for high intellectual endowments that a great brain must be enclosed in a thin, delicate skull, as if to facilitate the immediate cognition of external things, we saw, nevertheless, on the inspection of the remains a few years ago, in conformity with the entire skeleton, a skull of unusual thickness and firmness. So did nature guard in him a brain of extreme tenderness, in order that it might look towards the interior only, and carry on in undisturbed repose the world contemplation of a great heart. What that exceedingly robust strength enclosed and preserved was an inner world of such conspicuous delicacy that, left defenceless to the rough touch of the external world, it would have gently dissolved—as did Mozart's genius of light and love.

His anti-Semitism and screams for racial purity approached madness. He even compared Brahms's music to that of "a Jewish czardas player." In one of his last tracts, *Heldentum und Christentum*, he claimed that the Aryans had sprung from the gods. But inferior peoples had deprived the Aryans of their godhead, especially the Jews, "former cannibals, educated to be the business leaders of society." Christ was not a Jew. He was basically an Aryan. Small wonder that Hitler was to say: "Whoever wants to understand National Socialistic Germany must know Wagner."

. Work on *Parsifal* continued, alternating with racist treatises, studies of what had happened to Christianity, and a love affair with Judith Mendès, she about forty years younger than he was. Judith, noted for her beauty, was the daughter of Théophile Gautier, the French poet and critic who had been one of Wagner's earliest admirers. She was married to the poet Catulle Mendès, and they first met Wagner at Triebschen. He was fascinated with her, and when they met again during the first season in Bayreuth, the attraction became physical. She moved into Villa Wahnfried, and Cosima pretended not to notice. Judith returned to Paris and her husband, but she and Wagner corresponded until 1878. It was Wagner's last love affair, and it is hard to resist reading into the sensuous music of the second act of *Parsifal* the erotic stimulation that Judith had given him.

Parsifal, finished in 1882, is commonly taken to be a religious opera, and there is something ironic in the sight of audiences attending it as a Christian rite. It is, however, an opera capable of many interpretations. The accepted theme is that of Christian mysticism, purity, and redemption. Others have found in it the essence of anti-Christianity; and Robert W. Gutman, one of Wagner's recent biographers, has proved, to his satisfaction at least, that *Parsifal* is "an allegory of the Aryan's fall and redemption." In this interpretation, Klingsor represents not only the Jews but also the Jesuits. That, specifically, is what Wagner once said to Cosima. Debussy had his own ideas about *Parsifal*. He wrote, only half jokingly, that Klingsor was "the finest character" in the opera:

He knows what men are worth, and weighs the solidity of their vows of chastity in scales of contempt. From this one may safely argue that this cunning magician, this hardened old criminal, is not merely the only human character, but the only normal character in this drama which contains the falsest of moral and religious theories—theories of which the youthful Parsifal is the heroic and foolish champion. In fact, in this Christian drama, no one wants to sacrifice himself.

One thing can be said of *Parsifal* with complete accuracy. Its composer was not a religious man. Wagner detested religious orthodoxy of any kind, and he dismissed Christianity as stemming from the Jews. If he had any religious feeling at all, it was a vague pantheism, a longing for the heroic deeds of Teutonic myth. The pan-Germanism of Richard Wagner was one of the governing forces of his life.

Parsifal, Wagner decided, should be restricted to Bayreuth for thirty years, after which the work would be released to the world. (The Metropolitan Opera did not care to wait that long, and staged *Parsifal* in New York in 1903. "Heresy!" shrieked the Wagnerians in Bayreuth and elsewhere.) Wagner made an exception for King Ludwig, and there were several private performances in Munich. The world premiere took place at Bayreuth on July 26, 1882. Hermann Levi was the conductor. He was chief conductor at the Munich Opera—and he was a Jew. Wagner spent a great deal of time pleading with this son of a rabbi to undergo baptism. Levi was so disgusted that he wrote a letter asking to be relieved of the assignment, and Wagner who admired Levi's artistry, had to spend that much more time patching things up. After *Parsifal*, Wagner was exhausted, and he had premonitions of death. He went to Venice to recuperate, and it was there that he died, on February 13, 1883. His body was brought back to Bayreuth, and as the coffin was being lowered into the grave an orchestra played the funeral march from *Götterdämmerung*.

The years after Wagner's death—indeed, the years after the first Bayreuth season of 1876—saw Wagner's music penetrate the intellectual life of Europe. He was a potent influence on all composers who worked in the 1870's, and upon those who followed—on Richard Strauss, on Bruckner and Mahler, on the French school, on Dvořák, even on Debussy. Wagnerism lived on in Schoenberg's *Verklärte Nacht*, with its post-*Tristan* harmonies, and in such later Schoenberg works as *Erwartung*, which is a post-*Tristan* song of love that even has the equivalent of a *Liebestod*. Alban Berg's music is saturated with Wagner. Wagner lived on in the profusion of books that were, and still are, written about him: books to explain the leitmotifs, the message of the operas, the implications in them (from Schopenhauerian thought to Jungian psychology to the impact on National Socialism). In France, during the last two-thirds of the nineteenth century, Wagner was probably the supreme figure in all the arts. The symbolist poets took up his cause, and such important painters as Whistler, Degas, and Cézanne were Wagnerians. Redon and Fantin-Latour painted canvases based on the operas. Daudet described the phenomenon: "We studied his characters as if Wotan held the secret of the world and Hans Sachs was the spokesman for free, natural, and spontaneous art." Mallarmé and Baudelaire were enthusiasts, and the latter went around saying that Wagner in music was the equivalent of Delacroix in painting. The French literature of the day was full of allusions to Wagner.

Early in the twentieth century, strong anti-Wagnerian schools began to make themselves felt. Debussy, who originally has been a Wagnerian, broke away and defiantly signed himself "musicien français." Even Debussy, however, was not able to shake entirely free. He poked fun at the wordy librettos and their length—"All this is inadmissible for those who love clarity and conciseness"—but had to admit that the Wagner operas were full of passages of "unforgettable beauty" that "silence all criticism." Debussy fought the music of the siren from Bayreuth, and in his own scores did make a considerable breakaway. Stravinsky was probably the first completely successful anti-Wagnerian, in that he discarded the entire Wagnerian apparatus in favor first of Russian nationalism and then of neoclassicism.

With the prevalent antiromanticism in all the arts that set in after 1920, Wagner slipped a little from his position. Suddenly the Wagner operas were found by musicians and intellectuals to sound thick, old-fashioned, verbose, faintly (or not so faintly) ridiculous. Coincidentally, the delights of bel canto opera and early Verdi were rediscovered. As Wagner began to slip, the international repertoire began to include Verdi operas that in some instances had not been staged for generations. There was something in Verdi's emotional health, clarity and directness that appealed to the age. It was also realized that Verdi and Wagner, once considered so apart from each other, did have some points in common, and *Falstaff* was held up as an example—*Falstaff*, in which set arias are all but abolished, in which the orchestra is completely integrated with the text, in which something very close to leitmotifs glint, disappear and reappear. Thus was the circle closed. The two great men, so far apart, came near touching in *Falstaff*. In the future Wagner and Verdi will live together, as they have lived together in the past. But one thing seems certain. Verdi will never again be underrated, as he once was; and Wagner will never again be taken as seriously as he was taken at the turn of the century, when he all but dominated the intellectual life of the Western world.

18

Keeper of the Flame

JOHANNES BRAHMS

The only German composer of Wagner's lifetime who was big enough to stand with him on more or less an equal footing was Johannes Brahms. But they are antipodal. Wagner was the revolutionary, the man of the future. Brahms was the classicist who dealt with abstract forms and never wrote a note of program music in his life, much less an opera. Wagner was to exert enormous influence on the future. With Brahms the symphony as handed down by Beethoven, Mendelssohn, and Schumann came to an end. Brahms, like Bach, summed up an epoch. Unlike Bach, he contributed little to the development of music, though some of his textures and harmonies find a faint echo in Arnold Schoenberg. Even in Brahms's own day the progressives thought little of him. Mahler called Brahms "a mannikin with a somewhat narrow heart." Such Wagner-dominated hotheads as Hugo Wolf gleefully jumped on each new Brahms composition, poking fun at it. Wolf, reviewing the Third Symphony for the *Wiener Salonblatt*, proclaimed that "Brahms is the epigone of Schumann and Mendelssohn and, as such, exercises about as much influence on the history of art as the late Robert Volkmann [a once-popular, now forgotten academic composer], that is, he has for the history of art just as *little* importance as Volkmann, which is to say *no* influence at all. . . . The man who has written three symphonies and apparently intends to follow with another six . . . is only a relic from primeval ages and no vital part of the great stream of time."

But for a relic Brahms has turned out to have remarkable endurance. The major part of his *oeuvre* has remained an active part of the repertory, and shows no diminution in public favor. Quite the contrary. Brahms, in the 1960's, was elbowing Beethoven as the most popular of symphonic composers. His four symphonies, the two piano concertos, the Violin Concerto and even his Double Concerto are basic repertory, as are the *Haydn Variations* and the *Academic Festival Overture*. Pianists are regularly playing the

F minor Sonata, the *Handel* and *Paganini Variations* and the various rhapsodies, intermezzi, and caprices of his late period. Chamber groups find indispensable the Clarinet Quintet, the Piano Quintet, the three string quartets and other chamber music. His songs are regularly on recital programs. The *German Requiem* is steadily performed. Violinists would be lost without the three sonatas. Considering that the major percentage of Mendelssohn's, Schumann's, and Liszt's music lies untouched in the Collected Editions considering that great reputations have come and gone, Brahms's record is amazing. Clearly he had something very pertinent to say to future generations.

Brahms was a conscious classicist, occupying in the last half of the nineteenth century a position analogous to Mendelssohn's in the first half Like Mendelssohn, he was content with the old forms, and he knew more about them than anybody in his period. As conductor of the Gesellschaft der Musikfreunde he placed a great deal of early music on its programs, and he was one of the very few musicians of his day who refrained from romanticizing and rewriting. Only a man well versed in baroque counterpoint could have written the propulsive, heroic fugue that concludes the *Handel Variations*, and only so strong an individualist as Brahms could at the same time have kept it from being a mere copy of an old formula. Bach he loved above all. He wrote to Clara Schumann of the Chaconne: "On a system for a small instrument, a man writes a whole world of the deepest thoughts and the most tremendous emotions. If I could imagine that I could have accomplished such a thing, could have conceived it within myself, I know surely that the excitement and the shock would have driven me insane" And he told Eusebius Mandyczewski "When the new Handel edition comes out and is sent to me, I put it in my library and say, As soon as I have time I will look it over. But when a new Bach edition appears, I let everything else go" He knew the classic period almost as well, and was a profound student of Beethoven's music. The violent romantic currents around him, the 'music of the future," he largely ignored. He was content to work the way the old masters had worked, employing counterpoint, variation, and sonata form He had a strong feeling for German folksong and often used it, but his is not a nationalist music. It is a music of immense weight and solidity, especially at the beginning of his career; a music marked with Schumannesque cross-rhythms, with a Beethovenian feeling for development, with a Bachian feeling for polyphony.

Above all it is essentially a serious music, even if Brahms could be as lyric as any romantic composer when he wanted to be. From the beginning he set himself to write a "pure" music, an absolute music, a music that would be a corrective to the extravagant ideas of Liszt and Wagner. His music could be complicated and difficult, but it was never showy except in one bravura set,

251

the *Paganini Variations*, and even there the virtuosity is governed by strict musical logic. His music deliberately avoided anything suggestive of superficial prettiness. For many years Brahms had the reputation of being a "difficult" composer, a philosopher in sound.

Definitely he was an uncompromising composer; but, then again, he was an uncompromising man. Prickly, tough, ultrasensitive, cynical, bad-tempered, he created almost as much fear as the dyspeptic Hans von Bülow. He had his generous side; if he was interested in a composer, as he was in Dvořák or Grieg, he would move heaven and earth to help him. But he was interested in very few living composers. Liszt and Wagner were alien to him, and he had little respect for Bruckner, Mahler, Tchaikovsky, Verdi, or Richard Strauss. The contemporary composer he probably loved best was the Waltz King, Johann Strauss, the younger. He never had any hesitation speaking his mind, and sometimes his comments could be brutally contemptuous. Max Bruch, a well-thought-of composer of the day (his G minor Violin Concerto still is played), sent Brahms the manuscript of an oratorio, *Arminius*. Brahms looked it over. One day shortly thereafter, Bruch and Brahms were dining, and they heard a hurdy-gurdy across the street. "Listen, Bruch!" Brahms shouted. "That fellow has gotten hold of your *Arminius!*" Even Brahms's closest friends could be impaled on the spike of Brahms's testiness. At a party in the composer Ignaz Brüll's house, the poet and biographer of Brahms, Max Kalbeck, started making an anti-Wagner speech. Brahms suddenly shot forth: "For God's sake, stop talking about things you don't understand." Brahms's remark was that of the professional irritated by the amateur, but it was tactless, and Kalbeck left the room. The critic Richard Specht, who relates this story, says that he met Kalbeck a few days later, and Kalbeck bitterly complained of Brahms's ingratitude. "This is what I get for such devotion!" But, said Kalbeck, "This time I did not tolerate such an attack by the lord and master. I wrote him a long letter and told him off in no uncertain terms." Specht wanted to know what Brahms's reaction was. "Of course," Kalbeck grinned, "I never sent the letter." There was a story current in Vienna that Brahms left a party saying, "If there is anybody here I have not insulted, I apologize." The Viennese critic Max Graf says that while the story *should* be true, it was invented by a man named Béla Haas, a friend of Brahms and Hanslick.

All of Brahms's biographers are unanimous in saying that beneath the gruff exterior was a heart of gold. That appears to be true, but it did not make it easier for his friends, who had to put up with a kind of bluntness that often was all but antisocial. Even with such devoted and lifelong friends as Clara Schumann and Joseph Joachim there were occasional ruptures. Brahms knew the kind of man he was. "I let the world go the way it pleases. I am only too often reminded that I am a difficult person to get along with. I am growing accustomed to bearing the consequences of this." His frank and even crude way of talking, and his inability to see any point of view but his own, cost him many friends. He would blurt out things without thinking. On tour in Denmark in 1868 he was asked by his hosts if he had seen the Thorwaldsen Museum. "Yes, it's quite extraordinary. It's only a pity that it's not in Berlin." This tactless remark got out, and the public outcry was such that Brahms had to leave the country.

In his youth he was a handsome man, slim, with fair hair, very blue eyes, and a high voice that annoyed him. In his mature years he became a heavy set man with an enormous beard. He constantly smoked cigars and had an appearance of hopeless sloppiness. And he *was* sloppy. He hated to buy clothes, and his old, baggy, patched trousers were invariably too short. In Vienna, there were many who pointed out the resemblances with Beethoven (could Brahms have played these up?): both were short men, both loved the country, both had fierce tempers, both were bachelors. They even had a similar way of walking, head forward and hands clasped behind the back. Over his shoulders Brahms would wear a plaid shawl secured by a safety pin. In his hand, a hat that he seldom put on his head. All his life he observed humble habits. Even when he was financially well off he ate at cheap restaurants, lived very simply, and spent next to nothing on himself. Generally he could be found at his favorite tavern, The Red Hedgehog. He liked the coffee there. His biggest indulgence was his collection of original music manuscripts, among which could be found Mozart's G minor Symphony. He even owned the autograph score of Wagner's *Tannhäuser,* which he got as a gift from the pianist Karl Tausig. (It turned out that the score was not Tausig's to give away Wagner asked for its return and, with great and guarded politeness, Brahms did return it. Wagner sent him in its stead an autograph of *Das Rheingold.*)

Between Wagner and Brahms was a certain grudging admiration. They were the leaders of opposed schools, and while they had little to do with each other, there was no overt hostility between them. Wagner had a few ill-tempered remarks to make about Brahms, but for the most part ignored him as studiously as Brahms avoided *him* In a way that was surprising, for both were fighters, and as early as 1860 Brahms, with Joachim, Julius Otto Grimm, and Bernhard Scholz had signed a proclamation against the "so-called music of the future." Nobody paid any attention to the proclamation. The signers for the most part were young and unproved musicians. Brahms never again signed a manifesto or made a public utterance about music. If he was set up as the leader of the classic school, it was none of his own doing and Brahms even was exasperated with the whole thing. It was Eduard Hanslick, his friend and the influential critic of the *Neue freie Presse,* who was instrumental in casting Brahms as the "foe" of Wagner, as the flag-bearer behind whom marched the "pure" musicians—Clara Schumann, Joseph Joachim, and the other upholders of the classic tradition.

On the whole Brahms lived an uneventful life. Most of it was spent in Germany and Vienna. He did little traveling and little to promote his music. He was born in Hamburg on May 7, 1833. His father was a double-bass player. When Brahms was six years old it was discovered that he had perfect pitch and an extraordinary musical talent. By good luck he fell into the hands of Eduard Marxsen, a fine musician and teacher who gave him a heavy diet of Bach. It was clear to Marxsen that Brahms was something special, and his faith never wavered. When he heard of Mendelssohn's death in 1847, he said: "A master of the art has gone; a greater one arises in Brahms." Brahms was fourteen at the time, and it took a prescient man to make such an accurate prediction. Marxsen and Brahms remained close friends throughout life, and the Piano Concerto in B flat is dedicated to him. He died ten years before Brahms, in 1887.

At the age of ten Brahms was playing the piano in public. He also, to bring money into the family, played in waterfront dives and bordellos. This left psychic scars. All his life he was uncomfortable with virtuous women, and his sex life seems to have been confined to prostitutes. (Max Graf tells the story of the great Brahms coming into a dubious café in the 1880's and being asked by a well-known prostitute to go to the piano. "Professor, play us some dance music." The composer of the C minor Symphony obediently went to the battered upright and entertained the company.) The experiences he went through as a child undoubtedly kept him from marriage. He was tempted many times but always pulled back. Altogether characteristic was his relationship with Agathe von Siebold. After becoming engaged to her, he sent her a hysterical letter: "I love you. I must see you again. But I cannot wear fetters . . ." Naturally Agathe acted like any prudent girl, and broke off the engagement. A man who could write a letter like this would not have made a good husband. Later in life, in a confidential moment, Brahms told a friend about some of the things he had gone through as a child. "That was my first impression of women. And you expect me to honor them as you do!"

Brahms at the age of twenty had composed several major piano works, including the Scherzo in E flat minor, and the C major and F minor Piano Sonatas. Like all of the Brahms piano music up to the *Handel Variations*, they were serious and thick, with rumbling basses, awkward figurations, and an almost complete lack of charm. But they radiated bigness; there was something monumental about them. Not many pianists were interested in this kind of music. Like the late Beethoven works, they were written as much against the piano as for the piano. They spurned the virtuosity of Liszt and the sweet decoration of Chopin, and were concerned primarily with idea instead of texture. Brahms was not going to achieve overnight fame as a composer with such music.

He was, however, recognized as an accomplished pianist, and in 1853 he toured with Eduard Reményi as an accompanist. Reményi was a Hungarian violinist who played *à la tzigane*. A showman rather than a musician, he unabashedly catered to his audiences, and his repertory consisted mostly of short encore pieces and his own transcriptions of Chopin nocturnes and mazurkas. (As late as 1879, Reményi was touring the United States—not with Brahms—and he amused a critic no end: "This class of music was about what I expected to hear, but I was not prepared for *Swanee River* and, horror of horrors! must it be told? *Grandfather's Clock*.") What Brahms felt playing for this gentleman, history does not relate. It was on this 1853 tour with Reményi that Brahms met Joseph Joachim (1831–1907). The young but already famous violinist was very much impressed with Brahms's piano playing, and even more with his music. They became friends. At that time, Joachim was a member of the Liszt circle, and he took Brahms to Weimar with him. Brahms brought his music along, but was too shy to play it. Liszt, who gloried in acting as a patron of young composers, and who most likely was the greatest sight reader who ever lived, took Brahms's manuscripts to the piano and played at sight the E flat minor Scherzo and some of the C major Sonata. Whatever Brahms thought of Liszt as a composer, he had nothing but admiration for him as a pianist. "We others can play the piano," he later said, "but we all of us have only a few fingers of his hands." Liszt then played for Brahms his B minor Sonata. There is a story that Liszt looked at Brahms to see how the young man was taking it, and found him fast asleep. It sounds apocryphal. Nobody slept while the great Franz Liszt was storming up and down the keyboard.

If there was one living composer the young Brahms loved, it was Schumann. In 1853 the two men came together in Düsseldorf. Joachim had told Schumann about his new friend, and had been instrumental in arranging the meeting. There is a note in Schumann's diary dated September 30, 1853: "Brahms to see me (a genius)." Schumann was so impressed he wrote a long article about Brahms in the *Neue Zeitschrift für Musik,* calling him a young eagle and predicting that great things would come from him. It was Schumann's last article for the publication he had founded. Another concrete gesture by Schumann came when he introduced Brahms to Breitkopf and Härtel, who published his early works. So great was the attraction between Schumann and Brahms that he insisted the younger man move into his house. Brahms was at Clara's side after Schumann tried to commit suicide, and he was at her side after he died, in 1856. Brahms ended by falling in love with her. There are stories that the relationship between them was more than platonic, but it is hard to believe that Clara would have given herself to Brahms. Her mind, from everything we know about her, did not work that way. She was the widow of the great Robert Schumann, and she became a professional widow who wore mourning clothes all her life. That is not to say she and Brahms were anything but close. If nothing else, the memory of the man they both loved would have kept them together. They needed each other and they inspired each other. They also thought alike about music, had much the same ideals and aspirations, and were, intellectually and emotionally, much closer to each other than most husbands and wives.

The other great friendship of his life was with Joseph Joachim, who was to the violin what Clara Schumann was to the piano—an upholder of the faith, a bastion of classicism in the romantic kingdom. Joachim perceived the steel in Brahms as early as 1854, as witness a letter to a friend:

> With Brahms, who stayed with me for a few days, sleeping on the black couch, I could not feel perfectly at ease, even though I again recognized his good, even extraordinary, qualities. . . . Brahms is the most intransigent egotist imaginable, although he himself does not realize it. Everything oozes out of his sanguine nature quite spontaneously, but at times with a lack of consideration (not a lack of reticence, which would suit me fine!) that causes injury because it betrays uncouthness. . . . He recognizes the weakness of people with whom he deals, and he exploits them. . . . All he cares is to write music without interference; and his faith in a more sublime world of fantasy, and his manner of keeping all the unhealthy sensations and imaginary sufferings of others at arm's length borders on genius. . . . His compositions, so rich and ruthlessly rejecting all earthly woes, are such an effortless game in the most complex disguise. Never have I encountered such talent. He has surpassed me by far.

Brahms's first great orchestral work was the D minor Piano Concerto, which had its premiere in 1859 with the composer at the piano. Its opening, bold and daring, with a magnificent, defiant theme that still raises shivers, announced a major talent. It was not a work calculated to get many performances, for it was too difficult, too uncompromising, too big, too demanding intellectually. The initial consensus could be found in the remark of a critic that "the public was wearied and the musicians puzzled." At the Leipzig premiere another critic called the concerto "a symphony with piano obbligato" (not an original thought, for many years previously E. T. A. Hoffmann had called the concertos of Mozart and Beethoven "not so much concertos as symphonies with piano obbligato"). The critic went on to say that "the solo part is as ungrateful as possible and the orchestral part a series of lacerating chords." Leipzig was the headquarters of the neo-Mendelssohn party of archconservatives. But Leipzig's criticism was echoed elsewhere. Anton Rubinstein expressed what many musicians were thinking when Brahms's music first appeared: "For the drawing room, he is not graceful enough, for the concert hall not fiery enough, for the countryside not primitive enough, for the city not cultured enough. I have but little faith in such natures." Even such progressive composers as Édouard Lalo in Paris were bothered twenty and more years after the D minor Concerto was written. In a letter to the Spanish violinist Pablo de Sarasate, Lalo said that he had heard the D minor Concerto five times: "I maintain that when a soloist is set on the stage he must be given the main role and not be treated as a soloist within the orchestra. If the solo genre displeases the composer, then let him write symphonies or something else for the orchestra alone, but don't let him bore me with fragments of solo constantly interrupted by the orchestra." Many pianists felt that way. The D minor Concerto never received many performances, and not until the 1950's did it become one of the most popular of all concertos.

No matter what the critics and some of the musicians thought, it was evident that a new and powerful voice was being heard, and some important people in musical Germany took note. Little by little Brahms's reputation grew. Clara Schumann and Joachim played his music, and Julius Stockhausen began to sing his lieder. In 1862 Brahms visited Vienna, returned the following year, and made the city his home for the rest of his life. A decision by the Hamburg Philharmonic was instrumental in the move. Brahms wanted to become conductor of the orchestra, but was turned down—a rejection that rankled within him as long as he lived.

On his arrival in Vienna, Brahms became conductor of the Academy of Singing, and remained in that position for two years. After that, he concentrated on composing, breaking up his creative work by short concert tours as pianist or conductor. He made many friends in Vienna, including the pianist Julius Epstein, the violinist Joseph Hellmesberger, and the singer Amalie Weiss (whom Joachim married). Hellmesberger, who was the leader of a prominent string quartet, loudly acclaimed Brahms as Beethoven's heir. In the Brahms circle were also the great surgeon and amateur musician Theodor Billroth; the conductor Hermann Levi (who later moved to Munich, became a Wagnerian, and thus lost Brahms's friendship); the poet Max Kalbeck (who wrote the first important biography of Brahms); and the musicologist and Beethoven specialist, Gustav Nottebohm. Brahms lived in various apartments until 1871, when he took permanent lodgings at Karlgasse 4, over which his housekeeper, Frau Celestina Truxa, presided. It was in that house that he died, twenty-six years later.

The work that made Brahms famous was the *German Requiem*. It was first performed in Dresden in 1868 with one section missing, and the com-

257

plete work had its premiere the following year in Leipzig. The text is in German, from the Lutheran Bible, and has no relation to orthodox rites. Even the name of Christ is avoided. Brahms was a freethinker, and this disturbed his religious friends. "Such a great man! Such a great soul! And he believes in nothing!" lamented the appalled Dvořák. After the success of the *German Requiem*, Brahms all but stopped touring as a pianist. For several years, 1872–1875, he conducted the concerts of the Gesellschaft der Musikfreunde, and after that he no longer professionally conducted except to pick up the baton for his own music. He kept his publisher, Fritz Simrock, plentifully supplied with new material. Until 1876, he wrote in all forms except symphony and opera. Opera did not interest him, although every now and then he said he would like to write one. Nobody took him seriously. But symphony was another matter. His friends kept urging him to write one, but he held off. As with all the romantics, he had before him the fearsome specter of the Beethoven Ninth, against which all symphonies had to be measured.

Finally, in 1876, came his Symphony No. 1. Brahms had been working on it for years, and was not to be rushed. Beethoven at the equivalent age of forty-three had composed eight of his nine symphonies, but Brahms, who was being hailed as Beethoven's successor, was not going to put himself in competition with the greatest of all symphonists until he was sure of his command over the medium. "Composing a symphony is no laughing matter," he would tell those friends who kept insisting he must give birth. And, 'You have no idea of how it feels to hear behind you the tramp of a giant like Beethoven." Sure enough, musical Europe instantly set up the Brahms C minor Symphony against Beethoven, all the more in that a theme in the last movement of the Brahms bore some resemblance to the "Ode to Joy" theme in the Ninth. Hans von Bülow excitedly called Brahms's symphony "The Tenth." Brahms was half pleased, half irritated, by Bülow's outburst.

Having taken the plunge, Brahms followed with another symphony the next year. Then came masterpiece after masterpiece—the Violin Concerto in 1879, the B flat Piano Concerto in 1881, the Third Symphony in 1883, the Fourth Symphony in 1885, the Concerto for Violin and Cello in 1887. A large quantity of piano music and lieder, and three violin sonatas, came after the First Symphony. There was a remarkable series of works for the clarinet—the Clarinet Trio and Clarinet Quintet (both in 1891), and two clarinet sonatas (1894). These clarinet works were the result of Brahms's friendship with Richard Mühlfeld, the first clarinetist of the Meiningen Orchestra. In the 1880's, the greatest interpreter of Brahms's orchestral music was Hans von Bülow, who had taken over the Meiningen Orchestra in 1880 and proceeded to make it the precision instrument of European orchestras. Bülow was constantly on tour with the orchestra, and was constantly programing Brahms's music. All the devotion he previously had lavished on Wagner now was placed at the feet of Brahms. If a story related by Kalbeck is true, he, Brahms, and Bülow were walking in Vienna, Brahms a little ahead. Bülow clutched Kalbeck's arm, telling him to look at Brahms. "How broad and secure and healthily he stalks in front of us. I have him to thank for being restored to sanity—late, but I hope not too late—in fact, for still being alive. Three quarters of my existence has been misspent on my former father-in-law, that mountebank, and his tribe, but the remainder belongs to the true saints of art, and above all to him, to him." Bülow wrote to his fiancée, Marie Schanzer, that after Beethoven, Brahms was "the greatest, the most exalted of all composers. I consider his friendship my most priceless possession, second only to your love. It represents a climax in my life, a moral conquest." Unfortunately the friendship foundered on Brahms's tactlessness. Bülow had intended to conduct the Brahms Fourth Symphony on tour with the Meiningen Orchestra in Hamburg. It would have been the Hamburg premiere. Instead Brahms got there a few days earlier and conducted the premiere with the local orchestra. There undoubtedly was a psychological reason for this, for Brahms had a love-hate relationship with Hamburg, and on this occasion he must have been anxious to show the city how the local boy had made good. Nevertheless he did step on Bülow's toes, and the conductor was so insulted he not only refused to lead the Meiningen Orchestra in Hamburg; he also, in a typically quixotic gesture, resigned from the orchestra.

Bülow was not the only friend Brahms lost. Relations between him and the faithful Joachim were strained after the violinist's divorce from Amalie Weiss, in 1881. Brahms took Amalie's side, and Joachim was understandably hurt. In 1887 Brahms and Joachim were reconciled, though the friendship was never as close as it had been. Brahms tried to joke about it. "Now I know what I've missed all these years. It was the tone of Joachim's violin." (As a point of historical interest, it is worth noting that Joachim made a few recordings around 1905, and at least one of them, the first movement of Bach's unaccompanied G minor Sonata, shows the noble style and pure tone that made him the greatest classical violinist of the century.) Brahms grew more difficult, more sarcastic, as he grew older, and Billroth complained that Brahms made it impossible for anybody to come close to him, much less love him. In a letter to his daughter written in 1892 Billroth says that after all those years he still cannot figure out Brahms's behavior. "He occasionally enjoys baiting or teasing people. It seems to be a necessity for him. It may be a remnant of the resentment that remained in him from early youth, when he, knowing how serious his work was, was not recognized."

Clara Schumann died in 1896. It was a great blow to Brahms, who expressed his sorrow in the noble and brooding *Vier ernste Gesänge*. A greater blow came almost immediately afterward. Brahms developed cancer of the liver, the same ailment from which his father had died. He wasted away, and his friends sorrowed "It is tragic," wrote Heinrich von Herzogenberg, "that a forceful personality like Brahms is condemned to observe with a clear mind every phase of the destruction of his body. Brahms flat on his back!" The husky Brahms had never been seriously ill in his life. He dragged himself out of bed on March 7, 1897, to hear Hans Richter conduct the Fourth Symphony, and he received a great ovation. On April 3 he died

As with so many composers, there are three well-defined periods in Brahms's creative life. At the beginning he was preoccupied with a struggle for form. His music was big, had the utmost seriousness of purpose and a self-conscious nobility that was curiously engaging. It also was a music that did not flow with much ease. It could be clumsy, and even his admirers admitted as much. In 1863 a writer for the *Rezensionen* in Vienna had some words to say about the turgidness of Brahms's early music, and noted with satisfaction that Brahms had been able "to extricate himself from the mystical fogs of that somewhat dense and darkly seething cloudiness of feeling." The article, however, did settle on what was the central point of the Brahms style: "It is the awful dignity, the profound and, at the same time, honest seriousness with which Brahms devotes himself to all he undertakes that raises him above the ordinary level."

Later in life Brahms was just as happy if his early music was not played. Not only does his Beethoven fixation show too strongly, but such works as the three Piano Sonatas, the B major Trio, or the B flat Sextet tend to be controlled by formal ideas. Form dominates the composer rather than the composer dominating form. If the music is full of originality and striking ideas, it also sounds thick and labored. Even later, as in the great F minor Piano Quintet of 1864, there is a thickness that weights down the music; and granted that Brahms was not the least interested in making "pretty" sounds, there nevertheless are miscalculations in balances.

With the *Handel Variations* (1861) and the two books of *Paganini Variations* (1862–63), Brahms entered on a new phase of piano writing, culminating in the Eight Pieces of 1878 and the two rhapsodies of 1879. There is more security, confidence, and ebullience; more brilliance without any concession to frivolity. The eight short pieces of Op. 76 are the first he composed along that line, and all of his subsequent piano works were to be short. The pieces are varied, extremely sophisticated harmonically and rhythmically, and they carry Schumann's lovely sketches, such as in the *Davidsbündlertänze*, one step further. Another characteristic of the middle-period music of Brahms, as in the three string quartets, is grace. The early works of Brahms are too serious to be graceful, but in the middle-period music he is infinitely more relaxed, and a quality of unexpected charm can be felt. In the *Liebeslieder* waltzes, those lovely evocations of the Strauss family, Brahms carries this charm almost to excess. The music verges on the sentimental. In his songs, of which he composed some 250, Brahms strikes a perfect balance. His songs are very much in the Schumann tradition, even with the frequently thick piano parts, and they exhibit a lyricism comparable to Schumann's.

It is interesting to note that Brahms often composed in sets of two. Thus there were, only a few years apart, two sextets, two quartets, the two most famous sets of piano variations, two orchestral serenades, two sets of vocal waltzes, two overtures (the *Tragic* and the *Academic Festival*), two clarinet sonatas, two piano quartets, two symphonies. As he wrote the first, he seemed to get interested in the problems and they overflowed into a companion work. He kept this habit up to the very end. His late works take a different course than one might have expected. Where Beethoven went on to music of ever-increasing intensity and daring, Brahms seemed to relax more and more, and the word that invariably is used to describe his last works is "autumnal." His style became ever more gentle and reflective, especially after the Fourth Symphony of 1885.

The four symphonies are so familiar that no extended description is necessary. No. 1 in C minor came after years of anguished experiment. Bülow's nickname, "The Tenth," did more harm than good. Beethoven-lovers resented it, and took it out on Brahms rather than Bülow. The Second, in D major, the most lyric, came in 1877, a year after the First. It was criticized for being too light and superficial, and Brahms's admirers were disappointed. The second movement, however, sounded very mysterious and knotty to its contemporaries. At the London premiere in 1878, all of the critics dodged the issue of the slow movement. In the *Times* review could be read: "It is almost impossible to judge of this movement from a first hearing." The *Standard:* "Of the adagio we shall make no effort to speak in detail." The *Daily Telegraph:* "The boldest critic might well speak with diffidence after but one hearing." Only the *Daily Chronicle* made a flat statement: "In every respect a masterly composition." The D major Symphony is to the C minor what the Brahms A minor String Quartet is to the C minor, that is, lyricism after drama. But after the C minor Symphony something equally heroic had been expected, and everybody seemed much happier with the Symphony No. 3 in F of 1883. This was promptly named by some critics "The Heroic," a name that never took hold. Two points about this symphony are not generally known. At the very end of the last movement, Brahms brings back the opening theme of the first movement in a gentle, quiet reminiscence. Many think this was original with Brahms. But Joachim Raff, a composer of the Liszt school who wrote popular program-symphonies, had previously ended his *Im Walde* Symphony (1869) exactly the same way. (Until the end

261

of the century Raff's *Im Walde* together with Rubinstein's *Ocean* Symphony were the two most-played of all symphonic works in the repertoire.) It also has not been noticed that the theme with which Brahms starts his symphony, after the two opening chords, comes from Schumann, where it turns up twice. In the second movement of Schumann's First Symphony, measures 74–78, it is stated, never to reappear again during the course of the work. Exactly the same thing happens in the first movement of the Schumann Third (pages 49 and 50 of the Eulenburg score). In both cases the key of the movement is in E flat, and in both cases the mysterious theme is in G major. Presumably the theme had a special meaning to Schumann, although its symbolism is not known. Perhaps Brahms knew what Schumann was driving at. In any case, he used the theme for the F major Symphony. His last symphony, No. 4 in E minor, was relatively unsuccessful for a while. It was considered too "secretive," and its key of F minor—rather unconventional—bothered some musicians. Also its finale, a chaconne (variations over a recurrent bass), was considered dry.

Another complaint registered against the music of Brahms was that it was too hard to play. Both of the piano concertos and the violin concerto are full of unusual and uncomfortable stretches, and there are spots in each work that are all but impossible to negotiate. There also are extended sections of mixed rhythms, where the right hand may play threes against the left hand's fours. Listeners in Brahms's day said these rhythms made them seasick. ("But this was probably the start of the polyrhythmic structure of many contemporary scores," Arnold Schoenberg later was to write.) Brahms's instrumental technique is anything but flashy, and demands an ability to handle wide stretches and awkward figurations. But what can be played *can* be played, as later virtuosos proved. Eugen d'Albert, one of Liszt's greatest pupils, was the first to adopt the B flat Concerto. People were astonished that he could play so long and demanding a work by heart. Today all of the Brahms concertos and instrumental music are tossed off by the young. If the music no longer poses insuperable technical problems—though nobody would claim that the Brahms concertos are easy—it still poses musical problems that continue to challenge artists.

In his last years, Brahms wrote a very tender, personal kind of music. That does not mean the music lacks tension. But such works as the D minor Violin Sonata, the Clarinet Quintet, the Intermezzi for piano, and his very last work, a set of eleven chorale preludes for organ, have a kind of serenity unique in the work of any composer. The late Haydn symphonies, for instance, could still be the product of a young man, but there is nothing suggesting youth or ardor in the late music of Brahms. It is the twilight of romanticism, and the peculiar glow of this setting sun is hard to describe. It beams a steady, warm light, not flaring up as it does in the music of Mahler not looming big halfway over the horizon as in the symphonies of Bruckner, not erupting with solar explosions as in the music of Richard Strauss. It is the music of a creative mind completely sure of its materials, and it combines technique with a mellow, golden glow. In a day when the gigantic operas of Wagner dominated the opera house, when the shocking symphonic poems of Richard Strauss were the talk of Europe, the music of Brahms continued to represent in an intensified way what it had always represented—integrity, the spirit of Beethoven and Schumann, the attitude of the pure and serious musician interested only in creating a series of abstract sounds in forms best realized to enhance those sounds.

19

Master of the Lied

HUGO WOLF

The year of Brahms's death also saw the disappearance of the strange Hugo Wolf from the local scene. The greatest song composer of his day and, many think, of all time, was placed in a sanitorium—a euphemism for lunatic asylum. Wolf had burned himself out, and even had his nervous system not been affected by the syphilis he had picked up at the age of seventeen, he was the kind of manic-depressive who in any event could not have lasted long. There are many photographs of Wolf, and they all look much the same. He stares at the photographer with those burning and hypnotic black eyes mentioned by so many of his contemporaries, dressed usually in a velvet jacket and flowing artist's tie: slim, handsome. aristocratic-looking, unsmiling, consumed. He looked, and was, a man out of the ordinary. Within the space of a few years this tortured creature left the world a legacy that carried the German art song to its highest point

He did write other things than songs. There is an interesting opera. *Der Corregidor*, almost never staged. There are also some choral works. a long string quartet, and the *Italian Serenade* for string quartet (later expanded for string orchestra). a handful of piano works, and a long symphonic poem named *Penthesilea*, which hardly anybody knows but which Wolf authorities assure us is a masterpiece (it isn't). But it was as a song composer that Wolf achieved whatever little fame he had in his own day, and it is as a song composer that he lives.

No greater songs exist. Wolf, the rebel who led such a stormy life, the bohemian and malcontent. the genius who died mad at the age of forty three. was able to direct a musical stream of laser-bright strength on poetry In the 242 songs he wrote, there often is a serenity at complete odds with his day to-day life. And no composer had such an acute feeling for poetry It has been pointed out many times that where such great song writers as Schubert. Schumann. and Brahms were musicians with a feeling for poetry. Wolf

264

was a poet who thought in terms of music. Nobody has to be reminded of the extreme beauty of the great lieder from Schubert through Brahms. But the Wolf songs are not only more original and more advanced harmonically, they also have more point, a stabbingly intense correlation of text and music. Wolf achieved what the Elizabethan song writer, Thomas Campion, expressed as the ideal: to couple words and notes lovingly together. Wolf did this so unerringly that the term "psychological song" has been used to describe his music. Some of this extraordinary meeting of word and music —this ability to pick up the high point of a poem through an unexpected modulation, or through an accompaniment that heightens the verbal meaning, or through a melody that can be searing in its purity and rightness— some of this came from Wagner, who was Wolf's idol. Some came from Liszt, whose prophetic songs have been so unaccountably neglected by recitalists. In many respects the Liszt songs prefigure those of Wolf.

It might be that Wolf's admiration for Liszt and Wagner, and his detestation of Brahms, came about for personal reasons. Wolf was born in Windischgraz, Styria (now Slovenjgrade, Yugoslavia), on March 13, 1860. Over his father's objections he left home in 1875 to study at the Vienna Conservatory. While Wolf was a student there, Wagner visited Vienna. The fifteen-year-old Wolf hung around him and finally worked up the nerve to show the great man some of his music. Wagner was amused by the young man's hero-worship. But he did not dismiss Wolf out of hand, which Brahms apparently did. When Wolf approached Brahms, the older man suggested that Wolf study counterpoint with Nottebohm. Wolf was furious. "It's only Brahms's North German pedantry that makes him thrust Nottebohm on me." From that moment, Brahms was his enemy. Wolf amply paid him off during the three years he was music critic for the Wiener *Salonblatt*.

A friend got him the job. Wolf, highly strung and nervous, had never been able to hold down any position up to then. Nor could he stay long in any one place. At school in Windischgraz he easily became bored and did well only in the one subject that interested him, music. He left the Vienna Conservatory after only two years, telling Joseph Hellmesberger, the director, that he was forgetting more than he was learning. Hellmesberger immediately expelled him. Wolf always claimed he left before being expelled, though for a time he seriously considered bringing legal action against the Conservatory. He did not have the patience to teach, and when he did teach he was not very good at it. For the most part he moved from one cheap lodging to another, and lived on food parcels sent by his family. As amanuensis to the conductor Karl Muck at Salzburg, and then as assistant chorus master there, he made enemies, got into trouble, and left, calling the place a "pigsty." He probably was not good enough for the job. But he did seem to enjoy his work as a music critic, and he made a name for himself with his violent attacks on Brahms and the entire Viennese establishment. He wrote with fury and venom: "Through this composition"—the D minor Concerto of Brahms—"blows an air so icy, so dank and misty, that one's heart freezes, one's breath is taken away. One could catch a cold from it. Unhealthy stuff!" Or, on the Brahms Fourth Symphony, "He has, to be sure, never been able to raise himself above the level of mediocrity, but such nullity, emptiness and hypocrisy as prevail in the E minor Symphony have come to light in none of his other works. The art of composing without ideas has de cidedly found its most worthy representative in Brahms." It could very well be that Wolf's reviews were a corrective in a musical Vienna that was domi nated by the conservative opinions of Brahms's friend Hanslick. It also was a fact that Wolf's intemperately expressed opinions and his unabashed propa ganda for Liszt and Wagner were a decided setback to his career.

Being a composer-critic put him in an awkward position. On the one hand he was attacking the (to him) staid and uninteresting programs of the Vienna Philharmonic. On the other hand he was going, hat in hand, to such important members of the orchestra as its famous concertmaster, Ar nold Rosé, and the violinist-violist Sigismund Bachrich, both of whom he had roughly handled in print. He wanted their help in getting his music played; he wanted the Rosé Quartet to play his quartet, and he wanted the Philharmonic to play his *Penthesilea*. Rosé gleefully let him dangle and then polished him off with an insulting letter. 'We have attentively gone through your D minor String Quartet and unanimously resolved to leave the work for you with the doorman of the Opera House. Will you have the kindness to send for it as soon as possible? He may easily mislay it. With kindest greetings.' Finally *Penthesilea* was rehearsed by the Philharmonic under Hans Richter. According to Wolf, the conductor led it through to the end because, as he told the orchestra, he wanted to see for himself the work of the man "who dares to write in such a way about *Meister* Brahms." Richter later denied that he had said any such thing, but the story does sound true. In any case, Wolf was very naïve in thinking that an attacking critic would be welcomed by the people he attacked. He was only sticking his neck out. He also could be unethical about his critical work, ready to use his column to castigate enemies on a personal basis. After the *Penthesi lea* fiasco he ran about swearing vengeance. "I will publish an article about Richter that shall make the devil himself grow pale." And he did.

Wolf started writing songs around 1875, but he came into maturity thir teen years later. From 1888 to 1891 he composed over 200 songs to poems by Mörike, Eichendorff, Goethe, Geibel, Heyse, and Keller. From 1895 to 1897 there were another thirty or so songs. His mind snapped in 1897 and he spent the last four years of his life in an asylum. Thus his song writing ca reer is confined to seven years. The major collections are the fifty-three songs to Mörike poetry (published 1889), the *Gedichte von Eichendorff* (1889), the *Spanisches Liederbuch, nach Heyse und Geibel* (1891), *Alte Weisen: Sechs Gedichte von Keller* (1891), the *Italienisches Liederbuch, nach Paul Heyse* (2 volumes, 1892 and 1896), and *Drei Gedichte von Michelangelo* (1898). There are over a hundred additional miscellaneous songs set to Heine, Lenau, Chamisso, and others. The period of his mastery starts with the Mörike songs of 1888. He wrote them at white heat—two, sometimes three, songs a day. In three months he turned out forty-three songs. Later in the year he turned his attention to Goethe and in three and a half months composed fifty songs. It was as if an outside force had grabbed his pen and guided it. Wolf knew the songs were good. "What I now write, I write for posterity, too. They are masterpieces." He would get drunk on his songs and describe them as though intoxicated: "*Erstes Liebeslied eines Mädchen* is by far the best thing I have done up to now. . . . The music is of so striking a character and of such intensity that it would lacerate the nervous system of a block of marble." But the very next day: "I retract the opinion that *Erstes Liebeslied eines Mädchen* is my best thing, for what I wrote this morning, *Fussreise*, is a million times better. When you hear this song you will have only one wish—to die."

These songs were immediately recognized as great works by a discriminating group. Rosa Papier and Ferdinand Jäger began to sing them in public. Generally Wolf, a good pianist, accompanied them. Even Wolf's enemies admitted that he might have something to say. The music represented something new in lieder composition. Some Wolf songs, of course, are as easily assimilated as the songs of Schubert, Schumann, and Brahms. But there are some difficult ones in which the secrets do not reveal themselves on first hearing. They can sound austere, unmelodic, too declamatory. It is necessary to hear some Wolf songs many times before the exquisite joinings and subtle expressive content are clear.

Wolf worked on the theory that the form of the poem must dictate the form of the music. He summed up his ideas in a letter to Rosa Mayreder, the librettist of *Der Corregidor:*

> There's something gruesome about the intimate fusion of poetry and music in which, actually, the gruesome role belongs only to the latter. Music has decidedly something of the vampire about it. It claws its victim relentlessly and sucks the last drop of blood from it. Or one could also compare it with a greedy suckling, who relentlessly demands fresh nourishment and becomes plump and fat while its mother's beauty wilts away. But this comparison is valid only with regard to the effect that music, in league with poetry, has upon the public. . . . Nothing has shocked me more than this groundless injustice in the preference of one art over the other

In the process of sucking out the poetry the music itself filled out and took shape. Most song composers have always been interested in melody primarily as melody. Wolf was interested in melody as merely one of the elements needed to underline the meaning of a poem. It might be said that each of his songs is a tiny word painting. Each one is different; each one is subtle, each is full of unexpected ideas. In *Dass doch gemalt* there is the quiet and touching conclusion, where a less imaginative composer would have rattled the piano with chords after the declaration of love that ends the poem. There is *Wer rief dich denn*, where the singer says one thing and the accompaniment indicates that what she is saying is false. There is the hushed, almost monotonal vocal line of *Nun wandre, Maria*, where the accompaniment suggests—so delicately, yet so persistently—a kind of blind, purposeless walking. There is *Gesegnet sei*, where on the words *Erschuf die Schönheit* there is a blaze of glory. There are the last three songs he composed, the *Michelangelo Lieder*, where the circle comes full turn: in *Wohl denk' ich oft*, a *Meistersinger* theme is heard at the end, and in *Sag mir, wie ich's erwerbe*, a motive from *Tristan*. In his last songs, Wolf recalled the great musical influence of his life and paid homage.

He never had any luck with his opera. In 1895 he began work on *Der Corregidor*, friends donating money to subsidize him. He had to be subsidized, for never in his life did he have a cent. He did not even have a home. In an effort to correct the situation he would come up with all kinds of impractical ideas. Among them was emigration to the United States, a country in which, as every European knew, every citizen was a millionaire. Wolf said that he was going to settle in "the land of gold, to lay the foundations of a decent existence on a safe basis of dollars." Of course nothing came of it. For years he drifted from one friend to another and not until 1896 did he find an apartment of his own. He enjoyed it for only a year. Wolf, who had lived off his friends, did not hesitate to accept money from his friends to keep him going while he worked on his opera. 'High time' High time that occurred to somebody. Really it should be the cursed liability and obligation of the State to support musicians and poets. Schubert, whose life Wolf's so resembled in many aspects, had said the same thing. Wolf worked rapidly on *Der Corregidor* and had it substantially completed in fourteen weeks. He looked at it with characteristic joy and optimism. People will no longer talk about anything but this opera. All of them, Mascagni, Humperdinck e tutti quanti will be unable to compete and will fade away.

When *Corregidor* had its premiere at Mannheim in 1896, it achieved a modest success. But soon it was dropped, and it never has entered the repertory. The following year Wolf went mad. He had delusions that he had been appointed director of the Vienna Opera and he went around the city saying that Mahler had been discharged and that he, Wolf, would immediately reorganize the organization. He burst into the house of the opera singer, Hermann Winkelmann, introduced himself as the new director and said that he wanted to make use of his services that very afternoon. Winkelmann pretended to be called to the telephone, did not return, and Wolf was very angry. He shall suffer for that, refusing the first request of his director." Wolf's friends gathered around him, not knowing what to do, and Wolf looked at their glum faces. "A fine lot of friends you are. When one for once accomplishes something in life, you are not a bit pleased." When the carriage for the asylum drew up, Wolf thought it was going to take him to Prince Liechenstein, the intendant of the Court Opera, so he carefully got into his dress clothes. From the madhouse he wrote detailed reports of his plans, and discussed the operas he wanted to compose. He had been working on one, *Manuel Venegas*, when he was stricken. Only a fragment remains. Released in 1898, Wolf wandered from one place to another, tried to drown himself, and had himself recommitted. He died in the asylum on February 22, 1903. A death mask was made. The face, fanatic and beautiful, thin, with a pointed beard, high cheek bones, and sunken eyes, looks like the face of Don Quixote as conceived by Doré.

THE LIVES OF
THE GREAT COMPOSERS
Volume Two

Waltz, Polka, and Satire

STRAUSS, OFFENBACH, SULLIVAN

If a measure of a composer's music is its longevity, at least three creators of light music in the nineteenth century have survived time and fashion so triumphantly that they legitimately can be called immortals. The waltz and Viennese operetta of Johann Strauss, Jr., the opéra-bouffe of Jacques Offenbach, and the operetta of Sir Arthur Sullivan remain with us, as charming, pert, and inventive as they ever were. Meyerbeer is all but forgotten, Gounod lives primarily through one opera; such formerly great names as Goldmark, Rubinstein, Heller, and Raff are only names in the history books. But the world continues to be entertained and even enchanted by Strauss, Offenbach, and Sullivan.

The waltz came first. It stemmed from the Ländler an Austro-German dance in three-quarter time. Between 1770 and 1780 the waltz first appeared. Almost immediately it became the craze of Europe, and not only in Vienna, though that city was its headquarters. Michael Kelly, the Irish tenor who sang in the world premiere of Mozart's *Le Nozze di Figaro*, remarked on the craze when he came to write his memoirs in 1826. "The people of Vienna," he noted, "were in my time [the 1780's] dancing mad; as the Carnival approached, gaiety began to display itself on all sides. The propensity of the Viennese ladies for dancing and going to carnival masquerades was so determined, that nothing was permitted to interfere with their enjoyment of their favorite amusement." Kelly cited a Viennese arrangement to clinch his point. So overwhelming was the craze, he said, that "for the sake of ladies in the family way, who would not be persuaded to stay at home, there were apartments prepared, with every convenience, for their accouchement, should they be unfortunately required." Kelly, a connoisseur, thought the Viennese ladies graceful; but, "for my own part, I thought waltzing from ten at night until seven in the morning, a continual whirligig, most tiresome to the eye and ear."

Naturally the waltz became a commodity, and throughout the entire nineteenth century even the greatest composers were not too proud to help supply the demand. There had been a precedent. Haydn and Mozart had written quantities of dance music. Schubert wrote several volumes of waltzes to supply the demand for the new craze. Weber's *Invitation to the Dance* for piano solo (later it was orchestrated by Berlioz) established the concert waltz. Chopin wrote idealized waltzes, not for dancing. Brahms contributed a set for piano and two sets for vocal quartet. Dvořák wrote some pretty waltzes. Richard Strauss's *Der Rosenkavalier* makes much use of the waltz. Ravel wrote a great waltz for orchestra, and a piano set called *Valses nobles et sentimentales*. Debussy composed several waltzes. There even is a waltz in the grim *Wozzeck* of Berg.

There were cries of immorality soon after the waltz appeared. Its first great exponent was Johann Strauss the elder, and Puritan nations knew where to put the blame. "This fiend of German birth, destitute of grace, delicacy, and propriety, a disgusting practice," bellowed an English publication, referring not to the Austrian-born Strauss but to the waltz form itself. But the tide was irreversible. "In every house, on every piano in Vienna," wrote a French journalist in 1852, "lie Strauss waltzes." This time the reference is to the younger Strauss. "He has written over 200, all are favorites, all are sung and trilled, and played throughout Europe. Plebeian and aristocrat hum and pipe them; orchestra and barrel organ play them. We hear them on the street, at the ball, in the garden, and at the theater. The dancing Viennese carry him in triumph on their shoulders and shout 'Strauss forever!' The rest of Europe re-echoes the sound and cries 'Strauss forever!' "

But there was more to the waltz than entertainment, and the better musicians were tremendously impressed with what the elder Strauss was doing. Berlioz visited Vienna in 1845 and had a good deal to say about the technical innovations brought in by the waltz and other dance music. In his *Memoirs* he devoted a long paragraph to the subject:

The Redoutensaal takes its name from the great balls frequently held in the hall during the winter season. There the youth of Vienna gives rein to its passion for dancing. . . . I spent whole nights watching these incomparable waltzers whirling around in great clouds, and in admiring the choreographic precision of the quadrilles—two hundred people at a time, drawn up in two long lines—and the vivid character dances, which for originality and polished execution I have not seen surpassed anywhere except in Hungary. And there stands Strauss directing his splendid orchestra; and sometimes, when one of the new waltzes he writes for every society ball makes a special hit, the dancers stop to applaud and the ladies go over to his rostrum and throw him their bouquets, and they all shout "bis" and make him come back at the end of the quadrille (since dancing feels no jealousy and allows music its share in the triumph and the fun). This is no more than justice; for Strauss is an artist. It is not sufficiently recognized what an influence he has already had on the musical taste of Europe as a whole by introducing cross-rhythms into the waltz. (Their effect on the dancers themselves has been so stimulating that they have devised the two-step waltz in an attempt to imitate it, though the music keeps the triple rhythm.) If the public outside Germany is ever brought to appreciate the extraordinary charm that can on occasion result from combined and contrasting rhythms, it will be owing to him. Beethoven's marvels in this line are too exalted to have affected more than a small minority of listeners. Strauss, on the other hand, deliberately appeals to a popular audience; and by copying him, his numerous imitators are perforce helping to spread his influence.

Even Henry Fothergill Chorley, that ponderous Tory, that Colonel Blimp of music criticism, grudgingly admitted that there was some value in the music. He heard the Strauss orchestra in 1844 and decided that the waltz, as conducted by the Viennese master, contained "a truth for all musicians to ponder." Never had Chorley heard such variety and subtlety of orchestral playing. And never had he heard a type of music that lent itself to such niceties of interpretation. "The manner in which silences, breathing-spaces and like piquancies, can throw life into a movement without its becoming fragmentary, might be studied advantageously by the symphonic composer."

Chorley was referring to the orchestra of the senior Strauss, and he had a cogent point. Orchestral playing as it is understood today was still in its infancy in the early 1840's. At that date the phenomenon of the autocratic conductor, the father-figure who by the force of his personality bends the wills of individual musicians into an integrated whole, was just coming on the scene. Previously there had been divided leadership, in which the first violinist and the musician at the clavier shared the conducting responsibilities. Early conductors like Weber, Spohr, Spontini, Mendelssohn, Wagner, Berlioz, and François Habeneck (who had founded the Concerts du Conservatoire in 1828) had started to break the system of divided leadership, but even as late as the 1840's most orchestras in Europe were hit-and-miss affairs that gave relatively few concerts a season. The best orchestra in France during the 1840's, the Conservatoire orchestra, could be heard only six times a year. In all of Europe there might have been a half-dozen orchestras that were well drilled. The others exhibited a kind of discipline, intonation, ensemble, and interpretation of an order that would not be tolerated today. The 1850's were to see the growth and development of the symphony orchestra into powerful and efficient groups; but in the 1840's, it is safe to say, the dance orchestras of Paris and Vienna supplied a kind of virtuosity that was unique at the time. Men like the two Strausses in Vienna and Napoléon

Musard in Paris took a carefully selected group of players, trained them, and set them to work night after night. No wonder they were superior to symphony orchestras. In addition, they were conducted by despots who would stand for no nonsense. Adam Carse, the British student of orchestral life and manners in the early years of the nineteenth century, has pointed out that Musard and the elder Strauss were the first modern conductors in the sense that when Habeneck or Mendelssohn conducted an orchestra, the audience would come to hear the music; but when Musard or Strauss conducted, the audience would come to hear and see *them*.

Johann Strauss, Sr., was born in Vienna on March 14, 1804. He took up the violin as a child, and at the age of fifteen he was a professional, playing in various orchestras. In 1826 Strauss and one of his friends, the violinist Josef Lanner, formed a small group. It was a success, and soon the orchestra numbered twelve players. Strauss did the conducting, leading (as was customary in the day) with the bow. Lanner did the composing. Josef Lanner (1801–1843) was an unusually skillful composer, and some of his music, especially the *Hofballtänze*, with its insinuating melodies, its grace and, in one episode, sudden bursts of febrile energy (anticipating in a way the restlessness of Ravel's *La Valse*), is on a par with any work later composed by any of the Strausses. Stravinsky did Lanner the honor of inserting one of his waltzes into *Petrushka*. In the early 1820's, Strauss too felt the urge to compose, and that was where trouble developed between him and Lanner. The gossip in Vienna was that Lanner appropriated some Strauss music, introducing it under his own name. The two men actually came to blows at a concert in the *Zum Bock* ballroom. Strauss went off and formed his own orchestra, taking with him some of his best men, while Lanner celebrated the event with a waltz that he entitled *Trennung* ("separation"). Now Vienna had two fine dance orchestras, and sides were taken. As Eduard Hanslick wrote:

> One cannot imagine the wild enthusiasm which the two created. . . . Over each new waltz the journals used to fly into raptures. There appeared innumerable articles about Lanner and Strauss, enthusiastic, frivolous and serious ones, and longer, to be sure, than those devoted to Beethoven and Mozart. That the sweetly intoxicating three-four rhythm, which took hold of hand and foot, necessarily eclipsed great and serious music, and made the audience unfit for any intellectual effort, goes without saying.

Lanner's kind of music differed from Strauss's. It was more lyric, while Strauss's had fire, temperament, and showmanship. The Viennese had a saying: "With Lanner, it's 'Pray, dance, I beg you.' With Strauss, it's 'You must dance, I command you.' " Strauss never forgot that he was composing dance music, even when he expanded the form into the concert waltz. He also made the Viennese waltz a big business. Lanner's competition spurred him on. Much to Strauss's disgust, it was Lanner who in 1829 received the commission to supply music for the Redoutensaal. Strauss, however, came up with a contract for something almost as important, the Sperlsaal. Soon he was employing some 200 musicians, and he was able to supply music for as many as six balls a night. He composed steadily, producing such lovely and still-popular pieces as the *Donaulieder* and the *Radetzky* March. It was not only waltzes that the Viennese demanded. They also expected galops, polkas, quadrilles, and marches. Strauss gave them what they wanted.

Everybody in Vienna visited the Sperl, the large beer garden and dance hall where Strauss mostly held forth. The writer Heinrich Laube observed the scene and has left a picturesque pen portrait of Strauss in action:

> Under the illuminated trees and in open arcades people are seated at innumerable tables, eating and drinking, chatting, laughing and listening. In their midst is the orchestra, from which come the new waltzes, the bugbear of our learned musicians, the new waltzes that stir the blood like the bite of a tarantula. In the middle of the garden on the orchestral platform there stands the modern hero of Austria, the Austrian Napoleon, the musical director Johann Strauss. The man looks as black as a Moor; his hair is curly, his mouth energetic, his lips sneer, he has a snub nose. If his face were not so white he would be the veritable King of the Moors. . Typically African, too, is the way he conducts his dances. His own limbs no longer belong to him when the desert-storm of his waltz is let loose His fiddle-bow dances with his arms; the tempo animates his feet and the Viennese accept this passionate behaviour with unparalleled enthusiasm. And now begin the preparations for the real dancing. To keep the unruly crowds back, a long rope is put up, and all who remain in the center of the hall are separated from the actual dancers. . . These orgies last until the early morning; and then Austria's musical hero packs up his violin and goes home to sleep a few hours and dream of new battle stratagems and waltz themes for the next afternoon.

In the middle 1830's Strauss took his orchestra on tour: Hungary and Germany in 1834, Paris in 1837 and 1838, where he shared programs with Musard; London in 1838. Everywhere it was the same story. Strauss conquered. Everybody loved his music; everybody was awed by the brilliance, finish, precision, and power of his orchestra Musicians were fascinated with Strauss's rhythmic subtlety, and Berlioz wrote a long article about Strauss and rhythm in the *Journal des Débats*. The schedule of the Strauss orchestra was killing. In France, Strauss and his men gave eighty-six concerts in ninety-one days. In England, seventy-two in a hundred and twenty Strauss worked himself to collapse and dragged himself back to Vienna more dead than alive.

He had a home life, of sorts. His wife, Anna Streim, bore him a large family—Johann II (born on October 25, 1825), Josef, Nelli, Therese, Ferdinand, and Eduard. He was as despotic a parent as he was a conductor. The only things he lived for were his orchestra and to make money. He was not very much interested in his wife and family. But on one thing he was firm. He did not want any of his children to become a professional musician. Johann, Jr., his eldest son, was talented, but such was his father's antipathy to the life of a professional musician for any of his children that he had to take lessons on the sly. Then something happened that made it easier for young Johann's training, however hard it may have been on his mother. The elder Strauss moved out and took up with another woman, who bore him four children. It was a great scandal in Vienna. Strauss died on September 25, 1849, but not before he had seen his son established in his footsteps. There was nothing he could do about it. Though he raged and raved, in the end he had to give his grudging consent.

Johann II was nineteen years old when he decided to compete against his father. Vienna was agog. There were few secrets in the city, and everybody knew about the tensions in the Strauss household. Johann II got an engagement at Dommayer's Garden Restaurant and at his first concert tactfully ended the evening with his father's *Lorelei-Rheinklängen*. The debut was a complete success. "Good night, Lanner. Good evening, Father Strauss. Good morning, Son Strauss." So ran a review in a Viennese paper. Johann II and his father became reconciled, and when the older man died, Johann II took over his father's orchestra and combined it with his own. He eventually had six orchestras, running from one to the other every night, making a short appearance at each. Business was business. Strauss had to employ a full crew —musicians for the six orchestras, assistant conductors, a librarian, copyists, publicists, booking agents. Like his father, he took his best orchestra on tour and captivated Europe.

Soon he was in a position to stop his nightly jaunts. He concentrated on composing, leaving the conducting to his brother Eduard except for special occasions. The 1860's saw the beginning of his great series of concert waltzes, marches, and polkas—a series that was to include *Acceleration*, *Perpetuum mobile*, *Morning Papers*, *Tales from the Vienna Woods*, *Voices of Spring*, *Vienna Blood*, *Emperor*, *Artist's Life*. And, of course, *On The Beautiful Blue Danube*. These are more than dance music. With their elaborate introductions and codas, their melodic inspiration, their delicately adjusted orchestration, their fine and subtle rhythm, they are authentic contributions to the great musical repertory. Small wonder that Brahms autographed Frau Strauss's fan with the opening measures of the *Blue Danube* and signed them. "Alas, not by Johannes Brahms." It also was Brahms who said: "*There* is a master of the orchestra, so great a master that one never fails to hear a single note of any instrument."

In addition to the orchestral music there were the operettas. In 1871 came *Indigo, or The Forty Thieves* (eventually this was reworked as *1001 Nights*). In all, Strauss composed seventeen stage works, of which only two represent him at anywhere near his consistent best. Those were *Die Fledermaus* and *Der Zigeunerbaron*. Most of the others—*Der lustige Krieg, Eine Nacht in Venedig, Cagliostro in Wien, Waldmeister*—have impossible librettos. The music itself may be wonderful (sections of *Waldmeister*, indeed, are ravishing) but the books do not make sense even by the loose standards of operetta. Strauss never worried about librettos. He composed *Eine Nacht in Venedig* without knowing the plot, and was terribly unhappy when he finally got around to reading it. "I never saw the dialogue but only the words of the songs. Consequently I put too much nobility into some parts of it that did not suit the work as a whole. . . . At the final rehearsal, when I learned the complete story in its correct sequence, I was horrified." That was typical of Strauss's happy-go-lucky way of operetta composing. But *Fledermaus*, at least, is a work of genius; and in the second act of *Zigeunerbaron*, where the lovers join voices in "*Und mild sang die Nachtigall, ihr Liedchen in die Nacht: die Liebe, die Liebe, ist eine Himmels Macht*," it is the essence of nostalgia, of Viennese love and life.

Strauss visited America in 1872, when he was invited to participate in Patrick Sarsfield Gilmore's Peace Jubilee in Boston. Gilmore was a bandmaster who thought big, and he sponsored colossal festivals in Philadelphia and Boston. In line with the size of those undertakings, Gilmore promised Strauss an equally colossal fee—$100,000 for fourteen performances—to conduct his *Blue Danube*. Strauss arrived in New York and newspapermen descended upon him. "Johann Strauss," reported the *World*, "the waltz king, personally, is evidently a good fellow. He talks only German, but he smiles in all languages." Strauss continued on to Boston, went to the great coliseum where the jubilee was being held, and was told what was expected of him while conducting an orchestra of 1,087 musicians. Then he *knew* Americans were crazy. When he returned home he wrote about his experience:

On the musicians' tribune there were 20,000 singers, in front of them the members of the orchestra—and these were the people I was to conduct! Twenty assistant conductors had been placed at my disposal to control those gigantic masses, but I was only able to recognize those nearest to me, and although we had had rehearsals, there was no possibility of giving an artistic performance. . . .

Now, just conceive of my position, face to face with a public of 100,000

279

Americans. There I stood at the raised desk, high above all others. How would the business start, how would it end? Suddenly a cannon shot rang out, a gentle hint for us 20,000-odd to begin playing the *Blue Danube*. I gave the signal, my twenty assistant conductors followed as quickly and as well as they could, and there broke out an unholy racket such as I shall never forget. As we had begun more or less together I concentrated on seeing that we should finish together too. Thank heaven, I managed it!

Strauss collected his $100,000, then made a short tour, doubled his money, and returned to Vienna. By this time, what with his income from Europe, he was a millionaire. Back in Vienna, he continued his series of operettas. He also wanted very much to compose a serious opera, but he never succeeded. On June 4, 1899, he died, the composer of nearly 500 works, as assured of immortality as Beethoven and Brahms. His music has received universal praise—praise from the most naïve and innocent music lover, praise from the most sophisticated of musicians. Strauss's music seems to be beyond criticism, and Richard Strauss's appreciation is typical:

> Of all the God-gifted dispensers of joy, Johann Strauss is to me the most endearing. This first, comprehensive statement can serve as a text for everything I feel about this wonderful phenomenon. In particular I respect in Johann Strauss his originality, his innate gift. At a time when the whole world around him was tending towards increased complexity, increased reflectiveness, his natural genius enabled him to create from the *whole*. He seemed to me the last of those who worked from spontaneous inspiration. Yes, the primary, the original, the proto-melody—that's it.
>
> Also I saw him and talked with him in Munich at the *Vier Jahreszeiten*. But I really got to know and love the whole realm of his wisdom in Meiningen, through Hans von Bülow, who had a beautifully-bound copy of all [?] the Strauss waltzes. Once he played them for me an entire evening. For me alone! An unforgettable evening of waltzes. I also willingly admit to having sometimes conducted the *Perpetuum mobile* with far more pleasure than many a four-movement symphony. As for the *Rosenkavalier* waltzes . . . how could I have composed those without thinking of the laughing genius of Vienna?

Where Strauss's music was an evocative bow at almost a fairy-tale Vienna, a Vienna of young hussars and beautiful ladies, a Vienna of sentimentality and charm, a pretty-pretty and never-never Vienna of dance and romance, the music of Jacques Offenbach was much more realistic. It was music of social satire. Strauss was gentle and nostalgic. Offenbach snapped.

Like Strauss, Offenbach came in at the right time. Just as the waltz and carnival were the rage of Vienna, so the polka and the cancan were the rage of Paris. The cancan had probably been introduced by soldiers from Algeria and, as with the waltz, there was a great to-do about its immorality. Ludwig Rellstab, the German counterpart of Chorley, was appalled when he visited Paris and saw the cancan danced at carnival time: "When one sees with what gestures and movements of the body the masked men approach the masked women, press close to them and actually throw them backwards and forwards between themselves to the accompaniment of continued acclamation, laughter and ribald jokes, one can only be filled with disgust—nay, with horror and revulsion at this mass depravity." Napoléon Musard was the hero of polka, quadrille, and cancan. He was an untidy, homely little man, invariably dressed in black, whose promenade concerts were the hit of Paris. Musard while conducting would enliven the proceedings by firing pistols, smashing chairs, and throwing his violin in the air. Berlioz, in 1835, was bemused: "At present we sit dumb over the triumph of Musard who, puffed up by the success of his dancing-den concerts, looks upon himself as a superior Mozart. Mozart never composed anything like the *Pistol Shot Quadrille*, consequently Mozart died of want."

Jacques Offenbach, born Jakob Eberst in Cologne on June 20, 1819, was playing the violin at six, composing at eight, playing the cello at nine. His father, a Jewish cantor and amateur violinist, took him to the Paris Conservatory in 1833, but the boy did not stay long. A year later he left, to play in various orchestras and live a Bohemian life. Even in the reign of the Citizen King who carried an umbrella, and even under the bourgeois rule of the bankers, there was a Bohemian life. The boulevardiers had their own morality, their own set of rules, and Offenbach to the end was a citizen of the boulevards rather than a citizen of Paris. He was at home among the eccentrics and nonconformists, and there was something eccentric about him, too. He was nearsighted (blind without his glasses), skinny, with an enormous nose, and long, wavy hair. He looked like an intelligent scarecrow with the head of a parrot.

As a composer, Offenbach got nowhere at first. He knew he had a flair for the theater, but the Opéra-Comique was not interested. Not until Louis-Napoléon and the Second Empire did Offenbach get started. Despairing of the Opéra-Comique ever staging one of his works, he decided to strike off on his own. "It occurred to me," he wrote in his autobiography, "that comic opera was no longer found at the Opéra-Comique; that really funny, gay, witty music was gradually being forgotten, and that what was being written for the Opéra-Comique was really small-scale grand opera." And, "It was then that I got the idea of starting a musical theater myself, because of the continued impossibility of getting my work produced by anybody else."

Therefore on July 5, 1855, Offenbach opened the Bouffes-Parisiens. The opening program consisted of a pantomime on Rossini themes, and two works composed by himself—a sentimental idyll named *La Nuit Blanche* and a farce, *Les Deux Aveugles*. It was more than a success. It was a sensation and all Paris tried to crowd itself into the tiny theater on the Champs-Elysées. Within a few months Offenbach had to move to another theater, and this also turned out to be far too small. It was described by the New York *Tribune* in 1863

> There gapes a little cavernous opening which, though dim by day, by night is lighted with superior gas and brilliant promise of good cheer. Over the narrow entrance a modest inscription stands to notify the passers-by that the theater of the Bouffes-Parisiens is within. . It is the David of opera houses and, in an indirect way, scatters worse wounds among the Goliaths, its big rivals, than they would care to acknowledge. The Bouffes-Parisiens is so little as to be almost a joke. You laugh, when you get inside it, at its tiny proportions. Two great muscular jumps would almost clear the stage from wing to wing, and a gentleman in the orchestra stalls might converse in a whisper with his friends in the gallery. There is, in fact, hardly room enough to swing a cat in. People do not, however, go to the Bouffes for the purpose of swinging cats. They go to listen to the brightest and newest music, to witness the best acting, of its order, that the French stage affords. And they are never disappointed. Absolutely never.

Offenbach was joined by two significant figures –Ludovic Halévy, the nephew of the famous composer of *La Juive* and later one of the librettists of *Carmen*, and Hortense Schneider, the singing actress. Schneider was the sex symbol of her day. Buxom, full of personality and *joie de vivre*, she lived as tempestuous a life as any she ever acted on stage. Generous with everything, she gave herself with abandon to a long series of lovers. Generally her lovers were millionaires. Schneider's enthusiasms were always tempered with a good bourgeois sense of the value of money

Offenbach worked on two levels. He was a skillful composer with a knack for creating lively melodies. But more, he had a streak in him that satirized and parodied everything within sight. Meyerbeer and Wagner, the court, the Emperor himself, the army and politicians, the entire Establishment. So skillfully and wittily were Offenbach's satires put together that Napoléon III himself would laugh when he attended the Bouffes-Parisiens. Offenbach's most popular work, *Orphée aux Enfers* ("Orpheus in the Underworld"), is nominally a satire on the gods and goddesses of Olympus. In reality it is an attack on the French social system. *Orphée* had its premiere on October 21, 1858, and it was moderately successful until Jules Janin attacked it in the *Journal des Débats*. That started a controversy, and everybody rushed to the Bouffes-Parisiens to see for himself. There was a chance for all to attend, for the operetta ran for 228 straight performances. Rossini attended and put the seal of approval on Offenbach. He called him the Mozart of the Champs-Elysées. But one loud dissenting voice was heard. Wagner hated the Bouffes-Parisiens and everything it represented. Offenbach's music, he wrote with his characteristic delicacy, was "a dung heap on which all the swine of Europe wallowed."

Orphée aux Enfers was followed, among other operettas, by *La Belle Hélène* in 1864. It was another satire on the Greek gods and contemporary French life. Then came *Barbe-Bleue* in 1866, *La Vie Parisienne* also in 1866, *La Grande-Duchesse de Gérolstein* in 1867, and *La Périchole* in 1868. The *Grande-Duchesse* was a satire on the military, and ranked with *Orphée* in popularity. For some reason it rubbed the conservatives the wrong way. This was especially true of listeners who had Calvinism and Puritanism in their blood. The conservatives in England and the United States loved Strauss and doted on the Gilbert and Sullivan operettas; but Offenbach made them cough, stutter, and turn red in the face. There was an ever-present suggestion of naughtiness in the Offenbach comic operas. They were not "clean." When the *Grande-Duchesse* was performed in the United States, John S. Dwight of Boston all but got sick. As a moral exhibition, he wrote, the operetta was "the lowest we have ever seen upon the stage. . . . In very shame for the good name of our city that it should even *seem* to forget itself about a thing so shallow, so ambiguous. . . ." All the critical balloons inflated themselves and rose from the ground in wrath. "Offenbach," cried the Philadelpha *Evening Bulletin*, "might be forgiven for his want of genius, but his pruriency is inexcusable. . . . He is the purveyor of bald, bad indecency." Chorley in England was no less shocked, and ended his report on the *Duchesse* in the London *Athenaeum* with: "The vulgarity of some of the words passes all description."

No matter. Offenbach's popularity went up and up, in England and America as well as in France. In 1872 Paris saw three simultaneous Offenbach productions—*Fantasio*, *La Boule de Neige*, and *Le Corsaire Noir*. Meyerbeer was still dominating the grand opera stage, Offenbach was the king of light opera, and the violently anti-Semitic Vincent d'Indy sneeringly referred to the stranglehold of those two composers as "L'école judaïque." Offenbach was collaborating with the famous playwright Victorien Sardou at the time, and the Paris correspondent of the Augsburg *Allgemeine Zeitung* called the Offenbach-Sardou combination "the Egyptian plague of the last decade." But the plague, if that is what it was, did not last long after that. Offenbach's popularity had virtually run its course by 1873. His German birth had not made him welcome in Paris during the Franco-Prussian war, even though Offenbach considered himself French: "I hope that this William Krupp and his dreadful Bismarck will pay for all this. Alas! What terrible people these Prussians are, and what despair do I feel that I myself was born on the Rhine and am connected by many links to these savages! Alas! My poor France! How much do I thank her for accepting me among her children!" In addition, the public was beginning to tire of the Offenbach operettas and was looking for something new. Something new did turn up in 1873, with Charles Lecocq's *La Fille de Mme. Angot*. Then came Robert Planquette with his *Les Cloches de Corneville*, and, finally, André Messager with a series of charming light works that could well stand revival today, especially *Véronique* and *Monsieur Beaucaire*. The French had had enough of social satire, and turned to the romantic escapist operetta of Lecocq and Planquette.

Desperately Offenbach tried to hold his own. He took over the Théâtre de la Gaîté and started a series of spectacle productions. Soon he was bankrupt. He summoned his company "You shall be paid to the last sou, my children. If I have been careless, I shall at least remain honorable." To add to his troubles, Johann Strauss came to Paris and conquered the city with *Die Fledermaus*. Poor Offenbach found himself an anachronism. And so, like Strauss, he went to America where, as every good European knew, one could pick up vast sums of money in any convenient horse trough. Maurice Grau, the impresario, cabled him an offer of $1,000 a night for a minimum of thirty nights. Offenbach was happy to accept. On his arrival in New York he was greeted with an editorial in the New York *Times* of May 8, 1876.

> On Friday last, Europe, to the extent of one person of Hebraic origin but of rather vague nationality, arrived in this City with a view to attending the Centennial celebration [in Boston]. A proud and grateful country seized the opportunity to show how it can welcome a distinguished foreign guest. Two rival clubs sent committees to welcome the steamer which conveyed him to our shores, and it is not yet known which club first succeeded in offering him a complimentary dinner. Reporters swarmed around him before he had yet landed, and one of them, connected with a Tammany evening paper, was actually presented with one of the great man's private cigars, and testified with much feeling that "mortal man never smoked their superior in quality."

The editorial called Offenbach the creator of our "fleshly school of music," and then let its Puritanism peep through. It commented that while *Geneviève de Brabant* (an Offenbach operetta) was "not without musical merit," its melodies "appear to have been written for a Phallic festival. . . The opéra-bouffe is simply the sexual instinct expressed in melody." Then the *Times* took a stern---one is tempted to say stiff---stand: "What a shame! Such a reception is an insult to every great and honorable artist. . . Priapism is not on a level with music."

Offenbach's first concert, at Gilmore's Garden, turned out to be the greatest event since Jenny Lind had toured under Barnum's auspices in the early 1850's. Speculators were getting as high as $25 for a pair of tickets. It seems that everybody was convinced that the composer would dance the cancan while conducting the score of *Orphée*. This everybody had to see. Offenbach, of course, merely came out and conducted, and there was a general feeling of letdown. About a third of the audience, some disappointed and others insulted, left before the concert was over. Obviously Grau's press agents had promised a great deal more than Offenbach was prepared to deliver. Subsequent concerts were financial losses, and the only events that showed a profit were several staged performances of *La Jolie Parfumeuse*. Offenbach was not happy about his reception, but, then again, some critics were not happy about his appearances in the United States. The *Music Trade Review* of May 18, 1876, prefaced a long article with: "We don't mean, and we do not wish to be, uncourteous to a foreign guest, but we would ask Mr. Offenbach himself: Has he ever made five dollars in Europe as a conductor? What is there in his appearing as a *chef d'orchestre* that should so much interest the American public as to justify the hope that they would flock with eagerness to see him, and pay one dollar admission to a concert which offers nothing worth paying that dollar?" The article continued with an attack on the programs, on the music itself ("He is the outgrowth of the governing demi-monde epoch of the Second Empire, the froth of tisane, neither healthy nor nourishing"), and on the orchestra. Offenbach naturally resented these attacks and could not wait to get home. Back in Paris he announced, all but kissing the street, "I am Offenbach again." He promptly wrote a small and, under the circumstances, thoughtful book about his experiences in America. Among his observations was one about American womanhood. Womanhood was a subject upon which Offenbach could pronounce with decided authority, and he gave the American girls a high rating: "Out of every hundred you meet, ninety are lovely."

The last years of his life were spent in a race against death. He desperately wanted to finish his one opera, *Les Contes d'Hoffmann*, which he had started in 1877. The libretto was written by Barbier and Carré after their play, which Offenbach immensely admired, and was based on stories by E. T. A. Hoffman. Perhaps he identified with the hero, or, one might better say, anti-hero. He spent much more time on *Hoffmann* than on any of his operettas, and he pleaded with Carvalho, director of the Opéra-Comique, to hurry the production. "I have not much time left, and my only wish is to see the first night." But he never lived to see his remarkable opera on stage. He died on October 5, 1880, leaving some of the score unfinished. The recitatives and part of the scoring were finished by Ernest Guiraud, and the premiere took place on February 10, 1881. It would have been Offenbach's

102nd work for the stage. Of all the European critics, Eduard Hanslick struck the correct note in his obituary notice: "Much as he wrote, Offenbach was always original. We recognize his music as Offenbach-ish after only two or three bars, and this fact alone raises him high above his French and German imitators, whose buffo operas would shrivel up miserably were we to confiscate all that is Offenbach-ish in them. He created a new style in which he reigned absolutely alone." Nietzsche, who concurred with Hanslick about Offenbach's talent, actually set him up against—of all composers—Wagner. In *The Will to Power*, Nietzsche, who was at the height of his anti-Wagner frenzy, wrote that "If by artistic genius we understand the most consummate freedom within the law, divine ease and facility in overcoming the greatest difficulties, then Offenbach has more right to the title of genius than Wagner" (That is what happens to people, even great philosophers, when emotion conquers reason.)

Offenbach's music, despite the ethnic background of the man, is as French as Strauss's is Viennese. It is clean, uncluttered, unsentimental, pointed, classic. If it reflects the frivolity of the age, it does so with extreme wit and sophistication. No music has ever lived unless it has originality, and Offenbach, who could be hasty and formula-ridden, could also rise to moments of great melodic invention. As Hanslick said, he was different from all other composers. *The Tales of Hoffmann*, his most famous work today, is exceptional in his output. Its breadth alone would make it so, and it also has a curiously appealing libretto based on the figure of a loser—a poet who cannot win happiness in life or love. There is a strange air of finality about *Hoffmann*, even considering such extroverted excerpts as Olympia's coloratura aria and the Barcarolle. In this opera, man, no matter how hard he tries, is not the master of his fate. Through *Hoffmann* looms the sinister figure of a force of destiny named, variously, Lindorf, Coppélius, Dapper tutto, and Dr. Miracle. Against this force Hoffmann is lost. He is continuously skewered by this evil genius; he is a fish continually and compulsively biting at the same baited hook, always with the same dreadful results. Offenbach's music rises to eloquence in the last act; and the final scene, with Hoffmann drunk and helpless while Lindorf steals away to repeat once more the never-ending sequence, leaves a bitter taste in the mouth.

In England the team of Sir Arthur Seymour Sullivan and Sir William Schwenck Gilbert instituted a tradition comparable to those started in Vienna by Strauss and in Paris by Offenbach. The Gilbert and Sullivan operettas are much closer to Offenbach than to Strauss, in that they are often topical and satirical. But as musicians, Sullivan and Offenbach had little in common. Sullivan was a well-trained composer of the Mendelssohn school who by rights should have composed only stuffy oratorios, respectable operas, and strict sonata-form symphonies. Everybody expected him to do so;

and, as a matter of fact, his works do include a symphony, quantities of stuffy and conventional church music ("Onward Christian Soldiers" is his), and a long-forgotten grand opera, *Ivanhoe*. Great things were expected of Sullivan. He was the fairhaired boy of British music, and he did have great talent. The London *Times* in 1866 referred to the young Sullivan as a musician "who, if we are to expect anything lasting from the rising generation of national composers, is the one from whom we may most reasonably and on the fairest grounds expect it."

Born in London on May 13, 1842, Sullivan won the first Mendelssohn Scholarship at the Royal Academy of Music in 1856 and studied for two years at Leipzig. He composed, in addition to the D minor Symphony, two oratorios, much incidental music to plays, and a large number of successful ballads (one of them is *The Lost Chord*). But it was the operettas he composed with Gilbert that brought in the money, and to the Victorians there was something sinful about a composer getting rich with such material. Everybody, from Queen Victoria herself down, assured Sullivan that he was wasting his time composing operettas. After a while Sullivan came to believe it. But he had expensive tastes. He gambled at Monte Carlo, raced two thoroughbreds (Cranmer and Blue Mark), kept a mistress or two, liked to move with royalty and rich people. All that took money, and operetta was an easy way of making money. So Sullivan turned out operettas and went to his grave on November 22, 1900, with guilt feelings. He thought that he had prostituted his art.

His partner, W. S. Gilbert, had no such feelings. Gilbert was a prolific creator who wrote seventy-one works for the stage, of which sixty-nine were produced. There was also prose and poetry. Eighty-one of Gilbert's published verses were collected into the *Bab Ballads*, illustrated with amusing and completely professional pen drawings by the author (some of the *Bab Ballads* were developed into librettos for the Savoy operas). In his early years, Gilbert worked for the Civil Service. Then he was admitted to the bar Finally he found his true vocation, as humorist and satirist. He became a contributor to the magazine *Fun*, and by 1866 was writing successful farces and plays. From 1871 to 1880 he wrote thirty-three stage works and had thirty-two of them produced. Among the works in that prolific period were four operettas to music by Sullivan.

The fame of Gilbert and Sullivan primarily rests on their collaboration. It is true that each could function without the other, and each did achieve success on his own. But hardly any of their individual efforts have lived, while nearly everything they wrote as a team is as popular as ever. Never in the history of music has there been such a symbiotic relationship. And that even though the two men did not even particularly like each other. Gilbert, a touchy and irascible man, quarreled mightily with Sullivan toward the end, and their relationship, which had started in 1871, broke off with the unsuccessful *The Grand Duke* in 1896. Later Gilbert realized what the rupture had meant. "A Gilbert is no good without a Sullivan, and I can't find one," he wrote in 1903, three years after his partner's death. Sir William lived until 1911, when he died on March 29, trying to save a young lady from drowning.

The producing end of the Gilbert and Sullivan team was Richard D'Oyly Carte, a composer of songs and operettas who became a manager and then an impresario. A genius for publicity, and a man with an instinct for success, he had brought Gilbert and Sullivan together for their first successful collaboration, *Trial by Jury*, in 1875. Previously the two men had been thrown together in an operetta named *Thespis*, an Offenbachian work about the gods growing old. It had run for a month and then was forgotten. Nor was the score ever published. In 1875, D'Oyly Carte, then manager of the Royalty Theater, suggested to Gilbert that he write a one-act trifle to act as a curtain-raiser for Offenbach's *La Périchole*. D'Oyly Carte also suggested Sullivan as the composer. Gilbert quickly worked up a script and visited Sullivan. "He read it through," Sullivan recalled, "as it seemed to me in a perturbed sort of way, with a gradual crescendo of indignation, in the manner of a man considerably disappointed with what he had written. As soon as he had come to the last word he closed up the manuscript violently, apparently unconscious of the fact that he had achieved his purpose as far as I was concerned, inasmuch as I was screaming with laughter the whole time." *Trial by Jury* was such an immediate hit that D'Oyle Carte moved fast. He secured the services of Gilbert and Sullivan, formed a Comedy Opera Company to stage their works, and presented *The Sorcerer* in 1877. The series was launched, the world kept laughing at the operettas, and the three principals became very rich men.

The Sorcerer ran for 175 performances, but that was nothing against the run of *H.M.S. Pinafore* in 1878, which had a run of 700 consecutive performances. The English-speaking world went mad. In the United States *Pinafore* was enthusiastically pirated and produced everywhere. Remarked *Dwight's Journal of Music*, "Hundreds of companies, professional and amateur, have been acting and singing it. In the great cities, *Pinafore* has held the stage in half a dozen theaters at once. . . . It has been served up in every theater and hall, church choirs go around the country singing it, every child sings and hums it; the tuneful images repeat themselves as in a multiplying mirror, from every wall, through every street and valley." In Chicago, eleven companies staged *Pinafore* in 1879, some of them simultaneously. There were Negro performances of *Pinafore* and, for the German-speaking population in America, *Pinafore* in German. (After World War II there was, briefly, a Yiddish *Pinafore*, staged by a Hadassah group in Brooklyn.) Some hundred thousand barrel organs were built to play *Pinafore* selections. As a result, Gilbert and Sullivan themselves came to America to share the wealth. They staged an "authentic" *Pinafore* at the Fifth Avenue Theater in New York. On their return to England they saw to it that their next production, *The Pirates of Penzance*, would have simultaneous openings in London and New York. The London premiere of *Pirates* took place in 1879 at the Savoy Theater, newly built by D'Oyly Carte for the Gilbert and Sullivan operettas. Hence the terms "Savoy Opera" and "Savoyard."

After *The Pirates of Penzance* there followed *Patience* (1881), *Iolanthe* (1882), *Princess Ida* (1884), *The Mikado* (1885), *Ruddigore* (1887), *The Yeomen of the Guard* (1888), *The Gondoliers* (1889), *Utopia Limited* (1893), and *The Grand Duke* (1896).

These operettas are regarded by some as Victorian in the pejorative sense. In some respects they are. But they are redeemed by a gentle sense of satire and a keen sense of the ridiculous. As Establishment figures, Gilbert and Sullivan were not interested in social reform, there is in their work none of the fierce indignation that so animated writers like Dickens. But the Gilbert and Sullivan operettas are never conventionally moralistic, and they poke fun at some cherished notions of the Victorians. England during Victoria's day was a class-conscious nation, and seldom did anybody ever cross over. 'He knows his place' was an approving remark, and there was a famous hymn of the day:

> The rich man in his castle,
> The poor man at his gate,
> God made them high and lowly,
> And ordered their estate.

But *Pinafore* joked with this code of values. Captain's daughters did not, in real life, fall in love with simple sailors. They only did so in sentimental novels. Gilbert in *Pinafore* had his fun with this particular convention, but in the process there are shrewd thrusts at the Admiralty. The libretto is an example of topsyturvydom (a word commonly used with Gilbert and Sullivan) on a grand scale. *Trial by Jury* and *Iolanthe* put Parliament and the legal system through a series of absurd maneuvers; *Patience* took the aesthetic movement of the pre-Raphaelites, Wilde and Swinburne to a sort of reductio ad absurdum, *Princess Ida* poked fun at women's rights and female education, *The Gondoliers* satirized republican government; *Ruddigore*, one of the most parodistic, took off on the barnstorming melodramas so popular in their day.

The basic plots of the Gilbert and Sullivan operettas are in themselves simple and, frequently, farcical. Industrious researchers have pointed out that there is nothing particularly new in any Gilbert and Sullivan situation. Even one of the most famous *Pinafore* passages—"What, never?" "No, never!" "What, never?" "Well, hardly ever."—has a precedent. At least, S. J. Adair Fitzgerald pointed out, with great glee, that the following occurs in Persius: "Quis haec legat?" "Nemo mehercule." "Nemo?" "Vel duo, vel nemo." Which he translates as: "Who will read this?" "Surely nobody." "What, nobody?" "Well, hardly anybody." Persius died in 62 A.D.

From Gilbert and Sullivan came a body of work that has a significant place in the hierarchy of creative effort in Victorian times. Sullivan composed the only English music of his period worth talking about. Except for him it was a terrible age, musically speaking. The shadow of Mendelssohn had obscured England, just as the shadow of Handel had blocked sunlight from the English composers some hundred years previously. Sullivan may have been indebted to Mendelssohn (and to Schumann and Donizetti), but his workmanship was impeccable. He was a much better technician than Strauss or Offenbach. He also was a better musical parodist than Offenbach. Take the wonderfully funny Handelian sequences sung by that precious trio, Arac, Guron, and Scynthius, in *Princess Ida:* they are among the wittiest things in music, as are also the Handelian parodies in *Trial by Jury.* And a waltz like "Poor Wand'ring One" perfectly mocks the bel canto style. But beyond all the fooling around is the writing of a completely equipped, inventive musician. The fact that Sullivan's music flows so easily deceives some listeners, making them think it is second-rate. It is far from that. Sullivan was a supreme technician of the lyric stage, and there is something Mozartean about the effortless grace and purity of his music. And his ability to set the English language was of a transcendental order. Nobody has set English words to music with comparable ease and sheer rightness. But Sullivan needed the proper words to fire him, and those he received from Gilbert. The two men were indispensable to each other. Without Sullivan, no Gilbert. Without Gilbert, no Sullivan.

❦ 2 ❧

Faust and French Opera

FROM GOUNOD TO SAINT-SAËNS

The Paris Opéra, which had taken the lead in the 1830's, suddenly became an anachronism in the 1850's. Indeed, most French music seemed to stagnate. It was a bad period, and nothing seemed to be coming up. At the Opéra-Comique works by Boieldieu, Adam, and Auber, all composers of the 1830's and before, made up most of the repertory. Between 1852 and 1870, only five—*five!*—new French operas were added to the repertory of the Opéra. The management was not taking any chances on new works. Thus the new school of French composers had to turn elsewhere. Fortunately for them, Léon Carvalho, director of the Théâtre-Lyrique, was hospitable to new music. So was Jules Pasdeloup, who founded the Concerts Populaires in 1860 and saw to it that French music—and Wagner, too—got a hearing. It was ironic that the new French opera which turned out to be the most popular of its time, the opera that springs to most people's mind when French opera is mentioned—Charles Gounod's *Faust*—had its premiere not at the Opéra but at the Théâtre-Lyrique.

Faust was a triumph of bourgeois music applied to bourgeois taste. Its libretto by Jules Barbier and Michel Carré was adapted, in a milk-and-water fashion, from Goethe. Its music was nowhere so advanced as Berlioz. It had the stagiest of stage devils, and a heroine who ascended to heaven accompanied by the proper noises of the celestial choir. But it swept Europe and the United States. Between Verdi's Big Three of 1851-1853 and the Wagner craze that came after the first Bayreuth season of 1876, it was one of the very few operas to take Europe by storm. "*Faust, Faust, Faust,*" complained a British critic in 1863, "nothing but *Faust. Faust* on Saturday, Wednesday and Thursday; to be repeated tonight, on Tuesday, and 'every night until further notice,' as they say at the theaters."

Charles Gounod, who composed thirteen operas, is still represented in the international repertory by two other works, *Roméo et Juliette* and *Mireille*.

But neither has come near the popularity of the one work by which his name is known to most people. Born in Paris on June 18, 1818, Charles François Gounod was an interesting figure. His father was a talented though unsuccessful painter who died when Charles was four years old. His mother, a skillful artist herself, took over her late husband's classes and in addition gave music lessons. Charles picked up both arts with facility. He was a good draftsman, and at the age of twelve he also was starting to compose. He decided to leave art in favor of music when he was thirteen; the impetus was a performance of Rossini's *Otello* that he heard. "If they had attempted to prevent me from learning music," Gounod later stated, "I should have run away to America and hidden in some corner where I could have studied undisturbed." In 1836 he entered the Conservatory, winning the Prix de Rome three years later. Rome fascinated Gounod. He discovered a great deal of sixteenth-century ecclesiastical music there, and started to make a serious study of it. And, close to the fount of the Church, he became very religious. In fact, for a time he could not make up his mind whether or not to go on with music or to enter the Church.

He returned to Paris in 1843 by way of Vienna and Leipzig. In Vienna he arranged for performances of several of his religious works, thus launching his career; and in Leipzig, where he spent four days with Mendelssohn, he heard the choral music of Bach for the first time. It left an overwhelming impression. His first position in Paris was as musical director of the Chapel for Foreign Missions, and he immediately brought Bach, Palestrina, and other early composers into the services, over great objections.

At the Chapel for Foreign Missions he wore semiclerical dress, signed himself "Abbé Gounod," and then, in 1847, entered the Carmelite monastery as a novitiate. Like Liszt, he was torn between flesh and the devil, and in some quarters he was called "the philandering monk." He also was an outgoing kind of person who liked to be liked; and with his overpowering charm, there were few who could resist him. Those who could resist him found his behavior excessive, and they looked askance at his habit of kissing people indiscriminately. Edmund Got, the actor, wrote in his diary that Gounod was "as talented musically as he is exuberant and shamelessly pushy as a man. He actually kissed me on both cheeks the first time I ever met him!" Henri Meilhac, the writer and one of the *Carmen* librettists, told a friend: "Gounod spent all day Wednesday and Thursday with us. Never have I been kissed so often in so short a time."

The only way to fortune in the French musical establishment was through opera, and Gounod turned his hand to it starting in 1850 with *Sapho*, which was produced the following year. Several more operas followed and made no impression. He supported himself through his position as conductor of the Orphéon, a union of choral societies, for which he held a grand title. Superintendant of Instruction in Singing to the Communal Schools of the City of Paris. His father-in-law was instrumental in steering Gounod to the post. In 1852 Gounod married Anna Zimmerman, the daughter of a famous piano teacher in the Conservatory. Pierre Zimmerman trained many of the best pianists of the period, and has achieved an extra footnote in history from one pianist he did not train. He turned down Louis Moreau Gottschalk, the prodigy from New Orleans, in 1842 with the comment that no pianist could possibly come from America, a land of savages and steam engines.

Gounod started work on *Faust* in 1856, but broke it off to work on another opera, *Le Médecin malgré lui*. It was produced in 1858 and was a success. On March 19, 1859, *Faust* had its premiere at the Théâtre-Lyrique. From then on, Gounod was the most famous composer in France. The opera contained many of the elements that Massenet was to refine—spicy chromatic harmonies, sweetness of melody, sentimentalism, graceful orchestration, completely idiomatic writing for the voice. French opera of the latter half of the nineteenth century is an art of delicate adjustment, no matter how imposing the forces involved. A large orchestra may be used, but the scoring is much slighter than in a corresponding German work, where the pages are black with notes. *Faust* is grand opera, but a kind of grand opera that makes its best effect only when presented with style, rightness of proportion, and delicacy of sound.

Gounod spent the rest of his life trying to write another *Faust*. He never did, though he composed a great deal of music. His own favorite opera, *La Reine de Saba* (1862), made little headway. *Mireille* (1863) and *Roméo et Juliette* (1864) did better, but neither came anywhere near *Faust* in popularity. A relatively unexplored area of Gounod's *oeuvre* involves his songs. *Venise* and the *Biondina* cycle are characteristic—elegant, charming, sweet. They constitute an important part of the international song repertory and have been unjustly neglected outside of France. They also influenced the development of French song through Debussy, and Ravel in 1922 pointed out their significance: "The real founder of song writing in France was Charles Gounod. It was the composer of *Venise*, of *Philémon et Baucis*, and of the Shepherd's song in *Sapho* who rediscovered the secret of harmonic sensuality that had been lost since the French harpsichordists of the seventeenth and eighteenth centuries."

In the last part of his life, Gounod turned to religious music and achieved a great deal of success, especially in England, with such works as *Mors e Vita*, *La Rédemption*, and the *Messe à Sainte-Cécile*. Listeners responded enthusiastically to the disguised eroticism of the music. It was not for nothing that Gounod wanted to be known as the Musician of Love; and he was referring to things other than love in the Christian sense. "If a good

Catholic were to dissect me," Gounod once said in a candid moment, "he would be much surprised at what he would find inside."

The Franco-Prussian War sent Gounod to England, where he remained from 1870 to 1875, and it was there that he had his affair with Mrs. Georgina Weldon. She was born Georgina Traherne, married a Captain George Weldon, and lived in London at Tavistock House, which had once been the residence of Charles Dickens. It was a situation out of *Vanity Fair*. She was a sort of Becky Sharp and her husband the equivalent of Colonel Crawley. Georgina became Gounod's business manager, and Tavistock House became the scene of an amiable *ménage à trois* after Gounod's wife packed up and indignantly went back to Paris. Later she sent her son, Jean, to look into the matter. He promptly tried to seduce Georgina and she threw him out of the house. But Gounod finally tired of her and left England. Safely in Paris, he asked her for his scores, effects, and money he had loaned. Instead, the Weldons instituted a countersuit, including a large bill for room and board for three years. Eventually Gounod did get his music back, after settling for $50,000, but for years he lived in mortal fear that Georgina would descend upon Paris and claim him. That did not happen, and he died peacefully on October 18, 1893.

It was conceded that Gounod was an immortal, and that his great religious works would survive eternity itself. Saint-Saëns was impelled to write: "In the dim distant future when inexorable time has done its work and the operas of Gounod are forever at rest in the dusty sanctuaries of libraries, the *Messe à Sainte-Cécile*, the *Rédemption* and the oratorio *Mors e Vita* will still have life in them. They will show the coming generations what a splendid musician lent lustre and renown to France in the nineteenth century." Posterity has not endorsed Saint-Saëns's flattering estimate. Occasionally the *Sainte-Cécile* is heard, and it plods along in a saccharine, platitudinous manner, full of plagal cadences, full of choruses with harps sounding prominently in the accompaniment. As Martin Cooper has written, Gounod after 1870 "might as well have echoed Tennyson's despairing cry that he was the greatest master of English living and had nothing to say."

After *Faust*, the next great French opera was *Carmen*. The brilliantly gifted Georges Bizet, who died at the age of thirty-seven, is almost a one-work man—but what a work! *Carmen* was the only piece he wrote that represented him in full maturity. Had he lived, he might have revolutionized opera in France. As it was, *Carmen* soon became recognized as a work of genius, and some saw in it a corrective against Wagner. Nietzsche was one. "My favorite among the contemporary Frenchmen are Bizet and Delibes," he wrote. Léo Delibes (1836–1891) composed two of the most exquisite of all ballet scores, *Coppélia* and *Sylvia;* and his opera *Lakmé*, as well as that lovely song, *Les Filles de Cadiz*, still remains in the repertory. "Bizet's opera

Carmen," continued Nietzsche, "I know well. It is music that makes no pretensions to depth, but it is delightful in its simplicity, so lively, so unaffected and sincere, that I learned it all practically by heart, from beginning to end."

Nietzsche underestimated *Carmen.* It is a far deeper work than his rather condescending remarks would indicate, and its last act has something of the terror and inevitability of the last act of *Don Giovanni.* Carmen in a way is a female Don Giovanni. She would rather die than be false to herself, and that makes her an authentically great figure. The opera does not have a perfect libretto—Micaela is dragged in, and her contribution to the opera is entirely unconvincing—and there are also weak moments in the score; but the work is nevertheless a blazing conception and even to this day a startling one. When the great inspiration of the opera, the Fate theme, is heard in the orchestra, stark and threatening, it takes a most blasé listener not to feel his adrenalin surge.

It was no inspired dilettante who composed *Carmen.* Georges Bizet, born in Paris on October 25, 1838, was one of those children with all the musical gifts—absolute pitch, fast reflexes, everything. He was in the Conservatoire at the age of nine and took every prize in sight—piano, organ, composition, solfège. He easily won the Prix de Rome in 1857. Prior to that he had met Gounod, who exerted a strong influence on Bizet's development. Bizet's early and lovely Symphony in C is virtually a copy of Gounod's Symphony for Wind Instruments. But the melodies are Bizet's own. From the beginning he had a refined, superior melodic sense, and taste to go with it. He never wanted to be a heaven-stormer, and preferred Apollo to Dionysus. "I have the courage to prefer Raphael to Michelangelo, Mozart to Beethoven, Rossini to Meyerbeer," he once wrote. His talents attracted attention, and many professionals felt that he was the coming man. There was nothing in music he could not do—this plump, short-tempered young man, always elegantly dressed, constantly nibbling on sweets, cakes, chocolate, and *petits fours.* (To get on the good side of Bizet one had to cater to his sweet tooth.)

His first opera was *Les Pêcheurs de Perles,* and it had a terrible libretto. Michel Carré and Eugène Cormon (real name, Pierre-Étienne Piestre) supplied the book, and Cormon later said that had he and Carré realized Bizet's talents they would not have saddled him with "that white elephant." It had its premiere at the Lyrique in 1863, and such was the appeal of its music that it never entirely was dropped from the repertory. Even today it enjoys occasional revivals. It should be mentioned that *Les Pêcheurs de Perles,* with its action set in Ceylon, was one of the many operas of the time that reflected the vogue for exoticism. One could include Meyerbeer's *L'Africaine,* Gounod's *Reine de Saba,* Delibes' *Lakmé,* Bizet's *Djamileh*

The French were always fascinated by Near East and Oriental exoticism. In the last quarter of the century a great interest in the exotic music of Spain became manifest, to be represented by *Carmen* and explored by such composers as Chabrier, Debussy, and Ravel.

Bizet's next significant opera was *La Jolie Fille de Perth,* performed at the Lyrique in 1866. This too suffered from a poor libretto and it failed. Bizet was discouraged. He continued to compose operas, starting many he never finished. In 1869 he married Géneviève Halévy, daughter of the composer of *La Juive.* (She was Proust's model for the Princesse de Guermantes.) The Franco-Prussian War found Bizet a soldier in the National Guard. Nearly all of the prominent French composers did their bit. Saint-Saëns also joined the National Guard, while Massenet and Fauré were infantrymen. During the war Bizet composed one of his most delightful pieces, the *Jeux d'Enfants* for piano duet. In 1872 he completed *Djamileh,* an opera that had ten performances, was retired, and did not turn up again until 1938. That same year, 1872, Bizet composed the incidental music to Daudet's *L'Arlésienne* and started to think about *Carmen.* Henri Meilhac and Ludovic Halévy prepared the libretto, taken from the story by Prosper Mérimée. The Opéra-Comique was unhappy about the idea. "Mérimée's *Carmen?* Isn't she killed by her lover? And that background of thieves, gypsies, cigar-makers!" Or, "Death on the stage of the Opéra-Comique! Such a thing has never been seen. Never!" Camille du Locle, head of the Comique, had no faith in the work. He considered it too daring, risqué, unconventional. As it had spoken dialogue rather than recitative, it belonged to the Opéra-Comique, but du Locle was worried about the subject matter and its impact on audiences. France had the reputation abroad of being a naughty country, but the French middle class always has been sturdily moral and even Puritanical. Du Locle had visions of his entire clientele boycotting his house.

But du Locle had committed himself, and *Carmen* received its first performance at the Opéra-Comique on March 3, 1875. Bizet pronounced it "a definite and a hopeless flop," and became ill. Bizet always had a tendency to become discouraged when things did not go his way, and he would develop all kinds of psychosomatic ailments. It so happened that *Carmen* was not "a definite and hopeless flop." Neither was it a great success. The opera had forty-eight performances, but it played to smaller and smaller houses. Three months after the premiere, on June 3, 1875, Bizet died of cardiac complications. Not much later, Ernest Guiraud transformed the spoken dialogue into recitatives for the Viennese premiere, and it is in that form which *Carmen* is customarily heard. It took only a few years for *Carmen* to be played all over Europe. Even Wagner was impressed: "Here, thank God, at last for a change is somebody with ideas in his head." Tchaikovsky adored the opera, and Brahms said that he would have gone to the ends of the earth to embrace the composer of *Carmen*.

In a way, *Carmen* started the verismo school. It contained contemporary characters true to life and traced the disintegration of an honorable soldier. Carmen herself is a more subtle character than the usual leering, hip-swinging, soprano or mezzo-soprano (both sing the role) would suggest. Carmen, indeed, is moral rather than immoral because she is always honest with herself. She never violates her own code of conduct. If she does not follow bourgeois sexual codes, neither is she promiscuous. She belongs to only one man at a time. She knows her powers and does not hesitate to use them, but sexual power is not the most important element in her makeup. Indeed, a well-acted Carmen should suggest her contempt for most men, and for humanity in general.

Technically the score is full of original ideas. The orchestra is not a mere support for singing. It has its own life. *Carmen* is an opera of passion, power, and truth, and is infinitely superior to the carefully arranged, prettily served canapés of Gounod and Massenet. They were skilled professionals, but Bizet was a genius. He sought the kind of honesty that Mussorgsky sought in *Boris Godunov*. Art had to reflect life—not idealized life, but life as it actually was lived.

Jules Massenet, the most popular French opera composer of the last quarter of the nineteenth century, was a businessman musician who knew what the public wanted and decided to give it to them. He was an opportunist not very popular with his colleagues. He was too successful, too cynical, too preoccupied in pandering to public taste, too smug about his success. Bizet could see what was coming. "That little fellow is about to walk all over us," he said. Massenet's special mixture was a kind of sugared eroticism—an "*érotisme discret et quasi-religieux*," as Vincent d'Indy described it—and the international public could not seem to get enough of it. It was also strongly prevalent in Massenet's religious music, about which he was as cynical as he was about his operas. "I don't believe in all that creeping Jesus stuff," Massenet told d'Indy, "but the public likes it. and we must always agree with the public." No wonder Rimsky-Korsakov called him "a crafty fox"; no wonder that most of his colleagues considered him a jealous, ambitious, and hypocritical flatterer. Yet for some thirty years Massenet dominated French opera to a point where his kind of melody could be heard even in the music of such iconoclasts as Debussy. Romain Rolland was to say that in the heart of every French composer was a slumbering Massenet.

Massenet was born on May 12, 1842, and died on August 13, 1912. At the age of eleven he was in the Conservatoire, and he won the Prix de Rome in 1863. Four years later his first opera was produced—the first in a series of twenty-six. At the turn of the twentieth century such Massenet works as *Hérodiade, Le Cid, Thaïs, Sapho, Cendrillon, Le Jongleur de Notre-Dame, Don Quichotte, Werther,* and *Manon* were given everywhere. Not until the 1920's did their popularity begin to recede. Today, outside of France, it is primarily *Manon* on which Massenet's fame rests. His other operas are as dated as Meyerbeer's. In *Manon* everything coalesced. Massenet, a skillful musician, here used leitmotifs *à la* Wagner, sentimental melodies *à la* Gounod, an orchestra that produced soothing and sensuous sounds, a libretto that could titillate the tired businessman and yet send him out of the theater morally uplifted (Manon comes to a bad end).

It is curiously feminine music, and *Manon* has a great deal of feminine charm about it. "Massenet," wrote Debussy, "seems to have been the victim of the fluttering fans of his fair hearers, who flirted them so long to his glory; he yearned to reserve for himself the beating of those perfumed wings; unfortunately he might as well have tried to tame a cloud of butterflies." Debussy pointed out that music to Massenet was a delightful avocation rather than the cruel god who controlled Bach and Beethoven. Slim, courtly, elegant-looking, romantic, Massenet turned ladies' heads. He liked and understood women, and they reciprocated. Bessie Abbott, the opera singer, remembered how "he could make women so happy with his adroit verbal petting that one could listen to him forever. He had a pretty trick of telling his fair companions that she suggested a melody, and he would go to the piano and improvise some honey-sweet strain that really did suit the personality of the one so highly complimented." (Bessie's grammar is as vivid as her writing.) And so Massenet prospered. He made enormous amounts of money, invested wisely, and remained the perpetual charmer both in his music and in his life.

The obituary notice in the *Musical Courier* made a special point of trying to explain Massenet's extraordinary popularity: "It is pretty sure that if Massenet had not lived just when he did, when the world was thirsting for a little melody, and when few composers were attempting to write melody, that Massenet would have been a failure. But it just so happens that Massenet wrote melody, combined with a little modernism and just a touch of Wagnerism, at a time when most composers were trying to get beyond the old school. Therefore Massenet was appreciated. We welcome his poor melodies because we have no others."

No opera composer in France could compete with Massenet. Alfred Bruneau's *Le Rêve* (1891) had a run but was dropped and never returned. Camille Saint-Saëns wrote many operas but had only one success, and that an early one, with *Samson et Dalila* in 1877. Gustave Charpentier wrote several operas, and did create a furor with one, *Louise* (1900). This followed the lead of *Carmen* as a verismo work, and took it one step further into socialism and free love.

In advanced musical circles, *Louise* was hated as much as any Massenet opera. It was considered eclectic and cynical. Debussy all but became wild when discussing it, and the general attitude of musicians is summed up in the 1955 edition of *Grove's Dictionary of Music and Musicians*, where the writer calls *Louise* "superficial and spurious . . . depending for its appreciation on a mere passing curiosity." That may be, but the curiosity has had a long time to exhaust itself. *Louise*, composed in 1890 and not produced until 1900, is still in the repertory and has many admirers, which is not bad for a mere passing curiosity. It has its faults. It is sentimental (its verismo aspects nothwithstanding), it has too many touches of Massenet, and it is heavily Wagnerian (the influence of *Die Meistersinger* is strongly pronounced in *Louise*). Yet it has strength, and above all it has Paris.

Nominally the opera is about two lovers and the breakaway of a girl from her bourgeois background. In reality the opera is an evocation of Paris. "*Cité de force et de lumière! Splendeur première! Paris, ô Paris! cité d'amour.*" So sing the lovers (to Charpentier's own words; he wrote the libretto himself). And the very last word in the opera is "*Paris!*" Louise runs away for good and her father knows very well where the blame lies. It is not Louise's mother. It is not Julien the lover. It is Paris, and he shakes his fist at the great city.

Charpentier lives by this one work. He was an unusual type. Born in Dieuze on June 25, 1860, he went to Paris at the age of twenty-one as a music student from the provinces. His love affair with the city was spectacular, and he was never happy outside of Montmartre. He even lived his part, looking like something out of *La Bohème* with his flowing pantaloons, his long, black artist's tie and slouch hat. He was a socialist, and some of his own background went into the opera. Louise works in a dressmaking shop, while Charpentier himself had worked in a textile factory. He had taken up with a seamstress named Louise Jehan, who was employed in a dressmaking shop in the Rue Lepic. Charpentier even took her first name for his opera. *Louise* was a shocker in its day. Here was an opera that took place in the present, that contained working girls and a dressmaking shop, that made a plea for free love and the dignity of the individual, that castigated parents for holding too tightly to their children. Charpentier threw a rock through the glass window of French middle-class morality. Yet *Louise* became one of the most popular of French operas, and it does have some beautiful things in it. The Noctambulist scene is evocative of the city loved by all the civilized world; and when Julien and Louise sing their apostrophe to Paris, something very French and genuine comes through. There is, of course, *Depuis le jour*, that haunting, high-floating aria; and the twittering seamstress scene; and the rapturous first-act duet. None of this, to be sure, has the integrity of Bizet's one great opera. Charpentier was basically a sentimentalist; and while he based his opera on one or two episodes from his own life, he created a world that existed only in his own imagination and went no further. But *Louise* still has authentic period charm and something more

Charpentier lived until 1956. when he died on February 18 at the age of ninety-six. To the end he wore his nineteenth-century costume and was one of the sights of Paris. He was not one of the most polished of men. When he went to Vienna in 1903 to superintend the *Louise* premiere. the first thing he tried to do was make love to the beautiful Alma Mahler. wife of the composer-conductor who was the head of the opera house and in charge of the premiere. The Montmartre exponent of free love was so clumsy about it that the Mahlers were vastly amused and not at all angry. Alma Mahler wrote about him in her diary. "Spits under the table. chews his nails. draws your attention by a pressure of his knee or a nudge of his elbow. Trod on my foot last night to call attention to the beauty of *Tristan*. He's a socialist and wants to convert me." Eventually Charpentier wrote a sequel to *Louise* and called it *Julien*. It was as still-born as an opera could be. and after a few performances it disappeared for good.

A much greater composer—though his operas are not in the repertory—was Emmanuel Chabrier. one of the true originals of music. Among the oddities of his career is the fact that all of it was compressed into a ten-year period. Chabrier. born in Ambert on January 18. 1841. was playing the piano at the age of six. but his father opposed music as a profession. Therefore Chabrier took a law degree in 1862 and for the next eighteen years worked in the Ministry of the Interior. He moved in musical and artistic circles. was friendly with Manet and Verlaine. but for a long time did not compose. He collected paintings, and owned works by Manet. Renoir. Fantin-Latour. Sisley. Forain, and Monet. After his death. forty-eight paintings from his collection were sold at auction. on March 26. 1896. They brought a fair sum then. Today.

Not until the late 1870's did he appear as a composer. *L'Étoile*. an operetta, came out in 1877. and the one-act *Une Éducation Manquée* in 1879. Then he heard *Tristan* and was so impressed he decided to devote the rest of his life to music. He resigned from the Ministry in 1880. There followed, in rapid succession. a remarkable group of piano works named *Dix pièces pittoresques*. the orchestral rhapsody. *España*; a long opera, *Gwendoline*; a comic opera. *Le Roi malgré lui*. more piano music. and a group of songs. All of these were composed in the 1880's. Toward the end of the decade he had a mental breakdown and was incapable of writing. He died in Paris on September 13. 1894.

No composer in France at the time was more original. *Gwendoline*. which hardly anybody has ever heard. is supposed to be Wagnerian. and in some respects it is. though a study of the score shows music of unusual harmonic and melodic originality. But that is not what Chabrier stands for. He

300

brought, in his other works, something new to music—the notion of frivolity as an end in itself. Even in the early *L'Étoile* there are all the marks of what he was to represent—a breakaway from the Offenbachian kind of operetta into something much more sophisticated. There is in *L'Étoile* something of the music hall, something of the circus. It is Toulouse-Lautrec in tone. There are bubbling duets; there is one duet, between tenor and baritone, that is the funniest satire of a bel canto aria ever written; there are harmonies so sophisticated and even "bluesy" that they could have come from Gershwin; there is something that leaps the years and lands on Satie and the French group of the 1920's known as *Les Six*. Chabrier, not Satie, is the spiritual father of *Les Six*, both in his deliberate use of froth and his equally deliberate flight from Wagnerism. Though Chabrier had been influenced by Wagner, he soon tried to avoid all traces of German music. He even began to have the same approach as Debussy, *musicien français*. While working on his *Briséis*, an opera he never completed, he wrote to a friend, "I do not know whether the music will be French, but of one thing I am certain—it will not be German. For better or worse I must be of my country. It is my first duty!"

Chabrier never was one to go in for development or classic form. He had his own kind of unity, one that adhered to its own built-in logic, the kind represented by the later music of Berlioz. Chabrier greatly admired his famous predecessor. "Did Berlioz, a Frenchman above all (he wasn't old-hat in his time), put variety, color, rhythm into *La Damnation de Faust*, *Roméo et Juliette* and *L'Enfance du Christ*? But they lack unity, people say. I answer, *merde!* If in order to be *one* I am fated to be boring, I prefer to be 2, 3, 4, 10, 20—in short, I prefer to have ten colors on my palette and to break up all the lines. And to do that I don't necessarily want to do over and over again the devastating (1) act for the exposition, (2) act with silly women and vocal exercises by the queen, (3) act with a ballet, and the interminable ballet that reshuffles the cards, (4) the indispensable love duet, (5) the drunken orgy at twenty minutes before midnight, firing of muskets, Jews' cauldron, death of the leading characters." Chabrier clearly did not like Meyerbeerian grand opera.

His ideas are basically melodic. They appear and then disappear for good without the Germanic kind of development. In a way, Chabrier was an inspired amateur. "I am virtually self-taught," he wrote. "I belong to no school. I have more temperament than talent. There are many things that one must learn in youth which I shall never attain; but I live and breathe in music. I write as I feel, with more temperament than technique. But what's the difference? I think I am an honest and sincere man." Amateur or not, his piano music is very difficult to play. The figurations can be so unconventional that conservatory-trained hands have to learn different patterns and reflexes. It is wonderful piano music. with verve and wit; and the harmonies, with their constant ninth chords, anticipate Debussy. The *Trois valses romantiques* are masterpieces in miniature. and the last of the three waltzes is disquieting in its harmonic fluctuations. This is music that approaches decadence. *España*, on the other hand. is all brightness and ebullience, and leads directly into Ravel. Chabrier's masterpiece is *Le Roi malgré lui*, a lighthearted work of extraordinary sophistication. It should be revived. George Balanchine made use of some of the waltzes for his ballet *Bourrée fantasque* and they give an idea of the brilliance of the scoring and the vivacity of the melodic invention. But the public is still unfamiliar with the lovely vocal writing in *Le Roi malgré lui* Many previous composers could be light and amusing, but Chabrier was the first to be *serious* about being light and amusing, He raised his concept to the level of an aesthetic. Except for *Gwendoline* and the unfinished *Briséis*, he never aimed for big things. He was the apostle of spontaneity. of the short. elegant idea set forth in jewel-like manner. This he achieved perfectly. and within his restricted frame was one of the most remarkable composers of the period.

Quite different was Camille Saint-Saëns, the most perfect of technicians. A good deal of Saint-Saëns's music is still in the repertory. but his reputation outside of France is low. The common charge against Saint-Saëns's music is that it is all technique and no ideas. that it is empty form, that it is elegant but superficial. In a way he was the French Mendelssohn. His career is worth examining. for in his long life—October 9, 1835 to December 16, 1921—he spanned many of the musical revolutions of two centuries and he had his own contribution to make.

It is not generally realized that Saint-Saëns was probably the most awesome child prodigy in the history of music. His I.Q. must have soared far beyond any means of measurement. Consider at $2\frac{1}{2}$ he was picking out tunes on the piano. Naturally he had absolute pitch. He also could read and write before he was three. At three he composed his first piece. The autograph, dated March 22, 1839, is in the Paris Conservatoire. At five he was deep in analysis of *Don Giovanni*. using not the piano reduction but the full score. At that age he also gave a few public performances as a pianist. At seven he was reading Latin and interesting himself in science. especially botany and lepidoptery. He also collected geological specimens. His formal musical training started at seven, and he made his official debut at ten. As an encore at his debut recital he offered to play any of Beethoven's thirty-two sonatas from memory. His fame reached as far as the United States, and an item in the Boston *Musical Gazette* of August 3, 1846, states that "there is a boy in Paris, named St. Saëns, only ten and a half years old, who plays the music of Handel, Sebastian Bach, Mozart, Beethoven and the more modern masters, without any book before him." Saint-Saëns had total recall.

If he read a book or heard a piece of music it was forever in his memory.

He grew up to be one of the important pianists and organists of his day, a fine conductor, a brilliant score reader, a composer who worked prolifically in all forms, a sound musicologist, and a lively critic. Outside of music he dabbled in astronomy (he was a member of the Astronomical Society of France) and archaeology, looked into the occult sciences, published a volume of poetry, and tried his hand at playwriting. At the beginning of his career he was considered one of France's musical revolutionaries. As he grew older he was known as an archconservative. He admitted to being an eclectic, and said of his music: "I ran after the chimera of purity of style and perfection of form." He was a small, dandified, peppery man, and a dangerous one to cross despite his foppish looks. Pierre Lalo described him: "He was short, and always strangely resembled a parrot: the same, sharply-curved profile; a beaklike hooked nose; lively, restless, piercing eyes. . . . He strutted like a bird and talked rapidly, precipitately, with a curiously affected lisp."

For many years he was organist at the Madeleine (Liszt called him the greatest organist in the world). He took up the cause of Wagner and fought for *Tannhäuser* and *Lohengrin*. He also allied himself with the other progressives, Liszt and Schumann. In 1861 he became a teacher at the École Niedermeyer. Fauré was his most prominent pupil. He toured as a pianist, and in an age of flamboyant virtuosos, Saint-Saëns was an exponent of purity, clarity, refinement, and classicism. He gave a cycle of the Mozart piano concertos, probably the first pianist in history to do so. In the meantime his own music did not make much headway. Some were secretly pleased that this phenomenal but somewhat arrogant musical mind was having so little success. Berlioz, witty as ever, quipped of Saint-Saëns that "He knows everything but he lacks inexperience." Saint-Saëns began to make enemies. He could not stand Franck's music, and he feuded with Massenet. Massenet was elected a member of the *Institut,* an honor avidly desired by Saint-Saëns. Ever the flatterer, Massenet sent Saint-Saëns a telegram: "My dear colleague, the *Institut* has made a terrible mistake." Furious, Saint-Saëns wired back: "I entirely agree with you." A few years later Saint-Saëns was elected and became an Immortal. But, years later, he saw to it that Debussy was kept out of the *Institut.* He despised Debussy's music. "I've thtayed in Parith to thpeak ill of 'Pelléath and Mélithande,' " he told a friend. He also had bad things to thpeak about the music of d'Indy and Strauss.

The evil that he did lives after him. Many seem to have forgotten the good he did. He not only was a progressive force in his day. In addition he founded, with Romain Bussine (a voice professor at the Conservatoire), the Société Nationale de Musique in 1871. This organization stood godfather to the entire new generation of French composers. The purpose of the Société was to give new French music a hearing, and it did, for many years, introducing works by Franck d'Indy, Chabrier Bruneau, Chausson, Dukas, Lekeu Magnard and Ravel Romain Rolland called the Société the "cradle and sanctuary of French art" All that has been great in French music from 1870 to 1900 has come by way of it Without it the greater part of the works that are the honor of our music not only would have been unperformed but perhaps would not even have been written Nor was it only French music that interested Saint-Saëns. Aside from his propaganda for Liszt and Wagner it was he who introduced the music of *Boris Godunov* to French musicians, bringing back the vocal score after a trip to Russia He kept doing what he thought was best for music But by 1890 he was a bitter reactionary—sour ill-tempered, restless, with a compulsion to travel Perhaps he secretly realized he had never lived up to his glorious potential In addition his personal life collapsed. In 1878 he lost both of his children within a few months André fell out of a window and Jean died of an infantile disease Three years later Saint-Saëns walked out on his wife There was no divorce or separation, but they never met again (She died in 1950 at the age of ninety-four) Brooding, Saint-Saëns wrote a philosophical book entitled *Problèmes et Mystères* It was a study in pessimism that advocated atheism Art and science Saint-Saëns maintained, will take the place of religion. Life has no purpose "People have always been disappointed in their search for final causes. It may simply be that there are no such things." Existentialism in France had a spokesman in Saint-Saëns long before Sartre

Like any ambitious French composer of his day, he composed operas After two tries he succeeded with *Samson et Dalila* in 1877 It had its premiere not in Paris but in Weimar None of Saint-Saëns's twelve other operas came within remote distance of its popularity, though experts say that *Ascanio* (1890) is a better work But it is *Samson* that has remained in the repertory Indeed, considering the generally low repute of his music, it is amazing how much of his work does remain in the repertory There are the G minor and C minor Piano Concertos, with No. 5 in F sometimes performed: there is the Symphony No. 3 (*Organ*) in C minor there are the Violin Concerto in B minor and the Cello Concerto in A minor there is the *Carnival of the Animals*, from which comes *The Swan* The Introduction and Rondo Capriccio for violin and orchestra is heard very often. Of the symphonic poems the *Danse Macabre* is famous, and once in a while *Le Rouet d'Omphale* gets a hearing.

This is not a bad representation. It suggests that Saint-Saëns is a better composer than he is reputed to be There must be some vitality in the music to have kept it alive so long. There also is something aesthetically satisfactory about the logic of his music, its neatness, finish, clear outlines sheer professionalism. It is a music rooted in the classic tradition whatever its departures from orthodox form. A case can be made for Saint-Saëns as the first of the neoclassicists. Above all his music has classic elegance. Of all French composers of his time he was the most chaste, and his music completely avoids the supersensuous sounds of Franck and his school. The G minor Piano Concerto or the *Organ Symphony* may not probe very deeply, but at least they avoid the banality and bad taste of so much music of the period. His piano music, almost never played, verges on the salon but escapes triteness because of its brilliance and objectivity. It is very effective music. A good example is the C minor Toccata (the solo version of the last movement of the Fifth Concerto). It has the kind of glitter that bridges Liszt and Ravel. It may be that Saint-Saëns is due for a reassessment. A turn of the wheel might find his kind of consummate craft, and his lightweight but elegant and clear-cut musical ideas, worthy of revival. The trouble is that Saint-Saëns is best known by his worst music—*Samson et Dalila*, *The Swan*, the *Danse Macabre*—and not by the Septet for Piano, Trumpet and Strings, the D minor Violin Sonata, and the Piano Quartet in B flat.

From *Saint-Saëns and His Circle* by James Harding, Chatto and Windus Ltd., London

SAINT-SAËNS, CARICATURE BY "HIS RESPECTFUL PUPIL"
GABRIEL FAURÉ.

❦ 3 ❧

Russian Nationalism and the Mighty Five

FROM GLINKA TO RIMSKY-KORSAKOV

The idea of a country's aspirations being consciously reflected in its music was a nineteenth-century development and was most strongly pronounced in those countries a little outside the mainstream of European thought. Russia, Poland, Hungary, Bohemia, and Spain all produced at least one nationalistic composer of stature. The people in most of those countries had the most to aspire to. Rich countries with satisfied citizens do not normally produce nationalistic music, which in a way is propaganda—a spiritual call to arms. A country with a people under the domination of a foreign power, such as the Kingdom of Bohemia under Austrian rule, or a country where the people groaned under the iron fist of a czar and his entrenched, grasping aristocracy, was not capable of much in the way of social protest. But protests could be made in literature and music, and they were. Where the hands of the activists were tied, the musician at least could express his country's longing for freedom or his country's pride in its traditions. And all this was helped by the romantic identification with "the folk."

Nationalism in music is the conscious use of a body of folk music, appearing even in such extended forms as symphony and opera. Wagner is the most Teutonic of all composers, but he is not a nationalist composer because he never drew upon the heritage of German folk music. Even if a composer occasionally does write a piece in which folk elements are used, that does not necessarily make him a nationalist. Brahms wrote a set of *Deutsche Volkslieder* but that did not make him a national composer, no more than Schubert was when he composed his *Divertisement à la Hongroise*. Those pieces were outside the main body of their work, as were Liszt's *Hungarian Rhapsodies*. Nationalism in music is not a superficially applied patina of folk music. Rather it is an evocation of the folk spirit, of the songs, dances, and religious music of a people. The true nationalist does not have to quote that material directly. He is so impregnated by the *melos* that all of his music evokes, as a specific response, the music of his homeland. The *melos* of the composer's country is an essential part of his actual mental and aural processes, as much as the air he breathes, the food he eats, and the language he speaks.

Though neither Chopin nor Liszt were true nationalists, Chopin had shown the way in his mazurkas and polonaises, and Liszt in his rhapsodies. (The nineteenth century had a much higher opinion of the Liszt rhapsodies than later ages did.) When Russia began to stir, it was to Chopin and Liszt rather than the academic composers to whom most of her musicians looked. Chopin and Liszt represented freedom as opposed to the "rules" of the German and Austrian conservatories. And the Russian nationalists hated rules. Russian composers were the first ones in Europe to make an aesthetic out of nationalism. Mikhail Glinka (1804–1857) started it off with his opera *A Life for the Czar*, in 1836. It took only fifty years after that for Russia to produce a handful of nationalist composers who turned out to be among the most original and powerful in the history of music.

Russian music until Glinka had been dominated by the Italians. Such important eighteenth-century composers as Manfredini, Galuppi, Paisiello, and Cimarosa had worked in Russia. Opera in Moscow and St. Petersburg—as, indeed, in other European cities—meant Italian opera. The music of the few native-born Russian composers active before Glinka is known only to specialists. Russia was a mysterious nation at the turn of the nineteenth century—an immensely powerful one, as Napoleon found out, but just emerging from a medieval condition. The entire Western tradition of philosophical thought, culture, and science was largely unknown there except to a few enlightened members of the aristocracy. Musically the country had a rich heritage of folk song, but there was nothing in the way of a musical establishment. As late as 1850 there was no conservatory of music in all of Russia. There were very few teachers, very few music books and publications. In St. Petersburg there was an organization known as the Russian Philharmonic Society. It gave two concerts a year.

Musicians were second-class citizens. As Anton Rubinstein wrote before setting up the St. Petersburg Conservatory in 1862, "Russia has almost no artist-musicians in the exact sense of this term. This is so because our government has not given the same privileges to the art of music that are enjoyed by the other arts, such as painting, sculpture, etc.—that is, he who practices music is not given the rank of an artist." This is important. What Rubinstein is saying is that musicians literally had no social status. A painter could be recognized by the government and given the title of "artist of the state." Not a musician.

The history of Russian music as it is known today starts with Glinka, who wrote a large quantity of inferior, Western-influenced music before his two great operas *A Life for the Czar* and *Russlan and Ludmilla* Tchaikovsky for one could never get over Glinka's transformation "A dilettante who played now on the violin, now on the piano, who composed colorless quadrilles and fantasies on stylish themes, who tried his hand at serious forms (quartet, sextet) and songs, but composed nothing but banalities in the taste of the 30 s -who suddenly in the thirty-fourth year of his life produces an opera which by its genius, breadth, originality and flawless technique stands on a level with the greatest and most profound music!" Glinka, as the founder of the Russian national school, was deified by his successors. Tchaikovsky's remark is typical. All Russian composers, then and now, regarded Glinka much the way a disciple gazes upon the face of the Master Tchaikovsky again "The present Russian school is all in *Kamarinskaya*, just as the whole oak is in the acorn From *Kamarinskaya* all Russian composers (including myself) draw contrapuntal and harmonic combinations whenever they have to deal with a Russian dance tune."

Mikhail Glinka was born on June 1 1804, into a wealthy landowning family He had violin and piano lessons, including several piano lessons from the celebrated John Field, the Irish pianist composer who had settled in Russia in 1803 At best, however, Glinka's musical education was sketchy He became a civil servant in 1824, in the Ministry of Ways and Communication in St. Petersburg. In 1828 he resigned and traveled in Europe, spending nearly three years in Milan, where he met Bellini and Donizetti, and then spent a year in Berlin, studying theory under Siegfried Dehn The music he composed through this period is primarily cosmopolitan, and the Russian touches are not much more pronounced than Beethoven's use of Russian themes in his *Razumovsky* quartets Glinka's Sextet for Piano and Strings, for instance, is strongly Mendelssohnian Considering that it was composed in 1832, it has a strikingly romantic, idiomatic piano part, and it does quote a Russian folk song in an unadorned manner. But the musical materials can under no circumstances be called original

Back in Russia in 1834, friendly with Pushkin and Gogol, Glinka decided to compose an opera on a Russian subject He settled on a national hero, Ivan Sussanin (in Russia the opera is called *Ivan Sussanin* to this day, rather than *A Life for the Czar*), and he spent two years on the score. The opera is about the peasant Ivan Sussanin, who misdirected a body of the Polish army, thus saving the life of the first Romanov at the expense of his own Glinka said that he was inspired by the story "As if by magic, both the plan of the whole opera and the idea of the antithesis of Russian and Polish music, as well as many of the themes and even details of the working-out all this flashed into my head at one stroke" The opera had its premiere on December 9, 1836, in the presence of the Imperial family, and was a great success. There is no reason why it should not have been. The Court was habituated to Italian opera, and *A Life for the Czar* is strongly Italianate. Harmonically it poses no problems, and melodically it is attractive. To twentieth-century ears, it is a pleasant work but scarcely revolutionary, and it is hard to understand Tchaikovsky's all but hysterical eulogy. But the twentieth century is too far removed. To Russians in 1836 and for many years thereafter, *A Life for the Czar* stood alone—the first opera on a Russian subject, the first with a libretto that concerned peasants instead of nobles, the first to quote Russian folk song.

Glinka never had an equivalent popular success, though *Russlan and Ludmilla* is a much more interesting and important opera. Composed in 1842, it was strongly nationalistic, with Orientalisms, a use of the whole tone scale, some rugged dissonances, and with much more personality than *A Life for the Czar*. But it was a failure. At least one major European musician liked it. Liszt on a tour of Russia, read the full score at the piano and went around trumpeting its worth. Always alert to new talent and new sounds, Liszt was one of the few musicians outside Russia to keep a constant eye on that country's development. In later years he described exactly what Russian music represented. Having developed independently far from any foreign-born influence, the Russians (said Liszt) brought something new into music that delighted him in its rhythmic and fresh taste. One of the fresh concepts that the experienced ear of Liszt relished was the exotic quality of the Russian folk song that played so large a part in Glinka's late music and in the music of his successors. Rhythmically, Russian folk music is highly irregular, frequently in five-four or seven-four time meters used relatively little by Western composers until Stravinsky popularized them in the twentieth century. It was no accident that Stravinsky's rhythmic irregularity was so marked; as a pupil of Rimsky-Korsakov, he knew a great deal about Russian folk song.

Depressed by the lack of interest in *Russlan and Ludmilla*—a work too advanced for the Russians of his day—Glinka left in 1844 for an extended visit to France and Spain. The latter country entranced him, and he even tried to learn Spanish dancing. "My feet were all right, but I couldn't manage the castanets." The *Jota Aragonesa*, one of the first attempts of any European composer to use Spanish melodies and rhythms, was the result, as was an overture named *A Night in Madrid*. Nor did Glinka neglect his Russian-derived music; and in 1848 came the symphonic poem *Kamarinskaya*, the progenitor of an entire half-century of orchestral music based on Russian folk themes. But on the whole he did little composing. He traveled, he took up with a series of agreeable young ladies (his own marriage in 1835 had ended with separation in 1839 and divorce in 1846), he met and enter tained his colleagues all over the continent. He was bored. Finally he found a new interest—church music. He went to Berlin to study Bach and the church modes. There he caught a cold, and on February 15, 1857, he died. Immediately he became a national hero. "Beethoven and Glinka!" exclaimed Anton Rubinstein. Rubinstein's Russian contemporaries saw nothing exaggerated in the coupling.

The next development in Russian music came when a group of inspired amateurs gathered around a father-figure named Mili Balakirev, a short, squat, Asiatic-looking, largely self-taught composer. What resulted was one of the strangest things in musical history, and it could not have taken place anywhere else in the world.

Balakirev was born in Nizhny-Novgorod on January 2, 1837. At the age of ten he was taken by his mother to Moscow, where he studied piano and was more or less adopted by Alexander Ulibischev, an enthusiast who wrote books on Mozart and Beethoven. Ulibischev encouraged young Balakirev, who started composing before he knew anything about the rules of music. His friend and fellow student, the violinist Peter Dmitrievitch Baborikin, attested to the fact that Balakirev owned not a single book on harmony, orchestration, or theory. But Balakirev who had determination, who had a good musical mind and a good ear (including absolute pitch), persisted; and when he heard the Glinka operas, he decided to devote himself permanently to music. In 1855 he set himself up in St. Petersburg. There, encouraged by Glinka, he became active as a pianist and composer.

He was a man of strong opinions who expected to be obeyed, and he became the leader of Russian music after Glinka died in 1857. Not only the leader; he became the czar. Around him gathered a group of young musicians who were to be known as The Russian Five—a group of self-taught dilettantes active in other fields. Several of them remained part-time composers all their lives. César Cui, in 1856, was the first to be attracted to the Balakirev orbit. Cui (1835–1918) was an army officer and remained one to the end of his life. He was an engineer, and his specialty was fortifications. As a composer he was the least talented of The Five, and although he wrote a good deal none of his music has remained in the repertory except a salon piece named *Orientale*. He was more valuable to the group as a critic. His articles appeared in France as well as in Russia, and he was constantly explaining the nationalistic principles of The Five.

Modest Mussorgsky (1839–1881) was the next to enter the circle. He appeared to be an unlikely candidate for immortality. At that time, 1857, he was an eighteen-year-old ensign in the crack Preobrajensky Regiment, and had been taught what every good regimental officer of the Preobrajensky had to know—how to drink, how to wench, how to wear clothes, how to gamble, how to flog a serf, how to sit a horse. Of this set of accomplishments. Mussorgsky found drinking the most congenial. His other big accomplishment was an ability to play the piano. His mother had taught him, and his repertory consisted of fashionable potpourris of the day. Alexander Borodin, then an army medical officer, met him in 1856, while both were duty officers at the same hospital. In a letter to the critic Vladimir Stassov, many years later, Borodin wrote of his first impression of Mussorgsky:

I had just been appointed an army doctor and Mussorgsky was a newly hatched officer. Being on hospital duty, we met in the common room; and feeling bored and in need of companionship, we started talking and forthwith found one another congenial. The same evening we were invited to the army doctor's house. Having a grown-up daughter, he often gave parties to which the officers on duty were asked. Mussorgsky was at that time a very callow, most elegant, perfectly contrived little officer: brand-new, close-fitting uniform, toes well turned out, hair well oiled and carefully smoothed-out, hands shapely and well cared for. His manners were polished and aristocratic. He spoke through his teeth, and his carefully-chosen words were interspersed with French phrases and rather labored. He showed, in fact, signs of a slight pretentiousness; but also, quite unmistakably, of perfect breeding and education. He sat down at the piano and, coquettishly raising his hands, started playing delicately and gracefully, bits of *Trovatore* and *Traviata*, the circle around him rapturously murmuring "*Charmant! Délicieux!*"

Music was what Mussorgsky loved above all. So overwhelming was the impact of Balakirev upon him that he resigned his commission in 1857 and plunged madly into the study of music. There was money in the family, and thus Mussorgsky had no financial problems. Borodin ran into him two years later and was more impressed: "Nothing in his aspect recalled the quondam officer. His attire, his manners, were as dainty as ever, but no trace of foppishness remained." It was not until 1861, when the serfs were emancipated, that Mussorgsky began to have problems. Many landowning families, Mussorgsky's among them, were hard hit. Mussorgsky had to go it alone, without financial help from his family, and was forced to take a civil service job.

Into the Balakirev circle next came a young naval officer named Nicolai Rimsky-Korsakov (1844–1908). Like Mussorgsky, he came from an aristocratic family. Unlike Mussorgsky, he was not even a capable pianist, though he dabbled with that instrument and also the cello. He wanted to compose, but he did not know where to turn until he met Balakirev. They came together through Rimsky's piano teacher, one Feodor Canille. "Last Sunday," Rimsky wrote to his parents early in December, 1861, "Canille introduced me to M. A. Balakirev, a well-known musician and composer, and also to Cui, who has written an opera, *The Prisoner of the Caucasus.*" Rimsky-Kor sakov was overwhelmed, and didn't know how to thank Canille enough "for such a magnificent acquaintance." Balakirev saw something in Rimsky and clutched him to his heart. In a letter to Stassov, Balakirev wrote that Cui was "a talent but not a human being in the social sense," and that Mussorgsky was "practically an idiot." But Rimsky-Korsakov! "I put my trust in you," he told the young naval officer, "like an old aunt in a young lawyer nephew." Rimsky had already brought him sketches for a symphony in E flat minor. Balakirev urged the eighteen-year-old composer to finish it.

Alexander Borodin joined the Balakirev circle in 1862. Borodin (1833–1887), the illegitimate child of Prince Luka Gedeonoshvili, was trained as a scientist and remained one all his life. He went to the Academy of Medicine, graduated with honors, and went on to study at Heidelberg. Chemistry was his specialty. His doctoral thesis was entitled "On the Analogy of Arsenical with Phosphoric Acid." In the meantime, there was his music. Like Mussorgsky, he was an amateur pianist with an urge to compose, and his teachers at the medical school would upbraid him for devoting so much of his time to music.

So there they were—the army engineer, the ex-ensign, the naval cadet, and the chemist. There were also peripheral members of the circle, such as the art historian and music critic Vladimir Stassov; or the two talented Purgold daughters, one a singer and one a pianist. There was Alexander Dargomijsky (1813–1869), not a member of The Five but a composer with some original ideas who was closely associated with the circle. They were constantly meeting at his house, and he could have been the leader instead of Balakirev, but he was of frail health, without Balakirev's ability to command and inspire. There was Alexander Serov, the first important music critic in Russia and himself a composer. But the active workers were Cui, Mussorgsky, Rimsky-Korsakov, and Borodin. They sat directly at Balakirev's feet. Their curriculum and method of study would have brought tears to the eyes of a good German professor. Lacking books, lacking basic knowledge, they simply leaned on each other and against Balakirev. They would get whatever scores they could, from Bach through Berlioz and Liszt, playing through them, analyzing their form, taking the pieces apart and putting them together again. Perhaps that is not a bad way to study music. They criticized one another's works, helped one another compose, advanced in tiny steps. They were a close-knit group, and two of them, Mussorgsky and Rimsky-Korsakov, actually roomed together for a while. As Borodin wrote, "In the relations within our circle, there is not a shadow of envy, conceit or selfishness. Each is made sincerely happy by the smallest success of another."

Self-taught and proud of it, they defiantly made a virtue of their liabilities, and raised the flag of their doctrine in an uncompromising manner. As a group they preached spontaneity, "truth in music," nationalism, opposition to academism and Wagnerism. To them the villains of Russian music were the Rubinstein brothers and their conservatories, for they were the Enemy, representing the Western academic tradition. Anton Rubinstein (1830–1894), Russia's first great pianist, was a prolific composer who turned out piece after piece in the Mendelssohn-Schumann-Chopin tradition of early romanticism. His *Ocean Symphony* was probably the most popular orchestral work in Europe during the last half of the nineteenth century. As in his other music, there is not a trace of nationalism in the *Ocean Symphony*. Only recently has Rubinstein's music virtually disappeared, though the Melody in F is still known, the D minor Piano Concerto and a few solo piano pieces are still occasionally heard, and his opera, *The Demon*, is still performed in Russia. In 1862 Rubinstein founded the St. Petersburg Conservatory. Two years later his brother, Nicholas, founded the Moscow Conservatory. Nicholas Rubinstein (1835–1881) was also a fine pianist Tchaikovsky considered him superior even to his more famous brother

Both of the Rubinsteins were anathema to The Five. "It would be a serious error to consider Rubinstein a Russian composer," Cui wrote. "He is merely a Russian who composes." To The Five, the two conservatories represented the sterile, dead weight of the German conventions. Balakirev considered the St. Petersburg Conservatory a plot "to bring all Russian music under the yoke of the German generals." The Five were looking for something else. Their interest was primarily in dramatic music for the voice, or in orchestral music representing the traditions of their own country. Their idea of "truth" differed considerably from the Rubinstein idea of truth. As Cui explained their doctrine, "Dramatic music must have an intrinsic worth, as absolute music, independent of the text." And: "Vocal music must be in perfect agreement with the sense of the words. The structure of the scenes must depend entirely on the relation of the characters and on the general movement of the play." Away with coloratura roulades, away with those calling cards named "leit motifs," away with the "immutable stereotyped forms." Inspiration was the important thing, much more important than "rules" or sonata form

The dislike of The Five toward the academicians was fully reciprocated. To the conservatory-trained musicians, the Balakirev circle consisted of amateurs. Tchaikovsky, for one, was constantly ridiculing the (to him) outrageous and self-satisfied claims of The Five. "One must always *work*, and a self-respecting artist must not fold his hands on the pretext that he isn't in the mood. I have learned to master myself and am glad I've not followed in the footsteps of those Russian colleagues who have no self-confidence and no patience, and who throw in the sponge at the slightest difficulty. That is why, in spite of their great gifts, they produce so little and in such a desultory way." In a long, famous letter to Nadejda von Meck, his patroness, Tchaikovsky wrote exactly what he thought of The Five. The letter, dated January 5, 1878, is an important document, illustrative of what the "educated" Russian musicians of the day were thinking:

> All the newest Petersburg composers are very gifted persons, but they are all afflicted to the marrow with the worst sort of conceit and with a purely dilettantish confidence in their superiority over all the rest of the musical world. Rimsky-Korsakov has been the recent exception. He too was self-taught like the others, but a radical change has occurred in him [Rimsky had recently been appointed professor of composition at the St. Petersburg Conservatory] . . As a very young man he fell in with a group of people who first assured him he was a genius, then told him it was not necessary to *study*, that schooling kills inspiration, dries up creativity, and so on. At first he believed this. His first compositions reveal a very great talent devoid of any theoretical training. In the circle to which he belonged, every one was in love with himself and with one another. Cui is a gifted dilettante. His music is devoid of originality, but is elegant and graceful. . . Borodin is a 50-year-old professor of chemistry at the Academy of Medicine. Again a talent—even an impressive one— . . . he has less taste than Cui and his technique is so weak that he cannot write a line without outside help. Mussorgsky you very correctly call a has-been. In talent he perhaps exceeds all the others; but he has a narrow stature and lacks the need for self-perfection. . . . The most outstanding person of this circle is Balakirev. But he has grown silent after accomplishing very little. He has immense gifts; and they are lost because of some fateful circumstances that have made a saintly prig of him. . This, then, is my honest opinion of these gentlemen. What a sad thing! With the exception of Rimsky-Korsakov, how many talents from whom it is futile to await anything serious! And is not this generally the way in Russia? Tremendous powers fatally hindered by a sort of Plevna from taking the field and enjoining battle as they should. Nevertheless these powers exist. Even a Mussorgsky, by his very lack of discipline, speaks a new language. It is ugly, but it is fresh. . . .

Tchaikovsky was trying hard to be fair, but his distaste and prejudices show through. He was, however, honest enough and musician enough to see the elemental power of Mussorgsky. About Balakirev he was, on the whole, correct. Balakirev was more a catalyst than a composer, and very little of his music has survived. The only work that still has any currency is his tremendous piano piece, *Islamey*. Sir Thomas Beecham used to conduct Balakirev's First Symphony, and Serge Koussevitzky had a liking for the symphonic poem *Thamar*. Neither work has been much heard in the West since those two champions died.

The 1860's was the decade during which The Five worked together as a unit Balakirev in addition kept busy as the head of the Free School of Music, which he set up in opposition to the St. Petersburg Conservatory. The Free School sponsored concerts, and Balakirev conducted about twenty a year, introducing many new Russian scores (including several by Tchaikovsky). He continued to ride herd over his young friends, and Rimsky Korsakov referred time and again to his "iron-grip." Balakirev on the one hand was sincerely interested in their development. On the other hand he was a despot who had to have things his own way, and he resented it when the members of his circle started going off on their own, maturing, ignoring his advice. As he felt his influence decrease, his attitude became sharper and more domineering than ever. "I particularly dislike the one-sidedness of his musical opinions and the acerbity of his tone," Tchaikovsky, who had dealings with him, complained. Rather than take a secondary position, Balakirev began to avoid the circle, a fact that Borodin noted in 1871:

I don't understand why Balakirev turns away so stubbornly. Perhaps it's only his conceit gnawing at him. He is so despotic by nature that he demands complete subordination to his wishes, even in the most trifling matters. It doesn't seem possible for him to acknowledge freedom and equality. He cannot endure the slightest opposition to his tastes or even to his whims. He wants to impose his yoke on everyone and everything. And yet he is quite aware that we all have already grown up, that we stand firmly on our feet and no longer require braces. This evidently irks him. More than once he has said to Ludma. "Why should I hear their things; they are all so mature now that I've become unnecessary to them, they can do without me," etc. His nature is such that it positively requires minors around whom he can fuss like a nurse around a child. Meanwhile the alienation of Mili, his obvious turning away from the circle, his sharp remarks about many, especially about Modest, have considerably cooled those sympathetic to him. If he goes on like this he may easily isolate himself and, this, in his situation, would amount to spiritual death.

Borodin was an accurate prophet. Balakirev soon broke entirely from the circle. In 1872 he left music completely to take a job with a railroad company. He felt rejected and useless, and he became a religious fanatic. That lasted several years, and then he returned to the musical wars, resuming the directorship of the Free School and taking a new group of pupils, among them the talented Serge Liapunov. He also started to compose again, eventually finishing two symphonies and a huge piano sonata. (Balakirev previously had been notorious for starting but never finishing his compositions.) He became friendly with Tchaikovsky, bombarding him with suggestions and advice. But he no longer was the symbol he had been. He was respected, but his word no longer was law. The founding father of The Five was the last but one of the group to die (Cui outlived him by eight years). At his death in 1910 he was little more than a name to the younger generation of Russian composers. But without him the course of Russian music would have taken a completely different turn.

Mussorgsky was the first of The Five to come to fulfillment. Of the group, he was the most original and the most uncompromising. He lived only for music, and perhaps he drank so much because he never could achieve his vision. Certainly nothing but alcohol interfered with his quest. He paid next to no attention to his civil service position, he seems to have had no love affairs (suggestions that he was a homosexual are unsupported), he had no money, and he lived only to get on paper the sounds that were in his mind. He believed that an artist had to hew his own path and not follow the crowd. There is a revealing sentence in a letter he wrote to Rimsky in 1867. He was writing about Wagner, a composer he did not like very much, but he felt "Wagner is powerful, powerful, in that he lays hands on art and yanks it around." Little by little Mussorgsky worked out his philosophy. Basic to his ideas was the concept of the reproduction of human speech in musical terms, and he tried to achieve it in a setting of Gogol's *The Marriage*, of which he completed only one act. He called that act his Rubicon. "This is living prose in music . . . this is reverence for the language of humanity, this is a reproduction of simple human speech."

He became fixated on the subject. Time and again he referred to it, and he was obsessed with the problem. "I want to say that if the expression in sound of human thought and feeling is truly produced by me *in music,* and this reproduction is musical and artistic, then the thing is in the bag." Or: "If it is possible to tug at the heartstrings by the simplest of means, merely by obeying an artistic instinct to catch the intonations of the human voice —why not look into this matter?" Or: "I should like to make my characters speak on the stage exactly as people do in real life, without exaggeration or distortion, and just write music that will be thoroughly artistic. . . . What I project is the melody of life, not of classicism." Mussorgsky decided that he had a mission "unexampled in the history of the art: that of setting to music prose straight out of life, of turning out musical prose." He had not pulled these ideas from the empty air; they previously had been promulgated by Dargomijsky, whose opera *The Stone Guest* stood as a concrete example of sung speech in its pure state. Dargomijsky in 1857 had written: "I do not intend to debase music to the level of mere amusement . . . I want the notes to express exactly what the words express. I want truth." *The Stone Guest* was derided as "a recitative opera," and Dargomijsky never finished it. (Cui completed the final scene, and Rimsky-Korsakov scored it.) But the work, and Dargomijsky's theories, made an enormous impression on

Mussorgsky. The entire concept was new. No composer previously had thought of opera in that fashion, Wagner least of all. Wagner's *Stabreim* was a literary device, far removed from natural speech.

Allied to the Mussorgsky concept of sung speech was a strong national ism. He wanted to express the Russian people. "When I sleep I see them, when I eat I think of them, when I drink—I can visualize them, integral, big, unpainted, and without any tinsel." To achieve his ideal, Mussorgsky was prepared to break any rule, go to any length. He despised anybody—Saint-Saëns, for instance—who in his opinion took the easy way out by pandering to public taste, and his comments on Cui and Rimsky-Korsakov after the circle began to break up have an indignation that curiously anticipates the writings of Charles Ives: "When I think of certain artists who dare not cross the barrier, I feel not merely distressed but sickened. All their ambition is to detail, one by one, carefully-measured drops of prettiness. A real man would be ashamed of doing so. Devoid of wisdom and will power, they entangle themselves in the bonds of tradition."

Mussorgsky started working on his masterpiece, *Boris Godounov*, in 1868. The great score has a peculiar history. Mussorgsky adapted his text (he wrote the libretto himself) from a Pushkin play. It is a libretto that is more a series of pageants than anything else, but it is held together by the tremendous figure of Boris and, more, by an inexorable sweep that passes from the intrigue of the court to the life of the people. The opera may be named *Boris Godounov*, but it far transcends any one figure. It is Russia: the Russia of king and boyar, priest and intriguer, common man, field, city, and forest. The score was finished in December, 1869, after fifteen months of work. Mussorgsky submitted it to the theater and it was rejected on the grounds that it lacked a major female role. There were other reasons for the rejection, and it is a matter of record that the committee was shocked by the novelty of the opera and its bleakness—it's "truth." Stassov and other friends urged Mussorgsky to revise *Boris Godounov*, and he reluctantly set about it. He dropped a scene in St. Basil Square, cut sections from other scenes, inserted new arias of an almost orthodox nature, and composed an entirely new third act, the Polish act, which has a prominent part for soprano. Now the opera ended with the Peasant Revolt and the song of the Simpleton. The revision was completed in 1874. Some Mussorgsky experts, including his biographer, M. D. Calvocoressi, believe the second version to be weaker than the first.

In 1873, three scenes from *Boris* were staged at the Maryinsky Theater. The following year the vocal score was published by Bessel. Finally, on January 27, 1874, the entire opera was staged, though with a few cuts. It had a decided success with the public, and less of a success with the critics. Among the dissenting critics was Cui, who attacked *Boris* for its "feeble" libretto, its "Wagnerism," its "crude tone painting," its "immaturity," its "lack of technique." Mussorgsky was crushed. Then he became furious at Cui. *Boris Godounov* remained in the repertory for several years, disappearing in 1879. In five years it received twenty-one performances. After Mussorgsky's death the opera received five more performances and then, in 1882, was withdrawn.

The history of *Boris Godounov* does not end there. As a tribute to the memory of his friend, Rimsky-Korsakov undertook the preparation of all Mussorgsky manuscripts for publication. *Boris* came under his editorial supervision. Rimsky-Korsakov was a skilled composer, a devoted and honest musician, and a loyal friend; but he also had a conventional mind and certain things about the opera appalled him: "I worship *Boris Godounov* and hate it. I worship it for its originality, power, boldness, independence and beauty. I hate it for its shortcomings, the roughness of its harmonies, the incoherencies in the music." He knew there would be opposition: "Although I know I shall be cursed for so doing, I will revise *Boris*. There are countless absurdities in its harmonies, and at time in its melodies. Unfortunately, Stassov and his followers will never understand."

And so, Rimsky took it upon himself to edit, change, reharmonize, and reorchestrate *Boris Godounov*. It is the Rimsky-Korsakov edition that was promptly used in opera houses the world over, and is still generally in use, despite protests by musicologists and critics. Not until 1928 was the original full score published. There have been several attempts to present the "original" *Boris,* but most musicians believe that the original score has to be touched up to make it "sound." Thus when the Metropolitan Opera staged what purported to be the original, it was in a heavily touched-up version by Karol Rathaus. At least Rathaus left the original harmonies unchanged. Other adaptations have been made, including a version by Dmitri Shostakovich that out-Rimskys Rimsky. The fact seems to be that the original version of *Boris* has so many instances of inept scoring that some editorial work has to be done. The controversy about how much to do is still raging.

After *Boris Godounov,* Mussorgsky turned his attention to another opera, *Khovantchina.* He also went through a profound psychic upheaval. His private life became a mess, and his friends were frightened by his compulsive drinking. Mussorgsky had turned into a dipsomaniac. Borodin lamented. "This is horribly sad! Such a talented man and sinking so low morally. Now he periodically disappears, then reappears, morose, untalkative, which is contrary to his usual habit. After a while he comes to himself again—sweet, gay, amiable and as witty as ever. Devil knows what a pity!" Mussorgsky's friend, the artist Ilya Repin (whose frightening, unforgettable portrait of Mussorgsky in his last days is one of the masterpieces of nineteenth-century portraiture), has recorded the disintegration:

It was really incredible how that well-bred Guards officer, with his beautiful and polished manners, that witty conversationalist with the ladies, that inexhaustible punster . . quickly sank, sold his belongings, even his elegant clothes, and soon descended to some cheap saloons where he personified the familiar type of has-been, where this childishly happy child, with a red potato-shaped nose, was already unrecognizable. . . Was it really he? The once impeccably-dressed, heel-clicking society man, scented, dainty, fastidious? Oh, how many times V.V. [Stassov] on his return from abroad was hardly able to get him out of some basement dive, nearly in rags, swollen with alcohol.

Nevertheless Mussorgsky continued to compose and to work at his government position, though haphazardly. He managed to hold on to his job in the Forestry Department of the Ministry of State Property. Then he was transferred to Government Control, where he had an indulgent superior who turned his head aside when Mussorgsky showed up drunk. The piano score of *Khovantchina* was finished in 1874 (he never scored the opera, which was brought to completion by Rimsky-Korsakov), and from 1875 to 1877 Mussorgsky worked on, among other things, his opera *The Fair at Sorochintzi* and the cycle *Songs and Dances of Death*. He even pulled himself together to make a tour of Russia as piano accompanist for a singer. But his heavy drinking continued. In 1880 and 1881 he had fits of delirium tremens. Finally he had a stroke and died at the age of forty-two on March 16, 1881. At the unveiling of a monument to him in 1885, the other members of The Five lifted the four corners of the veil.

Mussorgsky's total output was small, and he lives today only by a handful of works. There is *Boris Godounov*, of course, with its epic sweep, real-life characters, and spirit of the Russian people. There are the four songs of the *Songs and Dances of Death,* one of the most powerful and terrifying cycles ever written. With its jarring harmonies, its mixture of recitative and melody, its poignancy, and its brooding atmosphere, it stands next to *Boris* as one of Mussorgsky's sublime achievements of "truth" in music. The specter of death throws a black shadow across every measure, and the *Lullaby* of the *Songs and Dances* is searing in its bleakness and pity—a pity that never descends to sentimentalism. There is the *Pictures at an Exhibition* for piano solo, a permanent concert-hall favorite (and also a favorite with conductors in the Ravel orchestration). There is a group of remarkable songs, including two cycles, *Sunless* and *The Nursery*. The two last operas, *Khovantchina* and *The Fair at Sorochintzi*, were completed by other composers. How much of Mussorgsky remains in them, and how much of Rimsky-Korsakov and Vissarion Shebalin respectively, is impossible to say. The Prelude to *Khovantchina,* a beautiful tone picture, occasionally appears on a symphony program, as does the early symphonic sketch *A Night on Bald Mountain*.

Mussorgsky did not live entirely unrecognized outside of Russia. Liszt was interested in his music, and in 1874 *Boris Godounov* created much talk in professional French circles when Saint-Saëns returned from Russia with the score. There were those then, as there are today, who came to the conclusion that Mussorgsky was an inspired dilettante. What many academically trained musicians failed to see was that while Mussorgsky's music could be awkward and even full of errors in relation to the rules, it was often *purposely* rough and awkward. The rules often were deliberately broken. Naturally, Mussorgsky's music would be of greatest interest to those composers who themselves broke the rules. Debussy, who knew the score of *Boris* and heard other music by Mussorgsky when he was Nadejda von Meck's pianist in Russia, was fascinated. Above all Western musicians, Debussy responded to Mussorgsky's modalism, irregular scales and rhythms, and asymmetrical patterns. Yet even Debussy implied that Mussorgsky was a kind of untutored savage: "He is unique and will remain so because his art is spontaneous and free from arid formula. Never has a more refined sensibility been conveyed by such simple means; it is like the art of an inquiring savage discovering music step by step through his emotions." Today it is recognized that Mussorgsky was by far the most original and modern of nineteenth-century Russian composers. He was of the future, and he probably knew it. "The artist believes in the future because he lives in the future," he wrote in his dedication of *Boris Godounov*.

As for Borodin and Rimsky-Korsakov, their destinies took different paths. Borodin never left science, and he composed even less than Mussorgsky. After his return from Heidelberg in 1862—he came back to St. Petersburg with a wife, a Russian pianist he had met in Germany—he was appointed to the faculty of chemistry in the Academy of Medicine. He moved into an apartment on the grounds. There he lived for the rest of his life with his wife, innumerable cats, and equally innumerable relatives, in a state of happy and maniacal disorder. He was an easy-going, kind-hearted man. Professor Borodin, one of the most respected chemists in Europe, was loved by his pupils. How he found time to compose *anything* remains a mystery. Students, friends, scientists, musicians, and in-laws were constantly wandering through the rooms of the Borodin apartment. The samovar was at a perpetual boil. Borodin never had any privacy. Often he found a relative or visitor in his own bed, and with a resigned shrug he would camp on the sofa for the night. He described himself as a Sunday composer. "Science is my work and music is my fun." A levelheaded man, he was not as disturbed as the others when The Five started to break up. "So far as I see, this is nothing but a natural situation. As long as we were in the position of eggs under a setting hen (thinking of Balakirev as the latter) we were all more or less alike. As soon as the fledgelings broke out of their shells, they grew feathers. Each of them had to grow different feathers; and when their wings grew, each flew to wherever his nature drew him." Borodin said that eventually everybody came to understand this but Balakirev.

Borodin's major work was the opera *Prince Igor,* which occupied him for some twenty years. But he never found the time to finish it. Rimsky-Korsakov and Alexander Glazunov had to reconstruct it from a mass of sketches and what they remembered when Borodin himself played and sang excerpts. There was not even an overture in notation, though Borodin had composed one, and Glazunov had to notate it from memory. The feat is not as difficult as it sounds. Glazunov had a remarkable ear and memory, watery as his own music is. *Prince Igor* is a beautiful work with the emphasis on folklore, and is more akin to the Rimsky-Korsakov operas than to *Boris Godounov.* Or is that because Rimsky edited *Prince Igor* as extensively as he had edited the Mussorgsky opera? There are, however, a handful of works that presumably are Borodin's own. One never really knows, for The Five were constantly tinkering with one another's scores, and Borodin was a very complaisant man. In any case, the Symphony No. 2 in B minor is a masterpiece. Borodin had a refined ear for orchestral sound and, working as closely with Rimsky-Korsakov as he did, knew the potentiality of each instrument in the orchestra as well as any composer in Europe. Rimsky would arrive at the Borodin house lugging three or four instruments, and the two men would spend a weekend experimenting with, and trying to play, the tuba, the English horn, the bassoon, or whatever instruments were at hand. Between the two of them, they worked their way through every instrument of the orchestra. In the B minor Symphony there is, besides the gorgeous, resilient, exotic-sounding melodies, a kind of bright orchestral sound of unusual personality. Rimsky-Korsakov is supposed to be one of the great masters of the orchestra, and he is, but his scores sound thick next to the wonderfully articulated sounds and mixtures of the Borodin B minor. There are those who, like Debussy and his friends at the conservatory, put that work at the top of all Russian symphonies, including the last three by Tchaikovsky.

Borodin's music achieved a sizable reputation outside of Russia. Often he would travel to scientific conferences, and at those times he would take the opportunity of meeting Europe's foremost musicians. He showed the manuscript of the B minor Symphony to Liszt, who was impressed enough to put it on a program. In Belgium the Countess de Mercy-Argenteau, a patroness who was greatly interested in Russian music, sponsored performances of Borodin's First Symphony. In Paris, his String Quartet in A major was played. Such success might have spurred other men, but Borodin continued to remain a Sunday composer, full of musical ideas and projects without the time to accomplish them. On February 2, 1887, he was at a party, had a heart attack, and died instantly.

Today he is remembered primarily by four works—*Prince Igor,* the

String Quartet No. 2 in D, the B minor Symphony, and a tone picture called *In the Steppes of Central Asia*. The opera, which has a static libretto, is a musical evocation of early Russia, with its heroes, boyars, and Asiatic tribes. The *Polovetsian Dances* occur in the second act, and at the turn of the century were considered an authentic representation of barbaric Russia. Time, and Stravinsky's *Sacre du Printemps*, have relegated the *Polovetsian Dances* to a form of light music, but the dances nevertheless remain effective, and the opera as a whole has some of the grandeur, if not the truth, of *Boris*. Of Borodin's two string quartets, No. 1 in A is long and rambling, but the D major is a jewel. Less nationalistic than much of Borodin's music, verging on the salon, it is a sweet, gentle, and attractive work, beautifully composed, and by far the single most popular piece of chamber music that has come out of Russia.

Nicolai Rimsky-Korsakov, born in the Novgorod district on March 18, 1844, became The Grand Old Man of Russian music. As a young man he had, while still a naval officer, worked under Balakirev's guidance and produced such interesting and individual works as the *Antar* Symphony, the symphonic poem *Sadko* (later to be the subject of one of his most famous operas), and the opera *The Maid of Pskov*. In the 1860's The Five would often gather at the house of Nicolai Purgold, a wealthy connoisseur. Of Purgold's ten children, two were talented musically. Alexandra was the singer and Nadejda the pianist. Those two girls were the first to see much of the new music produced by The Five, and they performed it at the many soirées held by the hospitable Purgold. Between Nadejda and Rimsky-Korsakov a romance sprang up, and they were married in 1873.

That was two years after he became associated with the St. Petersburg Conservatory. Rimsky-Korsakov had been invited to become Professor of Practical Composition and Instrumentation. He spent sleepless nights worrying about the invitation, as well he might. He already had a great reputation as a composer, but only he knew how little he knew. Balakirev's teaching had not included even the most elementary aspects of the art of music. As Rimsky-Korsakov wrote in his autobiography:

It was not merely that I couldn't at that time have harmonized a chorale properly, had never written a single contrapuntal exercise in my life, and had only the haziest understanding of strict fugue, but I didn't even know the names of the augmented and diminished intervals or of the chords, other than the tonic triad and the dominant and diminished sevenths. Though I could sing anything at sight and *distinguish* any conceivable chord, the terms "chord of the sixth" and "six-four chord" were unknown to me. In my compositions I strove after correct part writing and achieved it by instinct and by ear. My grasp of the musical forms (particularly of the rondo) was equally hazy. Although I scored my own compositions colorfully enough, I had no real knowledge of string technique or of the practical possibilities of horns, trumpets and trombones. As for conducting, I had never led an orchestra in my life.

This was the new professor He was allowed to remain in the navy, and he taught in uniform. What ensued was comedy on a grand scale. Rimsky started to study furiously, keeping just one step ahead of his classes. He went deep into counterpoint, harmony, and analysis. In a few years he became a fine teacher. But some of The Five, especially Mussorgsky, were furious. Rimsky-Korsakov had sold out; was considered a renegade who had joined the enemy, who was throwing over his Russian heritage to compose fugues and sonatas. "The Mighty Five have hatched into a horde of soulless traitors," snarled Mussorgsky.

And The Five did break up. But Rimsky-Korsakov, far from being a renegade, turned into the most national of all Russians except Mussorgsky himself. He composed a series of operas—*Snow Maiden* (1881), *Christmas Eve* (1895), *Sadko* (1896), *The Czar's Bride* (1898), *The Story of the Czar Saltan* (1898), *The Legend of the Invisible City of Kitezh* (1905), *The Golden Cockerel* (1907)—that were the essence of the Russian folk heritage. They are not as deep as *Boris Godounov*, they do not probe character, and their harmonies are very polite. But they open up a delightful new world, the world of the Russian East, the world of supernaturalism and the exotic, the world of Slavic pantheism and vanished races. Genuine poetry suffuses them, and they are scored with brilliance and resource. Rimsky was a master of orchestral color, and also of picture painting in music. Nobody has described his orchestral sound better than Serge Rachmaninoff, himself no mean orchestrator:

> In Rimsky-Korsakov's scores there is never the slightest doubt about the "meteorological picture" the music is meant to convey. When there is a snowstorm the flakes seem to dance and drift from the woodwinds and the sound holes of the violins; when the sun is high, all instruments shine with an almost fiery glare; when there is water, the waves ripple and dance audibly through the orchestra, and this effect is not achieved by the comparatively cheap means of a harp glissando. The sound is cool and glassy when he describes a calm winter night with a glittering starlit sky. He was a great master of orchestral sound-painting and one can still learn from him.

On the whole, the Rimsky-Korsakov operas are underrated works. A score with the devastating power of *Boris Godounov* can make an overwhelming impact sung in any language. But the more delicate Rimsky-Korsakov operas are so bound up with the Russian folk tradition that they wither in translation. Those who have seen *Sadko, Kitezh,* and other Rimsky operas in Russia can attest to a kind of vitality and charm that productions elsewhere are not able to muster.

In addition to the operas, Rimsky-Korsakov wrote much orchestral music. The *Capriccio Espagnol* was finished in 1887, *Schéhérazade* and the *Russian Easter* Overture in 1888. There was a one-movement, Lisztian, Piano Concerto (1883) based on Russian themes. There was a Symphony in E flat minor (1865) and also a Symphony in C (1873) that are no longer played. He also composed songs, piano pieces, choral works, and church music. When he was not composing, he was conducting, or traveling around the country as inspector of naval bands (although he had left the navy in 1873). He was assistant director of the court chapel (1883–1884), he continued to teach at the Conservatory, wrote a famous book on orchestration, fought off periodic bouts of Dostoievskian depression, made trips to France and Belgium as conductor and exponent of Russian music. From all accounts, he was not a very good conductor. Igor Stravinsky, who was his pupil from 1906–1908, offers a little picture:

> Rimsky-Korsakov was a tall man, like Berg or Aldous Huxley, and, like Huxley, too, he suffered from poor eyesight. He wore blue-tinted spectacles, sometimes keeping an extra pair on his forehead, a habit of his I have caught. When conducting an orchestra he would bend over the score and, hardly ever looking up, wave his baton in the direction of his knees. His difficulty in seeing the score was so great, and he was so absorbed in listening, that he gave almost no directions to the orchestra at all.

In the early 1880's there arose a new circle, this one gathered at the feet of Mitrofan Petrovich Belaiev. Belaiev (1836–1904) was the son of a wealthy timber merchant and a lover of chamber music. In 1885 he founded a publishing house, setting it up in Leipzig to secure international copyright, and in the same year he also sponsored the Russian Symphony Concerts in St. Petersburg. All of these activities were aimed at helping Russian composers. A new school was rising, and its members gathered in Belaiev's house, with Rimsky-Korsakov as adviser and old master. There were Anatol Liadov, Alexander Glazunov, Mikhail Ippolitov-Ivanov, Anton Arensky. All were pupils of Rimsky-Korsakov, as were, in his last days, Prokofiev and Stravinsky. The St. Petersburg Conservatory represented, and still does, the Russian national school, as opposed to the Moscow Conservatory, which stands for a more international, European style from Tchaikovsky through Sergei Taneiev and Sergei Rachmaninoff. In a way, the old Rimsky-Korsakov became the new Balakirev. When he died, on June 21, 1908, the great age of Russian music died with him—and a new one was to begin two years later, when Stravinsky's *Firebird* received its first performance.

❦ 4 ❧

Surcharged Emotionalism

PETER ILYICH TCHAIKOVSKY

The Mighty Five never knew exactly what to make of Peter Ilyich Tchaikovsky. He was a conservatory graduate and he composed symphonies more or less in the classic style with orthodox developments. That was enough to make one suspicious. On the other hand, he liberally quoted folk songs, and his music was undeniably Russian. That was good. So where did he stand? At first there was hostility between Tchaikovsky and The Five. Later Balakirev became interested in his music and introduced some of it to the Free School audiences. There was a truce. But Tchaikovsky never had a high opinion of Balakirev and his circle. Basically Tchaikovsky was a conservative and could not subscribe to the "truth" of Mussorgsky or to the loose organization of much of the music composed by the members of the circle.

It was not that Tchaikovsky himself was a complete master of form. But he was much more in the European tradition. And he had what many of The Five lacked—a sweet, inexhaustible, supersensuous fund of melody. It was this melody that was to make him famous, first in Russia, then internationally. It was a peculiarly Russian kind of melody, plangent, introspective, often modal-sounding, touched with neuroticism, as emotional as a scream from a window on a dark night. The music reflected the man. He was a nervous, hypochondriacal, unhappy man—unhappy at home, unhappy away from home, nervous in the presence of other people, terrified lest his homosexuality become open knowledge. He was largely successful at hiding his emotions, his fears and neuroses, from most of the persons with whom he came into contact. But to a few close friends and to his diary he confided everything. He could converse in an urbane way with people, and little did they know they repelled him. Thus he notes in his diary that he carried on "an unbelievably amiable and incredibly animated conversation. . . . But in my soul there was despair and a desire to flee from them to the ends of the world." When he arrived in New York in 1891 he went to his hotel. "I made myself at home. First of all, I wept rather long.' Then he bathed, dined, walked along Broadway and returned to his room, where he "took to whimpering again several times." In Paris he avoided, as much as possible, his colleagues. "Every new acquaintance, every fresh meeting with somebody unknown, has always been for me a source of suffering . . springing possibly from a shyness that has increased to a mania, possibly from a complete lack of any need for human society, possibly also from inability, without an effort, to say things about oneself that one doesn't think (which is unavoidable in social intercourse)—in short, I don't know what it is."

This surcharged emotionalism, implicit in almost every note he wrote, acted upon audiences in several ways. From the beginning, most listeners enjoyed the emotional bath in which they were immersed by the composer. Others, more inhibited, either rejected Tchaikovsky's message out of hand or despised themselves for responding to it. A composer is supposed to be more "manly." There is something embarrassing, even immoral, about such hysteria in music. For a long time Tchaikovsky, so loved by the public, was discounted by many connoisseurs and musicians as nothing but a weeping machine. In recent years there has been a new estimate, and musicians tend to find much more to admire in Tchaikovsky's music than they previously did. His orchestration is a subject of admiring comment—that dark-colored yet brilliant-sounding and perfectly calculated scoring. The structure of the last three symphonies is studied as a successful compromise between the demands of the classical symphony and the new forms imposed by the demands of a postromantic age. In any case, Tchaikovsky did as well without the approval of the learned musicians as he did with it. Of the late romantics, only Brahms has established himself so securely in the repertory. Tchaikovsky's last three symphonies, his three ballets (*Swan Lake, Sleeping Beauty, Nutcracker*), his Piano Concerto in B flat minor and Violin Concerto in D, his *Romeo and Juliet Overture* and two of his operas, *Eugene Onegin* and *The Queen of Spades*, are played everywhere. Almost as popular are such works as the *Manfred* Symphony (a program work based on the Byron drama and not listed among the six symphonies), *Francesca da Rimini*, the *Capriccio Italien*, the *Hamlet Overture-Fantasy*, and the Serenade for Strings. Each of his three string quartets and the Piano Trio in A minor has beautiful things in it. Recitalists still program his songs. And there are always the *Marche Slave* and the *1812* Overture . . .

As a creator Tchaikovsky developed slowly. Born in Kamsko-Votinsk of a well-to-do middle-class family on May 7, 1840, he was a precocious child, but the precocity showed itself in things other than music. At the age of six he could read French and German; at seven he was writing verses in French. He was very sensitive, and his governess called him "a porcelain child." Had his parents subjected him to intensive training he could have been a Wunderkind, for he was ultrasensitive to music and had a delicate ear. When he heard music—he was taking piano lessons at the age of seven —it stuck in his mind and kept resounding. "This music! This music! Take it away! It's here in my head and won't let me sleep!"

His family moved to St. Petersburg in 1850, and he went to school there. He had a mild interest in music and, though relatively untrained, was trying to compose when he was fourteen. In school he did not study music at all. After graduating from the School of Jurisprudence, in 1859, he entered the Ministry of Justice as a clerk first-class. Then in 1861 he went abroad, spending much more than he could afford. At this time there was little money in the family; his father had lost almost everything in a series of bad investments. "If ever I started on a colossal piece of folly," he wrote to his sister, "it was this journey.   You know, I have a weakness. As soon as I get any money, I squander it on pleasure. It's vulgar and stupid, I know, but it seems to be part of my nature." (Tchaikovsky never was able to hold on to money. He made a good deal during his life, but gave away much and spent the rest. He was once asked where he invested his money. Tchaikovsky laughed. "In the Kokorev Hotel when I stayed in Moscow." When he received an advance from New York for his trip to the United States in 1891, he sent out a note to friends and creditors: "I have just received good money. Come and get your share while it lasts.")

Not until he was twenty-one years old did he start to study music seriously. He worked with Nicolai Zaremba until the St. Petersburg Conservatory opened in 1862 Zaremba enrolled there, and Tchaikovsky followed him. Tchaikovsky joked about his studies, but secretly dreamed of being another Glinka, and in 1863 he resigned from the Ministry to devote his life to music. Anton Rubinstein, the director of the Conservatory, decided that Tchaikovsky had talent, and took a personal interest in him. Tchaikovsky went through the curriculum and even studied conducting. He was terrified when he stood in front of an orchestra, and he was terrified all his life, even when he was in constant demand as a guest conductor for his own music. He got the idea that his head was going to fall from his shoulders, and he actually would put his left hand under his chin to keep it attached. It is not surprising that he was not exactly a conductor who could inspire his players. But, aside from this, Tchaikovsky was one of the best Conservatory students, and in 1866 Anton Rubinstein recommended him to his brother Nicholas, who was looking for a harmony teacher for the Moscow Conservatory. The pay was small but Tchaikovsky had nowhere else to turn. He moved to Moscow and for six years lived with Nicholas, who swamped the wretched, homesick young man with kindness.

His life was quiet. He taught, composed, made friends. Within three years he had completed a Symphony in G minor (*Winter Daydreams*, 1866), some other orchestral music, and an opera, *The Voyevode* (1868). On a visit to St. Petersburg in 1868 he spent some time with the members of The Five. They liked his symphony, which he played to them from the manuscript. It had enough nationalism in it to interest them. As Rimsky-Korsakov wrote, "Our former opinion of him changed to a more favorable one, though his Conservatory education still placed a considerable barrier between him and us." Tchaikovsky meanwhile privately referred to The Five as "The Jacobin Club." Back in Moscow later that year, he had a flirtation with the Belgian soprano Désirée Artôt But she married a Spanish baritone, ending whatever hopes Tchaikovsky may have had for a more permanent relationship. They remained close friends, and Tchaikovsky always looked her up whenever he was in her vicinity on his travels.

Compositions steadily came forth. *Romeo and Juliet* was finished in 1869 and Tchaikovsky sent it to Balakirev, who rubbed his hands and proceeded to tear it to pieces. By 1875 Tchaikovsky had finished the Second Symphony (*Little Russian*) on Ukrainian themes, the symphonic poem *Fatum*, three operas, the Third Symphony (*Polish*), and the B flat minor Piano Concerto. He intended to dedicate the concerto to Nicholas Rubinstein, but that worthy criticized it in so devastating a manner that Tchaikovsky instead dedicated it to Hans von Bülow (whom he had never met), and Bülow gave the world premiere in Boston on October 25, 1875. John Dwight, Boston's leading critic, was predictably horrified. He could not understand "the extremely difficult, strange, wild, ultra-Russian concerto." He conceded that it was brilliant and exciting, but his review ended with a rhetorical question "Could we ever learn to love such music?" Dwight never could but others did, and Tchaikovsky's work began to be heard in Europe While there were pockets of opposition, especially from Hanslick in Vienna, Tchaikovsky's reputation steadily grew.

In 1877, there occurred two epochal events in Tchaikovsky's life. He married, and he entered into his curious relationship with Nadejda von Meck. His wife was a pretty girl named Antonina Ivanova Miliukova They had met at the Moscow Conservatory. She had a hero-worshiping crush on him, and presumably he married her thinking it would make him respectable He also felt sorry for the girl. Undoubtedly he must have thought they could arrive at some kind of working relationship. Things not only did not work out; the marriage was a positive disaster. Antonina turned out to be a stupid woman, and in addition she appears to have been a nymphomaniac —not the mate for a sensitive terrified homosexual. It took Tchaikovsky only a short time to realize he had made a colossal blunder "A few more days and I should have gone mad." As it was, he attempted suicide by immersing himself in a river, intending to catch pneumonia. Instead he caught only a monumental cold. His brother Modest, also a homosexual, rescued him and they fled to St. Petersburg, where Tchaikovsky promptly had a complete nervous breakdown. The marriage lasted nine weeks—that is, it broke up after nine weeks. He supported her, and she took up with a series of lovers. Finally in 1896 she was placed in an insane asylum where she died in 1917.

Nadejda von Meck, when she and Tchaikovsky first began to exchange letters, was a fabulously wealthy, music-loving widow of forty-six with eleven children. She loved Tchaikovsky's music and offered to subsidize him with the proviso that they were never to meet. Tchaikovsky accepted and for fourteen years received a generous allowance. They corresponded voluminously, and Tchaikovsky's letters to her provide a picture of a composer and his way of thinking and working unparalleled in the literature except for Mozart's letters. Why was she afraid of meeting him? Did she think she would be disillusioned? In one of the early letters in the correspondence, she writes: "There was a time when I was very anxious to make your acquaintance; but now, the more you fascinate me, the more I fear your acquaintanceship. I prefer to think of you from afar, to hear you speak in your music and share your feelings through it." Tchaikovsky was, of course, relieved. In his answer he wrote about misanthropy and his own problems: "There was a time when I was so possessed by this fear of mankind that I became almost insane." He said that he fully understood her position. "I'm not at all surprised that, in spite of your love for my music, you don't want to make my acquaintance. You are afraid you will fail to find in my personality all those qualities with which your idealizing imagination has endowed me. And in that you are quite right." They stuck to their pledge and never met, though they attended the same concerts and looked at each other out of the corner of their eyes. Once they came face to face. Both turned crimson with embarrassment. Tchaikovsky raised his hat, and she fluttered around and didn't know what to do. They fled from each other.

Psychiatrists can best discuss the relationship between the two. But from it came fourteen years of financial independence for Tchaikovsky. He was able to indulge himself and, as additional money from commissions and performances came in, to resign from the Conservatory in 1878 and buy himself a country home at Maidanovo. He was a rather striking figure—over average height, handsome, prematurely grey, with blue eyes and a neatly trimmed beard. He wore elegant clothes and his manners were exquisite. But his emotional problems did not cease with financial security. He suffered from incessant headaches, still wept easily, had constant doubts about himself and his music, and drank far too much. Liquor was one of his escapes. "It is said," he wrote in his diary, "that to abuse one's self with alcohol is harmful. I readily agree to that. But nevertheless I, a sick person, full of neuroses, absolutely cannot do without the alcoholic poison." He also was addicted to cards and had to have his nightly game of whist. Lacking that, he would lay out hands of solitaire.

In his diary and letters he wrote about his musical likes and dislikes. Wagner bored him, and he detested the music of Brahms. "It angers me that that presumptuous mediocrity is recognized as a *genius*. Indeed, in comparison with him, Raff is a giant, not to mention Rubinstein, who is still a big and vital personality." He had reservations about Beethoven: "I bow before the greatness of some of his works but I do not *love* Beethoven." The composer he adored above all others—and that was rare not only in the Russia of his time but also in the Europe of his time—was Mozart. He called Mozart "a musical Christ." The baroque period left him cold. "I play Bach gladly . . but I do not recognize in him (as some do) a great genius. Handel has for me an entirely fourth-rate significance and he is not even entertaining." Of two other great composers before Beethoven, "Gluck, despite the relative poverty of his creation, is attractive to me. I also like certain things of Haydn."

As a student of the music of Mozart and the classical composers, and as a creator who tried to clothe his music in appropriate forms, Tchaikovsky throughout his life struggled with architectural problems. Unlike The Five, he was greatly concerned with form. But his mind did not have the kind of logic and imagination that could weld various elements into an organic whole. In his early symphonies his developments are patchwork, full of uninventive padding in a desperate effort to keep things moving. Not until the Fourth Symphony did he develop a kind of form that would fit the rapturous, dancelike, essentially spontaneous and lyric nature of his music. Tchaikovsky was well aware of the problem, and he wrote about it to Nadejda in 1878:

What has been written with passion must now be looked upon critically, corrected, extended and, most important of all, condensed to fit the required needs of the form. One must sometimes go against the grain in this, be merciless, and destroy things that were written with love and inspiration. Although I cannot complain of poor inventive powers or imagination, I have always suffered from lack of skill in the management of form. Only persistent labor has at last permitted me to achieve a form that in some degree corresponds to the content. In the past I was careless. I did not realize the extreme importance of this critical examination of the preliminary sketch. For some reason the succeeding episodes were loosely held together and the seams were always showing. That was a serious defect, and it was years before I began to correct it. Yet my compositions will never be good examples of form because I can only correct what is wrong with my musical nature—I cannot change it intrinsically.

Analysts who use as a criterion the German symphonic form as laid down by Mozart and Beethoven have been citing "defects" in the Tchaikovsky symphonies ever since they were written. But strict application of formalistic criteria misses the point. Tchaikovsky's symphonies, even the first three, have such personality and such melodic appeal that they continue to sound eternally fresh. Despite the frequent naïveté of such works as the *Polish* and *Little Russian* symphonies, they are full of color, originality, and a very personal kind of speech. The last three Tchaikovsky symphonies break all of the rules as laid down by the textbooks, but here Tchaikovsky achieved a kind of synthesis that makes them as convincing structurally as any Brahms symphony—waltzes, march movements, and free forms notwithstanding. For they have a consistent emotional line and a consistency of workmanship, and the ideas progress surely and naturally. In his struggles with symphonic form, Tchaikovsky wrote three other symphonies and dodged the problem by calling them "suites." (The Suite No. 4, *Mozartiana*, is merely an orchestration of some piano pieces by Mozart.) The first three suites are generally neglected, but they have some gorgeous music in them, and they are permeated with the dance spirit—or, more specifically, the ballet spirit.

Ballet is implicit in a very large number of Tchaikovsky scores, even though he composed only three ballets proper. Much ballet music up to Tchaikovsky had been um-pah-pah music. A breakaway was made by Léo Delibes, who showed what a really skillful composer could do. Tchaikovsky admired Delibes's music a great deal, and in sections of *Swan Lake* the debt is apparent. Tchaikovsky's three ballets are close to opera, except that the "voice" parts are scored for dancers instead of singers. Each score has the equivalent of arias, duets, and ensembles. Tchaikovsky worked very closely with Marius Petipa, the choreographer for his ballets. During the creation of *Sleeping Beauty*, Petipa would write such instructions as: "Suddenly Aurora notices the old woman who beats on her knitting needles two-four measure. Gradually she changes to a very melodious waltz in three-four but then, suddenly, a rest. Aurora pricks her finger. Screams pain. Blood streams. Give eight measures in four-four, wide." For *Nutcracker* in 1891, Petipa's instructions were even more detailed. Tchaikovsky finished the score and looked at it with his usual pessimism. "No," he wrote, "the old man"—meaning himself—"is breaking up. Not only does his hair drop out or turn as white as snow; not only does he lose his teeth, which refuse their service; not only do his eyes weaken and tire easily; not only do his feet walk badly or drag themselves along; but he loses bit by bit the capacity to do anything at all. The ballet is infinitely worse than *Sleeping Beauty*—so much is certain."

Classic ballet is an idealized form of dance in which the ballerina, *en pointe*, tries to escape from the earth and its gravitational pull. The ballerina herself is idealized; she floats in the air; she is worshiped by the cavalier; she is young, radiant, and beautiful. There is no such thing as an old, ugly, or stout ballerina. Tchaikovsky identified himself with the idealistic qualities of ballet. There is a certain kind of homosexual who derides women; there is another, more feminine type, who loves women (except physically) and thinks like a woman. Tchaikovsky was one of the latter, and that helps explain the feeling of identification conveyed by the long-arched, proud, and sensuous melodies given to the ballerina—the *Rose Adagio* of *Sleeping Beauty* or the great *pas de deux* in *Nutcracker*. Tchaikovsky and the ballerina were one. The world of the ballet—the romantic, fairy-tale world of the ballet and its plush and gold surroundings, its beautiful women, its glamour, its homosexual ambience, its feeling of pomp and wealth, its intrigues, its association with royalty, its backstage gossip, its supple rhythms—this world comes up again and again in Tchaikovsky's music.

A good part of Tchaikovsky's career was spent in writing operas. When he could find a libretto that had a heroine with which he could identify, the result was excruciatingly beautiful music. In *Eugene Onegin* he found such a woman, and he composed his operatic masterpiece. Some consider the *Queen of Spades* a greater work, and it does have more intensity, a greater sweep, a mounting feeling of horror and inevitability. But the melodic materials are inferior to those found in the eternally lyric and elegiac *Onegin*, and the reason lies in the fact that Tchaikovsky was so attracted to Tatiana. *Eugene Onegin* is a quiet opera with a true-life ending—an ending that would have shocked every theatrical instinct of Verdi or the verismists. For the lover, who previously has spurned Tatiana, is simply sent away, and the curtain falls to quiet memories and nostalgia rather than a chorus shrieking vengeance or everybody in sight slaughtered.

Tchaikovsky's attitude toward opera was something like that of a Victorian's attitude toward sex. He loved it but at the same time had guilt feelings, thinking there was something sinful about it. Reflections about opera occupy a good deal of space in his letters. He could call opera "a false type of art" and in the same breath admit that there was in the form "something irrepressible that attracts all composers." Never a revolutionary, Tchaikovsky was content to accept the operatic conventions as they were. "The style of theater music must correspond to the style of scene painting: simple, clear, colorful." But unlike many composers of the time, Tchaikovsky was primarily interested in character rather than vocal effect or, indeed, any kind of effect. What he wanted was a libretto featuring strong human emotions, around which he could supply illustrative music. "I cannot write music with love and enthusiasm for any subject, however effective, if the characters do not compel my lively sympathy. If I do not love them, *pity* them, as living people love and *pity* . . ." Love and pity pervade *Onegin*, which has scarcely an inexpressive note in it, which has a piercing sadness and sweetness, and which is much more a singing opera than the *Queen of Spades*.

It may be this quiet sadness, this lack of sharp contour, that has held back the full success of *Onegin*. Tchaikovsky could write effectively for the voice, but he almost never supplied his singers with bravura work. Song is used to express character and mood, not to exploit the vocal cords. Verdi knew how to drive an audience to a frenzy, but Tchaikovsky constantly understates. Verdi and Wagner were musically tough; Tchaikovsky in his operas was uniformly gentle and yielding. Naturally Tchaikovsky's operas make less of an impression. But Tchaikovsky did not have to defer to anybody in his fund of melody and his knowledge of the orchestra; and, in its quiet way, *Eugene Onegin* can have an extraordinary impact. It has a continuous melodic wash, and idea follows idea: the exquisite opening duet (which grows into a quartet); the rapturous duet of Lensky and Olga followed by what surely is one of the great love arias in all opera, Lensky's *"Ya lyublu vas, Olga"*—"I love you, Olga." Tatiana's letter scene is the most familiar part of the opera (aside from the orchestral dances), and as one studies it there comes greater and greater respect for Tchaikovsky's powers as a craftsman. How surely he builds to the climax—Tatiana's outburst "Now I am alone!" with the orchestra welling up to one of those unforgettable, Tchaikovskian inspirations. Then there are the quarrel sequences, especially the bleak duel scene, with Lensky's great aria to his youth. At the end of the opera there is the muted but desperate confrontation between Tatiana and Onegin. All this is in a style that owed little to any composer. Tchaikovsky, who had analyzed the Wagner operas, did use a few leitmotifs, but in an elementary way. There is nothing the least Wagnerian about *Eugene Onegin*, and there certainly is nothing Verdian. The opera, which is based on Pushkin's poem, is in addition an altogether realistic picture of a certain stratum of Russian society. *Eugene Onegin* is to opera what *The Cherry Orchard* is to the legitimate stage.

As Tchaikovsky's music became well known throughout Europe, he traveled more and more. A blow came in 1890, when his annuity from Nadejda von Meck ceased. She thought she was going bankrupt, which did not happen to be the case. But she abruptly terminated the arrangement and refused to answer any of Tchaikovsky's letters. He was shattered. It was not the money; it was the fact that he felt soiled—the plaything of a capricious woman who could so bluntly sever so many years of emotional intimacy. He remained bitter for the rest of his life. "All my conceptions of mankind, my faith in the best of it, have been overturned." Later his brother, Modest, wrote: "Neither the triumph of the *Queen of Spades* nor the profound sorrow caused by the death of his beloved sister in April, 1891, nor even his American triumph served to soften the blow she had inflicted." What Tchaikovsky did not know was that Nadejda was going through a period of mental instability. Her relations with everybody had changed. Some writers hint that she severed relations with Tchaikovsky because she had learned of his sexual perversion. There is nothing to support such an assertion.

Tchaikovsky fled to the West. In 1891 he was invited to New York to share in the opening-week dedication of the Music Hall (renamed Carnegie Hall a few years later). The fee, $2,500 for four concerts, was handsome enough, and Tchaikovsky arrived toward the end of April. He was homesick, but the natives fascinated him. He was especially struck by the frankness and openhandedness of the people:

Amazing people, these Americans! Compared with Paris, where at every approach, in every stranger's kindness, one feels an attempt at exploitation, the frankness, sincerity and generosity of this city, its hospitality without hidden motives and its eagerness to oblige and win approval, are simply astonishing and, at the same time, touching. This, and indeed American customs, American manners and manners generally, are very attractive to me—but I enjoy all this like a person sitting at a table set with marvels of gastronomy, devoid of appetite. Only the prospect of returning to Russia can awaken an appetite within me.

He admired the skyscrapers, though he could not see how anybody could live on such a dizzy height as the thirteenth floor of a building. He described a dinner given for him by Morris Reno, the president of Music Hall. What struck him was that at the service of each lady was his portrait in a graceful frame; and, in the middle of the dinner, which lasted from 7:30 until 11, "an ice was served in some kind of small boxes to which were attached small slates, with pencils and sponges, on which excerpts from my works were finely written in pencil. Then I had to write my autograph on these slates." He visited Niagara Falls and Washington, conducted concerts in Philadelphia and Baltimore in addition to his four Music Hall appearances, and hastened back to Russia.

His last great work was the Symphony No. 6 in B minor, the *Pathétique*. He was going to make a mystery of it. "This time a program-symphony, but with a program that shall remain an enigma for everybody. Let them puzzle their heads over it. The work will be called simply *Program* Symphony (No. 6). The program is subjective through and through, and during my journey I often wept bitterly while composing it in my head." (At least one person thought he knew the secret program of the Sixth Symphony. Havelock Ellis called the work a "homosexual tragedy.") Tchaikovsky was happy at the speed and authority with which the symphony progressed. "You can't think of what a delight it is to feel that my time is not yet over." He claimed that he had "put his soul" into the work. It had its premiere in St. Petersburg on

October 28, 1893. After the premiere, at which the new work was received rather icily, Tchaikovsky gave up the idea of calling the score the *Program Symphony*. Modest Tchaikovsky suggested *Tragique* and then *Pathétique*, and Tchaikovsky decided on the latter. The next day he changed his mind again, but it was too late. "*Pathétique*" held. It is the greatest of his symphonies, and its last movement, which starts with a cry and ends with a moan, is the most unusual and pessimistic he ever wrote. Less than a week later he was dead. He had drunk a glass of unboiled water and contracted cholera. After a few days of suffering he died, on November 6, 1893.

Whether or not he is the greatest of all Russian composers, he has proved to be by far the most popular. No label fits him. He passed from nationalistic music to music of a more cosmopolitan kind, but nevertheless all of his music could have been written only by a Russian. Many music histories give the idea that Tchaikovsky was not a nationalistic composer. That is really a half-truth. As Stravinsky has written, "Tchaikovsky's music, which does not appear specifically Russian to everybody, is often more profoundly Russian than music which has long since been awarded the facile label of Muscovite picturesqueness. This music is quite as Russian as Pushkin's verse or Glinka's song. While not specifically cultivating in his art 'the soul of the Russian peasant,' Tchaikovsky drew *unconsciously* from the true, popular sources of our race." Tchaikovsky was strongly conscious of his folk heritage, and was constantly using it. In a letter to Nadejda in 1878 he expressed his attitude:

> As regards the Russian element in my works, I may tell you that not infrequently I begin a composition with the intention of introducing some folk melodies into it. Sometimes it comes of its own accord (as in the finale of our symphony [No. 4]). As to this national element in my work, its affinity with the folk songs in some of my melodies and harmonies comes from my having spent my childhood in the country and, from my earliest years, having been impregnated with the characteristic beauty of our Russian folk music. I am passionately fond of the national element in all its varied expressions. In a word, I am Russian in the fullest sense of the word.

Later in life he was not so consciously nationalistic. From the beginning, of course, his music was slanted more to the West than to the music of The Five. But it would be a mistake to eliminate Tchaikovsky entirely from the School of Russian nationalistic composers, different as was his approach from that of Mussorgsky and Rimsky-Korsakov. Where Rimsky-Korsakov spread out his arms to embrace Russian antiquity and folklore, where Mussorgsky spread out his arms to embrace the entire Russian people, Tchaikovsky spread out his arms to embrace—himself.

ꙮ 5 ꙮ

From Bohemia to Spain

EUROPEAN NATIONALISTS

After the Russians it was the Kingdom of Bohemia that, in Bedřich Smetana and Antonin Dvořák, turned out the most significant nationalistic composers in Europe. But unlike Russia, Bohemia (now part of Czechoslovakia) had a distinguished musical tradition. It had produced, at the turn of the nineteenth century, some internationally known composers and performers; and in 1811 it had opened one of the first musical conservatories in northern Europe. It was also the country that encouraged Mozart when he most needed encouragement.

Many of the early Czech composers, it is true, had left Bohemia to make their fortunes elsewhere. Austria dominated the Kingdom of Bohemia until concessions were made midway in the nineteenth century, and it was natural that many Bohemian musicians should settle in Vienna. Others went to Germany. Jiři Benda (1722–1795), who won praise from Mozart, was an émigré. So was Jan Ladislav Dussek (1761–1812), a fascinating composer, one of the most important pianists of his day and one of the first touring virtuosos, as much at home in St. Petersburg as he was in London. He lived a glamorous and even reckless life. In his youth he was extremely handsome (he was known as *le beau Dussek*) and his amours were the talk of Europe. Later in life he grew monstrously fat. It was Dussek (or Dusik, as his name sometimes is spelled) who contributed at least one immortal idea to the history of piano playing. He was the first to place his instrument sideways on the stage so that the public could admire his profile. As a composer, especially of piano music, he was prophetic. His ideas about piano technique were in advance of anybody at the time. More important was his preromanticism, and it is a romanticism that at times is not only "pre." His music, as in the Concerto for Two Pianos in B flat, can sound in part as though it had been composed by Schumann or even Brahms. *Grove's Dictionary* gives several startling examples of Dussek's advanced harmonies. Among other

336

Bohemian composers, Vaclav Tomášek (1774–1850) and Jan Voríšek (1791–1825) are mentioned in any Schubert biography as composers who strongly influenced the Viennese master's piano music.

But none of those composers were nationalists. Bedřich Smetana was the first to go to Bohemian folk song and use it as the basis for art music. Born on March 2, 1824, Smetana started out as a formidable prodigy. At the age of five he was a good enough violinist to take part in a Haydn quartet, and at six he played in public as a pianist. At eight he was composing. "I wanted to become a Mozart in composition and a Liszt in technique," he later said. But while he was a brilliant pianist, he did not go to the conservatory and was musically unlettered. As he wrote to Liszt, in 1848, "When I was 17 years old I did not know C sharp from D flat. The theory of harmony was a closed book to me. Though ignorant of this, yet I wrote music." His early music, mostly for piano, is a watery distillation of Liszt. Smetana was in Prague when the abortive revolution of 1848 was quashed. As he had sided with the patriots, he was under suspicion for many years. He could find no advancement at home and was glad to migrate to Sweden, where he was active from 1856 to 1861 as a teacher and as conductor of the Göteborg orchestra. In addition to conducting, he composed a great deal of piano music and three symphonic poems.

Smetana returned to Prague in 1862. There was a feeling of resurgence in the air. Austria's hold was weakening. The Provisional Theater was opened that year—it had been built specifically as a Bohemian home for the Bohemians—and Smetana conceived the idea of composing a national opera as a patriotic instrument. He had heard the Glinka operas, with their librettos on Russian subjects and their use of Russian-derived melodies, and they strongly impressed him. Smetana determined to write an equivalent kind of music for his own country. For the Provisional Theater in 1863 he composed his first opera, *The Brandenburgers in Bohemia*. This was followed three years later by *Prodaná nevèsta—The Bartered Bride*.

The Bartered Bride is a flawless work of comic art—spirited, jolly, sparkling. In it Smetana fell back upon the reservoir of Bohemian polkas and other dance music, though he did not quote directly. He invented all of the melodies. The opera is so spiced with the very spirit of the country that many find this hard to believe, but Smetana was proud of his ability to avoid direct quotation, and there is none of it in *The Bartered Bride*. Ralph Vaughan Williams, the British composer, tried to analyze Smetana's method of work and came to the conclusion that "Smetana's debt to his own national music was of the best kind, unconscious. He did not, indeed, 'borrow', he carried on an age-long tradition, not of set purpose, but because he could no more avoid speaking his own musical language than he could help breathing his native air." But strongly national though *The Bartered Bride* is, it is much more Westernized than the operas by Mussorgsky and Rimsky-Korsakov that were to come out of Russia. Prague, after all, was in the Western orbit. The exoticisms of the Bohemian musical language, however, were not in the Western musical consciousness until Smetana appeared. His language is, on the whole, a happy language. When Bohemian composers express melancholy, it is in a delicately elegiac way, without the crushing world-weariness and pessimism of the Russians. More often, Bohemian music expresses joy, happiness, dancing, festivals.

Smetana completed eight operas, of which *The Bartered Bride* is the only one in the international repertory. Most of his others are still performed regularly in Prague—*Dalibor, Libuše, Hubička* (*The Kiss*), *Dve vdovy* (*The Two Widows*) among them. In Czechoslovakia today Smetana is a national hero, much more so than Dvořák. For Smetana, more than any one man, made Czech music what it is, and not only by composing it. As pianist, conductor, teacher, and propagandist, he inspired his people and left a heritage of which they could be proud. Among his compositions still popular internationally are *Vlatava* (*The Moldau*) from the cycle of six symphonic poems, *Ma Vlast* (*My Country*), and his ever-fresh, autobiographical E minor String Quartet (*From My Life*). Occasionally his piano music is heard. Some of it is bombastic virtuoso rhetoric derived from Liszt and highly dated. The best piano pieces are the *Czech Dances,* inventive and charming sketches, often of considerable difficulty. There is also a Piano Trio in G minor that is of unusual loveliness.

In 1874, toward the end of his life, Smetana, like Beethoven, went deaf; and, like Schumann, mad. He wrote bravely but pathetically about his aural affliction to a friend in 1875: "The ear is quite healthy externally. But the inner apparatus—that admirable keyboard of our inner organ—is damaged, out of tune. The hammers have got stuck, and no tuner has so far succeeded in repairing the damage." He lost his memory and his speech, and was put in an asylum, where he died on May 12, 1884.

Smetana was the one who founded Czech music, but Antonin Dvořák, born on September 8, 1841, was the one who popularized it. His music has been played all over the world ever since Simrock published the *Moravian Duets* in the late 1870's. Since then Dvořák has not slipped from the repertory or showed any signs of doing so. And yet many music lovers accept him on sufferance. Only too often he is regarded as a minor nationalist, one of the better second-rank composers. It was not so in his own day, when he was the idol of Prague, when all Europe waited anxiously for his next work, when Hans von Bülow called him "next to Brahms the most Godgifted composer of the present day." (Bülow also described him as "a genius who looks like a tinker.") Brahms was not too proud to read proofs for Dvořák, whose fame was such that he was invited to New York in 1892 as

338

head of the National Conservatory of Music.

He wrote prolifically in all forms, and his was a unique voice. Those who call him a rustic second-rate severely underestimate him, possibly misled by the innocence and transparency of his music. Of course he was a rustic, a country boy from Bohemia who was apprenticed to a butcher. He was born of peasant stock and his music has a strong peasant strain. That is at once its strength and its weakness. Dvořák was far from the most subtle or intellectual composer of his day, nor was he in any sense a revolutionary. He respected classic forms, he thought in primary emotional colors, and life was a very wonderful, uncomplicated thing to him. He remained throughout his entire creative span the happiest and least neurotic of the late romantics. "God, love, motherland" was his motto. Brahms had his moments of black gloom; Tchaikovsky's neuroses were monumental; Mahler, whose neuroses made Tchaikovsky's neuroses look healthy, beat his chest and rent his hair (looking meanwhile at posterity out of the corner of his eye); Bruckner sat trembling, waiting for Revelation, a mystic and a natural (in the Elizabethan sense of the word); Wagner was a twisted egoist; Liszt was a complicated, paradoxical, Jesuitical poseur of genius. Only Dvořák pursued his simple, uncomplicated way. With Handel and Haydn, he is the healthiest of all composers.

Simplicity and emotional health, of course, are no guarantee of great music. They must be backed by something. In Dvořák's case they were backed by an inexhaustible melodic wealth and a feeling for modulation that are very close to Schubert. But Dvořák differs from Schubert in that nearly all of his best melodies are nationalistic. He was at his best when Bohemia took over; when, un-selfconsciously, he wrote music that expressed his native land and his love for it. He, like Smetana, seldom used actual folk themes, but his nationalism runs just as deep as Smetana's, and perhaps deeper. An absolute composer who happened to be a nationalist, he did not produce copies but created originals.

It is this un-selfconscious nationalism—broadly melodic, original, exotic, full of unexpected twists, enchanting in its harmony—that gives Dvořák's music its great charm and beauty. His nonnationalistic music, what there is of it, is relatively unimportant. That goes even for his Seventh Symphony in D minor (Op. 70). Many critics, especially the British ones (Dvořák and the British had a long association; the British were looking for somebody after Mendelssohn to admire, and they came up with Dvořák), seem to think that because the Seventh Symphony is Brahmsian and the most classically constructed of his works, it has to be the best. The academic mind is always with us. As a matter of fact, the Seventh Symphony up to the third movement is nothing but a façade, despite some lovely moments. Not until the third movement does Dvořák forget about Brahms and symphonic form,

339

and then he composes the most delightful individual movement of any of his symphonies. Here the classic formalities are off, and Dvořák breathes once more, singing forth one of those Bohemian-sounding melodies to which countermelodies cling in the most natural and unaffected polyphony. The D minor Symphony on the whole is nowhere near as good as the Eighth Symphony in G major, or even the early No. 3 in E flat major.

A musician and nothing but a musician, Dvořák was not widely read and, indeed, barely more than literate. In later life he would sporadically try to "improve" himself by reading a primer of some sort, but those efforts never went very far. The only passion he had outside of music was trains. The locomotive engine was to him one of the highest achievements of the human mind, and he often expressed the wish that he had invented it. He used to pay daily visits to the Franz-Josef Station in Prague, had all the timetables memorized, and was never so happy as when he could make friends with a locomotive engineer. He would send his pupils to the station to find out what engine was going on what train, or, when a pupil returned from a trip, would want to know what kind of train he had traveled on, and the name and model number of the locomotive. (Freudians have some things to say about the symbolism of the locomotive and its pistons.) Dvořák's pupils loved him, trains or no, though he could have a temper. They loved his sweetness, his gentleness, his dedication. When he launched on a subject he was oblivious to the world around him. One of his pupils has written about the time he, Dvořák, and several pupils were walking along the street and it started to pour. Dvořák, talking about his experiences in America, did not notice the rain. Everybody got soaked to the skin. Dvořák suddenly stopped, noticed water running from his hat, and said, "Now, children, run along home at once. I think it has started to rain."

Dvořák's talent was apparent from the beginning, and he started taking serious lessons at the age of twelve. His father was an innkeeper and kept a butcher shop, and for a while Dvořák worked in the family shop, but an uncle financed the boy's music studies and when he was sixteen he was sent to Prague. After graduating from the Prague Organ School in 1859 he took pupils and played the viola in various orchestras. As a player at the Provisionial Theater from 1862 to 1871 he participated in the first performances of several Smetana operas. He developed an enthusiasm for Wagner, he composed prolifically, and his music began to be played. His first public success came in 1873 with a strongly nationalistic choral work, *Hymnus*. In 1875 he won the Austrian State Prize for a symphony and came to the attention of two of the jurors, Brahms and Hanslick. Brahms wrote a letter to his publisher, Simrock: "On the recent occasion of allocating a state grant . . . I took much pleasure in the works of Dvořák of Prague. I have recommended him to send you his *Moravian Duets*. If you play them through, you will enjoy them as much as I have done. . . . Decidedly he is a very talented man. Besides, he is poor. Please take this into consideration." Simrock published the duets and had a hit on his hands. The infectious music swept Europe, as did the *Slavonic Dances* for piano duet that shortly followed.

Dvořák was launched. The German critic Louis Ehlert in 1878 wrote an enthusiastic review that was widely quoted: "Here at last is a hundred per cent talent; and, what is new, a completely natural talent." Ehlert went on to rave about the *Slavonic Dances*. Brahms was happy, and Dvořák was ecstatic about his new friend. Brahms could be prickly, but never was there the least hint of tension between the two. Dvořák to Simrock: "Brahms seems to be pleased by his connection with me; and as an artist and a man I am so overcome by his kindness that I cannot help but love him. What a warm heart and great spirit there is in that man! You know how detached he is from even his closest friends, at least where his compositions are concerned, and yet he has not been like that to me." When Brahms corrected proofs for Dvořák while he was away in the United States, Dvořák was overwhelmed: "In the whole world I do not think I could find another musician who would do the same." Dvořák may have been right; proofreading is a nasty, unrewarding job. As for Brahms, he felt very close to Dvořák. There was something in the younger man's personality that attracted him, aside from Dvořák's hero-worship. Brahms once wrote to a friend inviting Dvořák along: "We will eat from the same plate and drink from the same glass." It makes a pretty picture.

A steady series of works came from Dvořák: the *Slavonic Rhapsodies,* symphonies, choral music, considerable chamber music, operas, some piano music (the weakest part of his work), concertos. European audiences became familiar through Dvořák with Bohemian dance forms: the polka, the furiant (which Dvořák often used as a third movement instead of a scherzo), and the dumka, a slow and melancholy folk song. There was a great deal of talk in Europe about nationalism, and when Dvořák came to the United States the American newspapers picked up the subject.

He came to New York at the invitation of Mrs. Jeannette Thurber, the wife of a wealthy grocer. Mrs. Thurber had been instrumental in founding the National Conservatory of Music, and she wanted the famous Dvořák to head the institution. She was prepared to pay handsomely for his services. The terms of the contract specified an annual salary of $15,000, the equivalent of 30,000 gulden. (In Prague, his yearly salary had been 1,200 gulden.) For this, Dvořák was to teach three hours a day, prepare four students' concerts, conduct six concerts of his own music, and be granted a four-month vacation.

Dvořák arrived in New York in September, 1892. The reporters were on hand, and one of them left the following description:

341

He is not an awesome personality at all. He is much taller than his pictures would imply, and possesses not a tithe of the bulldog ferocity to be encountered in some of them. A man about 5 ft. 10 or 11 inches, of great natural dignity, a man of character, Dvořák impresses me as an original, natural and—as Rossini would say, to be natural is greater than to be original. . . . He is not beautiful in the forms of face, but the lines of his brow are so finely modeled, and there is so much emotional life in the fiery eyes and lined face, that when he lightens up in conversation, his face is not easily forgotten.

Mrs. Thurber helped spread the talk about nationalism. She was greatly interested in fostering a national American school of composition, and one of the reasons she had decided upon Dvořák as the head of the National Conservatory was the fact that he represented nationalism in his own music. She could point him out as an illustration of what American composers could aspire to. In the 1890's serious music in the United States was dominated by the German school, and there was very little that could be classified as "American" aside from some piano pieces by Louis Moreau Gottschalk. (There was a large amount of nationalistic popular music, but the serious composers paid no attention to it. The one breakaway came from Charles Ives, but he worked in a vacuum and his music was unknown.)

Dvořák, as Mrs. Thurber hoped, had strong things to say about the lack of an American nationalistic movement, and he pointed out what in his opinion could be done. "In the Negro songs I have found a secure basis for a new national music school. . . . America can have her own music, a fine music growing up from her own soil and having its own special character— the natural voice of a free and great nation," he told a New York *Herald* reporter. Stimulated by some of the native music he heard, Dvořák practiced what he preached. In his three years in the United States he produced several works that are known as "American," including the F major String Quartet, the E flat String Quintet, and the Symphony No. 9 in E minor, subtitled "From the New World." Most of the *New World* Symphony was composed in the five-room apartment that Dvořák and his family occupied at 327 East 17th Street. The scoring was completed in Spillville, Iowa, where Dvořák spent his summers. Spillville was a Czech settlement.

The *New World* Symphony started a controversy that was not clarified by Dvořák's own contradictory remarks about the score. At first he said that American music had played a part in his symphony: "It is the spirit of the Negro and Indian melodies which I have endeavored to reproduce in my new symphony. I have not used a single one of those melodies. I simply wrote characteristic themes incorporating in them the quality of Indian music." The first movement of the New World did use a Negro spiritual, "Swing Low, Sweet Chariot," and Dvořák also made use of the spiritual

"Goin Home." Everybody took it for granted that the work was not only an evocation of the American spirit, but that it was full of actual folk tunes or spirituals that Dvořák had encountered. There were those who saw the story of Hiawatha in the *New World*, and one of Dvořák's American pupils, Harry Rowe Shelley, said that he had it from the composer's own lips that a certain passage in the symphony represented the Indian girl's sobbing as she bade Hiawatha farewell. Soon Dvořák became rather annoyed with the fuss that the *New World* Symphony had created, and he flatly denied that there was anything specifically American in it. He described as "nonsense" the claim that the *New World* Symphony was the beginning of an American school, and decided that the music he had composed in America was "genuine Bohemian music," completely contradicting his initial exuberant remarks about Negro and Indian influences. His second thoughts were correct. There are traces of American thematic material and rhythms in the F major Quartet and the *New World* Symphony, but the music nevertheless is as American as St. Wenceslas. Dvořák could not have composed American national music had he tried. But despite his disclaimer, for years there was a controversy in the American press as to whether or not the *New World* was "American."

Among the works Dvořák composed in his last period, many of them written in America, were the dark-colored *Biblical Songs* (so different from his light-hearted *Gypsy Songs* of 1880), the radiant Cello Concerto in B minor, and the *Humoresques* for piano. The latter is worth mention if only for the G flat *Humoresque*, the one whose catchy tune was promptly whistled by everybody and arranged for every instrument and combination of instruments. Dvořák's last two string quartets, in A flat and G major, are his broadest and most serious pieces of chamber music, and possibly his greatest. These too he composed in the United States. On his return to Prague, he taught at the Conservatory and was appointed director in 1901. When he died, on May 1, 1904, it was an occasion for national mourning.

Although a great deal of Dvořák's music remains in the repertory, a great deal more remains to be investigated. The last three of the nine symphonies are frequently played, but No. 6 in D major is less familiar, and No. 5 in F is a total stranger to concert halls outside of Czechoslovakia, while the first four might not have been composed at all judging from their total neglect. Yet the F major Symphony is a gorgeous work; and of the early symphonies, No. 3 in E flat comes close to being a masterpiece. Its first movement is particularly striking. The work was composed in 1873, but already the full power of Dvořák's orchestration is in evidence—that buoyant sound, the golden horns, the instinct for putting each note in the right place. The English conductor Julius Harrison maintained that it is a rare thing to hear a lukewarm performance of any orchestral piece by Dvořák because "each instrumental part is instinct with life. Nothing stagnates, for Dvořák's ear was fully alive to every voice in the harmony." There is much orchestral music by Dvořák that should be heard with greater frequency—the *Scherzo Capriccioso*, the various serenades and the *Legends*, the Symphonic Variations. His symphonic poems are somewhat weaker, but *The Golden Spinning Wheel* is charming enough to warrant occasional performances.

His concertos remain alive. He wrote an attractive Piano Concerto in G minor with a rather ineffective piano part, a beautiful Violin Concerto in A minor, and a supreme Cello Concerto in B minor. Of his chamber music, the sunny Piano Quintet in A major, the String Quartets in F and E flat, and the *Dumky* Trio are familiar. Less known are the two massive last quartets, the propulsive E flat Piano Quartet, and the equally powerful F minor Piano Trio. Each ranks with the best chamber music of the late romantic period. Dvořák's operas are not in the repertory outside of Czechoslovakia, though *Rusalka* contains such lovely music, Wagnerisms and all, that one wonders why it is not in the steady repertory of an enterprising opera house. *The Devil and Kate* is a lusty comedy with some fine music in it. And, of the choral pieces, the *Stabat Mater* and the Requiem are among the grandest and most expressive works of their kind in the literature.

Last in the trilogy of great Czech composers is Leoš Janáček, born on July 3, 1854. He is a rather puzzling figure. For many years he was known outside of his homeland only by his one international success, the opera *Jenufa*. But after World War II his music, especially his operas, began to be heard in the capitals of the world, and slowly came the realization that Janáček was an original and important composer.

There were only thirteen years between him and Dvořák. But whereas Dvořák was purely an exponent of the late romantic tradition, Janáček, who died on August 12, 1928, reached well into the twentieth century, and his late music shows it. Even in his early years he exhibited a much more modern mind than Dvořák. He was not so great a composer and did not have Dvořák's pristine melodic sense, but he definitely was more powerful and biting, and in a way he was to Dvořák what Mussorgsky was to Tchaikovsky. Dvořák looked for beauty, Janáček looked for truth. Imagine the proper, religious, Victorian Dvořák taking a libretto like that of *Jenufa*, which deals with the murder of an illegitimate baby!

Janáček lived a quiet life, most of it in his own country, and most of *that* in Brno, where he directed a music school he had founded in 1881. Composer, theorist, conductor, and teacher, he started late. Not until he was twenty-two did he attempt composition, and he spent his life wrestling with the materials of music. His first significant work was not produced until he was forty. From that point he kept writing steadily until his death, with no falling-off in inspiration. The older he grew, the more terse, bleak, rugged, dissonant, and epigrammatic his music became. He was not an atonalist. Whether or not his music has a key signature, it always has a key center. But some of his harmonies are so harsh that they can suggest atonalism.

Janáček was a nationalist and a scholar of national music, which many of the early nationalists were not. Like Bartók and Kodály in Hungary, Vaughan Williams and Holst in England, he and František Bartoš investigated, catalogued, and edited collections of his country's folk songs. His own music, strongly influenced by his researches, has none of the heart-on-sleeve nationalism of Smetana, Dvořák, Rimsky-Korsakov, or Grieg. It is, like Bartók's, a nationalism that runs deeper. In his operas and vocal music it is a nationalism represented by declamatory patterns peculiar to folk song and speech. It is, in short, an elemental nationalism, one that goes to the raw, naked folk impulse rather than to the later, more smoothed-out, developed, and sophisticated material of the popular song. So closely wrapped up with speech patterns is Janáček's music that a listener must know the Czech language to achieve full identification with it.

Janáček worked out a theory of speech-in-music that is very close to Mussorgsky's, though he never heard a note of the latter's music until relatively late in life. "The study I have made of the musical aspects of the spoken language," he wrote, "has led me to the conviction that all of the melodic and rhythmic mysteries of music can be explained in reference to the melody and rhythm of the musical motives of the spoken language." At the beginning of the 1890's he was systematically notating the melodic and rhythmic qualities of the spoken word, and he discovered that with the help of these "speech-melodies" he could "form the motif of any given word." He could then, he maintained, "encompass the whole of every day life or the greatest tragedy" in music. Janáček became something of a mild fanatic on the subject of "speech melody," and wanted courses in it to be given in every conservatory and school of acting.

Allied to speech patterns was his feeling for nature. "I listen to the birds singing. I marvel at the manifestations of rhythm in its million different forms in the world of light, color and shapes, and my music remains young through contact with the eternally young rhythm of Nature." From anybody else this would be conventional and sentimental blathering, but Janáček did not write sentimental music, and a pantheistic strain does run through his music. Bartók had much the same feeling, and Janáček's nature music is echoed in the "night music" found in so many Bartók scores.

Although Janáček used many folklike materials in his work, it is not as a folklorist or melodist that he makes his impact. His music is recognizable more by certain idiosyncratic thrusts: by melismatic patterns evocative of folk song (his piano music is full of it); by a certain arch humor (as in the Capriccio for Piano and Winds); by a tight, pared-down harmony that often

345

sounds bare. In many respects he straddles the postromantic and the modern world. His harmonies, powerful as they are, are not adventurous enough to be fully modern, and yet are too unconventional to be postromantic. But his style is completely original. He worked out a system of composition that owed very little to previous musicians, and of few composers in the history of music can that be said.

Janáček's early works—*Jenufa* (1902) or the two-movement Piano Sonata (1905)—naturally speak a more conventional language than such late operas as *The Makropoulos Affair* (1924) or *From the House of the Dead* (1926). *Katya Kabanova* (1921) is the pivotal work that straddles the philosophies of two centuries. The very opening chord—F, D flat, B flat, B natural—is stark and modern, but it resolves to B flat minor. Juxtaposed to passages of pungent dissonances are sections that are all but Tchaikovskian, such as the C flat major episode on page 27 of the vocal score. (Janáček's system of composition was always getting him into such "impossible" keys as C flat, and his scores are terribly hard to read because of the profuse accidentals.) The dichotomy continues into the libretto itself. The plot, which deals with a married woman who has an affair and is driven to suicide by her conscience, is modern. Yet Janáček has no hesitation using the old-fashioned device of an interpolated song that has nothing to do with the action. Thus in the second act a character enters. "Nobody here yet? Then I'll sing a song while I'm waiting." And off he goes into a folk song—notated in D flat minor (another "impossible" key). None of these creaky devices occur in the late operas, works in which Janáček brought his "speech melody" to a logical conclusion. Characters declaim rather than sing, and it is the orchestra that has whatever melody there is. On the surface this would appear to lead to boredom, to plays with musical background rather than opera, but Janáček's rhythms are so fascinating, his sung speech inflections so precise, his integrity so great, that the operas exert a tremendous pull. So does the crude (purposely so) *Glagolitic Mass* of 1926, which puts the listener into a primitive Slavonic world.

No composer could be more unlike the grim Janáček than Norway's most important nationalist, Edvard Grieg. Where Janáček was carved from solid granite, Grieg was, in Debussy's words, "bonbons wrapped in snow." In his own time (he was born on June 15, 1841, and died on September 4, 1907) Grieg was tremendously popular. He rode on the wave of nationalism that produced the equally popular Dvořák. But whereas Dvořák composed in big forms, Grieg was primarily a miniaturist; and whereas Dvořák is as popular as ever, Grieg's reputation fell almost as rapidly as it had risen. Shortly after his death few musicians would take Grieg seriously. His once piquant chromatic harmonies, which had so titillated music lovers, were accused of being cloying. The new generation looked upon Grieg with the same condescension with which they gazed upon the photographs in great-grandfather's album. Grieg, in short, was as out of fashion as the stovepipe hats and velveteen jackets of his period. Along with Liszt and Mendelssohn, both of whom were also swamped by the antiromanticism of the period after World War I, Grieg was dismissed with a careless wave of the hand. In recent years, Liszt and Mendelssohn have made a comeback. But Grieg still languishes.

It is true that nobody can make a case for Grieg as one of the immortals. But he was one of the band of nationalists who did bring something new to music, and what Grieg had to say he for the most part said gracefully and prettily, with considerable style, and also with a compositional technique perfectly suited to his content. His music does not deserve the scorn with which it is so often received. At its best it is well made and often melodically distinguished. The G minor Ballade for solo piano is a good example. It uses a folk melody and starts with a slow, almost Franckian series of highly chromatic chords, after which it proceeds to a series of variations. The writing is a combination of nationalism with Schumann-inspired piano technique; but not until the glittering fourth variation, with its cadence of the raised sixth (typical of Norwegian folk music), does the nationalism take the upper hand. Throughout the work the writing is in beautiful taste, virtuosic without being vulgar. It is a lovely piece of music, infinitely above the cheap type of salon writing that flooded Europe at the time.

It is not an easy piece to bring to life, however, for the tradition it represents is gone. Pianists like Percy Grainger and Leopold Godowsky (who recorded the Ballade in the late 1920's) could bring freedom and feeling to Grieg's music. Pianists not trained in the romantic idiom are liable to vitiate the music by playing it too literally, destroying its spontaneity and delicacy, not knowing when to relax a tempo, when to use rubato, how to bring out the inner voices. Composers on a supreme level can survive almost any manner of performance, but lesser composers are peculiarly vulnerable to their interpreters.

Grieg, who studied (with great unhappiness) at the Leipzig Conservatory, was a good all-around musician—pianist, conductor, composer of course, a specialist in the music of his country. He had been strongly influenced by the now almost-forgotten Ole Bull (1810–1880). Bull was a Norwegian violinist who was largely self-taught, and who achieved a big reputation in Europe and the United States. Part genius, part charlatan, an eccentric man with strong opinions, he was a father-figure to Grieg. He himself was interested in Norwegian folk song, and in the 1840's composed a *Notturno* for string orchestra that bears all the marks of what Grieg later was to do. It is a lovely, evocative, and even haunting piece. It was Bull who urged that the fifteen-year-old Grieg be sent to Leipzig. In later years Grieg spoke vehe-

347

mently of his dislike for the Leipzig Conservatory. He said that his piano teachers were mostly inefficient and that his composition teachers gave him elaborate assignments long before he was ready for them.

He returned to Norway in 1862, gave piano recitals, and then went to Copenhagen, where he worked for a short time with Niels Gade, then the most important Danish composer. In Copenhagen he met his cousin, Nina Hagerup. They became engaged in 1864 and were married three years later. She was a singer who gave the premieres of many of his songs. Up to 1864, Grieg's compositions were in the style of Schumann, Mendelssohn, and the early romantic school. But in 1864 he became interested in Ole Bull's plea for a national Norwegian music, and he also became friendly with a young composer named Rikard Nordraak, who was actually writing in an idiom derived from Norwegian folk melodies. Grieg decided to devote the rest of his life to Norwegian nationalism. He returned to his own country, composed steadily, conducted, gave concerts, and within a few years became known as the brightest musical talent in Norway. Liszt heard some of his music and sent a warm letter of recommendation. Included in the letter was an invitation to visit Liszt at Weimar. The two men did meet in 1869, but in Rome, not Weimar. They became close friends. Later there was an evening in Weimar when Grieg showed Liszt the manuscript of his Piano Concerto in A minor. Liszt, with one of his typically flamboyant gestures, waved the composer away and read the concerto at sight, flawlessly.

When Grieg came to maturity, it was as a short, quiet, exquisite man who specialized in short, quiet, exquisite pieces of music. He had a busy life. In addition to his own creative work, he was active in Norway as a conductor and critic. He gave annual European tours as a pianist, playing his own music; and there were few more popular pianists or composers. Grieg was welcome wherever he went. He was a man with a levelheaded view of life, and he had a quiet wit that endeared him to his friends. There was the time he was made Knight of the Order of Orange-Nassau; he accepted with alacrity, because, as he wrote to a friend, "Orders and medals are most useful to me in the top layer of my trunk. The customs officials are always so kind to me at the sight of them." Always a delicate man, he suffered constantly from pulmonary trouble, but he had been too long before the public as a performer, liked the life and the people he met, and continued his tours almost to the day of his death. Indeed, he was all set to go to England when he was ordered to a hospital on September 3, 1907. He died the following day.

One of Grieg's troubles, as it was Saint-Saëns's trouble, is that he is known mostly by his worst pieces of music—*Peer Gynt*, say, or some of the more sticky *Lyric Pieces*, or several of his *Norwegian Dances*. There is much more to Grieg than those. One of his collections of national dances, the *Slåtter* (Op. 72), comprises bleak and unprettified pieces, amazingly close to what

348

Bartók was to do in his piano transcriptions of Hungarian melodies. Many of the *Lyric Pieces*, of which he composed ten books, are as good as some of Mendelssohn's *Songs Without Words*, and better than most. The G minor String Quartet served as a model for Debussy's String Quartet, as Gerald Abraham has so convincingly demonstrated. The three violin sonatas are beautifully laid out, appealing in content, graceful to play and hear. And the Grieg songs are of great beauty. He was an authentically distinguished song composer; in the *Haugtussa* cycle, or in such songs as *A Swan*, he achieved perfection in a small package.

Grieg never struck very deep and his range is admittedly narrow. Even the Piano Concerto in A minor, probably his most popular concert piece (*Peer Gynt* seldom turns up any more except in pop concerts), is closer to the fashionable virtuoso concertos of Rubinstein, Herz, Scharwenka, and Litolff than to the masterpieces of the literature. But it is a notch above Rubinstein and company because of its piquant melodies that reflect Grieg and no other composer, whereas the melodies of Rubinstein and the others could have been written by any composer. Grieg does not represent power or revolution. He represents charm, grace, sweetness, and still has a good deal to offer, bonbons and all. He was a minor master, and one of the finest.

Somewhat allied to Grieg were the two first important Spanish nationalists, Isaac Albéniz and Enrique Granados. Like Grieg, they took native melodies and superimposed upon them cosmopolitan techniques in a highly spiced chromatic idiom. Like Grieg, both composed largely in the smaller forms, with an emphasis on piano music. Like Grieg, their music verged on the salon. Unlike Grieg, each of the two composed a resplendent piano work that actually added something new to the repertory—Albéniz with his *Iberia*, Granados with his *Goyescas*.

Spain in the nineteenth century was one of the most backward and reactionary countries in Europe. Its intellectual life was limited, and it is hard to think of an important creative figure except Goya in the Spain of that period. In the country, however, was a body of vital folk song, and European composers would visit Spain, come away entranced with the native music, and write their *Jota Aragonesa*, *Caprice Espagnol*, and *España*. There was no serious music in Spain during most of the century, nor was there a place where Spanish musicians could be trained (the conservatory in Madrid had no professional standing). When a major talent turned up, such as Juan Arriaga (1806–1826), he had to go outside the country to study. (Arriaga, who died at the age of twenty, was very gifted, and a potentially great composer was lost at his untimely death.) The most popular form of Spanish music was the operetta, or zarzuela, and zarzuela composers spent most of their time copying Rossini and Bellini.

Not until after the middle of the nineteenth century was an effort made to survey the rich heritage of Spanish folk music. Felipe Pedrell (1841–1922) was the moving spirit. He was a composer, musicologist (he edited the works of the great sixteenth-century Spanish contrapuntist, Victoria), and a folklorist whose *Cancionero musical popular español* was for many years the basic guide to the field. Pedrell lived under the shadow of his scholarly work. "They have never done me justice," he told Manuel de Falla, "either in Catalonia or the rest of Spain. They have constantly tried to belittle me, saying I was a great critic or a great historian but not a good composer. It's not true. I *am* a good composer." But whatever reputation he has as a composer resides in Spain, for his music is unknown elsewhere. Throughout most of the century the best Spanish music continued to be composed by non-Spaniards. Glinka may have been the first to come under the spell of Spanish folk music, and he was followed by a battalion of others who became excited by the color, rhythmic snap, and exotic melodic appeal of Iberia. One of the composers most in love with the country was Chabrier: "We make the rounds of the café concerts, where they sing the *malagueñas*, the *soledas*, the *zapateados* and the *pateneras*; then the dances, which are positively Arabian, that sums it up. If you could see them wriggling their behinds, twisting and squirming, I don't think you'd care to leave." Everybody was taking advantage of Spanish music except the Spaniards.

It was in this period that Isaac Albéniz was born on May 29, 1860, and, a few years later, Enrique Granados, on July 27, 1867. There was a good deal in common between the two composers. Both were concert pianists of international reputation. Both were nationalistic composers who tried to create an authentic Spanish serious music. Neither was completely successful in that both *Iberia* and *Goyescas* remain influenced by Chopin, Liszt, the French turn-of-the-century school, and, possibly, the piano music of Leopold Godowsky. Godowsky (1870–1938) was a pianist's pianist who composed a great deal of keyboard music in which complexity and the movement of inner voices were almost an end in themselves.

Even if they were not originals, Albéniz and Granados did much to break new ground, and they worked on their masterpieces at much the same time, though without contact with each other. *Iberia* was composed between 1906 and 1909, *Goyescas*, 1909 to 1910. Both works are large-scale suites for large-scale virtuosos, full of the scent—there is no other word for it—of Spanish rhythms, Spanish melodies, Spanish life that nobody but a native-born composer could have evoked. Chabrier, Rimsky-Korsakov, and the others were merely tourists. *Iberia* and *Goyescas* were written by men who were at home. Technically the two pieces have much in common. They are extremely difficult, full of countermelodies, and the writing is characterized by exuberant rhythms, wide stretches, delicate pedal effects, textures so rich and thick they are quasi-orchestral, and elaborate ornamentation. Of the two, *Iberia* is the more direct, *Goyescas* the more romantic, dreamier, vaguer in outline, perhaps more haunting.

Albéniz led an interesting life. Exploited as a child prodigy (he was playing in public at the age of four), he was constantly running away from home. At the age of thirteen he made his way to Cuba, New York, and South America before the authorities and his parents caught up with him. His serious studies started at the Leipzig Conservatory in 1874, after which he went to the Brussels Conservatory. Then he had a few lessons with Liszt. In 1890 he studied composition in Paris under d'Indy and Dukas. His life thereafter was that of a touring pianist and composer. For a while he made his headquarters in London, where one of his operas was produced. Then he moved permanently to Paris. He turned out an enormous number of piano pieces, most of which are no longer heard. A few, however—the Tango in D is the most famous example—are known by everybody. Nothing else in his work suggested the scope of *Iberia*. It was of unprecedented difficulty, and the fine French pianist Blanche Selva was appalled when she looked at the music. "It is unplayable!" Albéniz, who was near death, assured her that it could and would be played. He died on May 18, 1909, leaving an unfinished trilogy of operas on the King Arthur legend. One of his operas, *Pepita Jiménez*, had a brief run in the 1890's. It is entirely forgotten.

Iberia is an abstract work based largely on Andalusian folk melody. *Goyescas*, which also uses Andalusian and flamenco elements, is based on etchings and paintings by Goya. Like Albéniz, Granados turned out a large number of pleasant, salonlike piano pieces, and nothing in his previous work would have suggested so grand a piece as *Goyescas*. Granados studied in Barcelona, then in Paris. He returned to Barcelona and settled down to the life of a piano teacher. Soon his compositions began to attract notice, and one of his operas, *María del Carmen*, was a success at its premiere in 1898. He also composed a series of exquisite, fragrant nationalistic songs called *Tonadillas*.

Then came *Goyescas*. Granados had been thinking about the music long before starting to compose it. "I am enamored with the psychology of Goya, with his palette, with him, with his muse the Duchess of Alba, with his quarrels with his models, his loves and flatteries. That whitish pink of the cheeks, contrasting with the blend of black velvet; those subterranean creatures, hands of mother-of-pearl and jasmine resting on jet trinkets, have possessed me." Granados wrote these words from the heart, and it is easy to see why. Those mysterious, beautiful, almost menacing "majas" that Goya painted, those aristocratic women peering behind fans, thinking their secret thoughts, that mixture of cruelty and decadence—all of this has stimulated imaginations much weaker than that of the sensitive Granados.

His suite originally had six pieces, to which was added *El Pelele*. By far the most famous, and the most often played in concert divorced from the suite, is *Quejas, o la maja y el ruiseñor*, known in English as *The Maiden and the Nightingale*. It contains one of the loveliest, most plaintive melodies that the period has to show; and, at the end, there are those wispy arabesques and trills of the singing nightingale. But this is far from nature painting; it is poetry in sound, the verses of a man of unusual sensibility.

Granados worked the pieces of *Goyescas* into an opera, to a libretto by Fernando Periquet. He had made a furor in Paris in 1914, playing his own music, and the Opéra commissioned the adaptation. But war came, and the Opéra was unable to stage the work. Giulio Gatti-Casazza at the Metropolitan Opera took it over, and the world premiere was given in New York in 1916. *Goyescas* was politely received, but it did not catch on, nor did it ever. The libretto is supposed to be weak, and it is, though worse librettos are still before the public. It is surprising that the little opera has not been picked up as a curtain raiser. It has authentic flavor.

Had not Granados come to the United States to supervise the production, he would have had many more years to live. As it happened, he was asked by President Wilson to play at the White House. Naturally he was happy to oblige. He canceled his return passage and arranged for a later ship. Finally, on March 24, 1916, he embarked for Dieppe on the S.S. *Sussex*, which was torpedoed in the English Channel. A survivor said that Granados was safe in a lifeboat when he saw his wife struggling in the water. He jumped in to save her, and both went down. The world was deprived of a composer just in the process of finding himself. Granados, after *Goyescas*, knew he was beginning to broaden. "I have a world of ideas," he said shortly before his death. "I am filled with enthusiasm to work more and more." But that was not to be. And so he lives today mainly by *Goyescas*, a few salon pieces, and some piercingly beautiful songs.

The work of Albéniz and Granados was carried on by Manuel de Falla. Falla, who was born in Cadiz on November 23, 1876, studied in Spain, won a national prize for his opera *La Vida Breve* in 1905, and then went off to Paris for seven years. The First World War sent him back to Spain, where he composed such popular pieces as the ballets *El Amor Brujo* and *El Sombrero de Tres Picos*. Also from that period came his *Noches en los jardines de España* (*Nights in the Gardens of Spain*) for piano and orchestra. After the war he composed a puppet opera, *El Retablo de Maese Pedro*, a harpsichord concerto, and a long piano piece named *Fantasia Bética*. After 1926 he composed very little. He moved to Argentina, lived in seclusion, and for the last twenty years of his life worked on a massive project, a sort of opera-oratorio, named *L'Atlántida*. He died on November 14, 1946.

Falla's total output is small, but everything he composed is jewel-like in its workmanship. At first his music resembled the music of previous Spanish nationalists, though it was more sophisticated, with an overlay of impressionistic techniques. It was based on *cante jondo*, Andalusian melodies and rhythms, flamenco, and other aspects of the Spanish *melos*, all filtered through a French-derived workmanship. *Noches en los jardines de España*, composed in 1916, is little more than a counterpart of d'Indy's *Symphony on a French Mountain Air*, composed in 1886. Both scores are for piano and orchestra, both exploit a piano technique abounding in arpeggios and harplike effects, both scores use national elements in a most sophisticated, concert-hall manner. Falla's *Noches*, his *La Vida Breve*, and *Seven Popular Spanish Songs* are none the worse for that, and they have been popular repertory pieces since they appeared. The music is not only charmingly evocative of Spain, but it is also the work of an extremely skilled composer with a subtle ear for color and absolute precision in technique. Falla was not only far above any Spanish composer of his day; he was the *only* Spanish composer of the day who rose above mediocrity.

After World War I there was a pronounced change in his style. The big influence on Falla was Stravinsky, who had composed *L'Histoire du Soldat* in 1918 and was investigating the possibilities of neoclassicism. Falla began to work in the same manner. His *El Retablo de Maese Pedro*, scored for an orchestra of twenty, with such unusual instruments as harpsichord, luteharp, and xylophone, is a counterpart to Stravinsky's little choreographed tale of the Russian soldier. Similarly, Falla's Harpsichord Concerto, with a small group consisting of flute, oboe, clarinet, violin, and cello, can be described as Hispanic neoclassicism. The music has never achieved the popularity of his earlier works, but it strikes much deeper into Spanish folk song, and in addition evokes the world of Scarlatti (who had spent so many years in Spain). His biggest work, *L'Atlántida*, for chorus, soloists, and orchestra, was left unfinished and seems to have died stillborn. Ernesto Halffter, the Spanish composer who studied with Falla, completed the score. It made very little impression when Ernest Ansermet conducted the American premiere in New York in 1962, and there have been few if any performances since then.

France, Italy, and Germany never had an important nationalistic composer. In England there was Ralph Vaughan Williams and in Hungary Béla Bartók, both to be discussed in later chapters. In Poland, Ignace Jan Paderewski (1860–1941) was turning out a commercial national product—a Chopin kind of nationalism expressed in late-romantic clichés: often graceful, but unimportant. A much stronger Polish nationalist was Karol Szymanowski (1882–1937), who passed from Russian to German to French schools, ending up an internationalist whose music was tinged with Polish folk elements and leaned heavily on late Scriabin. Very little of his work is heard in the West. In Denmark there was Carl Nielsen (1865–1931), a composer who in recent years has been attracting a great deal of attention. Nielsen, unlike Jean Sibelius (1865–1957) in nearby Finland, was not a true nationalist. Brahms and Mahler were stronger influences on his music than Danish folk song. But Nielsen worked out a strong and original style.

His talent showed up at an early age, he became a violinist, and was awarded a state subsidy for study. In all this his career paralleled Sibelius's (though Nielsen's state grant was nothing on the order of the generous one that the Finnish government gave Sibelius). He conducted the Royal Opera until 1914 and became head of the Royal Conservatory in 1915. While conducting a program of his own music in 1926 he had a heart attack and lingered a very sick man until his death in October, 1931.

Where Sibelius was influenced at first by Tchaikovsky and the Russian school, Nielsen looked to the German postromantics. His early works are very much in the postromantic tradition, and never did he entirely discard tonality. He even went so far as to give names to four of his six symphonies: No. 2 is *The Four Temperaments*, No. 3 the *Sinfonia Espansiva*, No. 4 the *Inextinguishable*, and No. 6 the *Sinfonia Semplice*. Actually, these titles did not indicate a Straussian kind of program music. Rather they were a Schumannesque, clue-giving device. Nielsen always was an "absolute" composer, and one whose music shows a steady growth. Like Janáček, he was a composer who had one foot in the nineteenth century, one in the twentieth. In his day he was accused of writing dissonance, of falling in with the atonalists. Today those attacks appear nonsensical. Nielsen was more adventurous than many composers of his day, but basically he was a traditionalist who accepted the classic forms, sometimes surrounding them with more biting harmonies than conventional ears could stand. Even in the Fifth Symphony, with its polytonal clashes, there is never any doubt about the underlying tonality.

While not as determinedly nationalistic as Sibelius's, Nielsen's music does have nationalistic echoes. But the thing that most impresses about it is its breadth. The man thought big. His rhythms are energetic, his melodies are long-breathed, his orchestration is generous. There is a great deal of individuality to his writing. In the 1930's, music lovers were hearing a great deal about the "bardic" qualities of Sibelius. It is ironic to realize that Nielsen, then all but unknown outside of Denmark, had just as much sweep, even more power and a more universal message. Sibelius's reputation fast dissipated after his death in 1957. In 1965, the centenary of his birth arrived with all the force of a feather against an iron anvil. There were a few memorial concerts in the United States, but the public did not seem to care much, one way or the other, and most professional musicians could not have been less interested.

It was different in the 1930's. At that time Sibelius was at the height of his fame, even though he had not composed a note since 1926. His Seventh Symphony of 1924 and *Tapiola* of 1925 were his last two important works. Like Rossini, he then sat back and watched the world go by. But whereas Rossini amused himself by composing jests and *aperçus*, Sibelius never once touched pen to music paper in the last thirty-one years of his life. There were rumors about an Eighth Symphony. Nothing happened. Sibelius clearly had made up his mind that he had nothing important to say any more. But he remained an important name. His music was especially venerated in England and the United States, where Sibelius had such champions as Sir Thomas Beecham, Constant Lambert, Serge Koussevitzky, and Olin Downes. Downes, music critic of the New York *Times*, was constantly reminding his readers about what Sibelius had done to revolutionize symphonic form, and he wrote article after article about the "strength," "masculinity," and "bardic" qualities of Sibelius. In England, Sibelius was taken with equal seriousness. When Lambert published his controversial *Music Ho!* in 1933, a book that looked upon modern music and found it not good, the only contemporary who came out well was Sibelius. "His Fourth Symphony," wrote Lambert, "is as unappreciated now as were the later sonatas and quartets of Beethoven in their day. Nevertheless, just as the later quartets of Beethoven have influenced modern thought far more than the fashionable works of Hummel and Czerny, so will the symphonies of Sibelius have a more profound influence on future generations than the *pièces d'occasion* of his contemporaries—the composers like Hindemith and Stravinsky who have made their compromise with vogue."

It did not work out as Lambert predicted. In the United States the decline of Sibelius started in 1940. Just as Downes had been instrumental in setting Sibelius on his pedestal, so another critic was instrumental in tearing him off. Virgil Thomson, in his first season as music critic of the New York *Herald Tribune*, heard the Sibelius Second Symphony and found it "vulgar, self-indulgent and provincial beyond all description." In a typical Thomsonian burst he wrote that he realized there were sincere Sibelius-lovers in the world, "although I must say I've never met one among educated professional musicians." Thomson was only echoing what many musicians were thinking. To them, Sibelius was little better than an anachronistic relic of postromanticism. In a way that is curious, for starting with the Fourth Symphony of 1911 Sibelius did bring something to music that was new, provocative, and antiromantic. Breaking away from the lush melodies and orchestration of his first three symphonies, breaking away from the long developments of the Mahler and Bruckner symphonic style, Sibelius instead worked with short motifs and a terse kind of development. It has been described as a mosaic style, and it succeeds in avoiding the romantic rhetoric.

The last four symphonies are not even specifically nationalistic, though commentators are eager to read into them the trees, snows, and mountains of the icy North.

Yet many professionals after World War II found Sibelius a dated bore. One reason was that music had taken a new departure. Schoenberg and Webern were the heroes; serialism had triumphed. (If Mahler was suddenly popular, it was because the serialists decided that in Mahler lay the seeds of the serial movement.) There may have been still another reason why Sibelius was scorned. Professionals look for consistency in a composer. They distrust a creator who constantly turns out music that is not on a high level, and are apt to regard as freaks those few works that do cause a ripple. How could the composer of *Valse Triste* and the *Romance* in D flat for piano be taken seriously? It cannot be denied that a large quantity of Sibelius's work —and he was a prolific composer—consists of ephemera. His violin works, apart from the D minor Concerto, are salon trifles, and his songs are competent without being striking. Sibelius composed only a handful of works that have any chance of survival. Yet even that is a better average than many composers can show, and in years to come the chances are that the music of Sibelius will occupy a more prominent place than it currently does. At the time of his death he was suffering from a bad name and an aesthetic that ran counter to the age. If a new age does produce a resurgent romanticism or neoromanticism, Sibelius could come back with it. He did, after all, talk with an individual voice when he was at his best, and he deserves to occupy an honorable place among the minor composers.

⚔ 6 ⚔

Chromaticism and Sensibilité

FROM FRANCK TO FAURÉ

"France! Great in all the arts, supreme in none." So mourned Anatole France. Be that as it may, the last quarter of the nineteenth century saw a large number of important French composers working in Paris, and in the closing decade the music of young Claude Debussy began to be discussed. But now there was a significant shift in their orientation. Through most of the century, France had stood for opera. With the exception of Berlioz—and he too would dearly have wished to be appreciated as a successful composer of operas—most French composers (at least, those of international reputation) had become famous as suppliers of very salable works for the lyric stage. Now appeared a group of composers whose ambition took in other things. Many of them did try their hand at opera, but opera was not the basic reason for their existence. They wrote symphonies, piano works, and chamber music, and they added significantly to the European ferment. Yet they turned out music that did not travel very well. César Franck and Gabriel Fauré, and then their pupils, composed fine works that somehow were for the most part not exportable.

Franck is today out of fashion; the delicate music of Fauré has never been able to secure a foothold outside of France; and the music of their followers --Vincent d'Indy, Ernest Chausson, Édouard Lalo, Paul Dukas, and the others —lies largely neglected, apart from one or two favorites by each composer. To most modern tastes this music is, in the case of Franck, too chromatic, too self-indulgent, too cloying; and, in the case of his followers, too derivative. It is also a music that is curiously ambivalent, in that it is strongly streaked with Wagnerism despite the efforts, sometimes frantic, of French composers to avoid Wagnerism. After the first Bayreuth Festival of 1876, the Wagnerian language swept French music, and every composer dutifully made his pilgrimage to the Festspielhaus, coming back bathed in Wagner's sensuous harmonies. One of Franck's most promising pupils, Guillaume Lekeu, actually fainted after the prelude to *Tristan* and had to be carried out of the theater. Wagner became the god of the symbolist poets, and a magazine, *La Revue Wagnérienne*, was started in Paris to preach the gospel of *Der Meister*.

Superficially there is little Wagner influence in, say, Franck's D minor Symphony or Chausson's *Poème*. Actually there is a great deal. Wagner's fluctuating harmonies, his reluctance to return to a home key, his incessant chromaticism—all that is reflected in French music of the post-Bayreuth period. Franck's chromaticism, indeed, carries Wagner's a notch forward, and a good deal of French opera of the day is a mirror of what Wagner was espousing at Bayreuth. Some French composers, at first enthusiastic Wagnerians, later started to wriggle out of Wagner's embrace. None was completely successful.

Franck was the dominating musical force of the period in France, both as composer and as teacher, and he gathered unto himself a group of pupils who did everything but put a halo over him and worship. There was something in the man that encouraged worship. While he was not the plaster saint d'Indy made him out to be, he was kind to a point of saintliness, serene, otherworldly. Never did a harsh word pass his lips, never a derogatory remark. He was not interested in honors or in money, and a stained-glass aura (reflected in his music) emanated from him. One of his greatest delights was to sit and improvise at the organ of Ste.-Clothilde in a religious ecstasy (in a way, Franck was a French Bruckner). People compared him with Fra Angelico. It was to Franck that the younger generation turned, much to the distress of such members of the Establishment as Saint-Saëns, Ambroise Thomas, and Massenet.

A Belgian who did not become a naturalized Frenchman until 1873, Franck was born in Liège on December 10, 1822. His father tried to exploit him as a child prodigy, and the boy did achieve something of a reputation. In 1835 the family moved to Paris, and at the age of fifteen César was sent to the Paris Conservatoire. He must have been a cocky lad, exultant in his talent. At the finals of the piano competition he was given a difficult piece to read at sight. For some reason he took it into his head to transpose the entire composition, and he played it in C major instead of E flat, transfixing the judges. A special meeting of the jury was held, and the decision, as reported in *La France Musicale* of August 5, 1838, was to give Franck a special prize:

First of all the jury awarded with one voice the first prize to M. Franck. But after that, the jury decided to look into the matter again. After some discussion, M. Cherubini announced with his customary grace: "The jury has now decided that M. Franck stands so incomparably far ahead of his fellow competitors that it is impossible to nominate another to share the prize with him. Accordingly, a second first prize will be given to those who would in ordinary circumstances have deserved the senior award.

A promising beginning; but after leaving the Conservatoire, Franck sank into obscurity. He taught, he concertized, he composed, and his music did come to the attention of Liszt, who praised a set of piano trios. Liszt met Franck and immediately sized him up: "I fancy he is lacking in that convenient social sense that opens all doors." Which, of course, was true. Franck was not an aggressive man. Indeed, his brother Joseph was a much better-known composer at the time. Today Joseph is completely forgotten.

Not until he was thirty years old did Franck switch from piano to organ. He specialized in church work and improvisation, and was considered to be by far the greatest improviser of his time. "Classical" organ playing—the correct performance of baroque organ music—was virtually a lost art in France until Franck and others headed the renaissance in the last half of the century. Jean-Bonaventure Laurens, writing in *La Gazette Musicale* of November 2, 1845, pointed out that whereas the piano music of Bach was well known (note the term "piano music"; nobody at the time would have thought of playing the *Well-Tempered Clavier* and other Bach clavier works on the harpsichord, assuming that a professional harpsichordist could have been found, which in itself is a doubtful assumption), the organ works were unknown, "since they all demand the use of the pedals, a technical feat that practically nobody in this country seems at the moment to have mastered." Not until Adolphe Hesse came to Paris and showed how the Bach organ works should really go was the attention of French musicians and organists turned to this sublime literature.

Franck's investigation into the resources of the organ was naturally accelerated when he became organist of Ste.-Clothilde in 1858. He started composing for the instrument, and his first important series of organ works came out in 1862 as *Six Pièces pour grand orgue*. They were by far the most significant compositions he had produced, and they have remained in the repertoire. But they did not make him famous. Franck at thirty-six was little known as a creative figure. In 1865 he moved with his wife and the four children to 95 Rue de Rennes (now the Boulevard du Montparnasse) and there spent the rest of his life. Mme. Franck was a virago. She was ambitious for her husband, but she did not like his music and she hated his experimentation. She knew just enough about music to be alarmed when Franck broke the rules and she made no secret of her dislike of the F minor Piano Quintet and the D minor Symphony. She was especially unhappy with the critical reception accorded those works. This was no way for a respectable

French organist to get ahead in the world. She argued and cried, nagged, and pestered. It was not a happy marriage.

Little of Franck's early music is played. He was one of those composers who develops late, and not until the 1880's did he compose most of the music by which he is known. (The *Six Pièces* of 1862 are an exception.) Prior to the 1880's, however, his music had been given occasional hearings. The Société Nationale de Musique, which had as its motto *Ars Gallica*, had put one of his works on its very first program, November 25, 1871. Only a year after that, Franck was appointed professor of organ at the Conservatoire. Very soon he became the most discussed teacher there, with a group of pupils who ran around Paris crying that Franck was the only progressive figure in that conservative institution. Those pupils were called the Franckists and, less politely, Franck's Gang. They included Lekeu (who died at the age of twenty-four), Henri Duparc, d'Indy, Guy Ropartz, Ernest Chausson, Gabriel Pierné, and Alexis de Castillon (another who died young). These young men were different from the general run of Conservatoire students. Many of them had money, one of them (Castillon) was a viscount, another (d'Indy) came from an aristocratic family, and they regarded the rest of the student body as rabble, much as an aviator regards the infantry. This kind of aristocracy and snobbery within the Conservatoire caused a great deal of resentment, all the more in that Franck was supposed to be nothing more than an organ teacher. The secretary of the Conservatoire had some tart words to say: "In this school we have at the present time a professor of organ who makes so bold as to turn his organ class into a composition class." There was grumbling, but nobody did anything about the situation.

As *de jure* teacher of organ and *de facto* teacher of composition, Franck passed to his pupils his ideas on harmony and form. He was uneasy when anybody stayed in the same key for any length of time. "Modulate! Modulate!" he would urge. As one of the pioneers in cyclic form—he had introduced it in his piano trios as early as 1842—Franck preached a kind of musical development in which initial material was subject to manipulation within an entire composition. Liszt, with his ideas of thematic transformation, had been doing much the same thing in the 1840's and '50's. Franck's ideas created strong centers of opposition, and his own music made little headway. When the Piano Quintet had its premiere in 1880 at a Société Nationale concert, Saint-Saëns, who was the pianist, hated every bit of it and stalked off the stage, refusing to return for applause. He even left the manuscript on the piano, although it was dedicated to him, and one of Franck's pupils rescued it. After the premiere of the D minor Symphony in February, 1889, Gounod's famous remark was "An affirmation of incompetence pushed to the length of dogma." Ambroise Thomas wondered why Franck called it a symphony in D minor when it passed through so many keys in so short a time. On the other hand, some important musicians—Chabrier, Théodore Dubois, Ernest Guiraud, and even Massenet—took Franck's side.

Around the mild, genuinely humble and modest Franck was a constant storm. During his lifetime, however, his music had very few performances. His oratorio *Rédemption* was a failure in 1873; his major choral work, *Les Béatitudes* (1869–79), was performed only once while he was alive, and that in his own apartment; his oratorio, *Rébecca* (1881), remains generally unknown to this day; and the D minor Symphony was a failure at its premiere. Critics lit into Franck for his "incomprehensible" way of writing. At his death, on November 8, 1890, he admittedly was the leader of a new French school, but not many observers would have given his music much chance for survival.

As things turned out, Franck became tremendously popular after his death, and it was a popularity that did not recede until the 1930's. Some of his music continues to be heard with regularity—the Symphony, the Symphonic Variations for piano and orchestra (1885), *Les Éolides* (1876), and, probably most famous of all, the A major Violin Sonata (1886). Not long ago his Prelude, Chorale and Fugue for solo piano (1884) and, to a lesser extent, his Prelude, Aria and Finale (1887), would have been included, but they seem to be slipping from the repertory. Organists, however, continue to play the Franck *Chorals* and other works, especially the *Grand Pièce symphonique*.

His music is noble and sincere, but what bothers many listeners is its saccharine quality. That, and a quality described as stained-glass religiosity. The music to them is too thick and its modulations too obvious. And some of the construction is demonstrably weak. When Franck worked in classic forms he was apt to go loosely along, as though improvising at the organ. Indeed his years of improvising strongly conditioned some of the formal elements of his music. The workmanship can be flabby. There is, too, an element of mysticism that repels some listeners. Mysticism is not fashionable any more in an objective, science-dominated age.

Franck had an extremely sensuous style. Pater Seraphicus, as he was called, could evoke some remarkably sophisticated rites in his music. Sections of the symphonic poems *Les Éolides* and *Les Djinns* (1884) have a coloring and sheen that anticipate some of Debussy's orchestral effects. The big Quartet in D (1889) and the Piano Quintet (1879) both aim high, and are broad, beautifully written and very striking works. One would not go wrong calling them masterpieces. Franck's music, basically, is loved by those who respond to the sensuous elements of sheer sound. Only those who have a physiological involvement with sound—a musical sweet tooth, to put it another way—can fully identify with the music of César Franck. Others find it so rich and sweetened that it can actually be sickening.

Of Franck's pupils, the talented Guillaume Lekeu (1870–1894) and Alexis de Castillon (1838–1873) died before they came to maturity. Experts in French music insist that Castillon's music is worth hearing, especially his chamber music. Henri Duparc (1848–1933) was a special case. Franck considered him his best pupil, but in 1885 Duparc had a mental breakdown and never composed another note though he lived for almost another half century. He had written a symphonic poem, *Lénore*, in 1875. That piece is no longer heard, and Duparc's fame rests entirely on thirteen songs (there are three others of less importance), each one unparalleled in France and, indeed, in Europe. Only Hugo Wolf was writing this kind of intense, psychological, rich-sounding and completely realized song.

Franck's two most famous pupils were Chausson and d'Indy. Chausson was the better composer, d'Indy the stronger influence. Those who love Franck's music also love Chausson's, for the music of both is ladled from the same rich, sensuous stream. Chausson was born in Paris on January 20, 1855, the overprotected child of a wealthy building contractor. The boy was given a private tutor and then sent to law school. He received his degree in 1877 but never practiced. All of his inclinations were toward the arts. "Ever since my childhood I have believed that I would write music. Everybody advises me against it. So I try painting and literature. Everybody gives me different advice." It was not until 1879, after exposure to Wagner's music, that Chausson made up his mind to be a composer. At the very late age of twenty-four he enrolled in Massenet's and Franck's classes, then dropped Massenet. In 1883 he left Franck and started to compose. He bought a house at 22 Boulevard des Courcelles and made it one of the artistic centers of Paris —the kind of brilliant salon that the Princess Belgiojoso had run fifty years previously. Painters, musicians, writers, and intellectuals were constantly there, and Chausson was friends with everybody who counted. (At his funeral, such figures as Degas, Rodin, Redon, and Louÿs were in the procession.) Chausson also more or less adopted the young Debussy, and the two men were very close. Chausson would lecture Debussy, and the touchy young fellow would not only take it but come back for more. "You are somewhat like a big, older brother in whom one has complete confidence," Debussy wrote, "and from whom one even accepts an occasional scolding." The generous Chausson befriended many other musicians as well. One was Isaac Albéniz. In fact, Chausson took in Albéniz and his whole family when the Spaniard was hard hit financially. Later Albéniz repaid the debt by privately paying Breitkopf and Härtel to publish Chausson's *Poème* in Germany.

Having no financial problems, Chausson could work when and where he pleased. He was a slow worker who could and did agonize for days over a single measure. His list of compositions is not large, and the important ones can be counted on the fingers of one hand. They are the Symphony in B flat (1891), the Concerto for Piano, Violin and String Quartet (1892), the *Poème de l'amour et de la mer* (1893), the *Poème* for violin and orchestra (1896), and the Piano Quartet (1898). His most ambitious work, the opera *Le Roi Arthus,* was composed between 1886 and 1895, and is not in the repertory. Experts describe it as Wagnerian. Chausson had some big projects in mind when his life was suddenly cut short by a bicycle accident on June 10, 1899. He lost control, crashed into a wall and was killed.

Strongly under Franck's influence, Chausson composed a luscious, opulently chromatic music in which the physiological action of pure sound occupies a major element. Is there anything in music, *Tristan* included, with the sensuous, almost tactile, feeling of the *Poème?* So rich is it that it is all velvet, and it definitely is not music for Puritans. It actually offends some listeners. This, and the Symphony in B flat, are unashamedly erotic, as much as music can be erotic. Chausson did for the symphony what Massenet was doing for the opera, though Chausson's music has more substance. The B flat Symphony is an underestimated work. It has more shape and discipline than the Franck D minor, its phrases are more pointed, its melodic content on an equally high level. The scented allure of Chausson's music is difficult to describe. It has the peculiarly French charm of a Pissarro painting—limited, perhaps oversweet, yet sensitive, purposeful, and powerfully evocative of a specific time and place in history.

All of the pupils of Franck worshiped their teacher, but it was Vincent d'Indy (1851–1931) who raised the worship to a cult. In his writings d'Indy even misrepresented Franck, so anxious was he to preserve the myth. He came to his teacher, like so many Franck pupils, at a surprisingly advanced age. D'Indy had plenty of talent—he had been a child prodigy—but he was essentially a dilettante until the age of eighteen, when he decided to study music seriously. He entered Franck's class in 1872, and his future life was set. It turned out to be one of the busier lives in French music. A man stubborn to the point of fanaticism, d'Indy was the propagandist for "Franck's Gang," and he helped further spread the message when he became director of the Société Nationale de Musique in 1890. In 1894 he founded the Schola Cantorum, along with Charles Bordes and Alexandre Guilmant. The Schola Cantorum originally was intended to be a society for the performance of sacred music, but it soon turned into a school for the study and restoration of old church music in general, and it also busied itself with scholarly work in French folk song. Many important French musicians were trained at the Schola Cantorum, the most prominent being Albert Roussel (1869–1937).

Little of d'Indy's vast output is heard today. The one work that still does make the rounds is the *Symphonie Cévenole* (1886), better known as the

Symphonie sur un chant montagnard français (*Symphony on a French Mountain Air*). It is a lovely work for piano and orchestra, brilliantly scored, haunting in its second movement, and with an ultrasophisticated use of folk elements. Much more direct than the music of Franck and Chausson, far less persistently chromatic, the *Cévenole* is one of the finest works of French postromanticism. Almost as good is the B flat Symphony (1909), which is seldom heard. French conductors of an older generation—Pierre Monteux was one—would program the B flat Symphony and the *Istar* Variations of 1897 (Koussevitzky was fond of the latter), but the current school of French conductors appears contemptuous of d'Indy's music. It is too bad for there are some beautiful things in the d'Indy *oeuvre.*

Two other French composers highly regarded in their day were Édouard Lalo (1823–1892) and Paul Dukas (1865–1935). Lalo still lives through his *Symphonie Espagnole* (1878) for violin and orchestra; and his opera, *Le Roi d'Ys* (1888), can still be heard in Paris. It is a much more forward-looking work than anything by Massenet and Gounod, and so is Dukas's *Ariane et Barbe-Bleue* (1907), a fascinating amalgam of Wagner and Debussy. Unfortunately Dukas is best-known by a potboiler, *The Sorcerer's Apprentice* (1897), while his fine C major Symphony (1896), his monumental Piano Sonata in E flat minor (1901), and his once-popular "*poème dansé,*" *La Péri* (1910), languish in near total neglect.

The composer who was the antithesis of Franck, and the greatest in France between Berlioz and Debussy, was Gabriel Fauré, and this despite the fact that Fauré worked primarily in small forms. He ranks with the greatest of all song composers, and he also concentrated on piano and chamber music. Because he never wrote a symphony or concerto, and because his one opera, *Pénélope* (1913), has never held the stage, he is apt to be dismissed out of hand. But to dismiss him, as so many outside of France tend to do, as a purveyor of Gallic *Kitsch* is to dismiss one of the most supple, elegant, and refined of all composers.

Fauré was a musician who was constantly developing. At the beginning he wrote charming songs in the style of Gounod and exquisite piano pieces à la Chopin and Schumann. As he grew older there came a deepening introspection and a curious harmonic palette. A quality that might be described as austere mysticism—the reverse of the voluptuous mysticism of Franck—entered his music, and some of his final works, sparse and enigmatic, are real puzzlers. Yet as one studies and lives with such music as the Thirteenth Nocturne (1922), or the E minor Violin Sonata (1917), or the song cycle *La Chanson d'Eve* (1907–10), it is with respect that becomes admiration and love. The writing is extremely fastidious, the textures much more transparent than in the early works, the harmonies almost bleak. Fauré, as he neared the end of his long life, was striving for a new kind of expression.

Never was there a more un-German composer. Of all the French composers of his day, Fauré was the most successful in his ability to ignore the siren sounds emanating from Bayreuth. It follows that music lovers whose orientation is to the German classics and to the big sounds of German postromanticism are the ones who like Fauré the least. They think in terms of orthodox structure and developments, and condemn Fauré's music for not being "deeper" or "more profound"—for not being the very thing it tried so hard not to be. This attitude is like condemning Robert Herrick for not being John Donne, and it irritates Fauré's admirers. Norman Suckling, author of the standard biography of Fauré in English, puts it as follows: "His music is, for instance, so transparent that the lovers of the turgid have no option but to accuse him of a lack of profundity. This charge comes with particular readiness from those who in various other connections are desirous of perpetuating the legend of French frivolity and who will therefore assume without further proof that so typical a French thinker as Voltaire was more shallow than, say, Fichte, because his writings are so much more transparent . . ."

Fauré was born in Paniers on May 12, 1845, and died in Paris on November 4, 1924. Mendelssohn, Chopin, and Schumann were alive at his birth, and thus his life spanned early romanticism, the Wagnerian music drama, the postromanticism of Brahms and Mahler, the neoclassicism of Stravinsky, the atonalism and dodecaphony of Schoenberg, and even the emergence of Aaron Copland, whom he conceivably could have heard when the young American was studying with Nadia Boulanger (herself a Fauré pupil). Amid all this, Fauré went his own quiet way. In successive eras of music dramas, bang-bang Straussian tone poems and Stravinsky ballets, he wrote intimate music—quartets, quintets, songs, piano pieces with the nondescriptive titles of Impromptu, Barcarolle, Nocturne, Prélude.

One of the few important French composers not trained at the Conservatoire, Fauré instead studied at the École Niedermeyer. Among his teachers was Saint-Saëns, and Fauré later said that he owed *everything* to his older colleague. In those days, the middle 1850's, Saint-Saëns was one of the progressives, and he introduced his pupils to Wagner and Liszt as well as to Bach and Mozart. Later he supported Fauré with encouragement and help, finding jobs and publishers for him. Fauré probably had a better musical education at the Niedermeyer than he would have received at the Conservatoire, which was largely a factory for producing virtuosos and fashionable composers. Thanks to Saint-Saëns, Fauré was introduced to the whole range of music. It should be remembered that Saint-Saëns, probably the most fabulous musical mind in Europe, was not only a musician who could instantly play anything. He also was a musicologist long before the term came into use. He knew more about old music than any performing musician of the 1850's, and he also was a purist who insisted that the old music be played as written, without romantic interpolations. At the Conservatoire, this kind of musical culture was unknown. As Fauré later wrote, "In 1853 the masterpieces of J. S. Bach, which constituted our daily bread [at the Niedermeyer] had still not found their way into the organ class at the Conservatoire; and in the piano classes at the same Conservatoire, the students still labored at the performance of Herz concertos, while Adolphe Adam shed his brilliant light upon his composition class."

Fauré left the École Niedermeyer at the age of twenty, with first prizes in piano, organ, harmony, and composition He had already written a large number of songs and piano pieces. From 1866 to 1870 he was a church organist in Brittany. Then he returned to Paris to become organist at St.-Honoré. He fought in the Franco-Prussian War, returned to the Niedermeyer as professor of composition, became choirmaster and later organist at the Madeleine, and finally, in 1896, entered the Conservatoire as a professor of composition. Fauré had previously been suggested for the post, but it would have been over the dead body of the director, Ambroise Thomas, who considered Fauré a dangerous revolutionary. "If he is nominated, I will resign." When Thomas finally did resign, in 1896, Massenet, who was teaching composition at the Conservatoire, pulled every string he could to get the position. But he would not take it unless it was a lifetime appointment. The Ministry of Public Information, however, decided that in the future no Conservatoire director would receive an appointment for life. Théodore Dubois was appointed, Massenet resigned in disgust, and Fauré was chosen to take over Massenet's class. Through the years, Fauré turned out such distinguished composers as Charles Koechlin, Florent Schmitt, Louis Aubert, Raoul Laparra, Jean Roger-Ducasse, and Maurice Ravel. He became director of the Conservatoire in 1905 and remained its head until 1920.

Fauré ran the Conservatoire with a firm hand. The small, mild, innocuous-looking Fauré proved to be an excellent administrator and a man of firm opinion. As head of the Conservatoire he started to introduce some reforms, and was faced with a revolt. The conservative professors could not see why things should not be done as they had been done in Cherubini's time. Fauré calmly got rid of the dissenters one by one. So numerous were the resignations that it began to be said of Fauré that he "needed his daily cartload of victims, like Robespierre." Théodore Dubois, whom Fauré replaced as head of the Conservatoire, was among those who resigned. Dubois, a hack, had remained on the board of directors as professor emeritus. He sent in his letter of resignation because "M. Fauré was transforming the Conservatoire into a temple for the music of the future." Fauré replaced him with two musicians who knew what it was all about—d'Indy and Debussy

At the age of sixty-four Fauré received one of France's supreme accolades

—a seat in the *Institut*. It was at this time, too, that he helped organize the Société Musicale Indépendante (S.M.I.), set up in opposition to the Franck-d'Indy-dominated Société Musicale Nationale. Nevertheless Fauré and d'Indy remained friends. Then tragedy. Deafness set in, complicated by distortion of pitch. High frequencies sounded flat, low ones sharp. It must have been agony. Yet Fauré continued to compose, and some of his best music comes from that time. News of his affliction became public, and in 1920 he was asked to resign from the Conservatoire. Almost to the day of his death he continued to compose, finishing his string quartet (the only one he composed) in 1924. He took to his deathbed wondering if he had written anything of value. "What of my music will live?" Pause. "But, then, that is of little importance." Charles Koechlin, in his little monograph on Fauré, claims those were his last words.

One of the major influences on Fauré was Chopin. He had in common with Chopin a delicate sensibility applied to every note, and his music has much the same feeling of melodic inevitability, refinement, taste, unerring judgment, and impeccable workmanship. Heroics had no place in his music. His feeling for delicate applications of tone color was remarkable, and Debussy learned much from him here. Yet Fauré's music is essentially masculine, whereas Debussy leans toward the feminine—or at least epicene—side. Both were masters of the song but worked in different directions. Debussy's songs were influenced as much by Mussorgsky's ideas of language as by earlier French composers. He tried to achieve natural speech patterns, and his vocal lines are often declamatory. Fauré worked much more closely within the traditions of European song, and his vocal lines are singing lines rather than attempts to reproduce speech patterns. From his very first song, *Le papillon et la fleur*, it was clear that Fauré had a genius for setting notes to words. How many composers—even Schubert, even Duparc and Wolf—can boast of so rapturous a song as *Dans les ruines d'une abbaye*, or the intensity and luxuriance of a cycle like *La Bonne chanson*? He composed about a hundred songs, ending with a masterpiece, *L'Horizon chimérique*, written in 1922.

His piano music is lyric and elegant, and difficult to play. There is little in the way of flashy virtuosity (as in Chopin, the ornamentation is functional), but the spread of the writing, its linear complexity and wide range over the keyboard, take it away from the amateur pianist. Fauré sent his Ballade for piano and orchestra to Liszt, and Liszt—Franz Liszt, who could read anything at sight, who was so hospitable to new music—returned the score with a curt note, saying it was too difficult. Fauré's piano music follows the development of his other music. As the composer grew older, the writing became more austere, far removed from the spontaneous lyricism of his youth and early middle age. Some think that Fauré's late music is too intellectual, too bleak to "work" in the concert hall. And it is true that the part of Fauré predominantly in the repertoire consists of those works that predate the problematic later ones. These include the A major Violin Sonata of 1876 (a rapturous work, much finer than Franck's in the same key, and composed ten years earlier), the simple, beautiful Requiem (1887), the C minor Piano Quartet (1879); the *Dolly* Suite for piano duet (1896); the songs; and a handful of early nocturnes, barcaroles, and impromptus. Once in a while the Ballade (1881), turned down by Liszt, is heard. It is a smoothly organized piece, enchantingly lyric, with a neat climax and a good measure of Fauré's delicate poetry. It may or may not have been orchestrated by him. Fauré never made any secret of the fact that he hated to compose orchestral music and that he would assign pupils to do the instrumentation Charles Koechlin, for example, orchestrated the popular *Pelléas et Mélisande* Suite.

Can there be such a thing as being too sensitive? Fauré was a master whose delicately adjusted music lacks the grand gesture and excitement that could give it mass popularity. The word "Hellenic" is often used to describe his music. "Civilized sensibility" is another description commonly found. It is music that contains the essence of everything Gallic—form, grace, wit, logic, individuality, urbanity. It is music that has attracted a small but fanatic band of admirers; and those who love the music of Fauré love it as a private, cherished gift from one of the gentlest and most subtle of composers

✻ 7 ✻

Only for the Theater

GIACOMO PUCCINI

Toward the end of his life, Giacomo Antonio Domenico Michele Secondo Maria Puccini wrote to a friend: "Almighty God touched me with his little finger and said 'Write for the theater—mind, only for the theater. And I have obeyed the supreme command." With such compliance and talent did Puccini submit to the inevitable that he composed three of the most popular operas ever written, died worth an estimated four million dollars, had all the opportunity he desired to play poker and to decimate the duck population around his lodge at Torre del Lago, and indulge his passion for fast boats, fast motor cars, and fast women.

That, in essence, is the story of Puccini's life. (He did compose other things than operas, but they are few in number and of supreme unimportance.) He once described himself as "a mighty hunter of wild fowl, opera librettos and attractive women." He also is on record as saying, "Just think of it! If I hadn't hit on music I should never have been able to do anything in the world!" He took no great interest in politics and the world around him. He was not particularly interested in the musical scene or in young composers. Or old ones, for that matter. He was neither a conservative nor a revolutionary. He belonged to no musical clique. He was not representative of the verismo, life-as-it-really-is school that so attracted the Italian composers of the 1890's, though verismo elements appeared in some of his operas. Polytonality, neoclassicism, futurism, impressionism, dodecaphony—to all those calls to battle he was indifferent, though he had looked at the music of such modern classics as Debussy's *Pelléas et Mélisande* and Schoenberg's *Pierrot Lunaire*, and was ready to incorporate what he liked of the new school into his own music. If certain aspects of verismo interested him, he used them in *Tosca* and *Il Tabarro*. If he was struck by Debussy's use of the whole-tone scale, he used it in *La Fanciulla del West*. Normally this kind of plundering would lead to eclecticism, but Puccini was not an eclectic. His own style was too pungent, too much his very own Whatever he was, he was completely outside the intellectual trend of his time. Musically speaking, Puccini owed little to anybody, and that is one of the miracles about the composer of *La Bohème, Tosca,* and *Madama Butterfly*

Born in Lucca on December 22, 1858, the last (as it turned out) in the line of five generations of respected musicians, he naturally grew up under the shadow of Verdi, the dominant force of Italian music in the last half of the nineteenth century. It was not that other composers did not compete; there are a few foothills at the base of the Verdian mountain. In the 1870's and thereafter, a few composers did write operas that became repertory pieces. It is amazing how many of those composers became one-work men outside of their native country and even, to a large extent, within Italy. There was Boito, with the revised version of his *Mefistofele* in 1875 Amilcare Ponchielli (1854–1906) came out with *La Gioconda* in 1876, and it was the only one of his nine operas with staying power. Alfredo Catalani (1854–1893) was much talked about in his day, but his two major operas, *Loreley* (1880) and *La Wally* (1892), were swept away by Puccini and the verismists, and are seldom heard outside of Italy.

The new school of verismo composers appeared in the 1890's, and at least two works of stature were the result. The verismists aimed for realism, often putting their characters into contemporary dress, using plots that contained humble people rather than aristocrats, delighting in raw violence on stage, and describing the action and emotional moods in music of stark emotion. Pietro Mascagni (1863–1945) was the first, with *Cavalleria Rusticana* in 1890. Ruggiero Leoncavallo (1858–1945) followed with *I Pagliacci* in 1892. In 1896 came *Andrea Chénier* by Umberto Giordano (1867–1948). Though *Chénier* is set in the French Revolution, it has so many verismo elements in it that it is included in the school.

Verismo opera did not last much more than a decade, and most of the verismo composers are in effect one-work men, much as their predecessors had been. Mascagni never wrote another opera anywhere near as popular as *Cavalleria Rusticana,* though *L'Amico Fritz* (1891) has some lovely things in it, and the "Cherry Duet" from that opera is pure gold from beginning to end. Similarly, Leoncavallo was never able to repeat the success of *Pagliacci,* even if his *Zazà* had a run for some years. Another one-work composer was Francesco Cilèa (1866–1950), whose *Adriana Lecouvreur* had its premiere in 1902. Modern taste tends to dismiss verismo opera as too hysterical and melodramatic, though it must be said that *Cavalleria Rusticana* and *Pagliacci* show no signs of any decrease in popularity.

Puccini grew up in this period but was singularly untouched by it. In his music is relatively little of the verismo blood and thunder. Nor is there any Verdi (except in the *Falstaff*-derived *Gianni Schicchi*), and there is no Wagner at all Somewhere. somehow, he evolved a personal, inimitable style that stands out among the Italian operas of his time like the song of a nightingale in a flock of starlings. The only composer of the day whose music could faintly be described as comparable was Massenet; and in a way Puccini is an Italian Massenet, though one with a greater feeling for drama and a superior melodic impulse Most of the Puccini operas have workable librettos, and he was fanatically concerned with the legitimacy of dramatic situation. But that is not what the Puccini operas stand for. Song, tender and sensuous song, is what Puccini offers Melody came naturally to him, and in this he may be called an instinctive composer, for everything in composition can be taught except how to create an immortal melody. Puccini may have been poor in fugue but he was rich in expressive melody, the thing that is basic to an opera composer Rosa Raisa, the great dramatic soprano who created the role of Turandot, said that after decades of singing Puccini and listening to his operas, she invariably came away deeply touched "At *Bohème* I start crying in the third act."

The Puccini operas may be naïve. and musicians have also accused them of pandering to a listener's baser instincts There is no denying that many Puccini operas are frank tearjerkers, and those who regard music as an art of spiritual betterment reject them out of hand. Their attitude can be expressed by Arnold Schoenberg's remark that "there are higher and lower means, artistic and inartistic. Realistic, violent incidents—as for example the torture scene in *Tosca* which are unfailingly effective should not be used by an artist, because they are too cheap, too accessible to everybody." Anybody who so desires can poke holes through any Puccini opera except, perhaps, the perfectly organized *Bohème* or *Gianni Schicchi* (and even there, in *Schicchi*, some critics pick on the pretty aria, *O mio babbino caro*, as a blot on an otherwise tight piece of operatic construction). The last acts of the Puccini operas are likely to be weak, and full of reprise melodies; and all of the operas have tunes so obvious and so sweet that they make some listeners gag. There are those who abominate the Puccini operas, and can cite all kinds of valid reasons why they should be abolished. None of this seems to matter in the least Puccini hit something that has made audiences strongly react, and he remains one of the most popular of all composers. He achieved his success through melody, plus a compositional technique that was more sophisticated than he is commonly given credit for

In addition to responding to Puccini's melody, audiences also respond to his characters, especially his heroines. Puccini always was much more convincing in his female characters than in his male ones. Puccini identified with women Mosco Carner, one of his biographers, puts it perfectly when he writes that "while the ground-bass of Verdi's operas is a battle cry, of Puccini's it is a mating call" Audiences, too, still respond to the Puccini li brettos, which are on broad lines and deal with elementals—love, hate, separation, death. The same could be said of the Verdi librettos, but Puccini's do aspire to, and on the whole achieve, a superior literary level (Verdi's *Otello* and *Falstaff* always excepted). Puccini would never get into the tortured complexities of a libretto like *Don Carlo* or *Simon Boccanegra*. His are straightforward, easy to follow, and peopled with characters who face problems that arouse an empathic reaction in all audiences. It may be hokum, but it is *nice* hokum: a dreamworld that never existed, in which emotions are expertly manipulated by composer and librettist. The four young men in *La Bohème* are the archetypes of all creative young men who ever shared a garret and dreamed their great dreams. (Some of this is autobiographical. As a student in Milan, Puccini shared a room with Mascagni. They lived *la vie de bohème*, eating on credit at the *Aïda* Restaurant, and protecting each other from creditors. Puccini even pawned a coat, as Colline does in *Bohème*; only Puccini needed the money to take a ballet girl out for a night on the town.) Cio-Cio-San stands for all women who have loved unselfishly. Mimì, the sweet but not too bright girl who finds herself entangled in a love affair that can only end in unhappiness, is intensely human in her way. And the flamboyant Tosca, that mixture of temperament, passion, and jealousy (she, like Cio-Cio-San and Mimì, is not a very bright girl, either), remains eternally interesting and provocative. Puccini, who knew women so well, seldom created a papier-mâché figure. His women are all too human.

Despite the great care Puccini lavished on detail, and despite his musical craftsmanship and sense of the theater, he was one of the most unintellectual composers who ever lived. Thus it is not astonishing that many learned musicians rail and shake their fingers at the stupid public that continues to support such "trash." A charter member of the Let's-Hate-Puccini Club was Fausto Torrefranca who, in 1912, prophesied that Puccini would be forgotten in a few decades. Puccini, wrote Torrefranca, was "decadent," a "manipulator" rather than a composer. And so on down to Joseph Kerman in 1956, who called *Tosca* a "shabby little shocker" and who insists that *Turandot* is more depraved even than *Tosca*, and that in general the operas of Puccini are "false through and through." The more intellectual the critic, the more he is apt to despise Puccini.

Yet the operas have if anything increased in popularity through the years. A season at a major opera house without the big three Puccini works—*Bohème*, *Tosca*, *Butterfly*—is most unusual. *Turandot* and *Manon Lescaut* are coming into their own, and even the once-despised *La Fanciulla del West* (*Girl of the Golden West*) is attracting attention again. *Gianni Schicchi*, one of the funniest operas ever written—what a shame Puccini so seldom exploited his talent for comedy!—is a repertory piece, and the dark-colored *Il Tabarro*, another of the three one-act operas of *Il Trittico* (the others are *Schicchi* and the relatively weak *Suor Angelica*), is a moody, gripping work. It is Puccini's only excursion into out-and-out verismo. Of the other Puccini operas, *Le Villi* and *Edgar* are prentice works, and *La Rondine* is seldom heard. *La Rondine*, commissioned by Vienna, is a bittersweet operetta and probably will be rediscovered. *Turandot* is his last and most massive, ambitious opera and invariably makes a thrilling effect if the soprano and tenor have enough voice.

When Puccini was born, it was expected that he would turn out to be a composer. Puccinis had been musicians and church organists in Lucca since 1712. But young Giacomo was anything but a prodigy. His teachers at the seminary were exasperated by his laziness. "He comes to school only to wear out the seat of his pants," one teacher reported. Anyway, he showed enough talent to be sent to the Milan Conservatory as a scholarship student. There his principal teacher was Ponchielli. Puccini's first success, *Le Villi* (1884), brought him to the attention of Giulio Ricordi, head of the famous publishing firm founded in 1808. Giulio stuck with Puccini through everything, and never made a better investment After the failure of *Edgar* in 1889 and the moderate success of *Manon Lescaut* in 1893, Puccini came up with *La Bohème* in 1896 and he became rich, Ricordi even richer Ricordi deserved it, for it was he who had subsidized Puccini through the lean years, and it was he who was always battling away at Puccini's laziness. During the composition of every opera, Giulio (and, after Giulio died, his son Tito) would write desperate letters: "The hunting season has begun. Go easy, Puccini! Don't let your passion for the birds seduce you away from music!"

Puccini married Elvira Gemignani in 1904 after having lived with her for many years. She, a married woman, had eloped with him from Lucca to Milan, and Puccini married her after the death of her husband. They were violently in love at the beginning. Later they had violent quarrels and split up for a time. That was during the Doria Manfredi incident. Doria was a servant at the lodge in Torre del Lago, near Florence, and Elvira got the idea that there was an affair between her and Puccini. She made the matter public, hurled all kinds of accusations at Doria, and hounded the poor girl to death. Doria poisoned herself. An autopsy revealed she was a virgin. Puccini rushed to Rome, locked himself up in a hotel room, and spent days weeping. For having driven Doria to suicide, Elvira was sentenced to five months' imprisonment "What a theme for an opera!" all Italy said. Eventually Puccini returned to Elvira, but it is doubtful if he ever again was close to her.

From all accounts, Elvira was not an interesting woman The baritone Titta Ruffo said that her jealousy was "near to lunacy." Musicians who worked with Puccini and were his friends always have been singularly loath to discuss her. One of Puccini's associates described her merely as "not a very literate woman." Another remembered her as "a heavy-set, rather dour sort of person who looked more Teutonic than Latin." She was in every way different from Puccini. As he grew older he became more handsome and urbane, more interesting to women—a fastidious dresser, fairly tall, aristocratic-looking, with an oval face, carefully trimmed moustache, heavily lidded eyes, and sensual lips. The man was a fashion plate, and on his first visit to America in 1907 he made a big impression on reporters used to the leonine thatches of a Paderewski or Gabrilowitsch. Here was a musician who actually had his hair cut. Puccini himself had slighting references to make about musicians "who think they have to have dandruff to be geniuses." Elvira, on the other hand, was dowdy, never a social success, and never helped her husband develop intellectually or emotionally. Had Puccini married the right sort of woman, many believe, he would have developed along more mature lines and perhaps might have lived longer (he died in Brussels on November 29, 1924, while being treated for throat cancer, undoubtedly caused by his excessive smoking, a nervous habit). Certainly he would not have found it so necessary to drift from the arms of one woman to another.

Many also think that it was because of Elvira that Puccini had so few—if any—close friends. Puccini was never close to anybody. Even his love affairs were concerned more with sex than with love. For a while Puccini was on good terms with Arturo Toscanini, who had conducted the *Bohème* premiere in 1896. It was a relationship that blew hot and cold. Giorgio Polacco, the conductor, liked to tell the story about the *pannetone* Puccini sent Toscanini one Christmas during a period of cold war. He suddenly realized that they were not on speaking terms at the moment, and wired Toscanini: PANNETONE SENT BY MISTAKE. PUCCINI. The next day he got an answer: PANNETONE EATEN BY MISTAKE. TOSCANINI.

On the whole, Puccini's life was uneventful. He brought out his operas at regularly spaced intervals, he kept his private life to himself (aside from the Manfredi incident his name never figured in any scandal), and he rarely spoke to reporters. Even in the United States, where reporters were continually besieging him, he had little to say, and desperate newspapermen could come up only with news instead of feature stories about the popular composer. They had fun with him on his departure for Italy on the *Lusitania* in 1910. Giulio Gatti-Casazza, the director of the Metropolitan Opera, and many of the singers saw him off. An army of reporters was present, and this is how the man from the *Telegraph* described the leave-taking. Italian emotionalism always tickled the American press:

> . . . In a body the Met group charged on Puccini. Like a brave man he met them with arms extended and lips pouted.
> A sound like somebody taking off a pair of wet galoshes in a hurry.

374

That was Gatti-Casazza's double kiss, one for each cheek of Puccini.

A sound like Bossie the Brindle pulling her hind foot out of the mud!

That was Amato's fervent salute.

A sound like somebody stropping a razor rapidly!

That was Scotti the basso putting seven or eight quick ones over

And so on for many more paragraphs.

Just as there was little for newspapermen to write about Puccini the man, so there was little for them to write about Puccini's music. His operas did not come in on clouds of controversy, as Wagner's did, and as *Salome* did in 1905. Most were immediate, secure successes, and the only failure was the world premiere of *Madama Butterfly* at Milan. Puccini quickly rewrote it, and success followed. Aside from *Il Tabarro* and *Gianni Schicchi*, his operas are pretty much of a piece. There is surprisingly little essential difference between *Bohème* of 1896 and *Turandot* of 1924, even if the latter is broader and somewhat more complex harmonically. Puccini's highly emotional and dramatically transparent works for the stage are in their way as cynical as Massenet's. Puccini knew very well how to stir the emotions of his audience, and he unabashedly did so. At least he was skillful enough to apply the same formulas without falling into self-parody. The operas that break the mold are *Il Tabarro*, with its sounds of the river, its *Cavalleria Rusticana* type of raw emotion and its verismo effects, and above all, the brilliant and scintillating *Gianni Schicchi*. There he composed an opera that is to his output what *Falstaff* is to Verdi's—a comic opera with very few set pieces, completely nonsentimental; an opera in which the orchestra comments on the action; an opera with a bubbling kind of gaiety that pokes affectionate fun at man and his works. It is as Italian as *Die Meistersinger* is German, and it carries its point in a fifth of the time. It is a marvelous work, but Puccini never again attempted anything like it. Instead he turned to grand opera. In *Turandot* he was going to evoke the Orientalisms of *Madama Butterfly*, but on an immense scale.

He died before finishing the last act. At the time of his death Puccini was discouraged. Opera, to him, had taken the wrong turning, and he could see no future. "By now the public for new music has lost its palate," he wrote in 1922. "It loves or puts up with illogical music devoid of all sense. Melody is no longer practiced—or if it is, it is vulgar. People believe the symphonic element must rule, and I, instead, believe this is the end of opera." He may have been right. *Turandot* is the last opera to be a steady repertory piece. The operas of Berg and Janáček are admired, but not by the public at large; the operas of Strauss composed after *Rosenkavalier* in 1911 have only a small following; the operas of Benjamin Britten—and, indeed, of every post-Puccini composer—have not been able to establish themselves

Turandot is the last of the operas that the public unreservedly loves.

Only the final pages were left incomplete, and the opera was finished by Franco Alfano. At the world premiere at La Scala, on April 25, 1926, Toscanini turned to the audience during the third act and said, "Here the master laid down his pen." There has been some difference of opinion as to whether or not Toscanini continued the performance. Rosa Raisa in 1959 put an end to the controversy by stating that Toscanini did not go on with the opera. Not until the second performance did he conduct Alfano's ending.

Neither a fast nor a prolific composer, Puccini took much time over his operas. Had he found suitable librettos he would have composed more. He considered many librettos and even started work on a few before discarding them. He kept nagging his friends to keep an eye out for suitable material, saying that he could not work if the libretto did not inspire him. While composing an opera, he spent much time on its historical and geographical background. His sense of theater and his passion for exactitude were much admired by singers who worked with him. "With Puccini, it's drama, drama, drama," said Rosa Ponselle. To Raisa, the essence of Puccini was "drama, accompanied by music." To make his dramas authentic, Puccini carefully checked every historic, physical, and psychological point of the libretto. As he wrote to Ricordi in 1899, "You know how scrupulous I am in interpreting the situation or the words and all that is of importance before putting anything down on paper." Working on *Tosca* he wrote to Father Pietro Panchelli, "In order to accentuate the contrast between the filthy desires of Scarpia and the mysterious atmosphere of the place, there should be a great Te Deum. Now, please let me know the exact tone of the church bells in the neighborhood of Castel Sant' Angelo and the exact tone of the big bell at St. Peter's." For *Butterfly* he studied Japanese music, had records made in Japan and sent to him, and did his best "to make B. F. Pinkerton sing like an American," whatever that may mean. For *La Fanciulla del West* he went through much early American popular and folk song "in order to get the atmosphere."

Nothing escaped his notice in his search for realism. Lucrezia Bori has told of the time she was notified by Ricordi that three gentlemen would be coming to Paris to hear her sing, and would she learn a few arias from *Manon Lescaut?* She did, and one day the three gentlemen presented themselves. They were Gatti-Casazza, Toscanini, and Puccini. "They looked at me from head to foot, and then from foot to head," Bori said. "They looked at me thoroughly." They must have been satisfied with what they saw and heard, for presently Bori was rehearsing *Manon Lescaut* with Caruso. She sang the role for the first time as a guest artist with the Metropolitan Opera, then, in 1910, touring Europe.

"I had new costumes made in Paris," Bori said. "They cost me a fortune.

You can imagine. After the dress rehearsal everybody came around to congratulate me. Soon Puccini came up, holding a cup of coffee. 'Bori,' he said, 'everything was perfect. Only in the last act, where Manon is starving and penniless, your costume is too clean.' So he threw the coffee on my gown.'

Working with singers, Puccini could be very demanding, but he never really lost his temper. When Edward Johnson sang the leading tenor roles in *Gianni Schicchi* and *Tabarro*, he coached with the composer. "He was worried about me," said Johnson. "After all, I was a foreigner." (Johnson was a Canadian-born singer who eventually became general manager of the Metropolitan Opera.) "When I rehearsed the *Tabarro* duet with the soprano, he couldn't get the quality of sound that suited him. Time after time he would make us change the key, always searching for added intensity." At the Rome premiere of *Il Trittico* the audience screamed for the composer. Johnson remembered the occasion very well. "He came backstage and we artists all rushed up to him. He got us all to line up and then he looked at me and said, '*Tira! Tira!*' meaning that he wanted us to drag him 'reluctantly' from the wings.'

Maria Jeritza was his favorite Tosca, and when she worked with him for the Viennese premiere she became worried because she was a blonde. Tosca in the opera is described as a brunette, and blonde sopranos wear wigs to be faithful to the role. Jeritza, proud of her blonde hair, hated to wear a wig. "Madame," Puccini said gallantly, "there are blondes in Italy, and they are the most beautiful women in the world." It was Jeritza, by the way, who started the tradition of singing *Vissi d'arte* flat on the floor. She claimed, in an interview given in 1926, that during the rehearsal the baritone accidentally pushed her off the sofa, and she did not have time to get up. "Never do it any other way!" shouted Puccini from the auditorium. "It was from God!"

Jeritza echoed all singers' remarks about Puccini's patience but firmness. "He would never take no for an answer. If a phrase had to be taken in one breath, he would keep me working on it until he got what he wanted." In Jeritza's opinion, Puccini knew more about the voice than most voice teachers, and while he might ask for difficult things, he never demanded the impossible. "He helped me technically. He also could insult you in the most gentlemanly way. We went over the music step by step, phrase by phrase. He molded me. I was his *creation*. Sometimes he would make me so angry I wanted to cry. Then he would get angry. 'Jeritza,' he would say, 'if I ever wake you at three in the morning and ask you to sing a high C, you *will* sing a high C!' "

Puccini also told Jeritza one thing she never forgot. To her, it summed up his entire musical philosophy.

"*Carissima mia*," he said to her, "you have to walk on clouds of melody."

Romanticism's Long Coda

RICHARD STRAUSS

From 1888, when *Don Juan* had its premiere, to 1911, when *Der Rosenka-valier* was staged, the most-discussed man of European music was Richard Strauss. His symphonic poems were considered the last word in shocking modernism and his *Salome* in 1905 and *Elektra* in 1909 caused riots and scandals. It was to be expected that the conservatives should dislike Strauss's new music. Saint-Saëns would have disappointed the world had he not waggled his beard and delivered a pronouncement: "The desire to push works of art beyond the realm of art means simply to drive them into the realm of folly. Richard Strauss is in the process of showing us the road." But, it was noted, even those allied to the progressives had nasty things to say. Gian-Francesco Malipiero in Italy, who should have automatically sided with Strauss's new "music of the future," curtly dismissed Strauss as "the Meyer-beer of the twentieth century." Gustav Mahler, on the other hand, called *Salome* a work of genius. Fauré, levelheaded as always, had some perspicacious things to say about the controversial opera. *Salome*, he decided, was a symphonic poem with vocal parts added, but: "Atmosphere and color are portrayed in their finest nuances, all by means of mediocre themes, it is true, but developed, worked, interwoven with such marvellous skill, that their intrinsic interest is exceeded by the magic of an orchestral technique of real genius, until these themes—mediocre, as I say—end by acquiring character, power and almost emotion." Strauss's brilliant orchestration bowled over his contemporaries. Dukas, on hearing *Salome*, said that he thought he knew something about the orchestra but now realized how much he had to learn.

To the public Strauss was The World's Greatest Composer and, incidentally, one of the world's great conductors. Everything he wrote received instant newspaper coverage the world over. What would he come up with next? For every new work was more sensational than the last. *Don Juan* had been succeeded by even more detailed story-telling tone poems, by bigger and bigger effects, by orchestras that grew in size until, in 1904, America heard the *Sinfonia Domestica*, which demanded the mightiest aggregation of players since Berlioz and his ideal orchestra. Sensation: that was the word for Strauss. An aura of sensation surrounded the slim, tall man and his outrageous music. Not only did he use a bigger orchestra than anybody else had used, not only was he the supreme master of that orchestra, he also wrote music that sounded excruciatingly dissonant. He told stories in his music, and you could hear the bleating of sheep or the sound of wind. More: the man undoubtedly was immoral. Who but a man of dubious morality would have set to music a text by Oscar Wilde, that British fellow who . . . you know . . . *Salome* in 1907 received a single performance at the Metropolitan Opera; the public outcry was such that the directors retreated pell-mell, removing it instantly from the boards. The New York reviewers were appalled. Lawrence Gilman, trembling with rage, wrote that he had been bored (an old critical ploy; when a reviewer is shocked to the very base of his fundament he can demonstrate his sophistication by saying he was bored). Henry Krehbiel called *Salome* a "moral stench." There were Letters to the Editor: "Are we to have our women, our children—sons and daughters—witness the spectacle?" In a newspaper headline in New York, *Salome* was called a "Loathsome Opera." The Baptists went on record as registering disapproval, as did the Archbishop of Vienna. Kaiser Wilhelm II of Germany, whose musical tastes ran more to Strauss (Johann) than Strauss (Richard), said he was sorry that Strauss had composed *Salome*. "I really like the fellow, but this will do him a lot of damage." The damage, Strauss noted many years later, "enabled me to build the villa at Garmisch."

Everything he did up until the time of *Der Rosenkavalier* seemed to make newspaper copy. It was not that he was eccentric. He was anything but. He was a good, solid, German bourgeois type, happily married, and never was there the least hint of scandal in his private life. Strauss would not have dared to have an affair. He was afraid of his wife, Pauline. Never was there a more henpecked husband. Perhaps it was this very lack of color that interested the public. It was hard to reconcile the wildness of the music with the sobriety of the man. When he unleashed the storms while conducting his own music he used a tiny beat and few motions; and critics could not get over the flamboyance of the music contrasted with the restraint of his gestures. Or perhaps it was that, like Puccini, he was of the new breed of composers who cut their hair short and dressed conservatively. The man who wrote such "modernistic" music looked like a banker.

Reporters and editors also seemed enchanted by the fact that great sums of money could be made from such music. When Strauss toured America in 1904, the Cleveland *Plain Dealer* ran a long article about Strauss's fees and royalties, figuring out that his income was at least $60,000 a year "and in five years he hopes to double that figure." The American magazine *The Theatre* reported in 1909 that "Richard Strauss is making so much money with his operas that he is likely to become the richest composer who ever lived." It was known that Strauss drove a hard bargain and liked the sound of crisp money as much as the sound of crisp strings. Alma Mahler sat with Strauss at the rehearsal of *Feuersnot* in 1901 "Strauss thought of nothing but money." she wrote in her diary. "The whole time he had a pencil in his hand and was calculating the profits to the last penny." In New York he gave two concerts in Wanamaker's Department Store, and the American press (also such stuffier American colleagues as Walter Damrosch) carried on in such a manner that one would have thought Strauss had given the concerts in a public comfort station The art of music was forever soiled, they implied

Strauss was unperturbed. There is nothing wrong for an artist to earn money for his wife and child, he said, pocketing his $1000 fee. It was not that he was mercenary, he told a reporter. He merely wanted to make enough to live comfortably for the rest of his days. The reporter did not ask him what he considered enough. Stories about Strauss's cupidity were constantly making the rounds. Strauss (so went one story) goes to Dresden for a *Salome* rehearsal On his return to Berlin he is met at the station by his son. "Papa, how much did you get for the rehearsal?" Strauss, weeping tears of joy, enfolds the boy. "Now I know you are a true son of mine."

The more serious, dedicated musicians of the day were disturbed, if not revolted, by Strauss's money-mania, and Fritz Busch, the eminent conductor, who knew Strauss well, hints as much in his autobiography: "The puzzle of Strauss, who in spite of his marvellous talents is not really penetrated and possessed by them like other great artists, but in fact simply wears them like a suit of clothes which can be taken off at will—this puzzle neither I nor anybody else has yet succeeded in solving: his decided inclination towards material things; and with his complete disinclination to any sacrifice, the sworn enemy of social change." Hans Knappertsbusch, another conductor, put it much more bluntly: "He was a pig."

Strauss's shrewd financial manipulations never failed to fascinate the New York press, which kept the public informed of all the composer's dealings. When *Der Rosenkavalier* had its Metropolitan Opera premiere, the New York *Sun* of December 8, 1913, broke the news that "the Metropolitan is said to be paying $1,500 a night or thereabouts for 'Rose Cavalier' in order to soothe the wounded feelings of Strauss after the affair of 'Salome' here. This is ten times what used to be paid for the most popular works of Puccini." Everybody in the world wanted to know the most intimate details, financial or otherwise, about The World's Greatest Composer or, as one newspaper put it, The Musical Man of the Hour.

And if nothing could be found for an article on Strauss, there always was good copy in his wife, Pauline. She was a grasping, strong, determined woman, once a singer, who went through life without thinking much about other people's feelings, least of all her husband's. She was a legend. For some reason, Strauss contentedly put up with her tantrums. He told the Viennese critic Max Graf that as a young man he had a tendency to dissipate and make nothing of himself. Pauline cured him of that. "Richard, go compose!" she would scream, and Strauss would shrug his shoulders, leave his game of skat (his favorite pastime), and go to the workroom. She had him well trained. Deems Taylor, the American composer-critic, once interviewed him at Garmisch. Before Strauss walked into the house, "he paused and wiped his feet carefully on a small square of dampened doormat that lay before the door. Advancing a step, he wiped his feet once more, this time upon a dry doormat. Stepping across the doorsill he wiped his feet for a third and final time upon a small rubber doormat that lay just inside the door."

Up through *Der Rosenkavalier* Strauss was a composer who generated a constant atmosphere of excitement and electricity. After *Der Rosenkavalier* something happened. Some critics consider all of Strauss's post-*Rosenkavalier* works a regression: pallid, repetitive music in which years of skill were operating from sheer habit. "A composer of talent who once was a genius," snorted Ernest Newman. Others insist that once having rid himself of the superficial sensationalism of the symphonic poems, Strauss started to compose the long series of operas that culminated in the "masterly" and "autumnal" and "profound" works of his old age. Strauss himself later indicated that in *Salome* (1905) and *Elektra* (1908) he had come too close to the Pit for comfort and hastily withdrew: "Both operas are unique in my life's works. In them I penetrated to the uttermost limits of harmony, psychological polyphony (Klytemnestra's dream), and of the receptivity of modern ears." The public reaction to Strauss's work after *Der Rosenkavalier*—and also the reaction of most of Strauss's colleagues—were in line with Newman's estimate of genius succeeded by talent. Strauss had existed as a sensationalist, successively topping one work with something even more *outré*. When he could not surpass any of his previous works in daring and sensationalism, there was an unprecedented falling-off in public response. No longer was the premiere of a Strauss opera an international event. The operas were politely received and no more; never again was there the excitement and brouhaha there used to be. Through the years after 1911 Strauss doggedly continued to compose much the same kind of opera, and his colleagues could not have cared less. To them, *Salome* and *Elektra* were the end of the line as far as Strauss was concerned. There were new heroes in international music—Prokofiev, Bartók, and especially Stravinsky. There was also much talk about Arnold Schoenberg, whose music made Strauss's once-revolutionary scores sound old-fashioned.

Richard Strauss was born in Munich on June 11 1864. His father, a peppery, opinionated, outspoken man, was the most celebrated horn player in Germany, and also a composer who thought that Wagner was subversive and that no true music had been written since Mendelssohn and Schumann. Franz Strauss was the horn player in the orchestra of the Munich opera, and had participated in the world premieres of *Tristan und Isolde* and *Die Meistersinger*. He was always getting into fights with Hans von Bülow and with Wagner himself. Franz simply loathed the horn parts of the Wagner operas, but he played them so beautifully that Wagner ignored his biting asides about the music. There must have been red hot moments when the martinet Bülow, the most dyspeptic conductor of his day, tangled with the fiercely independent Franz Strauss. One argument ended with Bülow telling Strauss to go and apply for his pension Strauss promptly packed his instrument and did exactly that, "because Herr von Bülow has so ordered." The incident was patched up. Some years later, when Bülow and the young Richard Strauss were working together, Bülow and Franz actually became friends.

Richard inherited his father's musical instincts. He was playing the piano at four and a half, the violin shortly afterward, and was composing at six. Franz Strauss kept his son on a very conservative musical diet, and the result was apparent in Richard's juvenile compositions. They were skillful, but they represented the early part of the nineteenth century. Richard could have been a touring prodigy *à la* Mozart, but his father kept him in Munich and put him into the *Gymnasium*, where the boy received a good general education. There was no rush. It was taken for granted in the Strauss family that Richard would be a musician, but all in good time. From the Gymnasium, Strauss in 1882 went to the University of Munich (he took some courses but never worked for a degree) and then spent some time in Berlin, making the rounds, playing the piano at musical parties. In 1884 Strauss met Bülow in Berlin, and the young composer's Serenade for Winds in E flat (Op. 7) was programmed by Bülow's Meiningen Orchestra. Bülow himself did not conduct; the assistant conductor took over and Bülow sat in the audience, vigorously applauding. So pleased was Bülow with the score that he asked Strauss to compose another like it. The result was the Suite for Winds in B flat (Op. 4). The score was rehearsed by Bülow in Meiningen but, in a pleasant gesture to the talented young composer, Bülow decided that the world premiere should take place in Strauss's own city, Munich. He also suggested that Strauss himself be the conductor. When Bülow "suggested," everybody obeyed. Up to then, Strauss had never held a baton in his hand, but conduct he did—in a state of shock, as he remembered in later years. All he knew was that he had committed no major blunders. After the performance, Franz Strauss thanked Bülow, and the famous conductor exploded in a typically Bülovian outburst: "You have nothing to thank me for. I have not forgotten what you did to me in this damned city of Munich. What I did today I did because your son has talent, and not for you." Suddenly, Strauss wrote in his little memoir about Bülow, "Bülow was in the best of spirits." His nasty remarks had soothed his bad humor and now he was happy.

The approval of so majestic a potentate as Bülow was enough to start Strauss on a promising career. Bülow even saw enough in Strauss to appoint him his assistant at Meiningen in 1885, and, at his debut, Strauss conducted his own F minor Symphony. He was well on his way—but as an academic composer.

The break in this continuity came with acquaintance with Alexander Ritter, a violinist in the Meiningen Orchestra. Ritter had known Wagner and had married Wagner's niece, Franziska. It was Ritter who introduced Strauss to the music of Berlioz, Liszt, and Wagner; who explained what The Music of the Future was all about; who encouraged Strauss to look for new ways of writing. That did not come immediately. The young composer wrote a Brahmsian Piano Quartet in C minor, and concentrated on perfecting his craft as a conductor. When Bülow resigned from Meiningen in November, 1885, Strauss was in sole charge of the orchestra. He finished out the season, went to Italy, returned to Munich, and composed a symphony called *Aus Italien*. The last movement caused great excitement at the premiere in 1887, and there were boos and cheers. Strauss did not worry about the opposition. "I now comfort myself with the knowledge that I am on the road I want to take, fully conscious that there never has been an artist not considered crazy by thousands of his fellow men." But he had not yet found himself, though the wild orchestration of the last movement of *Aus Italien*, in which Strauss quoted Luigi Denza's *Funiculì Funiculà* (under the impression it was a genuine folk song), gives more than a hint of the brilliance that was to come.

Strauss went to the Munich Opera in 1886 as third conductor. Meanwhile, during this period in his life, he continued to compose traditional works. One was the attractive *Burlesque* for Piano and Orchestra (1885). Another was the E flat Violin Sonata (1887)—charming, stylish, even masterly, but still essentially music of the past. In 1886 Strauss met Pauline de Ahna, the soprano he was to marry. She had sung in Munich several times under his direction, and the story goes that they had a violent argument at a rehearsal. Strauss disappeared into her dressing room, and they emerged with an announcement that they were engaged. Pauline was the daughter of a general, and she never let anybody forget that there was noble blood in *her* family. She always looked down at the Strausses and the bourgeois background they represented. Strauss's mother. Josephine Pschorr came from a wealthy family of brewers (Pschorr beer is still one of the popular brands in Munich). *Brewers!* Strauss's love for Pauline showed itself in the series of songs he composed specifically for her, and which she sang in public with him at the piano. One of those songs, the *Ständchen* of 1866, has remained among the most popular in the repertoire. Strauss continued to write songs all his life, and the world would be considerably poorer without such beautiful pieces of music as *Ruhe, meine seele; Cäcilie; Heimliche Aufforderung; Morgen; Freundliche Vision; Traum durch die Dämmerung* and—to many, the most beautiful of all--the four songs for voice and orchestra he composed in 1948. known as the *Vier letzte Lieder* or *Four Last Songs*.

The first major break in Strauss's music came in 1889, with the tone poem *Don Juan*. Everybody in Europe was writing symphonic poems. The symphonic poem was to the late romantic period what the concerto grosso had been to the baroque. There was prevalent unhappiness with symphonic form among the avant-garde. Beethoven, many felt, had said all there was to say, and had done all there was to do, with the symphony. One way around the problem was an extension of the Lisztian symphonic poem, and in Strauss the right man appeared to do it. On November 11. 1889, *Don Juan* received its premiere in Weimar, and a new force had arrived.

Don Juan was the score that made everybody recognize Strauss as Liszt's natural successor. and, to a point, Wagner's. The score required an orchestra of unprecedented size, handled with unprecedented virtuosity. Its melodic material, with its wide span and unexpected leaps, was something new. And although the work was tied to a specific literary program, the music was yet inventive enough and had enough structural integrity (free sonata form) to stand up as absolute music. *Don Juan* was followed by a series of symphonic poems that set all Europe on its ear: *Tod und Verklärung* in 1890 (the dates are the premieres, not the dates of composition), *Till Eulenspiegels lustige Streiche* in 1895, *Also sprach Zarathustra* in 1896, *Don Quixote* in 1898, *Ein Heldenleben* in 1899, the *Sinfonia Domestica* in 1904. *Eine Alpensinfonie* in 1915 was the last, and a failure. Each of these symphonic poems was progressively bigger and more sensational. It may also be that their musical worth is in inverse ratio to their size and dates of composition. A poll of musicians would probably show that the first four are the most highly regarded.

All of these scores derived basically from Liszt. But whereas the Liszt symphonic poems deal with very generalized programs, Strauss wrote explicit descriptive music: the labored breathing of a dying man, the trial of Till

Eulenspiegel, the hero in *Ein Heldenleben* fighting with his critics, the sun rising in *Zarathustra*, Don Quixote charging the windmill, and so on. His symphonic poems began to get more and more detailed, and the headline in a New York paper of 1904 about the *Sinfonia Domestica* was not far off the mark: "Home Sweet Home as Written by Richard Strauss—Pappa and Momma and Baby Celebrated in Huge Conglomeration of Orchestral Music." Strauss was on the defensive about the *Domestica*, and he wrote about it with characteristic lack of humor:

The symphony is meant to give a musical picture of married life. I know that some people believe the work is a jocular exposé of happiness in the home, but I own that I did not mean to make fun when I composed it. What can be more serious a matter than married life? Marriage is the most serious happening in life, and the holy joy over such a union is intensified through the arrival of a child. Yet life has naturally got its funny side, and this I have also introduced into the work in order to enliven it. But I want the symphony to be taken seriously, and it has been played in this spirit in Germany.

Strauss always blew hot and cold about the importance of the program in his symphonic poems. He supplied detailed scenarios for each one, yet was irritated when analysts and the public made too much of them. In 1905 he tried to explain his theories to Romain Rolland. He wrote a letter to the French writer and critic in which he said that "a poetic program is exclusively a pretext for the purely musical expression and development of my emotions." The program was not, Strauss emphasized, "a simple physical description of precise facts of life. For this would be most contrary to the spirit of music." Music, Strauss continued, has to be contained in "a determining form." But Strauss never felt dependent on classic forms in his series of symphonic poems. "New ideas must search for new forms," he kept on insisting. For the most part he was successful in his formal structures. Whatever the intrinsic value of the musical materials, Strauss put them into well-integrated free forms—modified sonata, variations, rondo. He was a superb technician, and one of the most resourceful orchestrators of all time. Even Debussy, who stood for everything Strauss was not, had to admit the "tremendous versatility of the orchestration, then the frenzied energy which carries the listener with him for as long as he chooses. . . . One must admit that the man who composed such a work [*Ein Heldenleben*] at so continually high a pressure is very nearly a genius." Yet, "modernistic" as his scores appeared to his contemporaries, they were the end of a period, not the beginning. After Strauss, very few composers wrote tone poems, and today practically nobody does. The symphonic poem as a viable medium currently appears as dead as the concerto grosso—deader, indeed, for the concerto grosso at least enjoyed something of a renaissance during the neo-classic period of 1920–1935.

Just as Strauss grew more famous as a composer, so grew his reputation as a conductor. In 1898 he succeeded Felix Weingartner as conductor of the Royal Opera in Berlin, and he remained there until 1918, after which he became co-director of the Vienna Opera. As a conductor, Strauss developed into an exponent of the revolt from romanticism that was beginning to take hold in the early 1900's. Romantic conducting was free, impulsive, often self-indulgent. Strauss, like Weingartner, like Karl Muck and Arturo Toscanini, kept himself out of the music much more than the romantics did. Using a tiny beat, he kept his rhythms regular, adhered closely to the score, and avoided flamboyance. Most of his conducting was done in the opera house, and it was not long before Strauss began to concentrate almost exclusively on composing as well as conducting opera.

During his run of symphonic poems Strauss had composed a Wagnerian opera named *Guntram*. It had its premiere at Weimar in 1894 and achieved only one performance. (Not until 1935 was it again heard, when it had a radio performance in Berlin.) Never was there such a failure. "It is incredible what enemies *Guntram* has made for me," Strauss wrote. "I shall shortly be tried as a dangerous criminal." Strauss was so discouraged that he waited for six years before writing another stage work. That too, an opera named *Feuersnot*, was a failure. At last with *Salome* of 1905 Strauss composed an opera that electrified the public as much as his symphonic poems had done. The subject matter of *Salome* had as much to do with its notoriety as the music. Everybody was eager to see Salome make love to the detached head of Jochanaan, and to watch her take off the seven veils one by one. (Marie Wittich, cast as Salome for the Dresden world premiere, at first refused to learn the role. "I won't do it, I'm a decent woman.") Everybody shivered to Strauss's shrieking, "decadent," near-atonal writing. Here, and in *Elektra*, which followed in 1908, Strauss moved out of the post-romantic castle to do battle with a new kind of harmony, a new and powerful kind of melody, and a progressive style that could have led him into still greater adventures. Both operas were, and to an extent remain, shockers. But, frightened by what he saw, Strauss withdrew, and never again experimented with the kind of jagged harmony and psychological underlining that make *Salome* and *Elektra* two of the most provocative operas of the century.

In its day *Elektra* posed tremendous problems for the singers and orchestra. Strauss wanted a new kind of singing, and the cry went up, just as it had gone up in Wagner's and Meyerbeer's day, that the result would be the permanent ruination of the human voice. Singers brought up in the earlier tradition were appalled. Ernestine Schumann-Heink, the great contralto, sang the role of Klytemnestra in the premiere, and she never got over it. "We were a set of madwomen, truly we were," she reminisced some years later. "He had written us so, and so we became in very truth. The music itself is maddening. He writes a beautiful, beautiful melody, five measures; and then he is sorry for writing something lovely and breaks off with a dissonance that racks you. He does not need singers because his orchestral scores so paint, so draw the picture." She ended with the statement that "If Mr. Hammerstein were to put on that opera tomorrow and offer me $3000 a night to sing Klytemnestra, I would say no. And $3000 is a great deal of money and I have many children."

Elektra brought Strauss and Hugo von Hofmannsthal together. In 1903, Max Reinhardt staged Hofmannsthal's translation of Sophocles' *Elektra*, and Strauss wanted to set it to music. Hofmannsthal made the adaptation, and in that librettist Strauss found his Boito and Lorenzo da Ponte. For almost twenty-five years Strauss and Hofmannsthal worked together, turning out *Der Rosenkavalier* (1911), the first version of *Ariadne auf Naxos* (1912), the *Josefslegende* ballet (1914), the revised *Ariadne* (1916), *Die Frau ohne Schatten* (1919), *Die ägyptische Helena* (1928), and *Arabella* (1933). It is a moot point whether or not Hofmannsthal's influence on Strauss was entirely healthy. Hofmannsthal led the composer away from the *Elektra* style into a kind of literary opera suffused with symbolism. Strauss's natural musical leaning was extroverted, violent, convulsive, sensational, but with Hofmannsthal leading the way, Strauss was diverted into a gray land of allegory and symbolism that did not fit his flamboyant approach. *Der Rosenkavalier* and *Elektra* are the only two of their collaborations that are still extremely popular. *Ariadne auf Naxos* (1916) also has a strong band of admirers, although this opera turns up less frequently. One of the problems with *Ariadne* is to find a competent cast. Strauss wrote here for voices of Wagnerian strength plus, in the role of Zerbinetta, a coloratura soprano who has to conquer incredible difficulties. The second-act aria of Zerbinetta, *Grossmächtigen Prinzessin*, is a set piece in which Strauss used bel canto procedures in twentieth-century terms, and very few singers have been able to sing the long aria with any degree of ease. The other Strauss-Hofmannsthal operas —*Die Frau ohne Schatten*, *Die ägyptische Helena*, and *Arabella*—even in Germany and Austria live mostly through a small band of fanatical admirers.

The two men had a curious relationship. Hofmannsthal, an Austrian, was one of Germany's most distinguished men of letters. He was quiet, shy, and sensitive, an idealist who at the same time was well aware of his worth. Strauss was his antithesis: hardheaded, practical, more interested in the concrete than the abstract. The two men clearly admired and respected each other. Yet they were never very close, and the relationship was strangely formal Their lengthy correspondence through the years is fascinating in many ways. Above all, it gives an idea of the eternal tussle between the demands of the music and the demands of the word. Strauss himself pondered the problem for decades, and his last opera, *Capriccio* (1942), to a libretto by Clemens Krauss and himself, is nothing but a long speculation on the subject of words and music. Which is of greater importance? Strauss could not make up his mind, and the opera ends with a question mark

The correspondence reveals that to Hofmannsthal, Strauss was a tremendous creative figure, one to be feared as much as admired. To Strauss, Hofmannsthal was something like a libretto factory. Strauss had no hesitation about stepping on his colleague's feelings, and during one sticky point in the preparation of *Ariadne* actually suggested that Hofmannsthal get a collaborator "Such things are usually done best by two people." Hofmannsthal, who stood in awe of Strauss, would never have suggested that the composer get a collaborator. He continued writing for Strauss because he was convinced that the composition of a libretto was as much an art as the construction of a play. "I know the worth of my work," he wrote to Strauss. "I know that for many generations past, no distinguished poet of the rank with which I may credit myself among the living, has dedicated himself willingly and devotedly to the task of working with a musician." He did bow to the music "I consider Dr. Strauss entirely as the principal partner, and the music as the dominant one of the elements joined together." And so he put up with a frequent lack of comprehension on Strauss's part. Some of his letters trying to justify his approach are sad to read. Strauss, as a practical man of the theater (and he was generally correct in specific criticisms of Hofmannsthal's librettos), would often raise violent objections Hofmannsthal would defend himself, as in his long account, in July of 1911, about the philosophical import of *Ariadne* Then, thirsting for some kind of praise, he continues in the vein of a jilted girl writing to the man she still loves: "All this, I must say, seemed to me to deserve some expression of appreciation from the one person for whom my work was visualized, conceived and executed. I doubt, moreover, if one could easily find in any other libretto for a one-act opera three poems of comparable delicacy, and at the same time equally characteristic in tone, as Harlekin's song, the rondo for Zerbinetta, and the Circe song of Bacchus. Not unnaturally, I would rather have heard all this from you than be obliged to write it for myself." One can imagine the exasperated, impatient shrug of Strauss's shoulders while reading this.

The tug of war between the man of words and the man of music was never settled, as it never is. Each considered his own contribution important, and each fought for it. Generally it was Hofmannsthal who gave way, with Old Testament groans and lamentations. Through the years of give and take it was Hofmannsthal who did most of the giving, Strauss most of the taking. By far their most successful collaboration was *Der Rosenkavalier*. After *Elektra*, Strauss decided to compose a comedy, and Hofmannsthal came up with an idea for a work with two main roles, "one for a baritone and one for a young and graceful girl dressed as a man, of the type of a Farrar or Mary Garden The period: Vienna at the time of Maria Theresa." The German operatic repertory badly needed a new comic work. There had been no internationally successful German comic opera since *Die Meistersinger* in 1868. *Der Rosenkavalier* came into being after much struggle on all sides. Strauss insisted on certain dramatic touches which Hofmannsthal, after a great deal of reluctance, inserted. He finally admitted that Strauss was right: "I see that it is all far more purely theatrical and very much better than the earlier version." One of the things Strauss insisted upon was to have the comic elements emphasized. "Don't forget that the audience should also laugh! *Laugh*, not just smile or grin! I still miss in our work a genuinely comic situation: everything is merely amusing, but not *comic!*" For a while the title of the opera was up in the air. As late as April, 1910, Strauss was thinking of calling it *Ochs*. Hofmannsthal suggested *Der Rosenkavalier* and proposed that it be called a "burlesque opera." Strauss objected to the word "burlesque." He said that once the public heard that word, it would think of Offenbach or Gilbert and Sullivan. They finally settled on *"Der Rosenkavalier*, Comedy for Music by Hugo von Hofmannsthal, Music by Richard Strauss."

Both also agreed that the opera should end not with Octavian the central figure, or even Ochs, but the Marschallin. "She is the central figure for the public," Hofmannsthal wrote, "for the women above all, the figure with whom they feel and *move*." It is interesting that in this letter Hofmannsthal wrote that *Der Rosenkavalier* was "a turning-away from Wagner's intolerable erotic screaming—boundless in length as well as in degree: a repulsive, barbaric, almost bestial affair, this shrieking of two creatures in heat as he practices it." Anti-Wagnerism was setting in, and *Der Rosenkavalier*, whatever Wagnerisms remain in it, follows a different aesthetic. *Die Meistersinger* has a libretto that is heavy German *Pfannkuchen*, while *Der Rosenkavalier* has a sophistication, especially in sexual matters, that Wagner never could have brought off. (Wagner, the great sensualist, was in his operas really a prude.) Hofmannsthal gently deals with young and old love in a civilized, urbane manner. Wagner's sex in *Tristan* is primal, like that of two whales gravely coming together In *Der Rosenkavalier* there are no Jungian archetypes, only the human condition. Instead of long narratives there are Viennese waltzes. Instead of a monumental *Liebestod* there is a sad, elegant lament from a beautiful, aristocratic woman who begins to see old age. Instead of death, we get a bittersweet and hauntingly beautiful trio that in effect tells us that life will go on as it always has gone on. People do not die for love in Hofmannsthal's world. They face the inevitable, surrender with what grace they can summon up, and then look around for life's next episode. As Strauss himself later said, the Marschallin had lovers before Octavian, and she will have lovers after him.

After *Der Rosenkavalier*, Strauss was an anachronism. European music was headed in a different direction while Strauss was still working his old formulae. Every composer does, in a way, for his music is the man; but a Beethoven, Mozart, Verdi, or Chopin continued to broaden and become deeper, more meaningful, more original. There is little of that kind of growth in Strauss's bland succession of operas, though *Die Frau ohne Schatten* has some exceedingly beautiful things in it (Strauss considered it his best opera.) Post-Hofmannsthal operas included *Die Schweigsame Frau* (1935), *Friedenstag* (1936), *Daphne* (1937), *Die Liebe der Danae* (1940), and *Capriccio* (1942). There also is a strange little opera called *Intermezzo* (1924), for which Strauss himself wrote the libretto. It is an autobiographical opera, a family joke about Strauss and Pauline's jealousy.

Time went on, the Nazis came into power, and Strauss was appointed president of the Reichsmusikkammer. The Nazis did not know exactly what to do with him. He *was* their most important composer, he did elect to stay in Germany, and yet he did and said things that would have put anybody else in a concentration camp. Then he would hastily resume friendly relations with the authorities. Strauss was opportunistic, amoral, and apolitical, and all he wanted was to be left alone to write his music and make money. He would gladly use a Jewish librettist, and did so in Stefan Zweig, much to the unhappiness of the Nazis. On the other hand he never put up much of a fight against the horrors of the Nazi regime. He wanted to have the best of all worlds.

During World War II he composed a series of reflective works mostly for small orchestra—the Oboe Concerto (1946), the Horn Concerto No. 2 (1942), the *Metamorphosen* (1945) for twenty-three solo strings. There also were the *Four Last Songs*, for soprano and full orchestra. About this music there are mixed feelings. Some listeners find in it what they also find in Strauss's late operas—the final flicker of postromanticism, the musings of a great composer in his full, venerable mastery. Others dismiss the music with actual irritation as works of tremendous skill that repeat past formulae and have nothing to say. Strauss died at Garmisch on September 8, 1949. The obituaries all paid tribute to his importance in the music of the late nineteenth and early twentieth centuries, but there was decided hedging about the post-*Rosenkavalier* works, and there still is. In any event, it is clear that Strauss exercised little or no influence on the new school of composers, most of whom disliked or even despised his work. Stravinsky's reaction is typical: ". bombast and rodomontade treacly the music [of *Capriccio*] chokes me. Strauss does not know how to punctuate. His musculature is without measure." To the new generation, his symphonic poems were vulgar. overorchestrated, ostentatious bores; and most of his operas tiresome, thick, repetitive works full of fake symbolism and fake philosophy. Which does not leave much of poor Strauss; and, in all truth, it is hard to take the huffings and puffings of the once-electrifying *Ein Heldenleben*, or the nature-painting of *Don Quixote,* or, indeed, most of the music that once meant so much to so many people. Nothing dates as fast as pure sensationalism, and the tragedy of Strauss is the tragedy of a superior musical mind flawed by the desire to put effect over substance.

❦ 9 ❧

Religion, Mysticism, and Retrospection

BRUCKNER, MAHLER, REGER

The year, 1911, of the premiere of *Der Rosenkavalier* was also the year during which Gustav Mahler died. Anton Bruckner had already been dead for fifteen years. Max Reger was to die five years later, in 1916. Those three composers in their day were completely eclipsed by Richard Strauss. Mahler was famous mostly as a conductor, as the central figure in the so-called "golden years" of the Vienna Opera, from 1897 to 1907. His symphonies were played, but performances were relatively few, and they became fewer after his death. Bruckner was regarded by many as some kind of pure fool (in the Parsifallian sense) who by some freak had managed to attract a small, devoted band of followers. Reger, on the other hand, was widely respected, and his music had a strong vogue in Germany for a decade after his death. Then it was dropped, and has remained dropped. To most musicians today, Reger, who was one of the few Brahms followers (as opposed to Mahler and Bruckner, who were Wagnerites out of Beethoven and Schubert), represents everything that is wrong and vulgar with postromanticism.

But the 1960's saw a remarkable renaissance of the music of Bruckner and Mahler. Mahler especially is regarded as a symbol of the second half of the twentieth century, and the process was accelerated when the scholars of the avant-garde decided that he was the spiritual father of dodecaphonism. Mahler's eternal questings, his seeking and searching, his inability to come to terms with society, his guilt complexes, his doubts and anxieties—all these made him, many believed, a prophet for an age riddled also with doubts and anxieties. Earlier ages at least had the comforts of orthodox religion. Mahler, the Jew turned Catholic, and neither a practicing Jew nor a practicing Christian, could find none of the answers. Most people of his time were able to make some kind of peace between themselves and the universe. Mahler never could, just as fewer and fewer people can today.

The meaning of life obsessed Mahler, and he was constantly asking questions. But the questions suggest that Mahler was more a neurotic than a Deep Thinker. There was something of the child in his plaintive queries. "Whence do we come?" he asked Bruno Walter. "Whither does our road take us? Have I really willed this life. as Schopenhauer thinks, before I was even conceived? Why am I made to feel that I am free while yet I am constrained within my character, as in a prison? What is the object of toil and sorrow? How am I to understand the cruelty and malice in the creations of a kind God? Will the meaning of life be finally revealed by death?" Why, why, why? Walter believed that each of Mahler's symphonies was a new attempt to answer the questions eternally plaguing him.

Bruckner too wrote symphonies that reflected an attempt to answer these questions. In Bruckner's case, however, no doubts are expressed. He was a devout man with a simplistic view of the world and the hereafter. God is good. Everything man does should reflect the glory of God. Music should honor Him. The old Bruckner once said to Mahler: "Yes, my dear, now I have to work very hard so that at least the Tenth Symphony will be finished. Otherwise I will not pass before God, before Whom I shall soon stand. He will say: 'Why else have I given you talent, you son of a bitch, than that you should sing My praise and glory? But you have accomplished much too little.'"

Temperamentally no two men could have been as far apart as Bruckner and Mahler. Yet they had certain things in common. Each composed nine symphonies: nine, that mystic Beethovenian numeral. Each composed long works—symphonies that in size, power, and orchestration far exceeded any of Brahms's and even the Beethoven Ninth. Both often fell back on the heritage of Austrian folk song, building entire movements on ländler-like melodies that can be traced back to Schubert. Both were strongly influenced by Wagner. And both were even more strongly influenced by Beethoven—the Ninth Symphony, specifically: the unapproachable ideal, the standard against which all music had to be measured.

In Bruckner's case the Ninth fixation could be seen in conscious or unconscious imitations of technical and melodic devices used in the Beethoven D minor. How many of Bruckner's symphonies start with a tremolo in the low strings, as does the Ninth, and then proceed to melodic material derived from the common triad, again as in the Ninth! How many slow movements of the Bruckner symphonies echo the soaring violin passages of the Beethoven adagio! Mahler had an even greater fixation. In the words of the psychoanalyst Theodor Reik, Mahler was an "obsessive neurotic" who was afraid of the thought of composing a ninth symphony. "The fact that Beethoven, Schubert and Bruckner had died after having touched the number nine in their symphonies made this number a menace." When Mahler did get to work on a ninth symphony, and actually finished it, he crossed out the number and published it as *Das Lied von der Erde*. Then, when composing his next symphony, he told his wife: "Actually, of course, it is the Tenth, because *Das Lied von der Erde* was really the Ninth." When it was near completion he said: "Now the danger is past." As a matter of fact, it was not past. He died a few months after finishing the work that was published as his Ninth Symphony, leaving only two substantially finished movements and a mass of sketches for the work that was to be his Tenth. This confirmed the dark feelings of those in the Mahler orbit. They *knew* that punishment awaited those who challenged certain forces. "It seems," wrote Arnold Schoenberg in 1913, "that the Ninth is the limit. He who wants to go beyond it has to leave. . . . Those who had written a Ninth Symphony were too close to the Beyond."

Whatever similarities Bruckner and Mahler had, their differences were huge. Their music stands for different things, for the opposing social and philosophical polarities of a period. Bruckner stands for repose, Mahler for unrest; Bruckner for certitude, Mahler for doubt; Bruckner for naïveté, Mahler for sophistication; Bruckner for provincialism, Mahler for internationalism.

Anton Bruckner, born in Ansfelden, Upper Austria, on September 24, 1824, studied at nearby St. Florian, where he became choirmaster and organist of the Foundation, a settlement of Augustine monks. In 1856 he moved to Linz as church organist. Once a week he went to Vienna to study counterpoint with Simon Sechter. This was the Sechter with whom Schubert was going to study in the last year of his life.

Bruckner was a simple man, incredibly rustic and naïve. He had a shaven head and a country dialect; he wore homespun and ill-fitting clothes and moved in constant awe of those great city people who knew so much more about everything than he did. A child of nature, he was not well read, was completely unsophisticated, would blurt out the first thing that came into his mind. He tipped the majestic and wealthy Hans Richter at the end of the final rehearsal of his Fourth Symphony. "Take this"—pressing a thaler into Richter's hand—"and drink a mug of beer to my health." The dumbfounded conductor looked at the coin, put it into his pocket, and later had it put on his watch chain. Antics like this amused some, irritated others. Wagner, for one, was amused. Bruckner went to Munich in 1865 to attend the premiere of *Tristan und Isolde,* and the music so overwhelmed him that he became one of the most enthusiastic Wagnerians in Europe. He met Wagner several times. On one occasion, Wagner gave him his hand, and Bruckner, overcome, bent down on his knee, pressed the Hand to his lips and said: "O Master, I worship you!" His Third Symphony shows some of this worship, though in his music Bruckner never was really a Wagnerian. Some analysts have a tendency to read things into it because it was dedicated to Wagner.

Through Johann Herbeck, the Viennese court conductor, Bruckner was appointed teacher of organ and theory at the Vienna Conservatory in 1868, and was made a professor there three years later. He also became organist of the court chapel and lecturer in theory at the University of Vienna. Several important conductors, among them Richter, Artur Nikisch, Hermann Levi, Felix Mottl, and Gustav Mahler, began to take an interest in his music. But whenever it was performed in Vienna, the Establishment critics, headed by Eduard Hanslick, tore it apart. Bruckner was convinced that Brahms was behind the attacks on him. What with the cool reception his music received, and his financial difficulties, his life in Vienna was not pleasant during his early years there. "Had to borrow money already in September, and again later, if I did not choose to starve," he wrote to a friend in Linz. "No man is helping me. Stremayr [the Austrian Minister of Education] promises—and does nothing. Fortunately there have come some foreigners who are taking lessons from me—otherwise I should have to go begging. Hear me further: I asked all the chief professors for pupils. They all promised, but except for some theory lessons I got nothing.   I should not have been brought to Vienna so long as I lived had I forseen this. It would be an easy thing for my enemies to drive me out of the Conservatory. I am surprised that this has not already happened.   "

Naïve as he was, Bruckner knew what was going on. In the wildly partisan Vienna of the time, there was the Brahms sect and there was the Wagner sect. Bruckner was classified as a Wagnerian. As the press was dominated by the Brahmsians, Bruckner found himself under constant attack. The story went that Bruckner was once asked by the Emperor if there was anything he could do for him. "Yes, Your Majesty, if you could only tell Mr. Hanslick to stop writing such terrible things about me," or words to that effect. The Emperor did grant him a pension, and in 1891 Bruckner was able to resign from the Conservatory, and from the University in 1894. He died on October 11, 1896.

To many, his clumsiness as a human being made him an object of derision. But those exposed to him for any length of time did not go away laughing. Bruckner inspired the same sort of devotion that César Franck did; and, indeed, Bruckner has been called a German Franck by more than one scholar. Max Graf attended several of his University lectures, and wrote that he went to Bruckner's class expecting to be amused. There was Bruckner, wearing the Upper Austrian loose jacket, his big head and wrinkled face peering at the students. When the Angelus would sound from the nearby church, Bruckner would stop his lecture, get on his kness and pray. Then he would resume the lecture. Occasionally he would pass Hanslick (who lectured on musicology) in the hall, and Bruckner would bow and scrape before that dreaded figure. But it did not take Graf long to become first impressed and then worshipful In Bruckner's theory lectures, the basis was Sechter. Graf, later to become Vienna's most important music critic, has written about Bruckner's approach:

> Sechter's doctrine, which was delivered to us by Bruckner like a holy heritage, was built on two strong pillars. The one that inspired Bruckner with greatest respect was the theory of the "Fundamental Basses," a world of spirits in the bass, which accompanied the harmonies like shadows in the depths; and the theory of "natural harmonies," which form the laws of all beauty of harmonic progression. Everywhere there was law and order, even holiness. The fundamental steps of the bass which Bruckner invariably noted in his scores under the last line of the staff, had cosmic importance. Thus we understood the greatness and sometimes the rigidity and solemnity of Bruckner's harmonies. Bruckner, the pupil of Sechter, who was a kind of architect of harmonies, pondered over chords and chord associations as a medieval architect contemplated the original forms of a Gothic cathedral. They were his path to the Kingdom of God.

It is this slow, inexorable, solemn procession of harmonies that is the essence of Bruckner's music. Everything was deliberate about the man's symphonies and choral music. The Viennese nicknamed him the "Adagio-Komponist"—the composer of adagios. Even his first movements were so big and stately, took so much time to get under way, that they sounded like adagios to the Viennese. Bruckner's music, with its Gothic arch, its tremendous spans, its organlike sonorities, its bigness in time and space, is essentially cathedral-like music of belief, and one probably has to be a believer to identify fully with it. The scherzo movements of the Bruckner symphonies often use Austrian dances, and these too involve belief. Mozart's third movements evoke the court; Haydn's, the peasants; Beethoven's, the gods at play. But Bruckner's evoke some kind of religious ideal involving nature. The religiosity of Bruckner's nine symphonies (and, of course, of his Masses and other religious choral music) suggests to his admirers a kind of message that is allied to the Infinite. Even unbelievers can find themselves carried away by the simple conviction of the man.

Just as Bruckner's music arouses an all but apocalyptic response in the faithful, so it is irritating and even meaningless to another group of listeners. Those who are not attracted to Bruckner's music are not necessarily bothered by its length. Rather they are bothered by the repetition of material that to them is not very stimulating to begin with. They tend to feel that Bruckner wrote the same symphony nine times. Not liking the message, or the thematic material to begin with, they are all but driven out of their minds as a Bruckner symphony makes its slow, inexorable procession. Bruckner admirers and Bruckner doubters are two armed camps glaring at each other, and the music evokes no middle response. What one camp finds noble and uplifting, the other finds long-winded and boring. Power to one is flabbiness to the other. In any case, Bruckner was an isolated figure. He had no followers, as Mahler did. But there is something in his music that appeals to one aspect of the modern psyche, and as a result his symphonies have in recent years become a basic part of the repertory. A good deal of their appeal lies in their unvarnished faith, their repose and unhurried serenity—qualities that so many people today long for. They can live the experience in Bruckner's music.

Bruckner's symphonies are full of textual problems. He was so anxious to get his music played that he would let conductors do anything with it—cut, alter, reorchestrate, smooth out rough harmonies. Bruckner said more than once that the correct performance of his music could await future generations. In the meantime, many of the first published editions of his symphonies, from 1878 to 1903, were unreliable and often actually corrupt. Well-wishers like the conductors Franz Schalk and Ferdinand Löwe decided to "help" the composer, and some of the first published editions are almost as much their work as his. Not until the formation of the International Bruckner Society in 1929 did correct editions of Bruckner's works begin to be issued in a projected twenty-two volume critical edition. Robert Haas and Alfred Orel were the first editors, and were succeeded by Leopold Nowak, who sometimes arrived at different interpretations of the scores. Today all literate conductors use either the Haas or Nowak editions.

If Bruckner's music arouses fanatical devotion in many listeners, Mahler's creates an actual frenzy. Again there are doubters, those who find Mahler's music too neurotic and often too banal for enjoyment. The dedicated Mahlerian regards these unregenerates the way St. Paul regarded the heathen. It is hard to think of a composer who arouses an equal loyalty. The worship of Mahler amounts to a religion. Any music critic will attest to the fact that a response of anything except rapture to the Mahler symphonies will bring long letters of furious denunciation. Much more than even Bruckner's music, Mahler's stirs something imbedded in the subconscious, and his admirers approach him mystically. Thus Arnold Schoenberg wrote:

> Actually everything that will characterize him is already present in the First Symphony. Here already his life-melody begins, and he merely develops it, unfolds it to the utmost extent. Here are his devotions to nature and his thoughts of death. He is still struggling with fate here, but in the Sixth he acknowledges it, and this acknowledgement is resignation. But even resignation becomes productive and rises, in the Eighth, to the glorification of the highest joys, to a glorification only possible to one who already knows these joys are no longer for him; who has already resigned himself; who already feels that they are merely an allegory for even higher joys, a glorification of the most supreme bliss

Life-melody . . . fate . . . resignation . . . joys . . . death . . . glorification. But this is not analysis. It is sentimental extrapolation, from the black and white symbols and spaces on music paper to a set of conclusions that Mahler's admirers would dearly like to believe; and it ends up making Mahler not merely a composer but a combination of Moses and Christ. Where Bruckner evokes a purely religious impulse, Mahler evokes a moral, psychic, mystic, Freudian one. Mahler's admirers find themselves talking about soul states, inner crises, ecstasy, apotheoses, transfiguration, fate, Nature with a capital N, spirit, the all-in-one and the one-in-all. Mahler's heroic and futile struggle to make sense out of life passes through his music to the listener. It is very easy to identify with the struggle. The question remains whether or not the struggle is worth the experience. Beethoven's struggles were expressed purely in music, and are those of an indomitable hero who not only triumphed but created his own hereafter. Mahler's struggles are those of a psychic weakling, a complaining adolescent who whimpered or blustered or grew hysterical rather than put up much of a fight. Mahler's music can, indeed, be sickening to a certain type of mind—a mind that prefers manliness to anguish. For Mahler was, down deep, a sentimentalist. He *enjoyed* his misery; he reveled in it; he wallowed in it, wanting the whole world to see how he was suffering. In him, the textbook definition of sentimentalism became a living example, for Mahler never transformed the self in terms of the object. He transformed the object in terms of his self.

Perhaps it was this weakness, this basic insecurity, that accounted for his external character. To compensate, he turned out to be an austere, despotic, querulous, and arrogant man, convinced of his moral and musical rectitude. His wife once remarked that he was always telephoning to God. "Thin, fidgety, short, with a high, steep forehead, long dark hair and deeply penetrating bespectacled eyes" (Bruno Walter's description), he was a manic-depressive with a sadistic streak. Musicians respected him but hated to play under his baton. He was the kind of conductor who would pick on individual players; the kind of conductor who would start a rehearsal of the *Lohengrin* Prelude and yell at the players, before a note was sounded, "Too loud!" He was nervous among people and had no small talk, none of the social graces. His musical honesty would not permit him to acknowledge the second-rate. Bruno Walter tells of the time a composer played his new score to Mahler, who hated it. He said nothing. The composer, a friend, was terribly hurt. A curt *"Auf wiedersehen!"* ended the scene. "An entire lifetime of personal relations of all kinds had not supplied Mahler with that modicum of social polish that would have brought the meeting to an ordinary end," Walter wrote regretfully. Of Mahler's dedication to music there was no doubt. He had an ideal, and his life was spent in search of it. As such, it was a noble life.

Mahler, indeed, put so much into his music—as composer, conductor, administrator—that there was very little time for anything else, and that included personal relationships. He ignored his wife, and she resented it. "I knew that my marriage and my own life were utterly unfulfilled," Alma Mahler wrote, many years later. Worried about himself and his wife, Mahler had a session with Sigmund Freud. In a letter to Theodor Reik, dated January 4, 1935, Freud recalled the event:

> I analyzed Mahler for an afternoon in the year 1912 (or 1913?) [it was 1910] in Leyden. If I may believe reports, I achieved much with him at that time. The visit appeared necessary for him, because his wife at that time rebelled against the fact that he withdrew his libido from her. In highly interesting expeditions through his life history, we discovered his personal conditions for love, especially his Holy Mary complex (mother fixation). I had plenty of opportunity to admire the capability for psychological understanding of this man of genius. No light fell at that time on the symptomatic façade of his obsessional neurosis. It was as if you would dig a single shaft through a mysterious building.

Reik concludes that Mahler's basic trouble was that in his passionate desire to achieve his ideal, Mahler neglected to live as other men did. While he was lost in his work, life passed him by. "He sought for the hidden metaphysical truth behind and beyond the phenomena of this world, for the ideal. He never tired in his search after that transcendental and supernatural secret of the Absolute and he did not recognize that the great secret of the transcendental, the miracle of the metaphysical, is that it does not exist."

Born in Kalist, Bohemia, on July 7, 1860, Mahler was the second of twelve children. In 1878 he went to the Vienna Conservatory, where he was a good pianist and where he discovered his talent as a conductor. When he was graduated, he started the slow climb from opera house to opera house that was the traditional path of an aspiring conductor. In 1880 he was musical director in the small city of Hall. The following year he went to Laibach (now Ljubljana), and in 1882 he worked in Olmütz. The year of 1883 saw him in Vienna (with an Italian opera company) and Kassel. In 1885 he was in Prague, and in 1886 the second conductor in Leipzig. Mahler remained in Leipzig for two years, but could not get along with Nikisch and left in 1888. His first big chance came in Budapest, where he was musical director of the Royal Opera from 1886 to 1888. Brahms heard him and was greatly impressed with his conducting of *Don Giovanni*. Richard Strauss also was impressed and passed the word to Bülow: "I have made a new, very attractive acquaintance in Herr Mahler, who appears to me a highly intelligent musician and conductor." The next step was Hamburg, from 1891 to 1897. Bülow heard him there and agreed with Strauss: "Hamburg has now secured a really excellent opera conductor in Gustav Mahler (a serious, energetic Jew from Budapest) who in my opinion equals the very best: Richter, Mottl, etc." Then in 1897, with the enthusiastic backing of Brahms, the thirty-seven-year-old conductor from Hamburg was named head of the Vienna Opera.

There, for ten years, Mahler imposed his despotic will. *He* was the opera. He chose the repertory and singers, conducted many of the performances, staged many productions himself, and had his finger in everything that had to do with the house. He even imposed his will on the audience. One stern glance from his thin, nervous, forbidding face, and quiet would mantle the hall. As a conductor, he appears to have been a precisionist on the order of Bülow and, again like Bülow, strongly intellectual in his approach. He insisted on strenuous preparation, driving himself and his singers and musicians to exhaustion. To him there was no such thing as a minor detail, for minor details were important—as every great conductor knows. Mahler would not tolerate inattentive or careless playing. Never in his life did he encounter an orchestra that satisfied him in his search for perfection. Some idea of his ear and musicianship can be gained from what he once wrote about orchestras:

> There are frightful habits, or rather inadequacies, which I have encountered in every orchestra. They cannot read the score markings, and thus sin against the holy law of dynamics and of the inner hidden rhythms of a work. When they see a crescendo they immediately play forte and speed up; at a diminuendo they become piano and retard the tempo. One looks in vain for gradations, for the mezzo-forte, forte, fortissimo, or the piano, pianissimo, pianississimo. And the sforzandos, forte pianos, shortening or extension of notes, are even less in evidence. And should one ask them to play something that is not written down—as is so necessary a hundred times when one accompanies singers in opera—then one is lost with every orchestra.

In the ten years of Mahler's administration the Vienna opera was revitalized and cleared of debt. Prominent stage directors, such as Alfred Roller, were brought in, often causing great controversy. Roller's production of *Tristan und Isolde*, with its free forms, advanced lighting effects, and general feeling of avant-garde expressionism, caused a furore. In Vienna, Mahler was a legend, and hansom drivers would single him out as one of the monuments, like St. Stephen's. "Der Mahler!" they would tell their fares, pointing to him in the street. He never stopped working. "I cannot do anything but work. I have unlearned all other things within the course of the years." Bruno Walter never could keep up with him. "At no time during the two years I spent with Mahler in the Hamburg theater or the six at the

Vienna Opera, did I note a lessening of that high-tension speed."

In 1907 he went to the Metropolitan Opera for two full seasons, then returned to New York in 1909 with a two-year contract as conductor of the Philharmonic Society. His American experiences were unhappy. His second season at the Metropolitan coincided with the first season of Giulio Gatti-Casazza and his star conductor, Arturo Toscanini. Friction developed between Mahler and the new management, especially when Gatti-Gasazza assigned *Tristan und Isolde* to Toscanini—after Mahler had already rehearsed the orchestra and prepared the production. It was also apparent that Mahler in New York was not the Mahler of the Vienna Opera. He allowed cuts, which he had not permitted in his own house; and as an excuse for some indifferent performances lamely said that the musicians would not play for him and that there was not enough rehearsal time. The New York critics did not like him, or he them. Worse was to happen when he took over the Philharmonic. His programming displeased the ladies of the board almost as much as his antisocial personality did. He was tactless enough to refer to the Philharmonic as "the true American orchestra—without talent and phlegmatic." That did not increase his popularity. Mahler had to defend himself at a board meeting, and his wife was appalled. "You cannot imagine what Mr. Mahler has suffered," she told the press. "In Vienna my husband was all-powerful. Even the Emperor did not dictate to him, but in New York he had ten ladies ordering him around like a puppet." Mahler already was fatally ill, and had only a few more months to live. He left New York without finishing his Philharmonic season, and died in Vienna on May 11, 1911.

As a busy and successful conductor all of his adult life, Mahler had a minimum of time for his own creative work. He referred to himself as a part-time composer, and indeed the list of his compositions is not large. It consists of the nine symphonies and the unfinished tenth, and *Das Lied von der Erde*, the *Kindertotenlieder*, and other songs with orchestral and piano accompaniment. Many of the songs, and some of the movements in the symphonies, were inspired by the poems of *Des Knaben Wunderhorn*, a collection of folk poetry published in 1805 by Ludwig von Arnim and Klemens Brentano. Like many city people, Mahler liked to get out into the country, persuaded that he was renewing himself; and the use of *Wunderhorn* poems gave him a feeling of identification with Austrian folk elements. There is no real nationalism in his music, however. Pantheism might be a better word to describe it.

As in so much of the music of Mahler's day, there is an implied program running through everything he wrote. These program elements are not specific, as in the Strauss tone poems. They are general, giving the psychic key to the score. Mahler was a child of his time, and the same impulse that made Clara Schumann describe the Brahms Third Symphony as the story of Hero and Leander, the same impulse that made Liszt supply a silly program to Chopin's F minor Fantasy, made Mahler look for an implied program in all music, not only his own. "Believe me," he wrote in 1896, "the symphonies of Beethoven too have their inner program, and when one gets to know such works better, one's understanding of the proper succession of the emotions and ideas increases. In the end that will be true of my works also." Elsewhere he wrote: "Beginning with Beethoven, there exists no modern music that hasn't its inner program." And, "It is therefore good that at the beginning, when my style is still foreign to him, the listener be provided with a few signposts and milestones along the journey, or shall we say a map of the stars to comprehend the night sky with its shining worlds." It naturally followed that he could write "My music is, everywhere and always, only a sound of Nature." By "Nature" Mahler meant the word in its widest sense—life and death, earth and universe. Of his Eighth Symphony: "Imagine the universe beginning to sing and resound. It is no longer human voices; it is planets and suns revolving." He went into great detail about his ideas of program music in a letter to Max Marschalk, dated March 26, 1896:

> . . . My need to express myself musically—symphonically—begins only where the *obscure* perceptions hold sway, at the gate that leads into the "other world;" the world in which things are no longer separable through the agency of time and place.
>
> Just as I think it is a platitude to invent music to a program, so I consider it to be unsatisfying and sterile to want to attach a program to a musical work. This is no way altered by the fact that the *occasion* for a musical creation is doubtless to be found in an experience of the author's, and an actual one, which for that matter might be specific enough to be clothed in words . . .
>
> Having expressed myself in the above terms, you can understand that I find it a little awkward to say something to you now about the C minor Symphony.—I have named the first movement "Funeral Rite," and if you want to know, it is the hero of my First Symphony that I am burying here and whose life I am gathering in a clear mirror, from a higher point of vantage. At the same time it is the great question: *Why have you lived?* Why have you suffered? Is all this merely a great, horrible jest?—We *must* resolve these questions somehow or other if we are to continue living—nay, if we are only to continue dying. Once this call has resounded in anybody's life, he must give an answer; and that answer I give in the last movement.

The letter goes on to describe in even fuller detail what the movements of the Second Symphony mean. All of Mahler's music has this kind of program, and every one of his symphonies can be described in terms of unrest, struggle, aspiration. Naturally there is a difference between Mahler's first and last works, between the buoyant and athletic writing of the First Symphony to the hushed, motionless pessimism that concludes the Ninth and *Das Lied von der Erde*. Aspiration finally gives way to resignation.

In Mahler's music are many unconventional harmonies, culminating with the mad, macabre *Burleske* of the Ninth Symphony, that weird march with its powerful dissonances and parodistic quality. But the harmonic daring of Mahler has been somewhat overplayed by those scholars too anxious to make him the link between Wagner and Schoenberg. Schoenberg's Five Orchestral Pieces of 1908 are already far more advanced than Mahler's last works of 1910 and 1911. As far as that goes, Alexander Scriabin around 1905 was dispensing with key signatures, using quartal instead of triadic harmonies, and using a type of dissonance that was more prophetic than anything in Mahler.

When history puts Mahler in perspective, it probably will be clear that he was, aesthetically and technically, much more a nineteenth- than a twentieth-century figure. He thought in terms of romanticism and composed in terms of romanticism. His concept of music as program, stemming from Wagner's idiotic exegeses on the Beethoven symphonies, was romantic. His big orchestra, like Strauss's, merely carried Wagner one step further. His harmonies were no more advanced than most of Strauss's, and not as advanced as those in *Salome* or *Elektra*. Schoenberg, Strauss, Scriabin, and Debussy were much more modern than Mahler even in his own day. Even though Mahler's symphonies illustrate the breakup of classical models, they remain symphonies "after Beethoven" in more ways than one, and some of Mahler's slow movements, like Bruckner's, are unconscious attempts to rewrite the adagio of the Ninth. The Mahler symphonies, of course, do not have the tight organization of the Beethoven symphonies. That they also lack the emotional discipline of the Beethoven symphonies goes without saying. The swollen dance movements of the Mahler symphonies are sentimental evocations of an earlier Austria, with its peasants and *Ländler*: those simple tunes, played so thickly by Mahler's immense orchestra, dripping with earnestness. (It may have been this kind of music to which Debussy was referring when he wrote that "The fashion for popular airs has spread quickly throughout the musical world: from east to west the tiniest villages have been ransacked, and simple tunes, plucked from the mouths of hoary peasants, find themselves, to their consternation, trimmed with harmonic frills.") The cosmic movements of Mahler are hysterical. A frightened, tortured Mahler shrinks from the Infinite. With all this, there are sections in most of his symphonies where the undoubted brilliance of Mahler the musician conquers Mahler the Deep Thinker. And in his most moving work, *Das Lied von der Erde*, Mahler for once created an edifice in which form and emotion match each other. The genuine sadness and otherworldly quality of the music do not sound artificial or forced, and the last song is as much a farewell to the end of romanticism in music as it is to the approaching end of Mahler's own life. But to make Mahler, as many have done, a modern symbol is to misunderstand modernism and to misunderstand Mahler. His questions about life were trite, no deeper than those of Dickens's Sairey Gamp: "Sech is life. Vich likewise is the hend of all things."

The turn-of-the-century composer in Germany who defiantly looked back rather than forward was Max Reger, the central figure of the "Back to Bach" movement. He worked almost alone, and outside of Germany his music is all but unknown; nor is it played much any more even in Germany. To most critics of the latter half of the twentieth century, who apparently know Reger only by such pieces as the *Mozart* or *Hiller* variations, he is a monster—a composer of swollen scores with pointless fugues. The mention of Reger's name arouses a conditioned reflex: "Fugue!" Mahler and Bruckner have enjoyed an enormous revival, but Reger, who worked and composed voluminously during the same period, is today ignored, except to appear on critics' lists of the ten most disliked composers.

In his day, Reger was well known. He was a bumptious, outspoken man who for some reason hard to discern today was considered an ultramodernist. A child prodigy, born in Brand (Bavaria) on March 19, 1873, he was a professional organist at the age of sixteen, a teacher in Munich for many years, a professor at the Leipzig Conservatory, and a pianist and conductor. At the age of forty-three he had a heart attack and died, on March 11, 1916.

It was Reger's mission in life to write music in the spirit of Bach and Beethoven. "I can say with good conscience," he wrote in 1914, "that of all living composers I am probably the one who is in closest touch with the great masters of our rich past." He inveighed against the "perverted rubbish of Wagnerites and Straussomania." Where most other German composers of the day followed the line from Berlioz through Liszt and Wagner, his ancestry started with Bach and worked through Beethoven to Mendelssohn and Brahms. As a romantic who flourished in the day of the great post-Wagnerian orchestra, Reger did not hesitate to put it to use. Where Brahms would write a series of orchestral variations on a theme by Haydn, keeping everything direct and lyrical, Reger did not hesitate to take the opening theme of Mozart's A major Piano Sonata and subject it to a series of gargantuan variations culminating in a colossal fugue. The idea was similar to that of Brahms; the execution suffered from gigantism. Some German-oriented musicians continue to admire this type of writing, but it is precisely scores like the *Mozart* Variations that have given Reger a bad name, and most musicians today consider them the epitome of shocking taste. Mozart's pretty, slender theme put through such elaborate, heavy-footed paces! Decked with such inappropriately scented, lush harmonies!

But the *Mozart* Variations are by no means typical of Reger's work. That score represents only one side of his output. A good deal of his music is devoid of counterpoint. His chamber music, of which the Clarinet Quintet is a representative example, is nothing more than an extremely chromatic Brahms, just as his F minor Piano Concerto is a massive work that goes the Brahms B flat Concerto one better in size and sonority. This is not to say that Reger was a mere imitator of Brahms. His intense chromaticism is handled in a very individual manner (some of his chromaticism sounds like, of all composers, Delius, who was very popular in Germany before World War I). Reger's melodies also manage to maintain purity despite their heavy lacquer of postromanticism. As a technician he was masterful. Still another side of Reger is encountered in the unaccompanied sonatas for violin. The composer who is associated in so many musicians' minds only with fugue and overloaded orchestral scores here composed a set of tiny sonatas, none much over five minutes long, of delicacy and charm. His songs and piano pieces, while they reflect the period, are elegant and often beautiful. Reger did not have the originality to be one of the great masters, but his secure workmanship and honest fund of melody should have prevented his music from falling so low in professional esteem. As with many of the minor romantics and post-romantics, a shift in aesthetic values from objectivism to subjectivism will have to take place before Reger's music begins to be reexamined.

Reger was a plucky man and a scrappy fighter who had no hesitation about speaking his mind. He has achieved a kind of fame through an episode that concerned his dismissal of a music critic: scatological but perfect. He read a review of one of his pieces that outraged him, and presently that critic received from Reger the following note: "Dear Sir: I am sitting in the smallest room of my house. Your review is before me. Shortly it shall be behind me." In his day, Reger did not lack champions. Arnold Schoenberg held his music in very high esteem; and in the conductor Fritz Busch, Reger found a musician who was frequently presenting his music. Busch believed that Reger was the greatest composer after Brahms. He described the composer as "an extraordinarily tall man with tiny feet and an ugly, child-like face." Busch once invited Reger to participate in a concert at Bad Pyrmont. He told Reger that there would be no fee, but that the Prince would give him a decoration. Reger had to know exactly what kind of decoration. "He wanted to know whether it would be the *gold* medal for art and science? Whether it would be the *large* gold medal? Whether it would be the large gold medal with the red ribbon?" During Reger's stay at Bad Pyrmont, the Princess asked him why he played an Ibach rather than a Steinway piano. Reger, as always, spoke his mind. "You know, Your Highness," he boomed, "they pay much more."

❧ 10 ❧

Symbolism and Impressionism

CLAUDE-ACHILLE DEBUSSY

"A tout Seigneur, tout l'honneur," runs the French proverb. Honor to whom honor is due. It is not that Claude Debussy lacked honors in his own day. After a slow start, this *musicien français* (so he described himself) was recognized as the greatest French composer of his time. But today he is more than that. He is considered not only the greatest French composer who ever lived; he is considered the revolutionary who, with the *Prélude à l'après-midi d'un faune* of 1894, set twentieth-century music on its way. The younger critics are ecstatic now when they discuss the contributions of Claude Debussy. He is, they say, the one who destroyed nineteenth-century rhetoric; the one whose harmonic and melodic innovations led to the breakup of the scale as used in the nineteenth century; the one whose new concepts of orchestration led straight into Webern; the one whose piano music gave pianists more to think about than any other composer since Chopin; the one who reinstated the power of sound for sound's sake: the Rimbaud, the Verlaine, the Cézanne of music. Pierre Boulez, that outspoken exponent of the serial school, has written that certain of Debussy's last works "will be almost more astonishing than the final works of Webern." To Boulez, these late Debussy works are pieces in which all elements of the past have been discarded, pieces illustrative of "the total overthrow of notions that had remained static up to that time." Even as early as in *L'après-midi*, Boulez says, "all of Wagner's heavy heritage was discarded. . . . The Debussy reality excludes all academism."

Debussy is the greatest of the musical impressionists, though symbolist might be a better word. The impressionist painters—Manet, Monet, Cézanne, Renoir, Pissarro, and the other members of the *Société Anonyme des Artistes, Peintres, Sculpteurs et Graveurs*—had three famous shows from 1874 to 1877, and after 1877 the term "impressionism" stuck. It was derived from a painting by Monet named *Sunrise—an Impression*. Debussy disliked the term in relation to his own music. As a matter of fact, his tastes in painting were more in the direction of Whistler and Turner than of the impressionists. The symbolist poets—Mallarmé, Verlaine, Rimbaud, Maeterlinck—meant more to Debussy than painting. Another writer who fascinated him, as he fascinated all the French symbolists, was Edgar Allan Poe. Debussy worked for a while on an orchestral work based on *The Fall of the House of Usher,* and in 1908 he actually signed a contract with the Metropolitan Opera for operas on *Usher* and *The Devil in the Belfry* (and also for one on a non-Poe subject named *The Legend of Tristan*). But impressionism and Debussy are forever intertwined, and with good reason. Just as the impressionist painters developed new theories of light and color, so Debussy developed new theories of light and color in music. Like the impressionist painters, and like the symbolist poets, he tried to capture a fleeting impression or mood, tried to pin down the exact essence of a thought as economically as possible. He was far less interested in classical form than in *sensibilité.* He was from the beginning a boy, then a man, of *sensibilité.* Even as a child he had the tastes of an aristocrat. At Bourbonneux's famous pastry shop, his friends would gorge themselves on the cheapest candy, the most they could get for a few centimes. Debussy would choose a tiny sandwich, or a little *timbale aux macaronis,* or a delicate bite of pastry. Later in life his tastes were equally exquisite. He had to surround himself with fine prints and books. He was a gourmet with a notable appetite for caviar. He dressed to the point of dandyism, complete with carefully selected cravat, cape, and broad-brimmed hat *à la* Western. He knew exactly what he wanted from life and he took it, ignoring the rest.

Born on August 22, 1862, in St.-Germain-en-Laye, just outside of Paris, he grew up to be a strange-looking boy with bony protuberances on his forehead—*un double front.* He became a brilliant pianist and was admitted to the Conservatoire at the age of ten. Two years later he was skillful enough to be playing Chopin's F minor Concerto. He also started to compose at that time. He had no close friends, and a fellow student described him as "uncommunicative, not to say surly; he was not attractive to his friends." He studied theory with Alfred Lavignac, piano with Antoine Marmontel, harmony with Émile Durand, composition with Ernest Guiraud. Even at that time he was a natural rebel, one with the kind of questioning mind that did not hesitate to ask embarrassing questions of his elders. At the Conservatoire he sat in on some of César Franck's classes and recoiled in horror. "*Modulez, modulez,*" Franck would say, looking over Debussy's exercises. Debussy shocked the class by facing directly up to the famous and venerable *maître.* "Why should I modulate when I am perfectly happy in the tonality I am in?" He poked fun at Franck, calling him a modulating machine. In Guiraud's composition class he would sit at the piano making up outlandish chords and refusing to resolve them. He was asked by an exasperated teacher what rules he followed. *"Mon plaisir,"* Debussy curtly answered. Nevertheless, his talent was recognized, and after winning many prizes he finally was awarded the greatest of all, the Prix de Rome, in 1884.

Debussy grew into a complicated and reserved man, one whose shell was hard to penetrate. He had few friends and fewer intimates. Erik Satie and Pierre Louÿs were among the few intimates. His private life was very private and rather deplorable—at least, according to customary canons of behavior. After returning from Rome in 1887 he lived with Gabrielle Dupont—Gaby of the green eyes—for ten years. Where she came from nobody knew. He settled in with her in a miserable room just off Montmartre and for those ten years she took care of him, supported him (What did she do? Was she a washerwoman? A *midinette?* Did she scrub floors? Nobody knows.), and shooed away creditors. He rewarded her in 1899 by marrying Rosalie Texier. Even before that, he had been unfaithful, and Gabrielle shot herself after an argument with him. She lived, briefly returned to him, and then disappeared as mysteriously as she had entered his life. Many years later, the pianist Alfred Cortot ran across her in a theater in Rouen. She was in the dress of a working woman.

Debussy's marriage to Rosalie did not last very long. After a while, Debussy once said, the sound of her voice made his blood run cold. He threw her over in 1904 for the married Emma Bardac, whereupon Rosalie, like Gaby, shot herself. When Debussy married Emma in 1905, most of intellectual Paris sided with Rosalie and felt that Debussy had married for money. Emma was older than Debussy and had several grown children. She bore Debussy a daughter—Chouchou, whom he adored—before her divorce from the banker Raoul Bardac. It is very possible that Debussy was interested in her money, but he also liked her as much as he could like anybody. Emma was a singer and a witty, sophisticated, artistic woman, where Rosalie had been a sweet, unintellectual provincial.

In every respect Debussy's tastes were not as other men's. While musical Europe was worshiping Wagner, Debussy had his brief fling with the operas of the German master and then fought Wagnerism for the rest of his life. Satie claimed credit for giving Debussy the final push from Wagner into a "purer" style. Erik Satie (1866–1925) was an eccentric pianist and composer who entertained the customers at *Le Chat Noir* and also managed to secure for himself a prominent position in French aesthetic life. He composed stripped-down, short pieces in "white-key" harmony, was an ardent anti-Wagnerian, and proclaimed a kind of music that in a way was antimusic, deliberately so. His *"musique d'ameublement"* was to be played without being listened to, like looking at wallpaper without seeing it. Satie was one of the early Dadaists and surrealists, and he composed music with such surrealistic titles as *Pièces en forme de poire* (*Pieces in the form of a pear*) or *Embryons desséchés* (*Desiccated embryos*). His music, which is a link between Chabrier and Poulenc, is of striking individuality. Throughout his life, Satie influenced the advanced French school, first Debussy, then the composers of *Les Six*. He represented a complete break from tradition.

Debussy and Satie first came together at *Le Chat Noir* around 1890.

When I first met Debussy [Satie later wrote] he was full of Mussorgsky and very deliberately seeking a way that wasn't very easy for him to find. In this problem I was well in advance of him. I was not weighted down by the Prix de Rome or any other prize, for I am a man like Adam (of Paradise) who never won any prizes—a lazy fellow, no doubt. At that time I was writing *Le Fils des étoiles* to a libretto by Joseph Péladan, and I explained to Debussy that I was in no way anti-Wagnerian but that we should have a music of our own—if possible, without any sauerkraut. Why could we not use the means that Claude Monet, Cézanne, Toulouse-Lautrec, and others had made known? Why could we not transpose those means to music? Nothing simpler.

Debussy himself was coming to the same conclusion independently. As early as 1894 he found his love affair with Wagner coming to an end. "Having been an impassioned visitor to Bayreuth for several years, I began to doubt the Wagnerian formula—or, rather, it seemed to me it fitted only the particular genius of that composer, who was a great collector of clichés that he summed up in a formula which seemed unusual only because people did not know music well enough." Debussy concluded that it was necessary to go beyond Wagner rather than follow in his path. More and more, Debussy began to find inspiration in Mussorgsky rather than in Wagner. He had heard Mussorgsky's music in Russia, where he had spent some time in 1881 as piano teacher to the children of Nadjeda von Meck, Tchaikovsky's patroness. (When he fell in love with Sonia, her eldest daughter, she sent him packing.) Another strong musical influence, one that immensely touched the nerves of his *sensibilité*, was the exotic ethnic music represented by the Javanese gamelan orchestra he had heard at the Grande Exposition Universelle, in 1889. At that time he noted that Javanese music employed a counterpoint "in comparison to which that of Palestrina is a child's game." Primitive and medieval music always interested him.

With these superrefined tastes ran a corresponding dislike of the academic composers. Brahms meant nothing to him, Tchaikovsky he disliked, Beethoven bored him. He seldom worked in sonata form, the prevailing form since Mozart. He believed that the symphony as a form was dead. "It seems to me that the proof of the futility of the symphony has been established since Beethoven. Schumann and Mendelssohn did no more than respectfully repeat the same forms with less power." His was a music of personal, all but tactile, sensation ("Formless!" cried the academicians), a music that lacked "proper" resolution of chords, a music in which tonality began to be broken up, in which certain twentieth-century ideas of form and technique were first put on display. He was the first of the post-Wagner composers to work in an entirely new style, and *L'Après-midi d'un faune* has a place in musical history comparable to the *Eroica* Symphony and Monteverdi's *Orfeo*. Each of those epochal works shook a fist at the past and made it clear that the old rules no longer applied.

Debussy *thought* in a new manner. "I am more and more convinced that music, by its very nature, is something that cannot be cast into a traditional and fixed form. It is made up of colors and rhythms. The rest is a lot of humbug invented by frigid imbeciles riding on the backs of the Masters—who, for the most part, wrote almost nothing but period music. Bach alone had an idea of the truth." There was very little music that Debussy liked, and he was as contemptuous of his French contemporaries and immediate predecessors as he was of some of the revered figures of the past. Massenet was "a master in the art of pandering to stupid ideas and amateur standards." *Faust* was "massacred" by Gounod, and Shakespeare's *Hamlet* was "most unfortunately dealt with by M. Ambroise Thomas." Charpentier was "downright vulgar." In general: "Our poor music! How it has been dragged in the mud!"

It was not for nothing that Debussy called himself *musicien français*. Mostly the label was a defiant affirmation of his anti-Wagnerianism, and later included his anti-German feeling during the First World War. In any case, his music is the essence of everything French. He once made a lengthy statement on what the Gallic ideals were, comparing French clarity and elegance with German length and heaviness. "To a Frenchman, finesse and nuance are the daughters of intelligence." A French musician should not pile sonority upon sonority: that would be un-French. Artists should use self-control. At that time, Debussy was looking for a libretto. "I am dreaming of poetry that would not condemn me to contrive long and heavy acts, poetry that would offer me scenes which move in their locality and character, and where the characters do not argue but submit to life and their fate."

These lines were written in 1889. In 1893 he found his dream poetry. It was Maurice Maeterlinck's play *Pelléas et Mélisande*, produced in 1892. Debussy saw it and was enraptured. It exactly fit his ideas of a libretto. Even as a conservatory student he had been looking for a libretto that had "no place, no time, no big scene." He told his teacher that the musical element in opera was far too prominent, that there was too much singing. "The blossoming of the voice into true singing should occur only when required. A painting executed in grey would be the ideal." There should be, Debussy

410

said, "no developments merely for the sake of development." *Pelléas et Mélisande* could have been written to order for Debussy, and he immediately asked the author's consent to set it to music—a brash request from a little-known composer to a world-famous playwright. The result, ten years later, was a masterpiece. It was also a sore period for Debussy and Maeterlinck, a comedy of errors and ruffled pride, of bitterness, heroics, and sheer silliness.

They got along very well at the beginning. Debussy paid Maeterlinck a visit to discuss the libretto. He wrote to a friend that at first Maeterlinck "assumed the air of a young girl being introduced to her future husband." Debussy found him charming, knowledgeable in general, but musically illiterate. "When he speaks of a Beethoven symphony he is like a blind man in a museum." Debussy finished the score in 1895, was dissatisfied, and rewrote it completely. It was not until 1901 that he wrote the last notes. In the meantime he had published his String Quartet, the three Nocturnes for orchestra, some amazing songs, and was by then a famous composer.

When he played the score to Maeterlinck, the dramatist almost fell asleep from boredom. His wife, Georgette Leblanc, kept prodding him awake. Leblanc was an actress who had achieved stardom in Maeterlinck's plays. She also was a singer, and she hoped to create the operatic role of Mélisande. That was where the trouble started. According to her story— and most people believed her—Debussy was "enchanted" with the suggestion that she sing the premiere, and they had a few rehearsals together. But Albert Carré, director of the Opéra-Comique, had different ideas. He wanted Mary Garden, and Garden got the assignment. Neither Maeterlinck nor Leblanc knew anything about it until they picked up the paper one day. Then there was an explosion. Maeterlinck immediately tried to stop the production. Debussy denied that he had promised Leblanc the role. Maeterlinck went to court, and the court decided for Debussy. On receiving this news, Maeterlinck's fine Belgian temper boiled over. He brandished his stick and threatened to thrash Debussy. In a roaring rage, Maeterlinck jumped out of the window of his home (not as grand a gesture as it sounds, for he lived on the ground floor) and hastened to Debussy, breaking into his apartment. Debussy cut something less than a heroic figure. Confronted by the furious and formidable Maeterlinck, he refused to fight and sank prostrate into an armchair while his wife rushed to him with smelling salts. The baffled Maeterlinck took his leave saying, "All crazy, all sick, these musicians." There was talk of a duel between Debussy and Maeterlinck, or Carré and Maeterlinck. But there was no duel. Instead, Maeterlinck went to a fortuneteller. He did not believe in clairvoyance, he said, but then again he did not disbelieve in it. The clairvoyant supplied him with an answer that nobody could dispute. "The forces of nature are well balanced," said the clairvoyant. "According to human logic it is impossible to predict the outcome."

The affair ended with Maeterlinck writing an open letter to *Le Figaro,* telling the world that the performance was going to be given against his wishes. He accused Debussy of butchering the libretto "with arbitrary and absurd cuts." In the circumstances, said Maeterlinck, "I am reduced to wishing its immediate and decided failure."

Maeterlinck's wish was almost granted. *Pelléas et Mélisande* was not a success at its premiere on April 30, 1902, though it caused a great deal of comment. It soon took hold, however, even if it puzzled some fine musicians, especially German musicians. It ran so counter to what the Germans of the day considered opera that there was nothing for them to hold on to. Richard Strauss attended a performance of *Pelléas et Mélisande* in 1907 with Romain Rolland, who has written a very funny account of the evening:

> Strauss arrived at the end of the first scene and seated himself between Ravel and myself. Jean Marnold and Lionel de la Laurencie [two music critics] sat behind. . . . In his usual uninhibited manner with no regard for conventional courtesy, Strauss hardly speaks to anybody but myself, confiding his impressions of *Pelléas* to me in a whisper. (Since all the gossip in the papers he has become distrustful.) He listens with the greatest attention and, with his opera glasses up to his eyes, follows everything on the stage and in the orchestra. But he understands nothing. After the first act (the first three scenes), he says, "Is it like this all the time?" "Yes." "Nothing more? There's nothing in it. No music. It has nothing consecutive. No musical phrases. No development." Marnold tries to bring himself into the conversation and says, in his usual heavy manner, "There are musical phrases, but they are not brought out or underlined in a way that the ordinary listener would appreciate." Strauss, rather put out but very dignified, replies, "But I am a musician and I hear nothing." . . .

To this day, listeners conditioned by orthodox singing opera respond as Strauss did. *Pelléas et Mélisande* has never been popular in the sense that the operas of Verdi, Puccini, and Wagner are popular. It is too refined, too lacking in red blood. These attributes are, of course, the very things that attract the minority who consider *Pelléas et Mélisande* the most subtle and atmospheric opera ever written. It is an opera in which all traditional arias are banished. Instead, the characters declaim in a kind of speech-song. Before the premiere, Debussy called the cast together and begged everybody to forget they were singers. Mussorgsky, not Wagner, is the progenitor of the vocal line in this opera, though it also is the kind of integrated opera, complete with leitmotifs (which Strauss gleefully pointed out), that in theory closely approximates the Wagnerian ideal of a fusion of music, drama, and décor. In sound and concept, however, *Pelléas et Mélisande* altogether differs from Wagner. It is set in a dream world, a world of pianissimo sounds, diaphanous colors, subtlety, and restraint. It is an opera of *sensibilité*. Debussy was content. "I have tried to beat out a path where others can follow by adding their own discoveries and by ridding dramatic music of the heavy constraint from which it has suffered for so long a time."

Some years after the premiere he wrote for the Opéra-Comique an introduction to *Pelléas et Mélisande* that is of unusual interest. He said that he had always wanted to compose an opera. "But the form I wished to employ was so unusual that after various efforts I had almost abandoned the idea. Previous research in pure music had led me to hate classical development, whose beauty is merely technical and of interest only to the highbrows of our class. I desired for music that freedom of which it is capable perhaps to a greater degree than any other art, as it is not confined to an exact reproduction of nature, but only to the mysterious affinity between Nature and the Imagination." Wagner's theories were not the answer. "The thing, then, was to find what came *after Wagner's time* but not *after Wagner's manner.*" Maeterlinck's play suited Debussy because "in spite of its fantastic atmosphere" it contained "much more humanity than the so-called *documents of life.*" In his opera, Debussy said, he tried

to obey a law of beauty which appears to be singularly ignored in dealing with dramatic music. The characters of this drama endeavor to sing like real persons, and not in an arbitrary language built on antiquated traditions. Hence the reproach levelled at my alleged partiality for monotone declamation, in which there is no trace of melody. . . . To begin with, this is untrue. Besides, the feelings of a character cannot be continually expressed in melody. Then, too, dramatic melody should be totally different from melody in general. . . . The people who go to listen to music at the theater are, when all is said and done, very like those one sees gathered around a street singer! There, for a penny, one may indulge in melodic emotions. . . . By a singular irony, this public, which cries out for something new, is the very one that shows alarm and scoffs whenever one tries to wean it from old habits and the customary humdrum noises. . . . This may seem incomprehensible; but one must not forget that a work of art or an effort to create beauty are always regarded by some people as a personal affront.

Pelléas et Mélisande had no followers. It was unique and has remained unique. Debussy himself never made much of an attempt to push his one opera or, indeed, any of his music. His attitude toward life was something of a sullen I-don't-care viewpoint. Anyway, he did not like people very much, and that alone would have prevented him from the personal contacts that most composers have found indispensable for promoting their music. When he won the Prix de Rome in 1894 and had to live in the Villa Medici, he was miserable. He hated the villa, hated his fellow students, hated Rome, and fled to Paris without finishing his three-year term of what he called "forced labor." He always was abnormally touchy—quick to take offense, sensitive to the point of mania, uncomfortable with people he did not know. Naturally he hated to appear in public, hated to conduct, hated to play the piano at concerts. He preferred cats to people, and was never without one or more Siamese cats. Perhaps he saw reflected in cats the reserve, independence, and lack of morality of his own nature. Debussy did have the habits and morals of a tomcat, and there was something feline about the character of the man, though there was nothing feline about his physique. He was short, plump, flabby, pale, and indolent; he had heavily lidded eyes under his huge, bulging forehead; he wore a beard that reminded many of Christ in Italian renaissance paintings. He trained his hair to hide the bulges, but it did not work, and he was called "*Le Christ hydrocéphalique.*" He was indeed an unusual-looking man, and Colette referred to his "Pan-like head. . . . In his unrelenting gaze the pupils of his eyes seemed momentarily to dart from one spot to another like those of animals of prey hypnotized by their own searching intensity." Like a cat, he pampered himself and thought only of himself. "I don't know whether his egoism will ever be subdued," his schoolmate Paul Vidal had written. "He is incapable of any sacrifice whatever. Nothing has any hold over him. His parents are not rich. Instead of using the money from his lessons to support them, he buys for himself many books, curios, etchings and all that sort of thing. His mother has shown us drawers full of them." When his friends gave him "loans," they knew they would never be repaid.

The chain-smoking Debussy was a sybarite, a sensualist, an ironist, and not the most pleasant of men. It followed that he would be very choosy about his friends. Marcel Proust admired him, wanted to know him better, and once even cornered him and drove him home in his carriage. The meeting between the two great exemplars of *sensibilité* was not happy. Proust complained that Debussy did not listen to him. Debussy thought Proust was "long-winded and a bit of the concierge." Nevertheless Proust, always the snob, persisted, and asked Debussy to a party he wanted to give in his honor. Debussy refused to attend. "I know I am a bear, I much prefer to see each other again in a café. Don't hold it against me. I was born that way."

And he was also born a genius with two of the most sensitive ears any musician ever had. No composer ever had a more infallible instinct for the one chord that would supply exactly the right touch of color. These touches of color make his music, and especially his piano music, unique. Debussy composed a great deal of piano music, from the rather conventional *Pour le piano* to the austere *Études*. His piano music was as original as his own way of playing the piano. Alfredo Casella, the Italian composer, was spellbound when he heard Debussy play: "No words can describe his playing of some of the Préludes. He did not have the virtuosity of the specialist, but his touch was extremely sensitive. One had the impression that he was actually playing on the strings of the instrument, without the mechanical aid of keys and hammers. He used the pedals as nobody else ever did. The result was pure poetry."

Debussy would have been pleased with these words. His entire approach was aimed at liberating the piano from its percussive sound. That meant an approach derived from Chopin rather than from Beethoven. "I became finally and completely convinced," he wrote in 1909, "that Beethoven definitely wrote badly for the piano." And to the pianist Marguerite Long, "I heartily detest the piano concertos of Mozart, but less than those of Beethoven." Chopin had showed how, through pedal effects and delicate varieties of touch, the piano could be made to "sing." Debussy carried this one step further. Indeed he insisted that the piano should sound as though it were an "instrument without hammers." The fingers should "penetrate into the notes." Effects were to be obtained through use of the pedal—Debussy called it a "breathing pedal." In 1903 he started his mature series of piano works. In *Estampes, L'Isle Joyeuse*, the *Images, Children's Corner*, the two books of Préludes and the two of Études, a new style of piano writing was invented, the most significant since Chopin. Often the music is technically difficult, but technique is the least of it. Pianists of the day had to struggle with a new type of fingering, new spacings, new sonorities, and the revolutionary use of the pedal. Tones and chords now floated in air; melodies darted through blocks of suspended harmonies. (Later musicians like Pierre Boulez who loftily say that in their interpretations they want to "burn the mist off Debussy" ignore the fact that Debussy very consciously set out to create that very mist.) The piano pieces of Debussy are as much "impressions" as the canvases of the impressionist painters. They had no "development." Instead, these pieces seized upon a single idea, saw it through, and stopped. Harmonically the music followed no rule. Debussy's exquisite ear was the only rule, and it was an infallible ear. Tonality was not abandoned, but it did verge on dissolution. Chords did not necessarily resolve. They were often an end in themselves. A work like *Voiles* seems to operate in three keys at once—A minor, C major, and B flat major.

Debussy's songs also have this kind of tonal ambiguity. In the songs, the exquisite feeling for declamation heard in *Pelléas et Mélisande* is even more refined. The vocal line is largely a form of recitative, in which the words take on a heightened value, perfumed by Debussy's unerring ear for prosody and the exotic-sounding, sensual accompaniments. Debussy was always the sensualist. Even when he used ancient devices—modal scales, Gregorian chant, orientalisms of a pentatonic nature—the music sounded sensual. Or it sounded sensual when he used the whole-tone scale, a new device in which the scale was built on major seconds. There is in Debussy's music a languorous kind of veiled sound and, in the orchestral music, an absolutely new kind of approach. Debussy's orchestration is subtle, resilient, and original. As in his piano music, he *heard* differently from other composers. He gives us a series of sense impressions; and even in *La Mer*, the closest he came to writing a symphony, there is a feeling of improvisation rather than development. Color, timbre, and rhythm take on an importance equal to harmony and melody. To many of today's younger generation, a score like *Jeux* of 1912 is more revolutionary than anything by Schoenberg or Stravinsky.

Of course, Debussy pondered his aesthetic a good many years before starting to produce his great sequence of works. He did not write anything really significant until he was past thirty. Ravel, thirteen years his junior, started producing around 1900 at twenty-five, and the careers of the two were parallel. By 1907 the Debussy and Ravel cliques were having at each other, and musical Paris rocked with the battle. Debussy, who usually stood aloof from public controversy, was disgusted. He met a friend in the street one day, and the man said something about being annoyed by the Debussyists. "They annoy you?" said Debussy. "They are killing me."

When Debussy did start composing steadily, it was clear that his was not an abstract musical mind. He needed a trigger to set off a chain reaction, and it is significant that almost all of his works have names—*Printemps, Iberia, Children's Corner, Estampes, La Mer, Suite bergamasque, En blanc et noir*, and so on. Each of the twenty-four Préludes has a name, though the titles are placed *after* the music, not before. By doing this, Debussy clearly showed that he did not intend to write program music. He never tells a story. Rather he gives an impression—an impression of the sea, of moonlight, of goldfish, of Spain. He is the musical painter and epigrammatist *par excellence*. Even his most ambitious orchestral work, *La Mer*, is almost completely unprogrammatic, much less programmatic than Beethoven's *Pastoral Symphony* (which was also an "impression" of nature), for Beethoven has specific indications of bird calls, a thunderstorm, and a peasant's frolic. *La Mer*, on the other hand, is a series of tonal impressions in which one does not see waves but feels them, a series of impressions in which the images are implied rather than specific. "I have the greatest contempt for music that has to follow a bit of literature which they've been careful to hand out when you come in," Debussy once wrote.

It is interesting to note that in this great score the free impressionism of

Debussy is tempered with something like classic form. There are three movements that bear a passing resemblance to the classical symphony. When he died on March 25, 1918, in Paris, while it was being bombarded by the Germans, Debussy was turning to a new idea of classical form and was germinating six instrumental sonatas, of which three had been completed. The Sonata for Cello and the Sonata for Flute, Viola and Harp are infrequently played, but the Violin Sonata is often heard and it is a lovely work that looks back to the early String Quartet. It might have been that Debussy would have revolutionized classic form as much as he had revolutionized other aspects of music.

He was irritated with the term "impressionism," much as Schumann three generations before him had been irritated by the term "romanticism." When he composed *Images* he tried to explain his theories. "What I am trying to do is something different—an effect of reality, but what some fools call impressionism, a term that is usually misapplied, especially by the critics who don't hesitate to apply it to Turner, the greatest creator of mysterious effects in the whole world of art." But what it comes down to is a matter of semantics. Whatever it be called—impressionism, superreality, or what you will—Debussy worked as did the great poets or painters, heightening reality by giving a new aural picture of the world. From his exquisitely sharpened sensibilities came a new vocabulary. His was not the grand-thewed music of a Bach or Beethoven, and some of it is even precious. But in its taste, color, and fragrance there never has been anything like it. His work has a texture—transparent, glowing, vaguely modal, exotic, unerringly precise—that is one of the most original in music. So is his harmony original, with its hitherto unheard-of parallel chordal movement, unresolved dissonances, arbitrary scales, and a new grammar.

It is the beginning of the twentieth-century breakup of music. No longer was there a great structure assembled like a cathedral. No longer were there to be set rules by which this modulation or progression was allowed, that one not. Debussy did to tonal relationships what Monet and Cézanne did to traditional color relationships. *Pouf!* and out they went. Art and music became insinuation rather than rhetoric or illustration, the haiku rather than the sonnet. One magical, spiced chord was enough to set the mood. Why bother about unnecessary development? Debussy never forgot the remark of Verlaine that one must wring the neck of eloquence.

❧ I I ❧

Gallic Elegance and the New Breed

MAURICE RAVEL AND LES SIX

Claude Debussy and Maurice Ravel were to each other in France what Anton Bruckner and Gustav Mahler were to each other in Austria. Their careers overlapped, and they had certain things in common, representing much the same backgrounds and traditions. Debussy and Ravel are classified as impressionists—indeed, the only two impressionists of importance. But, as with Bruckner and Mahler, their differences were vaster than the things they had in common.

Where Debussy was a sensuous composer, in the line from Chopin to Gounod to Massenet, Ravel was much the more objective, a precisionist whose line runs from Liszt to Saint-Saëns to Fauré. Debussy's music floats on a cushion of air. Ravel's ticks away like a well-assembled chronometer—Stravinsky once called Ravel "a Swiss watchmaker." His music contains a great deal of artifice, and he was accused in his day of being artificial. "Has it ever occurred to them," he said of his detractors, "that one may be artificial by nature?" Ravel never minded being called artificial, but he very much minded being called imitative. Many critics in the first decade of the twentieth century wrote that Ravel copied Debussy. Ravel deeply resented the charge.

The relationship between the two greatest French musical figures at the beginning of the new century is a little clouded, and not much is known about it. Debussy and Ravel did not even correspond; no letter is known to have passed between them. Debussy, in letters to other people, had some snide remarks to make about his younger colleague. Ravel, much more temperate, had nothing but praise for Debussy throughout his life, though sometimes the praise had a curious cutting edge.

Ravel and Debussy probably met in 1901. At that time, Ravel, who had been born in Ciboure in the Basses-Pyrénées on March 7, 1875 (and thus thirteen years younger than Debussy), was still in the Paris Conservatoire, which he had entered in 1889. Although he had started to play the piano at the age of seven, Ravel was not a child prodigy, and he remained in the Conservatoire for sixteen years, an unusually long time. In 1898 he began to be performed. and in 1901 he composed his *Jeux d'eau*, which was published the following year Debussy at that time had composed no piano music of any importance In later life Ravel, politely but firmly, kept insisting he had priority; that if it was a matter of copying, Debussy had copied from *him*. Thus, in a letter to Pierre Lalo in 1906: "You propound at length on a rather special kind of piano writing, the invention of which you ascribe to Debussy. But *Jeux d'eau* appeared at the beginning of 1902, when the only known piano works of Debussy were the three pieces forming the suite *Pour le piano* which, I hardly need say, I deeply admire but which from a purely pianistic point of view conveyed nothing really new." And, as late as 1928, ten years after Debussy's death, Ravel was still desperately anxious to keep the record straight:

> For Debussy the musician and the man, I have had profound admiration, but by nature I am different from Debussy, and while I consider that Debussy may not have been altogether alien to my personal inheritance, I should identify also with the earliest phases of my evolution Gabriel Fauré, Emmanuel Chabrier and Erik Satie. . . . I believe that I myself have always followed a direction opposite to that of Debussy's symbolism. . . . It has been claimed with some insistence that the earlier appearance of my *Jeux d'eau* possibly influenced Debussy in the composition of his *Jardins sous la pluie*, while a coincidence even more striking has been suggested in the case of my *Habanera*; but comments of this sort I must leave to others. It could very well be. however, that conceptions apparently similar in character should mature in the consciousness of two different composers at almost the same time without implying direct influence of either one upon the other.

At the beginning, Debussy seems to have encouraged Ravel. He is said to have sent a letter to Ravel about the String Quartet of 1904: "In the name of the gods of music, and in my name, do not touch a single note." This sentence is quoted in many biographies of the two composers, but nobody has come up with the actual letter. Ravel's reputation grew very fast, and Louis Laloy. the French musicologist and critic, said in his memoirs that the friends of Debussy and Ravel took sides so furiously, that there were so many "silly meddlers," that after a while the two men simply stopped seeing each other. It was Romain Rolland's opinion that the coolness stemmed mostly from Debussy, "who has, I know, a violent antipathy for the music (or the success) of Ravel. Ravel speaks of him with great dignity and modesty." Debussy, who was terribly catty about almost all music but his own, had some nasty things to say about Ravel when Laloy reviewed Ravel's *Histoires naturelles* in 1907. Laloy wrote that the songs were in the spirit of Mussorgsky, only better. Debussy was furious and sent Laloy a note. He wrote that he was "amazed to see that a man of your taste deliberately sacrifices such a pure, instinctive masterpiece as *The Nursery* to the artificial Americanisms of the *Histoires naturelles* of M. Ravel. Despite Ravel's unquestioned skill, these songs consist of music that we must call unwarranted." Ravel, on the other hand, never ceased to admire Debussy's music, and in 1909–10 transcribed for two pianos the Nocturnes and *L'Après-midi d'un Faune.*

Ravel in 1910 was a famous man and had been so ever since 1905, when a scandal erupted over his failure to win the Prix de Rome. He had first competed in 1901. Amused by the stuffiness of the text to which he had to write a cantata, he submitted a manuscript largely in waltz time. The jury huffed and puffed. "M. Ravel should not think he can ridicule us. M. Ravel may well consider us flatfooted pedants, but he will not go unpunished for taking us for imbeciles." Ravel was awarded the second prize, and comforted himself with all the publicity he had received. He remained at the Conservatoire and competed again in 1902 and 1903, receiving no prize at all. When he applied for the Prix de Rome in 1905 he was not permitted to compete, on the grounds that he was over thirty. There was an immediate uproar from the press, and the case became a *cause célèbre.*

For Ravel was not merely a young, talented composer. He was far more than that. He had proved himself, and already was the most-discussed young composer in France. As early as 1895 he was in print with his *Menuet antique,* a short piano piece that already had the sophisticated precision of his mature style. His *Les Sites auriculaires* had been played at a concert of the Société Nationale in 1898. Ricardo Viñes, the Spanish pianist who had been a classmate of Ravel's at the Conservatoire and who eventually was to play the premieres of nearly all of Ravel's and Debussy's piano music, had introduced *Jeux d'eau* in 1902. In 1903 Ravel composed the fine song cycle *Shéhérazade,* and in 1904 the String Quartet in F. This was the composer who was not considered competent enough for the Prix de Rome in 1903, and who was not allowed to compete in 1905. There was indignation not only in musical circles, and the newspapers seized the story, siding with Ravel. For a few months Paris buzzed with the dispute. Ravel was interviewed by *Le Temps* and issued a dignified statement:

> I am not going to Rome. This was decided by the institute, which is the only one with the power to open to young composers the road to the Villa Medici. This misfortune upsets me. The award of the second prize; my diligent work, encouraged and appreciated by my professor, M. Ga-

briel Fauré; my works, published and favorably received by the public, allowed me to hope, without any ridiculous presumption of writing a perfect cantata, or one superior to my comrades, that I would be permitted to join the competition. . . .

One result of *l'affaire Ravel* was the resignation of Théodore Dubois as director of the Conservatoire, and the appointment of Fauré in his stead. But none of this directly affected Ravel, who left the Conservatoire. From that point to the end of his life, he lived quietly as a composer. He was a tiny man, just about five feet tall, elegant, a natty dresser to the point of dandyism. "I would at any time rather have been Beau Brummel than Maurice Ravel," he once said. There was a good deal of gossip about him in his day. He claimed Basque ancestry through his mother, but nobody has been able to trace the family line far enough back to see if the claim had any validity. There were those who called Ravel a Jew. Again there is no proof, though it appears unlikely. It was whispered that he was a homosexual. Again there is no evidence one way or the other. He never married, and his name was never linked to a woman or a man.

For a long time he was a member of a group known as the "Apaches," along with the composer Florent Schmitt, the poet Tristan Klingsor, the pianist Viñes, the writer Léon-Paul Fargue, the critic Dimitri Calvocoressi, and others famous in French intellectual life. This was a French *Davidsbund*, and Schumann would have been delighted. Much of Ravel's music was first heard by the Apaches, and he listened very carefully to their criticisms. His Sonatine and the five *Miroirs* were composed in 1905; the Introduction and Allegro for harp, flute, clarinet, and string quartet was finished in 1906, the same year as the song cycle, *Histoires naturelles*. *Miroirs* puzzled the Apaches; and, indeed, only one of the set has achieved much popularity—*Alborado del Gracioso*, with its Spanish snappiness and brilliant piano layout. The other pieces—*Oiseaux tristes, Noctuelles, La Vallée des cloches*, and *Une Barque sur l'océan*—seemed to wander in a no-man's land between music and painting. Where *Miroirs* bored most listeners of the day, the *Histoires naturelles*, set to poems by Jules Renard, caused a scandal. Jane Bathori sang them early in 1907 at a Société Nationale concert, and it was a wild evening. The Debussyists screamed at the Ravelites, and vice versa. Newspapers referred to the concert and the commotion it created as the second *Affaire Ravel*. Lalo added to the fire with articles accusing Ravel of imitating Debussy without knowing what he was doing.

Ravel, after entering the dispute himself and writing a few letters to the newspapers, started work on a one-act comic opera, *L'Heure Espagnole*. He finished it in 1907 and then had to wait four years to see it on stage. Other major works up to the beginning of World War I included the three-movement *Gaspard de la Nuit* in 1908 and the *Valses nobles et sentimentales* in 1911 (both for solo piano), *Ma Mère l'Oye* in 1908 (piano duet), the *Rapsodie Espagnole* in 1907 (for orchestra), and the ballet *Daphnis et Chloë*. The ballet was composed for Diaghilev's Ballets Russes, receiving its premiere in 1912. Unlike Stravinsky's two blockbusters for Diaghilev—*Firebird* in 1910 and *Petrushka* in 1911—*Daphnis et Chloë* has never been a popular ballet. Its story is too static, its choreography by Vaslav Nijinsky is too awkward, and its Grecian poses do not go very well with Ravel's score. But the two orchestral suites arranged from the ballet immediately started to make the rounds, and the *Daphnis et Chloë* Suite No. 2 became one of the most popular orchestral works of the century. The ballet itself was soon withdrawn from the Ballets Russes repertoire. But Ravel's association with Diaghilev did result in one of the most spectacular orchestral scores of the twentieth century, and it also served to bring Ravel and Stravinsky together. The two composers admired each other and in 1913, even worked together on an orchestration of Mussorgsky's *Khovantchina* to be used for a ballet. Ravel and the Apaches all turned out for the premiere of Stravinsky's *Sacre du Printemps* on May 29, 1913, at the Champs-Elysées Théâtre, cheering their new champion.

The last work Ravel completed before the war was the fine Trio in A minor, one of his most polished and elegant scores (the opening theme of the first movement may well be his greatest lyric inspiration). Ravel tried to get into the army but was rejected. He was too short, and he was underweight. Finally, early in 1916, he was accepted as a truck driver and even got to the front lines. In 1917 he was transferred to Paris and discharged because of ill health. Among other symptoms, it was feared that he had developed tuberculosis. He went to Normandy to convalesce, and worked on *Le Tombeau de Couperin*, finishing both the piano solo version and its arrangement for orchestra in 1917. Then, back in Paris, he composed *La Valse* (1920), which he originally named *Wien*. *La Valse*, a "choreographic poem," was composed for Diaghilev, who paid for it but never used the music. Ravel was hurt. (The two men met in 1925, and Ravel refused to shake hands. Diaghilev was insulted and challenged Ravel to a duel. As customary, the challenger was talked out of it. They never met again.) He purchased a little villa, Le Belvédère, at Montfort l'Amaury and stocked it with a collection of mechanical toys, which he loved to wind up and operate for his friends. In 1920 he was awarded the Legion of Honor—and refused to accept it. He had not forgotten the way he had been finessed out of the Prix de Rome. Later, showing what he thought of the French government, he accepted a decoration from King Leopold of Belgium and an honorary doctorate from Oxford.

In the meantime, *Les Six* were coming into international attention. They were grouped around Erik Satie and represented an aesthetic that differed considerably from Ravel's. He showed them a thing or two in 1925 with his opera-pantomime, *L'Enfant et les sortilèges*, as sophisticated a work as any turned out by *Les Six*. There followed the *Chansons madécasses* (1926), a violin sonata (1927), a trip to the United States in 1928, the famous *Bolero* (1929), and two piano concertos (1931) One of those concertos, in D for the left hand alone, was commissioned by the Austrian pianist Paul Wittgenstein, who had lost his right arm during the war. The other was the more orthodox Concerto in G.

In 1932, perhaps as a result of an automobile accident, perhaps from a disease more deeply functional, Ravel had a nervous breakdown. His injuries from the crash appeared to be superficial, and Ravel made light of them: "a few cracks, an arched nose to persuade the Americans of my Hebrew origin, but particularly some bruises on my chest that force me to cough in a crooked way." The following year, 1933, he began to lose control of his arms and legs. This was followed by memory loss and an inability to coordinate. Though his mind remained normal, he could not compose or play the piano. In 1937 he underwent brain surgery, from which he never recovered. His malady has been kept secret. On December 28, 1937, Ravel died in a Paris hospital.

He left a small quantity of music, little of it large-scale. And a good deal of his orchestral music was originally composed for the piano. This includes *Ma Mère l'Oye*, the *Pavane pour une infante défunte*, *Alborado del Gracioso*, the third movement (*Habanera*) of the *Rapsodie espagnole*, *Le Tombeau de Couperin*, and the *Valses nobles et sentimentales*. One of his most popular pieces involves another piano work, his orchestration of Mussorgsky's *Pictures at an Exhibition*. The flashy *Tzigane* was originally composed in 1924 as a piece for violin and piano, and later that year transformed into one for violin and orchestra. All of this music is of a piece; there is very little variation in quality. From the very beginning, Ravel worked out an individual style, and it varied surprisingly little through the years. His early influences were Liszt, Chabrier, Mussorgsky, and Fauré and, of course, Debussy played a part in his development. No young composer growing up in Paris after *L'après-midi* could entirely escape those new sounds.

But in essence, Ravel's aesthetic worked on different premises from Debussy's. Ravel was more precise, and a more orthodox formalist, using sonata form and forms derived from classical and baroque models. His music, personal as it is, has a strong feeling of objectivity. Ravel's music never had the languorous sensuousness of Debussy's; it was an etching against the watercolors of his great contemporary. Debussy's forms were often evolved from colors and textures, and followed no known rules. Ravel worked from themes rather than colors and textures. Much more than Debussy he looked to his

423

predecessors, often writing pieces "in the manner of." His very first important work, *Jeux d'eau*, was a water piece inspired by Liszt's *Jeux d'eaux à la Villa d'Este*. "It should be played the way you play Liszt," Ravel told Viñes. Ravel never conceived of the piano, as Debussy did, as an instrument without hammers. In *Gaspard de la Nuit* he specifically set out to write a post-Lisztian virtuoso piece "to be more difficult than Balakirev's *Islamey*." *Scarbo*, the last of the three pieces of *Gaspard de la Nuit*, is one of the most prodigious finger-twisters of the repertory. It came into special favor after World War II. The new generation of pianists loved it and made *Gaspard* one of the most-performed of twentieth-century piano works.

Having been triggered by Liszt and Balakirev, Ravel next turned to Schubert in his *Valses nobles et sentimentales*. "The title. . . . shows clearly enough my intention to compose a chain of waltzes in the style of Schubert [who had composed a series named *Valses Nobles*]. In the place of the virtuosity that characterized *Gaspard de la Nuit*, there was a style clearer, brighter, that emphasized the harmonies and brought them into relief." The *Valses nobles et sentimentales* ended up as French as Schubert is Viennese. The idea may come from Schubert, but the execution is perfumed French, especially the last of the waltzes, which in a dreamlike manner reminisces about the previous waltzes. Schubert was not the only Austrian composer who prompted a Ravel work. There also were Johann Strauss and Mozart. *La Valse* stems from the former, the Piano Concerto in G from the latter. Ravel described *La Valse* as "a sort of homage to the memory of the Great Strauss, not Richard, the other—Johann. You know my intense sympathy for this admirable rhythm, and that I hold *la joie de vivre* as expressed by the dance in far higher esteem than as expressed by the Franckist puritanism. I am so little a Catholic." As for the G major Concerto, Ravel claimed that it was "a concerto in the truest sense of the word, very much in the same spirit as those of Mozart and Saint-Saëns. The music of a concerto should, in my opinion, be light-hearted, brilliant and not aim at profundity or at dramatic effects." Ravel makes it clear that he does not like the piano concertos of Brahms; he said that they are against the piano, not for it.

The restless, inquisitive Ravel looked elsewhere for other works. He went back to the clavecinists for *Le Tombeau de Couperin*. In the United States he met George Gershwin, listened to a great deal of jazz, and incorporated it, with other American devices, into his music. He said that he had tried to compose *L'Enfant et les sortilèges* "in the style of an American operetta." The slow movement of his Violin Sonata is named *Blues*, and there is some jazz in his G major Concerto. For the *Rapsodie espagnole* and *L'Heure espagnole* he turned to Spain, as so many French composers before him had done.

His prime period ended in 1914. Later, in ill health, he found it harder and harder to write. It bothered him. "I have failed in my life," he told the composer Claude Delvincourt. "I am not one of the great composers. All the great have produced enormously. There is everything in their work—the best and the worst, but there is always quantity. But I have written relatively very little . . . and at that, I did it with a great deal of difficulty. I did my work slowly, drop by drop. I have torn all of it out of me by pieces . . . . and now I cannot do any more, and it does not give me any pleasure." Nevertheless he went on during the following twelve years to compose some fine music that shows no diminution in his powers. Some critics maintain that the Piano Concerto for the Left Hand, one of his last works, is one of the most exciting and significant he ever composed.

All of this music, no matter what its inspiration (Liszt, Schubert, or Spain), ends up filtered through Ravel's imagination and technique into a consistent amalgam. It all has the Ravel sound. He was a musician pure and simple, working directly with the materials of music, and, unlike so many of the composers of the period, he had no theories about music, nor did he involve himself with the various aesthetic movements. There seldom is the feeling of instinct in his music; everything is too carefully arranged and balanced. It is even, in a way, a reticent music, in that Ravel seldom bared his emotions. Some critics have complained that Ravel was too detached, and he most definitely *was* detached. But with this objectivity, the music also has charm, extraordinary finish, wit (as in the *Histoires naturelles*), and color. As an orchestrator he was even more inventive than Debussy, from whom he learned a great deal. Compare Ravel's *Rapsodie espagnole* with Debussy's *Iberia*, two great scores inspired by Spain, and composed within a year of each other—1907 and 1908 respectively. The Ravel orchestration has a springier, lither quality.

Ravel was not a creator on the mighty level of a Debussy. His mind worked along somewhat more conventional paths, and he was just a shade too conscious of his own style. But in his range he worked with surety and perfection, and his music has dated very little.

It has dated far less than the music of most of the members of *Les Six*, the darlings of Paris in the 1920's, the youngsters who were really "modern," who were going to lead French music into new paths. The genesis of *Les Six* goes back to 1917, when Diaghilev staged *Parade*, with music by Erik Satie, book by Jean Cocteau, décor by Pablo Picasso. *Parade* created one of those scandals so dear to the hearts of the French public. A group of young composers, vociferous in their admiration of the score, gathered around Satie. These youngsters, whom Satie called his *nouveaux jeunes*, were the Swiss-born Arthur Honegger, Georges Auric, Louis Durey, and Germaine Tailleferre. A year later, Francis Poulenc and Darius Milhaud joined the *nouveaux jeunes*. "We were tired of Debussyism, of Florent Schmitt, of

Ravel," Poulenc wrote. "I wanted music to be clear, healthy and robust—music as frankly French in spirit as Stravinsky's *Petrushka* is Russian. To me, Satie's *Parade* is to Paris what *Petrushka* is to St. Petersburg." Under this aesthetic, the young composers joined forces. Milhaud has described how *Les Six* became consolidated:

> After a concert at the Salle Huyghens [in 1919], at which Bertin sang Louis Durey's *Images à Crusoë* on words by Saint-Léger and the Capelle Quartet played my Fourth Quartet, the critic Henri Collet published in *Comoedia* a chronicle entitled "Five Russians and the Frenchmen." Quite arbitrarily he had chosen six names: Auric, Durey, Honegger, Poulenc, Tailleferre and my own, merely because we knew each other, were good friends and had figured on the same programs: quite apart from our different temperaments and wholly dissimilar characters. Auric and Poulenc were followers of Cocteau, Honegger derived from the German romantics, and I from Mediterranean lyricism.   . But it was useless to protest. Collet's article excited such worldwide interest that the "Group of Six" was launched, and willy-nilly I formed part of it.
>
> This being so, we decided to give some *Concerts des Six*. The first was devoted to my works, the second to foreign music.   . Satie was our mascot. He was very popular among us. He was so fond of young people that he said to me one day: "I wish I knew what sort of music will be written by the children who are four years old now." The purity of his art, his horror of all concessions, his contempt for money and his ruthless attitude toward the critics were a marvellous example for us all.

Cocteau became the intellectual leader of Les Six, much as Satie was its spiritual leader. Stravinsky was the third guru, but only as an influence. *Les Six* admired his music more than the music of any other living composer. To them, Debussy was "dead," and Ravel's music was "arty," "excessively refined," "outworn." Music in general, they said, was sterile, living on formulae of the old masters. Intermarriage and fresh blood were needed: the intermarriage of "serious" music with jazz, popular music, vaudeville, music hall, the circus, commercial music. To be lowbrow was to be highbrow. One had to thumb one's nose at tradition. One did not write symphonies. Instead one wrote foxtrots, satires, burlesques, caricatures, short pieces, dance music. It was the Jazz Age: a merry period that produced some merry works, most of which are now forgotten.

Durey and Tailleferre soon dropped from sight, and Auric never produced anything of much value. The one who first came to international attention was Darius Milhaud (born on September 4, 1892). Honegger was slow developing, and the facile Poulenc was regarded as a clown. Milhaud attracted a great deal of attention in the early 1920's, especially for his polytonal experiments. Stravinsky had started things off with the famous F sharp major against C major episode in *Petrushka*. Milhaud took it from there, developing the concept. "I set to work to examine every possible combination of two keys superimposed and to study the chords thus produced. Then I did the same thing in three keys. What I could not understand was why, though the harmony books dealt with chords and their inversions and the laws governing their sequence, the same thing could not be done for polytonality. I grew familiar with some of these chords. They satisfied my ear more than the normal ones, for a polytonal chord is more subtly sweet and more violently potent."

Milhaud, incredibly fluent and industrious, applied his polytonal theories to every type of music, and his scores—*La Création du monde* (1923), *Le Boeuf sur le toit* (1919), *Les Choëphores* (1919), the so-called "minute operas"—were the last word in chic avant-gardism of the 1920's. They were spicy, they were clever, they were sophisticated, they were dissonant, they shocked the bourgeoisie. Endlessly inventive, Milhaud came up with effect after effect. But eventually the shock value and novelty wore off. Today the Milhaud scores of the 1920's and 1930's tend to sound like Stravinsky pressed through a filter made in Paris. Very little of Milhaud's music remains in the permanent repertory.

Arthur Honegger (March 10, 1892–November 28, 1955) became allied to *Les Six* despite pronounced differences in style and outlook. He was close to the Central European tradition, and he wrote in a busy, angry-man, tightly compressed kind of way. There is very little humor in his music, and that alone almost immediately separated him from *Les Six*. Another point of difference was his penchant for working in sonata form: five symphonies, three string quartets, and the like. In the early 1920's he became famous for an age-of-steel tone poem, *Pacific 2-3-1* (1923). That has long since disappeared from concert programs. His large-scale choral works—*Le Roi David* (1921) and *Jeanne d'Arc au bûcher* (1938)—attracted a good deal of interest in their day and are still occasionally heard. But on the whole Honegger has slid from his once-high position, and his music is vanishing fast from the halls.

It seems clear that Francis Poulenc (January 7, 1889–January 30, 1963) has emerged as the strongest and most individual member of Les Six. Nobody would have guessed it in the 1930's. The betting would have been on Milhaud or Honegger. Poulenc was considered the comic (he even had a marked facial and physical resemblance to the great French comic Fernandel), the court jester, the sophisticate. So charming and amusing! So lightweight! So chic! As a corollary, so unimportant, *au fond!* To the world Poulenc was the musical soft-shoe man, dancing away at his music-hall routines with not a care in the world, a grin permanently plastered on his face.

As it turned out, neither Milhaud nor Honegger had much staying power. Poulenc was the one who kept growing. From the *enfant terrible* of *Les Six* he developed into a skilled composer whose outlook and technique developed with the years. And even from the beginning it was apparent that Poulenc was a fine composer of songs. He developed into a great one. Some insist he was the greatest since Fauré, and that includes Debussy. He had style; he had taste; his ear for the accent of the word, for the patterns of prosody and its relationship with the note, was unparalleled. Above all, he had a fresh and original fount of melody. As a melodist, Poulenc was more than a mere entertainer. He had a distinguished gift. Never a composer comfortable with large structures until near the end of his life, Poulenc found the lyric forms—songs, piano pieces—best suited to his intense but narrow talent. Poulenc's songs soon became firmly established in the repertoire, and they promise to be a permanent fixture.

A great deal of his other music also seems to have become fixed in the repertoire. Perhaps this is because of the basic conservatism of his idiom. True, it is smart and undeniably modern, what with its constant references to Stravinsky's neoclassicism, its titillating dissonances, and unexpected harmonic darts. One of Poulenc's favorite devices, to the point of mannerism, was his use of unprepared modulations a half step down. It is his fingerprint, found in virtually every piece he composed. But Poulenc was conservative in that he never lost contact with the past—with Schumann, and Fauré, and Chabrier, and the mainstream of nineteenth-century harmony. Despite his flirtations with polytonality and other then-advanced devices, Poulenc thought tonally and composed tonally. As often as not he composed in triadic, tonic-dominant harmony. That is one reason the 1920's and 1930's refused to take him very seriously. Those were the great days of "modernism," and modernism was equated with dissonance (or what was considered dissonant in those days; ears have since been stretched). It had to follow that anybody bucking the trend and, in effect, composing "white-key music," could not conceivably be accepted as an important creator.

But Poulenc went his own way and had the last laugh in the long run, for he outlived certain revered twentieth-century figures just as Berlioz outlived Meyerbeer, Offenbach outlived Halévy, Sullivan outlived Stanford, and Fauré outlived d'Indy. Poulenc's talent might have been restricted, and nobody ever claimed that he was a universal composer in the sense that Beethoven and Mozart were; but at the same time there was something genuine, something very valuable, about his talent. He had something to say, and he said it with style and personality.

At the beginning of his career, from the end of World War I to the early 1930's, he wrote flip, fashionable, brittle, but jewel-like music. The *Aubade* for small orchestra, the ballet *Les Biches*, the *Mouvements perpetuels* for piano, *Le Bal masqué*, a series of songs including the cycle *Le Bestiaire*—all these were the work of a brash, talented young man with a propensity for teasing his elders and poking fun at the verities. So clever is this music that even today it continues to charm. A little later came more substantial works like the Mass in G (1937) and the Organ Concerto (1938), less flip, trying for more serious things. A superb series of song collections date from this period, including *Banalités, Chansons villageoises, Tel jour, telle nuit, Caligrammes*. During World War II Poulenc composed an opera named *Les Mamelles de Tirésias*. This was a throwback to his tomfoolery days. As such, it was exceptional, but it also turned out to be a neo-Offenbachian romp, naughty and delicious. During the last twenty years of his life he seldom worked this vein. There was a broadening-out, a new dimension, an emphasis on religious music. These religious works culminated in the simple and beautiful Gloria (1961), and in the opera *Les Dialogues des Carmélites* (1957).

The opera is, like most of his music, intimate. Poulenc was never one for the big gesture. Indeed, in a curious way, *Carmélites* recalls such earlier and light-hearted works as *Les Biches* and *Aubade*, in that Poulenc's melodic habits changed very little through the years. He had his little tricks and was constantly repeating them. But toward the end, his short-breathed, delicate melodies were put to new uses, intensified, made to express something more than easy badinage. In the first dialogue between Blanche and Constance in the *Carmélites*, the exquisite, tiny theme (almost a motto) that comes up whenever death is mentioned is startling in its emotional impact, its focus of concentration. But it happens to be first cousin to a theme that can be found in the salonlike Sextet of 1940, and later in the Gloria of 1961. In each case the theme has an entirely different emotional meaning.

Many musicians still refuse to take Poulenc seriously. Part of the trouble stems from our musical phylogeny, so closely imbred to Germanic ideas about form, structure, and "sublimity." Poulenc did not compose orthodox, completely developed sonatas and symphonies; he had little truck with fugue and canon; he specialized in pretty songs and sophisticated piano pieces. *Ergo*, he must have written *Kitsch*. But this kind of *Kitsch*, as represented in Poulenc's vocal music, will live as long as there are singers around to sing songs.

12

The Chameleon

IGOR STRAVINSKY

Igor Stravinsky, born on June 17, 1882 in St Petersburg, lived to be universally recognized as the world's greatest living composer. He all but started out at the top. There was no doubt of his stature after the three Russian ballets he wrote for Serge Diaghilev between 1910 and 1913 in Paris. *Firebird,* which had its premiere on June 25, 1910, was the first, and it made the twenty-eight-year-old composer famous overnight, as Diaghilev had predicted the day before the performance. The score was a brilliant exercise in Russian nationalism, derived from Rimsky-Korsakov in general and Rimsky's *Coq d'Or* in particular. But it was far more daring and original than any work by Rimsky, and everybody knew that an unusual composer had arrived. Debussy's keen ears picked out the essential quality of *Firebird:* "It is not a perfect piece, but from certain aspects it is nevertheless very fine, for here the music is not the docile servant of the dance. And at times you hear altogether unusual combinations of rhythms." On June 13, 1911, came *Petrushka,* and it solidified Stravinsky's position as the coming man of European music. Like *Firebird, Petrushka* was a ballet on a Russian subject, but it moved with more confidence and mastery, and it had some ideas that were to affect the course of European music, especially its polytonality. There was one section in which two unrelated harmonies, C major and F sharp major, joined forces, and the effect came as a revelation to young European composers. For the next two decades there were numerous polytonal experiments stemming from *Petrushka.* To listeners of 1911, the Stravinsky ballet had a barbarous quality eclipsing anything that had come out of Russia before, and the tiny composer took on the dimensions of a giant. Even Diaghilev had not expected the fuss raised by *Petrushka.* Its great success was a surprise.

But all the excitement was nothing against the impact of *Le Sacre du Printemps,* which had its premiere on May 29, 1913. Stravinsky had conceived the idea for it while working on *Firebird*. "I dreamed of a scene of pagan ritual in which a chosen sacrificial virgin danced herself to death." Work on *Le Sacre* was dropped for *Petrushka*, but Stravinsky soon resumed work on the new ballet. (He has said that *The Coronation of Spring* would be closer to his original meaning than the usual translation, *The Rite of Spring*.) Vaslav Nijinsky was the choreographer, and the premiere resulted in the most famous *scandale* in the history of music. Hardly anybody in the audience was prepared for a score of such dissonance and ferocity, such complexity and such rhythmic oddity. Nobody connected with the production had the faintest idea that the music would provoke a visceral reaction. As soon as the bassoon ended its phrase in the high register, at the very opening of the ballet, laughter broke out. Soon there were whistles and catcalls. Nobody could hear the music. Diaghilev had the electricians switch the house lights off and on, in an effort to restore order. Nijinsky, in the wings, yelled the rhythms to the dancers. The Comtesse de Pourtalès stood in her box, brandishing her fan, and shouted: "This is the first time in sixty years that anybody has dared make fun of me." People hurled insults at each other. The Apaches, headed by Ravel, shrieked their praise. Stravinsky himself, in his *Expositions and Developments*, has described the famous evening at the Théâtre des Champs-Elysées:

That the first performance of *Le Sacre du Printemps* was attended by a scandal must be known to everybody. Strange as it may seem, however, I was unprepared for the explosion myself. The reactions of the musicians who came to the orchestra rehearsals were without intimation of it, and the stage spectacle did not appear likely to precipitate a riot. The dancers had been rehearsing for months and they knew what they were doing, even though what they were doing often had nothing to do with the music. . . . Mild protests against the music could be heard from the very beginning of the performance. Then, when the curtain opened on the group of knock-kneed and long-braided Lolitas jumping up and down (*Danse des adolescents*), the storm broke. Cries of "*Ta gueule*" came from behind me. I heard Florent Schmitt shout "*Taisez-vous garces du seizième;*" the "*garces*" of the sixteenth arondissement were, of course, the most elegant ladies in Paris. The uproar continued, however, and a few minutes later I left the hall in a rage; I was sitting on the right near the orchestra, and I remember slamming the door. I have never again been that angry. The music was familiar to me; I loved it, and I could not understand why people who had not yet heard it wanted to protest in advance. I arrived in a fury backstage, where I saw Diaghilev flicking the house lights in a last effort to quiet the hall. For the rest of the performance I stood in the wings behind Nijinsky holding the tails of his *frac* while he stood on a chair shouting numbers to the dancers like a coxswain.

Le Sacre du Printemps hit Europe with unprecedented force. It was to the first half of the twentieth century what the Beethoven Ninth and *Tristan* were to the nineteenth. For decades there were repercussions as composers all over the world imitated the new Stravinsky rhythms and sonorities. In Prokofiev's *Scythian* Suite, in Bartók's *Miraculous Mandarin,* in the Milhaud "minute operas," in music everywhere one could hear *Sacre* rhythms. They entered the musical subconscious of every young composer. *Le Sacre du Printemps,* with its metrical shiftings and shattering force, its near-total dissonance and breakaway from established canons of harmony and melody, was a genuine explosion. After the score had its premiere in Boston, a poem appeared in the *Herald* that was widely reprinted. It presented a prevailing audience attitude toward the Stravinsky work:

> Who wrote this fiendish *Rite of Spring,*
> What right had he to write the thing,
> Against our helpless ears to fling
> Its crash, clash, cling, clang, bing, bang, bing?

> And then to call it *Rite of Spring*
> The season when on joyous wing
> The birds harmonious carols sing
> And harmony's in everything!

> He who could write the *Rite of Spring*
> If I be right, by right should swing!

Stravinsky became the new apostle of modernism, replacing the fading Richard Strauss. Stravinsky was being discussed much more even than Debussy. The French composer was jealous, and wrote of Stravinsky in a nasty way not to be surpassed until Stravinsky himself in the latter part of his life started writing about musicians in his series of books with Robert Craft as collaborator. Debussy and Stravinsky met and socialized, and it was to Debussy that Stravinsky bore the completed *Sacre* in a four-hand version. He and Debussy played it through (Debussy was a fabulous sight reader), and Debussy went to all of the *Sacre* rehearsals. Obviously he respected Stravinsky. He also may have noted in the *Sacre* some of his own music, as Stravinsky pointed out in his *Expositions and Developments* of 1962: ". . . *Le Sacre* owes more to Debussy than to anyone except myself, the best music (the Prelude) as well as the weakest (the music of the second part between the first entrance of the two solo trumpets and the *Glorification de l'Élue*)." The opening of the *Sacre*—the famous bassoon solo—is not far distant from the theme that opens *L'après-midi d'un faune.* Yet there was tension between Debussy and Stravinsky, as indicated in the curious letter, one that mixes pettiness with grudging praise, that Debussy wrote to Robert Godet in 1916:

> I have recently seen Stravinsky. He says, my *Oiseau de Feu*, my *Sacre*, just as a child says "My toy, my hoop." And that is exactly what he is—a spoiled child who sometimes cocks a snook at music. He is also a young barbarian who wears flashy ties and treads on women's toes as he kisses their hands. When he is old he will be unbearable, that is to say, he will admit no other music, but for the moment he is unbelievable. He professes a friendship for me because I have helped him to mount a rung of the ladder from which he launches his squibs, not all of which explode. But once again, he is unbelievable. You have really understood him and, even better than I, have been able to understand the unrelenting workings of his mind.

In St. Petersburg, it is safe to say, nobody would have guessed that Stravinsky would have developed into the *enfant terrible* of music. As a child, he showed some talent, but certainly not of a spectacular order; nor did his early compositions hint at the musical revolution to come. But from the beginning he was exposed to music. His father, who died in 1902, was a bass singer at the St. Petersburg Opera, and musicians from Russia and abroad were constantly visiting the house. Thus Igor heard a great deal of music, and had piano lessons, but until the age of twenty-three was a law student at the University. About 1900, while still a student, he was introduced to Rimsky-Korsakov, showed him some of his attempts at composition, and was taken on as a private pupil in 1903. The lessons continued until Rimsky's death in 1908. One of the results, finished in 1907, was a grand Symphony in E flat, a richly scored, traditional work that any diligent student could have produced. It contains nothing of the Stravinsky sound or the Stravinsky style. On the whole it is an essay in the sterile academism of Alexander Glazunov.

In 1908, Stravinsky composed an orchestral work named *Fireworks*, which brought him to the attention of Serge Diaghilev, who had a genius for spotting talent. The history of music in the first quarter of the twentieth century would be considerably poorer without his presence. An intellectual, a man who thought big, an impresario willing to gamble, a man vitally interested in all of the arts, Diaghilev became active in Paris, where in 1906 he sponsored a show of Russian art. The following year he presented five concerts of Russian music at the Opéra, and followed that in 1908 with a staged performance of *Boris Godunov* with Feodor Chaliapin in the title role. In 1909, Diaghilev introduced Paris to Russian ballet, and the success was such that he organized the Ballets Russes as a permanent organization. From this

433

company stemmed some of the great works of the century. Diaghilev made the Ballets Russes a center of the avant-garde. Debussy, Falla, Stravinsky, Prokofiev, Ravel—the greatest and most progressive composers of the day wrote for it. Picasso, Bakst, and other great artists were called in for scenery and costumes. The dancers of the company, headed by Nijinsky and Karsavina, were a legend. This was a company with style, glamour, *goût*, and imagination; and it all revolved around the figure of the saturnine, powerful, and aristocratic Serge Diaghilev.

For his 1910 season, Diaghilev wanted a Russian ballet to a scenario on the Firebird legend to be choreographed by Michel Fokine. Anatol Liadov was approached and accepted the assignment to compose the music. He delayed and delayed. In desperation Diaghilev, remembering the impression that Stravinsky's *Fireworks* had made on him, turned to the young composer. Stravinsky whipped out the score in short order and went to Paris to be present at the rehearsals. *Firebird*, to Stravinsky's eternal disgust, turned out to be the most popular work he ever composed. He went on to create greater works, but it is *Firebird* in its orchestral suite (the full-length ballet is seldom performed) that still leads all Stravinsky works in number of annual performances.

The first three Stravinsky ballets are examples of Russian nationalism. After them, Stravinsky proceeded to an entirely different kind of music, turning from superscores with superorchestras to scores for small groups and a pointed, precise way of writing. From these came the neoclassic works. Transitional compositions between Stravinsky's nationalism and neoclassicism were *L'Histoire du Soldat* (1918), the ballet *Renard* (1922), the one-act opera *Mavra* (1922), the *Symphonies of Wind Instruments* (1921), and the cantata *Les Noces* (1923). All of these still have nationalistic elements, but the forces employed were small, and the workmanship heading in a new direction. For *L'Histoire du Soldat*, Stravinsky used a tiny orchestra that had analogies to a jazz group; for *Les Noces*, the dance cantata on the subject of a Russian wedding, a percussion orchestra and four pianos. *Les Noces* has some of the primitive, earthy, Russian feeling of *Sacre*, and something of its rhythmic impact; but *L'Histoire*, a dance pantomime based on a Russian fairy tale about a soldier and the devil, points to something altogether new—a stylized treatment of various musical forms with a completely different rhythmic and textural organization. Everything is in miniature—a miniature waltz and tango, a miniature chorale, a miniature march. Jazz played a part. "My knowledge of jazz," Stravinsky wrote in 1962, "was derived exclusively from copies of sheet music, and as I had never actually heard any of the music performed, I borrowed its rhythmic style not as played but as written. I *could* imagine jazz sound, however, or so I like to think. Jazz meant, in any case, a wholly new sound in my music, and

L'Histoire marks my final break with the Russian orchestral school in which I had been fostered."

Those who complained of the complexity of *Le Sacre du Printemps* could not have found much to object to in *L'Histoire,* with its clean sound and modesty of means. This work, and the *Symphonies of Wind Instruments,* led to the Octet of 1923, in which Stravinsky for the first time since his E flat Symphony worked in sonata form. Stravinsky was launched on neoclassicism: historical manner expressed in contemporary language. The clear forms of the baroque and classic appealed to Stravinsky's logical mind, and the following years saw a series of works—the Piano Concerto (1924), *Oedipus Rex* (1927), the Capriccio for Piano and Orchestra (1929), the *Symphony of Psalms* (1930), the Violin Concerto (1931), the *Duo Concertante* (1932), the Symphony in C (1940), the Symphony in Three Movements (1945)—in which old forms were revitalized and transformed in the alchemy of Stravinsky's workshop. The forms were old; the treatment and modification of the forms were ultramodern. There also were works in which Stravinsky arranged music of other composers—Pergolesi, in the ballet *Pulcinella* (1919); and Tchaikovsky, in another ballet, *Le Baiser de la Fée* (1928). Whatever the source of the music, it had the typical lean sound, idiosyncratic orchestral spacings, spiky dissonances, and asymmetrical rhythms that represented Igor Stravinsky.

As early as 1921 Stravinsky, in the *Symphonies of Wind Instruments* (the term "symphonies" is used in the sense of instruments sounding together and has nothing to do with sonata form), predicted that he was embarked on a type of music that would not be as popular as the early ballets. He said of the *Symphonies* in his autobiography (1935) that "It lacks all those elements that infallibly appeal to the ordinary listener, or to which he is accustomed. It is futile to look in it for passionate impulse or dynamic brilliance. . . . The music is not meant to 'please' an audience, nor to arouse its passions. Nevertheless, I had hoped that it would appeal to some of those persons in whom a purely musical receptivity outweighed the desire to satisfy their sentimental cravings."

These words could stand as a summary of what all of Stravinsky's post-*Sacre* music represents. He was correct in his feeling that audiences would have trouble identifying with such antiromantic, antisentimental writing. Many of his admirers were disconcerted. Stravinsky's neoclassicism was taken up by some composers, and elements of his language entered the thinking of all composers, but his music after 1920 never caused the upheaval that his Russian ballets had caused. The new works were considered cosmopolitan and generally abstract, just as Stravinsky himself was a cosmopolitan, a Russian expatriate living mostly in Switzerland from 1914 to 1920, in France from 1920 to 1939 (he became a French citizen in 1934), and

435

in the United States from 1939 (he became an American citizen in 1945). Certainly the public did not especially care for the majority of Stravinsky's neoclassic scores, a fact of which he was well aware. As he noted in the autobiography:

At the beginning of my career as a composer I was a good deal spoiled by the public. . . . But I have a very distinct feeling that in the course of the last fifteen years my written work has estranged me from the great mass of my listeners. . . . Liking the music of *Firebird, Petrushka, The Rite of Spring* and *The Wedding,* and being accustomed to the language of those works, they are astonished to hear me speaking in another idiom. They cannot and will not follow me in the progress of my musical thought. What moves and delights me leaves them indifferent, and what still continues to interest them holds no further attraction for me.

What Stravinsky represented, among many other things, was a complete rupture with romanticism. Everything about the man and his music was antiromantic. In the 1930's there was a great stir when Stravinsky said that it was not music's job to "express" anything. For years those remarks were hurled back at him by the traditionalists. What he had meant was that music by its very nature cannot express anything but music. "Composers combine notes. That is all." It was a neo-Hanslickian notion. Hanslick, in his treatise *The Beautiful in Music,* had based his entire argument on the theory that music was a completely abstract art, incapable of painting pictures or conveying anything except broad emotions. His, and Stravinsky's, remarks are probably accurate, though aestheticians have devoted much study to the meaning of meaning in music, and have never been able to arrive at a satisfactory answer. Stravinsky was never reticent about his belief that music is primarily form and logic. His antiromanticism extended to fierce attacks on performers and conductors who overinterpreted his music. This sort of thing irritated Stravinsky as much as did most romantic music. His main interest continued to be in structure, in texture, in balance, in rhythm. His music is the work of one of the supreme logicians.

Everything about Stravinsky pointed to an intellectual tidiness, and that included his work habits. Those were tidy to the point of compulsion. In 1916, the Swiss writer C. F. Ramuz, who was working with Stravinsky on *L'Histoire du Soldat,* looked at Stravinsky's work table and marveled:

Stravinsky's scores are magnificent. He is above all (in all matters and in every sense of the word) a calligrapher. . . . His writing desk resembled a surgeon's instrument case. Bottles of different colored inks in their ordered hierarchy each had a separate part to play in the ordering of his art. Near at hand were india-rubbers of various kinds and shapes, and all sorts of glittering steel implements: rulers, erasers, pen-knives, and a rou-lette instrument for drawing staves, invented by Stravinsky himself. One was reminded of the definition of St. Thomas: beauty is the splendor of order. All the large pages of the score were filled with writing in different colored inks—blue, green, red, two kinds of black (ordinary and Chinese), each having its purpose, its meaning, its special use: one for the notes, another the text, a third the translation; one for titles, another for the musical directions. Meanwhile the bar lines were ruled, and the mis-takes carefully erased.

(Thirty years later, nothing had changed. Nicolas Nabokov visited Stra-vinsky in Los Angeles. "I believe," he noted, "Stravinsky has in his study all the instruments needed for writing, copying, drawing, pasting, cutting, clip-ping, filing, sharpening, and gluing, that the combined effects of a stationery and hardware store can furnish." Life in the Stravinsky workshop continued to revolve around the piano. "The piano itself is the center of my musical discoveries," Stravinsky has written. "Each note that I write is tried on it, and every relationship of notes is taken apart and heard on it again and again.")

After his early successes in Paris, Stravinsky was constantly on the move. Up to the beginning of World War I he was resident in Russia, France, and Switzerland. The war years he spent in Switzerland, remaining there until 1920. Because of the 1917 Revolution in Russia, he did not return there (and he stayed away permanently until a visit in 1962). From 1920 to 1939 he lived in France, making concert tours through Europe and the United States. World War II sent him to the United States for good, and he settled in Hollywood.

In the United States, Stravinsky entered on a fruitful relationship with the Russian-born choreographer George Balanchine, with whom he had pre-viously worked in Europe. There were the ballets *Jeu de cartes* (1936; originally choreographed by Stravinsky himself in collaboration with M. Malaïev), *Danses Concertantes* (1942), *Orpheus* (1948), *Agon* (1957), *Movements* (1958), and others. Several scores, including the *Danses Con-certantes* and *Movements*, were not originally composed as ballets, but in Balanchine's choreographic realizations they achieved a popularity denied them in the concert hall. There also was one bizarre Stravinsky-Balanchine collaboration, composed in 1942 for the Barnum and Bailey Circus. The dancers in Stravinsky's *Circus Polka* were elephants, and the event was ad-vertised as "a choreographic tour de force," a description against which few would argue. Collaboration with W. H. Auden and Chester Kallman re-sulted in a large-scale opera, *The Rake's Progress*. Friendship with the young American conductor, Robert Craft, resulted in a switch to serial composition and also a series of tart books in which Stravinsky had his say about everything from the genesis of everything he composed to his opinions of other composers and his observations on life. Stravinsky-Craft pulled no punches, and musicians approached the books, when published, as though a live hand grenade were under the covers. Some eminent music critics had special cause to shudder. These books provide an unusual look into a major composer's mind.

Until the end of World War II, Stravinsky was the symbol of progressiveness in music. Prokofiev, Bartók, Schoenberg, and Webern were still active, but to the public Stravinsky represented modernism in music. By and large, musicians were content to accept Stravinsky as the leader of the avant-garde. But with the rise of the serial movement and the emergence of an articulate group wedded to the ideas of Schoenberg and the serial school, Stravinsky for the first time came under attack by young composers and critics. His entire post-*Noces* body of work was questioned, especially by the polemicists of the school of Paris. André Hodeir and Pierre Boulez led the charge. They took the attitude that Stravinsky's aesthetic was invalid, that his scores, a case of "accelerated exhaustion," represented "a sclerosis of all realms: harmonic and melodic, in which one arrives at a faked academism; and even rhythmic, in which one sees a painful atrophy produced." Those words came from Boulez, who insisted that Stravinsky's neoclassicism was retrogressive rather than forward-looking. "Incapable by himself of reaching the coherence of a language other than the tonal one, Stravinsky dropped the unwisely-attempted struggle and began to employ his expedients—which became arbitrary and gratuitous gestures intended to delight the already perverted ear." Boulez charged Stravinsky—*Stravinsky!*—with "intellectual laziness, pleasure taken as an end in itself."

It was not long after these attacks that Stravinsky dipped partially into the waters of serialism and eventually took the plunge. Nothing in his career caused more gossip in musical circles than his entry into serial writing, into the world of Schoenberg and Webern. Stravinsky and Schoenberg had never been close, and Schoenberg had no great liking for Stravinsky's music. At least, Schoenberg wrote a satire about Stravinsky and his neoclassicism in 1926, and even set it to music:

> Ja, wer trommelt denn da?
> Das ist ja der kleine Modernsky!
> Hat sich ein Bubikopf schneiden lassen;
> sieht ganz gut aus!
> Wie echt falsches Haar!
> Wie eine Perücke!
> Ganz (wie sich ihn der kleine Modernsky vorstellt),
> ganz der Papa Bach!

Which Eric Walter White, in his biography of Stravinsky, translates as:

> But who's this beating the drum?
> It's little Modernsky!
> He's had his hair cut in an old-fashioned queue,
> And it looks quite nice,
> Like real false hair—
> Like a wig—
> Just like (at least little Modernsky thinks so)
> Just like Father Bach!

In Europe, Stravinsky and Schoenberg met a few times, but never after 1912. Stravinsky heard *Pierrot Lunaire* and admitted that "it was beyond me" as it was "beyond all of us at the time." For many years Stravinsky did not hear a note of Schoenberg's music. In Los Angeles, where they both lived, they never saw each other. Previously, Stravinsky never had anything favorable to say about serial music. But after being introduced by Craft to dodecaphonic music, and especially the music of Webern, he revised his opinion. In an interview in 1952 he said that while he himself was not interested in writing serial music, "the serial composers are the only ones with a discipline that I respect." Stravinsky made an intensive study of Webern's music. Then he experimented with serial elements in several works, notably the *Canticum Sacrum* (1955) and *Agon* (1957). Finally came *Threni* (1958), the *Movements* for Piano and Orchestra (1959), *A Sermon, A Narrative, and A Prayer* (1961), the Variations in Memory of Aldous Huxley (1964), and the *Requiem Canticles* (1966), all serial works.

Naturally there was a great outcry that Stravinsky had gone over to the "enemy." Stravinsky was accused of jumping on the serial bandwagon, of abdicating his position, of an unseemly ambition to keep his place as leader of the avant-garde. What was overlooked in the hubbub was that, serial or not, *Threni* and the other works still had the old Stravinsky sound; that his serial scores were no more Webernish than *Le Baiser* was Tchaikovskian, or the Violin Concerto was Bachian. Stravinsky merely did with serialism what he had done with any other form of style that passed his way: put it through the Stravinsky filter. No composer with the overpowering personality of a Stravinsky could suddenly begin to write music reflective of any other mind but his own. In any case, the serial compositions are only a very small part of his work.

Through the years Stravinsky's position has been, in a way, perplexing. From 1911 to the end of World War II he was the acknowledged leader of the musical avant-garde and by common consent the world's greatest living composer. To the public he remained the apostle of modernism. To his colleagues, he was the most precise and finished technician of the day. Certainly up to 1945 he was the strongest influence on the contemporary musical scene. That alone would be enough to make secure his place in history. Minor composers may achieve great popularity in their day, but they never influence the course of music. Stravinsky did. He always was at the end of the rope, pulling everybody along with him. (In this, his career greatly resembled that of his good friend Pablo Picasso. There are many parallels between the two: their almost simultaneous entry into various stylistic periods, their use of distortion for expressive purposes, their brilliant craftsmanship, the influence they had on the avant-garde.)

But the curious thing is that Stravinsky, after his post-*Sacre* works, was greatly admired more by fellow musicians and a handful of vociferous followers than by the public. It is not that Stravinsky lacked public performance. His stature and reputation were too great. Everything he composed was immediately performed, and recordings automatically followed. He is one of the few contemporary composers represented on records by, substantially, his complete works, most of them recorded under his personal supervision. Yet his music has always commanded more respect than love. The majority of his works after *Sacre* seem to hang around the rim of the repertoire rather than being down in the nucleus. Remove the three Russian ballets and his two other most popular works, *Oedipus Rex* and the *Symphony of Psalms*, and his music suddenly drops near the bottom of the annual list in the survey of American symphony orchestra programs published by the American Symphony Orchestra League and Broadcast Music, Inc. Stravinsky has ended up a musician's musician rather than one who was major musical box office. His music may be too sharp, pointed, reserved, balanced, intellectual (if you wish). It is not music to everybody's taste. "I've come to the conclusion," wrote Aaron Copland in 1943, "that Stravinsky is the Henry James of composers. Same 'exile' psychology, same exquisite perfection, same hold on certain artistic temperaments, same lack of immediacy of contact with the world around him."

Nor does Stravinsky's music have the kind of melody that would attract a wide following, though it is an error to say, as some have done, that there is no melody in his music. An aria like the Jocasta plaint in *Oedipus Rex,* or the melody that starts the slow movement of the Symphony in Three Movements, or the scene in *Orpheus* where the protagonist serenades the Underworld, or the *Sur le lit elle repose* from *Perséphone* (is this not an unconscious echo of Tchaikovsky's *June Barcarolle?*)—these are melodies as pronounced as *Casta Diva*. Stravinsky could be as melodic as any composer if he wanted to. But he has not always wanted to. He never was a heart-on-sleeve composer, and often he cold-bloodedly discarded an obvious type of melody in favor of other elements of music. Thus his scores have been called "intellectual,' in the pejorative sense. Nothing more aroused Stravinsky's anger than to be chastized for being intellectual. What's wrong with the intellect? he demanded to know. To condemn Stravinsky's music for being "intellectual" is to condemn it for the very thing for which it should be praised. Of course it is intellectual, in the best sense of the word. It is a music in which the formal elements are cunningly in balance, in which patterns are juggled with virtuosity, in which a strong mind, going out of its way to avoid nineteenth-century concepts, sets out to exploit certain musical ideas with brevity, objectivity, and unromantic notions. Has there been a composer in the history of music, Bach and Webern included, who has displayed the sheer logic of Stravinsky? One doubts it. Much of the pleasure in listening to his music comes from sharing the mental processes of a superbly organized mind—a mind with a good deal of perkiness, to be sure; a fascinating mind; a witty and aphoristic mind; but above all, an organized mind. In his music there is no padding, no inflated or uneasy "developments." Stravinsky's music can communicate strongly, but only to a certain type of mind, a kind of mind equivalent to Stravinsky's own—which means a mind that responds to form, technique, rhythm, stylization. Where a Beethoven, Schubert, or even Bach appears to appeal to all listeners on all levels, Stravinsky does not have that universal quality. He can all but hypnotize a music lover who has a high degree of sophistication; but the sophisticates are, after all, a minority of the musical public. It may be that Stravinsky, "the world's greatest living composer," will end up living more for what he did to music rather than for what his music did to the majority of his listeners.

✒ 13 ✒

The English Renaissance

ELGAR, DELIUS, VAUGHAN WILLIAMS

By rights, England in the nineteenth century should have developed as strong and individualistic a school of composers as Germany, France, or Russia did. The roots were there, the tradition was there, and in Henry Purcell (1659–1695) England had produced a major figure. Long before Purcell, however, English composers of importance had made their contribution to the development of music. Such skilled contrapuntists as John Dunstable, who died in 1453 (the date of his birth is unknown), John Taverner (1495–1545), and Thomas Tallis (c. 1505–1585) produced a strong body of church music. The latter part of the reign of Queen Elizabeth I saw a brilliant group simultaneously active in London. There were William Byrd, Orlando Gibbons, Thomas Morley, John Dowland, John Wilbye, and Thomas Weelkes, among others, composing madrigals, ayres, lute and other instrumental music, and church music. Shakespeare, Marlowe, Jonson, Donne, Herrick, and the rest of the galaxy of great Elizabethan writers often worked closely with these composers. What a wonderful period it was, and how exciting it must have been!

English music culminated in the figure of Purcell. In the thirty-six years of his life, he turned out an enormous quantity of music in all forms—church music, odes, incidental music to plays, the first English opera (*Dido and Aeneas*, 1689), chamber music, part songs (some of them deliciously naughty), works for the harpsichord. His music has an unusual degree of personality, and some of it is startlingly modern. Aside from Purcell's striking melodic ideas and a harmony that at times anticipated the chromaticism of the romantics, he was unusual for his day in that his music speaks directly to the modern listener. The Elizabethan madrigals, for instance, lovely as they can be, call for an acquired taste because of their archaic modalities. It takes a listener with a certain amount of sophistication to respond to them. But Purcell's music, to a large extent, speaks the language of

Everyman. His successors should have developed and refined his techniques, bringing English music to even greater heights. But, unfortunately, he had no successors. Instead, George Frideric Handel came to England.

Handel's impact on music in England was cataclysmic. One might even say catastrophic. The massive figure of the burly Saxon pressed heavily on his successors, to a point where creative effort seemed to be stifled. The English could not get enough choral writing in the Handel manner; and since Handel, not unexpectedly, composed in that manner better than anybody else, it was Handel who was constantly played. It is true that romanticism did finally come to England. Indeed, Wordsworth started the entire romantic school with his *Lyrical Ballads* of 1798. Had British musical romanticism been as imaginative and creative as literary romanticism, England would have taken the lead throughout the world. Instead, the musical romanticism that most of the British pursued was in the Mendelssohn rather than the Chopin-Liszt-Wagner line.

Mendelssohn exerted as strong a force upon British musical thinking in the nineteenth century as Handel previously had done. There was something about the bourgeois, competent, academic Mendelssohn with which musical England completely identified. He was more of a god there than he was even in Leipzig. England was a conservative country, rich, with a powerful upper class; and it feared change. Mendelssohn was undeniably a genius, but such a *proper* genius! He was a gentleman, he was wealthy, he was a conservative, and he did not rock the boat. It was inevitable that Mendelssohn and Queen Victoria should become friends. They had a great deal in common—caution, conventionality of mind, breeding, a very conservative outward surface, and they took to each other very strongly. There is something sweet, innocent, and charming about the relationship, about Queen Victoria and Prince Albert, both music lovers, joining forces with Mendelssohn for a musicale like a good middle-class family. Everything was polite and cozy at Buckingham Palace when the nice Mr. Mendelssohn dropped in to pay his respects:

Prince Albert had asked me [Mendelssohn wrote in 1842] to go to him on Saturday at two o'clock, so that I might try his organ before I left England. I found him all alone; and as we were talking away, the Queen came in, also quite alone, in a house dress. She said she was obliged to leave for Claremont in an hour. "But, goodness! how it looks here," she added, when she saw that the wind had littered the whole room, and even the pedals of the organ (which, by the way, made a very pretty feature in the room), with leaves of music from a large portfolio that lay open. As she spoke, she knelt down and began picking up the music. Prince Albert helped and I too was not idle. Then Prince Albert proceeded to explain the stops to me, and while he was doing it, she said that she would put things straight alone.

But I begged that the Prince would first play me something, so that, as I said, I might boast about it in Germany; and thereupon he played me a chorale by heart, with pedals, so charmingly and clearly and correctly that many an organist could have learned something; and the Queen, having finished her work, sat beside him and listened, very pleased. Then I had to play, and I began my chorus from *St. Paul*—"How Lovely Are the Messengers." Before I got to the end of the first verse, they both began to sing the chorus very well, and all the time Prince Albert managed the stops for me so expertly—first a flute, then full at the forte, the whole register at the D major part, then he made such an excellent diminuendo with the stops, and so on to the end of the piece, and all by heart—that I was heartily pleased. . . .

Queen Victoria wanted all music to sound like Mendelssohn's. Her subjects obliged, writing very proper and not very original music. Between the death of Handel in 1759 and the emergence of Edward Elgar in the 1890's, England did not produce one major musical figure. There were good composers in the country during the nineteenth century—William Sterndale Bennett, Arthur Sullivan, Alexander Mackenzie, Charles Hubert Parry, Charles Villiers Stanford. All were academicians, and the music of these worthy composers seldom was heard outside of England. This was true even of Schumann's protégé, Sterndale Bennett, while Sullivan lives only through his operetta music. The counterpart to this group of composers would be the Boston Classicists in the United States. Some accomplished and even lovely music came out of the London group, just as it came out of Boston, and the music in both cases is better than its reputation, but it is a music too powerfully dominated first by Mendelssohn, later by Schumann and Brahms.

Elgar, born in Broadheath on June 2, 1857, broke the mold. He became recognized as England's greatest composer, and his reputation in his day was enormous. Then it rapidly declined, to rise up again in the 1960's. During the modernism of the 1920–40 period, the great days of Stravinsky, Bartók, Prokofiev, and Milhaud, most musicians would have ridiculed the very idea of Elgar being an important composer. He was considered an inflated provincial, popular in his day only because England was so desperately anxious to claim an important composer for her own. He was Edwardian, stuffy, a relic of Colonel Blimp and Empire. What else could be expected of a man who indulged in fox-hunting, golf, fishing, and kite-flying? Even Elgar's very appearance was held against him. He was tall, straight, heavily moustachioed, with a hooked nose and flaring nostrils; he carried his umbrella at the furl; his entire bearing was military; his clothes were proper;

he was the very model of an Edwardian clubman. It followed that he was a musical wallah who composed vulgar and jingoistic music (*Pomp and Circumstance:* really!). His music could no more be listened to than the poetry of Kipling could be read. And so mounted the catalogue of sins.

It was not only the aesthetic of a neoclassic age, with its revulsion against romanticism, that helped put Elgar among the discards for several decades. There also was the interest in nationalism, as represented in England by Ralph Vaughan Williams and the revival of the Elizabethan school. Nationalism was sweeping the entire musical world, what with Bartók in Hungary, Janáček in Czechoslovakia, Nielsen in Denmark, Sibelius in Finland, and Ives in the United States (though hardly anybody knew Ives's music). The nationalists immersed themselves in the native font, piping their native wood-notes wild. But Elgar would have none of this. He believed that it was a composer's business to invent tunes, not to quote them or base them on the quaint sounds of the past. Like Strauss and Mahler, he was a composer who delighted in massive effects. "If a composer writes for forty harps, get him forty harps." But this kind of thinking was long out of fashion at the time of Elgar's death, in Worcester on February 23, 1934. All his contemporaries could see were the Wagner, Strauss, and Brahms derivations of his music. His major works—the two symphonies, the Violin Concerto and Cello Concerto, the enormous symphonic poem *Falstaff*—all went into prompt decline. Only his *Enigma Variations* and *The Dream of Gerontius* had much currency among his serious works, and *Gerontius* was seldom played outside of England. Young musicians went around calling *The Dream of Gerontius* a "nightmare."

Yet to the musicians of the 1890's, Elgar was an individualist, and one of the greatest living masters of the orchestra. He was almost a self-taught composer. His father, an organist, violinist, and piano tuner, encouraged his early experiments in composition, which started as a child. Young Elgar studied violin and piano, went to work in a lawyer's office, and then decided to concentrate on music. He became a violinist in the Worcester Philharmonic, taught as a provincial musician, and turned out a large quantity of music, much of it salon, all of it unimportant. There was nothing to distinguish him from any other hard-working but hack composer. If he had any reputation at all, it was through sentimental little pieces like the *Salut d'Amour* for piano, a work that occupied the position in the drawing rooms of Victorian England that the Gottschalk piano pieces of the *Last Hope* variety occupied in American drawing rooms of the period.

Then, in 1889, came the *Froissart Overture*, Elgar's first significant work, and it revealed a composer with a brilliant feeling for the sonorities of the big postromantic orchestra. The *Black Knight* (1893), *King Olaf* (1896), and *Caractacus* (1898), all for chorus and orchestra, attracted further interest. By

1900, Elgar was the most famous composer in England, especially after the tremendous success of the *Enigma Variations* in 1899. This orchestral work was a musical picture of his friends. Elgar also said that the main theme itself had for a counterpoint "a theme that is not heard." Nobody has identified that mysterious unheard theme, the enigma of the *Enigma*. Hans Richter conducted the premiere in London, and the work was taken up on the continent. Fritz Steinbach, the Brahms specialist, called Elgar "an unexpected genius and pathbreaker in the field of orchestration. . . . Entirely original effects with almost unique virtuosity." Which was indeed a compliment from a conductor in the land of Richard Strauss.

Elgar clearly was influenced by Strauss. Some of his melodies have the characteristic Strauss contour, with their skips, large range, and unexpected landing spots. Elgar's orchestration also owes something to the composer of *Ein Heldenleben*. But Strauss's orchestration, effective as it is, often makes its point through sheer size and volume. Elgar achieved a more luminous sound. As Vaughan Williams remarked: "I have found that with Wagner the extra instruments could almost be dispensed with altogether, with a little loss of color, it is true, but with no damage to the texture. But when it came to Elgar, the case was quite different. Even in the accompaniments to choral movements there was hardly anything that could be left out without leaving a hole in the texture."

Elgar followed the *Enigma Variations* with what many consider to be his greatest work, the oratorio *Dream of Gerontius* to Cardinal Newman's text. The premiere at the Birmingham Festival was little short of a disaster. Richter was unprepared, the chorus did not understand the music, and the soloists were not up to its demands. (From that point on Elgar himself conducted most of his premieres.) Subsequent performances of *Gerontius* went better, and England, with its tradition of choral singing, took to the score. (The English, George Bernard Shaw somewhere observed, always "took a creepy sort of pleasure in Requiems.") *Gerontius* does have moments of great nobility and beauty. It also has a pious stuffiness about it; and while it is Elgar's most ambitious score, it is not, despite the claims of his admirers, his best. It occupies the position in his music that *A Mass of Life* occupies in the music of Delius: a big attempt that does not always come off.

Cockaigne: In London Town came in 1901. Elgar never pretended to be a nationalistic composer. But in *Cockaigne*, as in his later *Falstaff* of 1913, he wrote a kind of music that strongly evokes a national spirit. It may be more Merrie England than the real thing, but nobody but an Englishman could have conceived it. The same can be said of the four *Pomp and Circumstance* Marches. No. 1 in D was to Elgar what the *Valse Triste* was to Sibelius and the Prelude in C sharp minor was to Rachmaninoff. To people everywhere, Elgar was the composer of *Pomp and Circumstance*. The first two marches had their premiere at a Proms concert in 1901. "I shall never forget the scene at the close of the first of them, the one in D major," Elgar wrote in his autobiography. "The people simply rose and yelled. I had to play it again—with the same result; in fact, they refused to let me go on with the program. . . Merely to restore order, I played the piece a third time." Not much later, Edward VII suggested that *the* tune be provided with words, and it was, as *Land of Hope and Glory*. If Elgar had been well-known before that, now he was wildly famous. Honors came his way, including degrees from American universities and, in 1904, a knighthood. That was the year that saw a three-day festival of his music at Covent Garden.

Pomp and Circumstance may have brought Elgar fame and money, but musically it did him much more harm than good. The march tarred him with a Kiplingesque kind of jingoism, and there were those who refused to take seriously any music by the composer of *Pomp and Circumstance*. Musicians would not accept it for what it was—a rattling good march. In the meantime, Elgar was producing a fine series of works—the superb Introduction and Allegro for string orchestra (1905), the First Symphony (1908), the Violin Concerto (1910), the Second Symphony (1910), and the Cello Concerto (1919). Elgar also worked on a major choral trilogy. *The Apostles* came out in 1903, and *The Kingdom* in 1906. Neither work is in the international repertory. Part III of the trilogy never was finished.

The two symphonies are broad postromantic works, vigorous, very much in the Brahms tradition with some touches of Strauss. Both are fine, sturdy pieces, redeemed from their obvious derivations by the gusto of the writing and the typically Elgarian kind of melody. These symphonies are coming back into favor again, and so is the Violin Concerto, even with its unconscious references to the Brahms Violin Concerto. Possibly the best of Elgar's late works is the Cello Concerto, an elegiac, strongly personal work with hauntingly beautiful themes. The sustained lyricism of the opening theme is unusual even for Elgar, who liked long-phrased melodies. It goes on, generating from itself, for an incredible length of time. The Elgar Cello Concerto ranks with Dvořák's in B minor as the greatest of its species.

With the Cello Concerto and the Piano Quintet of 1919, Elgar's creative period stopped. He did compose a few things in the fifteen years remaining to him, but none of those works is heard. Like Rossini and Sibelius, Elgar decided to call it a day at the height of his career. He never recovered from the loss of his wife, in 1920. And he did not like the direction music was taking. Very likely he considered himself an anachronism. Certainly he was made to feel so. The hectic age after World War I dismissed his music, and the public ignored it. At his seventieth birthday concert in Queen's Hall, the house was only half full. Elgar said that he had composed a third symphony but would not waste time scoring it, as nobody wanted his music any more. He was a lonely old man. He withdrew from all musical contact, never went to a concert, said that he disliked music, and preferred to talk about cricket or horse-racing.

What the 1930's could not see through Elgar's glowing postromanticism was that his music had something very special. Unlike his Victorian predecessors, Elgar spoke with an unusual degree of individuality. He may have based his orchestra on Strauss and Wagner, and his symphonic and concerto forms on Brahms, but his melodies and his handling of the forms were very much his own. An Elgar melody, with its curious tension, its wide intervals and exuberant leaps, its confident, strong, British feeling (hard to describe in words, but it is there), immediately stands out, recognizable as the work of but one composer and no other in the history of music. That alone would suffice to put his music above that of a better technician or a more advanced experimenter. For music without personality, no matter how skillful, does not live. Elgar's music may be Edwardian and bourgeois, it may celebrate British imperialism (explicitly or, more often, implicitly), it may even have its share of conventional rhetoric (*Gerontius* certainly does). But it abounds in vitality and personality. It is no coincidence that Elgar's rehabilitation started with the revival of Kipling and other figures of the period. The spate of Edwardian studies in the 1950's showed that those bearded gentlemen and bustled ladies could be quite interesting, if not to say racy.

The element of Edwardian rhetoric in Elgar's music can make it hard to conduct. He used an immense orchestra, and the conductor is tempted to overstress. Then the music really sounds vulgar. Elgar himself recognized the problem and was greatly concerned about it. He told the critic Ernest Newman that the expression was written into his music, and all a conductor had to do was follow directions. "If only," he wistfully said, "people would be content to play the music as it is written down in the score." Otherwise Elgarian sentiment, Newman observed, has a habit of slobbering over, for which Elgar wrongly was blamed. "Few composers," Newman wrote, "suffer as much in this way from their uncomprehending interpreters as Elgar does; his exquisite sensitiveness is turned into sentimentality, his high spirits into vulgarity, his *nobilmente* into theatrical bombast—all because the conductor does not know where to stop." To which it can be added that Elgar himself conducted the orchestra in recordings of his Violin Concerto (with the young Yehudi Menuhin) and both symphonies, among other works, and his tempos and phrasings are there for all to study.

Elgar was one of a trinity of British composers, all active at the same time, who lifted British music from its post-Handel and post-Mendelssohn doldrums. The other two were Frederick Delius and Ralph Vaughan Williams, and no three composers could have been more different. Elgar, hearty and exuberant, was content to accept the England around him and to glorify it in music. Vaughan Williams, the outspoken nationalist, went back to the Tudor England of the sixteenth century for his inspiration. Delius fled the country, and the only inspiration he found was in himself. He did not like England very much, he was more an intellectual aristocrat than a bourgeois or commoner, and he wrote an entirely personal music that was as close to pantheism as music can get.

In some respects Delius was a composer like Fauré—highly personal, sometimes delicate, elegant, traditional without being academic. He did not compose a large body of music, and he had to wait a long time for recognition. By the time he had reached the age of forty he had written some significant music, but nothing was in print except a few songs. Not until 1905 did his music begin to take hold, and in Germany. Even then he did not enjoy international fame. He kept writing, polishing, and repolishing his music in his home at Grez-sur-Loing, about forty miles outside of Paris. In 1924, paralysis and blindness set in. A dedicated British musician, Eric Fenby, offered his services to the stricken Delius, and they worked out a system so that the composer could dictate his music. Several works did result from this effort, but fortunately Delius by that time had already finished all the music on which his fame rests.

It is difficult to describe this music. Some have called it English impressionism, but that does not fit too well. Many influences went to make up the complex man known as Frederick Delius. He was born in Bradford, near Manchester, on January 29, 1862. His family, wool merchants of German descent, were wealthy. Delius showed an aptitude for music and wanted to devote himself to it. His father, instead, decreed that Frederick enter the family business. Delius did, and turned out to be the worst businessman since the invention of money. After a time, his father was glad to get rid of him. Delius and a friend went off to Florida in 1884 to make their fortune growing oranges. They settled in at Solano Grove, near Jacksonville. Very few oranges were shipped to market. Instead, Delius concentrated on music. He became acquainted with a musician from New York named Thomas Ward, and they became friends. Delius said that the only teaching of real value he ever received was from Ward, who appears to have been a sound theorist and harmonist.

For a while, Delius taught music in Jacksonville, and later in Virginia. He also spent some time in New York. Then, in 1887, he went to the Leipzig Conservatory, where he was financed by his father. Delius never had to worry about money. The attractive *Florida Suite* was composed in Leipzig. Next, in 1888, came a visit to Paris. He lived there for a while with an uncle, and decided to make France his home. In France he married the painter Jelka Rosen, and he composed two wonderful orchestral works—

Over the Hills and Far Away (1895) and *Paris* (1899). These two works mark his mature style. He was slow in developing, but once he found his *métier* it remained unaltered all his life. "It came to me very slowly what I wanted to do, and when it came, it came out all at once." There followed an opera, *Irmelin* (1892), which was not staged until 1953, long after his death, and a series of other operas, orchestral pieces, and a piano concerto. At the age of forty-one, Delius had composed five operas, six large works for orchestra, about fifty songs and miscellaneous works, but virtually nothing was in print. Suddenly he began to be played in Germany. His opera *Koanga* was produced in Elberfeld in 1904, and another opera, *A Village Romeo and Juliet*, was produced in Berlin in 1907. The choral works *Appalachia* (1902) and *Sea Drift* (1903) were taken up by German conductors. In England, Thomas Beecham became interested in Delius's music and did everything in his considerable power to further its cause. Little by little, Delius made headway in England. In Germany he was considered one of the most important living composers. Beecham states that only Richard Strauss was more popular in the decade preceding the war. The violent anti-English feeling in Germany after 1914 removed Delius from the German repertory.

A work that attracted great attention, and one that has been called Delius's masterpiece, was *A Mass of Life* (1905). In all truth it is not Delius's masterpiece, no more than *The Dream of Gerontius* is Elgar's, except to those who equate masterpieces with length and breadth. But it does aim high and has some tremendous moments. The text of *A Mass of Life* comes from Nietzsche, a writer Delius adored. He would take a chapter from Nietzsche's works and study it, perhaps for weeks on end, then turn to another. "I hail him as a sublime poet and a beautiful nature," Delius said.

The genesis of *A Mass of Life* was Nietzsche's *Night Song of Zarathustra*. Beecham conducted the premiere in 1905. It is not a religious work, nor was Delius a religious man. He told Eric Fenby that he had no use for religion or creeds. "There is only one real happiness in life, and that is the happiness of creating." (A surprising number of the great composers have been freethinkers or downright atheists. Verdi, Saint-Saëns, Debussy, Brahms, Wagner, probably Schubert, Berlioz, and Chopin, come to mind.) If anything, Delius was a solipsist. He and his music existed for themselves, feeding on each other, closed in a little circle.

Delius was a striking figure. When Beecham met him for the first time, he thought he was a cardinal or at least a bishop in mufti, for, as he wrote,

. . . his features had that mingled cast of asceticism and shrewdness one mentally associates with high-ranking ecclesiastics. I was also struck by a general air of fastidiousness and sober elegance rarely to be observed in artists of any kind. Unexpectedly contrasting, but not unpleasing, was his style of speech, of which the underlying basis was recognizably provincial. Not for him was the blameless diction so laboriously inculcated and standardized in our leading public schools and ancient universities. He loyally preserved his preference for the Doric dialect of that great northern country of broad acres, which looks down with compassion upon the niminy-piminy refinements of the softer south. Upon this had been grafted a polyglot mish-mash, acquired during his twenty-four years of self-imposed exile from England. Both French and German words interlarded his sentences, and he always spoke of the "orchester." . . . In public he was invariably dignified, reticent and well mannered; and of Bohemianism there was no visible sign.

The rest of his life, after the outbreak of World War I, Delius alternated between England and France, spending most of his time at Grez-sur-Loing, where he lived quietly with his wife. He never paid much attention to the music written during his day. Indeed, he actively disliked most music except his own. His career was fulfilled in some fifteen years, roughly from 1900 to 1915. On June 10, 1934, he died, at Grez.

Delius's music owed nothing to anybody. Like Debussy, he completely broke away from established form, and there is a free, improvisatory quality about his music that sounds as if it had resulted from experimenting with voluptuous, exotically chromatic chords at the piano. It is a rhapsodic kind of music, in free forms, and is altogether free of classicism. The harmonies can be overwhelmingly rich and even dissonant at times, but they were unlike the harmonies of any other composer. "I don't believe in learning harmony or counterpoint," Delius said. "Learning kills instinct. Never believe the saying that one has to hear music many times to understand it. It is utter nonsense, the last refuge of the incompetent. . . . For me, music is very simple. It is the expression of a poetical and emotional nature." To Delius, "a sense of flow" was the only thing that mattered. Music had flow or it didn't. If it had, it was good music. If it didn't, it was bad. In 1920 he reacted violently to the advanced music of his day, in a long article he wrote for *The Sackbut:*

> There is room in the world for all kinds of music to suit all tastes, and there is no reason why the devotees of Dada should not enjoy the musically imbecile productions of their own little circle as much as the patrons of musical comedy enjoy *their* particular fare. But when I see the prophets of the latest clique doing their utmost to pervert the taste of the public and to implant a false set of values in the rising generation of music lovers by sneering at the great masters of the past, in the hope of attracting greater attention to the *petits maîtres* of the present—then I say it is time to speak openly and protest. . .

This is an age of anarchy in art; there is no authority, no standard, no sense of proportion. Anybody can do anything and call it "art" in the certain expectation of making a crowd of idiots stand and stare at him in gaping astonishment and admiration. . . .

Music does not exist for the purpose of emphasizing or exaggerating something which happens outside its own sphere. Musical expression only begins to be significant where words and actions reach their uttermost limit of expression. Music should be concerned with the emotions, not with external events. To make music imitate some other thing is as futile as to try and make it say *Good morning* or *It's a fine day*. It is only that which cannot be expressed otherwise that is worth expressing in music.

Delius observed his own precepts. Basically he was a tone painter who expressed himself in rapturous improvisations. The tiny tone poems—*Brigg Fair* (1907), *Summer Night on the River* (1911), *On Hearing the First Cuckoo in Spring* (1912)—sound like improvisations; and more extended works sound merely like more extended improvisations. It is music "concerned with the emotions," and it expresses things "which cannot be expressed otherwise." Delius was a wonderful melodist, almost a Tchaikovskian melodist. But he never was as plangent as the great Russian, and his melodies do not have that kind of immediate impact. Delius, despite his defiant words about the immediate impact of good music, takes a little more time to assimilate. Once assimilated, his music never seems to wear off. And if the listener likes one Delius work, the chances are that he will like them all, for Delius wrote almost consistently in the same style. He was, of course, far from being a universal composer. His equivalents in the other arts might be a Gerard Manley Hopkins, a Mary Cassatt, or a James Branch Cabell. (The last-named, to some, might be the kiss of death; but how many more elegant prose stylists are there? Delius's magical landscapes are of the same romantic country as Cabell's Poictesme.)

What Delius did, he did perfectly, and he wrote beautifully of beautiful things. Above all, his music has an exquisite refinement, frequently with an undercurrent of tragedy. Often it is sensuous, sometimes strong, but always elegiac and elegant. It is never program music but it is at all times evocative music—music of lakes, sunsets, landscapes, of the Paris sky and the Atlantic Ocean off the coast of America. Even his operas are intimate. *A Village Romeo and Juliet* is not for big houses. Delius lived much of his life in privacy, and something of this reserve, this reluctance to wear his heart on his sleeve, comes out in everything he wrote. Delius was not a composer who went to the people. They had to come to him. Those who did, like Beecham, discovered that the music of Delius is a unique experience. "Opinions are bound to differ, and widely," Beecham wrote in his biography of the composer. "For myself, I cannot do other than regard him as the last great apostle in our time of romance, beauty and emotion in music."

Ralph Vaughan Williams, who followed Elgar by fifteen years and Delius by ten, was a big, burly, indestructible man who had one of the longest creative spans in history. He was born in Gloucestershire on October 12, 1872, and died in London on August 26, 1958, finishing his Ninth Symphony only a short time before his death at the age of eighty-six. As he was already in print when he was nineteen years old, his was a sixty-five-year record of productivity. There was money in the family, and Vaughan Williams was able to take his time before settling on the idiom he was so faithfully to pursue. As a boy, he learned several instruments, none of them professionally. "I had been taught the pianoforte, which I never could play, and the violin, which was my musical salvation." At the Royal College of Music he studied with Stanford and Parry, and was especially indebted to the latter. "We pupils of Parry have, if we have been wise, inherited from Parry the great English choral tradition which Tallis passed on to Byrd, Byrd to Gibbons, Gibbons to Purcell, Purcell to Battishill and Greene, and they in turn through the Wesleys to Parry. He has passed the torch to us, and it is our duty to keep it alight." Unlike Elgar, Vaughan Williams rejected the German nineteenth-century tradition in favor of the English folk song and choral tradition. Temperamentally he was never able to identify with the German school. "To this day the Beethoven idiom repels me," he wrote as an old man, adding, "but I hope I have at last learnt to see the greatness that lies behind the idiom that I dislike, and at the same time to see an occasional weakness behind the Bach idiom which I love."

For some strange reason, considering his opinion of nineteenth-century German music, he went to Berlin to have a few lessons with Max Bruch. Nothing much came of these. He took a degree of Doctor of Music in Cambridge in 1901. Shortly thereafter he joined the English Folk Music Society. That was to be the turning point of his life. Like Bartók and Kodály, Vaughan Williams and his friend Gustav Holst went into the field to collect native music in as pure a state as it could be found. Holst was a well-known composer in his day, though little of his music is heard any more. He was considered an aggressive modernist, and was one of an important group of post-Elgar composers—a group that included Samuel Coleridge-Taylor, Arnold Bax, John Ireland, and, a little later, Arthur Bliss.

Vaughan Williams saturated himself in folk song. Through these studies he was able to free himself of foreign influences, as he explained in a lecture:

> In the days when Elgar formed his style, English folk song was not "in the air" but was consciously revived and made popular only about thirty

years ago. Now what does this revival mean to the composer? It means that several of us found here in its simplest form the musical idiom which we unconsciously were cultivating ourselves. It gave a point to our imagination. . . . The knowledge of our folk songs did not so much discover for us something new, but uncovered something which had been hidden by foreign matter.

His attitude toward musical nationalism represented as much a conscious flight from foreign domination as from any philosophy of composition involving the music of a people. Vaughan Williams had seen too many British composers end up as captives dragged on a rope behind the chariot of German academism, and he fiercely resisted capture. "As long as composers persist in serving up at second hand the externals of the music of other nations, they must not be surprised if audiences prefer the real Brahms, the real Wagner, the real Debussy or the real Stravinsky to their pale reflections." Better a limited but honest music than imitation. "Every composer cannot expect to have a world-wide message, but he may reasonably expect to have a special message for his own people." Anybody can write in the style of Wagner or Strauss, but that should not tempt the British composer. "Is it not reasonable to suppose that those who share our life, our customs, our climate, even our food, should have some secret to impart to us which the foreign composer, though he be perhaps more imaginative, more powerful, more technically equipped, is not able to give us?" That, Vaughan Williams concluded, was the secret of the national composer. He got to the point, as do so many men riding a hobbyhorse, where only music with a national tinge interested him. Thus it followed that most of Stravinsky's music bothered him, except for such scores as *Les Noces* and the *Symphony of Psalms*, in which Stravinsky's Russian heritage was so strongly emphasized. Otherwise, Vaughan Williams argued, Stravinsky was merely a clever and fashionable composer who relied on a bag of sophisticated tricks. As for the atonality of Schoenberg and his school, Vaughan Williams stood away. "Schoenberg meant nothing to me—but as he apparently meant a lot to other people, I dare say that it is all my own fault."

Buoyed by his overriding interest in British folk music, Vaughan Williams started writing scores that he hoped would spearhead a national movement. Two of them—the three *Norfolk Rhapsodies* and *In the Fen Country*—attracted a great deal of attention in 1906 and 1907 respectively. But Vaughan Williams felt that he needed more study and decided to take some lessons with, of all people, Maurice Ravel. "In 1908 I came to the conclusion that I was bumpy and stodgy, had come to a dead end, and that a little French polish would be of use to me." Off he went to Paris—a big, stout, bearlike man, dressed with cheerful sloppiness (Vaughan Williams always dressed "as though stalking the folk song to its lair," somebody once remarked)—to confront the tiny, dandified Ravel, who did not know exactly what to make of the invader. He looked at some of Vaughan Williams's music and told him to write a little minuet in the style of Mozart. Vaughan Williams met this head-on. "Look here, I have given up my time, my work, my friends and my career to come here and learn from you, and I am *not* going to write a *petit menuet dans le style de Mozart.*" Ravel guided Vaughan Williams away from "the heavy contrapuntal Teutonic manner." After Ravel, Vaughan Williams considered his musical education complete.

He returned to England and started to compose in all forms. His series of symphonies was inaugurated with *A Sea Symphony* (1910), *A London Symphony* (1914), and the *Pastoral* Symphony (1922). There also was an opera, *Hugh the Drover* (1914), in addition to choral pieces, incidental music to plays, the *Fantasia on a Theme by Tallis* (1910) for double string orchestra (one of his most popular works), and the beautiful song cycle *On Wenlock Edge* (1909), for tenor, string quartet, and piano. A sharp break in his style came with the Fourth Symphony in 1935. This departed from the folk-derived idiom of the previous symphonies in favor of a knotty, dissonant, and all but abstract style. The music is supposed to reflect Vaughan Williams's agitation over the Italian invasion of Abyssinia. "I don't know whether I like it," Vaughan Williams said of this symphony, "but this is what I meant."

From that point there was an ever-increasing harmonic tension in his symphonies. Some, like the Sixth, were abstract. Others, like the Fifth and Ninth, reverted to the folk idiom. But even in the abstract symphonies there was an underlying Englishness, with harmonic and melodic transformations that could be traced back to the Tudors. It was not nice-Nelly music. Vaughan Williams was not interested in writing "pretty" evocations of the past or present, and no British composer has so managed to steer clear of Ye Tea Shoppe school of music. The Vaughan Williams symphonies are rugged affairs with a strong dose of dissonance and often a type of construction that turns "sonata form" upside down. It is uncompromising music that follows no fashion of the day and is, in the best sense of the word, original.

The Fifth Symphony of 1943, with its return to the folk tradition, pastoral-sounding, idyllic, might well be Vaughan Williams's orchestral masterpiece. The abstract Sixth Symphony has an amazing last movement marked "always pianissimo, without a crescendo." It is a crepuscular, spooky movement, and its only equivalent in sonata-form history would be the last movement of Chopin's B flat minor Sonata. For his Seventh Symphony, the *Sinfonia Antartica* (not Antarctica), Vaughan Williams in 1953 adapted music from his film score *Scott of the Antarctic*. The Eighth Symphony (1956) is an unconventional work that Vaughan Williams described as "seven variations in search of a theme." Four months before his death came the Ninth Symphony (1958), a retrospective work rich in reminiscence and full of the sublimated nationalism of his best music.

The Ninth Symphony is a big work in every way, but it is seldom played. There has been a reaction against Vaughan Williams's music equivalent to the reaction that set in against Elgar's. Elgar, however, has been rediscovered, and Vaughan Williams also will be. He may yet turn out to be hailed as the most important symphonist of the century. Neither an academic nor an avant-gardist, he wrote emotionally uncluttered music that was set forth in old forms considerably modified for expressive ends. It is easy to overplay his nationalism. If patriotism, as Dr. Johnson said, is the last refuge of a scoundrel, it is also true that nationalism in music can be the refuge of a chauvinist, as was proved so convincingly during the period of Socialist Realism in Russian music. It is the easiest thing in the world to write "national music" of a certain kind. All that is necessary is to take a folk tune and dress it in an orchestral coat of many colors. But Vaughan Williams did not operate that way. His nationalism, like Bartók's or Dvořák's, was as much the expression of the inner state of a man as of the outward state of his country's culture. Whatever the initial impulse that triggered Vaughan Williams's music, it ended up as music first, nationalism second—the music of a big man, a big spirit, and a very original thinker. Vaughan Williams was fond of a quotation of Gustav Stresemann, and it can serve as a summation of what he was trying to do: "The man who serves humanity best is he who, rooted in his own nation, develops his spiritual and moral endowments to their highest capacity, so that growing beyond the limits of his own nation he is able to give something of the whole to humanity."

♯ 14 ♯

Mysticism and Melancholy

SCRIABIN AND RACHMANINOFF

After Tchaikovsky and The Five came two Russian composers whose lives for a while were linked: Alexander Scriabin, born in Moscow on January 6, 1872, and Serge Rachmaninoff, born in Oneg, near Novgorod, on April 1, 1873. Both were students together, both were formidable pianists, and both were the most important men of Russian music in the two decades up to World War I. Scriabin died in Moscow on April 27, 1915, and Rachmaninoff, twenty-eight years later and almost half a globe away, in Beverly Hills, California, on March 28, 1943. Scriabin was a flaming, mercurial, probably insane (toward the end) man, who started as a composer of charming little piano pieces and ended up a mystic who wrote near-incomprehensible music that was going to pull together all the arts and religions. Rachmaninoff wrote his C minor Piano Concerto in 1901 and never deviated from the pattern, writing essentially the same kind of music throughout his life. The public liked his music, but to many professionals around the world he was a creative nobody, crying his Russian tears at the feet of Tchaikovsky. It was to Serge Prokofiev that the world looked in the 1920's when the subject of Russian music came up—Prokofiev, the meteor from the East, the age-of-steel composer, the cubist in music. And after Prokofiev there was his natural successor, Dmitri Shostakovich. Rachmaninoff? *Really!*

Rachmaninoff and Scriabin first encountered each other in the piano class of Nikolai Zverev. Rachmaninoff was twelve years old, Scriabin thirteen. Both were formidable talents, with perfect pitch, supple hands, all-encompassing memories, and creative aspirations. It was no easy life in Zverev's school. He was a hard taskmaster. His students were up at 6 A. M. to start the day, and they worked for the next sixteen hours. They wore uniforms, had to take language lessons, and were brought up as gentlemen. Zverev, who was rich, took no money for his lessons, and his pupils had to come from good families. He was a homosexual, and it was whispered in Moscow that he

457

taught certain of his pupils other things than music. Scriabin and Rachmaninoff, at any rate, apparently came through physically untouched. They entered the Moscow Conservatory, Rachmaninoff in 1887, Scriabin in 1888. Both were composing at the time. Scriabin was the more precocious. He was in a period of great love for Chopin, often slept with a volume of Chopin's music under his pillow, and at the age of fourteen composed his Étude in C sharp minor (Op. 2), Chopinesque, but a little masterpiece.

At the Conservatory, Rachmaninoff studied piano with Alexander Siloti. Scriabin went to Vassily Safonov. Both also had lessons in counterpoint with Taneiev, and with Arensky studied theory and composition. Among the Safonov pupils was the fabulous Josef Lhevinne, and Scriabin nearly ruined his right hand trying to emulate Lhevinne's thunderings in the Liszt *Don Juan Fantasy*. He had trouble with the hand for years. Rachmaninoff and Scriabin swept easily through the Conservatory, grabbing prizes as they went. Rachmaninoff won the Great Gold Medal in 1892 and Scriabin won the Little Gold Medal. Then after graduation, their paths diverged for some years. The slight, elegant, convivial, party-going, and alcoholic-prone Scriabin started to tour Europe as a pianist. Rachmaninoff stayed in Moscow for the most part, where he was better known as a composer and conductor than as a pianist. He was a completely different kind of man from Scriabin. Rachmaninoff was dour, serious, taciturn, and open to only a very few close friends. He was stubborn and would not be pushed around, even as a student. He was one of the few who dared stand up to Zverev; and in the Conservatory he insisted on his rights. When he was seventeen he composed his First Piano Concerto (later it was revised), and it had a tryout at the Conservatory the following year. His fellow student, Mikhail Bukinik, has left an account of that premiere:

At the rehearsals the 18-year-old Rachmaninoff showed the same stubbornly calm character that we knew from our comradely gatherings. Safonov, who ordinarily conducted the compositions of his students, would brutally and unceremoniously change anything he wished in these scores, cleaning them up and cutting parts to make them more playable. The student composers, happy to have their creative efforts performed did not dare contradict Safonov, and readily agreed to his comments and alterations. But Safonov had a hard time with Rachmaninoff. This student not only refused categorically to accept alterations, but also had the audacity to stop Safonov (as conductor), pointing out his errors in tempo and nuance. This was obviously displeasing to Safonov, but being intelligent, he understood the rights of an author, though a beginner, to make his own interpretation, and he tried to take the edge off any awkwardness. Besides, Rachmaninoff's talent as a composer was so obvious, and his quiet self-assurance made such an impression on all, that even the omnipotent Safonov had to yield.

Rachmaninoff's graduation work was a one-act opera, *Aleko*, which Tchaikovsky admired. Rachmaninoff had been introduced to Tchaikovsky by Zverev. "He listened to me, a young beginner, as if I were his equal," Rachmaninoff once said. Later Tchaikovsky arranged for the production of *Aleko* at the Imperial Theater, and did even more: "Timidly and modestly, as if he were afraid I might refuse, he asked me if I would consider having my work produced with one of his operas. To be on a poster with Tchaikovsky was the greatest honor that could be paid to a composer." There was much in common between the two composers, and Tchaikovsky may have seen his successor in Rachmaninoff. Both represented Russian melancholy expressed in German forms. Throughout his career Rachmaninoff was content to work within a completely traditional framework.

His career moved slowly. He did some teaching and playing, composed the famous Prelude in C sharp minor in 1892, completed a Symphony in D minor in 1895, and attended its premiere in St. Petersburg in 1897. The symphony was a fiasco. It was not that hardly anybody liked it. It was that *nobody* liked it. Rachmaninoff lost confidence and went through a terrible period. For almost three years he wrote nothing. "I felt like a man who had suffered a stroke and had lost the use of his head and hands." Instead of composing, he turned to the piano. When he appeared in London in 1899, he found that he was famous. His C sharp minor Prelude had preceded him. Still he could not compose. Finally he went to a Moscow specialist named Dr. Nikolai Dahl, who worked with him on a form of psychiatric treatment coupled with hypnosis and autosuggestion. Rachmaninoff would lie on a couch under hypnosis, and Dr. Dahl would repeat: "You will write your Concerto.   You will write your Concerto.   You will write your Concerto.   You will work with great facility.   The Concerto will be of excellent quality." The treatment worked. Rachmaninoff started his C minor Concerto and finished it in 1901. It remains the most popular work he ever composed. European and American tours followed. At these, Rachmaninoff played or conducted only his own music. He was at the piano for the world premiere of his D minor Concerto, in New York in 1909. Up to World War I he had composed three concertos, two symphonies (No. 2 in E minor has retained its popularity), the symphonic poem *Isle of the Dead,* and a large quantity of songs and piano music. The piano music was tailored to his own spectacular hands. It is extremely difficult, demands wide stretches, and has tremendous virtuosity without indulging in Lisztian pyrotechnics. On the whole it is an original body of piano music, owing little to the nineteenth-century romantic school, yet part of the family. It also is strongly Russian in flavor. If it has a predecessor, it would be the piano music of Balakirev and of Adolph Henselt, the Bavarian pianist-composer who settled in Russia in 1838.

In the meantime, Scriabin was making a different kind of sensation in

Russia and abroad. Subsidized by the publisher Mitrofan Belaiev, he was playing all over Europe and demonstrating a sensuous, colorful kind of pianism, one altogether different from Rachmaninoff's clear, precise, strong, and logical work at the keyboard. At the age of twenty-six he became a professor of piano at the Moscow Conservatory, his base of operations when he was not concertizing. (He resigned in 1903.) He also was turning out a series of neo-Chopin piano works—Chopin with a Russian undercurrent. These works were graceful, lyric, full of personality, aristocratic, and by no means mere Chopin imitations. They exuded their own kind of charm. He also composed the Piano Concerto in F sharp minor in 1897, a work that gave many ideas to Rachmaninoff.

In 1898 came a shift in his style. The Third Piano Sonata showed a tendency to break textures into pointillistic bits of color. Outlines became vague, the content began to sound cryptic. Scriabin called the work *États d'Ame.* It was a decided break not only in his music but in all music. Nobody had conceived of this kind of piano writing. Spurred by his work along these lines, he started to turn to big forms, composing two symphonies by 1901. He also started to read Nietzsche and from there drifted into mysticism, inspired by the theosophical writings of Helena Blavatsky. He began to think in terms of sound and ecstasy, of music as a mystic ritual. It was as if Parsifal had gone to the East. The jargon of theosophy entered his speech. "In these mysteries of antiquity there was real transfiguration, real secrets and sanctities."

His Third Symphony and Fourth Sonata of 1903 began to break free of all conventions. Scriabin experimented with harmonies built on fourths instead of thirds, and the writing, especially for piano, became incredibly difficult and complex. He developed his "mystic chord"—C, F sharp, B flat, E, A, D—and worked out entire compositions based on it. Key signatures were dropped, and dissonance was piled on dissonance. His music began to explore a rapprochement with the other arts. In the Third Symphony, named *The Divine Poem,* an immense orchestra was used, and the music had to do with "Man-God," sensual pleasures, divine play, the Soul, the Spirit, the Creative Will. Scriabin considered *The Divine Poem* the turning point in his career. "This was the first time I found light in music, the first time I knew intoxication, flight, the *breathlessness* of happiness." His scores became peppered with such markings as "Luminously and more and more flashing." It might be that Scriabin also suffered from a rare genetic peculiarity known as synesthesia, in which sound is translated directly into color. People with synesthesia cannot hear music without seeing colors.

Scriabin's private life underwent stresses as his mysticism developed. Some peculiar traits developed. He became a compulsive hand-washer, and would put on gloves before touching money. He spent as much time at his toilette as an actress, looking for wrinkles, worried about baldness. He developed extreme hypochondria. His amorality approached Wagner's; and, like Wagner, he found it easy to rationalize and justify his actions. "Since it is far more difficult to do all one wants to do than *not* do what one wants, it is nobler to do what one likes." He seduced a former pupil, and there was a major scandal in Moscow. He left his wife, Vera (she was also a pianist), and their four children for another woman, telling Vera that he was going to live with Tatiana Schloezer as "a sacrifice to art." His friends received strange letters from him: "I can't understand how to write only 'music' now. How uninteresting it would be. Music, surely, takes on idea and significance when it is linked to one, single plan within the whole of a world-viewpoint. . . . Music is the path of revelation." He kept notebooks in which he jotted down his musings in a kind of disturbed prose-poetry that shows a mind anything but normal:

Something began to glimmer and pulsate and this *something was one*. It trembled and glimmered, but it was one. I do not differentiate multiplicity. This *one* was all with nothing in opposition to it. It was everything. I am everything. It had the possibility of anything, and it was not yet Chaos (the threshold of consciousness). All history and all future are eternally in it. All elements are mixed, but all that can be is there. It exudes colors, feelings and dreams. I wish. I create. I differentiate. I distinguish unclearly. Nothing is delineated. I know nothing, but all seems foreboding and I remember. Instants of the past and future come together. Confused presentiments and recollections, frights and joys.

Scriabin began to think that he was absorbed into the rhythm of the universe, and became megalomaniacal on the subject. He identified with God:

I am freedom, I am life, I am a dream, I am weariness, I am unceasing burning desire, I am bliss, I am insane passion, I am nothing, I am atremble.
I am play, I am freedom, I am life, I am a dream, I am weariness, I am feeling,
I am the world. I am insane passion, I am wild flight, I am desire, I am light,
I am creative ascent that tenderly caresses, that captivates, that sears, Destroying,
Revivifying. I am raging torrents of unknown feelings, I am the boundary, I am the summit. I am nothing.

You, depths of the past born from the rays of my memories, and you, heights of the future and creations of my dreams! You are not you.

461

> I am God!
> I am nothing, I am play, I am freedom, I am life.
> I am the boundary, I am the peak.
>
>   I am God!
> I am the blossoming, I am the bliss,
> I am all-consuming passion,
>   all engulfing,
> I am fire enveloping the universe,
> Reducing it to chaos.
> I am the blind play of powers released.
> I am creation dormant, Intellect quenched.

From 1904 he lived openly with Tatiana. His wife would not divorce him, so he and Tatiana left Russia from 1904 to 1909. In 1906 he was invited to the United States by Modest Altschuler, a classmate of Scriabin's who had gone to New York and formed the Russian Symphony Orchestra. Altschuler was one of the less talented conductors of his time, or any other time, but he introduced a great deal of Russian music to America. Scriabin arrived in New York in December and promptly gave a recital. Immediately the newspapers referred to him as "The Cossack Chopin." Scriabin liked America but could not understand American morality as explained to him by Altschuler. It seemed that Maxim Gorky had a great deal of trouble when he came to the United States with his mistress, and was evicted by several hotels. Scriabin revealed his findings to Tatiana: "Altschuler says that if Gorky had had a different whore in his room every day, and they had known ALL about it, they wouldn't have thought a thing of it or persecuted him to such an extent. That would have been natural. However, it is considered a crime now to live faithfully with a beloved woman out of wedlock." Nevertheless, early in 1907, Tatiana joined Scriabin in New York. Newspapers found out about it. Altschuler, crying that he would be ruined, put Scriabin and Tatiana on the next boat to Europe. Scriabin had been in the United States only for about four months. He never returned, though his impressions of the country were not unfavorable. "America has a great future," he told friends. "There is a very strong mystic movement there."

Scriabin and Tatiana lived briefly in Paris and then, late in 1907, settled in Lausanne. There they heard that Altschuler had conducted the world premiere of *The Poem of Ecstasy* in New York on December 10, 1908. Altschuler notified Scriabin that the work had not been reviewed, which was not true. It had been poorly received, but Altschuler wanted to spare Scriabin the details of its reception. At that time, Scriabin was desperately short of money, but there was a turn in his fortune with his liaison with the wealthy (by marriage) conductor, Serge Koussevitzky. They met in the summer of 1908. Koussevitzky, in Berlin, had started the Russian Music Edition and was looking for important scores. He visited Scriabin in Lausanne, and also invited him to appear with his orchestra as piano soloist. Scriabin accepted and, as Faubion Bowers relates in his biography of the composer, "overflowed with plans. He spoke of tactile symphonies. He called incense an art which joins earth and heaven. He described the *Mysterium* [a work about which Scriabin had been thinking for many years]. He explained this great, final, cataclysmic opus as synthesizing all the arts, loading all senses into a hypnoidal, many-media extravaganza of sound, sight, smell, feel, dance, décor, orchestra, piano, singers, light, sculptures, colors, visions. Koussevitzky brought rights to it then and there." The two men worked out an agreement through which Scriabin would be paid 5,000 rubles a year for five years, the time necessary for the completion of the *Mysterium*. Koussevitzky also agreed to publish all of Scriabin's other compositions during that five-year period, at good royalty terms. One of those works was the Fifth Symphony, which Scriabin named *Prometheus: The Poem of Fire*. This had an elaborate program, ending with the world's beginning and a cosmic dance of the atoms. In addition to the full symphony orchestra, *Prometheus* used a piano, a chorus, and a color organ. It was Scriabin's first actual attempt to synthesize music and colors, and he worked out a chart:

Note	Vibrations per second	Color
C	256	Red
C sharp	277	Violet
D	298	Yellow
D sharp	319	Glint of steel
E	341	Pearly white and shimmer of moonlight
F	362	Deep red
F sharp	383	Bright blue
G	405	Rosy orange
G sharp	426	Purple
A	447	Green
A sharp	469	Glint of steel [for some reason, the same as D sharp]
B	490	Pearly blue

Koussevitzky conducted the world premiere of *Prometheus* in Moscow, on March 2, 1911. But there was no color organ; the instrument turned out to be impractical and was dropped. Scriabin was back in Russia for the premiere. He had broken up his Lausanne establishment in 1910 and returned to his own country for good. Naturally his path again crossed Rachmaninoff's. Russia was split into two musical camps. Scriabin and Rachmaninoff: which was the greater composer? the greater pianist? Scriabin was much the more discussed, if only because of the strangeness of his music. By now he was using the intervals of seconds and ninths in addition to fourths, and was living in a strange world of his own. "My Tenth Sonata is a sonata of insects. Insects are born from the sun . . . they are the sun's kisses . . . How unified world-understanding is when you look at things this way." He spent a great deal of time working on the *Mysterium*—not composing any music, but thinking about its locale and the extramusical accompaniments to the spectacle. The *Mysterium* involved the end of the world and the creation of a new race of man. At the climax of the *Mysterium* the walls of the universe would cave in. "I shall not die," Scriabin said. "I shall suffocate in ecstasy after the *Mysterium*." He thought of himself as the true Messiah and wanted his *Mysterium* to be performed in a temple in India, a temple hemispherical in shape. To prepare himself for India, he went out and purchased a sun helmet and a Sanskrit grammar. As Bowers describes the *Mysterium*:

Bells suspended from the clouds in the sky would summon the spectators from all over the world. The performance was to take place in a half temple to be built in India. A reflecting pool of water would complete the divinity of the half-circle stage. Spectators would sit in tiers across the water. Those in the balconies would be the least spiritually advanced. The seating was strictly graded, ranking radially from the center of the stage, where Scriabin would sit at the piano, surrounded by hosts of instruments, singers, dancers. The entire group was to be permeated continually with movement, and costumed speakers reciting the text in processions and parades would form parts of the action. The choreography would include glances, looks, eye motions, touches of the hands, odors of both pleasant perfumes and acrid smokes, frankincense and myrrh. Pillars of incense would form part of the scenery. Lights, fires, and constantly changing lighting effects would pervade the cast and audience, each to number in the thousands. This prefaces the final Mysterium and prepares people for their ultimate dissolution in ecstasy.

Goodness knows how far Scriabin would have gone with the project. Had not Wagner created Bayreuth against all inconceivable odds? But Scriabin died while all of the *Mysterium* was in his head. He died in a ridiculous manner. People like him should go up in a blaze of fire. Scriabin died from blood poisoning, the result of a carbuncle on his lip. Rachmaninoff sorrowed. He, who up till then had played only his music in public, gave a series of Scriabin recitals in his memory. The Scriabin fans honored the idea but did not like the execution. Rachmaninoff's playing was not to their taste. Young Serge Prokofiev was in the audience for one of the recitals. Rachmaninoff played, among other things, the Fifth Sonata. When Scriabin played it, the music was all allure and suggestion, in subtle tints. It flew, Prokofiev said. "But with Rachmaninoff, all its notes stood firmly and clearly on the ground." Scriabin's friends were outraged. Ivan Alchevsky, the tenor, had to be restrained from running to the stage and telling Rachmaninoff what he thought of him. Prokofiev tried to smooth things out, saying that there were more ways than one to play a piece of music. He went to the green room and, with his typical lack of tact told Rachmaninoff that he had played very well. That was all the young man had to say. "And you probably thought I'd play badly?" Rachmaninoff icily inquired. That ended Rachmaninoff's relations with Prokofiev for many years.

Shortly after the 1917 Revolution, Rachmaninoff left Russia for good and settled in Switzerland, starting a new life as a piano virtuoso. He was about forty-five years old and had virtually no repertory aside from his own music. His reputation as a conductor was good—he had been a first-line conductor at the Imperial Theater and the Moscow Philharmonic—and several major American orchestras offered him positions, but he decided to concentrate on the piano. It probably was the better choice, for he was one of the colossal pianists in history. In 1935 he settled permanently in the United States. Of course through the years he continued to compose as well as concertize. Significant works were the Piano Concerto No. 4 (1926), the Variations on a Theme by Corelli, for solo piano (1931), the Rhapsody on a Theme of Paganini, for piano and orchestra (1934), the Third Symphony (1936), and the Symphonic Dances (1940).

There was never a time when the music of Rachmaninoff was out of the repertory. This is in sharp contrast with the music of Scriabin, for there never was a time when the music of Scriabin was really in the repertory, though his early piano pieces achieved some popularity, and *The Divine Poem* and *The Poem of Ecstasy* were played once in a while. Not until the late 1960's was there the beginning of a Scriabin rediscovery. Scriabin has suddenly begun to be studied very seriously. But Rachmaninoff, so often played, has had hardly any critical appraisal at all. He was a composer who unabashedly used nineteenth-century models for his music, and as a result has been all but dismissed by scholars, historians, professionals, and tastemakers.

Typical of the attitude is the sneering reference in the fifth edition of Grove's *Dictionary of Music and Musicians*. It is one of the most outrageously snobbish and even stupid statements ever to be found in a work that is supposed to be an objective reference. Rachmaninoff rates only five para-

465

graphs in this august nine-volume encyclopedia. It is worth reproducing the last two paragraphs complete:

> As a pianist Rachmaninoff was one of the finest artists of his time; as a composer he can hardly be said to have belonged to his time at all, and he represented his country only in the sense that accomplished but conventional composers like Glazunov or Arensky did. He had neither the national characteristics of the Balakirev school nor the individuality of Taneiev or Medtner. Technically he was highly gifted, but also severely limited. His music is well constructed and effective, but monotonous in texture, which consists in essence mainly of artificial and gushing tunes accompanied by a variety of figures derived from arpeggios.
>
> The enormous popular success some few of Rachmaninoff's works had in his lifetime is not likely to last, and musicians never regarded it with much favor. The third pianoforte Concerto was on the whole liked by the public only because of its close resemblance to the second, while the fourth, which attempted something like a new departure, was a failure from the start. The only later work that has attracted large concert audiences was the Rhapsody (variations) on a Theme by Paganini for pianoforte and orchestra.

Much of this is nonsense, but it represents a prevalent view of Rachmaninoff and his music. It blames him for not being Mussorgsky. It comes up with the astounding statement that he did not have the individuality of Taneiev or Medtner. Sergei Taneiev (1856–1915) was a Russian academician and specialist in fugue, whose music, if his Second Symphony is a fair example, was devoid of life and character and is as individual as a toothpick nestled in a box of toothpicks. Nicolai Medtner (1880–1951) was another Russian eclectic who, like Rachmaninoff, was a pianist-composer and who did Rachmaninoff the great honor of imitating him. Medtner's music has all but disappeared from the repertory. He was a composer on the order of an Ernö von Dohnányi—a good craftsman who seldom came up with an original idea. To call these two men more individual than Rachmaninoff displays ignorance and a blind reluctance to accept an unpalatable verdict of history.

For the facts are that Rachmaninoff is as popular as he ever was; that his music stubbornly refuses to go away; that, far from regarding his music with disfavor, every young pianist has in his repertory the C minor and D minor Concertos; that the C minor has had (at the point of writing) almost seventy years of exposure and the D minor almost sixty, with neither one showing any perceptible signs of waning; that in addition to the concertos the E minor Symphony also continues to make a great effect; that a good deal of Rachmaninoff's solo keyboard music continues to be well represented on programs throughout the world; and that many of his songs are still be loved. What more does a composer have to do to prove himself?

The point about Rachmaninoff's music is this: within its limitations it moves with perfect security and, yes, with much individuality. As with any major composer, it takes but a few measures of his work to establish its identity (Medtner and Taneiev would fail this test). Rachmaninoff may have contributed nothing to twentieth-century form or harmony, but he did suffuse the old forms with something highly personal, as Tchaikovsky did; and, in addition, he was one of the better melodists of his time. Nor was his melody as sentimental as writers like that in Grove's would have us believe. A good case can be made that Rachmaninoff was less sentimental than Tchaikovsky or Mahler. It is his followers who have made him sentimental: those minor composers who drifted off to write hack or movie music and helped make Rachmaninoff's name anathema.

Nor is it even true that his music is international as opposed to national. A strong Russian quality is the essence of Rachmaninoff's music, and that is part of its appeal. But whether or not it is nationalistic, whether or not it "belongs to its time"—all that is beside the point. A lot of music that "belongs to its time" is trash, and in any period of history there has been significant music that looked back rather than forward. The important thing about any composer is how individual he is, how well he expresses himself, how strong his ideas are. Rachmaninoff comes out better than most. His ideas did not have the universality of the great composers. Emotionally (and technically, too) he was apt to repeat himself. But the ideas themselves have validity and strength—as well over a half-century of delighted listeners continue to testify—the melodies have authentic sweep, and they always evoke a response. Ferruccio Busoni, it is said, had ten times Rachmaninoff's intellect, and he may have been an even more interesting pianist. But it is Rachmaninoff's music that continues to live, while Busoni's is hardly alive at all. The reason is that Rachmaninoff expressed himself, while Busoni had a tendency to express everybody from Bach to Liszt. (Busoni's music has a fascination of its own, but for different reasons.) Rachmaninoff's music has been around for a long time. If it did not have something to say, it would have disappeared long ago.

Rachmaninoff's music, of course, poses no problems. Scriabin's does. Almost as much as Schoenberg's it illustrates a break from the musical thinking of the past. Indeed, there is a strong parallel between the music of Schoenberg and the late Scriabin. Neither was influenced by the other, but both at almost the same time started to break away from triadic harmony and explore a harmony based on fourths instead of thirds. In the process the music of both composers became more dissonant. Schoenberg made the plunge into atonality and Scriabin did not, but he came very close, and orthodox key relationships were abolished. Scriabin's late music is a black mass of accidentals, fearsome-looking chords, and murderously difficult piano figurations. A work like the Tenth Sonata, with its strange trillings, its quartal harmonies, its disjunct melodic line, its dissonance and complete disregard for the amenities, is amazingly close to Schoenberg. One section near the end of the Tenth Sonata sounds as though Webern were the composer.

Another aspect of Scriabin that interested the late 1960's was his use of supplementary media. The concept of mixed media fascinated composers after 1965, and they began to experiment with lights, tape, speech and other sounds, in their scores. Scriabin, of course, had done much the equivalent prior to 1910. One of the key words of the late 1960's was "psychedelic," and it was found that Scriabin was the most psychedelic of all previous composers, dealing with visions, hallucinations, colors, smells, and tastes. There even was an element of Dada in Scriabin's musical thinking. He spoke about writing a sonata based on the pain of a toothache, or of dissolving a melody into an aroma.

Yet with all Scriabin's wildness in his late music, there are aspects that link up with his early music. To the very end his harmonies—no matter how complicated, no matter how divorced from key relationships—have a sensuous quality. Scriabin's music can be called erotic. It may be that music by itself cannot be erotic; it becomes so only through association; but some composers have more of a feeling for rich harmonic combinations than have others, and this is often termed erotic. Scriabin had this quality as much as any composer in history. There also is a certain kind of melody characteristic of Scriabin, and those big, sweeping gestures of *The Poem of Ecstasy* or *Prometheus* are but expansions of such works as the early *Poème* in F sharp.

In his early works there sometimes is a nationalistic quality. Later that was to disappear. Scriabin is not one of the Russian nationalists, though he did influence some of them. Stravinsky has called Scriabin a case of "musical emphysema," and his music "bombastic," but when Stravinsky came to write his *Firebird*, he had not only Rimsky-Korsakov in his blood. He also knew *The Poem of Ecstasy*.

It would be idle to deny that Scriabin's music, especially his orchestral music, suffers from self-indulgence. It is also true that in his mysticism he can be all but incomprehensible. Richard Anthony Leonard, in his book on Russian music, suggests a parallel between Scriabin and William Blake. Both were mystics, both were actuated by a personal vision, both talked with God, both produced works of art that can be explained only in terms of religious ecstasy, and both invented their own symbolism. Thus neither can be approached superficially. Their work has to be studied, and an understanding of what they were trying to do involves an understanding of

468

what they thought about matters outside their art. Blake has won his battle in the eyes of posterity. Scriabin has yet to win his. But he was one of the most original, fascinating, enigmatic, revolutionary, and rewarding composers of the turn of the century.

Under the Soviets

PROKOFIEV AND SHOSTAKOVICH

In the days before World War I, when Rachmaninoff and Scriabin were riding high in Russia, there was a student at the St. Petersburg Conservatory named Serge Prokofiev. He was a stubborn, ill-tempered, obstinate, and surly young man of undeniable talent. Some said genius. He was born in Sontsovka, in the Ukraine, on April 23, 1891. At the age of six he was a facile pianist, and at nine he was trying to compose an opera. When he entered the Conservatory, at the age of thirteen, everything about him attracted attention, including his looks. His head was set on a pipe-stem neck; he had pink skin that would turn red when he was in a rage (which was often), piercing blue eyes, and thick, protruding lips. He brought along with him to the Conservatory four operas, a symphony, two sonatas, and other piano pieces. Rimsky-Korsakov, Nicolai Tcherepnin, and Anatol Liadov were among his teachers. "I don't show my compositions to Liadov," Prokofiev said, "because if I did he probably would expel me from the class." He studied piano with Annette Essipov. She had been one of the many wives of the famous teacher Theodore Leschetizky, from whose atelier had come such famous pianists as Paderewski, Schnabel, Gabrilowitsch, and Friedman; and she herself was recognized as one of the best pianists of the day.

Prokofiev disturbed little Essipov. He disturbed everybody. Prokofiev was like King Gama in *Princess Ida*, always ready with a crushing repartee, with an irritating chuckle and a celebrated leer. He was a man who never could temporize, and he did not suffer fools gladly. He had to say exactly what he thought, and even as a student he was alienating his superiors by his sharp judgments on their music or their teaching methods. (He was to be like that all his life, and had to be approached cautiously. If he took a dislike to anybody, he could be savage. Typical was his reply to an admirer, who gushed over him and shook hands saying "What an infinite pleasure to meet you!"

Prokofiev turned away, growling "On my part there is no pleasure.")

As one of the new breed of antiromantics in a romantically oriented conservatory, Prokofiev composed music that appalled his venerable betters. His *Suggestion diabolique* (1909) and Piano Concerto No. 1 (1911), both composed while he was at the St. Petersburg Conservatory, set the institution on its ears, and he was denounced as "an extreme leftist." At the piano, Prokofiev was an ice-cold demon—throwing out bleak dissonances (or what were in those days considered bleak dissonances) and propulsive rhythms with complete control and emotional detachment. He would have none of the tradition that stemmed from Chopin and Liszt. The piano, he insisted, was a percussion instrument and had to be played percussively. Anyway, Prokofiev did not like the music of Liszt and Chopin, and was constantly poking fun at them. "They say you can't give a recital without Chopin? I'll prove that we can do very well without Chopin." No wonder Essipov in her report called him "very talented but rather unpolished." Nevertheless he won the Rubinstein Prize for piano playing in 1914, and on his own terms. Instead of playing the prescribed classical concerto, he insisted on playing his own, No. 1 in D flat. There was grumbling, but somehow Prokofiev bulled his way through. One of the best descriptions of Prokofiev in action as a young man comes from the composer Vernon Duke, who in those days was named Vladimir Dukelsky and was making up his mind to be a composer. His mother took him to a concert to hear the St. Petersburg Gold Medalist play his own concerto. Reinhold Glière conducted:

Glière bowed and shortly reappeared with a tall young man of extraordinary appearance. He had white-blond hair, a small head with a large mouth and very thick lips. . . . (Prokofiev was then nicknamed the "White Negro") and very long, awkwardly dangling arms, terminating in a bruiser's powerful hands. Prokofiev wore dazzlingly elegant tails, a beautifully cut waistcoat, and flashing black pumps. The strangely gauche manner in which he traversed the stage was no indication of what was to follow; after sitting down and adjusting the piano stool with an abrupt jerk, Prokofiev let go with an unrelenting muscular exhibition of a completely novel kind of piano playing. The prevailing fashion in those days was the languorous hothouse manner of a Scriabin or the shimmering post-Debussy impressionist tinklings of harp and celesta. This young man's music and his performance of it reminded me of the onrushing forwards in my one unfortunate soccer experience—nothing but unrelenting energy and athletic joy of living. No wonder the first four notes of the concerto, oft-repeated, were later nicknamed *"po cherepoo"* ("hit on the head"), which was Prokofiev's exact intention. . . There was frenetic applause, and no less than six flower horseshoes were handed to Prokofiev, who was now greeted with astonished laughter. He bowed

471

clumsily, dropping his head almost to his knees, and recovering with a yank.

The Russian Revolution came, and Prokofiev headed for the United States by way of Japan. With him were some major compositions. The Revolution may have sent him out of the country, but 1917 was also a great creative year for him. It saw many of the *Visions fugitives* for solo piano, the D major Violin Concerto, and the *Classical Symphony*, all of which have remained among his most popular works. The *Classical Symphony* was a *jeu d'esprit*. "It seemed to me that if Haydn had lived in this century, he would have retained his own style of writing while absorbing certain things from newer music. I wanted to write the kind of symphony that would have such a style." The *Classical* also was Prokofiev's first work written away from the piano. "I wanted to establish the fact that thematic material worked out away from the piano is better."

In the United States, Prokofiev was greatly discussed, somewhat admired, and not generally liked. His sharp, brittle, percussive, wildly propulsive playing was something new, and so was his music. "The Bolshevik pianist," he was called. Or, "Steel fingers, steel biceps, steel triceps—he is a tonal steel trust." To those used to the romantic meanderings of the Liszt and Leschetizky pupils, Prokofiev's playing was poison. Here were no romantic landscapes but pistons, clankings, the machinery of a new age. America did not like him, and he did not like America, especially after the failure of his opera, *The Love for Three Oranges,* when it was staged by the Chicago Opera in 1921. Prokofiev had some hard words to say about the United States:

> I wandered through the enormous park in the middle of New York and, looking up at the skyscrapers bordering it, I thought with fury of the wonderful American orchestras that cared nothing for my music; of the critics who were repeating for the hundredth time, "Beethoven is a great composer," while balking violently at new works; of the managers who arranged long tours for artists playing the same hackneyed programs fifty times over.

In disgust, he went to Paris and made his headquarters there. Diaghilev became interested in the young Russian and commissioned two ballets from him, *Le Pas d'acier* (1925) and *L'Enfant prodigue* (1929). He worked on his opera *The Flaming Angel,* finished his Third Piano Concerto, did a good deal of concertizing, and became one of the most-discussed composers of his period. In some respects, he was *the* composer. His music was not played as often as he would have liked, but it nevertheless created an enormous stir in the 1920's, and it made a great many people uncomfortable.

Those who felt uncomfortable had good cause to be; their instincts were correct. For Prokofiev *was* the Age-of-Steel composer, and his music did reflect the new antiromanticism. In a day when Schoenberg's advanced theory was not understood and little encountered, in a day when Stravinsky had "retreated" into neoclassicism after the colossal explosions of *Petrushka* and *Le Sacre du Printemps,* Prokofiev was to many the exemplar of the new era following World War I and the Russian Revolution. People could despise his music, could hate it, could deride it, but it could not be dismissed.

Today we can see that Prokofiev composed within a traditional framework. He used, for the most part, nineteenth-century forms; and his music, despite the many pile-ups of dissonance, was tonal. It is music of a powerful personality, and has many qualities that set it apart. Among those qualities are celerity, dash, confidence, and an enormous athleticism. Prokofiev was not a profound composer, but at its best his lean, clear, pointed music has a remarkably bracing quality. He could invent fine melodies when he wanted to. Melody, however, is not what Prokofiev's music is about. What Prokofiev represented was a sharp, eager, slashing attack on the romantic musical conventions. If in the long run it did not prove to be as revolutionary as many people thought it was, it has remained powerful and muscular, outliving most music of its time.

While Prokofiev was in Paris, a new hero arose in Russia. Dimitri Shostakovich, born in Petersburg on September 25, 1906, was the first important musical child of the Revolution. Like Prokofiev, he had been admitted to the Conservatory at the age of thirteen. There he studied with Maximilian Steinberg and was encouraged by Glazunov. Thin, serious, bespectacled, nervous, shy, chain-smoking, he impressed everybody with his talent. As a senior at the Conservatory in 1925 he composed his First Symphony, which had its premiere the following year, and it bore out all the good predictions that had been made about him. The First Symphony is a remarkable work for a nineteen-year-old—a symphony on a grand scale, with wit and an irrepressible *joie de vivre,* with irony and elements of parody, with juicy melodic content and rich-sounding orchestration. Immediately Shostakovich was established as an important composer. He followed the First Symphony with a series of works that cemented the initial impression. There was the satirical opera *The Nose* (1928), after the Gogol story; and in one interlude of the opera, a section scored for percussion orchestra, Shostakovich showed that he could be as modern as any of his colleagues in the West. There was a smart-aleck Piano Concerto which suggested that Shostakovich could have followed in the footsteps of *Les Six* had he so wanted. There was a ballet named *The Golden Age* (1930), from which the Polka achieved a great deal of fame at one time. Shostakovich also composed a pair of symphonies based on recent Russian history. One was subtitled *October* (1927) and the other

May Day (1931). In 1932 he finished an opera named *Lady Macbeth of Mzensk*, a sort of Russian verismo based on adultery and murder, and expressed in music of powerful dissonance.

It was this opera that got Shostakovich into trouble, for the new leadership in Russia did not look kindly on either the morality or the musical idiom of *Lady Macbeth of Mzensk*. In the early 1920's, experimental work in all the arts had been encouraged in Russia. The theater, headed by such creative forces as Vsevolod Meyerhold, Vladimir Mayakovsky, and Nicolai Okhlopokov, was smashing every tradition in sight. Sergei Eisenstein was bringing new horizons to the cinema. In painting and sculpture, modernism all but became the official style, and the constructivists, headed by Naum Gabo, were emerging as a major force. The creators who came out of the Revolution honestly believed that their art and Russian politics were headed in the same direction. As the artist Kasimir Malevich said, "Cubism and futurism were the revolutionary forms of art in foreshadowing the Revolution in political and economic life of 1917." But by 1930 the entire scale of values had shifted. Through one of the ironies of history, revolutionary Russia began to turn out art of a banality and uniformity of expression that represented the antithesis of revolution.

Some of this shift represented the bourgeois character of Stalin. But more than that, it represented official Soviet doctrine stemming from the words of Lenin, and the words of Lenin meant sanctification. Russian aestheticians and bureaucrats took as their starting point Lenin's statement that "Art belongs to the people." Art was turned into a vehicle for Soviet propaganda, and Socialist Realism came into being. In dictatorships, art always is disposed of much the same way. Only the terminology is different. Where Hitler was to ban avant-garde art and music on the premise that it represented decadent cultural Bolshevism, Stalin banned it on the grounds that it represented decadent imperialistic capitalistic formalism. Any kind of adventurous music was banned in Russia. Composers could not write it, audiences could not hear it. All twelve-tone music, all Bartók and Hindemith, all Stravinsky after *Petrushka* (which did not leave very much), anything that had any hint of abstractionism was banned. The country was closed. No foreign publications were admitted, and all foreign radio broadcasts were jammed. Soviet composers had little way of knowing what was going on in the world. A dreadful pall of uniformity fell over Russian art, literature, and music; and critics—all official spokesmen of government doctrine—developed a weird jargon in which music was evaluated not on its own merits but on its doctrinal purity. Yuri Keldish, in his *History of Russian Music*, denounced Stravinsky's music as the "reactionary essence of modernism as an anti-folk end in art, reflecting the decadent ideology of the imperialist bourgeoisie." All Russian critics wrote like this. The most dreaded charge against a composer was "formalism." Nobody knew exactly what it meant, except that if a composer was accused of formalism he had better start mending his ways. In general, formalism in music was anything modern or dissonant, anything that was "pessimistic," anything that did not reflect the heroic ideals of the Soviet worker. "Formalism," said Prokofiev, "is the name given to music not understood on first hearing."

Prokofiev was back in Russia at that time. He had made a visit in 1927, was enthusiastically welcomed, and in 1932 returned for good. Stravinsky for one, in his *Memories and Commentaries*, flatly states that Prokofiev's return to Russia was "a sacrifice to the bitch goddess, and nothing else. He had no success in the United States or Europe for several seasons, while his visit to Russia had been a triumph. When I saw him for the last time in New York in 1937, he was despondent about his material and artistic fate in France. He was politically naive, however, and he had learned nothing from the example of his good friend Miaskovsky. He returned to Russia, and when finally he understood his position there, it was too late." Nicolai Miaskovsky (1881–1950) was a prolific composer of symphonies (he wrote twenty-seven) and an eminent teacher who learned to dance to the Russian tune.

At first, Prokofiev was happy. He was celebrated and honored, he was kept busy, and until 1937 he was allowed to leave the country for concert tours. He told his friend Vernon Duke that he was content:

> . . . I asked Serge a difficult question then uppermost in my mind. I wanted to know how he could live and work in the atmosphere of Soviet totalitarianism. Serge was quiet for a moment and then said quietly and seriously: "Here is how I feel about it: I care nothing for politics—I'm a composer first and last. Any government that lets me write my music in peace, publishes everything I compose before the ink is dry, and performs every note that comes from my pen is all right with me. In Europe we all have to fish for performances, cajole conductors and theater directors; in Russia they come to *me*—I can hardly keep up with the demand. What's more, I have a comfortable flat in Moscow, a delightful *dacha* in the country and a brand-new car. My boys go to a fine English school in Moscow. . .

But Prokofiev could not have been happy about the restrictions that were beginning to handcuff Russian musicians. Shostakovich was the first to feel the blow, and his antagonist was Stalin himself. The occasion that drew forth Stalin's wrath was a performance of *Lady Macbeth of Mzensk* in Moscow in 1936. Stalin is said to have stormed out of the theater in a fury after the first act, livid with rage about the "degenerate" music. He immediately postulated three criteria for Soviet opera: subjects must have a Socialist theme; the musical language must be "realistic," *i.e.*, without dissonance

475

and based on Russian folksong; and the plot must be "positive," *i.e.*, with a happy ending in which the State is eulogized. With these postulates came an attack on Shostakovich in *Pravda*. This was serious. A Soviet musician coming under official disapproval could lose his job and could find all outlets for publication and performance closed. He also could lose his home and such perquisites as a car and his *dacha*. In Stalin's day, he even could be jailed. Shostakovich rehabilitated himself in 1937 with his Fifth Symphony. But to all intents and purposes, he was ruined as a composer. Never again would he write with the dash, sparkle, and modernity he had shown in the First Symphony, *The Nose, Lady Macbeth,* and the Piano Concerto. Instead he was to write nothing but safe music, repeating old formulas, imitating some of Prokofiev's mannerisms.

In the 1930's and 1940's, with Shostakovich in full retreat, Prokofiev was the dominant force in Soviet music. His harmonic ideas and melodic idiosyncracies could be found echoed in the music of every important Soviet composer of the day—in Shostakovich, in Dmitri Kabalevsky, in Aram Khachaturian, in Tikhon Khrennikov. They all composed watered-down Prokofiev. Prokofiev himself composed watered-down Prokofiev. They all also acted as spokesmen for the State and its propaganda—all but Prokofiev, who was big enough and stubborn enough to do nothing but compose. And compose he did. He wrote film scores, of which *Lieutenant Kije* (1934) and *Alexander Nevsky* (1939) are the most popular. He finished his Violin Concerto No. 2 (1935), *Peter and the Wolf* (1936), and his ballet music for *Romeo and Juliet* (1935). All of these turned out to be international favorites. An opera, *Semyon Kotko* (1939), did not work out. Another opera, *Betrothal in a Monastery* (1931), adapted from Sheridan's *The Duenna*, received only a few performances. The war years saw a series of important works—the huge opera *War and Peace,* the Piano Sonata No. 7, the String Quartet No. 2, the Flute (Violin) Sonata in D, the ballet music to *Cinderella,* and the Fifth Symphony. These were clearly the scores of a master, and also somewhat different from the music of Prokofiev's French and American period. It carried all of Prokofiev's rhythmic, melodic, and harmonic mannerisms, but sounded less modern, less age-of-steel. Emotionally it was a gentler kind of music, staying close to the principles of Socialist Realism.

Yet even so famous and internationally respected a composer as Prokofiev was not immune to criticism, and in 1948 the roof fell in. Prokofiev and every important Soviet composer of the day were attacked by the regime. The event that touched off the explosion was the premiere, on November 7, 1947, of Vano Muradeli's opera *Great Friendship.* It was reviewed as historically and ideologically incorrect, with "inexpressive, poor, unharmonious, muddled music . . . confused and discordant, built on continuous dissonances and ear-splitting combinations of sounds." Three months later the

476

Central Committee of the Communist Party held a meeting at which charges were preferred against Muradeli, Prokofiev, Shostakovich, Khachaturian, Miaskovsky, Vissarion Shebalin, and others. The Central Committee published a Resolution accusing all these composers of formalism, "antidemocratic tendencies that are alien to the Soviet people and its artistic tastes," and of writing music "strongly reminiscent of the spirit of contemporary modernistic bourgeois music of Europe and America." For page after page the Central Committee's diatribe went on. Critics also came under attack. "Musical criticism has ceased to express the opinion of Soviet society." The document contained a threat to the effect that such music "cannot be tolerated any longer," and ended with a four-point program:

(1) To condemn the formalistic movement in Soviet music as anti-national and leading to the liquidation of music.

(2) To urge the Department of Propaganda and Agitation of the Central Committee and the Committee of the Fine Arts to correct the situation in Soviet music, to liquidate the defects pointed out in the present Resolution of the Central Committee, and to secure the development of Soviet music in the realistic direction.

(3) To call upon Soviet composers to realize fully the lofty requirements of the Soviet people upon musical art, to sweep from their path all that weakens our music and hinders its development, and assure an upsurge of creative work that will advance Soviet musical culture so as to lead to the creation, in all fields of music, of high-quality works worthy of the Soviet people.

(4) To approve organizational measures of the corresponding Party and Soviet organs, designed to improve the state of musical affairs.

That was on February 10, 1948. From February 17 to 26 there was a meeting of Soviet musicians in Moscow, at which Andrei A. Zhdanov, the Politburo spokesman for cultural ideology, amplified some of the Central Committee's points. Khrennikov added to Zhdanov's remarks, attacking his colleagues and accusing them of formalism. Khrennikov specifically cited Shostakovich's Eighth and Ninth Symphonies and Second Piano Sonata, and Prokofiev's *War and Peace,* Sixth Piano Sonata, and a number of other piano works, as formalistic. He said that Soviet composers "must reject as useless and harmful garbage all the relics of bourgeois formalism in musical art." (Khrennikov soon became a powerful figure in the Soviet musical bureaucracy.) One by one the composers under attack got up and apologized. Muradeli: "How could it have happened that I failed to introduce a single folk song into the score of my opera? . . . I have before me a definite task, to realize fully and unequivocally the seriousness of my creative errors, and to correct these errors with ideological honesty in my future work." Shostakovich: "I am deeply grateful for   . all the criticism contained in the Resolution. . . I shall with still more determination work on the musical depiction of the images of the heroic Soviet people." Khachaturian: "How could it happen that I have come to formalism in my art? . . I want to warn those comrades who, like myself, hoped that their music, which is not understood by the people today, will be understood by future generations tomorrow. It is a fatal theory. In our country, millions of people, the entire Soviet nation, are now arbiters of music. What can be higher and nobler than writing music understandable to our people and to give joy by creative art to millions?" Prokofiev: "The Resolution   has separated decayed tissue in the composers' creative production from the healthy part.   . The Resolution is particularly important because it demonstrates that the formalist movement is alien to the Soviet people.   ." All the composers wrote a joint letter to Stalin, thanking him for the public spanking: "We are tremendously grateful to the Central Committee of the All-Union Communist Party (Bolsheviks) and personally to you, dear Comrade Stalin, for the severe but profoundly just criticism of the present state of Soviet music. . . . We shall bend every effort to apply our knowledge and our artistic mastery to produce vivid realistic music reflecting the life and struggles of the Soviet people.

Small wonder that any lingering ideas of individuality were squashed after the 1948 Central Committee Resolution. If the skillful puerilities of Prokofiev's *War and Peace* were to be condemned as formalistic, what was left for the Soviet composer to do but orchestrate folk songs and let it go at that? A period of complete uniformity followed. Russian music, like Russian painting, had nothing to offer to the world. Even the best composers of the Soviet Union—Prokofiev and Shostakovich—were reduced to turning out pallid and uncontroversial scores of artistic inconsequence—the musical equivalent of the agriculture paintings that the artists were turning out. Shostakovich embarked on chamber music, more symphonies, and film scores. Prokofiev wrote such rehashed music as the *Stone Flower* ballet in 1948, the Cello Concerto No. 2 in 1950 (later revised as the Sinfonia Concertante for cello and orchestra), and the Symphony No. 7 in the last year of his life. He died in Moscow on March 5, 1953, the same day that Stalin died.

Prokofiev left a group of works that show no signs of diminished popularity. He is one of the most-played of twentieth-century composers. Two of his five piano concertos, both violin concertos, the Fifth Symphony, a good deal of piano music (especially the third and seventh sonatas), and at least three ballet scores of importance—*L'Enfant prodigue, Romeo and Juliet,* and *Cinderella*—are constantly heard. It may be that a large percentage of Prokofiev's music eventually will die. He often did feature effect above sub-

478

stance in his early works; while in his later ones he was forced to compose a bland, written-down kind of music that is actually cynical. Works like the Piano Sonata No. 7, the D major Violin Sonata, or the G minor Violin Concerto do not wear well. Prokofiev's emotional range was limited and often, as in *The Flaming Angel*, he deliberately set out to shock. Once the shock value wears off, there is not much left. But in his best music he did hit an exposed nerve of the century.

A more liberal artistic policy struggled to come into being after Stalin's death. The second All-Union Congress of Composers actually spoke up for more freedom in 1957. But Nikita Khrushchev, who came into power in 1958, continued to espouse the cause of Socialist Realism. At least there was, during the Khrushchev regime, a party decree of 1958 that exonerated Muradeli and the others who had been attacked in 1948. Shostakovich's *Lady Macbeth of Mzensk* was brought back with a few revisions and a new title, *Katerina Ismailova*, and a film was even made of it. Shostakovich grew a little more confident in the post-Stalin era, and composed a symphony—his thirteenth—based on five poems by Yevgeny Yevtushenko. One of those poems, "Babi Yar," dealt with the massacre of the Jews in Kiev during World War II. Word got out that Khrushchev disapproved of the subject matter, and the premiere in 1962 was an occasion of gloom. Government officials did not attend, even though the work was the product of two of the cultural stars of the Soviet Union. Official disapproval was unofficially expressed, and the symphony was retired after a second performance. It was again performed the following year, in revised form. But even in its first version it was music of Socialist Realism, an example of poster-propaganda music. It has received very few performances in or outside of Russia.

Not until Khrushchev was deposed by Alexei Kosygin and Leonid Brezhnev in 1964 was there a relaxation in artistic doctrine. Radio jamming was stopped, and students and young composers were able not only to listen to foreign broadcasts of the latest avant-garde music, but also to copy it on tape. A dozen or so composers even started to write a form of serial music, working without textbooks and getting as much information as they could from visiting musicians. The music of Stravinsky and Bartók could be heard once more, and the new generation of composers started to imitate *Le Sacre du Printemps* and *Music for Strings, Percussion, and Celesta* instead of Prokofiev and Shostakovich. But after the Czechoslovakian uprising of 1968 there followed a freeze in the Soviet Union, and a crackdown on artistic freedom. Once again a form of curtain descended, and radio jamming was resumed. The future of music in the Soviet Union again looks bleak. Not until there is a major upheaval and reorientation in the aesthetic and political thinking of the Soviet Union will the country produce music that has any chance of survival.

❧ 16 ❧

German Neoclassicism

BUSONI, WEILL, HINDEMITH

The early years of the twentieth century saw a few composers deliberately look back rather than forward. There was Stravinsky with his neoclassicism. There was Reger with his "Back to Bach" movement. There was Paul Hindemith and his evocation of the baroque. And there was Ferruccio Busoni, who was the apostle of Young Classicism (sometimes called New Classicism).

Busoni, one of the greatest and most original of pianists, an intellectual, a composer of music that was little heard in its day and is little heard in ours, was one of those transitional figures with a restless mind whose theories outstripped his actual music in interest. Such advanced composers as Debussy, Stravinsky, and Schoenberg were content to work within the traditional octave. But Busoni as early as 1906 was postulating that the octave could be divided into thirty-six intervals, and he was thinking of the creation of new instruments to play such finely graded microtones. (The idea of microtonal music goes back to the early Greeks, and some medieval composers discussed it, but their theories had long been forgotten.) Busoni, in his search for an extension of the musical vocabulary, also worked out 113 scales by raising and lowering normal intervals. Some examples: C, D flat, D, F flat, G, A, B, C; or C, D, E flat, F flat, G, A sharp, B, C; or C, D flat, E flat, F sharp, G sharp, A, B flat, C. In his *Sketch of a New Esthetic for Music* (1911) he called for "a wealth of harmonic and melodic expression" by splitting the tone into three parts. When Thaddeus Cahill in the United States invented an instrument called the Dynamophone, which transformed electric current into a fixed and mathematically exact number of vibrations, Busoni seized upon this as a possibility for microtonal music. More: the Dynamophone operated independently of any musical instrument, and therefore Busoni was the first to envisage the possibility of electronic music. Busoni's ideas led directly into the work of the Czech composer Alois Hába, who started experimenting with quartertones and sixth tones around 1920; and

Busoni also anticipated some of the work of Edgard Varèse.

But Busoni's own music is neither microtonal nor electronic. He was content to theorize, and he never composed the daring kind of music that his ideas would indicate. He was born in Empoli on April 1, 1866, and died in Berlin on July 27, 1924. His father was Italian, his mother half German, half Italian. Busoni was one of those fantastically gifted children who need no lessons because they already seem to know everything about music. He was playing in public at eight and was a veteran of the concert stage at ten. He had no piano teacher besides his mother, and his only instruction in composition came in 1886, during a short stay at the Leipzig Conservatory, when he was already twenty years old. He was a handsome, virile-looking young man who should have had the world at his feet as a hero of the keyboard, but there was something a shade reserved, a shade too intellectual for tastes of the day, that kept him from wide public success. For a long time he taught—in Helsingfors, in Moscow, in Boston—alternating his teaching with long concert tours. But Berlin was his real home, and he was active there from 1894 to 1914, composing and holding master classes. As a pianist he was the exponent of the grand manner. He had a colossal technique and specialized in the big works of the repertoire, playing them with a combination of neo-Lisztian virtuosity and twentieth-century intellectuality. He thought nothing of putting on one program the Beethoven *Hammerklavier* Sonata followed by the four Ballades of Chopin. The war brought an end to his activities in Berlin, and he settled in Zurich. After 1920 he returned to Berlin, where he taught composition rather than the piano.

It was Busoni's aim as a composer to combine Italian warmth with German forms. Despite his far-out theories, he was basically a traditionalist and even a conservative. When he coined the term Young Classicism in 1919 he wrote that it meant "the mastery, the sifting, the turning to account of all the gains of previous experiments and their inclusion in strong and beautiful forms." Part of Young Classicism was "the definite departure from what is thematic and the return to melody. . . . the casting-off of what is 'sensuous' and the renunciation of subjectivity and the reconquest of serenity." Among other things about Young Classicism, "It does not know the future at all but represents the present at its time of origin. . . . It is ripe through experience gained and supported by tradition." This was a mild call to arms compared to the manifestos that the Futurists, the Second Viennese School, and the Primitivists were putting out, and it is small wonder that not many paid much attention to Young Classicism.

Because of the avant-garde theories scattered through Busoni's prose writings and letters, some musicians have read into Busoni's music things that are not there. The fact is that his music, though often extremely interesting, represents an eclectic approach to the new problems of form that agitated

481

the first half of the twentieth century. Creators like Stravinsky and Schoenberg came up with a specific solution. Busoni, like Reger, offered an escape, the one with his Young Classicism, the other with his Back to Bach movement, but in essence they had little to offer that was of interest to the radicals of the day. Busoni's early music, much of which he later disavowed, is frankly postromantic, with a noticeable debt to Brahms. A transitional work was the tremendous Piano Concerto of 1904, which ends with a choral finale. The three composers who meant the most to Busoni were Bach, Beethoven, and Liszt. One of his aphorisms was: "Bach is the foundation of piano playing, Liszt the summit. The two made Beethoven possible." Busoni's idols, Bach, Beethoven, and Liszt, are all present in the Piano Concerto. There even is a hint of Tchaikovsky. If Tchaikovsky could write a popular piano concerto with smashing opening chords, Busoni could go him one better with a series of gigantic chords that go on ten times as long as Tchaikovsky's famous opening splurge. The piano writing is Liszt-derived, and one movement of the Busoni concerto is based entirely on a Liszt theme, the Tarantella from *Venezia e Napoli*. Busoni must have had a mind like a blotter, and he never seems to have forgotten a note he ever heard, nor could he entirely shake himself free from the themes and ideas of other composers. His Piano Concerto, despite what some critics have said, is nothing more than a large-scale, ambitious postromantic work in which Busoni was determined to outdo Liszt, Rubinstein, Tchaikovsky, and all the other composers of virtuoso concertos. The finale for male chorus is merely tacked on. Interesting as it is in itself, it has no place in this concerto, and it gives the work an air of fake sublimity.

Later Busoni was able to shake off the obvious postromanticisms of much of his music. He began to write a series of works that are reserved, enigmatic, and full of novel twists. It is a very personal kind of music that ran counter to every trend of the day. Where Stravinsky was startling the world with the rhythms and barbarisms of *Le Sacre du Printemps*, where Schoenberg was breaking off into atonalism and expressionism, where Debussy was creating a new world of sensuous, antiacademic color, Busoni was working in a medium that was more intellectual than sensuous: a medium that took old forms and translated them into more modern terms. But Busoni's was a timid kind of neoclassicism, unlike Stravinsky's revolutionary filtration of classic and baroque elements into a dissonant and polyrhythmic language. Busoni's harmonies and rhythms were of the past, never far removed from the nineteenth century.

Nevertheless his music has its own personality and probity. His idolatry of Bach is reflected in the remarkable *Fantasia Contrappuntistica* for solo piano (later arranged for two pianos). In its twenty-five minutes it takes Bach from the 1740's to the beginning of the twentieth century. Reger at that time was also writing Bach-derived pieces, but Reger's were all but Franckian, with their juicy chromatic harmonies and cheerful self-indulgence. Busoni's ideas about Bach were stringent, powerful, and intellectual. The *Contrappuntistica* is in twelve sections—a series of variations on Bach's *Ehre sei Gott in der Höhe*, followed by four fugues interspersed with an intermezzo and variations, and ending with a chorale and stretta. The first fugue is an attempt to finish the uncompleted fugue in Bach's *Die Kunst der Fuge*. This part of the *Fantasia Contrappuntistica* is severely Bachian. But then come some startling shifts. As the work progresses one can hear a Beethovenian development of the fugal subject: *Die Kunst der Fuge* heard through Beethoven's *Grosse Fuge*, full of enigmatic, dissonant trills and a few stabbing harmonies. Busoni eventually gets around to Busoni, and the end of the *Fantasia Contrappuntistica* is extremely personal. The harmonies become dry and somewhat dissonant, and the entire feeling passes from Bach baroque to Bach with something completely alien superimposed on it. Liszt shows up in some of the writing—the Liszt of the *Weinen, Klagen* Variations —especially in the version for two pianos. But what is heard is a modern Liszt—the Lisztian textures without the Lisztian glitter and exhibitionism. Difficult and virtuosic as the *Fantasia Contrappuntistica* is, it is not a showpiece. Still another composer figures in the piano writing of this work— Charles Alkan (1813–1888), the almost-forgotten French pianist-composer so admired by Liszt and Busoni. Alkan was called the Berlioz of the piano and composed eccentric, monstrously long and complicated works that Busoni played in public once in a while. The amalgam of Liszt and Alkan in Busoni's piano style leads to a massive, fluent, orchestral manner of writing. Some of Busoni's elegies can be traced back to the shorter Alkan pieces.

In addition to his considerable number of piano works, Busoni composed several operas—*Die Brautwahl* (1912), *Arlecchino* and *Turandot* (1917), and *Doktor Faust* (1925), which he left unfinished at his death. As such his last opera joins the company of Puccini's *Turandot*, Boito's *Nerone*, and Berg's *Lulu*. Busoni's pupil Philipp Jarnach, working from his master's sketches, finished the last scene. Busoni had written his own libretto in 1914, but he was a busy touring pianist with a heavy teaching schedule, and he could work on his ambitious opera only at intervals. Long gone were the days when a Rossini or Donizetti could whip out a full opera in three weeks.

Doktor Faust is a remarkable opera with some very modern ideas. Busoni himself had a good deal of Faust in his makeup, and also a touch of Hamlet: "a weak man, yet a stout wrestler, whom doubts drive hither and thither; master of thought, slave of instinct, exhausting all things, finding no answer." Thus Busoni himself wrote about his nature. *Faust* is in line with this summing up: a tortured, complicated work that looks to the past and yet has sections that are prophetic. Busoni has left some comments about his opera. He was afraid to touch Goethe, he said, but he had fallen under the fascination of the Faust idea. His solution was to incorporate features of the medieval puppet show, which he filled with symbolism. At the end of the opera Faust passes his own spirit into the body of his dead child by the Duchess of Parma. Busoni's explanation is that "after Faust in his last approach to God has also thrown away belief, he proceeds to mystical deeds, which renew his exhausted life."

Busoni would have nothing to do with opera composers who wrote merely descriptive music, as Gounod had done in his setting of *Faust*. Busoni, in his opera, sought for a large outline, creating "musically independent forms which at the same time suited the words and the scenic events, and which also had a separate and sensible existence detached from the words and the situations." Thus the scene of the demons is in variation form, the scenic intermezzo is a rondo, and so on. This is exactly what Berg was to do in *Wozzeck* and it is one of the most original things about *Doktor Faust*. The music itself is varied. There are certain obvious derivations. Berlioz, Liszt, Wagner, and Strauss play a part. The derivations are easy to point out. But even they are used in an unusual, original manner. The whole *feeling* of the opera is original, derivations and all, nineteenth-century harmonies and all. It is post-Wagnerism without Wagner, post-Straussian without Strauss. It has a melodic line that resembles early Schoenberg here and there. And in one startling instance, in the second Prelude (starting with section 2 of the Breitkopf vocal score), there is an anticipation of the Dr. Schoen love motive in Berg's *Lulu*.

Like Mahler, Busoni believed that his music was for a later day, and he indicated as much in the epilogue of *Doktor Faust:*

> Still unexhausted, all the symbols wait
> Still in this work are hidden and concealed.
> Their germs a later school shall procreate
> Whose fruits to those unborn shall be revealed.
> Let each take what he finds appropriate:
> The seed is sown; others may reap the field.

But Busoni, unlike Mahler, has never had his day, although the late 1960's saw a slight interest in his music. His *Doktor Faust* has received very few performances in Europe and no staged performance at all (thus far) in the United States. The opera composer in Germany who achieved the smash hit of the 1920's was not Busoni but his pupil Kurt Weill, whose *Die Dreigroschenoper* (*The Three-Penny Opera*) was a wild international success that has yet to run its course.

Weill was born in Dessau on March 2, 1900, and died in New York on April 3, 1950. At first he composed respectable "modern music" that always turned up at the various festivals of the International Society for Contemporary Music. These works were well received and were never heard of again. (After Weill's death an attempt was made to revive them, but they were much too weak to gain a foothold.) It was not until Weill collaborated with Bertolt Brecht that he found his métier. In 1928 Brecht adapted—very closely indeed; it was actually a rewrite—John Gay's ballad opera of 1728, with new music by Weill, who scored the work for a small jazz combination. *Die Dreigroschenoper* had a predecessor in Ernst Krenek's jazz opera *Jonny spielt auf* (1927), but that work, so popular for a decade or so, has vanished for good and is much too dated to be revived, whereas *Die Dreigroschenoper* continues to retain its fierce and venomous punch. In a way *Die Dreigroschenoper* was a German equivalent of what *Les Six* were doing at the same time in Paris. But where the music of *Les Six* was Stravinsky-derived, often neoclassic, light and entertaining, Weill's little opera was bitter, anti-Stravinsky, anti-Wagner, anti-everything that was considered opera. It also was as much a social as a musical document, reflecting the terrible postwar period in Germany. It was to German music what the line drawings of George Grosz were to German art.

Weill never duplicated the success of *Die Dreigroschenoper*, though he composed several works in the same vein, including the longer and more ambitious *Mahagonny*. All are in essence rewrites of his great success. In 1933 Weill left Germany, went to France, then settled in New York, where he became a very popular composer for the Broadway stage. He also tried his hand at "American opera," and both *Street Scene* and *Down in the Valley* are attempts along that line. They do not work, and the composer of the biting *Dreigroschenoper* descended into cheap platitudes. At least in that opera Weill added a remarkable work to the lyric stage, and the word masterpiece is not too strong.

The most important man of German music in the 1920's was neither Busoni nor Weill but the short, bald, cherubic-looking, incredibly gifted Paul Hindemith. Germany was full of composers at the time, but the music of very few has lived. Eugen d'Albert, Hans Pfitzner, Franz Schmidt, Paul Graener, Walther Braunfels, Max von Schillings, Manfred Gurlitt, Artur Schnabel, Heinrich Kaminski—where is their music today? Hindemith and Weill are virtually the only ones of the period whose music has survived.

If ever there was a musician's musician it was Paul Hindemith. The man had perfect pitch, was a professional violinist and violist, a good pianist, could play virtually every instrument in the orchestra (if he was unfamiliar with one he would take off a week or so and master it), was a good musicologist, could compose with incredible facility, and had stored in that bald head of his an overwhelming knowledge of music. In the 1920's he was to German music what Prokofiev was to Russian music—a young revolutionary, impatient with the postromantic tradition, who was composing music that was regarded as the last word in acid dissonance and atonality (he never composed atonal music, but that is how it sounded to his contemporaries). His sharp, even savage, scores made him the *enfant terrible* of the decade. Well known is Richard Strauss's complaint to Hindemith: "Why do you have to write this way? You have talent." Less known is the cocky Hindemith's answer: "Herr Professor, you make your music and I'll make mine."

If Busoni represented a diluted form of neoclassicism, Hindemith represented the neobaroque. He worked in old classic forms—fugue, sonata, suite —and produced an enormous quantity of music, just as the baroque composers did. Throughout his entire creative span—he was born in Hanau on November 16, 1895, and died in Berlin on December 28, 1963—he represented the baroque. Like the baroque composers he adopted a utilitarian, practical view toward music. His philosophy was antiromantic and so was his music, which had its roots in the great German tradition of Bach through Beethoven. In his youth he was an avant-gardist, and his severe, dissonant music was never really close to the public's heart, even though his great talent was recognized almost immediately. He went on to compose a handful of scores that have become repertory items—the *Mathis der Maler* Symphony (1934), the *Kleine Kammermusik* for Wind Quintet (1922), the song cycle *Das Marienleben* (1924), the Violin Concerto (1939), *The Four Temperaments* (1944), the *Symphonic Metamorphoses* on Weber themes (1943), the Third String Quartet (1922), the *Ludus Tonalis* for piano (1943), the ballet *Nobilissima Visione* (1938)—but on the whole he was more admired by professionals than by the public. For professionals respond to craft; and Hindemith was one of the century's greatest craftsmen and most learned musicians.

His music was a model of workmanship in the mainstream of baroque and classic German music. Bach was probably the composer to whom Hindemith was closest. From the very beginning Hindemith shunned program music, just as he derided the theories of Schoenberg and Stravinsky. He was an academician and proud of it. And, working academically, he did put his mark on the music of the twentieth century. He showed that the German tradition was not exhausted and that it had vitality when properly approached. The old forms were generally his means of expression. But those old forms sounded anything but old as treated by Hindemith. Unlike the eclectic Busoni, who also was interested in old forms, Hindemith evolved a most unusual harmonic and melodic language, and any phrase he wrote can instantly be recognized as his. He evolved a tonal system based on the natural laws of sound, on the fundamental note and its overtone series; and it was as distinctive in its way as Scriabin's fourths and mystic chords, or as Stravinsky's rhythmic legerdemain. Above all, there was in his writing that sheer expertise. Of all the great figures of his day, he may have been the most complete musician *qua* musician.

As a theoretician, Hindemith was the author of some valuable and provocative books. Nor was he merely an ivory-tower theoretician. For several years after 1933—he did very little work in Germany after the Nazis branded his music as degenerate art—he busied himself reorganizing musical education in Turkey. In 1939 he settled in the United States, becoming head of the music department at Yale University in 1942 and an American citizen in 1946. In 1953 he returned to Europe.

Throughout his career, Hindemith was desperately anxious to write music that would be played not only by the professional but also by the amateur. It was Hindemith who was responsible for the term *Gebrauchsmusik*, or utilitarian music. As early as the 1920's Hindemith had become concerned about the ever-increasing schism between composer and public. Consequently he started composing, in addition to concert works, a long series of scores intended for amateur players. For them he wrote pieces for virtually every instrument, singly or in combination. It is not, in this case, important whether or not this kind of utility music is great. The significant thing is that a major composer turned his attention to it; and even the slightest work of a major composer is of greater musical value than the slickest work of a hack.

As it happens, much of Hindemith's *Gebrauchsmusik* is better than it sounds, as is so much of his other music. A good deal of Hindemith's music on first hearing is forbidding: pungent in its dissonance, austere in its form, acerbic in its melodic content. It is anything but loveable music. Indeed, it can impress one as downright unloveable. But, somehow, exposure to Hindemith's music always brings its own rewards. What at first seems forbidding soon turns out to be strong, subtle, curiously fascinating, and highly stimulating in its logic, organization, and integrity. It was only toward the end that Hindemith began to turn out scores almost by rote, much like Milhaud—competent but dry scores in which the flywheel seemed disconnected from the motor.

It is difficult to guess Hindemith's ultimate place in music. Perhaps he will end as the Max Reger of the 1920–40 period. Or it may be that a future age will put greater stress than the 1960's has done upon his solidity, impeccable workmanship, evocation of the baroque, and reserved but nevertheless pronounced melodies. After 1945 his music had little to offer to the new generation. Anything derived from the baroque or classic (and that included even the music of Stravinsky) was frowned upon. But fashions and fads change, while craft—real craft—will always be appreciated. Purely as a craftsman, Hindemith was on a transcendental level. True, it must be conceded that craft alone, unsupported by cogent ideas, is not enough; and Hindemith in the last years of his life was often guilty of mechanically stringing together notes. But at his best he was a strong creative figure with something positive to offer. The urgency and propulsion of some of his *Kammermusik* writing, the big conception of the symphony extracted from the opera *Mathis der Maler*, the lean, medieval-impregnated quality of such a score as *Der Schwanendreher*, the fascination of the deft contrapuntal writing in *Ludus Tonalis*—all these are reflective of an art and a mind that will live when most of the ephemera around it is long dead.

Rise of an American Tradition

FROM GOTTSCHALK TO COPLAND

While Europe was busily producing great composers, the United States during most of the nineteenth century was occupied in opening its frontiers. Muscles were bunched for a mighty effort, and amazing things were accomplished, but the national spirit was turned to matters other than the development of a serious musical culture. It was not that the United States lacked music. There was a strong body of folk music derived from the English, from the African slaves, and from the Caribbean area. At least two composers did take advantage of that material—Louis Moreau Gottschalk and Stephen Foster. Foster (1826–1864), who has come down in history as "America's minstrel," was one of the few composers to suggest something specifically personal and American in his music. He also was extremely popular. The whole country was singing "Old Folks at Home," "Old Black Joe," "Camptown Races," "Come Where My Love Lies Dreaming," and the other Foster favorites. Foster was a true lyricist, and his songs have never lost their authentic, gentle beauty.

But during the nineteenth century in the United States, "serious" music was by and large a foreign art, practiced by imported professors. The major symphony orchestras were staffed mostly by foreign-born musicians. Soloists and teachers were immigrants, many of them German, who represented a tradition stemming from Beethoven and his successors. American composers based their work on foreign models. When William Mason (1829–1908) wrote piano music, it was a synthesis of Schumann and Chopin. When William Henry Fry in 1845 composed the first American grand opera, *Leonora*, he went to Bellini for inspiration. Not until the appearance of Charles Ives late in the century did an American composer begin to speak with an individual, powerful voice. But Ives had been preceded by the fascinating Louis Moreau Gottschalk, a composer who trembled on the verge of a breakthrough but who never fully lived up to his potential.

Gottschalk might have been an American Glinka, but a combination of circumstances prevented it. Among those circumstances was his death at the early age of forty. In Rio de Janeiro, where he died in 1869, he was beginning to compose large-scale works, and had he had more time he conceivably could have added significantly to the repertory. As it is, he was a very interesting figure whose music started to be rediscovered in the United States after the Second World War.

He was born in New Orleans on May 8, 1829, the son of a British father and a Creole mother. Soon he learned everything his local teachers could give him, and at the age of thirteen was sent to Paris, where he was refused admittance to the Conservatoire on the grounds of his nationality. Pierre Zimmerman, head of the piano faculty, refused to listen to the boy. "America is only a country of steam engines." Gottschalk had to take private lessons, first a few with Charles Hallé, then with Camille Stamaty. Among the pupils in Stamaty's class was the seven-year-old Camille Saint-Saëns, and one wonders what young Gottschalk's reaction must have been the first time he heard the genius of an infant. But Gottschalk's talent at the keyboard also was of a supreme order. He soon became not only a good pianist, but a great and celebrated one. Among his admirers were Berlioz and Chopin, and for a while he had a tremendous vogue in Europe. He was slim, handsome, aristocratic, extraordinarily talented, and he blazed a trail through early romantic pianism. Many competent critics called him the equal of Liszt and Thalberg. The flashy young American, the first internationally famous pianist to come out of the United States, was the man of the hour.

In the late 1840's Gottschalk started to compose. In his background were the plantation melodies with which he had grown up, and also the snappy Cuban and Caribbean rhythms he had heard in New Orleans. Inspired by the nationalistic quality of the Chopin mazurkas, Gottschalk began to write music that was reflective of *his* ethnic background and environment. Native tunes and rhythms were put into a sophisticated piano layout stemming from Chopin and Liszt, to which Gottschalk added a device of his own later to be described as the "style pianola." It was so called because it resembled the tinkling of the player piano. Gottschalk had a great fondness for the upper two octaves of the piano keyboard, and was constantly producing from it cascades of silvery sound. His initial series of piano pieces, which he started to compose in Paris when he was sixteen years old, was based mostly on Negro and plantation melodies, with titles like *Bamboula*, *Le Bananier*, and *La Savane*. Later Gottschalk was to spend much time in the West Indies and South America, where a different type of nationalism entered his music. Even today some of his nationalistic music sounds sophisticated; it has dated very little, and the rhythmic flair of the writing, with its sharp syncopations, is surprisingly modern. A work such as *Souvenir de Porto*

Rico, written in the middle 1850's, is not very different from many pieces in Milhaud's *Saudades do Brasil*, written about seventy years later.

When Gottschalk's music began appearing in Europe, audiences could not get enough of it, and celebrated pianists jostled one another in their rush to play these exotic, colorful pieces from the New World. For several decades there was a run on them. Gottschalk was the first composer with the imagination to take advantage of the American and Caribbean folk material, and he had the skill to touch it up without losing its basic quality.

Gottschalk returned to the United States in 1853. He lived a busy life, concertizing steadily, writing large quantities of music, traveling through the country and in the West Indies, getting mixed up in love affairs (one of those, with the actress Ada Clare, shook the foundations of New York society). He loved the West Indies, Havana in particular, and he absorbed the native music he constantly was hearing. He kept a diary, posthumously published as *Notes of a Pianist*, in which a very literate, appealing personality comes through. Gottschalk was a good reporter, and his book is source material on the America of the Civil War period. As a composer, he was very popular with his countrymen. He wrote a good deal of salon music, and two of his salon pieces—*The Last Hope* and *The Dying Poet*—graced the pianos of every genteel household in the country. He was constantly on the move, as though fleeing from something. Before and during the war he toured the eastern and central states (always with supporting musicians; there was no such thing as a solo recital in those days). In 1865 he went to the Far West, playing in San Francisco and the mining towns. In San Francisco he got into trouble. The citizens were stirred up when there were reports that Gottschalk had made free with one of the respectable young ladies of the city. He hadn't, but rather than face a posse of vigilantes, he fled to a ship and sailed to South America. Beating his way through the continent, he ended up in Rio de Janeiro. There he arranged big concerts —"monster festivals," they were called—that would have made his friend Berlioz proud. Romantic to the end, he collapsed at the piano while playing one of his pieces, a work named *Morte*. Shortly after, he died. Some said it was of yellow fever. Some said that he had been assassinated by a jealous husband. The true cause appears to have been peritonitis.

A large part of Gottschalk's music was ephemeral. His dated salon pieces have little to offer except a nostalgic glimpse at a type of music that so delighted our forebears. More interesting are his big virtuoso pieces, which are in the mainstream of romantic pianism. Some of them are worth revival. Most important of all are his nationalistic works for piano, for orchestra, even for voice. These are prophetic. Gottschalk wrote them to entertain and probably had no delusions about their worth, but they have come down the generations not only as an authentic whiff of a vanished America but as significant creations in their own right. Probably no composer in the world at the time, not even Berlioz or Liszt, had Gottschalk's rhythmic freedom. His rhythms were profoundly original because he was working in an Afro-Cuban rhythmic world that had not been explored by any serious composer up to that time. Unfortunately, he lacked the independence of mind to follow this to its logical end; and he was too restless, too careless, a person to make full use of his natural abilities. At that, he could sometimes write with a breathless disregard for the amenities, as in the crazy discords at the end of the four-hand version of *La Gallina*, which all but anticipate Ives. He could also attempt works on a big scale, and his two-movement symphony (a symphony only because he called it so), *A Night in the Tropics,* has a broad, well-planned and rich-sounding first movement in which Berlioz figures, as well as the Félicien David of *Le Désert*. This movement is followed by a Cuban dance that crackles its jaunty, irresistible way.

Naturally this music was scorned within a few decades after Gottschalk's death, and all of it slipped into obscurity. It was considered trash, and serious composers were ashamed of it. Could such lightweight, commercial stuff represent American music? The trend was toward weighty writing in the German manner. In the last quarter of the century rose the group known as the Boston Classicists. Nearly all of them went abroad to complete their musical education in Germany, and they returned to the United States eager to pass on to their pupils the thrilling precepts of the Leipzig, Berlin, or Munich professors. John Knowles Paine (1839–1906) studied with Karl August Haupt in Berlin and in 1862 became director of music at Harvard. George Chadwick (1854–1931) worked under Solomon Jadassohn in Leipzig and Josef Rheinberger in Munich. Arthur Whiting (1861–1936) was a Rheinberger product, and so was Horatio Parker (1863–1919). Others in the group were Arthur Foote (1853–1937), who did *not* study in Europe, and Charles Martin Loeffler (1861–1935), the Alsatian-born violinist who came to Boston at the age of twenty. All of these composers were active in the New England area, all were conservatives, all but Loeffler were influenced by Brahms, and all composed good academic music that at the very least ranked with the good academic music of Europe.

All were put in the shade by Edward Alexander MacDowell, who was born in New York on December 18, 1861, and died there on January 23, 1908. Few composers have been so idolized during their lifetime. MacDowell occupied a position in the United States like Elgar's in England. He was not only hailed as America's greatest composer; he was firmly believed to be the equal of any composer anywhere. That was while he was alive. Few composers of equivalent fame in their day have been so soon forgotten. Of MacDowell's rather large output, what remains in the active repertoire? The D minor Piano Concerto (1890), a few of the *Woodland Sketches* (1896), the

Indian Suite (1897). That is about all. Every once in a great while there is a revival of one of the big symphonic poems. *Lamia* (1908) might turn up, or *Hamlet and Ophelia* (1895). They sound like faded, forgotten curiosities. Even the four piano sonatas, which used to appear occasionally, seem to have vanished.

The irony about MacDowell is that he was accepted as America's greatest composer without in reality having anything specifically American about his music. He realized that as well as anybody, and one can understand why he protested violently, in speech and in print, against being called a national-ist. Time and again he insisted that his music had to be accepted on its own terms, and he raised a fierce row when his music was included on an Ameri-can program. MacDowell energetically rejected the idea of nationalism in music. "So-called Russian, Bohemian or any other national music has no place in art, for its characteristics may be duplicated by anyone who takes a fancy to do so. On the other hand, the vital element in music—personality —stands alone." MacDowell did not want to be judged as an American composer; he wanted to be judged as a composer, without any special or chauvinistic favors. Another reason he so strongly railed against nationalism was his eagerness to justify his use of German models. There is very little local color in MacDowell's music. Works like the *New England Idylls* (1902) or *From Uncle Remus* (1898) could have been written by any Ger-man composer of the period.

This is not surprising, for aside from a year spent at the Paris Conserva-tory (1876), MacDowell was German-trained—at Stuttgart, Wiesbaden, Frankfurt, and, briefly, with Liszt at Weimar. His big inspiration was Joachim Raff, a very popular composer of the day. MacDowell studied with him in Frankfurt, and Raff showed great interest in the handsome, tall, red-headed American. In 1881 MacDowell became head piano teacher at the Darmstadt Conservatory and produced a great deal of music that interested Liszt. Liszt also enjoyed MacDowell's clever piano playing. It was not until 1888 that MacDowell returned to America for good. He had been in Europe for twelve years. Now he settled down in Boston, taught privately, and com-posed. In 1896 he went to New York to become chairman of the newly formed Department of Music at Columbia University. Seven years later he clashed with Nicholas Murray Butler, the president of Columbia, and re-signed in 1904, charging Butler and Columbia with "materialism." Mac-Dowell, a brokenhearted and emotionally shattered man after this experi-ence, died in 1908 feeling that he had failed in life.

A through-and-through romantic, MacDowell was perfectly content to write scores that were safely derived from Schumann, Liszt, Grieg, Raff, and Rubinstein. Especially Rubinstein. MacDowell's two piano concertos have often been compared with the Grieg A minor, but in fact they are closer to the conventional display concertos that Rubinstein had written. And they —the MacDowell as well as the Rubinstein—are very good concertos of their genre, though in MacDowell's case, his D minor is a much better realized and more spontaneous-sounding work than the companion A minor. The last movement of the D minor has a snappy buck-and-wing hint of the American scene rare in MacDowell's music.

Conventionality: that is the word that is, unfortunately, descriptive of MacDowell's music. He had gifts, but daring did not go with them. His harmonies are always derivative, and what saves his music from total extinction is an unusually sweet and genuine melodic power. It is in salon music like the *Woodland Sketches* that this kind of melodic gift best comes through. Of course, at the turn of the century, the tastemakers were apt to sneer at the *Woodland Sketches*, which contained works like *To a Wild Rose* and *To a Water Lily*. These were considered unimportant chips, sentimental effusions, and MacDowell was going to live by his great *Sonata Tragica* (1893) or *Sonata Eroica* (1895). It is easy to see how those two works commanded the respect they once did. MacDowell had ambitious dreams here, and attempted an equally big canvas. Critics spoke of his four piano sonatas—the other two are the *Norse* (1900) and the *Keltic* (1901)—in terms reserved for the Liszt B minor. They raved about the workmanship, the brilliant pianistic layout, the depth and passion of the music. What they did not see, because they were too close, was that the workmanship creaks, the passion is sham, and the difficulties are unsupported by cogent musical ideas.

But there is nothing sham about the lovely *Woodland Sketches* and some of the other piano pieces. Some of his songs, too, are of real beauty and would repay the attention of recitalists. For MacDowell, who so desperately wanted to be a "big" composer, was essentially a miniaturist. And, curiously, it was here that whatever national traits there were in him came out. The *Woodland Sketches* are much more than period pieces (just as Mendelssohn's *Songs Without Words* and Grieg's *Lyric Pieces* transcend their period). They are more than period pieces because they are perfect and individual of their kind, and have a melodic flavor that is altogether honest. *To a Wild Rose* is worth all the four sonatas rolled together, on the premise that an honest dime is worth more than a counterfeit $100 bill.

Thus, where MacDowell's orchestral music is mostly embarrassing, and where his large-scale compositions (the D minor Piano Concerto excepted) are mostly rhetoric unsupported by content, his shorter piano pieces and songs do deserve a niche in the repertory. It remained for Charles Ives, born thirteen years after MacDowell, to be the first great American national composer; but what MacDowell did was to show the world that the United States was not devoid of creative musical talent; and to show the United States that the career of a composer was one that could command a respected social status. Through his activities as a composer of world-wide reputation, and as pianist and as teacher, he crystallized an emergent national pride. He came on the scene just as America was conquering its last frontiers and for the first time beginning to think of things that were beyond pure materialism. It was the time when the industrial barons were beginning to separate Europe from its art treasures; when some wealthy people banded together to make for themselves a great opera house in New York; when there was great talk of a national academy of music; when Theodore Thomas was bringing the best in symphonic music to the people. The pot was ready to boil, and Edward MacDowell was one of the chief cooks.

Charles Ives, whose early career coincided with MacDowell's last period, cannot be judged in any rational manner. His music was so far ahead of its time that it was mutated rather than composed. He was everything MacDowell was not, and was a bewildering combination of seer and practical man, mystic and democrat, sentimentalist and businessman. His music is a constant reflection of his New England youth: remembrances of life in a simpler age. He yearned for the virtues of an older, town-hall-meeting, village-band, transcendentalist, Emersonian America, and expressed those yearnings in the most advanced, unorthodox, ear-splitting, grating music composed by anybody anywhere up to that time.

This was the composer who, with his partner Julian Myrick, ran one of the most successful insurance agencies in the country at the time (forty-eight million dollars worth of new business in 1929, the year he retired). This was the composer who was captain of the baseball and football teams at Danbury High School, who pitched a winning ten-inning game against the Yale freshmen, and later made the Yale football team. This was the composer who avoided most professional musicians, seldom went to a concert, published his own music, refused royalties and copyrights, delved into atonality before Schoenberg, into dissonances that made most contemporary music sound Victorian, into tone clusters long before Henry Cowell, into polytonality long before Stravinsky and Milhaud, into polyrhythms that remained for the postserialists to investigate. Quarter tones, asymmetrical rhythms, disjunct melodies, jazz and ragtime elements, anticipations of aleatory—name it, and Ives was doing it, usually long before anybody else.

So advanced was his idiom, so convulsively dissonant and complicated, so full of unusual textures and devices, that hardly anybody could grasp its significance. Stravinsky's reaction was typical. He first heard music by Ives in 1942. "I wish I could say that I was attracted by what I heard, for I respected Ives as an inventive and original man, and I wanted to like his music. It seemed to me badly uneven in quality, however, as well as ill proportioned." On further exposure to Ives, Stravinsky decided that though his original objections had not changed:

I think I now perceive the identifying qualities which make those objections unimportant. The danger now is to think of Ives as a mere historical phenomenon, "The Great Anticipator." He is certainly more than that but nevertheless, his anticipations continue to astonish me. Consider, for example, the "Soliloquy, or a Study in 7ths and Other Things." The vocal line of this little song *looks* like Webern's *Drei Volkstexte*, albeit the Ives was composed a decade and more before the Webern. The retrogrades are of the sort Berg was concerned with in the *Kammerkonzert* and *Der Wein*, though the "Soliloquy" was composed a decade and more before the Berg pieces. The rhythmic devices such as "4 in the time of 5" are generally thought to be the discoveries of the so-called post-Webern generation, but Ives anticipates this generation by four decades. The interval idea itself, the idea of the aphoristic statement, and the piano style all point in the direction of later and more accepted composers. But Ives had already transgressed the "limits of tonality" more than a decade before Schoenberg, had written music exploiting polytonality almost two decades before *Petrushka*, and experimented with polyorchestral groups a half century before Stockhausen.

Small wonder that Ives has been canonized as the saint of American music. Very few composers write in his style, but he has become one of the spiritual fathers of all composers active in America. To them, he is the symbol of daring and independence, of uncompromising genius decades ahead of his time, of a complete break from academism; and also, incidentally, as the composer of a body of music that finally has come into its own—a body of music unique in the literature, sometimes flawed but always vital. Ives's music in a way reflects the American unconscious, drawing together as it does the hymnodists from Billings on, the Negro and his music, Stephen Foster, the American folk music, even the academic tradition. Ives's music is also the history of American music.

He was born in Danbury, Connecticut, on October 20, 1874, and died in New York on May 19, 1954. At a time when all good American composers were going to Leipzig and Munich, dutifully studying the mysteries of fugue and sonata under Rheinberger and other academicians, Ives was putting two bands against each other, each band playing different American tunes in a different key. At the age of twenty, he composed a *Song for Harvest Season* for voice, cornet, trombone, and organ pedals, each in a different key: complete polytonality in 1894. MacDowell and Paine, the then leading American composers, with their *allegros* and *quasi sostenutos* and *andante con motos*, spoke a different language from Ives, who was writing such musical directions as "roughly and in a half-spoken way," or "The piano should be played as *indistinctly* as possible," or "In a gradually excited way." One of his songs is named *A Son of a Gambolier*, and toward the end Ives inserts a "Kazoo chorus with flutes, fiddles and flageolets." A few measures on, he directs: "And piccolos, ocarinas and fifes."

He did not expect the singer to run out and collect kazoo players. He wrote the direction because it was an indication of the type of tone color he wanted (though he would have been delighted had the singer actually come on stage with kazoo and ocarina virtuosos). Leopold Stokowski, who in the 1950's wanted to program an Ives piece, had a hard time locating a jew's harp player for a certain effect that Ives requested. Local 802 of the American Federation of Musicians had thousands of members, but not a single jew's harp player. Stokowski had to advertise before one was found.

The bulk of Ives's music falls between 1896 and 1916. His work was so unconventional and eccentric, and so impossibly hard to perform, that he did not get a public hearing of an orchestral work until 1927. It took John Kirkpatrick about ten years to learn the Piano Sonata No. 2 (the *Concord*). In 1947 Ives was given a Pulitzer Prize for his Third Symphony—forty-three years after he composed it. He was seventy-three years old then, and his style had been substantially formed by the middle 1890's. "I found I *could not* go on using the familiar chords early," he once explained. "I *heard* something else." In Yale, he had taken a composition course with Horatio Parker in 1898. Parker would look sorrowfully at the exercises submitted by the young maverick. "Ives, *must* you hog all the keys?" he would ask, with a sigh.

Very little of Ives's music has been published. His manuscripts, a wild collection of scarcely decipherable notes, prose (he had a worse handwriting than Beethoven's), marginalia, erasures, and scratches, are all but impossible to decipher. There are completed compositions, rough drafts, compositions started and abandoned, ideas of genius, and ideas of banality. On one manuscript he scribbled: "May not be good music, but true sounds make beauty to me." He writes, at the end of one of the *Tone Roads*, "There are many Roads, you know, besides the Wabash." One of his most haunting pieces is *The Unanswered Question*. The strings, Ives wrote, "are to represent the Silences of the Druids—Who Know, See and Hear Nothing." The trumpet intones "The Perennial Question of Existence," while "The Flying Answerers (flutes and other people)" run around in vain trying to discover the invisible reply to the trumpet. Nonsense? Profundity? Mysticism? Tongue in cheek? All things to all men, perhaps; but all men would agree that this was strange language indeed to emanate from the Ives and Myrick agency of Mutual Life.

He starts a composition in wedge formation after seeing a Yale-Princeton football game. "Trumpet running halfback," he suggests. Another unfinished composition is named *Giants vs. Cubs, August, 1907, Polo Grounds*. Partly decipherable among the frenzied scribblings are: "A—1st Mike jaunts [?] out to CF. Johnny at bat. Hits over Mike's head. Pitcher on mound. Ball. Strike. Ball. Ball. Strike." The classic 3-and-2 situation. "Johnny comes sliding home safe. Tune: *Johnny Comes Marching Home*." A little pleasant research in newspapers of the day reveals that Ives probably went to the Polo Grounds on Saturday, August 17, 1907. The Cubs played the Giants only one series at the Polo Grounds that August There were no Sunday games in the National League on August 18, and the chances are that Ives, a working man, could attend only the Saturday game of the series. The score was 3-2 in favor of the Cubs; they won when the great Christy Mathewson weakened in the twelfth inning. Ives, incidentally, appears to have been a little off the mark in his description of the action The only player in that game who slid home (the only player, indeed, in the four-game series between August 17 and August 21) was William "Spike" Shannon, the left fielder of the Giants.

Ives did not especially care if his music was considered unplayable "The impossibilities of today are the possibilities of tomorrow," he insisted. Himself an individualist, he did not even care if musicians bobbled the notes as long as they understood what the composer was trying to say and the general effect he was trying to achieve. At one of his infrequent performances, in 1931, the orchestra, struggling with his adventurous way of writing, ended up in chaos. "Just like a town meeting—every man for himself. Wonderful how it came out!" he admiringly said. Like Beethoven, whom he so greatly admired, Ives pursued an Idea, in the Platonic sense. But he was not an ivory-tower composer. He accepted art as a natural function of humanity, and looked forward to the day when "every man, while digging his potatoes, will breathe his own Epics, his own Symphonies (Operas if he likes); and as he sits of an evening in his own back yard in shirt sleeves, sucking his pipe and watching his children in *their* fun of building *their* themes for *their* sonatas of *their* life, he will look over the mountains and see his visions, in their reality." Above all, he despised the "pretty music" admired by the public. The typical music-lover, he who sits and inhales the "pretty sounds," he called Rollo, a name taken from the series of books for children written by the Reverend Jacob Hallowell Abbott between 1834 and 1858. Rollo was a nice, dull, mama's boy. Rollos *en masse* Ives called ladybirds. "Keep up our fight—*art!*—hard at it—don't quit because the ladybirds don't like it." He accuses "Richie Wagner" of false nobility. Debussy to him was "a city man with his week-end flights into country esthetics." Chopin was "soft . . . with a skirt on." Ravel was "weak, morbid, and monotonous." Stravinsky's *Firebird* kept "going over and over and it got tiresome." Mozart was effeminate and a bad influence on music.

Ives stands for a fierce musical integrity and a unique type of nationalism. He had been brought up on Emerson, idolized the man and his philosophy, and tried to express an Emersonian kind of transcendentalism in his music. Almost every Ives work contains references to his own New England background—to the tunes, hymns, patriotic songs, dances, and marches he heard in his youth. His entire approach can be summed up in his own notes to his Fourth Violin Sonata: "The subject matter, such as it is, is a kind of reflection, remembrance, expression, etc., of the children's services at the outdoor summer camp meetings held around Danbury and many of the farm towns in Connecticut in the Seventies, Eighties and Nineties . . ." *Reflection, Remembrance, Expression:* that is the key to Ives, whether to his Second Symphony, Second String Quartet, *Three Places in New England,* or the *Concord* Sonata. The Second Symphony tries to express "the musical feelings of the Connecticut country around here in the 1890's. . . . It is full of the tunes they sang and played then. . . . The part suggesting a Steve Foster tune, while over it the old farmers fiddled a barn dance with all its jigs, gallops and reels, was played in Danbury on the old Wooster House bandstand in 1889." The movement of the *Holidays* Symphony named *Washington's Birthday* describes a "barn dance at the Centre. The village band of fiddles, fife and horn keep up an unending 'break-down' medley. . . ." *Central Park in the Dark* is "a picture in sounds of the sounds of nature and of happenings that men would hear thirty or so years ago (before the combustion engine and radio monopolized the earth and air)." Some of those sounds are street cries, night owls from Healey's, the elevated train, newsboys yelling "uxtry!" pianolas, fire engines, a runaway horse, an echo over the pond—"and we walk home."

Everything Ives heard as a child seems to have made a permanent impression on him. Once, at a baseball rally in Danbury, he heard two marching bands, playing different music, approach and recede. As they came together there was a frightful dissonance. Ives thought the sound delightful, and he reproduced it again and again in his music. He would attend revival meetings where singers yowled lustily out of tune. This to Ives was life; people sounded like this, so why shouldn't his music? In the preface to the Fourth Violin Sonata he explains ". . . The second movement is quieter and more serious except when Deacon Stonemason Bell and Farmer John would get up and get the boys excited. But most of the movement moves quietly around that old favorite hymn of the children—'Yes, Jesus Loves Me, the Bible Tells Me So,' while mostly in the accompaniment is heard something trying to reflect the outdoor sounds of nature on those summer days. . . ." All this is in the music. Yet it is not at all program music. It has flavors and colors rather than story content.

Reflection, Remembrance, Expression. It all sounds simple enough as described. Hearing it and understanding it is not so simple. Ives was not out to make what he called "sissy sounds" for Rollo. It is true that he is constantly using familiar tunes—tunes like "America"; "Columbia the Gem of the Ocean"; "Tenting Tonight on the Old Camp Ground"; "Rule, Bri tannia", "Good Night Ladies"; favorite hymns and ragtime melodies. But what he does with them is another matter. The ending of the Second Symphony has fragments of "Columbia the Gem of the Ocean," some barn fiddling, and "De Camptown Races" all going on in different keys at once. But familiarity with the Ives idiom permits the listener to pull the polyphony apart. This unselfconscious, unabashed handling of the sentimental old melodies (never quoted in full but always allusively) put through a sieve of dissonance is what separates the Ives national idiom from that of the other American composers. Compared to him, Roy Harris is a tub-thumping chauvinist, Virgil Thomson a Parisian aesthete who dreams of the Middle West while sipping tea, and Copland is a cowboy from Brooklyn. Ives had an authentic Yankee voice, speaking the accent pure and communicating the belief and dignity of an entire people.

He had a right to his Yankee accent. His ancestors had come to New England in 1653. Ives's father, George, was a remarkable man who had been a bandmaster during the Civil War and later a bandmaster and teacher in Danbury. "Pa taught me what I know," Ives was to say. Part of his father's instruction was completely orthodox. He insisted that Charlie learn the rules before breaking them. But the better part of George Ives's instruction was unheard-of in his day. He was interested in new tonal relationships and had a completely open mind about them. "Nothing but fools and taxes are absolute," he said. He tried to work out a system of microtones, with twenty-four notes to the octave. Like his son, he was impatient with people who thought and heard conventionally. When Charles was ten years old, his father would make him sing "Swanee River" in the key of E flat and accompany him in C major. This was, Ives said many years later, "to stretch our ears   to be less dependent on customs and habits."

With this kind of background it is no wonder that Ives developed as he did. (Henry Cowell, his biographer, suggests that Ives was really writing his father's music for him.) But Ives soon gave up the idea of becoming a fulltime composer. "Father felt that a man could keep his music interest stronger, cleaner, bigger, and freer if he didn't try to make a living out of it." Ives never regretted going into the insurance business, and came to believe that there was more open-mindedness in the business world than in the music world. "My work in music helped my business, and my work in business helped my music." He married in 1908, adopted a daughter, went to the office, composed industriously on weekends and holidays (he had a farm in West Redding, near Danbury), and shrugged off the laughter his few public performances evoked. His wife, Harmony Twitchell, was the daughter of a Hartford clergyman. "She never told me to be good and write something nice that people would like," he said gratefully. In 1951, when Leonard Bernstein conducted the New York Philharmonic in Ives's Second

Symphony, Mrs. Ives, who had had sad experiences with audiences and her husband's music, timidly sneaked into a box. The symphony created a furor, and Mrs. Ives could not at first accept the idea that a work of Charles's was being applauded. Ives did not attend the concert. He heard the Sunday broadcast in his home on East Seventy-fourth Street, listening in the kitchen to the maid's table radio. (That was the only radio in the Ives home.) When the symphony was over, Ives, according to Henry Cowell, "did an awkward little jig of pleasure and vindication."

The Second Symphony was the first of Ives's four to come into favor. His First was a graduation piece, tuneful enough, full of reminiscences of Beethoven, Brahms, and Dvořák. The Second, composed in 1902 and not performed until Bernstein "discovered" it in 1951, moves with much more assurance. It is one of Ives's blander works, but it is authentic Americana, sweet and flowing. The Third, composed in 1911 and not performed until 1945, is something like a hymn-tune symphony, and it too is a sweet, flowing score written with spiky harmonic independence. It would have sent listeners of 1911 screaming out of the hall. The Fourth Symphony is wild. It is Ives's biggest, most sonorous, and most complex. He finished it in 1916, and its first complete performance came with Leopold Stokowski and the American Symphony Orchestra in 1965. Copyists had to work for a long time to get it into shape; the notation frequently was all but undecipherable, and there were no parts. The symphony is a compendium of what Ives was trying to do, alternating massed dissonance and polyrhythms with moments of Sunday-to-church calm (Stokowski had to use two assistant conductors at the premiere). It is an amazing work, and by far the greatest symphony ever composed by an American.

During his creative period Ives heard only a tiny handful of the scores he had written. When he did begin to receive performances, he was an old man with a bad heart and sight diminished by cataracts, and he was unable to leave his house to attend concerts. To the public he was an unknown figure. There are very few photographs of him, and he shunned publicity. Only once in his long life, in 1949, did he ever give a newspaper interview. As nobody wanted to hear his music, Ives published some of it himself: "privately printed and not to be put on the market. Complimentary copies will be sent to anyone as long as the supply lasts." Among his few supporters were the poet-novelist Henry Bellamann, the pianist E. Robert Schmitz, the composer Henry Cowell, and the composer-conductor Nicolas Slonimsky. Slonimsky programmed the *Three Places in New England* for a Town Hall concert on January 10, 1931. The music was resoundingly booed, and Carl Ruggles's *Men and Mountains,* on the same program, got an even more uproarious reception. Ives bore his own failure stoically, but during the screaming over the Ruggles he got to his feet and yelled "Stop being such a

God-damned sissy! Why can't you stand up before fine, strong music like this and use your ears like a man!" (Ives really spoke like this.) Slonimsky later conducted some Ives music in Europe, and while it was ridiculed, it also caught the ears of some responsible musicians and critics. The one major American critic to take up the Ives cause was Lawrence Gilman of the New York *Herald Tribune*. When fame and recognition finally did come, during the last decade of his life, Ives may have had some resentment about its tardy appearance. He did accept the Pulitzer Prize in 1947 for his Third Symphony, but told the committee that "Prizes are for boys. I'm grown up." He told a reporter that "Prizes are the badges of mediocrity," and he gave away the $500 he received for the award. He also said that many composers, perhaps of genius, had been started on the downward path by trying to win a $10,000 prize for an opera. The reference here was to Horatio Parker, whose opera *Mona* won a $10,000 prize offered by the Metropolitan Opera in 1911.

This attitude is basic Ives. It can, of course, be pooh-poohed away by pointing out that he was independently wealthy and could afford to scorn commercialism. (Mozart or Beethoven would have been the last men in the world to turn down $10,000 commissions.) But Ives's remark cannot be thrown aside so easily. What he meant was that pretty-pretty music for the Rollos of the world flourishes under conditions of patronage, that he who pays the piper calls the tune, and that a gifted composer would be tempted to prostitute himself. As far as Ives was concerned, there was no such thing as a part-time prostitute: you were pure, or you were not. Pretty-pretty music meant compromise. Ives considered it his duty as a Yankee and a Puritan to scorn comfort in listening; and he also believed that the public, which was spoiled enough as it was, had a similar duty to listen hard to new tonal relationships. What he did musically—those amazing innovations—he did despite himself. He did not have a very good technique; in some respects he had a terrible technique. What he had was genius and a new way of hearing. It is fascinating to speculate on how Ives would have composed had he received performances, worked with orchestras and musicians. Would he have gone into a smoother kind of writing? Would his notation have been clearer? It is hard to say, but probably not. Ives was too stubborn a man, and he came from a background where, as he noted on the manuscript of his *Tone Roads No. 1*, people "got up and said what they thought regardless of the consequences."

With Ives an almost unknown factor until his discovery in the 1950's, the composer who best represented the United States in the public and professional eye was Aaron Copland, born in Brooklyn on November 14, 1900. Copland made the break that took American music away from the tarnished provincialism of MacDowell into a powerful, modern, very personal kind of speech. He also helped break the stranglehold of the German domination on American music. As a young pianist and aspiring composer, he did at first study with Rubin Goldmark (nephew of Karl Goldmark, the composer of *The Queen of Sheba*), but abruptly shifted and went to Paris in 1921. There he studied with Nadia Boulanger at the new School of Music for Americans at Fontainebleau. Those studies with Boulanger were later described by Copland as the most important musical experiences of his life. Boulanger became the teacher of virtually every important American composer of the period from 1920 to 1940; she was to those two decades what Rheinberger and Jadassohn previously had been to theirs. So numerous were her students that it was said every American town had two things—a five-and-dime, and a Boulanger pupil.

Boulanger led her pupils away from nineteenth-century models. She was just as much interested in Mussorgsky and Stravinsky as she was in Brahms and Beethoven, and she was fully in sympathy with the new experiments springing up all over the world. Copland was in Paris at a good time, and was intellectually stimulated. Stravinsky, Ravel, Prokofiev, *Les Six*, the Ballets Russes—all had their headquarters there. Picasso, Hemingway, Gertrude Stein and her circle, Joyce, and the other heroes of the Left Bank made Paris in the 1920's the most exciting city in the world. Copland, brash, breezy and confident, full of ideas about music, interested in American jazz, started turning out a kind of music that was his own. It was a music that reflected the new age. Copland was not the only American to work in an avant-garde style. Henry Cowell had experimented with tone clusters and sound for sound's sake. Leo Ornstein, the brilliant young pianist, was smashing keyboards and getting a good deal of publicity about his rhythmic, dissonant music. But Ornstein soon disappeared, and Cowell seemed at best to be a minor talent. Copland was the one who had the brains, determination, and skill to arrive at his goal.

At first he was influenced by Stravinsky and *Les Six*, and composed polyrhythmic music that played with jazz elements. The ballet *Grohg*, later worked into the *Dance Symphony* (1925), belongs to this period, and so do *Music for the Theater* (1925) and the Piano Concerto (1927). It was clear that a major talent had arrived. After 1927, Copland dropped jazz. "With the Concerto I felt I had done all I could with the idiom, considering its limited emotional scope. True, it was an easy way to be American in musical terms, but all American music could not possibly be confined to two dominant jazz models: the 'blues' and the snappy number." Many other composers of the period had come to the same conclusion. During the 1920's some of the international stars, including Stravinsky, had a brief fling with jazz, but nothing much came of it.

After the Piano Concerto, Copland turned to a completely different form of expression, one that stimulated every young American composer. With the Piano Variations (1930), the *Short Symphony* (1933, later reduced to a Sextet), and *Statements* for orchestra (1935), Copland became the leader of the new American school

These new products from Copland's pen were stripped-down scores, dissonant, percussive, powerful, abstract. Pattern and rhythm were the main preoccupations, much more than melody. The Russians would have called them "formalistic." A strong mind was at work, manipulating the musical elements in forms that amounted to pure logic. Even Stravinsky had not gone so far. "They are difficult to perform, and difficult for an audience to comprehend," Copland said of this music. The public did not respond; it seldom does to abstract music—that is, music in which the rigorous development of an idea occupies more importance than melody (in the traditional sense of the word). To many audiences, this kind of music is considered too "intellectual," abstruse, and ungrateful. But elements of the new Copland style crept into the writing of many American composers. These were the days when everybody was desperately anxious to be "modern," and Copland was the most modern of all the Americans.

Suddenly Copland changed his style once again. He shifted from abstractionism to a more popular idiom. Copland felt that the new music could be dangerous in that it might end up completely alienating the public. In *The New Music* he pointed out that during the early 1930's

> I began to feel an increasing dissatisfaction with the relations of the music-loving public and the living composer. The old "special" public of the modern music concerts had fallen away, and the conventional concert public continued apathetic or indifferent to anything but the established classics. It seemed to me that we composers were in danger of working in a vacuum. Moreover, an entirely new public for music had grown up around the radio and the phonograph. It made no sense to ignore them and to continue writing as if they did not exist. I felt that it was worth the effort to see if I couldn't say what I had to say in the simplest possible terms.

Thus came into being the music by which Copland is best known and best loved. With *The Second Hurricane* (1935), *El Salón México* (1936), and above all with his three "American" ballets—*Billy the Kid* (1938) for Eugene Loring, *Rodeo* (1940) for Agnes de Mille, and *Appalachian Spring* (1944) for Martha Graham—he moved out of a small circle into a position as not only the most respected American composer, but also the most popular, by far. Other works that can be added to this list would include *A Lincoln Portrait* (1942), the opera *The Tender Land* (though it was not a success when it was produced in 1954), *Quiet City* (1940), and the *Twelve*

Poems of Emily Dickinson (1950). All of these are sophisticated, tuneful, and atmospheric scores, popular but not written-down. All bear the Copland imprint, with his characteristic harmonies and rhythmic breaks. In other words, Copland did not follow the material; he bent it to his will. Once again young American composers rushed to imitate the Master.

The 1930's saw a group of prominent American composers attracting attention with Copland. Few have had his staying power. It was hoped in those days that Copland, Roy Harris, Walter Piston, William Schuman, Samuel Barber, and Virgil Thomson would spearhead the new American school. Things did not work out that way, and history will put the group (Copland excepted) in an analagous position to the Boston Classicists—worthy and skillful musicians who lacked the individuality to create a lasting body of music. Harris turned out work after work, but only his Third Symphony achieved much currency, and today that work is only on the fringe of the repertory. Piston turned out polite, well-tailored classistic music of no particular urgency or individuality. Schuman's music, lean and athletic, well-organized and smartly orchestrated, was discussed but never much liked. Perhaps its melodic inhibition was the reason. Thomson at least composed two operas to Gertrude Stein librettos—*Four Saints in Three Acts* (1934) and *The Mother of Us All* (1947)—that had something sweet and genuine. They are rather precious works and not to everybody's taste but, with all their Satie-like "white-key" harmonies, they are immensely sophisticated and appealing. Barber, the most traditional of all, enjoyed great popularity and still remains very much in the repertory, though he composed less and less after 1960.

Music had changed. Instead of being the spearhead of the American movement, Copland and the other big American composers of the 1920–40 period found themselves in the backwash. The younger men turned to serial music and its derivatives, and instead of an American style there suddenly was an international style. Copland, never a very prolific composer, made a few attempts at a form of serial composition, as in the Piano Fantasy and the *Connotations* for orchestra, composed in 1962 for the opening concert at Philharmonic Hall, in New York's Lincoln Center. Neither work has had many performances, and Copland too has composed less and less. He busied himself other ways. As the most articulate of spokesmen for American music and musicians, he has been writer, critic, analyst, educator, and administrator. In his books and articles he has for years been explaining new music; as an educator he has guided the young students at the Berkshire Music Center in Tanglewood, which he headed from its inception in 1940 to 1969. Counselor and elder statesman, Aaron Copland is the urbane, respected symbol of a half century of American music.

✤ 18 ✤

The Uncompromising Hungarian

BÉLA BARTÓK

It is generally agreed that the three greatest post-Debussyian composers of the first half of the twentieth century were Igor Stravinsky, Arnold Schoenberg, and Béla Bartók each a powerful individualist, each a significant innovator If Stravinsky represents logic and precision in music, and if Schoenberg represents the break from tonality into an entirely new philosophy of musical composition, Bartók represents the fusion of nationalism and nineteenth-century musical forms into a convulsively powerful means of expression

Bartók was a tiny, frail man with explosive psychic force, prepared to go his own uncompromising way even if his music was never played. A stubborn integrity and an all-encompassing humanism animated the man, and he would not swerve from his ideal of truth, even when it involved resisting the Nazis and making a new home elsewhere. He was prepared at all times to stand up to the Establishment in defense of his music and in defense of his liberty. In this determination to maintain his personal and artistic integrity he was much like Schoenberg, and some of his letters even read like Schoenberg's. In 1915, when Bartók was getting hardly any performances, his First Suite was played, but in a mutilated form. Bartók immediately got off a letter of protest to the directors of the Budapest Philharmonic Society, pointing out that "the thematic interdependence of each movement is so close that there are measures in certain movements that simply cannot be understood unless they have been preceded by the earlier movements." Bartók added a final paragraph; and the directors of the Budapest Philharmonic Society, who probably honestly thought they were doing Bartók a favor by programming several movements of his Suite, must have been startled to read the composer's *fiat*

I must, under the circumstances, declare that I should be exceptionally grateful to you if you would never again perform any of my works. I can

506

make this request all the more, since the regrettable state of musical affairs in Budapest has in any case forced me to withdraw completely from public participation as a composer for the past four years, and to refrain from producing any of the compositions I have written during that period.

Bartók was a nationalist composer, probably, with Mussorgsky, the greatest who ever lived, and there is scarcely a note of his music that is not impregnated with the feeling of the Hungarian *melos*. It was not that he invented or quoted folk melodies, though once in a while that could happen. It was something far deeper than that. As one of the world's most knowledgeable ethnomusicologists — Bartók had an international reputation for his scholarly researches in folk music — the sound, rhythms, and scales of the music of his native Hungary were so much a part of him that he automatically thought in those terms. And what he expressed was the real, undiluted thing. Most nationalists of the previous century used a westernized, smoothed-out version of folk elements. Bartók went down to basics, to the raw material, the *Ur*-folk. He often put these materials into forms derived from the mainstream of Western music. "Kodály and I," he said, "wanted to make a synthesis of East and West." Zoltan Kodály too used folk elements in his music. But his works sound tame next to Bartók's. Kodály had a more polite and more conventional mind, and while he was a fine composer, he could not break entirely away from the academic or nineteenth-century formulae. Bartók did, changing the sonata and other forms as suited him, and using folk elements in a new and daring manner.

From the beginning he was exposed to folk music. He was born in Nagyszentmiklós, in the Torontál district of Hungary (now Rumania), on March 25, 1881. He was a serious child who developed into a serious man, and though his figure was slight, and his features delicate, he nevertheless gave the impression of unyielding strength. His father died when he was seven years-old, and his mother, a piano teacher, moved around the country. Bartók thus during his childhood had the opportunity of hearing several varieties of folk music. His mother started him on piano when he was five, soon discovering that he had absolute pitch and amazing aptitude. At the age of eleven he was playing in public. In 1899 he entered the Budapest Academy of Music. Those were the days when the major Hungarian talent was Ernö von Dohnányi (1877–1960). Dohnányi was a remarkable pianist, and a composer who worked skillfully in the Brahms tradition. Later he became the czar of Hungarian music. He and Bartók were rivals, and their paths were to cross many times throughout the years. When Bartók was graduated in 1901 and gave his public concert, the critics could find no higher words of praise than to say that Bartók was the only piano student at the Academy who might follow in Dohnányi's footsteps. (Dohnányi had been graduated from the Academy in 1897, winning a great number of prizes.)

Bartók had started to compose as a child. He stopped for a while, to concentrate on the piano In 1902 he heard Strauss's *Also sprach Zarathustra*, and became wildly excited. "Straightaway I threw myself into a study of Strauss's scores and began again to compose." The pieces he wrote in those days, such as the *Kossuth* Symphony (really a symphonic poem in ten parts), reflected the German tradition in general and Strauss in particular. More work at the piano followed, including some lessons with Dohnányi. There also were periods of bad health; throughout much of his life, Bartók was ailing in one way or another. In 1904 he composed his Op. 1, a Rhapsody for piano and orchestra. This again was a German-derived work, though with a strong nineteenth-century type of Hungarian nationalism. Liszt might have written it had he lived another twenty years; it is somewhat in the style of Liszt's *Hungarian Fantasia*. Bartók composed it as a vehicle for himself. Like any pianist-composer from Mozart on, he needed material to demonstrate his own wares, and it was this work, among others, that Bartók carried with him in 1905 to Paris, to compete for the Rubinstein Prize. He took second place in composition, to an Italian named Attilio Brignoli; and in the piano competition he lost out to Wilhelm Backhaus, which was no disgrace.

The big break in Bartók's line of development came in 1905, when he and Zoltán Kodály went into the field to collect folk music. They had with them an Edison machine on which they recorded hundreds of cylinders, and they took voluminous notes. The study and classification of folksong was to occupy a good part of Bartók's energy for the rest of his life. His first publication, with Kodály, was the collection named *Twenty Hungarian Folksongs*, which came out in 1906. Bartók and Kodály discovered that there were several categories of Hungarian folksong—the old style, largely pentatonic in melody; a new style, with mixed modes and heptatonic scales; and a class in which both elements were combined. To his friend Stefi Geyer, the violinist, Bartók wrote an amusing letter in dialogue form, discussing the difficulties in pulling old music out of the peasants. Bartók is "T" (The Traveler):

T . The neighbor's wife here said you'd know the sort of old, old songs you learned in your youth from the old folks.

P . Me?! Old songs?! The gentleman mustn't pull my leg. Hee-hee-hee-hee-hee!

T : But look here, this isn't a lark! I'm speaking quite seriously. I've come from far away, very far away, from Budapest, just to look for these old, old songs that are known only hereabouts!

P.: Well, and what do they do with those songs then—are they going to be put in the newspaper?

T.: Not at all! The point of this work is to preserve these songs, to put them down in writing. Because if we don't write them down, people won't know, later, what used to be sung here in our day. Because, you see, young folk know quite different songs; they don't even have any use for the old ones, they don't even learn them, though they're much lovelier than the ones made nowadays. Well, isn't that right? So fifty years from now, no one will know that they even existed, if we don't write them down now.

P.: Is that so? [Pause.] Bruhahahaha—heeheeheehee! No, I still don't believe it!

T. (desperately): But just look at this booklet, Auntie—see, I've written down all this. [He whistles a tune.] This one was sung by Mrs. András Gegö [he whistles another] and this by Mrs. Bálint Kosza. Well, you know them also, don't you?

P.: Eh, my day is over. It's not for an old woman to spend her time singing such songs; all I know now is church songs.

Bartók can get nothing from the lady but church songs, which he does not want, and adulterated folk songs, which he wants even less. He goes away "crushed," but he has squeezed out of Auntie an introduction to Mrs. Gyurka Sándor, who lives up the street at the corner and knows so many old songs she could sing them from sunup to sunset without repeating any.

In what he called "peasant music," Bartók found a rejuvenating force. He argued (in a long article in the German magazine *Melos*, published in 1920) that at the beginning of the twentieth century there was a turning point in music: "The excesses of the romantics began to be unbearable to many." But where to turn? "Invaluable help was given this change (or rather let us call it rejuvenation) by a kind of peasant music unknown up till then." In the best of this music, said Bartók, the forms were varied but perfect. In addition, the expressive power was "amazing," and at the same time the music was "devoid of sentimentality and superfluous ornaments." Here, claimed Bartók, was "the ideal starting point for a musical renaissance, and a composer in search of new ways cannot be led by a better master." What the composer has to do is "assimilate the idiom of peasant music so completely that he is able to forget all about it and use it as his mother tongue." Ralph Vaughan Williams in England at much the same time was arguing along the same lines. The concept of assimilation was integral to Bartók's way of thinking, as it was to Vaughan Williams and the other nationalists of the day, including Janáček, with his Czech speech patterns in music. All agreed that peasant music had to be studied in the field, as it actually existed, and that life had to be shared with the peasants. "It is not enough," wrote Bartók, "to study it as it is stored up in museums." Using peasant music in a superficial manner will only supply music with a few new ornaments and gewgaws: nothing more. An entirely new approach to folk music had to be developed, Bartók insisted. For instance, take the strange notion of the nineteenth century that only simple harmonizations were suited for folk melodies. That is all very wrong. "It may sound odd, but I do not hesitate to say that the simpler the melody, the more complex and strange may be the harmonizations and accompaniments that go well with it."

But if a composer wanted to work in this idiom, it was necessary for him to work in a tonal medium. That was where Bartók and the Viennese atonalists parted company. Bartók was adamant about the "truism" that folk music, which was tonal, could not be reconciled with Schoenberg's atonality. Bartók, anyway, was a little irritated by the claims of Schoenberg and his followers, who were insisting that there was One method and One method only. "Far be it from me to maintain that the only way to salvation for a composer in our day is for him to base his music on folk music," Bartók wrote in 1931. "But I wish that our opponents had an equally liberal opinion of the significance of folk music." Bartók tried to clarify a few points. Nationalist composers were charged by the atonalists with using borrowed materials. But the use of borrowed materials has nothing to do with the artistic results of a piece of music. When you come down to it, Bartók pointed out, Shakespeare borrowed, and so did Molière, Bach, and Handel. Everybody has his roots in the art of some former time. It so happens that in Bartók's case, "It is peasant music that contains our roots." It is no sign of barrenness or incompetence if a composer bases his work on folk music rather than taking Brahms or Schumann as his model. On the other hand, it is just as bad if a composer takes folk music and puts it into stereotyped musical forms. In both cases the basic conception is a mistake, for "It stresses the all-importance of themes and forgets about the art of form that alone can make something of those themes." Ultimately, of course, the merit of any piece of music is in direct ratio to a composer's talent. "In the hands of incompetent composers, neither folk music nor any other musical material will ever attain significance. The result will in every case be nothing."

Bartók's theories worked for him. The Viennese atonalists could not have been less interested. They of course went their own way and, as it turned out, history was on their side. After World War II and Bartók's death, his music, while popular, exerted very little influence upon the thinking of young composers. Exponents of the serial school found Bartók's music interesting only in those areas where a relationship could be traced with the work of Schoenberg and his school. Thus Pierre Boulez has dismissed Bartók as "a kind of synthesis of late Beethoven and the mature Debussy," and has praise only for that Bartók music which "arrived at a phase of very specially chromatic experiments not far from Berg and Schoenberg." Otherwise Bartók's music, to Boulez, "lacks interior coherence;" and as for the Bartók works that have found most favor with audiences—the Piano Concerto No. 3 and the Concerto for Orchestra—they exhibit "doubtful taste." Bartók's nationalism is described by Boulez, rather sneeringly, as "only a residue of the nationalistic thrusts of the nineteenth century."

So doctrinaire an approach toward the Bartók aesthetic ignores the fact that starting in 1906 Bartók began to compose a body of music in which folk elements were transmuted into something universal. His style did not evolve all at once, and there was a period of consolidation. As he became less interested in the music of Strauss, he became more interested in the music of Liszt and Debussy, and in the Russian music of Stravinsky up to *Les Noces* He became a piano teacher at the Budapest Academy (never did he teach composition) and started composing—the *Portraits* (1908), the *Bagatelles* (1907), the First String Quartet (1908), and a great deal of piano music in which the instrument was treated with a sharp, percussive attack. A one-act opera, *Bluebeard's Castle* (1911); the ballet-pantomime, *The Wooden Prince* (1917); and a ballet, *The Miraculous Mandarin* (1919) were among his bigger works. None of these achieved much popularity, and the ballet, with its neo-*Sacre* rhythms, ferocious dissonance, and sex-ridden plot, was universally condemned. Other works of the period from 1907 to the early 1920's include two Violin Sonatas (1921–1922) and the Second String Quartet (1917).

If Bartók received few performances, at least his music made a strong impact upon European professionals. It was much more discussed outside of Hungary than in his own country, where he was very much a prophet without honor. His music was considered atonal, which it was not despite its powerful dissonance. Not until 1920 did Bartók write a work that had any degree of popularity. That was his *Dance Suite*. The latter half of the 1920's saw Bartók's style come to full maturity. A series of major works ensued: the *Cantata Profana* (1934), the first two Piano Concertos (1927 and 1931), the last four String Quartets (1927, 1928, 1934, and 1939), the Sonata for Two Pianos and Percussion (1938), the *Music for Strings, Percussion, and Celesta* (1937, considered by many his masterpiece), the Violin Concerto No. 2 (1939), and the Divertimento for String Orchestra (1940). The music of this period had enormous thrust, personality, and virility, all enclosed in a savage kind of dissonantal nationalism. It was more dissonant than anything Stravinsky, Prokofiev, or the French school were writing, and its slashing sound was immediately recognizable as Bartókian. Only the Viennese atonalists and Charles Ives were capable of such uncompromising dissonance.

Naturally Bartók was attacked because of his lack of melody. He liked to build works from motto themes, sometimes only a few notes long, and from Liszt he developed a kind of cyclic form that would unify all elements. As Halsey Stevens, in his biography of Bartók, has written: "His motives, frequently of two or three notes only, are in a constant state of regeneration. They grow organically; they proliferate; the evolutionary process is kinetic. No doubt many motivic manipulations which seem carefully calculated were brought about intuitively: the line between reason and intuition is never sharply defined, but the compact thematic logic cannot be denied."

A politically sensitive man, Bartók was appalled by the spread of Nazism. After the *Anschluss* on March 11–13, 1938, Bartók knew that he would be forced to leave his country, for after Austria would come Hungary. As he wrote to a friend in Switzerland, "There is the imminent danger that Hungary will also surrender to this system of robbery and murder. How I could then continue to live or—which amounts to the same thing—work in such a country is quite inconceivable." Yet Bartók was fifty-eight years old and was supporting his mother in addition to his wife and family. He made some wry remarks about the Nazis and their ideas of racial purity. His publisher was Universal, of Vienna, and when the Nazis took Austria, all composers on the Universal list received a questionnaire—"an infamous questionnaire," Bartók exploded—asking "Are you of German blood, racially related, or non-Aryan?" Bartók and Kodály refused to fill it out on the grounds that such questions were illegal and unconstitutional. It was, in a way, a pity they so decided, Bartók wrote, because one could make such lovely jokes:

> For example, say that we are non-Aryan—for, after all, "Aryan," as my dictionary tells me, means "Indo-European." We Hungarians, however, are Finno-Ugric, indeed perhaps even North Turkic, racially, and so in no way Indo-European, consequently not Aryan. Another question goes: "Where and when were you wounded?" Answer: "On 11, 12, and 13 March in Vienna."

Bartók left Universal to go to the British publishing firm of Boosey and Hawkes. In 1939, when his mother died, he decided to leave Hungary, and the following year he was in the United States, where he was to spend the last years of his life. Before he left, he wrote a will, and in it is one paragraph that fully illustrates Bartók's libertarianism and hatred of dictatorship:

> If after my death they want to name a street after me, or to erect a memorial tablet to me in a public place, then my desire is this: as long as what were formerly Oktogon-tér and Körönd in Budapest are named

512

after those men for whom they are at present named [Hitler and Musso-lini], and, further, as long as there is in Hungary any square or street, or is to be, named for those two men, then neither square nor street nor public building in Hungary is to be named for me, and no memorial tab let is to be erected in a public place.

In the United States, he was given a position at Columbia University, where he worked on a collection of folk songs. He had very little money, but stories of his sheer penury are a romantic invention. He was never in actual want. For a while he lived in Forest Hills, in an apartment house, and on Christmas Eve, 1940, wrote a charming letter to his sons in Budapest describing his new home and his American experiences:

On Dec. 7 we moved into a furnished apartment at the above address. It is 16 km. from the center of New York, but the subway (express) station is in front of our door, so that for 5 cents we can be in the city in 20 minutes, at any time. Trains run constantly, and day and night without interruption.   There are shops and all conveniences nearby. The heating is so excessive that we have to turn off ¾ of the radiators; we can keep one of our bedroom windows wide open (if there's no wind). We are beginning to be Americanized, e.g., in the matter of food. In the morning, grapefruit, puffed *wheat* (!) with cream, brown bread and butter, eggs or bacon or fish.   My head is filling up with all sorts of new words: subway stations, street names, subway-system plans, a mass of possibilities for changing trains: absolute necessities in order to live here . We've had enough trouble learning how to cope with various gadgets of the electric, gas, corkscrew, can-opener type, etc., and with means of transportation, but we are managing now. Only once in a while is there any inconvenience; so, for inst., we recently wanted to take the subway to New York's southernmost part: I didn't know exactly where to change to what (the directions aren't much in evidence; in fact, they are sparse and muddled), so that we jaunted around for 3 hours under the ground; finally, our time having run out, we sneaked shamefacedly home, under ground of course, without having achieved our purpose.

In addition to his job at Columbia, Bartók composed and did some concert work. But bad health set in, and his last public appearance took place in New York, on January 21, 1943. He and his wife Ditta played his Two-Piano Concerto (originally the Sonata for Two Pianos and Percussion) with the New York Philharmonic under Fritz Reiner. Doctors could not diagnose the cause of the illness, or so they told Bartók. He had leukemia, and no cure was possible. Bartók's weight dropped alarmingly, down to 87 pounds, and he also suffered from a constant fever. The American Society of Composers, Authors and Publishers (ASCAP) supplied money to see him through his bad period. Serge Koussevitzky came to Bartók with a commission of one thousand dollars for an orchestral work. (This was done at the promptings of Reiner and the violinist Josef Szigeti.) The Concerto for Orchestra resulted; it turned out to be Bartók's most popular orchestral work. For Yehudi Menuhin he composed a Sonata for Unaccompanied Violin; and for his wife he worked on the Third Piano Concerto. At the end of 1944, things were looking up. Money from royalties and performing fees was coming in; a new agreement with Boosey and Hawkes promised a great deal more; he worked on a Viola Concerto for William Primrose; and he started thinking about a concerto for two pianos for Bartlett and Robertson. But as his prospects began to improve, he grew progressively weaker. Desperately he tried to finish two large-scale works at the same time—the Viola Concerto, which was left incomplete, and the Third Piano Concerto, of which all but a few measures of scoring were finished. On September 26, 1945, he died in New York. On his deathbed he lamented, like Schubert, "The trouble is that I have to go with so much still to say."

Within a few years after his death Bartók was among the most-played of all modern composers. The Concerto for Orchestra not only entered the repertory, it almost elbowed aside *Petrushka* and the *Classical* Symphony. Beginning pianists began to cut their eyeteeth on the six volumes of *Mikrokosmos*, those 153 pieces ranging from simple to difficult, all intended to introduce youngsters to modern keyboard sounds. They became standard teaching material. Young virtuosos began to play the last two piano concertos, especially the Third. There was a run on that work, and it vied with Prokofiev's C major Concerto and the ones by Rachmaninoff as the most popular of twentieth-century works for piano and orchestra. Especially admired were the six string quartets. Cycles of the six were played with increasing frequency after Bartók's death, and they were considered by many the greatest body of chamber music after the last quartets by Beethoven.

The first two Bartók quartets, of 1908 and 1917, are relatively conventional, though the harmonies are of a dissonant type of chromaticism. The third of 1927, and the three after that, are in a new, wild, cataclysmic world, full of chamber-orchestra sonorities and a series of effects that frightened listeners and players of the day. Bartók asks for glissandos for all instruments, *ponticello* bowings (close to the bridge), harmonics, *col legno* (using the wooden part of the bow), complicated multiple stoppings, quarter tones, and a variety of percussive sounds that include the famous "Bartók snap"—the rebound of the string against the finger board. Coming to this music unprepared, with the quartets of Brahms or even late Beethoven in mind, can be a disconcerting experience for listeners. These quartets can no more be understood on one hearing than the Beethoven quartets can be. The same can be said of Bartók's *Music for Strings, Percussion, and Celesta* and of the Sonata for Two Pianos and Percussion. The opening movement of the former, with its muted polyphonic flow and rarefied, austere world, has been compared with the opening of the Beethoven Quartet in C sharp minor. The idiom of these works has to be absorbed, and it takes many hearings to do so. Once it is, the music clears up. Rich and complicated as it is, it is nowhere near so difficult as it sounds at first. The ever-present Magyar rhythms and fragments of folklike melody come strongly to the fore, and the dissonances begin to sound pungent instead of fearsome. Those grating seconds and sevenths, those big interlocking chords, those harmonies stemming from the modalities of peasant music, those savage and eccentric rhythms in fives and sevens—all clear up into a direct emotional utterance.

As Bartók himself was so careful to point out, he was not primarily a "nationalist." He was a composer who merely happened to believe that folk music in its pure state was a fructifying force. Thus he wanted to be assessed as a composer, not as a folklorist. He composed rugged music that asked no quarter of anybody, and his best works are the reflection of one of the strongest musical minds of the twentieth century.

✣ 19 ✣

The Second Viennese School

SCHOENBERG, BERG, WEBERN

The first decade of the twentieth century saw a series of convulsive changes in human thought. So radical were those changes that the implications of their full impact were not recognized at the time, and they took years to make their effect. In 1900, Sigmund Freud published *The Interpretation of Dreams*, after which mankind found a new way to probe into the human mind. In the same year, Max Planck published his quantum theory, which destroyed Euclidean geometry and Newtonian physics. Working with Planck's equations, Albert Einstein in 1905 evolved his special relativity theory, after which mankind's understanding of the rules governing the universe were changed. In 1903 the Wright brothers got an airplane into the air, ending man's ages-old search for powered flight. In 1910, Vassily Kandinsky painted his first fully nonrepresentational work, after which painting could never be the same. For the first time, a painting could be regarded purely as a formal assemblage of shapes and colors without reference to anything in nature. And in 1908 Arnold Schoenberg composed his *Buch der hängenden Gärten*, destroying the ages-old concept of tonality as effectively as Einstein had destroyed Newton's macrocosmos. All this in one decade, perhaps the most revolutionary decade in recorded history.

Arnold Schoenberg, who was born in Vienna on September 13, 1874, was a revolutionary who all his life kept insisting he was a traditionalist. Even though he had to admit that he had discarded the musical aesthetic of the past, he nevertheless maintained that all of his works had "arisen entirely from the traditions of German music. . . . My teachers were primarily Bach and Mozart; secondarily Beethoven, Brahms and Wagner." Or, "I am a conservative who was forced to become a radical!" He was a short, bald-headed man with the face of a fanatic: a strong, heavily lined, messianic, uncompromising face; a face with a mouth twisted into a tight-lipped grimace of permanent distrust; a face with huge, glaring, magnetic eyes. "His eyes were

protuberant and explosive, and the whole force of the man was in them"
(Stravinsky).

Schoenberg felt himself to be a man with a mission. "Once, in the army, I
was asked if I was the composer Arnold Schoenberg. 'Somebody had to be,'
I said, 'and nobody else wanted to be, so I took it on myself.'" He conceived of music as an art that conveyed "a prophetic message revealing a
higher form of life toward which mankind evolves." Schoenberg, of course,
was the prophet bearing the message. A higher force was directing him.
When he finished his Chamber Symphony he told his friends that he had
now established his style. "But my next work showed a great deviation from
this style; it was my first steps toward my present style. . . . The Supreme
Commander had ordered me on a higher road." His letters are full of an insistence on the unalterable rightness of his music. Schoenberg's egomania
approached Wagner's. ". . . I believe what I do and do only what I believe;
and woe to anybody who lays hands on my faith. Such a man I regard as an
enemy, and no quarter given! You cannot be with me if you are also with
my opponents." Or, "Views divergent from my own are something I should
never resent, as little as I resent anyone's having any other disability! one
short leg, a clumsy hand, etc. I could only be sorry for such a person, but I
couldn't be angry with him." In 1942 he was asked by a candidate for a
master's thesis to supply certain information about himself and his music.
His reply was devastating: "The composer of *Pierrot Lunaire* and other
works which have changed the history of music thanks you for the honorable
invitation of participating in the production of a Master Thesis. But he
thinks it is more important that he writes those works which candidates for
a master degree will never know; and, if they know them, will never feel the
distance which would forbid them to bother him with such questions." It
followed that very little—if any—of the music composed in his time satisfied him. He poked fun at Stravinsky's neoclassicism and satirized him personally. For those composers who piled discords on discords, "like gluttons
(wishing to pass as 'moderns') but do not have the courage to draw the consequences from them," he had nothing but contempt. He jeered at the
"pseudo-tonalists," and at such neobaroque composers as Busoni and Hindemith, "who claim to make 'a return to So and So'" (though, inconsistently, he regarded Reger, the leader of the Back-to-Bach movement, as a genius). His dislikes included the folklore school headed by Bartók, "who try
to apply to the ideas of popular music, which are by nature primitive, a
technique that is only appropriate to a more evolved type of thought." Finally, as if to make sure he had not overlooked anybody, Schoenberg in one
sweeping condemnation attacked "all the 'ists,' whom I can see only as man-
nerists."

In the beginning Schoenberg wrote more or less conventional music of a lush chromatic texture that stemmed from Wagner and Mahler. Yet from his first scores Schoenberg was regarded as a subversive. In 1900 a group of his songs created a public outburst at a recital. "Since then," Schoenberg said many years later, "the scandal has never ceased." Even *Verklärte Nacht* caused a near-riot at its premiere in 1903. Today a score like *Verklärte Nacht* is regarded as the essence of late romanticism, but audiences at the turn of the century did not see it that way, and the lack of firm tonality was unsettling to them.

Schoenberg came to music as a self-taught composer. Although he was playing the violin at the age of eight, he had very little training. When he tried to compose, as a teen-ager, it was in imitation of music that he had heard. For a while he worked in a bank, though he became part of the intellectual life of Vienna, mixing with artists, writers, and musicians. He met the composer and conductor Alexander von Zemlinsky and took some counterpoint lessons with him. As far as anybody knows, Schoenberg never had any other instruction. He is one of the few important composers in history who was a complete autodidact. Schoenberg married Zemlinsky's sister in 1901. (She died in 1923, after which Schoenberg married the sister of the violinist Rudolf Kolisch.)

Schoenberg's early works included a string quartet and a group of songs. In 1899 he composed the voluptuous string sextet *Verklärte Nacht*, which is a long, languorous post-*Tristan* sigh. (In 1941 Schoenberg rescored it for string orchestra.) One oddity about *Verklärte Nacht* is that it is a piece of chamber music set to a program (the only other example that comes readily to mind is Smetana's E minor Quartet, *Aus meinem Leben*). The story came from a poem by Richard Dehmel. Schoenberg later went on to compose music that ruptured all the "rules," and eventually he created an organizational system—the so-called "twelve-tone method"—that was to be the most important single influence on the musical thinking of the generation after World War II. But, ironically, the rather conventional *Verklärte Nacht* is the Schoenberg work that has remained the most popular, just as of all the Stravinsky scores *Firebird* is first in public favor.

For a brief time after his marriage Schoenberg worked in Berlin, conducting music-hall and operetta performances. He worked on his symphonic poem *Pelleas und Melisande* and on the enormous *Gurrelieder* in 1900, which was not scored until many years afterwards. In 1903 he returned to Vienna and began to teach. Among his first pupils were Anton von Webern and Alban Berg. Webern was born on December 3, 1883. He was a quiet, scholarly man who in 1906 took a doctorate in musicology. For many years he made his living as conductor of the Vienna Workers' Symphony Concerts. Berg, born on February 9, 1885, was a tall, handsome, aristocratic young man whose family had money. As a musician, he was a complete dilettante when he came to Schoenberg. "The state he was in," Schoenberg wrote in 1910, ". . . was such that his imagination apparently could not work on anything but songs. Even the piano accompaniments for them were song-like in style. He was absolutely incapable of writing an instrumental movement or inventing an instrumental theme. You can hardly imagine the lengths I went to in order to remove this defect in his talent." Schoenberg had other talented pupils, but none on the order of a Berg or Webern. They worshiped him, which was just as well, for Schoenberg exacted worship. Schoenberg's teaching was rigorous and demanding, but not doctrinaire. He insisted on the pupil's using his own imagination, even as a beginner. Exercises were not to be written by rote. They were, even in their simplest form, to be exercises in expression. "Hence," Webern later wrote, "he [the pupil] must actually create, even in the most primitive beginnings of musical construction. What Schoenberg explains to the student is altogether bound up, then, with the work in hand. He brings no external dogmas. Thus Schoenberg educates actually through creating. He follows the traces of the students' personality with the utmost energy, tries to deepen them, to help them break through . . ." Schoenberg all his life remained the spiritual father of Berg and Webern. He preached, they obediently listened.

Schoenberg's music soon began to drift away from the colossal orchestral concepts of *Pelleas und Melisande* and *Gurrelieder*. It became more compact, aphoristic, and dissonant. The Chamber Symphony of 1906 experimented with fourths, much as Scriabin was doing at the same time in Russia. In 1908 Schoenberg had arrived at the point where tonality was abolished. He realized that the songs in the *Buch der hängenden Gärten* (Op. 15) had led to something new:

With the songs Op. 15 I have succeeded for the first time in approaching an ideal of form and expression that has hovered before me for years. . . . I am conscious of having removed all the traces of a past esthetic; and if I am in the process of going towards a goal which seems certain to me, I already feel the opposition I shall have to overcome. . . . I think that even some people who have believed in me up to now will not realize the necessity of this evolution.

These songs were followed by the short one-act opera *Erwartung*, the Five Orchestral Pieces (both in 1909), the Six Little Piano Pieces of 1911 and, above all, *Pierrot Lunaire* in 1912. Schoenberg was now writing expressionistic rather than postromantic music. This was no accident. He was closely allied with the German painters of *Die Brücke*, the group that put expressionism on the rails; and he himself even painted some intense, though amateurish, canvases, including a self-portrait. Kandinsky's definition of expressionist painting contained the statement: ". . . the presentation of an internal expression in external, visible form;" and Schoenberg very consciously tried to do in music what the expressionists were doing in painting. "Everything I have written has a certain inward similarity to myself." Expressionism is intensified romanticism, the exploration of inner states. All expressionistic art and music are very serious. Expressionism avoids the superficially pretty and attempts to transcend nature. It often deals with social commentary, psychological commentary, the soul, the psyche, the subconscious. Kokoschka once painted a portrait. "Those who knew you will not recognize you," he told the sitter, "but those who do not know you will recognize you very well." Where the impressionists tried to evoke an ideal state through transparent and sensual textures, and an avoidance of black pigments ("Black does not exist in nature"), expressionism is stark, often brutal, purposely distorted in line and texture, full of nervous tension. Impressionistic music is smooth and never entirely breaks away from tonality (=nature): expressionistic music is dissonant, atonal, with jagged melodic leaps, and deals with an intensified realism rather than idealism.

Schoenberg was steadily moving toward completely atonal textures—"the emancipation of the dissonance," as he put it—and he realized them in the Op. 11 piano pieces and *Pierrot Lunaire*. His opera *Erwartung* was a significant step in the aesthetic that finally resulted in Berg's *Wozzeck*. Schoenberg composed *Erwartung* in seventeen hectic days, between August 17 and September 12, 1909. (Then he had to wait fifteen years for a staged performance of the 30-minute-long work.) The text is by Marie Pappenheim. A woman seeks her lover in the forest. She finds him dead, near the house of the woman who has stolen him from her. That is all the story. The music reflects the woman's states of mind, in a vocal line that is largely declamatory, and in a harmony that is largely fourths and altered fourths, sevenths, and complexes of notes. The entire work is athematic. That is, there is no repetition of any theme, and melody in the accepted sense has disappeared. Yet the work, after one has become immersed in its idiom, looks back as much as it looks forward. Indeed, it is heavily Wagnerian. Wagner is apparent in the big orchestra, in the rich textures, and in many aspects of the libretto. *Tristan und Isolde* is full of night-and-day symbolism, and so is *Erwartung*. *Tristan und Isolde* ends with a love-death, and so does *Erwartung*: when the woman in the Schoenberg opera finds her dead lover, she sings a long passage that is nothing less than a *Liebestod*. Through Schoenberg's new and unconventional language, something very traditional can be experienced.

Just as *Erwartung* looks back to Wagner, so it also looks forward to *Pierrot Lunaire*, which many consider to be Schoenberg's most significant score.

Pierrot Lunaire is composed for speaker (it was commissioned by an actress rather than a singer), flute (doubling on piccolo), clarinet (doubling on bass clarinet), violin (doubling on viola), cello, and piano. For the twenty-one songs of *Pierrot Lunaire* Schoenberg used a poem by Albert Giraud in a German translation by Otto Erich Hartleben. The poem is a parallel to T. S. Eliot's later *Waste Land* and is a series about the decadence of modern man. Schoenberg's settings were unprecedented for their daring and novelty, and for the first time the words *Sprechstimme* (literally, "speak voice") and *Sprechgesang* (literally, "speak song") entered the language. The vocal line calls for a heightened kind of song-speech—*Sprechgesang*—in which speech patterns rise and fall. It is not singing, nor is it speaking, but it is something in between, with the voice at times swooping up and sliding down in sounds of approximate pitch (and, here and there, also ascending to an unearthly high falsetto sound). Some of the music in *Pierrot Lunaire* is based on traditional forms—passacaglia, canons, and the like. But where the forms may be classically precise, the harmonic and melodic idiom break all the known rules. Musicians immediately realized that here was a new world of sound. But it is more than that. *Pierrot Lunaire* is a magical and evocative score that inhabits a ghostly, miniature, imagery-ridden world full of blood symbolism. Today it is recognized as being as seminal a work as *Le Sacre du Printemps*, Joyce's *Ulysses*, Picasso's *Les Demoiselles d'Avignon*, and the reasoning that led to $E = mc^2$. In particular, the vocal style of *Pierrot Lunaire* exerted an overwhelming influence on many composers of the post-World War II period.

In his book, *Style and Idea,* Schoenberg traced his development from the composer of *Verklärte Nacht* through *Pierrot Lunaire* and dodecaphony. One important passage deals with the concepts in Schoenberg's mind that led to *Pierrot:*

> In the last hundred years the concept of harmony has changed tremendously through the development of chromaticism. The idea that one basic tone, the root, dominated the construction of chords and regulated their succession—the concept of *tonality*—had to develop first into the concept of *extended tonality.* Very soon it became doubtful whether such a root still remained the center to which every harmony and harmonic succession must be referred. Furthermore it became doubtful whether a tonic appearing at the beginning, or at the end, or at any other point really had a constructive meaning. Richard Wagner's harmony had promoted a change in the logic and constructive power of harmony. One of its consequences was the so-called *impressionistic* use of harmonies, especially practiced by Debussy. His harmonies, without constructive meaning, often served the coloristic purpose of expressing moods and pictures. Moods and pictures, though extra-musical, thus became constructive ele-

ments, incorporated in the musical functions; they produced a sort of emotional comprehensibility in practice, if not in theory. This alone would perhaps not have caused a radical change in compositional tech nique. However, such a change became necessary when there occurred si multaneously a development that ended in what I call the *emancipation of the dissonance*

The term, "emancipation of the dissonance," Schoenberg explains, re fers to the comprehensibility of dissonance, "which is considered equiva lent to the consonance's comprehensibility. A style based on this premise treats dissonances like consonances and renounces a tonal center. By avoid ing the establishment of a key, modulation is excluded, since modulation means leaving an established tonality and establishing *another* tonality." It was in 1908, says Schoenberg, that the first compositions in this style were written by him and, soon afterward, by Webern and Berg.

Needless to say, this kind of music encountered tremendous hostility, and it still does. Even in the 1960's, during the height of the Schoenberg and Webern craze among composers, their music seldom was performed. In the first decades of the century, nearly every Schoenberg premiere was accompa nied by a *scandale*. Not that there were many premieres. The music was strange, very difficult, not liked by audiences, and therefore most musicians and conductors avoided it. Schoenberg was confident that his music would become the normal language. "In ten years," he wrote in 1910, "every tal ented composer will be writing this way, regardless of whether he has learned it directly from me or only from my works." Later he was not so confident. "Today," he wrote in 1924, "I realize that I cannot be under stood, and I am content to make do with respect." Several years before his death he was resigned to his fate. In a letter written in 1947 he said that "I am quite conscious of the fact that a full understanding of my works cannot be expected before some decades. The minds of the musicians, and of the audiences, have to mature ere they can comprehend my music. I know this, I have personally renounced an early success, and I know that—success or not—it is my historic duty to write what my destiny orders me to write."

Like any composer, Schoenberg eagerly sought performances. Unlike most composers, he insisted that performances be true to the music— that is, thor oughly prepared—or else no performances would be allowed. "I will not be bullied by anyone," he wrote to his publisher in 1913, after the composer conductor Franz Schreker threatened to cancel a performance. "I am not *so* eager for success. In particular: what I am interested in is not *a* perfor mance, only a good performance. Please do not hesitate to cancel the performance." He would not permit his operas, *Erwartung* or *Die glück liche Hand*, to be given once and then dropped. "I would let a theater have them only for inclusion in the repertory." Irritated and insulted because the Vienna Philharmonic had never played his music, he notified Wilhelm Furt-wängler that "I would not let a new work have its first performance in Vienna. The fact is I am the only composer of any reputation at all whom the Philharmonic has not yet performed. And it may as well rest at that!" In the United States he learned that Otto Klemperer had expressed a dislike for his music, that Klemperer had said it was "alien" to him. When Klemperer got in touch with Schoenberg about conducting a work, he received a letter bitterly accusing him of the alleged statement. "I then consider that you should cease to conduct my works. For what can a performance be like if the music has become alien to you?" In 1922 Edgard Varèse decided to perform *Pierrot Lunaire* and received a stiff letter from Schoenberg. Among other things, there was this paragraph:

What offends me equally, however, is that without asking me whether you *can and may* do so, you simply set a definitive date for my *Pierrot Lunaire*. Have you already got a suitable speaker; a violinist, a pianist, a conductor, etc.? How many rehearsals do you mean to hold, etc., etc. In Vienna, with everyone starving and shivering, something like 100 rehearsals were held and an impeccable ensemble achieved with my collaboration. But you people simply fix a date and think that's all there is to it! Have you any inkling of the difficulties, of the style, of the declamation, of the tempi, of the dynamics, and all that? And you expect me to associate myself with it? No, I'm not *smart* enough for that. If you want to have anything to do with me, you must set about it quite differently. What I want to know is: 1. How many rehearsals? 2. Who is in charge of the rehearsals? 3. Who does the *Sprechstimme*? 4. Who are the players? If all this is to my satisfaction, I shall give my blessing. But for the rest I am, of course, powerless and you can do as you like. But then kindly refrain from asking me about it. I regret not being able to say anything more obliging. But I must reject this exclusively business approach. I sincerely hope that another time I may have occasion to be more cordial.

During World War I, Schoenberg was in service for two spells, between 1915 and 1917. He composed very little, not publishing again until 1923. Of his two famous pupils, Berg was in the army for three years, and Webern for a short time. The big, handsome Berg, healthy looking but never a well man, was discharged because of his asthma. Webern was released because of bad eyesight. Berg, Webern, and Schoenberg remained in constant touch during the war years and afterward, when Schoenberg moved to Berlin, always corresponding, describing, and analyzing one anothers' latest compositions. Berg was the most romantic of the three, the one most suggestive of

Wagner, Mahler, and postromanticism Like Schoenberg, Berg had his roots in the German tradition and was constantly working in old forms. He did not compose much In 1912 came the *Altenberg* songs, in 1914 the Three Orchestral Pieces, and in 1914 he started work on *Wozzeck*, adapting the Georg Büchner play to his purposes. He finished the libretto in 1917, the score in 1922. It was characteristic that Berg erect his opera on classical and preclassical forms This atonal, expressionistic opera was described by its composer as a sonata, the first act being an exposition, the second a development, and the third a form of recapitulation Act I, in five scenes, contains a suite, rhapsody, military march, lullaby, passacaglia, and rondo. The five scenes of Act II are in effect five movements of a symphony, sonata movement, fantasy and fugue, largo, scherzo, and rondo (with an introduction) Act III, also in five scenes, is a series of inventions on a theme, on a tone, on a rhythm, on a chord, on a tonality.

Few are conscious of this construction when listening to *Wozzeck*. It had its premiere in 1925 at the Berlin State Opera, Erich Kleiber conducting, after an unprecedented series of rehearsals. It cannot be said that the opera was liked, but it created such a furor that other European opera houses hastened to produce it. Critics attacked it as degenerate art and chaos in music, but *Wozzeck* also had its admirers and defenders. So powerful and original an opera naturally had some perceptive listeners on its side. The more sensitive listeners decided that there was method in Berg's madness. Max Marschalk, in the *Vossische Zeitung*, pointed out that in *Wozzeck* dissonance had been elevated to a very principle, that "forms resolve into continuity, colors coalesce, and there results something which, by its very oscillation and nebulous atmosphere, is probably exactly the music which justifies the transformation of *Wozzeck* into an opera." Adolf Weissman in *Die Musik* wrote about the spiritual values of the opera and its 'instinctive perception.'

Other critics felt uneasy. "The listener attains an hypnotic state in which he believes the walls of the theater are about to crash down on him," wrote Erich Steinhardt in *Der Auftakt* And, of course, there were the old-line critics who frothed at the mouth. Paul Zschorlich of the *Deutsche Zeitung* was one: "As I was leaving the State Opera, I had the sensation of having been not in a public theater but in an insane asylum. On the stage, in the orchestra, in the stalls—plain madmen. We deal here, from a musical viewpoint, with a capital offence." Naturally the Soviet critics saw in *Wozzeck* the decline of the West, and expressed their opinions in the approved ideological language. "Berg's opera reveals the helplessness of the Western-European petty-bourgeois intellegentsia before oncoming fascistization, and demonstrates the crisis not only in the individual consciousness of the Western-European bourgeois composer, but in Western-European musical culture in general" (Boris Asafiev, in *Sovietskava Musica*).

Berg in 1928 explained what he was trying to do, in language that goes back to Gluck and Wagner:

> I never entertained the idea of reforming the artistic structure of the opera with *Wozzeck*. . . . I wanted to compose good music, to develop musically the contents of Büchner's immortal drama, to translate his poetic language into music; but other than that, when I decided to write an opera, my only intentions, including the technique of composition, were to give the theater what belongs to the theater. In other words, the music was to be formed as consciously to fulfill its duty of serving the action at every moment. Even more, the music should be prepared to furnish whatever action needed to be transformed into reality on the stage. . . .
>
> That these purposes should be accomplished by use of musical forms more or less ancient (considered by critics as one of the most important of my ostensible reforms of the opera) was a natural consequence. For the libretto, it was necessary to make a selection from twenty-six loosely constructed, sometimes fragmentary, scenes by Büchner. Repetitions that did not lend themselves to musical variations had to be avoided. Finally the scenes had to be brought together, arranged and grouped in acts. The problem therefore became, utterly apart from my will, more musical than literary, one to be solved by the laws of musical structure rather than by the rules of dramaturgy. . . .
>
> No matter how cognizant any particular individual may be of the musical forms contained in the framework of this opera, of the precision and logic with which everything is worked out, and the skill manifested in every detail, from the moment the curtain parts until it closes for the last time, there must be nobody in the audience who pays any attention to the various fugues, inventions, suites, sonata movements, variations and passacaglias—nobody who heeds anything but the idea of this opera, which by far transcends the personal destiny of *Wozzeck*. This I believe to be my achievement.

Webern, meanwhile, was exploring a different kind of world—the world of the microcosm instead of the macrocosm; a world of delicate, ephemeral, pointillistic sounds, silences, new pitch relationships, constant aphoristic distillation, daintily shimmering orchestration. In his Passacaglia for Orchestra, in the *Stefan George* songs, in the Five Movements for String Quartet and Six Pieces for Orchestra, all composed between 1908 and 1909, he worked with tiny fragments, mottos, and cells rather than themes. He worked out a new method of scoring, in which almost every note of a phrase was given to a different instrument, with consequently changing colors. Webern got the idea from Schoenberg, who had talked about "a melody of tone colors," or *Klangfarbenmelodie*. Webern's music continued to become more and more compact and brief. With his song cycles of 1914–17 he all but (in the estimation of Pierre Boulez) anticipated the serial system with his "assimilation of rigid counterpoint to fundamental serial forms." To Boulez, Webern here created a new dimension: sound-space "The ge nius of Webern appears unprecedented, both for the radicalism of his points of view and for the novelty of his sensibility."

In 1923 Schoenberg again started composing, and gave to the world a new way of musical organization. "I called this procedure 'Method of Com posing with Twelve Tones Which are Related Only with One Another.' " A composer named Josef Matthias Hauer had been evolving a comparable sys tem, but it was Schoenberg's that took hold. Briefly, Schoenberg's twelve tone (or dodecaphonic) method involved basing a composition on a "series" made up from the twelve notes of the chromatic scale, arranged in such a way that no note was repeated within the basic set, or tone-row, or series (hence the term "serial composition"). Thus no single note was more impor tant than any other note. This basic set, the tone-row, functioning in the manner of a theme or motive, could be manipulated in three ways. It could be played upside down (inversion), backwards (retrograde), and backwards upside down (retrograde inversion). All these are mirror forms, and are not new. Bach had used them in the *Kunst der Fuge* and elsewhere. What Schoenberg was looking for—as, indeed, what Bach was looking for—was a way to achieve complete unity within a piece of music. Schoenberg felt that his new method "corresponds to the principle of *the absolute and unitary perception of musical space.*" But however the music was composed, what ever its system, Schoenberg insisted that listeners and musicians should for get about the system and judge the music as music, "I can't say it often enough: my works are twelve-tone *compositions*, not *twelve-tone* composi tions."

This new music was, basically, horizontal (contrapuntal) as against the vertical (harmonic) writing of the romantics. Its melodic line was disjunct, with wide leaps. The tone-row was arranged so that there was no feeling of triadic (traditional) harmony, (Berg was to break this rule.) Instruments and the voice were used in unusual registers. Instead of recognizable themes, there were cells derived from the tone-row. The last movement of Schoen berg's Piano Pieces (Op. 23) and sections of the Serenade, both published in 1923, contained twelve-tone elements; and the Piano Suite (Op. 25), also published in 1923, was a twelve-tone work throughout. (British writers refer to "twelve-note" rather than "twelve-tone" music. Schoenberg himself, in let ters and essays written in English, and in conversation, used the term "twelve-*tone*." The difficulty comes with the German word *Ton*, which can be translated as "tone" or "note.")

Schoenberg's two disciples enthusiastically adopted the new technique. Berg never entirely divorced himself from postromanticism, and later serial purists have called his work a hybrid, because even within the serial technique it often sounds tonal. Berg set to work on the *Lyric Suite* for string quartet, and on the Chamber Concerto, both of which incorporate serial principles. He then started a serial opera, *Lulu;* and his last work, the Violin Concerto, was also serial. For *Lulu,* Berg brought together two dramas by Frank Wedekind—*Erdgeist* and *Die Büchse der Pandora.* Lulu is an embodiment of Lilith: an amoral temptress who ruins all she touches; and yet she has a curious innocence because she is unconscious of her evil. She is the serpent in the menagerie of life. Berg derived the entire opera from the initial row of twelve tones, but as customary with him, the note to note relationships often have a feeling approaching tonality. He never finished the last act, though many sketches and a short score are in existence. Berg scholars claim that Act III of *Lulu* could easily be completed in a manner entirely faithful to the composer's intentions, but permission to do so has not been granted by the Berg estate.

Webern during the 1920's kept refining his style into what Boulez calls "a new manner of musical *being*." Webern, he says, "was the first to explore the possibilities of a dialectic of sound and silence," with silences as integral parts of the rhythmic cells. Webern also evolved a new structure of pitches, rethinking "the very idea of polyphonic music on the basis of the principles of serial writing" (Boulez). Where Schoenberg and Berg never could discard romanticism, Webern was the one who worked in pure tonal organization, rejecting completely the romantic rhetoric. It could be said that there was no rhetoric at all. So condensed was the writing that a piece might last only a few minutes, and every once in a while under a minute. Forms so highly concentrated cannot stand lengthy developments. Boulez, Webern's most articulate spokesman, points out that Webern's adoption of serial technique helped unify his vocabulary but did not fundamentally alter his musical thinking: his style had been revolutionary before dodecaphonism and remained revolutionary after it. Boulez claims that in Webern's mature works, between 1927 and 1934—those works would include the String Trio, the Symphony, and the Concerto for Nine Instruments—"each sound becomes a phenomenon in itself, linked to the others . . . He aerates his positionings in time and space as well as in their instrumental context." Instrumentation itself takes on a structural function. Boulez summarizes Webern's contributions as an art of unprecedented refinement and concentration of musical materials, in which relationships are so rigorously organized that melody, harmony, and even rhythm become indissoluble from each other. From there it was only a short step to the totally organized music of Olivier Messiaen, Milton Babbitt, and Boulez himself, which came into being shortly after World War II. In totally organized music, even dynamics, tone colors, and silences are serially handled.

The transition from serial music to totally organized music might have come earlier had not the Nazis and seven years of war intervened. With Hitler's rise to power, the music of the Second Viennese School—as the Schoenberg-Berg-Webern group came to be known—was banned as cultural Bolshevism. Berg died in 1935, before the full impact of the Nazi horror became apparent. Webern was forced to live in obscurity, doing editorial work for Universal Edition. He was accidentally shot and killed in Mittersill during the night of September 14, 1945, by an American soldier who was working on a black market case in which Webern's son-in-law was involved. Schoenberg, who was a Jew, had to flee from Berlin in 1933. He had been there since 1926, teaching at the Prussian State Academy of the Arts. He went to France and then to the United States, where in 1933 he settled in Boston as a teacher in the Malkin Conservatory. Because of ill health, he went to Los Angeles a year later, where he taught at the University of California in Los Angeles and gave private lessons. He became an American citizen in 1941 and changed his name from Schönberg to Schoenberg. "My name is to be spelled with 'oe.' I changed it when I came to America because few printers have the 'ö' type, and I wanted to avoid the form 'Schonberg.' " In 1944, at the age of seventy, he had to retire from the University, but his pension— $38 a month—was so small, because he had been a faculty member for only eight years, that he was forced to continue private teaching. During the seventeen years he lived in California he was so busy as a teacher that he had relatively little time for composition, though he did finish the Violin Concerto, the String Quartet No. 4, the Theme and Variations for band, the Piano Concerto, and *A Survivor from Warsaw* for speaker, men's chorus, and orchestra. He also worked on his opera *Moses und Aron*, which he had started in 1927 Two acts had been completed by 1932. Schoenberg was anxious to complete *Moses und Aron*, but he never did. He died in Los Angeles on July 13, 1951

There is a good deal of Schoenberg himself in *Moses und Aron*. At the end of his life he was a bitter man, acutely conscious of his worth and resentful of his neglect: a man of the highest ideals who tried to give the world a message that most found unpalatable or incomprehensible. Small wonder that he should have identified with Moses. Schoenberg had left his religion, but as anti-Semitism mounted in Germany, he returned to it, proudly proclaiming his Jewishness. There are two fascinating and revealing letters he wrote to Kandinsky in 1923. Kandinsky had been one of the founders of the *Blaue Reiter*, a group of avant-garde artists (Franz Marc used to paint blue horses, hence the name, "Blue Riders") with whom Schoenberg had been associated, and he and Kandinsky were close friends. After World War I, Kandinsky entered the Bauhaus group, and there were reports that some of the Bauhaus members were anti-Semitic. But they rationalized their beliefs, and some of their best friends were Jews. On April 20, 1923, Schoenberg wrote an anguished letter to Kandinsky: "I have at last learned the lesson that has been forced on me during the years, and I shall not ever forget it. It is that I am not a German, not a European, indeed perhaps scarcely a human being (at least, the Europeans prefer the worst of their race to me), but I am Jew. . . . I have heard that even a Kandinsky sees only evil in the actions of Jews and in their evil actions only Jewishness, and at this point I give up the hope of reaching any understanding.

I should like the Kandinsky I knew in the past and the Kandinsky of today each to take his fair share of my cordial and respectful greetings." Kandinsky answered, explaining that Schoenberg was not representative of most Jews. Schoenberg exploded:

Dear Kandinsky:

I address you so because you wrote that you were deeply moved by my letter. That was what I hoped of Kandinsky, although I have not yet said a hundredth part of what a Kandinsky's imagination must conjure up before his mind's eye if he is to be my Kandinsky. Because I have not yet said that for instance when I walk along the street and each person looks at me to see whether I'm a Jew or a Christian, I can't very well tell each of them that I'm the one that Kandinsky and some others make an exception of, although of course that man Hitler is not of their opinion.

This was in 1923, and *Moses und Aron* was still to come. Schoenberg, after finishing the second act in 1932, never could figure out how to end the opera. He ran into the problem of how to reconcile what he called "some almost incomprehensible contradictions in the Bible." In any event, Schoenberg was not trying to compose a Biblical opera *à la Samson et Dalila*. With that kind of opera, all kinds of liberties can be taken with the text. In an opera that seeks a philosophical truth, as does *Moses und Aron*, there has to be some kind of support for the conclusions. And while Schoenberg became strongly religious after World War I ("In these years religion has been my only support—I confess that here for the first time"), his was a religion based on ethical teaching, not external conformity. What seemed to interest Schoenberg particularly about Moses was a little passage in the Bible where Moses says to the Lord: "I am not eloquent, neither heretofore, nor since Thou has spoken unto thy servant, but I am slow of speech, and of a slow tongue." Schoenberg in his libretto set up a dualism between Moses and his brother Aaron. Moses sees and understands the God of the Jews, but cannot convey his vision. Aaron, a man of less vision and insight, is a politician-demagogue who can act as Moses's tongue and sway his people. But he can act only as long as Moses is at his side to prompt him.

Thus there are God and Moses on one side, Aaron and the people (mob?) on the other. A conflict ensues. Moses understands the Oneness of God. But such understanding is given to few men. Perhaps it is an understanding at which the masses will never arrive. Even Aaron, so close to Moses, is ready not only to compromise but to go back to idol worship when the spiritual leader is not beside him. Aaron realizes that the masses have "naught but their feeling." To Moses this is anathema. "My love is for the idea. I live only for it." Aaron points out that the tablets containing the Ten Commandments are also images, "just part of the whole idea." Then, says Moses, "I shall smash to pieces both these tablets, and I shall also ask Him to withdraw the task given me." At the end of the second act, Moses falls to the ground in despair. It is not that he doubts the existence of the One God. It is that he despairs of ever being able to explain the Idea to the people. "Oh word, thou word that I lack." The allegory is clear enough. Will Moses-Schoenberg ever find the Word?

Schoenberg did try to finish the opera, rewriting the last act four times. "Here," he wrote to an expert on the Bible, "I have so far encountered great difficulties because of some almost incomprehensible contradictions in the Bible. For even if there are comparatively few points on which I strictly adhere to the Bible, still, it is precisely here that it is difficult to get over the divergence between 'and thou shalt smite the rock' and 'speak ye unto the rock.' You have worked on this material for so long: can you perhaps tell me where I could look up something on this question? Up to now I have been trying to find a solution for myself. . . . It does go on haunting me."

But Schoenberg never did find the solution, and thus *Moses und Aron* remains a torso. It also remains, however, one of the most personal operas ever written; and, unfortunately, so static, wordy, and unoperatic an opera that it probably never will command much of an audience. Through it is seen the figure of Moses-Schoenberg pleading mutely for the people to follow him, never beset by doubts concerning the Message he was carrying, but wondering if the Message would ever be accepted. Could spiritual principle ever triumph over matter and the Golden Calf? Schoenberg himself never doubted the eventual triumph of principle. And he died just as his vision was beginning to come true for him, just at the moment when his Message was beginning to dominate the thoughts of every avant-garde composer in the world. If the period from 1830 to 1860 was the Early Romantic Period, if the latter half of the century was the Age of Wagner, if the period from 1915 to 1945 was the Age of Stravinsky, then the decades from 1950 were the period of Schoenberg and his school; and the final returns are not yet in.

❧ 20 ❧

Postlude

Many things happened to music after World War II, but they are not within the scope of this book. It will take a generation or more to sort out the new theories, to separate the real from the ephemeral. The period after World War II was a period of unrest, and music, like the other arts, reflected that unrest. Old values no longer applied, and on all sides there was a search for style. Some composers found it in rigid control over all aspects of music. Some found it in precisely the opposite manner, by relaxing all controls. Some looked toward the electronic medium. A new kind of music developed, and also a new terminology. There was much talk of post-Webernism, post-serialism, *musique concrète*, open forms, closed forms, Dada, total organization, indeterminacy, randomness, stochastic music, environmental music, total theater, aleatory, improvisation, rock. So radical were some of the changes, so unusual the new sounds, that a new definition was needed for music. Stravinsky suggested "meta-music." Whatever it was, a good deal of it stemmed from the theories of Schoenberg and Webern, and a good deal of it also resulted from technological advances in electronics. Machines were developed by means of which composers could synthesize their own sounds—dispensing altogether, if they so wanted, with the performer.

But there came about a schism between the avant-garde composer and the public. With all the activity that went on in the international avant-garde, with all the publicity that the new music received, with all the many recordings available, it remained a frightening fact that hardly any music in the new idiom was able to establish itself in the permanent repertory of symphony orchestras, opera houses, and concert halls of any country in the world. Explanations were suggested for the breakdown in communication. Perhaps the conductor Ernest Ansermet was correct in the conclusions he drew in his book *Les fondements de la musique dans la conscience humaine*

(1961); perhaps the new music was so alien to the normal processes of thought and aural experience that it was based on a faulty aesthetic. Or perhaps, on the other hand, there was a great composer working under everybody's nose, with a message too subtle for his contemporaries. Perhaps music was developing into a collective effort, in which composer, sound engineer, physicist, film expert, and theater man pooled talents. Perhaps music was passing through a period of agonized experimentation, waiting for the new Berlioz or Wagner to fuse everything into an expression of power and personality that would also mean something to the public. But whatever the complex of reasons, it seemed apparent twenty-five years after the end of World War II that there was a hiatus in the mighty line of powerful, individualistic composers that extended from Johann Sebastian Bach through Igor Stravinsky and Arnold Schoenberg.

A Selected Bibliography
of Books in English

FOR VOLUME ONE

1

Blume, Friedrich   *Renaissance and Baroque Music* (New York, 1967)
Bodky, Erwin   *The Interpretation of Bach's Keyboard Works* (Cambridge. Massachusetts, 1960)
Bukofzer, Manfred   *Music in the Baroque Era* (New York, 1947)
Dart, Thurston   *The Interpretation of Music* (New York, 1963)
David, Hans T., and Mendel, Arthur   *The Bach Reader* (New York, 1966)
Donington, Robert   *The Interpretation of Early Music* (New York, 1963)
Geiringer, Karl   *The Bach Family* (New York, 1954)
             Johann Sebastian Bach (New York, 1966)
Hutchings, A. J. B.   *The Baroque Concerto* (New York, 1961)
Rothschild, Fritz   *The Lost Tradition in Music   Rhythm and Tempo in J. S. Bach's Time* (New York, 1953)
Schweitzer, Albert   *J. S. Bach.* 2 vols. (New York, 1966)
Spitta, Philip   *Johann Sebastian Bach* (London, 1884–85)
Terry, Charles Stanford   *Johann Christian Bach* (London, 1933)

2

Abraham, Gerald (ed.)   *Handel. A Symposium* (London, 1954)
Burney, Charles   *A General History of Music*, ed. Frank Mercer   2 vols (New York, 1967)
Dean, Winton   *Handel's Dramatic Oratories and Masques* (London, 1959)
Dent, Edward J.   *Handel* (London, 1934)
Deutsch, Otto Erich   *Handel: A Documentary Biography* (New York, 1954)
Lang, Paul Henry   *George Frideric Handel* (New York, 1966)
Myers, Robert Manson   *Handel's Messiah* (New York, 1948)
Pleasants, Henry   *The Great Singers* (New York, 1966). See chapter on the castratos.

3

Asow, Hedwig, and E. H. Mueller von *The Collected Correspondence and Papers of Christoph Willibald Gluck* (New York, 1962)

Berlioz, Hector *Memoirs*, ed. David Cairns (New York, 1969)

Burney, Charles *An Eighteenth-Century Musical Tour in France and Italy*, ed. Percy A. Scholes. 2 vols. (London, 1959)

Cooper, Martin *Gluck* (London, 1935)

Einstein, Alfred *Gluck* (London, 1936)

Grout, Donald Jay *A Short History of Opera*. 2 vols. (New York, 1965)

Howard, Patricia *Gluck and the Birth of Modern Opera* (New York, 1963)

Nettl, Paul *The Book of Musical Documents* (New York, 1948). See excerpts from the Mannlich memoirs.

Tovey, Donald *The Main Stream of Music and Other Essays* (New York, 1949)

Weisstein, Ulrich *The Essence of Opera* (New York, 1964)

4

Geiringer, Karl *Haydn: A Creative Life in Music* (New York, 1963)

Nettl, Paul *Forgotten Musicians* (New York, 1951). See pp. 161–203 for autobiography of Karl Ditters von Dittersdorf, which has source material on Mozart and Haydn.

Newman, William S. *The Sonata in the Classic Era* (Chapel Hill, North Carolina, 1963)

Robbins-Landon, H. C. *The Symphonies of Joseph Haydn* (New York, 1956)
  The Collected Correspondence and London Notebooks of Joseph Haydn (New York, 1959)

Somfai, Laszlo *Joseph Haydn: His Life in Contemporary Pictures* (New York, 1969)

Tovey, Donald *The Main Stream of Music and Other Essays* (New York, 1949). See pp. 1–64 for essay on the string quartets of Haydn.

Anderson, Emily (trans. and ed.) *The Letters of Mozart and His Family*. 3 vols. (London, 1938)

Badura-Skoda, Paul and Eva *Interpreting Mozart on the Keyboard* (London, 1962)

Brion, Marcel *Daily Life in the City of Mozart and Schubert* (New York, 1962)

Dent, Edward J. *Mozart's Operas* (London, 1947)

Deutsch, Otto Erich *Mozart: A Documentary Biography* (Stanford, California, 1965)

Einstein, Alfred *Mozart: His Character, His Work* (New York, 1945)

Girdlestone, Cuthbert *Mozart and His Piano Concertos* (New York, 1964)

Kelly, Michael *Reminiscences*. 2 vols. (London, 1826)

King, A. Hyatt *Mozart in Retrospect* (London, 1955)

Medici, Nerina, and Hughes, Rosemary (eds.) *A Mozart Pilgrimage: Being the Travel Diaries of Vincent and Mary Novello in the Year 1829* (London, 1955)

Nettl, Paul *Mozart and Masonry* (New York. 1957)

Ponte, Lorenzo da *Memoirs* (New York, 1929)

Robbins-Landon, H. C., and Mitchell. Donald (eds.) *The Mozart Companion* (New York, 1956)

Rothschild, Fritz *Musical Performance in the Times of Mozart and Beethoven* (New York, 1961)

Schenk, Erich *Mozart and His Times* (New York, 1959)

Turner. W J. *Mozart· The Man and His Works* (New York, 1954)

6

Anderson, Emily (trans. and ed.) *The Letters of Beethoven* 3 vols. (New York, 1961)

Chorley, Henry F *Modern German Music* (London, 1954). Also valuable for impressions of Schumann, Wagner, Verdi, and Mendelssohn.

Cooper, Martin *Beethoven· The Last Decade* (New York, 1970)

Marek, George *Beethoven: Biography of a Genius* (New York, 1969)

Misch, Ludwig *Beethoven Studies* (Norman, Oklahoma, 1953)

Moscheles, Ignaz *Recent Music and Musicians* (New York, 1873). Also valuable for impressions of Chopin, Mendelssohn, Liszt, and the early romantics.

Pleasants, Henry (trans. and ed.) *The Musical Journeys of Louis Spohr* (Norman. Oklahoma, 1961)

Schindler, Anton Felix *Beethoven as I Knew Him* (London, 1966)

Sonneck, O. G *Beethoven: Impressions by His Contemporaries* (New York, 1926)

Spohr, Louis *Autobiography* (London, 1878)

Sterba, Richard and Edith *Beethoven and His Nephew* (New York, 1954)

Thayer, Alexander Wheelock *The Life of Beethoven, revised and ed. by Elliott Forbes.* 2 vols. (Princeton, New Jersey, 1964)

Tovey, Donald Francis *Beethoven* (London, 1945)

7

Abraham, Gerald (ed.) *The Music of Schubert* (New York, 1947)

Brown, Maurice J. E. *Schubert: A Critical Biography* (New York, 1958)
Essays on Schubert (New York, 1966)

Capell, Richard *Schubert's Songs* (London, 1928)

Deutsch, Otto Erich *The Schubert Reader* (New York, 1947)
Schubert: Memoirs by His Friends (New York, 1958)

Einstein, Alfred *Schubert· A Musical Portrait* (New York, 1951)

Grove, George Article on Schubert in his *Dictionary of Music and Musicians.*

Schumann, Robert *Music and Musicians.* 2 vols. (London, 1891). Also valuable for reviews and commentaries on Mendelssohn, Berlioz, Chopin. Liszt, and many of the minor early romantics.

8

Carse, Adam *The Orchestra from Beethoven to Berlioz* (New York, 1949)

Courcy, G. I. C. de *Paganini.* 2 vols. (Norman, Oklahoma, 1957)

Einstein, Alfred *Music in the Romantic Era* (New York, 1947)

Hallé. Charles   *Life and Letters* (London, 1896) Valuable for source material on many of the early romantics.

Lenz, Wilhelm von   *The Great Pianists of Our Time* (New York, 1899)

Newman. William S   *The Sonata Since Beethoven* (Chapel Hill, North Carolina. 1969)

Schonberg, Harold C.   *The Great Pianists* (New York, 1963)

Stevens, Denis (ed.)   *A History of Song* (New York, 1961)

Warrack, John   *Carl Maria von Weber* (New York, 1968)

9

Barzun, Jacques   *Berlioz and the Romantic Century.* 2 vols. (Boston, 1950)

Berlioz, .Hector   *Evenings With the Orchestra,* trans Jacques Barzun (New York, 1956)

Berlioz, Hector   *The Memoirs of Hector Berlioz,* trans. David Cairns (New York, 1969)

10

Abraham, Gerald (ed.)   *Schumann: A Symposium* (London, 1952)

Brion, Marcel   *Schumann and the Romantic Age* (New York, 1956)

Chissel, Joan   *Schumann* (London, 1948)

Cooper, Martin   *Ideas and Music* (London, 1965) See pp. 163–208 for essay on Schumann songs.

May, Florence   *The Girlhood of Clara Schumann* (London, 1912)

Pleasants, Henry   *The Musical World of Robert Schumann* (New York, 1965)

Sams, Eric   *The Songs of Robert Schumann* (New York, 1969)

Schumann, Robert   *Music and Musicians.* 2 vols. (London, 1891)
                        Early Letters (London, 1888)

11

Abraham, Gerald   *Chopin's Musical Style* (London, 1939)

Boucourechliev, A.   *Chopin: A Pictorial Biography* (New York, 1963)

Chopin, Frédéric   *Selected Correspondence,* trans. and ed. Arthur Hedley (London, 1962)

Cortot, Alfred   *In Search of Chopin,* trans. Cyril and Rena Clarke (New York, 1952)

Delacroix, Eugene   *The Journal of Eugene Delacroix,* trans. Walter Pach (New York, 1937)

Hedley, Arthur   *Chopin* (New York, 1962)

Holcman, Jan   *The Legacy of Chopin* (New York, 1954)

Huneker, James   *Chopin: The Man and His Music* (London, 1901)

Liszt, Franz   *Frédéric Chopin,* trans. Edward N. Waters (New York, 1963)

Walker, Alan (ed.)   *Frédéric Chopin* (New York, 1967)

Wierzynski, Casimir   *The Life and Death of Chopin* (New York, 1949)

12

Beckett, Walter   *Liszt* (London, 1956)

Fay, Amy   *Music Study in Germany* (New York, 1903)

Friedheim, Arthur   *Life and Liszt* (New York, 1961)

Grove's Dictionary of Music and Musicians, 1955 edition The catalogue of Liszt
  works compiled by Humphrey Searle is indispensable.
Huneker, James *Franz Liszt* (New York, 1911)
Liszt, Franz *Letters to Marie zu Sayn-Wittgenstein,* trans. Howard E. Hugo (Cam-
  bridge, Massachusetts, 1953)
Mason, William *Memories of a Musical Life* (New York, 1901)
Newman, Ernest *The Man Liszt* (New York, 1934)
Searle, Humphrey *The Music of Liszt* (New York, 1966)
Sitwell, Sacheverell *Liszt* (New York, 1956)
Walker, Bettina *My Musical Experiences* (New York, 1893)

13

Glehn, M. E. von *Goethe and Mendelssohn* (London, 1874)
Haweis, H. R. *My Musical Life* (London, 1888)
Jacob, Heinrich Eduard *Felix Mendelssohn and His Times* (Englewood Cliffs,
  New Jersey, 1963)
Mason, Lowell *Musical Letters from Abroad* (New York, 1854)
Mendelssohn, Felix *Letters from Italy* (New York 1865)
            Letters (New York, 1945)
Moscheles, Ignaz *Recent Music and Musicians* (New York, 1873)
Petitpierre, Jacques *The Romance of the Mendelssohns* (New York n.d.)
Radcliffe, Philip *Mendelssohn* (London, 1954)
Werner, Eric *Mendelssohn* (New York, 1963)

14

Dwight's Journal of Music, 1852–1881 41 vols. Reprinted by Arno Press (New
  York, 1968)
Fitzlyon, April *The Price of Genius A Life of Pauline Viardot* (New York, 1964)
Moscheles, Felix *Fragments of an Autobiography* (New York, 1899) See pp
  271–299 for essay on Rossini.
Pleasants, Henry *The Great Singers* (New York, 1966)
Russell, Frank *Queen of Song The Life of Henrietta Sontag* (New York 1964)
Schultz, Gladys Denny *Jenny Lind, the Swedish Nightingale* (New York 1962)
Stendhal *Life of Rossini* (New York, 1957)
Toye, Francis *Rossini* (New York, 1947)
Weinstock, Herbert *Donizetti* (New York, 1963)
             Rossini (New York, 1968)

15

Crosten, William L. *French Grand Opera An Art and a Business* (New York,
  1948)
Dieren, Bernard van *Down Among the Dead Men* (London 1935) See pp
  142–174 for essay on Meyerbeer
Dwight's Journal of Music, 1852–1881 41 vols. Reprinted by Arno Press (New
  York, 1968)
Goldman, Albert and Sprinchorn, Evert (eds.) *Wagner on Music and Drama*
  (New York, 1964) See pp. 111–121 *et passim* for essay on Meyerbeer

16

Abraham, Gerald   *A Hundred Years of Music* (Chicago, 1964)

Dwight's Journal of Music, 1852–1881. 41 volumes. Reprinted by Arno Press (New York, 1968)

Gatti, Carlo   *Verdi: The Man and His Music* (New York, 1955)

Hussey, Dyneley   *Verdi* (New York, 1962)

Martin, George   *Verdi: His Music, Life, and Times* (New York, 1963)

Osborne, Charles   *The Complete Operas of Verdi* (New York, 1970)

Shaw, George Bernard   *London Music in 1888–89* (London, 1937)
                                    Music in London, 1890–94. 3 vols. (London, 1949)

Toye, Francis   *Giuseppe Verdi: His Life and Works* (New York, 1946)

Walker, Frank   *The Man Verdi* (New York, 1962)

Werfel, Franz, and Stefan, Paul (eds.)   *Verdi: The Man in His Letters* (New York, 1942)

17

Bekker, Paul   *Richard Wagner* (London, 1931)

Bülow, Hans von   *Early Correspondence* (London, 1896)

Burk, John (ed.)   *Letters of Richard Wagner* (New York, 1950)

Donington, Robert   *Wagner's Ring and Its Symbols* (New York, 1963)

Dwight's Journal of Music, 1852–1881. 41 vols. Reprinted by Arno Press (New York, 1968)

Goldman, Albert, and Sprinchorn, Evert (eds.)   *Wagner on Music and Drama* (New York, 1964)

Gutman, Robert W.   *Richard Wagner: The Man, His Mind, and His Music* (New York, 1968)

Hanslick, Eduard   *Vienna's Golden Years of Music*, trans. and ed. Henry Pleasants (New York, 1950)

Jacobs, Robert   *Wagner* (New York, 1962)

Newman, Ernest   *The Life of Richard Wagner*. 4 vols. (London, 1933–46)

Shaw, George Bernard   *London Music in 1888–89* (London, 1937)
                                    Music in London, 1890–94. 3 vols. (London, 1949)
                                    The Perfect Wagnerite (London, 1898)

Wagner, Richard   *My Life*. 2 vols. (New York, 1911)

Zuckerman, Elliott   *The First Hundred Years of Wagner's Tristan* (New York, 1964)

18

Barkan, Hans (trans. and ed.)   *Johannes Brahms and Theodor Billroth: Letters from a Musical Friendship* (Norman, Oklahoma, 1957)

Gal, Hans   *Johannes Brahms: His Work and Personality* (New York, 1963)

Geiringer, Karl   *Brahms* (New York, 1947)

Hill, Ralph   *Brahms* (New York, 1948)

Latham, Peter   *Brahms* (New York, 1949)

Mason, Daniel Gregory   *The Chamber Music of Brahms* (New York, 1933)

May, Florence   *The Life of Johannes Brahms* (London, 1905)

Schauffler, Robert Haven   *The Unknown Brahms* (New York, 1933)

Schoenberg, Arnold   *Style and Idea* (New York, 1950). See pp. 52–104 for essay on Brahms.

19

Newman, Ernest   *Hugo Wolf* (London, 1907)
Rolland, Romain   *Essays on Music* (New York, 1948). See pp. 341–361 for essay on Wolf.
Sams, Eric   *The Songs of Hugo Wolf* (New York, 1962)
Walker, Frank   *Hugo Wolf* (New York, 1968)

FOR VOLUME TWO

1

Darlington, W. A.   *The World of Gilbert and Sullivan* (New York, 1950)
Fitz-Gerald, S. J. Adair   *The Story of the Savoy Opera* (New York, 1925)
Gilbert and Sullivan   *Complete Plays* (Modern Library, New York, n.d.)
Goldberg, Isaac   *The Story of Gilbert and Sullivan* (London, 1928)
Hughes, Gervaise   *The Music of Gilbert and Sullivan* (New York, 1960)
Kracauer, S.   *Offenbach and the Paris of His Time* (London, 1937)
Pastene, Jerome   *Three-Quarter Time* (New York, 1951)
Sitwell, Sacheverell   *La Vie Parisienne: A Tribute to Offenbach* (London, 1937)

2

Bovet, M. A. de   *Charles Gounod* (London, 1891)
Cooper, Martin   *French Music* (London, 1951)
                        Georges Bizet (London, 1938)
Curtiss, Minna   *Bizet and His World* (New York, 1958)
Finck, Henry T.   *Massenet and His Operas* (New York, 1910)
Glinka, Mikhail   *Memoirs*, trans. R. B. Mudge (Norman, Oklahoma, 1963)
Gounod, Charles   *Autobiography* (London, 1875)
Hewes, Arthur   *Saint-Saëns* (London, 1921)
Harding, James   *Saint-Saëns and His Circle* (London, 1965)
Saint-Saëns, Camille   *Musical Memories* (London, 1921)
                           Outspoken Essays on Music (New York, 1922)

3

Calvocoressi, M. D.   *Modest Mussorgsky: His Life and Works* (London, 1956)
Calvocoressi, M. D., and Abraham, Gerald   *Masters of Russian Music* (New York, 1936)
Diehl, A. M.   *Musical Memories* (London, 1897)

Garden, Edward   *Balakirev* (New York, 1967)

Leyda, Jay, and Bertensson, Sergei   *The Mussorgsky Reader* (New York, 1947)

Rimsky-Korsakov, Nikolai   *My Musical Life* (New York, 1923)

Rubinstein, Anton   *Autobiography* (London, 1890)

Seroff, Victor   *The Mighty Five* (New York, 1948)

4

Abraham, Gerald (ed.)   *The Music of Tchaikovsky* (New York, 1946)

Bowen, Catherine Drinker, and Meck, Barbara von   *Beloved Friend. The Story of Tchaikovsky and Nadejda von Meck* (New York, 1946)

Lakond, Wladimir (trans. and ed.)   *The Diaries of Tchaikovsky* (New York, 1945)

Newmarch, Rosa   *The Life and Letters of Peter Ilich Tchaikovsky* (London, 1906)

5

Abraham, Gerald (ed.):   *Grieg: A Symposium* (London, 1948)
   The Music of Sibelius (New York, 1947)

Clapham, John   *Antonín Dvořák* (New York, 1966)

Finck, Henry T   *Grieg and His Music* (New York, 1929)

Fischl, Viktor (ed.)   *Antonín Dvořák: His Achievement* (London, 1942)

Gray, Cecil   *Sibelius* (London, 1931)

Johnson, Harold E.   *Jean Sibelius* (New York, 1959)

Robertson, Alex   *Dvořák* (London, 1945)

Simpson, Robert   *Carl Nielsen: Symphonist* (London, 1952)

Stefan, Paul   *Anton Dvořák* (New York, 1941)

Trend, J. B.   *Manuel de Falla and Spanish Music* (New York, 1929)

Vogel, Jaroslav   *Leos Janáček* (London, 1962)

6

Barricelli, Jean-Pierre, and Weinstein, Leo   *Ernest Chausson* (Norman, Oklahoma, 1955)

Cooper, Martin   *French Music* (London, 1951)

Demuth, Norman   *César Franck* (New York, 1949)

Indy, Vincent d'   *César Franck* (London, 1910)

Koechlin, Charles   *Gabriel Fauré* (London, n.d.)

Meyers, Rollo   *Emmanuel Chabrier and His Circle* (London, 1969)

Northcote, Sydney   *The Songs of Henri Duparc* (New York, 1950)

Suckling, Norman   *Fauré* (New York, 1951)

Vallas, Léon   *César Franck* (New York, 1951)

7

Carner, Mosco   *Puccini: A Critical Biography* (New York, 1959)

Fiorentino, D. del   *Immortal Bohemian: An Intimate Memoir of Giacomo Puccini* (London, 1952)

Hopkinson, Cecil   *A Bibliography of the Works of Giacomo Puccini* (New York, 1968)

Marek, George R.   *Puccini* (New York, 1951)

Seligman, Vincent   *Puccini Among Friends* (New York, 1938)

Specht, Richard   *Giacomo Puccini* (London, 1933)

8

Hammelmann, Hans, and Osers, Ewald (trans.)   *A Working Friendship: The Correspondence Between Richard Strauss and Hugo von Hofmannsthal* (New York, 1961)

Mann, William   *Richard Strauss: A Critical Study of the Operas* (New York, 1966)

Mar, Norman del   *Richard Strauss.* 2 vols. (New York, 1962 and 1969)

Marek, George   *Richard Strauss: The Life of a Non-Hero* (New York, 1967)

Strauss, Richard   *Recollections and Reflections* (London, 1953)

9

Engel, Gabriel   *The Life of Anton Bruckner* (New York, 1931)

   The Symphonies of Anton Bruckner (Iowa City, 1955)

Graf, Max   *Legend of a Musical City* (New York, 1945)

Mahler, Alma   *Gustav Mahler: Memories and Letters* (New York, 1946)

Mitchell, Donald   *Gustav Mahler: The Early Years* (London, 1958)

Newlin, Dika   *Bruckner, Mahler, Schoenberg* (New York, 1947)

Reik, Theodor   *The Haunting Melody* (New York, 1953)

Schoenberg, Arnold   *Style and Idea* (New York, 1950). See pp. 7–36 for essay on Mahler.

Walter, Bruno   *Gustav Mahler* (New York, 1941)

10

Boulez, Pierre   *Notes of an Apprenticeship* (New York, 1968)

Cortot, Alfred   *The Piano Music of Debussy* (London, 1922)

Debussy, Claude   *Monsieur Croche* (New York, 1948)

Lockspeiser, Edward   *Debussy* (New York, 1949)

   Debussy: His Life and Mind. 2 vols. (New York, 1962 and 1965)

Meyers, Rollo H.   *Erik Satie* (London, 1948)

Seroff, Victor   *Debussy: Musician of France* (New York, 1956)

Vallas, Léon   *The Theories of Claude Debussy* (London, 1929)

11

Demuth, Norman   *Ravel* (New York, 1962)

Hell, Henri   *Francis Poulenc* (New York, 1959)

Honegger, Arthur   *I Am a Composer* (New York, 1966)

Lockspeiser, Edward   *Debussy: His Life and Mind.* 2 vols. (New York, 1962 and 1965). See Vol. II, pp. 36ff., for study of Debussy and Ravel.

Myers, Rollo H.   *Ravel: His Life and Works* (London, 1960)

Seroff, Victor   *Maurice Ravel* (New York, 1953)

12

Boulez, Pierre   *Notes of an Apprenticeship* (New York, 1968)

Duke, Vernon   *Listen Here!* (New York, 1963). See pp. 149–189 for essay on Stravinsky.

Lambert, Constant *Music Ho! A Study of Music in Decline* (London, 1934)

Lang, Paul Henry (ed.) *Stravinsky: A New Appraisal of His Work* (New York, 1963)

Lederman, Minna (ed.) *Stravinsky in the Theatre* (New York, 1949)

Lifar, Serge *Serge Diaghilev: An Intimate Biography* (New York, 1940)

Stravinsky, Igor *Autobiography* (New York, 1936)
                 Poetics of Music (New York, 1956)

Stravinsky, Igor, and Craft, Robert *Conversations With Igor Stravinsky* (New York, 1959)

Dialogues and a Diary (New York, 1963)

Expositions and Developments (New York, 1962)

Memories and Commentaries (New York, 1960)

Themes and Episodes (New York, 1966)

Retrospectives and Conclusions (New York, 1969)

White, Eric Walter *Stravinsky: The Composer and His Works* (Los Angeles, 1966)

13

Beecham, Thomas *Frederick Delius* (New York, 1960)

Colles, H. C. *Essays and Lectures* (London, 1945)

Day, James *Vaughan Williams* (New York, 1961)

Fenby, Eric *Delius as I Knew Him* (London, 1936)

Foss, Hubert *Ralph Vaughan Williams* (New York, 1950)

Holst, Imogen *The Music of Gustav Holst* (London, 1951)

Howes, Frank *The Music of Ralph Vaughan Williams* (London, 1954)

Kennedy, Michael *Portrait of Elgar* (New York, 1968)
                 The Works of Ralph Vaughan Williams (New York, 1964)

Schwartz, Elliott *The Symphonies of Ralph Vaughan Williams* (Amherst, Massachusetts, 1964)

Vaughan Williams, Ralph *National Music* (New York, 1964)

Vaughan Williams, Ursula *R.V.W.* (New York, 1964)

Walker, Ernest *A History of Music in England* (London, 1952)

14

Abraham, Gerald, and Calvocoressi, M. D. *Masters of Russian Music* (New York, 1936)

Bertensson, Sergei, and Leyda, Jay *Sergei Rachmaninoff* (New York, 1956)

Bowers, Faubion *Scriabin: A Biography of the Russian Composer.* 2 vols. (Palo Alto, California, 1969)

Culshaw, John *Rachmaninov: The Man and His Music* (New York, 1950)

Seroff, Victor *Rachmaninoff* (New York, 1950)

15

Duke, Vernon *Passport to Paris* (Boston, 1955)

Hanson, Lawrence and Elizabeth *Prokofiev: A Biography in Three Movements* (New York, 1964)

Martynev, Ivan   *Shostakovich* (New York, 1947)
Nabokov, Nicolas   *Old Friends and New Music* (Boston, 1951)
Nestyev, Israel V.   *Prokofiev* (Palo Alto, California, 1960)
Slonimsky, Nicolas   *Music Since 1900* (New York, 1949). See pp. 684–712 for documentation of 1948 Zhdanov Decree.

16

Austin, William W.   *Music in the 20th Century from Debussy Through Stravinsky* (New York, 1966). See pp. 396–416 for essay on Hindemith.
Busoni, Ferruccio   *The Essence of Music* (New York, 1957)
                    A Sketch of a New Esthetic of Music, in *Three Classics in the Aesthetic of Music* (New York, n.d.)
Busoni, Ferruccio   *Letters to His Wife* (London, 1938)
Dent, Edward J.   *Ferruccio Busoni: A Biography* (London, 1933)
Hindemith, Paul   *A Composer's World* (New York, 1961)

17

Broder, Nathan   *Samuel Barber* (New York, 1954)
Chase, Gilbert   *America's Music* (New York, 1966)
Copland, Aaron   *Copland on Music* (New York, 1963)
                The New Music (New York, 1968)
Cowell, Henry (ed.)   *American Composers on American Music* (Stanford, California, 1933)
Cowell, Henry and Sidney   *Charles Ives and His Music* (New York, 1955)
Gilman, Lawrence   *Edward MacDowell: A Study* (New York, 1909)
Gottschalk, Louis Moreau   *Notes of a Pianist* (New York, 1964)
Hoffman, Richard   *Some Musical Recollections of Fifty Years* (London, 1910)
Howard, John Tasker   *Our American Music* (New York, 1954)
Ives, Charles   *Essays Before a Sonata and Other Writings* (New York, 1962)
Lang, Paul Henry (ed.)   *One Hundred Years of Music in America* (New York, 1961)
Loggins, Vernon   *Where the Word Ends: The Life of Louis Moreau Gottschalk* (Baton Rouge, Louisiana, 1958)
Lowens, Irving   *Music and Musicians in Early America* (New York, 1954)
MacDowell, Edward   *Critical and Historical Essays* (Boston, 1912)
Mathews, W. S. B.   *A Hundred Years of Music in America* (Chicago, 1889)
Reis, Claire R.   *Composers, Conductors and Critics* (New York, 1955)
Smith, Julia   *Aaron Copland* (New York, 1955)
Thomson, Virgil   *Virgil Thomson* (New York, 1966)

18

Austin, William W.   *Music in the 20th Century from Bach Through Stravinsky* (New York, 1966). See pp. 223–242, 319–329.
Fassett, Agatha   *The Naked Face of Genius: Béla Bartók's American Years* (Boston, 1958)
Hodeir, André   *Since Debussy* (New York, 1961). See pp. 83–96.
Stevens, Halsey   *The Life and Music of Béla Bartók* (New York, 1964)

19

Boulez, Pierre   *Notes of an Apprenticeship* (New York, 1958)

Leibowitz, René   *Schoenberg and His School* (New York, 1949)

Moldenhauer, Hans   *The Death of Anton Webern* (New York, 1961)

Newlin, Dika   *Bruckner, Mahler, Schoenberg* (New York, 1947)

Perle, George   *Serial Composition and Atonality* (Los Angeles, 1963)

Redlich, H. F.   *Alban Berg: The Man and His Music* (New York, 1957)

Reich, Willi   *Alban Berg* (New York, 1965)

Rufer, Josef   *The Works of Arnold Schoenberg* (New York, 1963)

Schoenberg, Arnold   *Style and Idea* (New York, 1950)

Stein, Erwin (ed.)   *Arnold Schoenberg Letters* (New York, 1965)

Stuckenschmidt, H. H.   *Arnold Schoenberg* (New York, 1959)

Wörmer, Karl H.   *Schoenberg's 'Moses and Aaron'* (New York, 1963)

20

Cage, John   *Silence* (Middletown, Connecticut, 1961)

Hodeir, André   *Since Debussy* (New York, 1961)

Lang, Paul Henry (ed.)   *Problems of Modern Music* (New York, 1960)

Mitchell, Donald   *The Language of Modern Music* (New York, 1963)

Pleasants, Henry   *The Agony of Modern Music* (New York, 1955)

Salzman, Eric   *Twentieth Century Music: An Introduction* (Englewood Cliffs, New Jersey, 1967)

Yates, Peter   *Twentieth Century Music* (New York, 1967)

Index

Kallman, Chester: 437
Kaminski, Heinrich: 485
Kandinsky, Vassily: 516, 520, 528, 529
Karsavina, Tamara: 434
Keiser, Reinhard: 40
Keldish, Yuri: 474
Keller, Gottfried: 266, 267
Keller, Maria Anna: 57
Kelly, Michael: 273
Kenner, Josef: 100
Kerll, Johann Caspar: 23
Kerman, Joseph: 372
Khachaturian, Aram: 476, 477, 478
Khrennikov, Tikhon: 476, 477
Khrushchev, Nikita: 479
Kinsky, Prince Ferdinand Johann Nepomuk: 86
Kipling, Rudyard: 448
Kirkpatrick, John: 497
Kleiber, Erich: 524
Klemperer, Otto: 523
Klingsor, Tristan: 421
Klopstock, Friedrich Gottlieb: 103
Knappertsbusch, Hans: 380
Köchel, Ludwig: 76
Kodály, Zoltán: 345, 453, 507, 508, 512
Koechlin, Charles: 366, 367, 368
Kokoschka, Oscar: 520
Kolisch, Rudolf: 518
Kosegarten, Ludwig Gottfried: 103
Kosygin, Alexei: 479
Koussevitzky, Serge: 314, 355, 364, 462, 463, 514
Kozeluch, Leopold: 61
Krause, Johann Gottlieb: 19, 20
Krauss, Clemens: 388
Krehbiel, Henry: 379
Krenek, Ernst: 485
Krupp, William: 283
Kupelwieser, Leopold: 101
Kurzrock, Johann Baptist: 101

Lablache, Luigi: 111, 152, 188, 195, 197
Lachner, Franz: 98

Lafont, Charles: 171
Lalo, Edouard: 257, 357, 364
Lalo, Pierre: 303, 419, 421
Laloy, Louis: 419–420
Lamartine, Alphonse: 152, 167, 200
Lambert, Constant: 355
Lamond, Frederick: 171
Landon, H. C. Robbins: 61
Lang, Paul Henry: 41
Lanner, Josef: 276, 277, 278
Laparra, Raoul: 366
Lassus, Orlando: 182
Laube, Heinrich: 277
Laurencie, Lionel de la: 412
Laurens, Jean-Bonaventure: 359
Laussot, Jessie: 238
Lavignac, Alfred: 407
Leblanc, Georgette: 411
Lecocq, Charles: 284
Legouvé, Ernest: 125
Legrenzi, Giovanni: 23
Lehmann, Lilli: 198
Lekeu, Guillaume: 304, 357–358, 360, 362
Lenau, Nikolaus: 267
Lenin, Nikolai: 474
Lenz, Wilhelm: 119
Leo, Leonardo: 182
Leonard, Richard Anthony: 468
Leoncavallo, Ruggiero: 370
Leopold II, Emperor: 79
Leschetizky, Theodore: 470, 472
Levasseur, August: 201
Levi, Hermann: 166, 238, 248, 257, 395
Lhevinne, Josef: 458
Liadov, Anatol: 324, 434, 470
Liapunov, Serge: 315
Libani: 222
Liechenstein, Prince: 269
Liennowsky, Prince Karl: 86
Lind, Jenny: 195, 197, 217, 285
Lipausky, Joseph: 29
Liszt, Adam: 166
Liszt, Cosima (see Wagner, Cosima): 169, 241, 242
Liszt, Franz: 30, 80, 110, 111, 113, 114, 115, 118, 119, 123,

127, 128, 135, 136, 142, 145, 148, 149, 151, 152, 155, 156, 158, 159, 160, 161, 164, 165–177, 178, 181, 182, 183, 185, 186, 193, 234, 236, 237, 241, 245, 251, 252, 254, 255, 262, 265, 266, 292, 303, 304, 305, 306, 307, 308, 309, 312, 319–320, 321, 337, 338, 339, 347, 348, 350, 351, 359, 360, 365, 367, 368, 383, 384, 402, 404, 418, 423, 424, 425, 443, 467, 471, 472, 482, 483, 484, 490, 492, 493, 494, 511, 512
Litolff, Henri: 152, 349
Lobkowitz, Prince Franz Joseph von: 85: 86
Locke, John: 167
Locle, Camille du: 296
Loeffler, Charles Martin: 492
Long, Marguerite: 415
Loring, Eugene: 504
Lortzing, Albert: 120, 200
Louis-Napoléon: 281
Louis-Philippe: 152
Louÿs, Pierre: 362, 408
Löwe, Ferdinand: 397
Ludwig II, King: 241, 242, 243, 244, 248
Lübeck, Vincent: 23
Lully, Jean-Baptiste: 23, 40, 50

MacDowell, Edward: 171, 492–495, 496, 502
Mackenzie, Alexander: 444
Maeterlinck, Maurice: 407, 410–412
Magnard, Albéric: 304
Mahler, Alma: 300, 380
Mahler, Gustav: 95, 115, 123, 149, 171, 248, 250, 252, 262, 268, 339, 354, 355, 356, 365, 378, 392–404, 418, 445, 467, 518, 524
Mainwaring, John: 33, 34, 35
Maiorano, Gaetano (see Caffarelli): 39
Malaïev, M.: 437
Malevich, Kasimir: 474
Malibran, Maria: 111, 152, 171, 197, 201
Malipiero, Francesco: 378

550

554

MAHLER

Alma Mahler

'I lived his life. I had none of my own. He never noticed the surrender of my existence. He was utterly self-centered by nature, and yet he never thought of himself. His work was all in all.'

Both Alma's devotion to Mahler and her own forceful character shine through her recollections of the ten intense years they shared from 1901 to 1911. Her lively account of these last days of the Habsburg Empire mixes domestic detail with anecdotes of such figures as Richard Strauss, Debussy, Freud and Schoenberg, personal moments with musical analysis, and paints a vivid picture of the years when Mahler brought the Vienna Opera to the highest pitch of perfection in its history. Alma was herself a gifted musician and helped her husband considerably with his work when he forbade her to continue with her own. Combined with a collection of Mahler's letters and photographs, her memories contribute much to our understanding of one of the greatest composers of this century.

Donald Mitchell is an eminent music scholar and the author of the definitive Mahler biography. This new edition of *Gustav Mahler: Memories and Letters* takes account of recent scholarship and incorporates previously unpublished material.

'The narrative is fascinating; the complex mind and temperament of Mahler are convincingly evoked. And Alma can write in a way that re-creates the moment'
Guardian

'Cannot fail to enthrall anyone with a taste for Mahler and the cultural flowering that marked the last years of the Habsburg monarchy'
Observer

'An extraordinarily vivid and convincing account of a unique relationship'
TLS

0 7474 0317 1
BIOGRAPHY

THE LIFE AND DEATH OF MOZART

Michael Levey

'Essential reading for all Mozartians'
The Times

Mozart's reputation as a composer continues in the ascendant, yet, curiously, our understanding of the man has been clouded: his personality has been seen as irreconcilable with the musical genius. This picture is unsatisfactory and unsatisfying. Michael Levey sees behind that darkened varnish the clear image of a man of immense liveliness and great humanity not at all at odds with the genius we acknowledge in the music. Simply, Michael Levey reveals the real Mozart.

'He succeeds in showing us a new Mozart, quite different from the innocent, child-like, almost infantile character so often presented by "musical" writers' *Sir Charles Mackerras*

'Rings true . . . in a manner that gives the book unusual strength and authority'
Yorkshire Post

'An original and scholarly biography which succeeds in bringing Mozart alive'
Contemporary Review

'Uncommonly fresh, vivid and touching'
The Scotsman

0 7474 0150 0
BIOGRAPHY

Abacus now offers an exciting range of quality titles by both established and new authors which can be ordered from the following address:

Little, Brown and Company (UK) Limited,
P.O. Box 11,
Falmouth,
Cornwall TR10 9EN.

Alternatively you may fax your order to the above address. Fax No. 0326 376423.

Payments can be made as follows: cheque, postal order (payable to Little, Brown and Company) or by credit cards, Visa/Access. Do not send cash or currency. UK customers and B.F.P.O. please allow £1.00 for postage and packing for the first book, plus 50p for the second book, plus 30p for each additional book up to a maximum charge of £3.00 (7 books plus).

Overseas customers including Ireland, please allow £2.00 for the first book plus £1.00 for the second book, plus 50p for each additional book.

NAME (Block Letters) ....

ADDRESS ....

....

☐ I enclose my remittance for _____

☐ I wish to pay by Access/Visa Card

Number ☐☐☐☐☐☐☐☐☐☐☐☐☐☐☐☐☐

Card Expiry Date ☐☐☐☐